Introductory Econometrics

This book constitutes the first serious attempt to explain the basics of econometrics and its applications in the clearest and simplest manner possible. Recognising the fact that a good level of mathematics is no longer a necessary prerequisite for economics/financial economics undergraduate and postgraduate programmes, it introduces this key subdivision of economics to an audience who might otherwise have been deterred by its complex nature.

The main features of *Introductory Econometrics* include:

- A non-mathematical exposition of the key issues and topics
- Focus on economic/financial models and their empirical analysis
- Econometric analysis as it is carried out in practice
- Inclusion of worked examples involving real economic data
- An introductory but rigorous exposition of modern econometric topics, including qualitative response models, panel data regression and cointegration analysis
- An introduction to financial econometrics, including modelling volatility and correlation in financial time series.

This text treats econometrics as a subdivision of economics, rather than that of mathematical statistics. It is designed to explain key economic/econometric issues in a non-mathematical manner and to show applications of econometric methods in practice. It should prove to be invaluable to students at all levels venturing into the world of econometrics.

Hamid R. Seddighi (BA Mathematical Economics, Essex; MSc. Economic-Statistics, York; DPhil. Economics, York) is a senior lecturer in Applied Research Methods for Business and Management at the Faculty of Business and Law, University of Sunderland, UK. As a Senior Lecturer in quantitative economics and a Reader in applied economics, he has taught Econometrics at the Universities of Sunderland, York and, more recently, at the University of Durham, UK. He has supervised to successful completion PhD candidates in applied econometrics and has published many articles in the field of applied econometrics in international journals. He has co-authored four text books in the area of economic theory and modelling, econometrics, and international trade.

Introductory Econometrics

A practical approach

Hamid R. Seddighi

Routledge
Taylor & Francis Group

LONDON AND NEW YORK

First published 2012
by Routledge
2 Park Square, Milton Park, Abingdon, Oxon OX14 4RN

Simultaneously published in the USA and Canada
by Routledge
711 Third Avenue, New York, NY 10017

Routledge is an imprint of the Taylor & Francis Group, an informa business

British Library Cataloguing in Publication Data
A catalogue record for this book is available from the British Library

Library of Congress Cataloging in Publication Data
Seddighi, Hamid R.
Introductory econometrics : a practical approach / Hamid Seddighi.
p. cm.
1. Econometrics. I. Title.
HB139.S414 2011
330.01′5195—dc23
2011020638

ISBN: 978–0–415–56687–2 (hbk)
ISBN: 978–0–415–56688–9 (pbk)
ISBN: 978–0–203–15768–8 (ebk)

Typeset in Times NRMT
by RefineCatch Limited, Bungay, Suffolk

MIX
Paper from
responsible sources
FSC
www.fsc.org   FSC® C004839

Printed and bound in Great Britain by
TJ International Ltd, Padstow, Cornwall

To the memory of my mother and for my wife

Contents

List of figures & tables

Figures

Tables

Preface

This is the second edition of *Econometrics: A practical approach* by H.R. Seddighi, K.A. Lawler and A.V. Katos. In this revised edition further attempts have been made to provide a thoroughly modern, mainly non-mathematical, and accessible exposition of basics of econometrics, without sacrificing rigour and depth. Key chapters of the previous edition have been retained but thoroughly revised, new material has been added to them and the book has been reorganised to aid a structured teaching and learning approach.

New chapters on qualitative response regression models, panel data regression models and aspects of financial econometrics have been included in this edition. The book has been organised into five teaching units to facilitate a structured teaching and learning approach to modern econometrics as follows:

1. Unit 1 Single-equation regression models (Chapters 1–7).
2. Unit 2 Simultaneous equations regression models (Chapter 8).
3. Unit 3 Qualitative variables in econometrics and panel data regression analysis (Chapters 9–11)
4. Unit 4 Time series econometrics (chapters 12–15)
5. Unit 5 Aspects of financial time series econometrics (chapter 16).

Each unit can be taught separately depending on the nature of the programme/module being offered. Units 1, 2 and 3 are suitable for one/two semester undergraduate/post graduate programmes in economics, business, and relevant MBA programmes. Units 4 and 5 are suitable for one/two semester programmes, covering advanced undergraduates in economics, finance, and relevant MBA programmes.

Acknowledgements

I would like to thank my students past and present for their comments and reactions to some of the material included in this book. Thanks are due to anonymous referees who reviewed an earlier edition, providing suggestions for improvements. Some of these have been incorporated into this edition. Thanks are also due to Dr Dennis Philip of Durham Business School, University of Durham, for undertaking the work on Unit 5 of this new edition. I also wish to thank Jeff Evans of Sunderland Business School, University of Sunderland, for preparing the statistical tables included the Appendix.

Finally I wish to acknowledge the contributions of K.A. Lawler and A.V. Katos to an earlier edition of this book. In particular, special thanks are due to A.V. Katos for his contributions to some of the key chapters of the previous edition. Some of the key material of the earlier edition have been revised but retained in Units 1, 2 and 4 of this new edition. This is greatly appreciated and acknowledged by the author.

Dr Hamid R. Seddighi

Unit 1

Single-equation regression models

- This unit introduces the reader to the traditional approach to econometric analysis, focusing on the formulation, estimation and evaluation of single-equation regression models.
- The unit explains the traditional specific to general (SG) methodology of econometric analysis and demonstrates this methodology in a step by step fashion via a number of applied econometric examples.
- The emphasis throughout this unit is on understanding the key concepts and issues and on applying key ideas to modelling and empirically evaluating economic models.
- Chapters 1 and 2 explain the process of economic modelling and modification of the economic models into econometric models for the purpose of empirical analysis.
- Chapter 3 explains the concept of estimators, sampling distributions, properties of 'good' estimators, and the OLS estimators and their properties.
- Chapter 4 explains the criteria for evaluation of the regression results, focusing on hypotheses testing and tests of significance.
- Chapter 5 explains the diagnostic testing procedures used in practice to test and to detect breakdown of the standard assumptions, including several tests for autocorrelation and heteroscedasticity. Unlike conventional texts, which typically devote several chapters to these issues, and, therefore, give the impression that each of the breakdowns occurs independently of other problems, this chapter follows what typically happens in practice, explaining all key problems together under one roof to re-emphasise the methodological problems of the traditional approach.
- Chapter 6 explains the phenomenon of spurious regression, frequently encountered within the framework of the traditional (SG) methodology. It discusses how this methodology deals with this problem in practice and explains the modern approach to dealing with this problem.
- Chapter 7 provides detailed coverage of the traditional approach to converting static econometric models to dynamic econometric models, explaining the distributed lag and the autoregressive dynamic models.
- This unit shows key aspects of the traditional methodology to single-equation econometric analysis, including modelling, estimation, evaluation and spurious regression phenomenon, providing a sound foundation for the modern approach to time series econometric analysis, to be discussed in Unit 4.
- This unit is suitable for an introductory course/module in econometrics to be delivered over one semester.

- To better understand key elements of this unit, students are encouraged to model various economic variables, making use of the review questions at the end of each chapter, collect relevant data (for example, from various online sources), and use an appropriate regression package to estimate, evaluate and analyse single-equation regression models.

1 Economic theory and economic modelling in practice

INTRODUCTION

Econometrics is a branch of economics dealing with the empirical evaluation of abstract economic theories and models. The principle aim of econometrics is to check the validity of the economic models against data, and to provide empirical content to economic theories and models. The key component of an econometric analysis is therefore an economic theory specifically in the form of an economic model suitable for empirical evaluation. This chapter provides an introductory discussion of the methods of economic modelling and econometric analysis. To this end, a number of simple economic models are developed step by step to illustrate the key features of economic modelling and to demonstrate the need for empirical evaluation of the models via econometric analysis.

Key topics

- Economic modelling in practice
- The econometric approach
- The specific to general methodology of econometric analysis

1.1 Economic theory and modelling

Economic theories are developed to provide logical and coherent explanations of economic issues. These issues range from the activities of households and firms, to the activities of government relating to employment, inflation and economic growth.

Typically, economic theory consists of a set of conceptual definitions about the economic variables under consideration and a set of assumptions about the behaviour of economic agents, including households, firms and the government. Economists then follow a process of logical deduction deriving the implications of the assumptions. These implications are the predictions of the economic theory. They are usually reported as conditional statements in the form of testable hypotheses concerning the issues and causal linkages.

The implications of theory when configured as economic hypotheses constitute an economic model. Economic models are, therefore, derived from theoretical arguments and are, essentially, a simple representation of the complex real-world economic relationships. Economic models can be represented verbally, geometrically or algebraically. In this latter form, the relationship among economic variables implied by theoretical arguments is expressed by mathematical symbols and equations. These three types of presentation of economic models are frequently combined to explain various economic phenomena under examination.

Algebraic presentations of economic models have, however, a number of advantages. These are that they provide:

- frameworks within which the relationships among economic variables are expressed in consistent and logical sequences;
- the frameworks for the model builder to generalise theoretical arguments and ascertain implications;
- frameworks for the empirical investigation of economic hypotheses.

1.2 Economic modelling in practice

To illustrate the process of economic model building we develop two economic models. These are: (a) a model of household consumption expenditure, and (b) a model of demand for competitive imports.

1.2.1 A model of household consumption expenditure

This model is designed to explain factors influencing the planned consumption expenditure of a household. That is, the amount of expenditure that a household plans to spend out of income. There are a number of important theoretical contributions in this field. The simplest of these theories is the Keynesian absolute income hypothesis (AIH). In developing this theory, Keynes argued that, of the many factors that influence the level of household consumption expenditure, the most important is the level of household current disposable income. The way in which consumption expenditure is influenced by the disposable income is, according to what Keynes called 'the fundamental psychological law', that, 'men are disposed, as a rule and on average, to increase their consumption as their income increases, but not by as much as the increase in their income' (Keynes, 1936). The change in consumption expenditure per unit of a change in income is called 'marginal propensity to consume' (MPC). According to Keynes, the MPC is less than unity. Furthermore, Keynes argued that the proportion of income saved would increase as household income increased. The proportion of income consumed is called the 'average propensity to consume' (APC). Given Keynes' view, the average propensity to consume falls as real income rises. Moreover, Keynes argued that the marginal propensity to consume would be less than the average propensity to consume.

To derive an algebraic model from these theoretical arguments, we define two variables:

- Y = consumption expenditure of household
- X = household income.

Economic theory identifies income to be the major determinant of household consumption expenditure Y. This statement may be expressed mathematically as follows:

$$Y = f(X).$$

That is, Y depends on X (Y is a function of X) and the direction of causation is from X to Y, so X influences Y, but Y does not influence X. In this presentation, Y is called *the dependent variable* and X the *independent variable* of the model.

This mathematical relationship is the maintained hypothesis of the theory, from which theoretical reasoning is used to explain the nature of the relationship between Y and X.

According to AIH, households increase consumption as disposable income increases, but not by as much as income. In other words, as income changes, consumption also changes, but the corresponding change in consumption expenditure is assumed to be less than the change in income. Mathematically, we may define:

ΔY = a change in income
ΔX = a change in consumption expenditure
$\Delta Y/\Delta X$ is assumed to be less than one.
Or equivalently:
$\Delta Y/\Delta X \leq 1$

where the ratio $\Delta Y/\Delta X$ is the marginal propensity to consume (MPC). This shows the change in consumption per unit of a change in income. Hence, the average propensity to consume (APC) can be written as:

$APC = Y/C$
where APC > MPC and APC falls as real income rises.

The algebraic form of the model may now be summarised as:

$Y = f(X)$
$0 \leq MPC = \Delta Y/\Delta X \leq 1$
$MPC < APC; APC = Y/X.$

In general, economic theorists do not specify the exact functional forms that are likely to exist among economic variables. The specification of functional forms is left to the model builder. It is, however, customary to consider an initially linear relationship, because of the ease of presentation and analysis. Following this tradition, the AIH in a linear form may be presented as:

$Y = a + bX; a \geq 0; 0 \leq b \leq 1.$

Where a is the intercept term and b is the slope of the linear function. Both a and b are unknown constants and are called *parameters of the model*. An important task for econometrics is to provide estimates of the unknown parameters of the economic models on the basis of economic data on economic variables. This model can be presented graphically by assuming certain hypothetical values for the unknown parameters: a and b. This is done in Figure 1.1, where the dependent variable is measured along the vertical axis and the independent variable along the horizontal axis.

According to Figure 1.1, there exists a one-to-one relationship between Y and X. That is, given a value for X, such as X_1, there is a unique value for Y, which is shown in Figure 1.1 as Y_1. That is, within the framework of economic models, the relationship between economic variables is represented by deterministic equations. We return to this point in subsequent sections.

1.2.2 *A model of demand for competitive imports*

Economic theory identifies three major factors determining a country's demand for competitive imports, that is, those imports for which there are domestic substitutes.

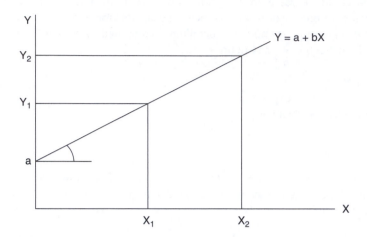

Figure 1.1 A one-to-one deterministic relationship for consumption and income.

The first factor is level of final expenditure, that is, total expenditure in a given period in an economy. The composition of total expenditure is also important given the degree of the import content of the different components of total expenditure (consumption, expenditure, investment expenditure and expenditure on exports). In developing a model of competitive imports, we allow for a general case and distinguish between the three broad categories of final expenditure, namely, total consumption expenditure by the private and public sectors, investment expenditure and expenditure on exports. The underlying assumption being that each aggregate component of final expenditure has a different impact on imports.

The second factor developed by theory is the price of imports relative to the price of domestic substitutes. Where the price of imports is measured in the units of domestic currency and expressed in index form, the domestic price level is also expressed in index form, for example, in the form of wholesale price indices or GDP price deflators. A rise in the relative prices would normally lead to a fall in demand for competitive imports. In most cases, to explain how prices are determined, it is usually assumed that the supply elasticities are infinite, which implies that whatever the level of domestic demand for imports, these are supplied and, therefore, that import prices are determined outside the model, through the interactions of demand and supply. The domestic price index is also usually taken as given and is assumed to be flexible, thereby eliminating excess demand at home. Theory also identifies the capacity of the import substitution sector to produce and supply the goods as an important factor in determining the demand for imports. However, the capacity variable is essentially a short-run phenomenon and is relevant only if excess demand at home cannot be eliminated by a change in domestic prices. To generate an algebraic model we begin by defining the economic variables considered to be important in determining the demand for competitive imports. These variables are defined as follows:

M	= the volume of imports (imports in constant price)
CG	= the sum of private and public sector consumption expenditure in real terms (constant prices)

INVT = expenditure on investment goods, including gross domestic fixed capital
        formation and stock building in real terms (constant prices)
EXPT = expenditure on exports in real terms (constant prices)
PM   = an index price of imports in units of domestic currency
PD   = an index price of domestically produced goods
PM and PD may be measured by price deflators as follows:

$$PM = \frac{\text{imports in current prices}}{\text{imports in constant prices}}$$

$$PD = \frac{\text{GDP in current prices}}{\text{GDP in constant prices.}}$$

Having defined these variables, we are now in the position to present the general form of the algebraic model as follows:

$$M = f(CG, INVT, EXP, PM/PD) \qquad (1.1)$$
$$(+ve)\ (+ve)\ (+ve)\ (-ve)$$

Hence, according to theoretical arguments, the demand for competitive imports depends on ('is a function of') the main components of aggregate demand: CG, INVT and EXP. Each of these has a separate impact on import demand. Moreover, one expects that the relationship between each one of these variables and imports to be positive. That is, a rise/fall in any of these variables would result in a rise/fall in the level of demand for competitive imports. With regard to the relative price term, we expect that a rise/fall in this term to lead to a fall/rise in the level of imports. We indicate this negative relationship by using a negative sign below the relative price variable in the previous equation. In this particular presentation of the model, M is the dependent variable, and CG, INVT, EXP, PM/PD are the independent variables.

To analyse in more detail the nature of the interactions between the dependent variable and each one of the independent variables for any economic model, we need to assume a certain functional form for the general economic model presented by Equation (1.1). This will be done as follows.

1.3 Mathematical specification of the economic models

Generally, the exact specifications for economic models are best left to model builders. Ease of presentation and interpretation, in most applications, means that model builders tend to use either linear or log-linear specifications. We consider each of these specifications in turn.

1.3.1 A linear specification

In a linear specification, the dependent and independent variables of the model are linked together via a linear equation in which the parameters of the model appear in linear form. In applying this type of specification to the model of demand for imports outlined above, a linear model may be obtained as follows:

$$M = \alpha_1 + \alpha_2 CG + \alpha_3\ INVT + \alpha_4\ EXP + \alpha_5(PM/PD) \qquad (1.2)$$

where α_1, α_2, α_3, α_4, α_5 are unknown constants and are called *the parameters* of the model; α_1 is the intercept term of the linear equation and α_2, α_3, α_4, α_5 are slope parameters.

In this linear presentation of the model, each slope parameter shows the impact of a marginal change (a one unit change) in a particular independent variable, while other independent variables are constant, on the average value of the dependent variable. For example, α_2 shows the impact of a one unit change in CG, while INVT, EXP and PM/PD are kept constant, on the average value of import demand. Symbolically:

$$\alpha_2 = \frac{\Delta M}{\Delta CG} \Big| INVT, (EXP, PM)/PD(constant) \tag{1.3}$$

α_2 may be termed marginal propensity to import out of aggregate consumption. It is expected that its value lies between 0 and 1.

Similarly, α_5 shows the impact of a one unit change in the relative price variable, while all components of aggregate demand are kept constant, on the average level of demand for competitive imports. That is:

$$\alpha_5 = \frac{\Delta M}{\Delta \left(\dfrac{PM}{PD}\right)} \Big| INVT, EXP, CG(constant) \tag{1.4}$$

According to theory, one expects α_5 to be negative.

1.3.2 A log-linear specification

In log-linear specifications, the logs of the dependent and independent variables are linked via a linear equation in which all parameters appear in a linear form. Equation (1.5) demonstrates a log-linear specification of the model of demand for imports:

$$\log M = \beta_1 + \beta_2 \log CG + \beta_3 \log INVT + \beta_4 \log EXP + \beta_5 \log (PM/PD) \tag{1.5}$$

where β_1 is the intercept term and β_2–β_5 are the slope parameters.

The slope parameters β_2, β_3, β_4 and β_5 are *partial elasticities*, each showing the percentage change in the dependent variable with respect to a percentage change in any one of the independent variables under consideration.

For example:

The parameter β_2 shows the percentage change in the dependent variable per unit of a percentage change in the independent variable CG, ceteris paribus. So:

$$\beta_2 = \frac{\%\Delta M}{\%\Delta CG} \text{ (all other independent variables constant).}$$

Note that in a log-linear specification each slope parameter shows the percentage change in the dependent variable (and not its log) per unit of a percentage change in any one of the independent variables. In economic analysis such a parameter is called an 'elasticity'. Here, β_2 is the partial elasticity of import demand with respect to consumption expenditure, showing the percentage change in the level of imports for every one per cent change in the level of CG. For example, if β_2 is found to be 5 per cent, it implies that, for every single per cent change in CG, (all other independent variables are kept constant), demand for import changes by 5 per cent. This implies that the demand is highly price elastic. Log-linear economic models are extremely popular in applied economic/econometric analysis due to the ease of specification and interpretation of results.

A summary of key steps required for economic modelling

Step 1 Give a clear statement/explanation of the economic theory underlying the economic phenomena under consideration. Pay particular attention to the assumptions, noting implications and limitations.

Step 2 Use simple linear relationships in parameters to present the economic model in algebraic form. Use linear relationships to model/link economic variables to measure the impact of marginal changes on the dependent variables.

Step 3 Use log-linear specifications when you want to measure elasticities. Make sure you understand how the variables are linked through the log-linear specification. Remember that a slope coefficient in a log-linear specification shows the percentage change in the dependent variable per unit of a percentage change in an independent variable (to which the slope coefficient is attached).

1.4 The need for the empirical evaluation of economic models: the econometrics approach

Economic models, presented in an algebraic form, provide the starting point for an econometric enquiry. An econometric enquiry basically aims to: (a) quantify the relationship among economic variables, providing numerical estimates for the unknown parameters of the model, and (b) to test to see whether the economic hypotheses derived from theory are consistent with facts in the form of economic data.

For example, in the previous examples, the objective of the study is to determine estimates of the parameters of the models. Specifically referring to the household consumption and income model, it is interesting to find the value of the household marginal propensity to consume, so as to predict the impact of a marginal change in household income on household average consumption expenditure. Similarly, with respect to the model of competitive imports, researchers are interested to estimate the model to establish the value of various partial elasticities. For example, it is of research interest to know the partial elasticity of demand for imports with respect to each component of final expenditure. Robust estimates of the partial elasticities would have solid policy implications in terms of inflation and/or balance of payment issues.

In addition to parameter estimation, researchers are also interested to know how well deductive/theory-based algebraic models explain real-world economic relationships. Thus, if we cannot find evidence against a particular model, we can say that the theory/model conforms to the available facts. If this is the case, the model may then be used for policy analysis/economic forecasting by practitioners. Alternatively, if we find empirical evidence against a particular model, we can conclude that the model does not conform to the reality and, therefore, the economic theory upon which the model is based should either be discarded or modified. Moreover, we need a procedure for choosing between competing economic theories. Often there are a number of competing economic theories designed to explain the same economic phenomena. For example, in order to explain price inflation, there are demand-pull, cost-push and monetary theories of inflation. The key question is which one of these, if indeed any, best explains price inflation in a given country over a period of time. The only way to answer these types of question is to resort to empirical investigation.

For these reasons there is a vital need to conduct empirical analysis in economics, providing empirical content to abstract economic models. To this end, we need a framework/ mechanism for confronting economic models with economic data. This framework is provided by econometrics. Thus, a working definition of econometrics would be:

> Econometrics is a branch of economics dealing with empirical measurement of economic relationships. The term 'metrics' signifies measurement. It aims to provide empirical content to abstract economic models, with the purpose of verifying or refuting them.

Given this definition, the question which now arises is how does one carry out econometrics work/research in practice? In other words, what is the methodology of econometric/ empirical analysis in economics. There are three major rival methodologies for empirical work/analysis in economics; these are 'specific to general' (SG), 'general to specific' (GS), and co-integration methodologies. In this text we will follow two key methodological approaches: (a) the well-documented and applied specific to general methodology (SG), and (b) the recently popularised co-integration methodology. We start with the traditional approach to econometric modelling, often termed the specific to general (SG) approach to econometric modelling. In Chapters 12–15 we will discuss in detail the co-integration methodology.

1.4.1 The traditional approach to econometric analysis: specific to general (SG) methodology

The specific to general (SG) approach to econometric modelling is the earliest methodology used to carry out empirical research in economics. It is called the traditional approach and it dates back to the 1930s when the Econometric Society was established to encourage and promote empirical work/research in economics. From the 1930s up until the late 1970s, the SG approach to econometric analysis dominated research work in applied econometrics.

The SG approach begins procedures with economic theory and applies this to the issues under investigation. In this situation, the practitioner using this strategy must be careful in explaining the theory to be utilised in the analysis. There are, however, occasions when a relevant economic theory/model concerning a particular economic issue has not yet been developed. In this situation, care has to be taken to ensure that the economic model/hypothesis underlying the empirical analysis is explained. Once an economic hypothesis is selected for the purposes of empirical investigation, its algebraic form must be specified. There are no concrete guidelines as to how to specify the algebraic forms. In practice, it is customary to use a linear-in-parameter specification, particularly when one is interested in measuring the impact of marginal variations in the dependent variable with respect to small changes in the independent variables. Log-linear specifications are also extremely popular for measuring various partial elasticities, in both time series and cross-section analysis. However, mathematical models are exact relationships and are not compatible with inexact economic data. To reflect the inexact nature of the data, economic models are transformed into 'econometric models'. We discuss in detail, subsequently, the nature of such modifications. Once an econometric model is developed, the assumptions are explained. Nowadays, there are many specially designed software packages for the estimation of econometric models (e.g. Microfit, EViews, Give, SPSS). In subsequent chapters, procedures governing the estimation and confirmation of econometric models are explained. If the model is found to be adequate, passing all key diagnostic tests/checks designed for confirmation, it may then be used for policy simulation. If, however, the model is found to be inadequate, it should either be modified or discarded. These steps are summarised below.

1.4.2 Key steps of the specific to general (SG) econometric methodology

- Begin with theories (or falsifiable hypotheses derived from theories) which are drastic abstractions of reality;
- Formulate highly simplistic relationships (linear-in-parameter) to represent the hypotheses which reflect the theories;
- Estimate the linear equations from the data set using techniques which are 'optimal' only on the assumption that the econometric model is properly specified;
- Test a few of the 'explicit' assumptions or utilise tests for 'implicit' assumptions such as tests for auto-correlation;
- Revise the original specification in the light of a restricted number of diagnostic tests;
- Re-estimate the model, as sets of hypotheses, accordingly.

The approach, nonetheless, has obvious drawbacks. These are that:

- Since each and every test is conditional on arbitrary assumptions which are tested later, then if any of these are rejected, at any given stage in the investigation, all previous inferences are invalidated.
- Given the restricted number of diagnostic tests conducted, it is accordingly not always known if the 'best' model has been achieved by using this iterative methodology.

Figure 1.2 schematically shows key stages in a traditional econometric investigation based on the SG methodology.

1.4.3 The general to specific (GS) methodology

In contrast to the specific to general (SG) approach, the general to specific (GS) approach starts with a general model loosely based on theory and seeks to derive a specific model explaining the data generation process. The key steps of this methodology are summarised below:

1 Begin with the most general specification which is reasonable to maintain within the context of theory.
2 Conduct the simplification process, which is undertaken by way of a sequence of tests, which aim to avoid the charge of measurement without theory or empirical foundation. Moreover, within the context of the GS approach it should be noted that:

    a   the significance levels for the sequences of testing is known;
    b   the sequential testing procedures are used to select a data coherent model of economic relationships.

Nevertheless, there still remain drawbacks with the GS approach. These can be generally stated as being that:

1 The chosen general model might only actually comprise a 'special' case of the data generation process, so that diagnostic testing remains vitally important.
2 Data limitations and inconsistencies weaken the approach.
3 There still remains no universally agreed uniquely optimal sequence for simplifying the 'general' model in practice.

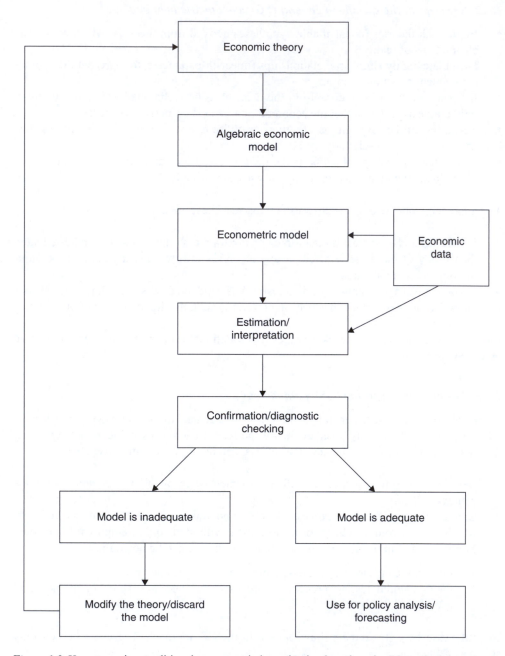

Figure 1.2 Key stages in a traditional econometric investigation based on the SG methodology.

Despite a number of key shortcomings, as outlined above, the SG methodology has dominated the majority of empirical work in economics since the mid-1930s. It is currently used
in econometric texts to introduce students to econometric analysis. We will follow this tradition in Chapters 1–8 to introduce basic concepts, models, analysis and limitations. However,

in Chapters 12–16 we will focus our discussion on new methodologies for time series investigations, particularly on co-integration analysis.

1.4.4 Economic data

A data set constitutes a key ingredient of econometric modelling and analysis (see Figure 1.2 above). Typically, a data set contains a set of observations on the variables of the economic/financial model. These observations may be collected in a number of different ways, to generate the following types of data:

1   *Time series data* These are observations collected on the values of the variables of the model over time. Time series data are typically collected from official public/private secondary data sources. For example, in the UK the Economic Trends and the London Stock Exchange market databases are well-known sources of reliable time series data for time series econometrics investigations. The Economic Trends Annual Supplements are excellent sources of time series data on key UK macroeconomic variables (gross domestic product, aggregate consumption expenditure by private and public sectors, imports, exports, etc.), in quarterly and in annual frequencies. The Economic Trends Annual Supplements are available online. For financial econometrics analysis, The London Stock Exchange (LSE) market databases and *The Financial Times* (FT) provide high-frequency time series financial data on stocks/shares prices, the volume of financial transactions and the pattern of demand and supply of stocks and shares. Time series data are used for modelling, model evaluation and forecasting in time series econometrics studies.

2   *Cross-section data* These are observations collected on variables of the model at a point in time. Cross-section data may be collected from public/private data collection agencies, which collect cross-section data via surveys on various aspects of individuals, consumers, and producers. For example, various published surveys and data on households' monthly expenditures (expenditure over a specific month), on companies' annual investment outlays (over one particular year) and on a sample of stock returns. In cross-sectional econometrics studies, typically a sample is chosen by the researcher from a population of interest and cross-section data is then collected via questionnaire for detailed econometrics investigation.

3   *Panel data sets* These provide observations on a cross-section of individuals, firms, objects or countries over time. Typically, in a panel data set, a long cross-section data set is mixed with a short time series to generate a combined cross-section/time series data set. For example, a panel data set on:

- the daily prices of a sample of (say 100) stocks over 3 years;
- the monthly expenditure of a group of households (say 1000) over time (say 3 years);
- the annual R&D expenditure of manufacturing companies located in the NE over a 5-year period;
- problem: examining effectiveness of negative income tax (thousands of households over 2–3 years);
- earning potential of university graduates: a large data set on graduates' characteristics, age, type of degree, employment, etc. The graduates are then followed over time (say 1–4 years) and time series data are collected on earnings and promotions.

As was pointed out above, in a panel data regression analysis, a large cross-section data set is normally mixed with a short time series data set, for the purpose of empirical analysis.

1.5 A summary of key issues

- Economics uses deductive methodology to explain real-world phenomena. Modelling the relationship between economic variables is a key aspect of economic analysis. Economic theory is developed on the basis of logical reasoning and a set of plausible assumptions to explain how key economic variables are determined in the real world.
- When economic theory is expressed in mathematical form, the economic theory is formulated within the framework of a mathematical model.
- Mathematical models are typically formulated as linear models. These types of models depict straight linear lines, have an intercept term and slope parameters.
- Log-linear specification is another popular form of economic models. In this type of model, the slope parameters are various elasticities.
- Economic models show causation between variables. The variable to be explained by the model is called the dependent variable (regressand) and those explaining it are independent variables (regressors).
- Economic theory and models lack empirical content. They must be empirically tested to see whether they are capable of explaining the data and are consistent with facts.
- Econometrics is a branch of economics dealing with empirical evaluation of economic theories and models, to establish whether a theory is capable of explaining the data for which it is designed.
- Specific to general (SG) methodology is the traditional approach to conducting empirical analysis in economics. This is a positivist approach to empirical analysis, based on deductive reasoning and theory, using quantitative data, focusing on ensuring reliability and precision in analysis.
- There are many good sources of economic data available online, including the Economic Trends Annual Supplement, the OECD databases, the EU databases, and various central banks publications.
- Economic data are collected in three different forms: time series data, cross-section data and panel data.

Review questions

1   Explain the meaning of each of the following terms:

   a   economic theory
   b   economic model.
   c   econometric model.

2   Explain what is meant by:

   a   a deterministic model
   b   a stochastic model.

3   Which type of data is suitable for use with an economic model? Explain your answer.
4   Distinguish between the specific to general (SG) and the general to specific (GS) methodologies of econometrics. Which one of these two approaches do you find more attractive? Explain your answer.

5　Explain what you understand by each of the following:

    a　a linear model
    b　a log-linear model
    c　dependent variable
    d　independent variables.

6　Explain the nature and types of economic data. What are the key sources of economic data?

7　Compare and contrast times series data with panel data. Give examples of each type of economic data to illustrate your answer.

2 Formulating single-equation regression models

INTRODUCTION

Economic models are by their nature deterministic. That is, given a set of values for the independent variables of the model, only one value can be generated for the dependent variable, from any one of this type of model. This is in contrast to economic data, which are not deterministic. That is, for any given set of values for the independent variables, there is likely to exist a range of values for the dependent variable under investigation. Before any empirical analysis and evaluation, in order to explain the data generation process (DGP), the deterministic economic models must therefore be modified to reflect the stochastic nature of the data. This chapter explains in detail how this modification is done using a number of examples to illustrate key ideas.

Key topics

- The two-variable linear regression model
- The disturbance term, its role and assumptions
- The multiple linear regression model (the classical normal linear regression model: CNLRM)

2.1 Towards developing an econometric model

To investigate the relationships among economic variables captured by an algebraic model, and to confirm, or otherwise, the underlying economic theory, the algebraic model has to be confronted with appropriate economic data. There is, however, a problem associated with this process, which has to be resolved before the process of measurement and confirmation can begin. The problem arises from the fact that, whereas an algebraic economic model intrinsically portrays an exact relationship among a number of variables, the data seldom exhibits such exact relationships. The economic data, however, have to be taken as given and cannot be modified. The solution, therefore, lies in the algebraic economic model, which needs to be modified to reflect the nature of economic data. To undertake this modification to the algebraic model, we need to establish the likely role of the economic model in generating the economic data. In other words, we need to explain the particular feature of the relevant data which the model purports to show. This is a deductive process. To perform the necessary modifications, we need a set of assumptions concerning a feasible data generation process in the underlying economic model. To fix these ideas we consider the simple household consumption/ income model again. Thus, when:

$$Y = a + bX$$

This algebraic relationship is an exact one, showing a one-to-one relationship between income X and consumption Y. So, given a value for X (income), the model generates a unique value for Y (household consumption). In other words, for a particular level of income, according to this relationship, there can be only one level of household consumption expenditure. This is inconsistent with the underlying data, which show that households with identical income levels seldom have identical consumption levels over specific periods of time. What could be a true picture is that at any specific level of income, there is a distribution, or a range, of unknown consumption expenditure levels. This type of relationship is depicted in Figure 2.1, which shows a hypothetical distribution of monthly consumption levels at different levels of monthly income.

For each level of income, it is reasonable to assume that there would be a probability distribution of associated consumption levels for households. Notice that we talk about likely probability distributions because we do not know the exact level of monthly consumption expenditure of each household. The proposition here is that households with the same level of income, say X_1, are likely to have different levels of consumption. Consumption levels are likely to be different because there are many factors other than income (interest rates, size of family, location, habits, savings behaviour, etc.) which influence monthly expenditure. It is difficult to measure the net influence of all these economic and behavioural factors, but they do exist, leading to probability distributions of consumption expenditure at each level of income. We aim to go deeper, making assumptions concerning how each of these probability distributions could have been generated. A probability distribution is identified by three basic characteristics. These are the shape, the central value, and a measure of dispersion of values around the centre of the distribution.

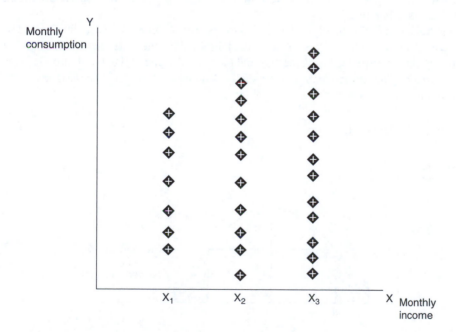

Figure 2.1 Consumption and income.

2.2 The standard assumptions of the data generation process (DGP)

1   *The normality assumption* In the absence of any specific information concerning the shape of the distribution, it is customary to assume that for each level of the independent variable (income levels), the dependent variable (consumption expenditure) is normally and independently distributed. This assumption is depicted in Figure 2.2.

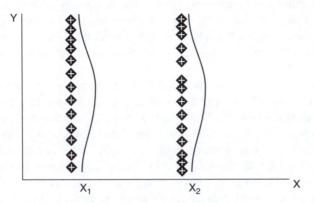

Figure 2.2 Normally distributed levels data for the variables.

Characteristics of a normal distribution

A consideration of the basic features of a normal distribution allows further exploration of the normality assumption. A normal distribution is bell-shaped and symmetrical around its central value (see Figure 2.3).

The central value of the distribution is called the *expected value* and is usually denoted by $E(X)$. Half of the distribution lies to the left of $E(X)$, with the other half to its right. A measure of average dispersion of values around the central value of the distribution is given by the *variance of the distribution* and is usually denoted by Var (X). The variance of the distribution is defined as:

$$\text{Var}(X) = E[X - E(X)]^2 \tag{2.1}$$

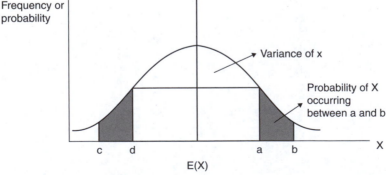

Figure 2.3 A normally distributed variable.

The variance of the distribution has no meaningful unit of measurement, so to generate a meaningful measure of the dispersion of values around the central value, the square root of variance is used in practice. This is called the *standard deviation* of the distribution, denoted by SD(X), and the unit of measurement is the same as X, the variable under consideration. The area under the curve between any two points shows the probability of X occurring between those two points (see Figure 2.3).

Hence, $Pr(a \leq X \leq b)$ = area under the normal curve between a and b.

An important property of the normal distribution is that the probability of X occurring between a and b would be the same as X occurring between c and d, provided the distance of these points from the centre of the distribution is the same (measured in units of standard deviations). That is, the probability of X occurring between c and d to the left of E(X) is the same as the probability of X occurring between a and b to the right of X, as long as (c–d) and (a–b) are the same distance from the centre of distribution. What are the implications of these characteristics of the normal distribution for the data generation process concerning the household consumption/income model? First, it is assumed that most of the consumption expenditure is concentrated around the average consumption expenditure, or expected expenditure, at any particular income level. Second, the consumption expenditure of households occur 'above average' or 'below the average', depending on each household's circumstances and behaviour. However, the probability of consumption levels occurring 'above average' is the same as the probability of consumption levels occurring below the expected consumption level for each class of income. Third, at each level of income, the probability that household consumption expenditure lies between a certain range, say above expected consumption, is the same as the probability of that household consumption expenditure being between a certain range below the expected consumption expenditure, provided that the two ranges of consumption expenditure have the same distance/difference from expected consumption. These are the main implications of the normality assumption. They can only be considered valid if the normality assumption is confirmed through diagnostic testing.

2   *The expected value of each distribution is determined by the algebraic economic model*
   This is an important assumption, and it is being made to bring the economic model to the forefront of analysis. If the model is correctly specified and is consistent with the data generation process, then its role is to show the central value/expected value for each distribution. Given this framework, the algebraic economic model represents the average value or the expected value for the dependent variable, at any specific value of the independent variable. Using the consumption/income model, the expected level of consumption for any given level of income is assumed to be determined by this simple relationship. Given X_1 is a level of income, the expected level of consumption expenditure $E(Y/X_1)$ (reads expected consumption given X_1 level of income) is determined by the algebraic model as follows:

$E(Y/X_1) = a + b\,X_1$ [at the centre of distribution of Y given X_1], similarly the expected level of consumption expenditure given the level of income of X_2 is:

$$E(Y/X_2) = a + b\,X_2 \qquad (2.2)$$

The straight line $E(Y/X) = a + b\,X$ then goes through the centre of each distribution, connecting the expected levels of consumption expenditure at various income levels. This is depicted in

Figure 2.4. The line $E(Y/X) = a + bX$ is called the *population regression line* or *function*. This line is unknown and it is to be estimated on the basis of a set of observations/data on Y and X. Notice that this assumption has to be tested and confirmed later using appropriate diagnostic tests. All that is being said is that, provided the algebraic model is correct or is based on a valid economic theory, then it shows the average level for the dependent variable, at various levels for the independent variable. This assumption also enables us to represent each observation in terms of the expected value of each distribution and the deviation of the data points from the expected level of distribution. For example, the consumption expenditure of the ith household, corresponding to the income class X_i can be represented as follows:

$$Y_i = E(Y/X_i) + u_i \tag{2.3}$$

where u_i shows the deviations of the *i*th household's consumption expenditure from the expected/average expenditure of households with the income of X_i. The u_i term can be positive, in which case households consume more than average, or it can be negative, implying that the *i*th household consumes less than expected consumption for the income group X_i. We can substitute for $E(Y_i/X_i)$ in terms of the algebraic model to obtain:

$$Y_i = a + bX_i + u_i \tag{2.4}$$

$a + b X_i$ = the algebraic economic model showing expected consumption at income level X_i, and u_i = deviation of *i*th household consumption expenditure from the expected consumption for the income group of X_i.

In this simple model, u_i represents the net influence of all factors/variables other than income on the *i*th household consumption expenditures. Some of these factors are economic factors influencing consumption such as interest rates, wealth, and possibly rates of inflation. For household consumption expenditure, family size is also an important factor. In a more sophisticated model, these factors should be included. In such cases, there are a number of independent variables, (income, interest rates and wealth) each influencing consumption expenditure independently. Other factors that are captured by u_i, however, cannot be measured quantitatively; these include tastes and the behavioural patterns of households. These factors essentially influence the consumption expenditure in unsystematic, random ways. In other words, we cannot precisely measure all these net influences. Given this, the econometric relationship is stochastic in nature. That is, given a level of income such as X_i we are likely to get a range of values for consumption expenditure, because the influence of random factors, as captured by the term u_i, are different for different households. The term u_i is called a *random disturbance term*. Its value occurs randomly and its inclusion into analysis disturbs an otherwise deterministic algebraic economic model.

Using the idea/concept of the disturbance term, we can now present the consumption expenditure of each household (the data points) as follows:

$$Y_i = a + bX_i + u_i \tag{2.5}$$

$i = 1, 2, 3,...; $ (n = number of observations)

Hence, each observation obtained from household consumption expenditure population can be decomposed as a sum of two elements. The expected consumption for the income class (i.e. $E(Y/X_i)$ and the deviation from the expected value which reflects the special characteristics/behaviour for that household. This model is called an *econometric model*. It is a modified economic model. The economic model is modified through inclusion of the disturbance term u_i, to reflect the stochastic/random nature of economic data. This econometric model is compatible with the data and although it is based on a deterministic algebraic economic model, it can be used with stochastic economic data to quantify the underlying economic relationships.

Note that the data generation assumptions can also be made in terms of the distribution of the disturbance term. In particular, the probability distribution of each consumption expenditure is generated through the probability distribution of the disturbance term. In other words, if we assume that consumption expenditure is normally distributed, then by implication, the disturbance terms associated with each value of the independent variable are also normally distributed. With regard to the second data generation assumption, this implies that the expected value for each distribution of the disturbance term must be zero. To see this, consider the simple econometric model again:

$$Y_i = E(Y/X_i) + u_i \tag{2.6}$$

Now taking the average/expected value of both sides, we have:

$$E(Y_i/X_i) = E(Y/X_i) + E(u_i/X_i) \tag{2.7}$$

Notice that the average of Y_i, given X_i, is $E(Y_i/X_i)$ and that the average/expected value of $E(Y_i/X_i)$ is in fact itself, since there is only one expected value! Therefore, by implication, $E(u_i/X_i)$ must be zero, for (2.7) to hold. This is called the zero mean assumption. So the net influence of all factors other than the independent variable (income), when averaged out, are zero, provided that the underlying model is correctly specified.

3   *The independence assumption* How are the data points/observations of the consumption expenditure generated? The standard assumption here is that the dependent variable (consumption) and, by implication, the disturbance term, are independently distributed. In other words, the consumption expenditure of different households is independent of each other. Therefore, factors captured by the disturbance terms for different households are independent of each other. For example, consumption expenditure of the ith household is independent of consumption expenditure of the jth household; symbolically, the assumption of independence is usually written as follows:

$$Cov(u_i, u_j) = 0 \quad i \neq j \tag{2.8}$$

Where cov is short for covariance. Covariance measures the degree of association between two random variables. This assumption is often termed the non-autocorrelation assumption, which implies no association between the values of the same variable (disturbance term).

4   *The constant variance assumption* Now we need an assumption concerning the dispersion of the values around the central value of each distribution. In the absence of any information concerning the variance of each distribution and the way it might be determined, the standard assumption usually made is that the variance of the distribution

of the dependent variable/disturbance term is constant and does not change across distributions. In terms of the consumption/income model, this assumption implies that the spread/variance of distribution of the consumption expenditure does not change across the different income groups. In other words, the variance of the distribution does not change with the level of independent variable income. This is a strong assumption, and in practice it often breaks down, particularly when using cross-section data. This is because, in this type of data, independent variables tend to change significantly from one distribution/group to the next. Significant variations in the levels, or scales, of the independent variables might well in turn influence the variance/spread of each distribution, generating changes in the variance across distributions. As with the other assumptions about the data generation process, we therefore need to check/test the appropriateness of this assumption when analysing the empirical model.

2.3 The two-variable classical normal linear regression (CNLR) model and its assumptions

We are now in position to present the classical normal two-variable linear regression model, which we have developed on the basis of the above assumptions. This model shows:

- a linear relationship between two economic/financial variables;
- the direction of the causation is from right to left, that is the independent variable, according to the theory, directly causes/influences the dependent variable and not the other way round;
- the data generation process is stochastic, determined by the assumptions concerning the distribution of the disturbance term/the dependent variable;
- the classical normal model is distinguished by the normality assumption made to explain the shape of the probability distribution of the data generation process. We use the same notation as the consumption/income model, representing the dependent variable by Y and the independent variable by X. The model may be presented as follows:

$$Y_i = a + bX_i + u_i \qquad i = 1, 2, 3, ..., n \text{ (n observations)} \qquad (2.9)$$

Y_i is distributed normally and independently around the expected value of $E(Y_i/X_i) = a + bX_i$, with a constant variance. We use some standard notation to present the standard assumptions as follows:

$$Y_i \sim NID(a + bX_i, \sigma^2)$$

where   N = normal
   I = independently
   D = distributed
   $E(Y_i/X_i) = a + bX_i$, the expected value of each distribution
   σ^2 = notation for a constant variance

Alternatively, we may state the assumption in terms of the distribution of the disturbance term u_i:

$$u_i \sim NID(0, \sigma^2) \text{ ; where}$$

$$E\left[Y_i - E(Y/X_i)\right]^2 = E[ui]^2 = \sigma^2 \text{ (constant variance)}$$

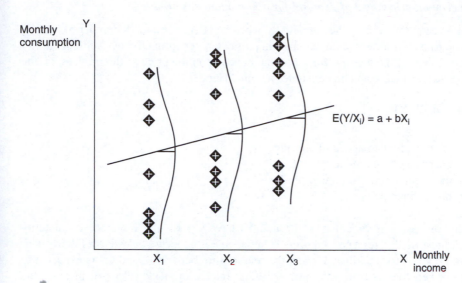

Figure 2.4 A linear consumption-income model.

Notice that the expected value of the disturbance term associated with each of the independent variables is assumed to be zero. This model is depicted in Figure 2.4.

The straight line $E(Y/X_i) = a + bX_i$ is called the *population regression line* or, sometimes, the population regression function. The aim of the analysis is to estimate this population regression line, that is, to estimate a and b, on the basis of a set of observations on Y and X. Before we consider this issue, we first expand the theoretical model to include more independent variables. In practice, it is seldom the case that only one independent variable influences the dependent variable.

2.4 Towards the formulation of a general single-equation regression model

The two-variable linear regression model presented above is essentially a theoretical model with little practical use. It is used to explain the basic features of an econometric model and assumptions. Because there are only two variables involved, one can use a simple two-dimensional diagram to present the model. In practical applications, it is seldom the case that a particular economic variable under consideration (dependent variable) is determined on the basis of only one other economic variable (independent variable). The relationships between economic variables are much more involved and complex and one needs to make use of all the information provided by economic theory to specify an econometric model. In most applications, the model under consideration is determined by a number of other variables, based upon logical reasoning and economic theory.

For practical purposes, we must therefore abandon the restrictive features of the two-variable model in favour of models where there are two or more variables that appear as regressors. These models form the basis for almost all empirical investigations in economics. The main feature of these models is that there are a number of variables, each exerting a systematic influence on the dependent variable under consideration. For example:

2.4.1 *An econometric model of demand for a homogeneous product*

According to economic theory the demand for a product depends upon a number of factors, each exerting a partial influence on demand. In particular, according to the traditional utility maximisation theory, the demand for a product depends on the price of the product, on the prices of related products, and on consumer income. Hence:

$$Q^D = f(P, P^*, Y)$$

where:
Q^D = the quantity demanded of a product
P = the price of the product
P^* = the average price of related products
Y = money income.

Each of the independent variables (P, P^* and Y) have a particular influence on quantity demanded. In particular, for a normal product, a rise in P is expected to lead to a fall in quantity demand (Q^D), ceteris paribus. Hence, the relationship between P and Q^D is expected to be inverse or negative. A rise in the price of other related products (P^*) will increase the demand for the product if these are close substitutes, and reduce demand if these goods are complementary. Finally, a rise in income is expected to lead to an increase in quantity demanded (a positive relationship).

We now modify this model to generate a simple econometric model for the purpose of empirical analysis. The necessary steps in this modification are as follows:

1   *Specification of the economic model* We specify the functional form of the economic model. There are many options; however, the two most popular forms are linear and log-linear models of demand.

A linear model of demand may be specified as follows:

$$Q^D = \beta_1 + \beta_2 P + \beta_3 P^* + \beta_4 Y \qquad (2.10)$$

Notice that the model is linear in terms of its parameters β_1, β_2, β_3 and β_4

In a log-linear specification each variable is expressed in a natural logarithmic form, as follows:

$$\log Q^D = \beta_1 + \beta_2 \log P + \beta_3 \log P^* + \beta_4 \log Y \qquad (2.11)$$

Notice that the model is linear in its parameters since there are no powers.

The 'correct' functional form is not known at this stage and we therefore conduct a number of diagnostic tests to see whether or not the chosen functional form is consistent with the data.

2   *Data generation process (DGP) assumptions* The next step in developing an econometric model is to specify the data-generating assumptions. That is, we need to explain how each observation on quantity demanded might have been generated. The basic idea is the same as in the case of the two-variable model. We assume that for each set of values of the regressors (P, P^* and Y), we get a probability distribution for quantity demanded. These probability distributions are generated as a result of influences of random factors on quantity demanded. For example, random factors such as changes in

tastes, fashion and the behaviour of buyers. The net influence of these factors is captured by the disturbance term u. The data generation assumptions are then concerned with the shape of each conditional probability distribution, the expected values of each distribution, and the variance of each distribution.

Following the standard assumptions developed previously, we assume that for each set of values of the regressors (P, P*, Y), the associated disturbance term will be normally and independently distributed with a zero mean and a constant variance, say σ^2. Given these assumptions, an econometric model of demand, based on a log-linear specification may be written as follows:

$$\log Q_t^D = \beta_1 + \beta_2 \log P_t + \beta_3 \log P_t^* + \beta_4 \log Y_t + u_t \tag{2.12}$$

With $u_t \sim NID(0, \sigma^2)$; for $t = 1, 2, \ldots n$

Thus, each observation on quantity demand (or its log) can be written as the sum of two components: a systematic component showing the expected level of demand for the product at any given level of prices and incomes, so:

$$E(\log Q_t^D / \log P_t, \log P_t^*, \log Y_t) = \beta_1 + \beta_2 \log Pt + \beta_3 \log P_t^* + \beta_4 \log Y_t \tag{2.13}$$

and a stochastic component, u_t, showing the net influence of factors other than prices and incomes on quantity demanded. These random factors, for example, changes in the behaviour of buyers, might generate deviations from the expected level of demand, causing the level of demand to be less/more than expected levels. The disturbance term u_t is added to the expected level of demand to account for these random deviations. We can present the model graphically, using a two-dimensional diagram, by allowing only one regressor (e.g. P_t) to change and keeping the other two regressors constant.

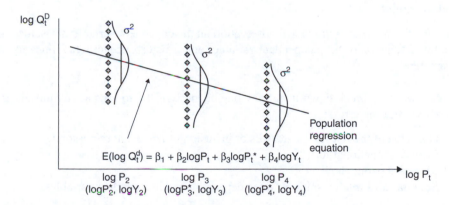

Figure 2.5 A log-linear model of demand.

2.5 The multiple linear regression model and its assumptions: the classical normal linear regression model (CNLRM)

We are now in the position to generalise the presentation of the multiple linear regression model. It is customary to present the dependent variable by 'Y', the regressors by 'X' and the parameters of the model by β.

According to economic theory, the dependent variable Y is a function of 'k' regressors:

i.e. $Y = f(X_1, X_2, X_3, ..., X_k)$.

To present a general linear econometric equation, we assume that there exists a linear relationship between the dependent and independent variables (linearity in parameters). Hence:

$$Y = \beta_1 X_1 + \beta_2 X_2 + \beta_3 X_3 + ... + \beta_k X_k \tag{2.14}$$

With this specification, each observation on the dependent variable can be written as the sum of two components, as follows:

$$Y_t = \beta_1 X_{1t} + \beta_2 X_{2t} + \beta_3 X_{3t} + ... + \beta_k X_{kt} + u_t \tag{2.15}$$

where subscript 't' indicates the relevant observation at time 't'. To allow for an intercept term, we allow the value of X_{1t} to be unity, i.e.

$$Y_t = \beta_1 + \beta_2 X_{2t} + \beta_3 X_{3t} + ... + \beta_k X_{kt} + u_t; \qquad (t = 1, 2, 3, ...) \tag{2.16}$$

Alternatively, we can use the subscript of 'i' instead of 't', i.e. (cross-section data)

$$Y_i = \beta_1 + \beta_2 X_{2i} + \beta_3 X_{3i} + ... + \beta_k X_{ki} + u_i; \qquad (i = 1, 2, 3, ...) \tag{2.17}$$

2.6 A summary of the key assumptions of the multiple linear regression model

1   *The specification assumption* Each observation on the dependent variable is assumed to be a linear function of 'k' independent variables and a disturbance term (u) (linearity in parameters).

This assumption may break down under any one or more of the following circumstances, producing specification errors:

    a   Omission of the relevant regressors or inclusion of irrelevant regressors;
    b   Incorrect functional form;
    c   Changing parameters;
    d   Simultaneous relationships between dependent and independent variables.

2   *Zero mean assumption* The expected value of each distribution of the disturbance term is zero, i.e. $E(u_t | X_{1t}, X_{2t}, ...) = 0$ for all 't', which implies that the expected value of the dependent variable is determined by the linear economic model, i.e.

$$E(Y_t | X_{2t}, X_{3t}, ...) = \beta_1 + \beta_2 X_{2i} + \beta_3 X_{3i} + ... \tag{2.18}$$

The breakdown of this assumption occurs with incorrect specification of the economic model, such as the omission of relevant regressors.

3   *The homoscedasticity (constant variance) assumption* The variance of each conditional distribution of the disturbance term (or the dependent variable) is the same and equal to an unknown constant variance (σ^2) i.e.

$$\text{Var}(u_t \mid X_{2t}, X_{3t}, ...) = \sigma^2 \text{ for all 't'} \tag{2.19}$$

also $\text{Var}(Y_t \mid X_{2t}, X_{3t}, ...) = \sigma^2$ for all 't'   (2.20)

The failure of this assumption is known as heteroscedasticity. Heteroscedasticity usually occurs in cross-sectional data analysis where changes in the magnitude of one or more regressors cause variations in the variance of the dependent variable/ disturbance term.

4   *The non-autocorrelation assumption* The disturbance terms are not correlated, so there is no association between any pair of disturbance terms 't and s', hence:

$$\text{cov}(u_t, u_s) = 0 \text{ for all } t \neq s \tag{2.21}$$

This assumption implies that the values of the dependent variables are independent of each other. The breakdown of this assumption is known as *autocorrelation*. It usually occurs in time series analysis due to prolonged influence of random shocks which are captured by the disturbance terms. Autocorrelation could also be due to the specification errors known as dynamic misspecification.

5   *Independent variables are non-random and are fixed in repeated sampling*. In practice, this assumption can fail due to:

a   One or more of the independent variables being measured with random errors. This phenomenon frequently occurs in empirical analysis and there is a need to check for random errors by statistical tests.

b   Some or all of the independent variables contained in the model may not be independent of the dependent variable. This phenomenon occurs when dependent and independent variables are *jointly determined*. In this situation, a single-equation model is not an adequate presentation of the data generation process and the independent variables may not be fixed in repeated sampling.

6   *Lack of perfect multicollinearity assumption*. Multicollinearity occurs when there exists a near, or perfect, linear association between any two or more of the explanatory variables in the model. In this situation, it is not possible to measure the separate impact of each independent variable on the dependent variable. Multicollinearity essentially reflects problems with data sets rather than the model. It usually occurs when there are little variations in the values of the regressors over the sample period. To reduce the extent of the multicollinearity we must ensure that there are sufficient variations in the values of the regressors.

There is, however, always a certain degree of multicollinearity existing in econometric models due to the nature of economic data. The stated assumption implies that it is possible to measure the separate impact of each regressor on the dependent variable.

7   *The normality assumption*. For each set of values of independent variables/ regressors, the dependent variable/the disturbance terms are normally distributed. In certain

situations, especially where the data contains a significant number of outliers, the assumption of normality fails and the normal procedures of model evaluation are no longer valid.

The model and the assumptions may be written as follows:

Time series data: $Y_t = \beta_1 + \beta_2 X_{2t} + \beta_3 X_{3t} + ... + \beta_k X_{kt} + u_t, u_t \sim NID(0, \sigma^2)$ (2.22)

Cross-section data: $Y_i = \beta_1 + \beta_2 X_{2i} + \beta_3 X_{3i} + ... + \beta_k X_{ki} + u_i$, for $t = 1, 2...$

$u_i \sim NID(0, \sigma^2)$ for $i = 1, 2,...$ (2.23)

This model and its assumptions constitute the general form of a single-equation regression model. This general specification of the regression model is sometimes referred to in the literature as the *classical normal linear regression model* (CNLRM).

2.7 A summary of key issues

- Economic models are deterministic, representing simple one-to-one relationships between variables. That is, given a set of values for the independent variables, they are formulated to generate only one specific value for the dependent variable under consideration.
- Economic data are stochastic and random. That is, for each given set of values for the independent variables of the model, a range of values for the dependent variable is likely to be observed in the real world. For example, given a level of household income of say £2000 per month, there would be a range of values of household monthly consumption expenditure associated with this level of income, for example, a range of monthly expenditure between £1500–£2100. Given this observation, we say that for each set of values of the independent variables, there is likely to exist a probability distribution of the dependent variable, showing the probability of each particular range of values of the dependent variable.
- The probability distribution of each dependent variable is generated due to the fact that in the real world where data is generated and collected, there are many factors other than those specified in a regression model, as independent variables that influence the dependent variable. Many of these factors are randomly generated, giving rise to a probability distribution of the dependent variable. The combined impact of these variables is assumed to be captured by a random term called a random disturbance term.
- The probability distribution of the dependent variable for each set of values of the independent variables is similar to the probability distribution of the random disturbance term. It is common practice to specify the assumptions of the model in terms of the probability distribution of the disturbance term.
- Given that we do not have any information about these probability distributions and, therefore, about how the observed data are generated, we need a set of assumptions about the characteristics of these probability distributions. It is assumed that the mean of each distribution is on the regression line. This line is called the population regression function. Under this framework, the linear economic model shows the average (expected) value of the dependent variable for each set of values of the independent variables. The aim of the analysis is to estimate this average relationship.

- Other assumptions about the data generation process, which are necessary to start the process of empirical analysis, are: (a) the variance of each distribution of the dependent (or disturbance term) is constant, (b) the distributions are independent of each other, and (c) the shape of each distribution can be approximated by normal distributions. These assumptions, together with the linear regression model, give rise to the classical normal linear regression model.

Review questions

1 Distinguish between a deterministic and a stochastic relationship. Explain why economic models must be modified for use with economic data for the purpose of empirical analysis?

2 Explain what you understand by each of the following:

    a   a random variable
    b   dependent variable
    c   independent variables (regressors)
    d   intercept term
    e   slope parameter.

3 Explain what you understand by each of the following:

    a   a probability distribution
    b   the expected value/mean of a probability distribution
    c   the variance of a probability distribution
    d   observations are distributed independently of each other.

4 Explain the key characteristics of a normal distribution. Why is this distribution so popular in empirical analysis?

5 Explain what you understand by the data generation process (DGP). Why do we need assumptions about the DGP?

6 Explain what you understand by a disturbance term. Why is this term included in economic models? What does it represent and what is its role?

7 Explain the meaning of each of the assumptions of the classical normal linear regression model (CNLRM). Why are these assumptions necessary?

8 Construct a simple econometric model for each of the following:

    a   aggregate personal consumption expenditure in an economy
    b   aggregate investment expenditure in an economy
    c   demand for beef
    d   household monthly consumption expenditure.

In each case explain the role of any disturbance term included in the model. Why are these terms necessary? Explain the meaning of each one of the standard assumptions concerning this term and discuss what might happen in the event that each one of these assumptions breaks down.

9 Construct a log-linear econometric model of demand for textiles. Explain the underlying economic theory and discuss the meaning of each one of the parameters included in your model. Explain why a log-linear specification of the model is normally preferred in applied work. Discuss the role of the disturbance term included in your model and explain the meaning of each one of the standard assumptions concerning this term.

3 Estimating single-equation regression models

Basic ideas, concepts and methods

INTRODUCTION

Having developed an econometric model, the next task of the econometrician is to estimate the unknown parameters of the model. To this end, the econometrician must collect a data set containing observations on the dependent and independent variables of the model, and use the data for the estimation purposes. Choosing a right method of estimation is critical and merits special attention. This chapter explains how a method of estimation is chosen and is used in practice.

Key topics

- Estimators and point estimates
- The sampling distribution of estimators
- The ordinary least squares (OLS) method of estimation
- Monte Carlo studies
- The maximum likelihood (ML) method of estimation

3.1 Estimation of a single-equation regression model: basic ideas and concepts

Consider the following general linear regression model introduced previously.

$$Y_t = \beta_1 + \beta_2 X_{2t} + \beta_3 X_{3t} + ... + \beta_k X_{kt} + u_t; \ (t = 1, 2, 3, ...), \ u_t \sim \text{NID}(0, \sigma^2) \tag{3.1}$$

The model implies that each observation on the dependent variable Y, can be written as a linear sum of 'k' independent variables (linear in parameters) and a disturbance term (u).

Moreover, the expected value of Y, for any given values of the independent variables, is determined by the deterministic part of the model:

$$E(Y_t \mid X_{2t}, X_{3t}, ...) = \beta_1 + \beta_2 X_{2i} + \beta_3 X_{3i} + ... + \beta_k X_{kt} \tag{3.2}$$

Each slope parameter, $\beta_2, \beta_3, \ldots \beta_k$, measures the impact of a marginal change in the corresponding independent variable on the expected value of Y, while the other regressors are held constant. For example, β_2 shows the impact of one unit (a marginal change) in X_2 on the expected value of Y, while $X_3 \ldots X_k$ are held constant, i.e.

$$\beta_2, = \frac{\Delta E(Y_t \mid ...)}{\Delta X_{2t}} \quad \bigg| \quad X_3 \, ... \, X_k \, (\text{constant})$$

or in general:

$$\beta_i, = \frac{\Delta E(Y_t \mid X_{2t} ... X_{kt})}{\Delta X_{it}} \quad \bigg| \quad \begin{array}{l} \text{all other regressors} \\ \text{for } i = 2, ... \, k \end{array}$$

Given this interpretation, the slope parameters are sometimes called the *partial regression coefficients*. These parameters, along with the intercept parameter, are unknown. The first task of the empirical analysis is to quantify, or estimate, each of the unknown parameters, on the basis of a set of observations on the dependent and independent variables. For example, the estimated parameters for β_1, β_2, β_3 and β_k can be denoted as $\hat{\beta}_1$, $\hat{\beta}_2$, $\hat{\beta}_3$ and $\hat{\beta}_k$.

These are point estimates of the unknown parameters and are obtained from a sample of observations on the dependent variable and the independent variables. The actual process by which the numerical values of these parameters are obtained is discussed subsequently. At this stage it is sufficient to say that our aim is to generate estimates for the unknown parameters from a sample of observations on the dependent and independent variables. Recall that the expected value of the dependent variable is given by the expression:

$$E(Y_t \mid X_{1t}, X_{2t}, ...) = \beta_1 + \beta_2 X_{2i} + \beta_3 X_{3i} + ... + \beta_k X_{kt} \tag{3.3}$$

Once the intercept term (β_1) and partial regression coefficients ($\beta_2 \, ... \, \beta_k$) are estimated, we substitute for these estimates into Equation (3.3) to generate the expected value of the dependent variable for any given values of the independent variables. The estimated expected value of the dependent variable is denoted by $\hat{Y}_t$ and can be expanded as follows:

$$\hat{Y}_t = \hat{\beta}_1 + \hat{\beta}_2 X_{2t} + \hat{\beta}_3 X_{3t} + ... + \hat{\beta}_k X_{kt}; \qquad t = 1, 2, 3, ... ; \tag{3.4}$$

In practice, $\hat{\beta}_1^*$, $\hat{\beta}_k^*$ are numerical values and to generate the estimated expected value of the dependent variable we also need to substitute into Equation (3.4) the values of the independent variable. For example, let us consider the following hypothetical example. Suppose there are four parameters, and on the basis of a set of observations on the dependent and independent variables, we obtain:

$$\hat{\beta}_1 = 1, \hat{\beta}_2 = 2, \hat{\beta}_3 = 3, \text{and } \hat{\beta}_4 = 4$$

Thus, the estimated expected values for Y is:

$$\hat{Y}_t = 1 + 2X_{2t} + 3X_{3t} + 4X_{4t} \tag{3.5}$$

To generate a specific value for the $\hat{Y}_t$ variable, we substitute a specific set of values for the independent variables in Equation (3.5). For example, the estimated expected value of the dependent variable ($\hat{Y}_t$) when $X_2 = 100$, $X_3 = 300$ and $X_4 = 400$ can be calculated as follows:

$$\hat{Y}_t = 1 + 2(100) + 3(300) + 4(400) = 1 + 200 + 900 + 1600 = 2701 \qquad (3.6)$$

In addition, knowledge of the parameter estimates enables us to provide information on the impact of a marginal change (a one unit change) in the value of any one of the regressors on the estimated expected value of the dependent variable, while all other regressors are held constant. In the hypothetical example, $\hat{\beta}_2 = 2$.

$$\hat{\beta}_2 = \frac{\Delta \hat{Y}_t}{\Delta X_{2t}} \bigg| = 2$$

Therefore, when X_2 changes by one unit, $\hat{Y}_t$ changes by two units in the same direction as X_2. Similarly:

$$\hat{\beta}_3 = \frac{\Delta \hat{Y}_t}{\Delta X_{3t}} \bigg| = 3$$

$$\hat{\beta}_4 = \frac{\Delta \hat{Y}_t}{\Delta X_{4t}} \bigg| = 4$$

The reliability of the parameter estimates depends crucially upon whether or not the econometric/regression model and its assumptions are consistent with the data. In particular, only when each of the assumptions is found to be consistent with the observed data, can we consider the point estimate to be reliable. The second aim of an empirical investigation is therefore to test to see whether each assumption is consistent with the data. These assumptions include those concerning model specification as well as data generation assumptions. The testing procedures that are used in practice are based on a series of diagnostic tests designed to confirm the model and its assumptions. Based upon the results of the diagnostic tests, two situations can arise:

1   We may fail to falsify each one of the assumptions. In this case, the model is consistent with the data and we proceed to test economic hypotheses implied by the economic theory/model and use the model for empirical analysis.

2   One or more assumptions will not be consistent with the data. This is pretty much a normal occurrence in practice. In this situation, on the basis of the empirical results obtained, our task is to improve the econometric model. There is, therefore, a link between economic theory and empirical analysis. Econometric analysis not only provides empirical content to abstract economic models but also helps us to understand complex economic relationships. This process means that we modify and improve economic theories to achieve a better understanding of the data generation process and, hence, economic issues.

3.1.1 Estimation

Given a multiple linear regression model of the form:

$$Y_t = \beta_1 + \beta_2 X_{2t} + \beta_3 X_{3t} + \ldots + \beta_k X_{kt} + u_t \;,\; u_t \sim \text{NID}(0,\, \sigma^2) \qquad \text{for } t = 1, 2, \ldots n \qquad (3.7)$$

The task is to estimate the unknown parameters β_1, β_2, β_3 . . ., β_k on the basis of a set of observations (such as those presented in Table 3.1) on dependent and independent variables (i.e. Y_t and X_{2t} . . . X_{kt}). A general data set is presented in Table 3.1, as follows:

Table 3.1 A general data set

Y	X_2	X_3	X_4	....	X_k
Y_{t1}	X_{21}	X_{31}	X_{41}	....	X_{k1}
Y_{t2}	X_{22}	X_{32}	X_{42}	....	X_{k2}
..	..	..	..	....	..
..	..	..	..	....	..
Y_{tn}	X_{2n}	X_{3n}	X_{4n}	....	X_{kn}

Each row depicts the observations obtained on the dependent and independent variables (for example, the first row is the first set of collected observations on the dependent and independent variables).

3.2 Estimators and their sampling distributions

We need to convert the observations on the dependent and independent variables into numerical values for the unknown parameters β_1, β_2, β_3 . . ., β_k. A mechanism useful for this purpose is called an *estimator*. In particular, an estimator is a mathematical formula which is used to convert the observations on the dependent and independent variables into numerical values of the unknown parameters. The resulting numerical values are called *point estimates*. Each parameter has its own estimator which can be used to generate point estimates. Conventionally, estimators are shown by a hat (^) on top of the parameter.

$\hat{\beta}_1 = f_1$ (observation on dependent and independent variable) = point estimate of
    unknown β_1

$\hat{\beta}_2 = f_2$ (observation on dependent and independent variable) = point estimate of
    unknown β_2

. . .

$\hat{\beta}_k = f_k$ (observation on dependent and independent variable) = point estimate of
    unknown β_k

where f_i (i = 1 . . . k) denotes a particular mathematical formula.

How do econometricians determine these estimators? Econometricians seek reliable point estimates of the unknown parameters. The reliability of an estimator cannot be judged on the basis of only one point estimate since the actual value of the parameter is unknown. Under this condition, the only way to judge an estimator is to look at the performance of the estimator under repeated estimation/sampling procedures.

This is a hypothetical procedure used to generate the sampling distribution of each estimator. Econometricians will then select an estimator whose sampling distribution has a number of desirable/optimum properties.

3.2.1 The sampling distributions of estimators

To fix these ideas, let us investigate how to generate the sampling distribution of an estimator by a hypothetical repeated sampling procedure.

The basic idea is to retain the value of the regressors fixed from sample to sample, obtaining data on the dependent variable. In general, because of the influence of factors other than regressors on the dependent variable (captured by the disturbance term), we are likely to get different values for the dependent variable from sample to sample, although the values of the regressors are fixed. If we repeat this procedure a large number of times, we obtain a large sample data containing the same values of the regressors, but different values for the dependent variable, as in Table 3.2.

In Table 3.2, the values of the regressors are fixed at certain levels. Each column shows the observations on the dependent and independent variables in this hypothetical sampling procedure. The first row shows the first set of observations, the second row the second set of observations and the final row the *m*th set of observations. The interesting point here is that although the values of the regressors are kept fixed from sample to sample, as it is shown in Table 3.2, we are likely to obtain different values for the dependent variable from sample to sample due to the fact that the dependent variable contains the influence of the random disturbance term. These values of the dependent variable are presented by Y_{ij}, where 'i' is the number of observations and 'j' is the number in the sample. For example, Y_{21} is the second observation on Y in the first sample, and so on.

In this hypothetical experiment, if we substitute for each sample data in an estimator (say $\hat{\beta}_k$ – the estimator of β_k) we get a large number of point estimates for β_k. More specifically, we can write:

$$\hat{\beta}_k = f_k(Y_{11},\dots,Y_{n1}; X_{21},X_{22},\dots,X_{2n}\dots) \rightarrow \hat{\beta}_{k1} \text{ point estimate obtained from sample 1}$$

(3.8)

$$\hat{\beta}_k = f_k(Y_{12},\dots,Y_{n2}; X_{21}, X_{22},\dots,X_{2n}\dots) \rightarrow \hat{\beta}_{k2} \text{ point estimate obtained from sample 2}$$

(3.9)

$$\hat{\beta}_k = f_k(Y_{1m}.,Y_{nm}; X_{21},X_{22},\dots,X_{2n}\dots) \rightarrow \hat{\beta}_{km} \text{ point estimate obtained from sample m}$$

(3.10)

Table 3.2 Sample values of regressors and independent variables

Sample 1				Sample 2				Sample m			
Y	X_2	X_3	X_4	Y	X_2	X_3	X_4	Y	X_2	..	X_m
Y_{11}	X_{21}^*	X_{31}^*	X_{41}^*	Y_{12}	X_{21}^*	X_{31}^*	X_{41}	Y_{1m}	X_{21}^*		X_{m1}^*
Y_{21}	X_{22}^*	X_{32}	X_{42}	Y_{22}	X_{22}^*	X_{32}		Y_{2m}	X_{22}^*		X_{m2}^*
..	..	..	..	..	..	..	..	..	..		..
..	..	..	..	..	..	..	..	..	..		..
..	..	..	..	..	..	..	..	..	..		..
Y_{n1}	X_{2n}^*	X_{3n}^*	X_{4n}^*	Y_{n2}	X_{2n}^*	X_{3n}^*	X_{4n}^*	Y_{nm}	X_{2n}^*		X_{mn}^*

By arranging the point estimates into class intervals, it is possible to generate the sampling distribution of estimator of β_k as follows:

Class Interval	Frequency
$\beta^*_{k1} < \hat{\beta}_k < \beta^*_{k2}$	f_1
$\beta^*_{k2} < \hat{\beta}_k < \beta^*_{k3}$	f_2 ...
...	...
...	...

By measuring the relative frequency on the vertical axis and the corresponding class interval on the horizontal axis, we can obtain the histogram corresponding of the hypothetical sampling distribution, and thus generate the sampling distribution of the estimator. Figure 3.1 represents one such sampling distribution. (Note: the mid-points of each bar of the histogram are connected together to form the sampling distribution.)

   An estimator whose sampling distribution has a number of desirable characteristics given the data generation assumptions, is then considered to be 'optimal' to be used for the purpose of estimating parameters of the econometric/regression models. These desirable characteristics or properties of the sampling distributions are discussed below.

3.2.2 *Desirable properties of the sampling distribution of an estimator*

1   *Unbiasedness properties* The expected value of a distribution represents the central value of the distribution. It is considered desirable for the expected value of the sampling distribution to coincide with the true value of the unknown parameter (i.e. $E(\hat{\beta}_k) = \beta_k$). In other words, if we were to repeat the process of sampling a large number of times, the

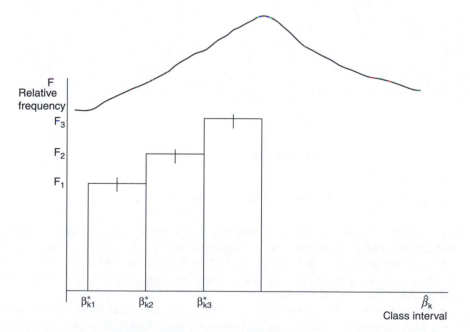

Figure 3.1 The sampling distribution of an estimator.

estimator has the property that its average/expected value (i.e. the expected value of its sampling distribution) is the same value as the unknown parameter.

The bias of the estimator in this case will be zero and the estimator is said to be unbiased. Hence: $E(\hat{\beta}_k) - \beta_k = 0$ (where $E(\hat{\beta}_k) - \beta_k$ is defined as the bias of the estimator).

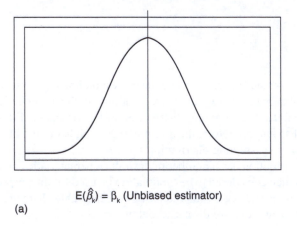

$E(\hat{\beta}_k) = \beta_k$ (Unbiased estimator)

(a)

Figure 3.2a Sampling distribution of an unbiased estimator.

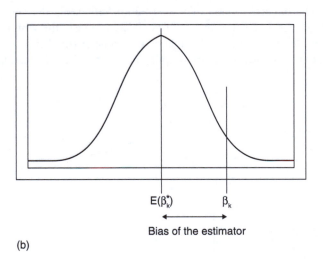

$E(\beta_k^*)$ β_k

Bias of the estimator

(b)

Figure 3.2b Sampling distribution of a biased estimator.

2   *The minimum variance property of sampling distribution* The variance of sampling distribution of an estimator provides a measure of average dispersions of values of the estimator around the expected/central value of the distribution. The standard deviation/standard error is the square root of this variance showing the dispersion of the values either side of the mean of the distribution.

It is desirable for the variance of the sampling distribution of an unbiased estimator to be as small as possible. The smaller the variance, the narrower is the sampling distribution and the more reliable an unbiased estimator would be. Neither the property of unbiasedness nor the minimum variance property on their own are sufficient to enable selection amongst the estimators. However, when they are combined, they provide a powerful criterion for selection. In particular, it is desirable for the sampling distribution of an estimator to be unbiased as well as possessing the minimum variance property. So:

$$E(\hat{\beta}_k) = \beta_k \, (\text{unbiased property})$$

$$Var(\hat{\beta}_k) = E[\beta_k - E(\beta_k^*)]^2 \, (\textit{as small as possible})$$

Such an estimator is called an *efficient* estimator. The standard deviation (i.e. the error associated with the sampling distribution) of the minimum variance estimator is less than any other unbiased estimator. Hence, most of the points generated by such an estimator would cluster around the expected value of the distribution. Such an estimator would be more reliable, that is, it is more likely to produce point estimates which are close to the true values of the unknown parameters compared to other methods of estimation, if one repeats the process of estimation many times. This is how a 'good' estimator is normally selected for the estimation of the regression models.

3   *The sufficiency property* In addition to the efficiency property, it is desirable for an estimator to make use of all sample data to generate point estimates. An estimator which uses all observations on the dependent and independent variables to generate point estimates is known as a *sufficient* estimator. All observations, including extreme values, are used to generate point estimates and no information is discarded.

A 'good' estimator is therefore defined as a sufficient estimator whose sampling distribution has a mean value that is located on the parameter to be estimated, and the dispersion of values about this central value is as small as possible. In many cases, however, it is difficult to ascertain amongst many unbiased estimators, which estimator has the smallest variance. To overcome this problem, another requirement is added to that of efficiency. In particular, it is desirable for an estimator to be a linear function of observations on the value of the dependent variable. Through linear manipulation of the data on the dependent variable, a point estimate can be generated. Such an estimator is called the *best linear unbiased estimator* (BLUE).

3.2.3 The asymptotic properties of estimators

The above properties of the sampling distribution of estimators provide a powerful selection criteria for a 'good' estimator. In particular, amongst all linear unbiased estimators, we select an estimator whose sampling distribution has the smallest variance. Such an estimator is called an efficient estimator and given the assumptions of the econometric model, we need a method of estimation which generates an efficient estimator.

In many econometric applications, however, it is not possible to identify the properties of the sampling distribution of an estimator when the sample size is small and, consequently, these selection criteria no longer apply. However, we can determine what happens to the sampling distribution as the sample size becomes larger and larger. In practice, we need to know if the estimator becomes unbiased as the sample size increases and whether the variance of the estimator has a tendency to become smaller and smaller as the sample size becomes larger and larger. The properties of the sampling distribution of an estimator obtainable only when one allows the sample size to become extremely large are called *asymptotic properties*. These properties provide the criteria for the selection of a 'good'

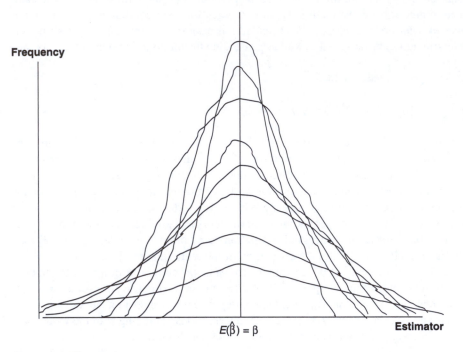

Figure 3.3 The consistency property.

estimator when the sampling distribution of the estimator and other properties cannot be determined due to the small size of the sample. In particular, the following asymptotic properties are desirable:

1   *The consistency property* The estimator is such that its asymptotic distribution becomes concentrated on the true value of the parameter as sample size becomes extremely large. So, as the sample size becomes larger and larger, the centre of the sampling distribution of the estimator shifts towards the true value of the parameter. Moreover, the spread of the distribution becomes smaller and smaller as sample size increases. In the limit, the sampling distribution simply becomes a vertical line concentrated on the true value of the parameter. This is shown in Figure 3.3.

2   *Asymptotically efficient estimator* An asymptotically efficient estimator is such that its variance approaches zero faster than any other consistent estimator. In situations where small sample properties of the sampling distribution of the estimator cannot be determined, the usual practice is to consider asymptotic properties, and select an estimator which is asymptotically efficient. In practice, the properties of the sampling distribution of the estimator and their asymptotic characteristics are determined using Monte Carlo simulation/studies. We will explain this method later on in this chapter.

3.3 Estimation methods: the OLS and the ML estimators

We are now in a position to develop a method for estimating the parameters of the multivariate linear regression model. We seek estimators which are efficient, given the model's assumptions. Amongst all methods of estimation available, there are only two types which satisfy the efficiency criterion, given the assumptions. These are:

1　*The ordinary least squares (OLS) estimators*
2　*The maximum likelihood (ML) estimators.*

The OLS estimators can be obtained without reference to the normality assumption, whilst ML estimators require the assumption of normality to hold. Both methods generate identical estimators of parameters.

3.3.1　The ordinary least squares (OLS) method

Let us begin by considering a k-variable linear regression model such as:

$$Y_t = \beta_1 + \beta_2 X_{2t} + \beta_3 X_{3t} + ... + \beta_k X_{kt} + u_t, \ u_t \sim \text{NID}(0, \sigma^2), \text{ for } t = 1,2 \ ... \tag{3.11}$$

We aim here to generate efficient estimators of the unknown parameters β_1 to β_k so that each parameter can be estimated given a set of observations on the dependent and independent variables. We denote the estimators as follows:

		uses		generates	
$\hat{\beta}_1$	$\rightarrow$ estimator of β_1	$\rightarrow$	a set of observations on Y and $x_1...x_k$	$\rightarrow$	
$\hat{\beta}_1$	(a point estimate)				

		uses		generates	
$\hat{\beta}_2$	$\rightarrow$ estimator of β_2	$\rightarrow$	a set of observations on Y and $x_1...x_k$	$\rightarrow$	
$\hat{\beta}_2$	(a point estimate)				

. . .

		uses		generates	
$\hat{\beta}_k$	$\rightarrow$ estimator of β_k	$\rightarrow$	a set of observations on Y and $x_1...x_k$	$\rightarrow$	
$\hat{\beta}_k$	(a point estimate)				

The conditional expected value of the dependent variable is given by the following expression:

$$E(Y_t) = \beta_1 + \beta_2 X_{2t} + \beta_3 X_{3t} + ... + \beta_k X_{kt} \tag{3.12}$$

and the estimated expected value is obtained by substitution of the point estimates into Equation (42):

$$\hat{Y}_t = \hat{\beta}_1 + \hat{\beta}_2 X_{2t} + \hat{\beta}_3 X_{3t} + ... + \hat{\beta}_k X_{kt}, \text{ for } t = 1,2,3,...... \tag{3.13}$$

where $\hat{Y}_t$ is the estimated expected value of Y or simply fitted values. In the theoretical model the difference between each individual value of the dependent variable and the expected values of the dependent variable is known as the disturbance term, i.e.

$$Y_t - E(Y_t) = u_t \text{ for all } t = 1, 2, 3,... \tag{3.14}$$

The empirical counterpart of the disturbance term (u_t) is known as *the residual* and is usually denoted as e_t. It can be obtained as follows:

$$e_t = Y_t - \hat{Y}_t = Y_t - \hat{\beta}_1 + \hat{\beta}_2 X_{2t} + \hat{\beta}_3 X_{3t} + ... + \hat{\beta}_k X_{kt}, \text{ for } t = 1,2,3,... \tag{3.15}$$

Each residual shows the difference between an observed value of Y and the estimated expected value of Y and it is in this sense that a residual may be considered to be the empirical counterpart/estimate of a disturbance term.

The OLS method makes use of the concept of the residuals to obtain parameter estimates. In particular, under the OLS method, the parameter estimates are obtained such that the sum of the squared residuals is minimized. Note that a residual can be positive or negative, depending upon whether or not the estimated expected value of the dependent variable is greater than or less than a particular value of Y. We can square each residual and then sum up the squared residuals to obtain the residual sum of squares (RSS) as follows:

$$\text{Residual Sum of Squares} = \text{RSS} = e_1^2 + e_2^2 + e_3^2 + \ldots e_k^2$$

$$\text{or simply} \ldots \sum_{i=1}^{n} \sum_{i=1}^{n} e_i^2 \tag{3.16}$$

where Σ is the summation operator. We can substitute for e_i into the above expression and we arrive at the following equation:

$$\text{RSS} = \Sigma e_i^2 = \sum_{i=1}^{n} [Y_t - \hat{\beta}_1 + \hat{\beta}_2 X_{2t} + \hat{\beta}_3 X_{3t} + \ldots + \hat{\beta}_k X_{kt}]^2 \tag{3.17}$$

Under the OLS method, $\hat{\beta}_1 \ldots \hat{\beta}_k$ are obtained in terms of observations of the dependent and independent variables $Y_t, X_{1t} \ldots X_{kt}$, such that the residual sum of squares is minimised, i.e. we find the OLS estimators such that $\Sigma e_i^2 = \Sigma[Y_t \ldots]^2$ is as small as possible. This procedure yields the OLS estimators $\hat{\beta}_{1ols} \ldots \hat{\beta}_{kols}$. Each estimator is a particular function of the dependent and independent variables, yielding point estimates for each set of observations on Y and $X_1 \ldots X_k$, i.e.

$$\hat{\beta}_{iOLS} = f_i (Y_t, X_{1t} \ldots X_{kt}); \quad i = 1,2,3,\ldots, K \tag{3.18}$$

The exact mathematical formula of each estimator can be obtained by the matrix algebra and minimisation procedures. In practice, one uses regression packages (e.g. Microfit 4/5 or EViews) where the OLS method is routinely used to generate point estimates. The main reason for the popularity of the OLS method is that under repeated sampling procedures, and given the assumptions of the model, the sampling distribution of each OLS estimator has a number of desirable/optimal properties. In particular, it can be shown that if all assumptions of the model are consistent with the data then:

1   The OLS estimators are unbiased, i.e. the expected value of the sampling distribution of an OLS estimator is equal to the unknown parameter. Symbolically:

$$E(\hat{\beta}_{kOLS}) = \beta_k \quad \text{for } k = 1,2,3\ldots \tag{3.19}$$

This is a conditional property dependent upon the validity of the zero mean assumption, which in turn depends upon the model to have been specified correctly.

In particular, there are no omitted variables from the regression model. The omitted variables give rise to biased and therefore unreliable OLS estimators.

2   The OLS estimators have minimum variance. This sampling property of the OLS estimators is conditional on the validity of the assumption of non-autocorrelation and homoscedasticity. Symbolically:

$$\mathrm{Var}(\hat{\beta}_k) = \mathrm{E}[\beta_k - \mathrm{E}(\hat{\beta}_k)]^2 \quad \text{is as small as possible} \qquad (3.20)$$

If all data generations assumptions explained above are satisfied, it can be shown that among all linear unbiased estimators, the OLS estimators have the smallest variance. That is, they are BLUE. The mathematical proof of this statement is beyond the scope of this introductory text. The proof of this proposition is provided by the Gauss-Markov theorem, which provides formal justification for the use of the OLS methods of estimation. Note that the normality condition is not required for the Gauss-Markov theorem to hold.

Given the properties of (1) and (2), the OLS estimators are said to be efficient. However, it should be noted that the efficiency property depends crucially on the validity of the model's assumptions. If any of the assumptions fail, then the OLS method is no longer efficient and another method of estimation would need to be found. It is therefore important that we verify the assumptions at stages in the empirical analysis.

3.3.2 Properties of the sampling distribution of the OLS estimators

The data generation assumptions identify important features of the sampling distribution of the OLS estimators. The shape of the distribution depends upon the assumption concerning the shape of the distribution of the dependent variable. If we maintain the assumption of normality, the sampling distribution should also be normal. This is because the sampling distribution is obtained from the values of the dependent variable which are consistent with the normal distribution. The sampling distribution of an OLS estimator $(\hat{\beta}_k)$ is presented below:

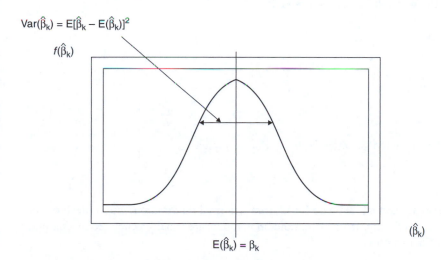

Figure 3.4 Sampling distribution of an OLS estimator.

Symbolically, $\hat{\beta}_k \sim \mathrm{N}(\beta_k, \mathrm{Var}(\hat{\beta}_k))$.

If all data generation assumptions outlined above are to hold, then the OLS estimators are efficient and sufficient. Moreover, these estimators are asymptotically efficient.

3.4 Monte Carlo studies

A Monte Carlo study/experiment is a practical method for checking the properties of the sampling distributions of the estimators.

We discussed above that estimators are selected on the basis of their performance under the repeated sampling/estimation procedures. This hypothetical sampling procedure generates sampling distributions of the estimators. A 'good' estimator is then identified as one whose sampling distribution has a mix of desirable properties, including unbiasedness, efficiency and consistency. Given the assumptions in the classical linear regression model, the Gauss-Markov theorem provides a theoretical foundation for the use of OLS estimators. In particular, the theorem demonstrates that amongst all the unbiased estimators, OLS estimators have the smallest variance and in this sense they are the *best linear unbiased estimators* (BLUE).

In addition to theoretical reasoning, econometricians also employ Monte Carlo simulation experiments to understand the sampling properties of estimators. A Monte Carlo experiment provides a framework within which econometricians have complete control of the way the data is generated. Within this controlled experimental environment, a practitioner sets the values of the unknown parameters from the outset to see how well a particular method of estimation can track values. This is in fact the reverse of the estimation procedure. Within the framework of a Monte Carlo study, the value of the parameters are known from the start. However, what is not known is how close a particular method of estimation generates these known values.

In what follows, we demonstrate the steps undertaken in a Monte Carlo study with reference to the OLS estimators.

1   Set specific values for the parameters of the model to begin the process. For example, in a simple two-variables regression model:

$$Y_t = \beta_1 + \beta_2 X_t + u_t$$

Set: $\beta_1 = 0.5$

$\beta_2 = 0.8$

2   Collect data on independent variable X_t. For example:
$$\begin{bmatrix} X_1 \\ X_2 \\ ... \\ X_n \end{bmatrix}$$

3   Generate some random numbers for u_t from a normal distribution with a mean of zero and a variance of unity. In practice, random numbers are usually generated by computer software. For example:

$$\begin{bmatrix} U_1 \\ U_2 \\ . \\ U_n \end{bmatrix}$$

Random numbers for u_t.

4   Use values of X_t and random numbers for u_t to generate a set of observations for Y_t, the dependent variable of the model.

For example:

$$Y_1 = 0.5 + 0.8X_1 + U_1$$
$$Y_2 = 0.5 + 0.8X_2 + U_2$$
$$\ldots$$
$$Y_n = 0.5 + 0.8X_n + U_n$$

5   Choose a particular estimation method, for example, OLS. Use the value of X_t and Y_t (generated in step 4) to generate point estimates for the parameters of the model.

For example, using the OLS method with a regression package, the point estimates for β_1 and β_2 are generated via two OLS formulae given below:

$$\hat{\beta}_2 = \frac{\sum_{i=1}^{n}(Y_i - \bar{Y})(X_i - \bar{X})}{\sum(X_i - \bar{X})^2} \ldots\ldots[point\ estimate]$$

$$\hat{\beta}_1 = \bar{Y} - \hat{\beta}_2\bar{X}\ldots\ldots[point\ estimate]$$

where $\bar{X}$ is the sample mean of observations on X and $\bar{Y}$ is the sample mean of generated data for Y.

Note: the above OLS formulae are derived from the minimisation of the residual sum of squares. Unlike conventional texts, we have deliberately not used unnecessary maths and numerical examples in this chapter to derive these estimators. In our view, this does not meet any purpose. In practice, almost certainly one uses an appropriate regression package, which produces the point estimates in a matter of seconds.

6   Compare the point estimates with the set parameter values. Are these closely matched?
7   Repeat this controlled experiment from step 3 many times to generate 'sampling' distributions for the OLS estimators (i.e. $\hat{\beta}_1$ and $\hat{\beta}_2$).
8   Check the following properties of the 'sampling' distributions:

a   Shape: are the distributions symmetrical around their central values?
b   Expected value: are the expected value/central values close to or the same as the set parameter values? So:

$$E(\hat{\beta}_1) = 0.5\ and;\ E(\hat{\beta}_2) = 0.8$$

c   Variance: is the variance of each distribution 'relatively' small?
d   Consistency: are the 'sampling' distributions becoming narrower and narrower as the sample size of the controlled experiment increase?

Using a Monte Carlo study such as this, it can be shown that OLS estimators are: unbiased, possess minimum variance, and are efficient and consistent. However, these properties depend crucially on the generation of random data from a normal distribution with a mean of zero and a constant variance. Through a Monte Carlo simulation experiment, econometricians have been able to investigate the impact of a change in any one of the data generation conditional assumptions on the behaviour of the estimators. This type of analysis enables the investigators to select a 'best' estimation method to fit the type of data available in different situations.

3.5 Maximum likelihood (ML) estimators

Maximum likelihood (ML) estimators are frequently employed by practitioners for the estimation of single equations and, particularly, systems of equations. The intuitive idea underlying the ML methodology is quite appealing: estimators are derived such that the likelihood/probability of obtaining all data points on the dependent variable is the maximum.

For example:

$$Y_t = \beta_1 + \beta_2 X_t + \beta_3 Z_t + u_t$$

$$\text{observations on } Y = \begin{bmatrix} Y_1 \\ Y_2 \\ .. \\ .. \\ Y_n \end{bmatrix}$$

We find β_1, β_2 and β_3 such that the probability/likelihood of observing $\begin{bmatrix} Y_1 \\ Y_2 \\ .. \\ .. \\ Y_n \end{bmatrix}$ is maximised.

To derive ML estimators we need the normality assumption to hold. Given this assumption, the ML estimators are derived from the joint probability density function of the dependent variable in the model. The mathematical derivation of these estimators, in our view, is beyond the scope of this introductory text. However, in the subsequent chapters we will revisit the ML estimators and show their applications in practice. The key point is that the ML estimators are in fact the same as OLS estimators. In this respect, the OLS estimators are also ML estimators. That is, provided, the normality assumption holds, the OLS estimators generate the highest probability of obtaining any sample observations on the dependent variable. This is yet another theoretical justification for the popularity of the OLS estimators.

3.6 A summary of key issues

- The aim of regression analysis is to estimate econometric models to provide empirical content to abstract economic theories and models. To this end, the key objective is to find estimators capable of estimating the parameters of the regression models.
- An estimator of a parameter is a mathematical formula which can generate point estimates for that unknown parameter on the basis of a set of observations on the dependent and independent variables of the model. It basically converts these observations into a point estimate for the parameter.
- An estimator is selected on the basis of the properties of its sampling distribution, given the data generation assumptions underlying the regression model. The sampling distribution of an estimator is obtained via a repeated hypothetical sampling procedure.
- A 'good' estimator is an estimator whose sampling distribution has the following properties, given the regression model's assumptions: (a) the expected/mean value of the distribution is the same as the parameter to be estimated, (b) the variance of the sampling

distribution is as small as possible, and (c) the estimators use all the sample information to generate point estimates.

- An unbiased estimator whose sampling distribution is as small as possible, given assumptions, is called an efficient estimator. An estimator which uses all available sample information to generate point estimates is called a sufficient estimator. Estimators with these two properties are considered to be 'good' estimators, that is, under repeated sampling procedures they tend to generate point estimates which are close to the true value of the parameters.

- Sometimes it is not possible to evaluate the properties of the sampling distributions of the estimators with normal size samples; in this situation, the large sample or the asymptotic properties of the sampling distributions are considered. An estimator which is consistent and asymptotically efficient, given the regression model's assumptions is considered to be a 'good' estimator, in this case.

- Given the data generation assumptions of the classical normal linear regression model, there are only two estimation methods, the OLS and the ML estimators, capable of producing estimators whose sampling distributions have all the desired properties.

- The OLS estimators can be derived without the assumption of normality. These are obtained such that the residual sum of squares (RSS) (this is sometimes called the sum of squared residuals (SSR)) is minimised.

- Within the framework of the CNLRM, the Guass-Markov theorem is used to prove that the OLS estimators are best linear unbiased estimators. That is, they are BLUE.

- Monte Carlo experiments are carried out to establish properties of the estimators under repeated sampling procedures. These experiments have indeed demonstrated that OLS estimators are the best, given the regression model's assumptions.

- The maximum likelihood (ML) estimators are obtained such that the probability of observing the sample points is maximised. The ML estimators require the assumption of normality. These estimators are identical to the OLS estimators and are BLUE, given the data generation assumptions.

Review questions

1   Suggest a regression model for the estimation of each one of the variables listed below:

   a   demand for tourism in a particular country
   b   aggregate investment expenditure in an economy.

   Explain how you would measure each variable included in your model. Explain the role of any disturbance term included in your model and outline and discuss the standard assumptions concerning this term. Why are these assumptions necessary?
      Collect a sample of observations on the variables included in your model (use an appropriate secondary source of data), and use a regression package (e.g. Microfit) to estimate the parameters of your regression model. Explain the meaning of the point estimates reported by the regression package.

2   Discuss the role of empirical analysis in economics.

3   Explain what you understand by the sampling distribution of an estimator. How is the sampling distribution used in the search for a 'good' estimator?

4   Explain the ordinary least squares (OLS) method. What do you understand by the statement that OLS estimators are 'BLUE'?

5   Explain what you understand by a Monte Carlo study. Devise your own Monte Carlo experiment to check the properties of the sampling distributions of the OLS estimators.

6   Explain what you understand by each of the following:

a   an unbiased estimator
b   minimum variance property
c   standard deviation/standard error of an estimator
d   efficiency property
e   sufficiency property

7   Explain the meaning of each one of the following:

a   consistent estimator
b   asymptotically efficient estimator
c   maximum likelihood (ML) estimators.

Key terms: Chapters 1–3

- *Econometrics* A branch of economics dealing with empirical measurement and confirmation of economic models.
- *Traditional/conventional approach (SG)* An empirical methodology based on specific economic theory/model.
- *Disturbance term/error term* A random variable included in economic models to change a deterministic model into a stochastic framework compatible with economic data.
- *Multicollinearity* A high degree of linear association between two or more variables.
- *OLS method* The ordinary least squares (OLS) method – based on minimisation of the residual sum of squares.
- BLUE The best linear unbiased estimator.
- *Monte Carlo study* A controlled experiment designed to generate/determine properties of estimators.

4 Evaluation of the regression results

Hypothesis testing and tests of significance

INTRODUCTION

In the previous chapters we developed the theoretical arguments underlying linear regression models. In this chapter and the next we put these ideas into practice by estimating and empirically evaluating a multiple linear regression model. In practice, the computations are carried out by the regression packages (Microfit 4/5 and EViews), which are widely available. These packages generate various diagnostic test results, which are used to evaluate the regression models in practice. We consider a number of key diagnostic tests, including those used for the detection of autocorrelation, heteroscedasticity and specification errors. Unlike conventional texts, which have traditionally dealt with these issues in several separate and disjointed chapters, and therefore give the impression to the reader that diagnostic testing and model evaluation in practice is also carried out in a similar disjointed fashion, this text takes a modern approach to empirical evaluation of the regression models, dealing with diagnostic testing procedures collectively, but in a step by step fashion. To this end, we have devoted two key chapters to the explanation of the procedures used for model evaluation in practice. This chapter deals with modelling, data requirement, estimation, criteria for model evaluation and some basic statistical procedures using a single-equation model of competitive imports to illustrate the basic idea and procedures. In the next chapter we deal with key diagnostic testing procedures used collectively in practice, to empirically evaluate single-equation regression models.

Key topics

- Criteria for empirical evaluation of regression models
- Hypotheses testing procedures and statistical tests of significance

4.1 Econometric modelling in practice: a model of demand for competitive imports

The first step in developing an econometric model involves the consideration of theoretical relationship about the variable. Thus, on the basis of assumptions and deductive reasoning, economic theory provides a framework from which the main variables influencing an economic phenomenon are linked in a causal way. We therefore begin by considering the economic theory concerning the demand for imports. We have discussed features of this model in the previous chapters. In what follows, some of the basic assumptions of this model are reviewed once again.

Economic theory focuses on three major variables determining the demand for competitive imports. For example, imports of manufactured goods to the UK are competitive imports, since the UK produces all types of manufactured goods. An economic factor influencing the import of competitive goods is the level of final expenditure, that is, total expenditure in a given period in the economy. Since total expenditure on goods and services in a given period reflects the level of gross domestic product, this first variable is usually measured by the level of gross domestic product (GDP). It should, however, be noted that the composition of total expenditure might also be important to the extent that the import content of different components of total expenditure/GDP differs. We therefore have two options concerning the treatment of total expenditure: (a) to use GDP as proxy for final expenditure, or (b) to allow for each component of GDP (i.e. consumption, investment, exports), to appear separately under the assumption that each macro component of final expenditure may have a different effect on imports (see Abbott and Seddigh, 1997). In this chapter we follow the simpler model to assist exposition.

A second variable influencing the demand for imports, ceteris paribus, is the price of close substitutes. In particular, a rise in relative price levels is expected to lead to a fall in demand for imports. In most studies of import functions it is assumed that supply elasticities are infinite and therefore import prices are taken as being determined outside the theoretical model. Moreover, it is usually assumed that the domestic prices are flexible and change to eliminate excess demand. Under these conditions, import prices and the domestic price levels are determined outside the model through the interaction of world demand and supply. Moreover, infinite supply elasticities assumed means that income distribution is unaffected. The third factor is the capacity of the country to produce and supply the goods domestically. However, the capacity factor is essentially a short-run phenomenon and is relevant only if excess demand at home cannot be eliminated by a change in domestic prices (Thirwall, 1991).

Given this reasoning, the import demand function may be written symbolically as follows:

$$M = f(GDP, PM/PD) \tag{4.1}$$
$$(+)\quad(-)$$

where M = aggregate imports in units of domestic currency/constant prices

GDP = gross domestic product at constant prices

PM = an index price of imports expressed in domestic currency

PD = an index price of domestically produced rival goods.

On theoretical grounds, we expect a positive relationship between M and GDP. So a rise/fall in the level of GDP, with PM/PD unchanged, is expected to lead to a rise/fall in the level of aggregate imports. On the other hand, a rise/fall in relative price term, PM/PD, (with GDP held constant) is expected to lead to a fall/rise in the level of aggregate imports. More specifically, we expect to see a positive relationship between aggregate imports and GDP and a negative relationship between aggregate imports and the price of imports relative to the price of domestic goods, where the prices of imports are expressed in domestic currency.

4.1.1 Aims of empirical studies

Before we go any further, it is useful to state the aims of the empirical study. In most empirical studies of economic phenomena based on the traditional (SG) approach, the aims may be stated as follows:

1   To provide empirical content to abstract economic theories/models. To this end, we aim to quantify/estimate the relationship between aggregate competitive imports, M, and main determinants.
2   To evaluate the theoretical explanation of the data generation process.
3   In light of the results, the economic model is enhanced as an explicator of the observed phenomena.
4   To use the econometric model for policy simulations and forecasting.

4.1.2 Modelling requirements

Given the above aims, the basic tools are:

1   An econometric model, designed to explain observations concerning aggregate competitive imports.
2   A set of observations (a data set) of the variables included in the model. In this example, these are: M, GDP, PM and PD.
3   A method of estimation which can be used to convert the data set into point estimates of the parameters of the model. Given the data generation assumptions, the estimators are required to have desirable properties, these include: efficiency, sufficiency and consistency features.
4   A set of criteria for the evaluation of the regression results and a set of diagnostic tests designed to test assumptions. These assumptions include specification and data generation assumptions.
5   A regression package (e.g. Microfit 4/5 or EViews) which generates the desired diagnostic tests/information. These basic requirements are now discussed.

4.1.3 Specification of the econometric/regression model

The econometric model is derived from an economic model to explain observations. To this end, the economic model must be modified in two respects: (a) we must suggest a specific functional form for the model, in other words, we must state a specific mathematical relationship between aggregate imports, M, and its main determinants; (b) the model must be data admissible. This requirement implies that a deterministic economic model must be modified to reflect the stochastic nature of the data.

The model $M = f(GDP, PM/PD)$ is a general mathematical relationship, saying that, based on the theoretical reasoning, aggregate imports depend mainly on total expenditure and relative prices. The economic model must be given a specific functional form. Unfortunately, theory does not help in specifying an exact mathematical relationship.

In this situation, the practitioner has no option but to assume a certain functional form from the outset. The assumption of the specific functional form chosen can then be tested later on. In studies of the demand for aggregate imports, most practitioners have either used a linear specification or, alternatively, log-linear specification. In a linear specification, variables under consideration are connected to each other by a set of linear parameters. The model is said to be linear in parameters.

$$M = \alpha_1 + \alpha_2 GDP + \alpha_3 \left(PM/PD \right) \tag{4.2}$$

In this specification, α_1 is the intercept term, and α_2 and α_3 are the respective slope parameters.

In a log-linear specification the log values (expressed as natural log) are connected to each other through a set of linear parameters, as follows:

$$\log M = \beta_1 + \beta_2 \log GDP + \beta_3 \log \left(PM/PD \right) \tag{4.3}$$

Both linear and log-linear models are frequently used in practice.

The choice between the two is essentially an empirical one and can be resolved by diagnostic testing. However, in the analysis of import functions, practitioners tend to prefer the log-linear specifications for some, or all, of the following reasons:

1   In log-linear specifications the slope parameters are the partial elasticities. Thus, β_2 and β_3 represent the partial elasticity of imports with respect to GDP and the relative price term, respectively. The income elasticity and elasticity of imports with respect to relative prices are estimated directly.
2   It is easy to interpret estimated slope parameters as these show percentage changes. Moreover, the units by which the variables are measured do not influence the magnitudes of estimated coefficients, unlike linear specifications.
3   Log transformations of variables reduce the variability in data. This potentially reduces the likelihood of heteroscedasticity.

Given these properties, we also make use of a log-linear model to estimate partial elasticities of demand for imports with respect to income and relative prices, as follows:

$$\log M_t = \beta_1 + \beta_2 \log GDP_t + \beta_3 \log \left(P_M/P_D \right)_t + u_t \qquad \text{for } t = 1,..., n \tag{4.4}$$

where u_t is a random disturbance added to the equation to capture the impact of all other variables omitted from the regression model. These influences include random variables such as sudden change in taste, political upheaval, natural disasters, etc. The equation suggests that each observation obtained on logs of imports are made up of two components, namely: (i) the 'average' expected value of imports at any specific level of GDP and PM/PD, given by:

$$E\left[\log Mt \right] = \beta_1 + \beta_2 \log GDP_t + \beta_3 \log \left(P_M/P_D \right)_t \tag{4.5}$$

and (ii) a term showing the deviations from the expected value given by u_t. Moreover, the expected value of imports is determined by variables suggested by economic theory. The deviations from the average are essentially due to random factors. We start the process by making some standard assumptions concerning how data are generated. These assumptions concern the distribution of the disturbance term or, equivalently, the probability distribution of the dependent variable, competitive imports. This may be presented symbolically as:

$$u_t \sim NID\ (0,\ \sigma^2); \text{ for } t = 1, ..., \text{ n}. \tag{4.6}$$

Hence, the disturbance term is normally and independently distributed around a mean of zero with a constant variance. The regression model may therefore be written as follows:

$$\log M_t = \beta_1 + \beta_2 \log GDP_t + \beta_3 \log\left(P_M / P_D\right)_t + u_t \tag{4.7}$$

$$u_t \sim NID\ (0, \sigma^2); \text{ for } t = 1, ..., \text{ n}$$

4.2 Definition of variables, time series data, and the OLS estimation method

The way in which each variable is measured and used in the model has important implications for the results. Occasionally, economic theory provides insights regarding the appropriate definition and the use of economic variables. Practitioners must be fully aware of these insights and, wherever possible, use them. Regarding the model of imports, the variables may be defined as:

M = volume of imports. This yields the total value of imports at constant prices. Imports in a given year are measured in a particular base year.

GDP = gross domestic product at constant prices.

P_M = a price index of imported goods with prices measured in domestic currency. This is typically calculated as:

$$P_M = \frac{\text{imports in current prices}}{\text{imports in constant prices}}$$

P_D = A price index of domestic goods, including GDP deflator/wholesale price index.

In this example we have defined P_D to be the GDP deflator as:

$$P_D = \frac{\text{GDP in current prices}}{\text{GDP in constant prices}}$$

4.2.1 Time series data for the estimation of the model

For the purpose of illustration, we have used the UK quarterly time series data covering 1980 (Q1) to 1996 (Q4). There are 68 quarterly observations taken from the Economic Trends Annual Supplement (1998). The reason for selecting this particular period to illustrate key issues is because the UK competitive imports grew rapidly during this period due to a significant shift in the UK economy from manufacturing to services. This is a period of some rapid growth in UK competitive imports and it seems therefore useful to estimate the income elasticity and price elasticity of demand for imports over this period. These estimates are taken into account when devising appropriate macroeconomic policies to deal with the growing balance of trade deficits. Of course, you can use the above regression model with any other appropriate time series data (many suitable data sets are available online), including data collected from other countries, to estimate and to evaluate a similar regression model. Note that the Economic Trends Annual Supplement is a reliable source of the UK macroeconomic data. This data bank is readily available online and we have presented the data collected from this source in Appendix 1. You are, however, strongly advised to consult this online data source and run similar regressions to the one reported here. The Economic Trends Annual Supplements contain detailed time series data on the UK macroeconomic variables and are particularly suitable for use in the regression analysis of the type discussed in this text.

Estimation

The model was estimated by the ordinary least squares method using Microfit 4/5. Under the OLS method, the parameters are estimated so that the residual sum of squares is minimised. The reason for using the OLS method is that the OLS estimators are BLUE, provided that all data generation assumptions are in fact valid. We need to test the validity of these assumptions to ensure this is the case.

The Microfit 4/5 regression package produces a set of diagnostic tests designed to test the adequacy of the model. In what follows, these are discussed in a step by step fashion.

4.2.2 Presentation of the regression results

$$\text{Log } \hat{M}_t = -13.4337 + 2.025\text{logGDP}_t - 0.905 \text{ log}\left(P_M / P_D\right)_t \qquad (4.8)$$
$$\phantom{\text{Log } \hat{M}_t = } (0.78558) \ (0.066527) \qquad (0.74096)$$

$R^2 = 0.98109$

F-statistic (2, 65) = 1683.3

DW = 0.55343

SE of regression = 0.035263

This is a popular way of presenting regression results, with estimated parameters being the coefficients attached to each corresponding variable, estimated standard errors written below corresponding coefficients, followed by R^2 (coefficient of determination), the F-statistic, the Durbin-Watson (DW) test statistic and, finally, the standard error of regression. Each of these computer-generated numbers have implications for the adequacy of the model and are used in the evaluation of the regression results. Before we consider these in detail, we first discuss the types of criteria used in practice to empirically evaluate regression results.

4.3 Criteria for the evaluation of the regression results

There are three criteria: economic, statistical and econometric, used to evaluate regression results in practice and all have to be met and satisfied for the regression model to be considered to be adequate. In what follows, we consider the economic and statistical criteria, leaving the econometric criteria for the next chapter.

4.3.1 Economic criteria

This is a simple but powerful criteria of the model evaluation. Economic criteria are concerned with the *sign* and *size* of the estimated parameters (coefficients). One needs to check that the sign and size of coefficients are consistent with economic theory. It is important to point out that we are quantifying economic relationships linked by some linear parameters. All parameters with the exception of the intercept term, which is usually added to the econometric model for computational convenience, have economic meanings. Given this observation, if the economic model is well defined, it is expected that the sign and size of the estimated parameters follow consistent theoretical arguments. Applying these criteria to the estimated model of imports, we observe that the partial elasticity of imports with respect to GDP/income is estimated as 2.025. The sign is positive and consistent with economic theory. The magnitude suggests that for each 1% change in the level of GDP, with relative prices constant, we expect the volume of imports, on average, to change by about 2%. In other words, import demand is highly elastic with respect to income. Economic theory does not provide us with guidance concerning the magnitude of this parameter. It is advisable to check the magnitude of estimated parameters against other published work. The price elasticity of demand is estimated at −0.905. The sign is negative and consistent with the predictions of economic theory. The size of the coefficient suggests that, for each 1% change in the relative prices of imported goods compared to domestically produced goods, it is expected that imports fall by only 0.9 of 1%. This value suggests that the demand for imports could be unit elastic. We need to consider this seriously when conducting further analysis. The economic criteria appear to be satisfied. This is only one yardstick of the evaluation and we need further analysis. If, on the other hand, the sign and the magnitude of coefficients were found to be contrary to what is suggested by the economic theory, we should resolve this problem before going further. This, for example, could be done by checking the adequacy of the data set and the regression model.

4.3.2 Statistical criteria

Statistical criteria are used to provide statistical underpinnings for the econometric model. In particular, we test to see if statistical evidence exists, against or in favour of inclusion of each regressor. These individual/single tests are called *tests of significance* and are routinely carried out in applied work. We also test to see if there exists any evidence in favour of inclusion of all the regressors in the model. This is a joint test of significance and, in this case, we are testing for the *overall significance* of regression.

In addition to tests of significance it is also useful to know how close the estimated line (plane) is to the scatter of observations which have been used to estimate it. This is a measure of 'goodness of fit' of the estimated line and is usually called the *coefficient of determination* or R^2. We begin by considering R^2.

4.3.3 Coefficient of determination R^2 and the adjusted coefficient of determination $\bar{R}^2$

The coefficient of determination R^2 provides a measure of 'goodness of fit' of the estimated line to the sample data. In particular, it shows the percentage/proportion of total sample variation in the dependent variable which is due to sample variations in all independent variables of the model. The higher the value of R^2, the better would be the fit of the estimated linear relationship to the sample data points. To see these issues, we make use of a simple two-dimensional diagram corresponding to the model of import demand. For illustrative purposes we treat relative prices as a constant in the equation, so that the import equation can be drawn in a straight line in a two-dimensional diagram:

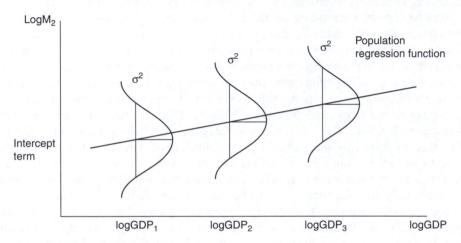

Figure 4.1 Population regression line.

Figure 4.1 shows the population regression line corresponding to the log-linear model of import function. At each level of GDP we expect to find a range of demand levels for imports, due to the influence of factors other than GDP on demand. Some of these could be random. The distribution of import demand levels are symmetrical around the expected values given by the model. Note that each observation has two components: a deviation from the expected value captured by the disturbance term and the expected value of imports, given by the model. The aim is to estimate the population regression line. To do this we select a sample of data values from the population data set and use the OLS method to estimate the line. The sample data set is shown in Figure 4.2.

Remember that the population regression line and the disturbance terms are non-observable; all we have is a set of observations on the dependent and independent variables of the model. These observations are first converted into the OLS estimates of the unknown parameters, giving rise to a sample repression line, such as the one depicted in Figure 4.2. The vertical distances between observed values and the estimated line are the OLS residuals. These may be thought of as being the *empirical counterpart* of the associated disturbance terms. The smaller the residuals, the better would be the fit of the estimated line to the data points and the sample regression line would be a better 'fit' to the unknown population regression line.

To find a measure of the 'goodness of fit' based on these observations, we notice that variations in the value of the dependent variable, from one observation to the next, is due to changes in either the values of the independent variables/regressors, or the influence of the disturbance term, or both. If we can separate these two influences, finding the percentage of the sample variations in the imports (or logs of imports) which can be explained by variation

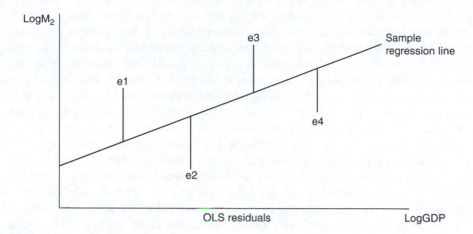

Figure 4.2 Sample regression line.

in the regressors, then the higher this percentage is, the better should be the fit of the sample regression line to the sample data. Therefore, it would be closer to the population regression line. The total sample variation in the dependent variable is defined as the sum of the squared deviations of each observation from the sample mean value of the dependent variable. That is:

Total sum of squares (TSS)   =   sum of (observation on the dependent variable – sample mean of the dependent variable)^2

or, symbolically:

$$TSS = \sum_{t=1}^{68} \left(\log M_t - \log \bar{M}_t \right)^2 \tag{4.9}$$

It can be shown, given model's assumptions, that this sum can be divided into the sum of two squared components, as follows:

Total sum of squares   =   sample variation due to changes in the regressors + sample variation due to changes in factors other than regressors = explained sum of squares (ESS) + residual sum of squares (RSS)

The coefficient of determination, R^2, is then:

$$R^2 = \frac{\text{explained sum of squares}}{\text{total sum of squares}} = \frac{ESS}{TSS} \tag{4.10}$$

or, alternatively:

$$R^2 = \frac{(1 - \text{residual sum of squares})}{\text{total sum of squares}} = \frac{(1 - RSS)}{TSS} \tag{4.11}$$

Multiplying the R^2 value by 100% gives the percentage of sample variations in the dependent variable which can be explained by joint sample variations in the independent variables of the model. R^2 takes only positive values between zero and one. It shows the extent of linear association between the dependent and all the independent variables of the model. Note that the coefficient of determination is only a measure of the 'goodness of fit' of the linear relationship and in the case of non-linear relationships, the R^2 value could be zero, even if there is a perfect non-linear relationship between variables. Moreover, the value of R^2 is highly sensitive to the validity of assumptions. In particular, when autocorrelation/heteroscedasticity are present, the R^2 value is highly unreliable. In practice, one has to be sure that all assumptions are consistent with the data before seriously considering the value of R^2. In the above regression, the value of R^2 is calculated as 0.98109%. That is, it appears that over 98% of sample variations in the dependent variable over the period 1980 Q1 to 1996 Q4 can be explained by the regressors, log GDP and the log PM/PD. Only 2% of total variation appears to be due to change in the factor captured by the disturbance term. The model appears to fit the data very well. We must not put too much emphasis on this value at this stage since the validity of the assumptions have to be tested. Occasionally R^2 is adjusted for the degrees of freedom of the RSS and the TSS to yield the $\bar{R}^2$, the adjusted $\bar{R}^2$. This is shown below:

$$\bar{R}^2 = 1 - \left(\frac{RSS}{TSS}\right)\left(\frac{n-1}{n-k}\right)$$

or

$$\bar{R}^2 = 1 - \left(1 - R^2\right)\left(\frac{n-1}{n-k}\right)$$

4.3.4 The adjusted coefficient of determination $\bar{R}^2$

This is used mainly for comparing regression models to which new variables are added. R^2 will always increase if a new explanatory variable is added to a regression model, even if the new variable is useless in explaining the dependent variable. $\bar{R}^2$ will normally fall, however, if the new variable does not belong to the regression model. In this situation, the adjusted coefficient of determination penalises the inclusion of unnecessary regressors to the model, occasionally carried out incorrectly to increase R^2!

4.4 Tests of significance

Let us consider the regression model again:

$$\log M_t = \beta_1 + \beta_2 \log GDP_t + \beta_3 \log\left(P_M/P_D\right)_t + u_t \tag{4.12}$$

The dependent variable ($\log M_t$) is assumed, on theoretical grounds, to be dependent on two independent variables/regressors, GDP and log PM/PD, respectively. The question is: is it possible to provide some statistical support for the inclusion of each variable in the model? If the answer to this question is positive, and provided that all assumptions are valid, statistical tests provide underpinning for the regression model.

The first step in performing statistical tests of hypotheses is to state the null and alternative hypotheses. In the tests of significance, the null hypothesis is the statement that contrary to the suggestion of economic theory, there is no relationship between the dependent and each one of the independent variables. In other words, the economic model is false. The model is treated as being false, unless contradictory evidence is found through statistical procedures. This is very much like trial by jury. The person is treated as innocent unless evidence is found to 'contradict' the person's presumed innocence. This type of procedure may be called the process of falsification. The test is designed to falsify the economic relationship.

We now state the null and alternative hypotheses concerning the economic model in hand. The null hypothesis is usually denoted as H_0 and the alternative H_1, and may be stated as:

H_0: there is no relationship between imports and GDP

H_1: H_0 is not true

Notice that the objective of the test is to test the null hypothesis against the alternative H_1. There is an alternative way of presenting the null hypothesis; in particular, it can be presented in terms of parameters of the model. More specifically, we notice that parameter β_2 links the dependent variable of the model to the independent variable GPD. Moreover, the value of this parameter is unknown. If the value of this parameter is zero, it is then implied that there is no relationship between the dependent variable and the GDP.

The null hypothesis may therefore be written as:

H_0: $\beta_2 = 0$ [no relationship between M & GDP]

The alternative hypothesis can be written more specifically. In particular, in forming the alternative hypothesis we should make use of information that we have concerning the value of this parameter. According to theory, the relationship between imports and GDP is positive in nature. Hence, movements in imports are in the same direction as those of GDP. Making use of this information, the alternative hypothesis may be written as:

H_1: $\beta_2 > 0$ [imports and GDP are positively related]

We therefore have:

H_0: $\beta_2 = 0$

H_1: $\beta_2 > 0$

or, alternatively:

H_0: $\beta_2 \leq 0$

H_1: $\beta_2 > 0$

4.4.1 The logic of hypothesis testing

The question that now arises is how to test the null hypothesis. The only information that we have concerning β_2 is its point estimate obtained from an OLS estimator $\hat{\beta}_2$.

Moreover, given the assumptions made, we know that $\hat{\beta}_2$ is an unbiased estimator with a minimum variance, provided the data generation assumptions are in fact valid. In short, $\hat{\beta}_2 \sim N(\beta_2, Var(\hat{\beta}_2))$.

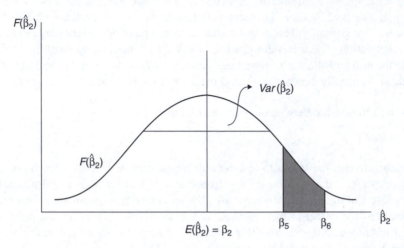

Figure 4.3 The sampling distribution of $\hat{\beta}_2$.

This distribution can be used for finding the probability that the estimator lies between any two specific values. For example, if one wishes to find the probability of the estimator to lie between β_5 and β_6 (any two specific values), we need to find the area under the normal curve between these two values, as shown in Figure 4.3. Mathematically, the area is found by finding the integral of the normal distribution, between β_5 and β_6. An important property of the normal distribution is that the value of the area under the curve between any two points depends only on the distance of each point from the mean of the distribution where each distance is expressed per unit of standard error, rather than the mean and the variance of the distribution. In other words, for all values of mean and variance of a normal distribution, as long as the deviations of the points from the mean per unit of standard error are the same, the probabilities are also the same. Making use of this property to calculate the probability that an estimator, or a random variable, lies between any two points, we use the standard normal distribution. The standard normal distribution is centred around a mean of zero and has a variance of unity. Statisticians have calculated these probabilities for various values of random variables and tabulated these in the table of standard normal distribution (see Appendix). Any normal distribution can be converted to the standard normal distribution, by expressing the values of the random variable in terms of deviation from the mean of the distribution per unit of the standard error. This standard normal distribution is commonly known as the Z-distribution. For example, one can convert the distribution of $\hat{\beta}_2$ into a standard normal (Z-distribution) as follows:

$$Z = \frac{\hat{\beta}_2 - \beta_2}{SE(\hat{\beta}_2)} \sim N(0,1)$$
(4.13)

or, diagrammatically:

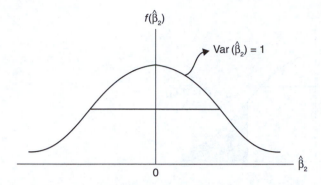

Figure 4.4 A standard normal distribution.

A specific value of Z, under H_0, obtained from (4.13) is called a Z-score. The probability that $\hat{\beta}_2$ (OLS estimator) lies between any two specific Z-scores can be calculated by converting the units of distribution into the units of standard normal distribution and then finding the area under the standard normal curve, from the tabulated table of Z distribution. This is called a confidence interval for this estimator.

4.4.2 The P-value approach to hypothesis testing

How does the discussion help in testing the null hypothesis? Remember that the process of hypothesis testing is essentially a process of falsification. We can therefore argue that, if H_0 is false, the probability that the Z-score would be more than or equal to the value that Z takes under H_0 ($\beta_{-2} \leq 0$) would be low, based on the observation that a false proposition should not occur frequently. To see this, consider the null and alternative hypothesis and the way Z-scores are calculated:

H_0: $\beta_2 <= 0$

H_1: $\beta_2 > 0$

$$Z = \frac{\hat{\beta}_2 - \beta_2}{SE(\hat{\beta}_2)} \qquad (4.14)$$

Z score under H_0 ($B_2 = 0$) is:

$$Z_1 = \frac{\hat{\beta}_2}{SE(\hat{\beta}_2)} \qquad (4.15)$$

If H_0 is false then β_2 would take positive values and Z-scores would tend to be less than Z_1 quite frequently. Therefore, if H_0 is false, the probability that Z-scores would be greater than, or equal to Z_1, under repeated sampling would be small, say less than 5%, as in Figure 4.5.

In Figure 4.5, the shaded area shows Pr ($Z \geq Z_1$). If H_0 if false, this probability would be small. The convention is to set this probability from the outset at some predetermined values, usually as 1, 5, or 10%. These are called the level of significance of the test. The practitioner then calculates the Pr ($Z \geq Z_1$). If this probability is less than 5%, say, one would be inclined to reject the null hypothesis.

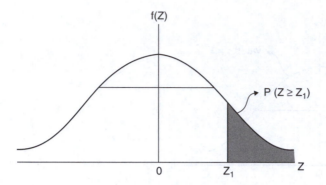

Figure 4.5 Hypothesis testing using the standard normal distribution.

This approach to hypothesis testing is called the p-value approach/method. The p-values are usually reported by regression packages. In practice, we do not know the standard error of the estimator SE (β_2). We need therefore to replace $SE(\hat{\beta}_2)$ with an estimator $S\hat{E}(\hat{\beta}_2)$, in the Z-score formula. Doing this, however, changes the shape of the normal distribution. The resulting distribution is called Student's t-distribution. It is centred on a mean of zero; however, it is slightly flatter than the standard normal distribution, as the variance of the distribution is slightly more than unity, for small numbers of observations, e.g. $n \leq 30$. However, as the number of observations increases to more than 30 and beyond, t-distribution converges to the standard normal/Z-distribution and the two distributions are not distinguishable for large samples. The t-distribution is therefore a small sample distribution closely related to the Z-distribution.

In practice we look at the p-values. If any one of these is less than the 5% level of significance, we can reject H_0, concluding that the independent variable in question is not statistically significant.

A test of significance for the slope parameter β_2 using the p-value approach

H_0: $\beta_2 \leq 0$

H_1: $\beta_2 > 0$

The p-value reported by the regression package is 0.032. In other words, if H_0 is true, there is only a 3% chance that the value of t-statistic that is $t = \dfrac{\hat{\beta}_2}{S\hat{E}(\hat{\beta}_2)} = \dfrac{2.0253}{0.06652} = 30.44$ will occur under repeated sampling. Using the conventional 5% level of significance, since the p-value is less than the chosen level of significance, we reject H_0. This result is, however, only reliable if all assumptions, including those concerning the disturbance term are consistent with the data. We therefore need to confirm all assumptions before arriving at an appropriate conclusion.

4.4.3 An alternative method based on critical values

There is an alternative way of conducting a test of significance using the table of the t-distribution. Under this method, once the level of significance of the test is set at, say 5%, practitioners then use tables of the t-distribution to find the so called critical value of the test. This is a particular value of the test statistic for which the probability that the t-ratio is equal to, or greater than that value, is 5%:

$$\Pr(t \geq c.v) = 0.05$$

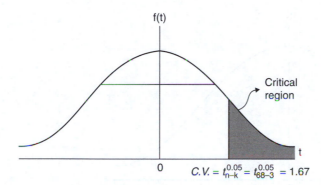

Figure 4.6 Significance testing and the critical region.

The shaded area is called the critical region of the test, because if the t-ratio falls in this region, we reject H_0 at a 5% level of significance. Notice that the method is very similar to the p-value approach. Under the p-value approach, we use the reported probability for rejecting/not rejecting H_0, whereas under this method, we use the critical value and critical region of the test to arrive at a decision. Both imply the same conclusions. We now perform the t-test under the alternative method.

Under H_0:

$$t = \frac{\hat{\beta}_2}{S\hat{E}(\hat{\beta}_2)} = \frac{2.0253}{0.061527} = 30.4413 \qquad (4.16)$$

With the critical value of the test being 1.67 (from the table of t-distribution (see Appendix)), we reject H_0, concluding that β_2 is significantly different from zero and the log GDP is a significant regressor.

4.4.4 A significance test for the slope parameter β_3

The null and alternative hypotheses may be stated as:

H_0: $\beta_3 = 0$ [no relationship between log M and log P_M/P_D]

H_1: $\beta_3 < 0$ [a negative/inverse relationship between log M and log P_M/P_D]

1 *The p-value approach* The p-value for the test is calculated at 0.0923, which is greater than 0.05. Therefore, we do not reject H_0, concluding that there is no statistical support

for the inclusion of P_M/P_D as a regressor in the model. This is an unexpected result. However, as was pointed out, the t-test is only reliable if all assumptions are valid. We cannot, therefore, express a firm opinion on the results, at this stage.

2　*The critical value approach*　Under H_0, The t-value is calculated as:

$$Z = \frac{\hat{\beta}}{S\hat{E}C\hat{B}_3} = \frac{-0.905}{0.74096} = -1.2213 \tag{4.17}$$

The C.V of the test of 5% level of significance is -1.67.

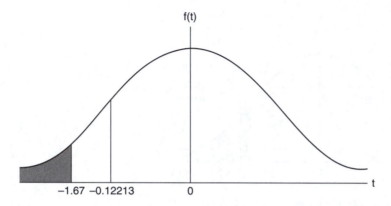

Figure 4.7 Conventional significance testing.

Decision rule:

$$t = -1.2213 > t_{65}^{0.05} = -1.67, \qquad |t| = 1.2213 < t_{65}^{0.05} = 1.671$$

We cannot reject H_0 at a 5% level of significance, concluding that the relative price term is not statistically significant. Notice that under H_1, β_2 takes only negative values, the appropriate critical region of the test is the shaded area, as is shown in Figure 4.7.

4.4.5 A significance test for the intercept term parameter β_1

We can perform a test of significance on the interrupt term to see whether or not it is statistically significant. In practice, it is advisable to carry out this test, as inclusion of an intercept term is essentially indicated by the type of functional form used. To perform this test we can state the null and alternative hypotheses, as follows:

H_0: $\beta_1 = 0$

H_2: $\beta_1 \neq 0$

Note that in the absence of any information concerning the value of the intercept term. The alternative hypothesis is stated such that β_1 can take either positive or negative values.

Under H_0, the t-ratio is calculated as:

$$t_2 = \frac{\hat{\beta}_1}{S\hat{E}C\hat{\beta}_1} = \frac{-13.4334}{0.78558} = -17.1 \tag{4.18}$$

Given the way H_1 is formulated, we need to consider both positive and negative values of the t-distribution using a 5% level of significance and dividing it equally between the two tails of distribution; the critical values of the test are 2.0, as shown in Figure 4.8 below.

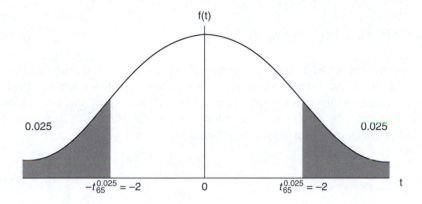

Figure 4.8 Two-tailed significance testing using the t-distribution.

A decision rule:

Because $\left|t = 17.1\right| > \left|t_{65}^{0.025} = 2\right|$, reject H_0 at the 5% level of significance, concluding that the intercept term is statistically significant and is different from zero.

4.5 Testing for linear restrictions on the parameters of the regression models

Before we test the joint significance of regressors, it is useful to first consider a general test procedure which can be used to test the validity or otherwise of one or a number of linear restrictions on parameters. For example, in the model under consideration, we may be interested to test the hypothesis that the income and price elasticities of imports are of the same magnitude. We can state this hypothesis as follows:

H_0: income elasticity of demand for imports = price elasticity of demand for imports

H_1: H_0 is not true

or, in terms of parameters of the model:

H_0: $\beta_2 = \beta_3$

H_1: H_0 is not true

In this formulation, the null hypothesis imposes a linear restriction on parameters in the model. This type of test where one, or a number of linear restrictions, are imposed on parameters, is very popular in practice. How is such a test conducted? We use the example below to give a basic insight into the procedure. In this example we have one linear restriction on the parameters of the model. We now impose this restriction. The restricted model can be written as:

$$\log M_t = \beta_1 + \beta_2 \, \log GDP_t + \beta_2 \log \left(P_M / P_D \right)_t + u_t \tag{4.19}$$

or

$$\log M_t = \beta_1 + \beta_2 \left[\log GDP_t + \log \left(P_M / P_D \right)_t \right] + u_t \tag{4.20}$$

We estimate the restricted model by OLS to obtain the R^2 and the associated residual sum of the squares (RSS). Now if the restriction is valid, what would be the relation between the R^2 or RSS of the restricted and the unrestricted (original model)? We expect, in this situation, these two sets of values to be very similar, as both models should fit the data equally well. Any observed differences are due to estimation procedures.

Symbolically:

$$R^2_{H0(unrestricted-model)} \cong R^2_{H1(restricted-model)} \tag{4.21}$$

or that the observed differences between the restricted and unrestricted residual sum of squares is small. That is:

$$RSS_R - RSS_U = \text{a 'small' magnitude.}$$

To be able to conduct a statistical test, however, what we need is a test statistic which utilises the difference between the two residual sum of squares. Assuming that the assumptions concerning the data generation process are met, under repeated sampling procedures, the difference between the two residual sum of squares divided by the number of restrictions on the parameters follows a chi-squared distribution. The chi-squared distribution starts at the origin and is defined only for positive values of a random variable. The shape of a chi-squared distribution changes with sample size. As sample size increases, this distribution becomes more symmetrical, approaching a normal distribution shape as sample size approaches infinity.

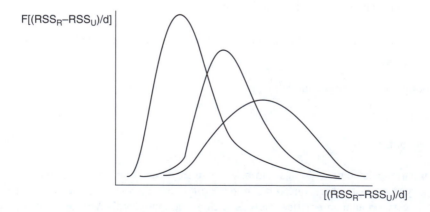

Figure 4.9 A chi-squared distribution.

The vertical axis is the frequency/probability of occurrence of values of $(RSS_R - RSS_U)/d$ under repeated sampling, and the horizontal axis is the value of $(RSS_R-RSS_U)/d$. Here d denotes the number of restrictions on the parameters of the model. In our example there is only one linear restriction, i.e. $\beta_2 = \beta_3$ and d is therefore equal to one. The denominator d also represents the degrees of freedom of the chi-squared distribution, which is the number of independent observations utilised to estimate a parameter. The problem with the use of $(RSS_R - RSS_U)/d$, as a test statistic is that the residual sum of squares are sensitive to the units of measurement of the dependent variables. It therefore does not provide an unambiguous measure when the difference between the residual sum of squares is small/large. Statisticians have overcome this problem by making the value in question a relative magnitude. More specifically, the difference between the two residual sum of squares is measured relative to the residual sum of squares of the unrestricted model per degrees of freedom, so:

$$F = \frac{[RSS_R - RSS_U]/d}{RSS_U/(n-k)} \sim Fd, n-k \tag{4.22}$$

if the assumptions are valid, under the repeated sampling exercise, $RSS_U/n-k$ also follows a chi-squared distribution with n-k degrees of freedom.

It can be shown that the ratio of two independent chi-squared distributions follow an F-distribution. The F-distribution is skewed and starts from the origin, and ranges to infinity. Since this distribution is related to a pair of chi-squared distributions, there are two associated degrees of freedom, d and n-k, degrees of freedom in the numerator and denominator, respectively. Figure 4.10 illustrates an F–distribution. Like the chi-squared distribution from which it is derived, an F-distribution becomes symmetrical with increases in the sample size. The F-distribution converges to a chi-squared distribution with large sample sizes.

There are tables of the F-distribution produced for different levels of significance, e.g. 1%, 5% and 10% (see Appendix). To find a desired F-value it is necessary to first select the table with the desired probability in the right tail, and locate the entry that matches the appropriate degrees of freedom for the numerator and denominator.

The F-statistic may also be written in terms of the R^2 values of the restricted and unrestricted models. This can be done only if the dependent variable of the model remains the same after the imposition of linear restrictions.

Figure 4.10 An F-distribution.

To convert the F-statistic into R^2 format, all we need is to divide both the numerator and denominator by the total sum of squares TSS. We have:

$$F = \frac{[RSS_R - RSS_U]/d}{RSS_U/(n-k)} \sim Fd, n-k$$

(4.23)

$$F = \frac{\left(\dfrac{RSS_R}{TSS} - \dfrac{RSS_U}{TSS}\right)}{(RSS_U/TSS)}(n-k)d$$

(4.24)

Assuming that the dependent variable of the model remains the same after imposition of the linear restriction, so that TSS for both restricted and unrestricted models are the same, we have:

$$F = \frac{\left(R_R^2 - R_U^2\right)}{\left(1 - R_U^2\right)}\left(\frac{n-k}{d}\right) \sim Fd, n-k$$

(4.25)

4.5.1 Testing for linear restrictions in practice

To perform a test of parameter restriction, we use the following steps:

1   Estimate the unrestricted model by the OLS and record RSS_U or R_U^2.
2   Impose the linear restrictions and estimate the restricted model by the OLS to obtain RSS_R or R_R^2.
3   Calculate the F-statistic and compare the value with the critical value of the test, obtained from F-distribution tables. Note that an F-distribution is identified by two degrees of the freedoms, one corresponding to the chi-squared distribution in the numerator and one corresponding to the chi-squared distribution in the denominator.
4   If the calculated value of F is greater than the critical value of the test we reject H_0 at a pre-specified level of significance, concluding that the linear restriction/s are not statistically significant.

An illustration of the use of the F-test follows, where it is applied to test the overall significance of the regression.

4.5.2 Testing the overall significance of regression

Given that there are usually more than one regressor in regression models, it is necessary to perform a joint test of significance in addition to t-tests. A joint test of significance is designed to test the significance of all regressors/independent variables of the model, jointly, in contrast to a t-test, which tests the significance of each regressor/independent variable of the model one at a time.

To begin the process we need to state the null and the alternative hypothesis of the test.

H_0: all regressors taken jointly/ collectively are not significant.

H_1: H_0 is not true

alternatively:

$H_0: = \beta_2 = \beta_3 = 0$ (independent variables GDP and P_M/P_D are not significant)

H_1: H_0 is not true

Notice that our aim here is to test the null hypothesis. The H_1 of the test may therefore be stated in a general form which encompasses alternatives.

Under H_0 we have two linear restrictions on the parameter of the model, therefore d = 2, which is the same as the number of parameters of the model minus one. So k–1= d, or parameters 3–1= 2 = d.

Since the dependent variable, log Mt, remains the same after imposing the linear restriction, we use the R^2 form of the F-test as follows.

$$F = \frac{\left(R_R^2 - R_U^2\right)}{\left(1 - R_U^2\right)}\left(\frac{n - k}{d}\right) \sim Fd, n - k \qquad (4.26)$$

The coefficient of determination of the restricted model is zero, since under H_0, the two independent variables are deleted. The test statistic, therefore, takes a simpler form, as follows:

$$F = \frac{\left(R_U^2\right)}{\left(1 - R_U^2\right)}\left(\frac{n - k}{d}\right) \qquad (4.27)$$

Upon substitution for corresponding the values into (4.26), we have:

$$F = \frac{0.98109}{\left(1 - 0.98109\right)} \times \frac{(68 - 3)}{2} = 1683.3 \qquad (4.28)$$

Note that in practice, we do not need to calculate the value of F for the test of significance, as it is normally reported by the regression packages.

Using the 5% level of significance, the critical value of F at the 5% level of significance is 3.15 (see Table in Appendix). Decision rule: because F = 1683.3 > $F_{3.15}^{0.05}$ = 3.15, we reject H_0 at the 5% level of significance, concluding that independent variables, jointly, are highly significant. The reliability of this test depends crucially on the validity of assumptions, which are to be tested in the next chapter.

4.6 A summary of key issues

- The regression results are evaluated by the economic, statistical and econometric criteria.
- The economic criteria checks to see whether the estimated coefficients have the 'correct' sign and appropriate magnitudes using economic theory as guideline. The statistical criteria are concerned with the tests of significance to provide statistical evidence in support of the regression model.
- Hypothesis testing is the main procedure of the statistical criteria. Individual tests of significance, based on t-distribution are carried out to see if each independent variable on its own is statistically significant and therefore impacts the dependent variable.

- To carry out hypothesis testing the sampling distribution of the OLS estimators are used. Given the assumption of normality, each OLS estimator has a normal distribution. Moreover, provided data generation assumptions are all in fact valid, each distribution is centred on the true value of the parameter with a minimum variance.
- A normal distribution can easily be converted into the standard normal distribution, with mean zero and variance equal to unity. This distribution is sometimes called Z-distribution. A particular value of Z-statistic is called a Z-score. There are tables of standard normal distribution used to find the probability of Z falling between any permissible range of values.
- A closely related distribution to the standard normal distribution is Student's t-distribution. This distribution emerges when one replaces the unknown standard error of the OLS estimator in the Z-statistic with its OLS point estimate. Under a repeated sampling procedure, this statistic has a sampling distribution with a mean zero and a variance slightly more than unity. This new statistic is called a t-statistic. A t-distribution is a small sample distribution (number of observations less than 30), and as the number of observations increases, a t-distribution converges to a Z-distribution.
- Each null hypothesis is formulated to indicate that each slope parameter is not significantly different from zero. A t-test is then used to falsify the null. Using either a p-value approach or a critical value testing procedure, if the null is rejected, it is concluded that the parameter is not zero and is statistically significant. This in turn is taken to imply that the corresponding independent variable/regressor is significant. The so-called t-ratios refer to the values of the t-statistic under null hypotheses; these are routinely reported by almost all regression packages. Each t-ratio shows the value of t-test statistic under the null hypothesis. As a rule of thumb, if the value of t-ratio is greater than two, the parameter is likely to be statistically significant.
- To test for the significance of a linear restriction (or a set of linear restrictions) on the parameters of a regression model, an F-test is employed. The null hypothesis is that the linear restriction is valid. If the null is true, then the residual sum of squares under the restricted and unrestricted versions of the regression model must be similar under a repeated sampling procedure. Using this idea, the difference between the restricted and unrestricted residual sums of squares is calculated and then divided by the number of restrictions. To generate an F-distribution this value is divided by the residual sum of the squares of the unrestricted model, which is in turn is divided by its degrees of freedom. The numerator and the denominator each having an independent chi-squared distribution, resulting in an F-distribution. Using a 5% level of significance, if the value of F-test statistic falls into the critical region of the test, we reject the null, concluding that the linear restriction on the parameters is not true.
- An F-distribution emerges from division of two independent chi-squared distributions. It is skewed towards origin and can only take on positive values. The F-distribution tables are available for calculating the probability of the F-statistic falling in a particular permissible range.
- To test for the overall significance of regression, an F-test is used. The null hypothesis is that slope parameters, taken jointly, are not different from zero. This is the same as the F test of linear restriction, but can be carried using the coefficient of determination version of the test as the dependent variable would not change after imposing the restriction. The F-test statistic is routinely reported by the regression packages. If the value of this test statistic under the null hypothesis is greater than the critical value of the F-test at, say 5%, reject the null concluding that the regression is significant.

- Note that the F-test is a joint test of overall significance and it is possible that the regression model is significant according to an F-test, but each individual t-test is not significant. That is, each individual parameter is not different from zero, but all, jointly, are different from zero. This situation might arise due to inadequacy of the data, particularly if the sample size is small and is taken as an indicator of multicollinearity in the data. In this situation it is advisable to increase the sample size and sample variation.

Review questions

1   Explain why it is necessary to empirically evaluate econometric models. What are the main criteria used in practice to evaluate econometric models? How would you use these criteria?

2   Explain what you understand by each of the following:

  a   hypothesis testing
  b   level of significance of the test
  c   test of significance
  d   test of overall significance
  e   critical value of the test.

3   Explain the logic of hypothesis testing. How does a p-value approach to hypothesis testing differ from the conventional testing procedures based on critical values? Explain.

4   Explain the key features of each one of the distributions below and point out under what circumstances you would use each one of these in practice:

  a   normal distribution
  b   Student's t-distribution
  c   F-distribution
  d   chi-squared distribution.

5   Collect 60 UK quarterly data from the Economic Trends Annual Supplement (available online) on aggregate imports, relative price of imports to price of domestically produced goods, and the real GDP, for a period of your own choice. Use the example covered in this chapter as a guide to carry out the following:

  a   Specify a log-linear regression model to estimate the price elasticity of demand and the income elasticity of demand for imports.
  b   Explain the role of any disturbance term included in your model and discuss the meaning of each standard assumption of concerning this term. Why are these assumptions necessary?
  c   Use a regression package to estimate the regression model. Present the regression results in a standard format.
  d   Use economic and statistical criteria to evaluate the regression results. Include in your analysis, individual tests of significance and a joint test of overall significance. Can you rely on these tests at this stage? Explain.
  e   Test for the parameter restriction that the sum of price elasticity of demand for imports and the income elasticity of demand for imports is equal to unity. Explain each step of this test carefully.

6   Carry out a similar exercise as above using a data set for a country of your own choice.

5 Autocorrelation, heteroscedasticity and diagnostic testing

INTRODUCTION

Econometric models are constructed on the basis of a number of simplifying assumptions necessary to start the process of empirical analysis. For example, to conduct an empirical analysis of the import demand function in the previous chapter, we made the following simplifying assumptions:

1   The relationship between imports and its determinants can be adequately presented by a log-linear equation (specification assumption).
2   The disturbance term is normally and independently distributed around a mean of zero, with a constant variance.
   Note that there are in fact four assumptions included in this statement. These are:

   a   the normality assumption;
   b   the non-autocorrelation assumption;
   c   the zero mean assumption;
   d   the homoscedasticity assumption.

3   The regressors are non-stochastic and are measured without errors.
4   There is no exact linear relationship among the regressors/independent variables.

The regression results are then obtained via the OLS method on the basis that each one of these assumptions is in fact valid. Given this framework, before considering the regression results as reliable, we need to test the validity of each one of these assumptions. The reliability of the OLS regression results depends crucially on the validity of these assumptions. The *econometric criteria* deal with testing and evaluation of the data genera-tion assumptions of non-autocorrelation, homoscedasticity, normality and specification errors. Although we have divided the criteria of the evaluation of the regression results into economic, statistical, and econometric criteria, in practice, these criteria are strongly linked and are collectively used to evaluate the results. The regression results can only be considered reliable when all three criteria simultaneously are satisfied. In this chapter we focus our attention on the econometric criteria of evaluation. In particular, we explain the phenomenon of *autocorrelation* and *heteroscedasticity* and explain in detail the detection and testing procedures used in practice for each one of these key problems. Unlike other introductory econometric texts that devote several separate chapters to these issues, in applied work, these issues are typically investigated collectively, but in a step by step fashion. We follow this practice and investigate the validity of the data generation assumptions, collectively, and in a step by step fashion in this chapter. To illustrate key issues, we will continue with the regression results of the UK demand for competitive imports.

Key topics

- Econometric criteria of model evaluation, the specification and misspecification tests
- Causes and consequences of autocorrelation and detection procedures
- Causes and consequences of heteroscedasticity and detection procedures
- Testing of the normality assumption

5.1 Econometric criteria of evaluation and diagnostic testing procedures

Econometric criteria are concerned with the data generation assumptions, which include the assumptions of specification of the model, as well as the assumption of normality, independence, zero mean, and constant variance of the disturbance term. In what follows we will look at a number of diagnostic tests commonly used in practice to test the validity of these. For illustrative purposes we continue to use the model of demand for imports. To begin the process, it is useful to consider the regression model and assumptions:

$$\log M_t = \beta_1 + \beta_2 \log \text{GDP t} + \beta_3 \log \left(\text{Pm}/\text{Pd} \right) t + u_t \tag{5.1}$$

$$\left(\text{specification assumption} \right); \qquad u_t \sim \text{NID}(0,\ \sigma_t^2);\ \text{for all t}$$

(where NID signifies normally independently distributed)

Within the framework of the traditional specific to general (SG) approach, there are no accepted benchmarks regarding the correct order of diagnostic tests to be used; choice of the tests and the order by which they are performed are left to the practitioner. In what follows, we utilise a Microfit 4/5 output regarding the types of diagnostic test and the order of testing, distinguishing between specification and misspecification tests.

5.1.1 Specification and misspecification tests

Specification tests involve a specific alternative/form of the regression model. For example, significance tests, either of the 't' or 'F' variety are specification tests. These tests are designed to confirm or refute a known specification given by the model under consideration, against a specific alternative. Misspecification tests, on the other hand, do not involve a specific alternative form of the model. They are essentially used to detect an inadequate specification. That is, they tell us that a particular assumption under consideration is inadequate (cannot be confirmed), but how to correct this inadequacy is left to the practitioner. It should also be pointed out that the reliability of a specification test crucially depends on the validity of the data generation assumptions. The practitioner therefore needs to carry out the required misspecification tests first before considering specification tests. In applied work, econometric criteria are therefore investigated before statistical criteria in arriving at a conclusion regarding the adequacy of the model.

5.2 Autocorrelation: causes, consequences and detection – the Durbin-Watson test

The Durbin-Watson (DW) (1951) test is perhaps the most celebrated misspecification test in applied econometrics. It was originally developed to detect serial correlation in the data. Serial correlation is used to describe a situation where the values of the same variable are connected to each other. Another term used in econometrics describing the same phenomenon is autocorrelation. Serial correlation and autocorrelation are both used to indicate the breakdown of the assumption of independence. The assumption of independence is made from the outset to describe the independence of the distributions of disturbance terms/ dependent variable. This means that a disturbance term/dependent variable corresponding to a particular observation does not depend on a disturbance term/dependent variable corresponding to another observation. For example, in a time series study of output, we can use the disturbance term to take into account the influence of random factors, such as breakdowns of machinery, climatic changes, and labour strikes, on the level of production per period. In this example the assumption of independence implies that a breakdown of machinery/strikes/climatic changes, or, for that matter, any random changes only affect the level of production in one period: the period during which the random event has actually occurred. In other words, the influence of a random shock does not persist over time; it has only a temporary influence on the dependent variable. Notice that the only way that a prolonged influence of random events can occur in econometric models is when the disturbance terms are correlated over time; so that when a random shock occurs in a particular period, it can also influence the dependent variable in other periods, through interdependency and correlation/connection with the disturbance terms in other times. The assumption of independence or no autocorrelation/no serial correlation, even when the model is correctly specified, often breaks down in practice because of the prolonged influence of random shocks on the economic variables. In time series applications, practitioners should expect the presence of autocorrelation and the breakdown of the assumption of independence. This is particularly the case when the econometric model is incorrectly specified to begin with, which is normally the case within the framework of the traditional methodology. Let us explore the connection between autocorrelation and incorrect specification of the model a bit further. Recall how the systematic part of an econometric model is developed on the basis of economic theory, which is used as a guide in the selection of the independent variables for inclusion in the model. In applied work there could be other variables, not suggested by the economic theory under consideration, influencing the dependent variable. For example, in developing a model of aggregate consumption expenditure using the Keynesian hypothesis of the absolute income hypothesis (AIH), we are guided by the theoretical arguments that real income is the main determinant of short-run consumption. In a modern economy there are other variables, equally as important. These variables include interest rates and rates of inflation. Moreover, there are competing theories of aggregate consumption expenditure over time, recommending the inclusion of excluded variables. If a practitioner omits one or more of these variables whose effects are captured by the data, the econometric model would be inconsistent with the data and so is *misspecified*. The cause of misspecification, in this case, is omission of relevant economic variables in the econometric model. A particular indication of this type of specification error is the breakdown of the independence assumption and the presence of autocorrelation. This is because one or more of the excluded variables could be autocorrelated variables. For example, if the interest rate is left out of the model of consumption expenditure, we get autocorrelation, because interest rate time series are autocorrelated. What happens in this situation is that the disturbance term picks up the influence of the excluded variable/s which are autocorrelated. We therefore get autocorrelation in the model. A test for autocorrelation is, therefore, essentially a general misspecification test, as the practitioner is unable to determine the exact cause of autocorrelation from test results. Further work would be needed to deal with the problem of autocorrelation in order to discover the exact cause.

In the light of this discussion, the Durbin-Watson test may be regarded as a general misspecification test, in the sense that it can detect the autocorrelation, but is incapable of identifying its cause. The test is easily carried out in practice and is routinely reported by regression packages. It therefore provides an early warning device concerning the specification of the model. Before we consider this test and the way it is used in practice it is useful to look at the consequences of autocorrelation for the OLS methods of estimation.

5.2.1 *Consequences of autocorrelation for the OLS estimators*

Recall that we use the OLS method of estimation because it generates efficient estimators. So, under repeated sampling, the OLS method generates estimators whose distributions have the properties of unbiasedness, minimum variance and consistency. The problem is that these properties are highly sensitive to the data generation assumptions made from the outset. They will be generated only if these assumptions are in fact consistent with the data. In the case of autocorrelation, the consequences for the OLS estimators are serious. It can be shown that while they are still unbiased, they tend to have large variances and become inefficient. In fact there are other estimators (for example, generalised least squares (GLS)) which are efficient and should be used instead. Moreover, the OLS method tends to underestimate the standard errors of the estimators. In this situation, the t-ratios become highly unreliable. In addition, OLS methods underestimate the standard errors of regression, which in turn leads to unreliable R^2 and F-statistics. In short, all the basic tools of analysis, including the t and F-tests and R^2 become highly unreliable. In practice, it is advisable to test for the presence of autocorrelation as a matter of routine before reporting the results of statistical tests of significance.

5.2.2 *The Durbin-Watson (1951) test*

The Durbin-Watson (DW) test is a simple test designed to deal with first-order autocorrelation. First-order autocorrelation is a term used to describe a situation where the successive values of the same variable are interrelated/correlated. This is perhaps the simplest form of autocorrelation. We can present first-order autocorrelation, using mathematical notation, as follows:

$$u_t = \rho u_{t-1} + \varepsilon_t \qquad \varepsilon_t \sim NID\,(0,\,\sigma_e^2); \qquad \text{for all } t \qquad (5.2)$$

where, ε_t is a white noise process satisfying all standard assumptions. In this specification of autocorrelation, the successive values of the disturbance term are correlated. The extent of the linear relationship between these successive values is captured by the term ρ. This term ρ could take on any value between -1 and $+1$. When it is a positive value, autocorrelation is said to be positive. This basically means that the difference between successive values of the disturbance term will be positive or negative for a long period. The disturbance terms do not alternate in sign over a long period of time. This form in turn implies that the nature of the influence of a random shock on the dependent variable remains the same over successive periods. For example, if the disturbance term is added to a model of production, to capture the impact of random events on output, positive autocorrelation implies that the impact of a breakdown on output will be the same over time. It essentially reduces output over a number of time periods. Its sign in this case is negative and will remain so for a period of time. On the other hand, if ρ is negative, we say that we have negative autocorrelation. In this case the disturbance term alternates in sign, so one period it is negative, and the next period it is positive, or vice versa. In other words, the impact of a random shock on the dependent variable of the model changes from one period to the next. In one period it has a positive impact on the dependent variable, and in the next period it has a negative impact. Note that in the case of positive autocorrelation the difference between the successive disturbance terms, over periods of time, is either positive or negative. Whereas in the case of negative autocorrelation, the sign of the difference between successive values of the disturbance term would alternate in sign. This simple observation provides the basis for the DW test. Given that the disturbance terms are not observable, any test based on this observation must use the empirical counterpart of a disturbance term; in the case of the OLS estimation the empirical counterparts are the OLS residuals. A simple detection method based on these residuals would be to look at the signs over the sample period. If the residuals do not change sign over a relatively long period, this could indicate positive autocorrelation. Alternatively, if the residuals tend to change signs from one period to the next, this could be a sign of negative autocorrelation. Durbin and Watson extended this idea a bit further to generate a test statistic. They reasoned that in the case of positive autocorrelation the difference between successive OLS residuals tends to be small (because both residuals have the same sign). On the other hand, in the case of a negative autocorrelation the difference between the successive OLS residuals tends to be relatively large (because the residuals alternate in sign). Taking this idea one step further, in order to make all differences positive they square each of the residual differences. Moreover, to take into account all differences, they add all squared differences. They then reasoned that in the case of a positive autocorrelation this sum would be relatively small, whereas in the case of a negative autocorrelation it would be relatively large. Symbolically:

$$\sum_{t=2}^{n} (e_t - e_{t-1})^2 \text{ is relatively small, if positive autocorrelation exists; is relatively large, if}$$
negative autocorrelation exists

where e_t is the OLS residual for period t, showing the difference between the observed value and the fitted value of the dependent variable. Note that when calculating the above sum we lose one observation, hence t starts from the second observation.

The pressing question which arises now is what constitutes a relatively large/relatively small value in this context? Before we answer this question, however, it is important to recognise that the value of this sum depends on the units by which the variables of the model are measured. The first task is therefore to eliminate this problem. Durbin and Watson dealt with this problem by dividing the above sum by the sum of the squares of the OLS residuals, hence:

$$DW = d = \frac{\sum_{t=2}^{n} (e_t - e_{t-1})^2}{\sum_{t=1}^{n} e_t^2} \tag{5.3}$$

Both the numerator and the denominator have the same unit of measurement and so this ratio is unit free. We can now get back to the question of the magnitude of this ratio. To deal with this problem, Durbin and Watson expanded the ratio as follows:

$$Dw = d = \frac{\sum\limits_{t=2}^{n} e_t^2}{\sum\limits_{t=1}^{n} e_t^2} + \frac{\sum\limits_{t=2}^{n} e_{t-1}^2}{\sum\limits_{t=1}^{n} e_t^2} - 2\frac{\sum\limits_{t=2}^{n} e_t e_{t-1}}{\sum\limits_{t=1}^{n} e_t^2} \tag{5.4}$$

They then argued that the value of each of the first two ratios is approximately equal to one and the sum of the first two is therefore approximately 2. The third ratio is in fact the OLS estimator of the correlation coefficient. This coefficient lies between −1 and +1. We therefore have:

$$DW = d \cong 2(1-\hat{\rho})$$

It is now possible to determine the range of the values of the Durbin-Watson (DW) ratio, as follows:

1   In the case of a perfect positive correlation, the value of $\hat{\rho}$ would be approximately +1, and the value of the DW ratio is approximately zero.
2   In the case of a perfect negative correlation, the value of $\hat{\rho}$ would be approximately −1 and the DW ratio would be approximately 4.
3   Finally, in the case of no autocorrelation, the value of $\hat{\rho}$ would be approximately zero and the DW ratio would be approximately 2.

The range of the values for the DW ratio is therefore (0 and 4). As a quick guide, zero could indicate a strong positive autocorrelation, 4 a strong negative autocorrelation and 2 a lack of autocorrelation. This is a quick guide and what is needed is a test statistic which can be used in all situations. For this purpose we need the sampling distribution of the DW ratio, and some critical values. Durbin and Watson showed that their test statistic has not got a unique critical value, but rather it lies between two limiting values under repeated sampling procedures. These limiting values are called the upper and the lower bound values and are denoted by du and d_L, respectively. Durbin and Watson then calculated these values for different sample sizes and alternative numbers of independent variables. These values are tabulated in the table of the DW test.

5.2.3 Key steps in the DW test

We illustrate this test, step by step, as follows:

1   We start the test by specifying the null and the alternative hypotheses:

H_0 = there is no autocorrelation in the model/data

H_1 = autocorrelation does exist

or, more specifically:

$H_0: \rho = 0$

$H_1: \rho \neq 0$

Although the test is essentially two-sided, in most applications H_0 is tested against a positive alternative, to reflect the kind of autocorrelation that is expected.

2   The DW test statistic is calculated as:

$$DW = d = \frac{\sum\limits_{t=2}^{n}(e_t - e_{t-1})^2}{\sum\limits_{t=1}^{n} e_t^2} \tag{5.5}$$

3   We choose a particular level of significance for the test, say 5%, and find the corresponding upper and lower bound values from the table of DW.

The decision rule of the test is as follows:

1   If the DW test value is less than d_L, reject H_0 in favour of positive autocorrelation.
2   If the DW test value is between d_L and du, the test is inconclusive. In this case use the du as the critical value of the test; this assumes autocorrelation exists. It is, however, recommended in this case to use an additional test for autocorrelation to confirm this result.
3   If DW is between du and 4-du, do not reject H_0. In other words, autocorrelation does not exist.
4   If DW is between 4-du and 4-d_L the test is inconclusive. In this case, use 4-d_L as the critical value, in other words, assume negative autocorrelation exits. It is advisable to carry out an additional test to confirm this result.
5   If the DW value is between 4-d_L and 4, do not reject H_0, negative autocorrelation is present. In practice, the value of the DW test statistic is calculated by the regression package and is routinely reported. All we need to do is to look at this value; if the value is close to 2, it is a good indication that autocorrelation does not exist, any other value signifies autocorrelation. We then need to confirm these results, using the tables for the DW test statistic.

There are some shortcomings in this simple misspecification test. In particular, although the test is a first-order test, a significant value of the DW test statistic is also consistent with higher-order autocorrelation. In other words, if H_0 is rejected, practitioners should not take this to mean that first order autocorrelation exits, but that the order of the autocorrelation is not known. Moreover, the test is highly unreliable when a lagged value of the dependent variable appears as a regressor in the model. In this case the value of the DW test statistic would be biased towards 2, indicating no autocorrelation, despite the fact that autocorrelation is present. There are a number of alternative tests available that are appropriate for use in this situation.

5.2.4 The DW test in practice

To illustrate the DW test, we apply this test to the regression results of the import demand function presented in the previous chapter (in 4.8).

We start by assuming a first order autoregressive process as follows:

$$u_t = \rho u_{t-1} + \varepsilon_t \qquad \varepsilon_t \sim NID\ (0,\ \sigma_e^2); \qquad \text{for all } t$$

Given this process, the H_0 and H_1 of the test may be written as follows:

H_0: $\rho = 0$

H_1: $\rho \neq 0$

The test statistic is:

$$DW = d = \frac{\sum\limits_{t=2}^{n}(e_t - e_{t-1})^2}{\sum\limits_{t=1}^{n}e_t^2} \tag{5.6}$$

The value of this statistic is reported by the Microfit 4/5 software to be 0.55343.

Using a 5% significance level, the lower and the upper bound values for $n = 68$ and $k = 3$ and $\acute{k} = 3-1 = 2$ (where k is the number of parameters including the intercept term), are respectively:

$d_L = 1.54$ and $du = 1.66$.

Decision criterion: because DW = d = 0.55343 < d_L =1.54, we reject H_0 at d = 5%. H_0 is not consistent with the data. Positive autocorrelation appears to be present.

As it appears that there is autocorrelation in the model, the OLS regression results should therefore be treated as unreliable. This is what usually happens in practice. It is seldom the case that, within the framework of the traditional approach to econometric modelling, we succeed in the first attempt. The question now is how to respond to a significant value of the DW test statistic. We consider this next.

5.2.5 How to respond to a significant value of the DW test Statistic: the traditional (SG) approach

A significant value of the DW test statistic implies that autocorrelation exists.

However, neither the cause nor the order of the autocorrelation are known. In applied work within the framework of the specific to general (SG) approach to econometric modelling and analysis, autocorrelation is usually generated due to a model's misspecification, caused by one or more of the following factors:

1 Omission of one or more relevant regressors;
2 Dynamic misspecifications, for example, exclusion of lagged values of dependent and independent variables;
3 An incorrect functional form of the model, for example, the correct model could be non-linear in parameters.

There are other causes of autocorrelation. For example, the prolonged influence of random shocks. This could be responsible for autocorrelation. In these situations we need to test for the specification errors first, correct the model using theory, then deal with any residual autocorrelation left in the model.

Given that the nature and causes of autocorrelation are not clear, in practice we need to follow a particular strategy to deal with the problem of autocorrelation. There is no specific strategy recommended and used by all practitioners. The strategy that we recommend follows the specific to general methodology based on the diagnostic testing as follows:

1   Attempt to find the order of autocorrelation first. For this purpose we use a general diagnostic test for autocorrelation, such as the Lagrange multiplier (LM) test.
2   Use a general misspecification test for incorrect functional form, such as Ramsey's regression specification error test (RESET).
3   Use another misspecification test, this time for heteroscedasticity, which may be the cause of misspecification, particularly in using cross-section data.
4   If the diagnostic tests indicate the model is misspecified, try to correct the model starting from theory. This is particularly useful when the cause of the problem is omitted variables. In time series analysis, the cause of specification errors is often *dynamic misspecification*. In this type of study, researchers concentrate on the dynamics of the model and try to correct for it by using an adjustment mechanism such as a partial adjustment model.

We next discuss these diagnostic tests applied to the model of competitive imports.

5.2.6 The Lagrange multiplier (LM) test for the detection of autocorrelation

The Breusch-Godfrey (1978) (BG) test is commonly known as the Lagrange multiplier (LM) test. This is a general test for autocorrelation, used by practitioners to detect the order of autocorrelation. This test is a large sample test and is reliable when a sufficiently large number of observations are available. Moreover, the larger the number of observations, the more reliable the results of this test tend to be. To demonstrate the test, suppose that we wish to test for autocorrelation up to the 4th order. Under this specification, the disturbance term in any particular period depends on the disturbance terms in each of the previous four time periods. More specifically:

$$u_t = \rho_1 u_{t-1} + \rho_2 u_{t-2} + \rho_3 u_{t-3} + \rho_4 u_{t-4} + \varepsilon_t \tag{5.7}$$

$$\varepsilon_t \sim NID\,(0, \sigma_t^2); \qquad \text{for all t.}$$

This pattern of autocorrelation could emerge, for example, when one is using quarterly data.

The disturbance term in a particular quarter would depend on the disturbance terms in the previous four quarters.

We start the test by specifying the null and the alternative hypotheses as:

$$H_0:\ \rho_1 = \rho_2 = \rho_3 = \rho_4 = 0$$

$$H1:\ H_0 \text{ is not true}$$

If autocorrelation of up to the 4th order exists, the regression model takes the following form:

$$\log M_t = \beta_1 + \beta_2 \log GDP_t + \beta_3 \log\left(P_m / P_D\right)_t + \rho_1 u_{t-1} + \rho_2 u_{t-2}$$
$$+ \rho_3 u_{t-3} + \rho_4 u_{t-4} + \varepsilon_t \tag{5.8}$$

We may call this equation the unrestricted form of the model, in a sense that there are no restrictions imposed on the parameters of the model.

If the null hypothesis could not be rejected, the model would be the regression equation we started with, hence:

$$\log M_t = \beta_1 + \beta_2 \log GDP_t + \beta_3 \log\left(P_m / P_D\right)_t + \varepsilon_t \tag{5.9}$$

We call this equation the restricted form of the model, in the sense that there are four parameter restrictions on parameters of the model (four zero restrictions), compared to the unrestricted form of the model. We are therefore essentially testing for parameter restrictions. We have already considered the F-test for linear restrictions in the previous chapter. The test statistic is as follows:

$$F = \frac{[RSS_R - RSS_U]/d}{RSS_U/(n-k)} \sim Fd, n-k \tag{5.10}$$

Decision rule: using the 5% level of significance, if F(d, n-k) > F(critical value at 5%), reject the null hypothesis at the 5% level of significance, concluding that autocorrelation up to the 4th order exists. Notice that we still do not know the exact order of autocorrelation. All we can say at this stage is that autocorrelation could be up to the 4th order. To find the order of autocorrelation we need to test down. That is, we start from a sufficiently high order, say the 5th order, and then test down, using this procedure. If there is no autocorrelation of the 5th order, we test for the 4th order, and so on, until the order of autocorrelation is identified. We are now in the position to apply this test to the model. We do this in a step by step fashion:

5.2.7 *Key steps of the LM test for detection of autocorrelation*

1   Set up the null and the alternative hypotheses. Since we are dealing with quarterly data, we test for up to 4th order autocorrelation in the model/data. In fact, Microfit 4/5 automatically tests for up to 4th order autocorrelation when inputted data is quarterly. In the case of annual and monthly data, Microfit automatically tests for 1st and up to 12th order autocorrelation, respectively. A 4th order autoregressive model may be written as:

$$u_t = \rho_1 u_{t-1} + \rho_2 u_{t-2} + \rho_3 u_{t-3} + \rho_4 u_{t-4} + \varepsilon_t \tag{5.11}$$

$\varepsilon_t \sim NID(0, \sigma_t^2)$; for all t.

The null and the alternative hypotheses can now be written as:

$H_0: \rho_1 = \rho_2 = \rho_3 = \rho_4 = 0$

$H1: H_0$ is not true.

2   The test statistic is

$$F = \frac{[RSS_R - RSS_U]/d}{RSS_U/(n-k)} \sim Fd, n-k \tag{5.12}$$

The value of this statistic is computed as $F(4,61) = 17.4855$, where $d = 4$; $n = 68$; $k = 7$.

3   We next choose a particular level of significance, say 5%, and find the critical value of the test from the table of the F-distribution. The critical value is $F(4,61) = 2.53$. Now because $F(4,61) = 17.4855 > F(4,66) = 2.53$, we reject the null hypothesis at the 5% level of significance, concluding that there is autocorrelation up to the 4th order in the data/model.

The LM test therefore indicates a significant amount of autocorrelation in the model/data. Note that we have not yet determined the correct order of autocorrelation, all we have done is to confirm the result of the DW test that autocorrelation exits and it could be up to the 4th order. We now go to the next step in the analysis and carry out a general misspecification test.

5.2.8 *The Ramsey regression specification error test (RESET)*

The RESET test is a popular misspecification test developed by J. B. Ramsey (1969). It is used to test whether some unknown variables have been omitted from a regression model. The test can also be used to detect incorrect functional forms. This test is routinely carried out in practice by the econometric packages. For example, Microfit 4/5 reports the results of this test after the LM test as a main diagnostic test. We demonstrate this test with reference to the model of demand for imports. The regression model is:

$$\log M_t = \beta_1 + \beta_2 \, \log GDP_t + \beta_3 \, \log(P_m/P_D)_t + u_t \tag{5.13}$$

If the model is correctly specified, the expected value of the dependent variable is determined by the variables suggested by the theory; in this situation the disturbance term is a random variable capturing only the influence of the random terms on the dependent variable. In other words, if the model is correctly specified, there should not be a relationship between the expected value of the dependent variable and the disturbance term. However, if the model is not correctly specified, either due to omission of relevant regressors or incorrect functional form, the disturbance term would not only capture the influence of random terms on the dependent variable, but it also captures the influence of omitted variables. In other words, there are some variables included in the disturbance term which would have a systematic influence on the dependent variable. These unknown omitted variables, captured by the disturbance term, are the cause of model misspecification.

Following this line of reasoning, in developing a misspecification test, Ramsey recommends adding a number of additional terms to the regression model and then testing the significance of these additional terms. More specifically, he suggested that one needs to include in the regression model some functions of the regressors, on the basis that, if the model is misspecified, the disturbance term would capture these variables, either directly or indirectly through other variables omitted from the regression. All we need to do is to test for the significance of these additional terms. If these additional variables are found to be significant, then the model is misspecified. Notice that the test does not tell us how to correct the model, it is designed to show that the model is misspecified. To correct the model, we need to use theory. In time series investigation it is advisable to consider the dynamic structure of the model and correct accordingly.

The question which now arises is how to perform a RESET in practice? In particular, what are these additional variables to include in the model to start the process? The additional variables are some function of the regressors. Therefore, we need a variable which depends on the regressors used in the model. An obvious candidate variable is the estimated expected value of the dependent variable (fitted values) obtained from the OLS estimation of the regression model under consideration.

With reference to our model of demand for imports, we have:

$$\log \hat{M}_t = \hat{\beta}_1 + \hat{\beta}_2 \log\text{GDP}_t + \hat{\beta}_3 \log\left(P_m/P_D\right)_t \tag{5.14}$$

The estimated expected value of the dependent variable ($\log M_t$), depends on the regressors. Following Ramsey's recommendation we need a function of this variable to include as an additional variable in the model. In practice, we normally include a number of the powers of this variable as additional variables in the regression model to obtain the so-called expanded equation; we then test for the significance of these additional variables using the F-test for linear restrictions. If the additional variables are found to be significant, one concludes that the regression model is misspecified. Regression packages, and in particular Microfit 4/5, carry out this test automatically using the second power of the fitted value of the dependent variable as an additional regressor. In practice, however, it is useful to look at the graph of the OLS residuals against the fitted values to see whether we can detect a relationship. We can also count the number of turning points on the graph as a guide to the power of the fitted values to be included as additional variables. For example, normally, one turning point in the graph suggests a quadratic relationship, so we include the second power of the fitted value as an additional variable. Two turning points could be indicative of a third-degree polynomial relationship, so we include both the second and the third powers of the fitted values as additional variables in the regression, and so on.

5.2.9 Key steps of the RESET test

1   Estimate the regression model by the OLS and make a note of the residual sum of squares. Call this RSS_R.
2   Include a number of the powers of the fitted values (the squared values) as additional variables in the regression to obtain the expanded equation. With reference to the regression model, the expanded equation is:

$$\log M_t = \beta_1 + \beta_2 \log\text{GDP}_t + \beta_3 \log\left(P_m/P_D\right)_t + \beta_4 \left[\widehat{\log M_t}\right]^2 + u_t \tag{5.15}$$

3   Estimate the expanded equation by the OLS and record the residual sum of squares and call this RSSu. Notice that the original regression model is in fact a restricted form of the expanded equation where the coefficient of the additional variable is set to zero.
4   Using the expanded equation as the unrestricted form of the model, and the original regression equation as the restricted form of the model, we test for the significance of additional variables. With reference to our model, we can specify the null and alternative hypotheses:

$H_0: \beta_4 = 0$

$H_1: \beta_4 \neq 0$

5   This is the F-test of linear restrictions. The test statistic is:

$$F = \frac{[RSS_R - RSS_U]/d}{RSS_U /(n-k)} \sim Fd, n-k \tag{5.16}$$

where d = number of parameter restrictions (the difference between the number of the parameters of the unrestricted model and the number of the parameters of the restricted model).

n = number of the observations

K = number of the parameters of the unrestricted model.

6   We need to compute the value of this test statistic. This is F(1, 64) = 2.6145, where d = 1 and n–k = 64.

7   Decision rule: choosing a 5% level of significance, the critical value of the F-test is approximately 4. Because F(1, 64) = 2.6145 < $F_{1,64}^{0.05}$ = 4, we do not reject the null hypothesis at the 5% level of significance. The RESET test appears to indicate that the model is not misspecified. In the light of the results of other misspecification tests (notably the DW test), this is surprising. However, the RESET result cannot be relied on, because of the significant amount of autocorrelation in the data/model already detected by the DW and LM tests. This situation clearly demonstrates one of the major shortcomings of the traditional (SG) approach to econometric modelling. In this approach, the reliability of each diagnostic test depends crucially on the results of all other tests carried out, and if any one of these tests breaks down, they all fail. Only when all the diagnostic test results are consistent and all assumptions are confirmed, can we consider that the regression is reliable.

5.3 Heteroscedasticity: causes, consequences and detection

One of the main assumptions of the linear regression model is the assumption of homoscedasticity, or constant variance. This assumption implies that the variance of the distribution of the dependent variable of the model, corresponding to each set of values of the independent variables, is constant. In other words, variations in the values of the independent variables are assumed not to affect the variance of the dependent variable. Symbolically, the assumption of the homoscedasticity may be written as:

Var (dependent variable) = σ^2 for all t = 1,. . ., n.

Alternatively, in terms of the variance of the distribution of the disturbance term, the assumption of homoscedasticity implies that the variances of the distributions of all the disturbance terms are the same. Symbolically:

Var $(u_t) = \sigma^2$ for all t = 1,. . ., n.

Notice that variance (dependent variable) = var $(u_t) = \sigma^2$.

The failure of this assumption is called heteroscedasticity. In practice, heteroscedasticity could occur due to one, or combinations, of the following factors:

1   In cross-sectional work, it is often the case that the values of the independent variables change significantly from one observation to the next. Significant variations in the independent variables cause the variance of the dependent variable/disturbance term to change, resulting in heteroscedasticity. This particular form of heteroscedasticity is said to be caused by scale effects spilling over from independent variables. For example, in the regression model of consumption/income relationship, as income changes significantly from one observation to the next, the variance of the expenditure (the dependent variable) tends to change with it. In particular, the higher the level of income, the higher is the variance of the distribution of the consumption expenditure. This is because at higher levels of income consumers have greater scope/freedom to spend. The variance of consumption expenditure rises with income as the pattern of expenditure becomes more unpredictable.

2   Although heteroscedasticity usually occurs in cross-sectional analysis due to scale effects, it can also be present in time series analysis. In particular, the variance of the disturbance term could become smaller with the passage of time to reflect learning from the past errors, or better data collection procedures. Both these tend to reduce the variance of the disturbance term over time.

3   Specification errors, due to omission of relevant regressors or incorrect functional form, can also cause heteroscedasticity. For example, if a regressor has been left out of the model its influence is captured by the disturbance term, which, in turn, could become heteroscedastic if the omitted variable is itself heteroscedastic. In practice, it is therefore advisable to follow up a general misspecification test (e.g. RESET), with a test for heteroscedasticity, such as the Koenker-Bassett test, routinely carried out by Microfit 4/5.

5.3.1 Consequences of heteroscedasticity for the OLS estimators

Before we consider a number of tests carried out in practice to detect heteroscedasticity, it will be useful to discuss briefly the impact of heteroscedasticity on the OLS estimators. Generally speaking, these estimators are no longer best in the class of unbiased estimators and are not, therefore, reliable. In fact, it can be shown that another estimator, the generalised least squares (GLS), is a superior estimator. More specifically, when heteroscedasticity is present it can be shown that:

1   The OLS estimators are unbiased but are no longer efficient, that is, they tend to have relatively large variances.

2   The OLS estimator of the error variance is biased. The direction of the bias depends on the relationship between the variance of the disturbance term and the values taken by the independent variable causing heteroscedasticity.

3   The test statistics which make use of the OLS estimate of the error variance, including t and F-tests, are unreliable, generating misleading results.

4   The coefficient of determination, R^2, will also be unreliable, usually overestimating the extent of a linear relationship between the dependent and the independent variables.

Given the serious nature of these consequences, it is clearly necessary to test for the heteroscedasticity in applied research, particularly when cross-section data is used. We next consider a number of statistical tests designed to detect heteroscedasticity.

5.3.2 Detection: the Koenker-Bassett (1982) (KB) test

This is a simple diagnostic test done automatically by regression packages, for example, Microfit 4/5. We demonstrate this test by using the regression results of the model of import.

Heteroscedasticity implies that the variance of the disturbance term is not constant over the data range. The Koenker-Bassett (KB) test assumes, in particular, that the variance of the disturbance term is a function of the regressors. The actual functional form need not be specified. To get the test operational, we need a proxy for the non-observable variance and a variable which is influenced only by the regressors. The squares of the OLS residuals are usually used as a proxy for the variance. As for the other variable, the KB test uses the fitted values of the dependent variable (in this example logM). The test then assumes a certain relationship between these two variables. Specifically, it is assumed that the squared residuals (the proxy for variance) is a linear function of the squared fitted values of the dependent variable, used here to capture the variations in all the regressors.

5.3.3 Steps in the KB test

1   Specify the auxiliary equation of the test as follows:

$$e_t^2 = a_0 + a_1 [\widehat{\log M_t}]^2 + \varepsilon_t \qquad (5.17)$$

$$\varepsilon_t \sim NID (0, \sigma_t^2); \qquad \text{for all t}$$

where e_t is the OLS residual.

2   Set out the null and alternative hypotheses, focusing on the significance of the slope parameter a_1 in (5.17) that is:

$$H_0: a_1 = 0$$

$$H_1: a_1 \neq 0$$

The test is a simple t-test, which is:

$$t = \frac{\hat{a} - a}{S\hat{E}(\hat{a})} \sim t_{n-k} \qquad (5.18)$$

3   Decision rule: given that the t-test has only one degree of freedom, it can be shown that the squared value of the t-value is distributed as an F-distribution with one degree of freedom. In practice, one usually uses the F-version of the test. The value of this statistic for the model of competitive imports is $F(1, 66) = 4.9546$. The critical value of the test at the 5% level of significance is approximately 4. We therefore reject H_0, concluding that there is evidence of heteroscedasticity present. Given the nature of the time series model it is likely that heteroscedasticity is due to the model misspecification, as it is indicated already by the DW test.

5.3.4 The White test for the detection of heteroscedasticity

This is yet another popular test for heteroscedasticity, developed by H. White (1980) as a general test for the detection of heteroscedasticity. It is routinely carried out in practice and is reported by regression packages. It does, however, need a large data set and it is essentially a large sample test. In principle, it is similar to the KB test, in that it aims to detect whether the variance of the disturbance term is a function of the regressors. More specifically, it tests to see if error variance is affected by the regressors. To use the test, the square of the OLS residuals in the regression model is taken as a proxy for the unobserved variance and is regressed on the regressors of the model, their squared values, and their cross products. The R^2 of this equation times the number of observations, n, that is nR^2 can be shown to be distributed as a chi-squared distribution for large samples with degrees of freedom equal to the number of the regressors used in the auxiliary equation, excluding the intercept term. For a large value of this test statistic we reject the null hypothesis of homoscedasticity and conclude that heteroscedasticity is present. Note that the test cannot identify the cause of the problem, it just indicates that the heteroscedasticity problem does exist.

5.4 A test of normality assumption: the Bera-Jarque (1987) (BJ) test

An important assumption of the classical linear regression model is the assumption that the dependent variable/disturbance terms are normally distributed. Given this assumption, the OLS estimators are also normally distributed and the specification/misspecification tests outlined have associated 't', 'F' and chi-squared distributions. Given the crucial role of the diagnostic tests in the analysis of the results, it is important to carry out tests to confirm the assumption of normality. A popular test for this purpose is the Bera-Jarque (BJ) test. The BJ test is designed to track departures from the normal distribution by checking the skewness and the kurtosis of the distribution of the OLS residuals. The BJ test statistic is given as follows:

$$BJ = \left[n/6 \; SK^2 + n/24 \left(EK - 3 \right)^2 \right] \tag{5.19}$$

where n = the number of observations, SK = a measure of skewness of the distribution, and EK = a measure of kurtosis of the distribution.

It can be shown that the BJ test statistic, under repeated sampling, and the null hypothesis that the OLS residuals are normally distributed, has a chi-squared distribution with 2 degrees of freedom. Microfit 4/5 reports the value of the BJ test statistic with other diagnostic tests. In practice, all we need to do is to compare the BJ test value with the theoretical value of chi-squared distribution with 2 degrees of freedom, at a pre-specified level of significance. If the BJ test statistic is greater than the corresponding critical value at a pre-specified level of significance, for example, 1% or 5%, we reject the normality assumption.

The BJ test is highly sensitive to the presence of the outlier observations which generate large OLS residuals. The rejection of the normality assumption could therefore signal the existence of the outlier observations, or breaks in the data.

5.4.1 Steps of the BJ test

1   Specify the null and alternative hypothesis of the test as follows:

H_0: the disturbance terms are normally distributed (the OLS residuals are normally distributed).

H_1: H_0 is not true

2   Calculate the test statistic.

$$BJ = \left[n/6 \; SK^2 + n/24(EK - 3)^2 \right] \sim \chi_2^2 \tag{5.20}$$

3   Decision rule: the value of the BJ test statistic reported by Microfit 4/5 is 0.81353. Because $BJ = 0.81353 < \chi_2^{2\,(0.05)} = 5.99$, we do not reject H_0 at $\alpha = 5\%$, concluding that the normality assumption is maintained. This result implies that the normality assumption of the shape of the data generation process is consistent with evidence.

5.5 A summary of key issues

- The traditional approach to econometric analysis is based on the specific to general (SG) methodology. Within this framework a simple regression model based on theory together with a number of assumptions designed to explain the data generation process are first specified. The regression model is estimated by the OLS, since if all assumptions are valid this method generates the best linear unbiased estimators (BLUE).
- In practice, almost all data generation assumptions are likely to break down. In this case the OLS estimators are likely to lose their desirable properties, generating misleading results.
- To deal with this problem, the SG approach recommends a battery of diagnostic testing to be carried out on each one of the data generation assumptions. If problems are detected then correction should be carried out using theory and logical reasoning to guide this process. Within this framework a general model/theory is to be derived from the original specific model.
- This framework seems sound in theory, but is not all that successful in practice. Misspecification tests detect problems, but are incapable of identifying corrections. All corrections and modifications are to be carried out within the framework of the theory. This is a difficult task and in applied work one frequently is not able to arrive at a satisfactory model by using this iterative methodology.
- Note that within this framework, each and every test is conditional on arbitrary assumptions, which are to be tested later, and if any of these are rejected at any given stage in the investigation, all previous inferences are invalidated.
- Because of these issues the SG methodology has focused mainly on how to formulate 'good' estimators using mathematical and statistical methods to come up with alternative estimators to the OLS to deal with problems. Although this approach has been fruitful for mathematicians and statisticians, it has not been all that beneficial for economists and economic analysis.
- The problem is that this iterative methodology has been seldom able to correct the structure of the economic models or to come up with new innovative theories consistent with data and evidence.
- Autocorrelation is the breakdown of independence assumption. In regression analysis it is taken to mean that the values of the dependent variable/disturbance term are not independently distributed. Disturbance terms are correlated and can no longer be considered to be randomly distributed. Although autocorrelation could be due to prolonged influence of random events, in almost all time series applications, it is an indication misspecification. This could be due to omission of relevant variables, including incorrect dynamic specification.

- The consequences of autocorrelation for the OLS estimators are serious. These estimators are no longer efficient and regression results are, by and large, misleading and unreliable.
- The DW test is a simple, but powerful, misspecification test. It is used to detect autocorrelation, assuming that successive values of the disturbance term are correlated (first-order autocorrelation). If autocorrelation is detected, however, it could be of a higher order. In this case, an LM test is used to establish the order of autocorrelation. This could be followed by a RESET test to provide further evidence of specification error. These tests are not capable of indicating as to how to correct the model.
- Heteroscedasticity is the breakdown of the assumption of homoscedasticity or constant variance. It implies that the variance of the probability distribution of the dependent variable/disturbance term no longer remains the same across all observations. In cross-section regression, it could be due to a scale effect. That is, it could be caused if values of the independent variables change significantly in the data set. Variation in independent variables generates variability in the variance of the dependent variable/disturbance term. In time series data it could be another indication of incorrect specification. The KB test or the White test are routinely used for detection. If heteroscedasticity is detected, the OLS estimators are no longer efficient and the OLS results are typically misleading and unreliable.

Review questions

1 Explain the difference between the specification tests and misspecification tests. Why are both types of test necessary when evaluating a regression model?
2 Explain the causes and consequences for the OLS estimators of each of the following:

   a   autocorrelation
   b   heteroscedasticity
   c   multicollinearity.

3 Explain the Durbin-Watson Test for autocorrelation. What are the shortcomings of this test? How would you react to a significant value of this test in a regression analysis?
4 Explain how you would test for the heteroscedasticity in practice. What would you do if you find that heteroscedasticity is present in the model?
5 Collect a time series data set consisting of 70 annual observations on each of the following:

   a   aggregate personal consumption expenditure C
   b   national income NI
   c   annual rate of inflation P*.

6 Use economic theory to specify a suitable regression model for the aggregate personal consumption expenditure, in terms of national income and the rate of inflation. Define your variables carefully and use your data set with a regression package to estimate the model.

   a   test for autocorrelation, including the DW and the LM tests
   b   test for specification errors using a RESET test
   c   test for heteroscedasticity, and explain all procedures
   d   use economic, statistical and econometric criteria to evaluate the regression results
   e   are the regression results satisfactory?
   f   explain how you would attempt to improve the regression results.

6 The phenomenon of the spurious regression, data generation process (DGP), and additional diagnostic tests

INTRODUCTION

Regression models derived from economic theory are long run-equilibrium models. Based on theory, they show functional relationships among a number of variables in the long run. The time series data that are used in regression models are, however, dynamic, showing the magnitude of economic variables over specified intervals of time. There is no guarantee that these observed magnitudes are long-run values for the variables under consideration, or that interactions among economic variables are completed over one time period. There could be some lagged responses between the dependent variable and the regressors specified in the model, due to slow adjustment processes. The data captures the lagged responses, but the regression model excludes them. There is, therefore, inconsistency between long-run static econometric models and the data used for estimation. This is detected by the diagnostic tests, the DW and the RESET, as a specification problem. This chapter continues with the specific to general (SG) methodology and explains how this methodology attempts to introduce a dynamic lag structure into the regression model in response to the specification error problem indicated by the diagnostic tests. Closely linked to this correction procedure is the phenomenon of the spurious regression and the way the traditional (SG) approach attempts to deal with this problem. This chapter also includes additional diagnostic tests used in practice for the evaluation of regression models.

Key topics

- The phenomenon of the spurious regression
- The partial adjustment and the autoregressive short-run dynamic model
- Testing for the structural break and parameter stability: the Chow test
- Testing for measurement error: the Hausman test

6.1 The phenomenon of the spurious regression

The inconsistency between econometric model and the data generation process typically manifests itself via the results of diagnostic tests, which, usually, in time series analysis, indicate inadequacy of the static econometric model in capturing the main features of the dynamics of the data generation process. There is of course a good chance that the data generation processes are non-stationary and that the data generation process changes over time from one observation to the next. The non-stationary time series implies that the mean and variance of the data generation process (DGP) will not remain constant over time. In this case, to attempt to model these processes using simple static econometric models is futile, as there are no relevant stationary data generation processes to support the long-run static econometric model. That is, unlike the long-run equilibrium economic models, which link several variables in a model together, there are no relevant stationary data generation processes tending to move together towards an equilibrium state supporting this specification. In other words, the regression would be *spurious* and is in fact meaningless. Within the framework of the traditional approach, this problem usually manifests itself via diagnostic tests results indicating model misspecification. A good sign of this phenomenon is a low value of the DW test statistic, indicating a high degree of autocorrelation, coupled with a high value for the coefficient of determination R^2, indicating a good fit, but this is because of autocorrelation in the data, and not because the model is a good fit! Moreover, in applied work, one also typically obtains significant values for t and F-test statistics, when autocorrelation is present. It is therefore tempting to consider the model to be adequate, but the model is in fact totally meaningless and what we are observing is due to non-stationary data generation processes generating meaningless and conflicting regression results. This is termed the *spurious regression phenomenon*, and within the framework of the traditional approach is frequently encountered in practice. Granger and Newbold (1974) recommend the following rule of thumb to detect spurious regression: if the coefficient of determination, R^2, is greater than the DW value, then it is likely that the regression is *spurious*.

6.1.1 Detecting a spurious regression

Let us apply this rule to the regression results of the UK demand for competitive imports (presented in 4.8). The coefficient of determination and the DW test value are reported as 0.98 and 0.55, respectively. Applying this rule of thumb, we are therefore led to suspect that the regression is spurious and the model is incapable of identifying the competitive imports data generation process.

This implies that all regression results of this static model are in fact meaningless and should be discarded.

The traditional specific to general (SG) methodology of dealing with the problem of spurious regression, such as the one suspected in the above example, may be summarised as follows:

- Assume, without further investigation, that the data generation processes are in fact stationary and the fault lies with the specification of the regression model.
- The model builder therefore focuses on improving specification of the model, including the dynamic specification of the regression model, attempting to introduce lags into the relationship, and hoping things work out, ignoring the data generation processes and their characteristics.
- The focus is on making the model dynamic by simply including various types of lags into the regression model (see Chapter 7), without a theoretical and empirical foundation.

The modern approach, encapsulated by the cointegration analysis, takes a completely different approach to the problem of spurious regression:

- The immediate focus is on the data generation process of each variable, rather than the regression model.

- It first investigates to check whether the variables are stationary. This is done via unit root testing procedures, which are discussed in detail in Chapter 13.
- If any one of the variables in the regression model is not stationary, the regression is likely to be spurious.
- If the variables can be made stationary, they can be combined together in a regression model. If that is the case, then it focuses on the estimation and empirical evaluation of the underlying economic model and its dynamic structure. The short-run dynamic adjustment process is uniquely determined via an error correction mechanism, if the long-run economic model is consistent with the data.

We will explain in detail the modern approach to time series econometric analysis in Chapters 12–15. For now, in what follows, for illustrative purposes only, we continue with the traditional framework, modifying the model's specification and its dynamic structure in search of the data generation process (DGP).

6.2 Making the regression model dynamic via a partial adjustment process: estimation and evaluation

To modify the model and to replicate the data generation process, the first step is to look for dynamic misspecification as the cause of inadequacy. In particular, attempts are made to introduce lags among economic variables to capture the short-run dynamic nature of the data generation process. A particular procedure, used frequently by practitioners of the traditional methodology, is to assume partial adjustment mechanisms, which are then linked to the long-run regression model. The practitioner then estimates the short-run dynamic model and uses the results to derive the implied long-run parameters.

There are other lag and dynamic structures used by practitioners. We will deal with these in detail in the next chapter. In what follows, we demonstrate the partial adjustment method by using the log-linear model of imports demand of the previous chapter.

The static econometric model under consideration can be seen as portraying the long-run paths of desired levels of imports. In other words, theory suggests that in the long run, desired levels of imports depend on the level of expenditure/income and relative price terms. The desired, or the long-run level of imports are not observable and we need a mechanism which can be used to convert the model into data values in the data set. One such mechanism is a partial adjustment scheme. The basic ideas are as follows. The actual change in the dependent variable suggested by the data values is assumed to be a fraction of the desired change, due to sluggish conditions in the economy and slow adjustment processes among economic variables. Symbolically, in terms of model of imports, we can write:

$$\left(M_t - M_{t-1}\right) = \alpha\left(M^D t - M_{t-1}\right) \tag{6.1}$$

actual change   desired change

where $0 < \alpha \leq 1$ is the speed of the adjustment parameter. The closer α is to unity, the quicker the response of economic variables are to changes in economic conditions and the faster would be the adjustments towards equilibrium. Moreover, the closer α is to unity, the more efficient the economy. Market economies with institutional rigidities, labour market rigidities and inefficient market mechanisms tend to be sluggish, reacting slowly to required/desired changes. For these economies the parameter α tends to be close to zero, indicating a slow and prolonged adjustment process within the above framework. We can now combine the partial adjustment process with the regression model to generate a short-run model, as follows:

$$M_t = \alpha M_t^D + (1-\alpha) M_{t-1} \tag{6.2}$$

The long-run regression model showing the desired level of imports is:

$$M_t^D = \beta_1 + \beta_2 \, GDP_t + \beta_3 \left(P_m / P_D\right)_t + u_t \tag{6.2a}$$

Where all variables are measured in logs (for the ease of presentation we have not included the log notation).

Substitution for M_t^D from the regression model into (6.2) results in:

$$M_t = \alpha \, [\beta_1 + \beta_2 GDP_t + \beta_3 P_t + u_t] + (1-\alpha)M_{t-1} \tag{6.3}$$

$$M_t = \alpha \, \beta_1 + \alpha\beta_2 GDP_t + \alpha\beta_3 P_t + (1-\alpha)M_{t-1} + \alpha u_t \tag{6.4}$$

where all variables are in logs and $P = P_M/P_D$

The appearance of the M_{t-1}, the lagged dependent variable, as a regressor, implies that this is a short-run dynamic model. This model is called an autoregressive dynamic short-run model, and we will discuss its properties in detail in the next chapter. Notice that if u_t is NID $(0, \sigma^2)$, αu_t would also be a white noise process. We can therefore estimate the short-run model by the OLS, find the estimates of the short-run parameters and then use the values to estimate the implied long-run parameters. This two-step method is what has been done frequently in practice, within the SG framework.

We now illustrate the procedure:

Table 6.1

SR	LR
$\alpha_1 =$	$\alpha \beta_1$
$\alpha_2 =$	$\alpha \beta_2$
$\alpha_3 =$	$\alpha \beta_3$
$\alpha_4 =$	$(1-\alpha)$
$v_t =$	αu_t

Where SR= short run and LR= long run. Short run parameters are estimated first, then using the short run and long run relationships identified above, the long run estimates are generated.

The SR model may now be written as:

$$M_t = \alpha_1 + \alpha_2 GDP_t + \alpha\beta_3 P_t + \alpha_4 M_{t-1} + v_t \tag{6.5}$$

The regression results corresponding to (6.5) from Microfit 4/5 are reported in Table 6.1.

The dependent variable is log M_t and 67 observations were used for estimation from 1980 Q2 to 1996 Q4.

Table 6.2 OLS estimation from Microfit 4/5

Regressor	Coefficient	Standard error	T-ratio
C	−5.5571	1.2243	−4.5391
LogGDP	0.81046	0.17343	4.6731
log p	−0.011308	0.056721	−0.1993
log mt−1	0.6178	0.084666	7.2969
R-squared	0.98973	**F-statistics**	F(3,63)=2023.1
R-bar squared	0.98924	**SE of regression**	0.026132
Residual sum of squares	0.04302	**Mean of dependent variable**	10.3558
SD of dependent variable	0.25189	**Maximum of log likelihood**	151.1823
DW – statistic	1.8125		

Test Statistics	F Version
A: Serial correlation	F(4,59) = 2.2653
B: Functional form	F (1, 62) = 0.3023
C: Normality	χ^2 (2) = 4.95
D: Heteroscedasticity	F (1, 65) = 3.65

where:–
A: Lagrange multiplier test for serial correlation
B: Ramsey's RESET test using the squared fitted values
C and D: based on the regression of squared residuals or squared filled values

6.2.1 Evaluation of the regression results

1   First, we note that the estimated slope coefficient signs are in accordance with economic theory. In particular, the estimated (partial) income elasticity of demand for imports is positive (0.81046) and price elasticity of demand is negative (−0.011308). The magnitudes of these coefficients are, however, quite small, reflecting the short-run nature of the model. Nevertheless, the SR price elasticity of demand is estimated at only −0.011308, which indicates a very small response in demand for imports due to changes in relative prices. Moreover, the T-ratio corresponding to the coefficient of log p appears to be very small indeed (−0.19937) and statistically insignificant. This result suggests that UK demand for imports appears to be non-price sensitive. This is a surprising result and at odds with economic theory. It is worth reviewing literature concerning the estimate of the price elasticity of demand for imports, before accepting/reporting this result.
2   Diagnostic tests. The DW test is inappropriate in this case, as the lagged dependent variable is a regressor. In this situation we can either consider the result of the Lagrange multiplier test or carry out Durbin's h-test, which is a test for the first-order autocorrelation in the autoregressive models. We first explain Durbin's h-test and then consider the LM test statistic.

6.2.2 The Durbin h-test for autocorrelation

This is a test for first-order autocorrelation and is carried out when the lagged dependent variable is one of the regressors of the model. The test, suggested by J. Durbin (1970), is essentially a large sample test, and the more observations are used, the more accurate the test results should be. Given a first-order autoregressive process, the null and the alternative hypotheses of the test are written as follows:

Given AR(1)

$$u_t = \rho u t - 1 + \epsilon t \tag{6.6}$$

where

$$\epsilon t \sim NID\ (0, \sigma^2)$$

$$H_0 : \rho = 0$$

$$H_1 : p \neq 0$$

It can be shown that, under H_0, the following test statistic, when a large data set is used, has a standard normal distribution:

$$h = \hat{\rho} \sqrt{\frac{n}{1 - n\,\hat{var}(\alpha_4)}} \sim N(0,1) \tag{6.7}$$

where $\hat{\rho}$ = estimate of first-order correlation coefficient given by $\hat{\rho} = 1-(DW/2)$, n is the sample size, and var(α_4) with a hat, is the estimated variance of the lagged dependent variable. For example, in the model of imports, $\widehat{var}(\alpha_4)$ is $(0.084666)^2$. To apply the test we need to calculate the value of the h-statistic and then compare it with the critical values, at a pre-specified level of significance, of the normal distribution. For example, at $\alpha = 5\%$, the critical values are ± 1.96. Now if $-1.96 \leq h \leq 1.96$, we do not reject H0, concluding that H0 is consistent with the data and first-order autocorrelation does not appear to be present.

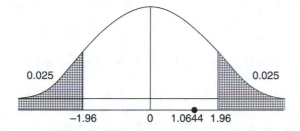

Figure 6.1 The Durbin 'h' test.

We now apply this test to the model under consideration:

$$h = \left(1 - \frac{1.8125}{2}\right) \sqrt{\frac{67}{1 - 67(0.084666)^2}} = 1.0644 \tag{6.8}$$

Decision rule: because h = 1.0644 falls in between 1.96 and −1.96, we do not reject H_0. The null hypothesis is consistent with the data at $\alpha = 5\%$ and first-order autocorrelation does not appear to exist in this modified short-run model.

6.2.3 The Lagrange multiplier (LM) test on the short-run model

The LM test is frequently used to test for higher order autocorrelation. Again, it is a large sample test and its use should be restricted to when a large data set is available. Given that we have used quarterly observations, (Microfit 4/5) automatically tests for up to 4th order autocorrelation chi-sq (4) or F(4,57). The first number, 4, is the number of linear restrictions which have been imposed on the parameters of the model. The underlying assumptions and steps are as follows:

Assume AR (4):

$$u_t = \rho_1 u_{t-1} + \rho_2 u_{t-2} + \rho_3 u_{t-3} + \rho_4 u_{t-4} + \epsilon; \quad \epsilon_t \sim \text{NID } (0, \sigma^2_t), \text{ for all } t$$

under this specification the unrestricted form of the model is:

$$\log M_t = \alpha_1 + \alpha_2 \log \text{GDP}_t + \alpha_3 \log P_t + \alpha_4 \log M_{t-1} + \rho_1 u_{t-1} + \rho_2 u_{t-2}$$
$$+ \rho_3 u_{t-3} + \rho_4 u_{t-4} + \epsilon_t \tag{6.9}$$

H0: $\rho_1 = \rho_2 = \rho_3 = \rho_4 = 0$ [4 linear restrictions]

H_1: H0 is not true

The restricted form of the model is, thus, the original model:

$$\log M_t = \alpha_1 + \alpha_2 \log \text{GDP}_t + \alpha_3 \log P_t + \alpha_4 \log M_{t-1} + u_t$$

The test statistic is the familiar F-test, as follows:

$$F = \frac{\left(RSS_R - RSS_U \right) \Big/ d}{RSS_U \Big/ (n-k)} \sim F(d, n-k) \tag{6.10}$$

This value is reported as F(4, 59) = 2.2653. Note: we have 67 observations and K = 8 (parameters in the unrestricted model).

   Decision rule: because F(4, 59) = 2.2653 < $F^{0.05}_{4,59}$ = 2.53, we do not reject H0 at α =5%. H0 is not consistent with the data. Therefore, according to this result, autocorrelation of up to 4th order does not exist in this model. [Note $F^{0.05}_{4,59}$ = 2.53 is the theoretical value of F(4,59) at 5%, obtained from the F-distribution table.]

6.2.4 The RESET test on the short-run model

This is a misspecification test. As pointed out previously, the square of the fitted values are added to the original equation to generate an expanded equation. One then tests for the significance of the addition terms. These procedures are demonstrated below:

$$\log M_t = \alpha_1 + \alpha_2 \log \text{GDP}_t + \alpha_3 \log P_t + \alpha_4 \log M_{t-1} + \alpha_5 \left[\widehat{\log M_t} \right]^2 + u_t \text{ (expanded equation)}$$

H0: $\alpha_5 = 0$

H1: $\alpha_5 \neq 0$

The test statistic is:

$$F = \frac{\left(RSS_R - RSS_U\right)\Big/ d}{RSS_U \Big/ \left(n-k\right)} \sim F(d, n-k) \tag{6.11}$$

The value of this test statistic is computed as $F(1, 62) = 0.30323$.

Note that the first degrees of freedom (one) is the number of linear restrictions on parameters in the model (d=1). The theoretical value of $F_{1,62}$ at $\alpha = 5\%$, is approximately 4.

Decision rule: since $F(1,62) = 0.3023 < F_{1,62}^{0.05}$, we do not reject H0 at $\alpha = 5\%$. H0 is therefore consistent with the data and the model appears to be well specified, according to the RESET test.

6.2.5 The Koenker-Bassett (KB) test on the short-run model

This is another diagnostic/ misspecification test. It is specifically designed to detect heteroscedasticity in the data, but is also used in time series analysis to indicate misspecification. It is based on the regression of the squared residuals on squared fitted values. It can be demonstrated as follows:

$$\text{Var} \left(V_t\right) \quad = F \left(\text{logGDP}, \log P, \log M_{t-1}\right)$$
$$\Big| \text{ Proxy} \qquad\qquad\qquad \Big| \text{ Proxy}$$
$$e^2 \left(\text{OLS}\right) \qquad\qquad\qquad \left(\log\hat{\ } m_t\right)$$

The auxiliary regression is specified as:

$$e^2 = \beta_1 + \beta_2 \left[\widehat{\log M_t}\right]^2 + u_t$$

The null and alternative hypotheses are as follows:

H0: $\beta_2 = 0$

H1: $\beta_2 \neq 0$

The test statistic is:

$$F = \frac{\left(RSS_R - RSS_U\right)\Big/ d}{RSS_U \Big/ \left(n-k\right)} \sim F(d, n-k) \tag{6.12}$$

The value of the above test statistic is computed as $F(1, 65) = 3.65$. The critical value of $F(1, 65)$ at $\alpha = 5\%$ is approximately 4.

Decision rule: since $F(1,65) = 3.65 < F_{(1,65)}^{0.05} = 4$, we do not reject H_0. H_0 is therefore consistent with the data. It appears that there is no evidence of heteroscedasticity/ misspecification in the model/data.

6.2.6 *The BJ test for normality*

Finally, we perform the BJ test on the short-run regression.

The BJ test for normality is conducted as follows:

H_0: Disturbance terms are normally distributed

H_1: H0 is not true

The BJ test statistic is:

$$BJ = \left[n/6 \; SK^2 + n/24 \left(EK - 3 \right)^2 \right] \sim \chi_2^2 \qquad (6.13)$$

The BJ statistic is computed by Microfit 4/5 as 4.95. The chi-squared value with 2 degrees of freedom at $\alpha = 5\%$ is 5.99. Decision rule: because $BJ = 4.95 < \chi_2^{2\,(0.05)} = 5.99$, we do not reject H0, concluding that H0 is consistent with the data. The normality assumption is therefore consistent with the data.

Within the framework of the traditional approach, and based on the results of the above diagnostic tests, the short-run partial adjustment model appears to be 'well specified' and explains the short-run data generation process. The only point of concern is the statistical insignificance of the relative price term, which needs further investigation.

We can now use the short-run estimated coefficients to derive the long-run parameters, as follows:

$\hat{a}_1 = -5.5571$

$\hat{a}_2 = 0.81046$

$\hat{a}_3 = -0.011308$

$\hat{a}_4 = 0.61780$

Since $\alpha_4 = (1-\alpha)$, $\hat{\alpha} = 1 - 0.6178 = 0.3822$ $\qquad (6.14)$

The coefficient of adjustment /speed is indicating a fairly sluggish adjustment process. The estimate of other long-run parameters are as follows:-

$\hat{\beta}_1 = -5.5571/0.3822 = -14.54$

$\hat{\beta}_2 = 0.81046 / 0.3822 = 2.2$

$\hat{\beta}_3 = -0.011308 / 0.3822 = -0.03$

where $\hat{\beta}_2$ *and* $\hat{\beta}_3$ are the estimates of long-run income elasticity and the price elasticity of demand for imports, respectively. While the long-run income elasticity appears to be consistent with previous studies, the price elasticity of demand, however, is only estimated at -0.03, reflecting very little response in demand for import to changes in relative prices. While the sign of this coefficient is consistent with the theoretical consideration, the magnitude appears to be too small. In conclusion, income seems to be the main variable influencing the level of imports, both in the short and long run. In particular, according to the empirical results, for every 1% change in the level of national income/ GDP, we expect, on average, imports to change by 2.2%. Imports are, therefore, considered to be highly income elastic. Given this result, unless exports also increase at the same rate per period, the economy could be faced with a balance of trade problems. Moreover, devaluation, the traditional remedy to deal with balance of payment problems would not be an effective policy option, given the above estimate of the price elasticity of demand for imports.

6.2.7 Further comments

This is where, within the framework of the SG methodology of single-equation regression, the analysis typically stops. The regression results appear to be passing the diagnostic tests and the parameter estimates appear to be consistent with the theoretical restrictions. There are a few 'minor problems' with the regression results and the underlying theory, but, overall, the model appears to be adequate. However, no attempt is made to explain why, for example, the relative price variable is not significant. Moreover, there is no theoretical justification given for the use of the partial adjustment process. The focus is on efficient estimation, using the OLS, not on underlying theory, nor on the data generation process of each variable included in the regression model. This example illustrates the SG methodology of single-equation regression analysis in practice. It is basically a hit and miss procedure; the above regression model may not be the 'best' model, just because it passes a few diagnostic testing procedures, and there is no theory underlying the short-run dynamic adjustment mechanism. It is just that the results appear to be adequate based on the criteria of evaluation. This is the point of departure for the modern approach to time series econometrics, which uses a completely different methodology to regression analysis, and which is based on the cointegration methodology. We will provide a detail analysis of the modern approach in Chapters 12–15.

Additional diagnostic tests

In what follows, we consider the key features of a number of additional diagnostic tests routinely carried out in applied research, to identify specific problems, including structural breaks and measurement errors.

In time series applications it is advisable to test for the parameter stability over the period of investigation. This is particularly important when long-run time series data are being used for estimation. The fundamental motive for this is to see whether the underlying regression model has remained unchanged. For this to be the case, the parameters of the model must have remained constant over time. Econometric models do fail and, as a result, the parameters linking the variables do change drastically. A breakdown in economic relationships occurs due to structural breaks in the economy. For example, significant currency crises, or external economic shocks, such as oil embargos, and sanctions. Or, due to political changes which usually bring about structural changes in the economy. Whatever the causes, a structural break results in the failure of economic relationships, misspecified econometric models, and faulty inference. In practice, it is therefore advisable to routinely carry out diagnostic tests for parameter stability.

There are two types of diagnostic tests available:

1   The Chow 'type' test: designed to test for parameter stability when a possible break point in the data/model can be identified 'a priori'.
2   Tests based on recursive estimation methods. These tests include CUSUM and CUSSUM Q tests, and are carried out when the break point in the data/model is not known 'a priori'.

We now provide a brief outline of each type of test.

6.3 The Chow test for parameter stability

The Chow test (1960) is designed to test for parameter stability. In this situation, the aim of the analysis is to see if the parameters of the model have been constant over the period of investigation. Suppose that there are (n) observations available and it is thought a structural break in the economy has occurred at the end of period (n_1). The structural break divides the data set into (n_1) observations before the possible break in the data and (n_2) observations after the possible break in the data, where $n_1 + n_2 = n$, the total number of observations. Provided that we have sufficient degrees of freedom (i.e. n_1 and n_2 are long periods of time), the Chow test for parameter stability is carried out as follows:

1   Estimate the model by OLS, using n observations, to generate the residual sum of squares RSS.

    a   Estimate the model by OLS, using n_1 observations, to generate the residual sum of squares, for the period before the 'break', RSS_1.

    b   Estimate the model by OLS, using n_2 observations, to generate the residual sum of squares, for the period after the 'break', RSS_2.

In the absence of a structural break, the residual sum of squares of the entire period, RSS, must be approximately the sum of the residual sum of squares of the two sub-sample periods, so:

$$RSS \cong RSS_1 + RSS_2 \tag{6.15}$$

Or, simply, the difference between RSS and $(RSS_1 + RSS_2)$ must not be statistically significant. A test statistic is therefore needed based on $RSS - (RSS_1 + RSS_2)$. Chow showed that the following test statistic has an 'F' distribution:

$$F = \frac{\left[RSS - (RSS_1 + RSS_2) \right] / K}{(RSS_1 + RSS_2) / (n - 2K)} \sim F, K, n - 2k \tag{6.15a}$$

where the numerator has a chi-squared distribution with K degrees of freedom and the denominator has a chi-squared distribution with n–2k degrees of freedom. K is the number of parameters of the model (including the intercept term) and n is the number of observations. The 'F' test statistic is used to test for the stability of the regression parameters. The test, however, is only reliable when the variance of the disturbance term has remained unchanged over time. It is therefore customary to carry out a test to check for changes in the variance of the disturbance term, and then use the Chow test. This is illustrated below:

6.3.1 The Chow test in practice

To illustrate the Chow test, we consider the regression model:

$$Y_t = \beta_1 + \beta_2 X_{2t} + \beta_3 X_{3t} + u_t \tag{6.16}$$

with

$u_t \sim NID\ (0, \sigma_2)$; for $t = 1, 2, \ldots, n$.

For illustrative purposes, suppose that a possible break point in the data is at the end of period n_1. The regression model for the period $n_{1+1}, \ldots, n$, may be expressed with 'new' parameters as follows:

$$Y_t = \alpha_1 + \alpha_2 X_{2t} + \alpha_3 X_{3t} + u_t \tag{6.17}$$

with

$u_t \sim NID\ (0, \sigma_2^2)$, for $t = n + 1, \ldots, n$.

Key steps of the Chow test are as follows:

1   Specify null and alternative hypotheses.

$H_0: \sigma_1^2 = \sigma_2^2$

$H_0: \sigma_1^2 \neq \sigma_2^2$

2   We first test for H_0. If H_0 is not rejected, we then test for the parameters' stability. The test statistic for this is based on the estimation of the error variance, using n_1 and n_2 observations in turn. Hence:

$$F = \frac{RSS_2 / (n_2 - k)}{RSS_1 / (n_1 - k)} \sim F(n_2 - k, n_1 - k) \tag{6.18}$$

where:

RSS_2 = residual sum of squares obtained from the OLS regression of the model over the period $n_{1+1}, \ldots, n$ (using n_2 observations).

RSS_1 = residual sum of squares obtained from the OLS regression of the model over the period $t = 1, \ldots, n_1$, (using n_1 observations).

If $F > F^{\alpha}_{n_2-k,n_1-k}$ reject H_0 at α% level of significance.

3   If H_0 is not rejected, use the Chow test for the parameter stability, as follows:

H_0: $\beta_1 = \alpha_1$; $\beta_2 = \alpha_2$; $\beta_3 = \alpha_3$;

H_1: H_0 is not true

The test statistic is:

$$F = \frac{\left[RSS - (RSS_1 + RSS_2)\right]/K}{(RSS_1 + RSS_2)/(n-2K)} \sim F,K,n-2k \tag{6.19}$$

where in this example K=3,

if $F > F^{\alpha}_{n_2-k,n_1-k}$ reject H_0 at α% level of significance, concluding that H_0 is not consistent with the data and parameters have changed over the sample period.

Comments

Note that the Chow test is essentially a joint test requiring a constant variance for the disturbance term over the sample period. There are occasions when the break point in the data is such that it does not provide sufficient degrees of freedom for two separate OLS regressions. This situation occurs when either $n_1<k$ or $n_2<k$. Supposing $n_2<k$, the Chow test procedure may be summarised as follows: ($n_1<k$ may be dealt with in the same way):

1   First, test for constant error variance:

$H_0 : \sigma_1^2 = \sigma_2^2$

$H_0 : \sigma_1^2 \neq \sigma_2^2$

The test statistic for this test is:

$$HF(n_2) = 1 / \frac{(RSS_1)}{(n_1 - k)} \bullet \sum_{t=1}^{n_2} e_{2t}^2 \sim \chi_{n_2}^2 \tag{6.20}$$

where $\sum_{t=1}^{n_2} e_{2t}^2$ is the sum of squares of the one-step-ahead forecast errors. To obtain e_{2t}, we first estimate the regression by OLS over the n_1 sub-sample. We then use these parameter estimates together with the value of the regressors in each period, over $n+1...n$, (n_2 observations) to obtain one-step-ahead forecast errors.

Decision rule: If $HF(n_2) > $ (chi-Sq (n_2)) or $\chi_{n_2}^{2(\alpha)}$, reject H_0 at α% level of significance. This test is known as the Hendry forecast (HF) test. If H_0 cannot be rejected, go to the next step, as follows:

2   Second step.

H$_0$: $\beta_1=\alpha_1$; $\beta_2=\alpha_2$; $\beta_3=\alpha_3$;

H$_1$: H$_0$ is not true

Test statistic:

$$F = \frac{\left[RSS - (RSS_1 + RSS_2)\right]/K}{(RSS_1 + RSS_2)/(n-2K)} \sim F, K, n-2k \tag{6.21}$$

If $F > F^\alpha_{n_2-k,n_1-k}$ reject H$_0$ at α% level of significance concluding that H$_0$ is not consistent with the data.

6.4 Recursive estimation

The key shortcoming of the Chow test is that in practice one possible break point in the data/model must be identified from the outset. In many applications, such a priori information is not available. In these situations, it is advisable to complement the Chow test with one or more diagnostic tests based on the recursive estimation methods. Recursive estimation involves a series of OLS estimations. In practice, we start with a minimum number of observations, usually as low as the number of the parameters of the model, k. We then estimate the model on the basis of k, k+1, k+2,. . ., up to n. This procedure generates a time series of OLS estimates. If the model is structurally stable, the variations in all parameter estimates must be small and random. On the other hand, if parameter estimates tend to change significantly and systematically, it could indicate a structural break and some underlying misspecification. The recursive estimation methods generate recursive residuals, upon which a number of diagnostic tests have been based.

6.4.1 *CUSUM and CUSUM Q tests for parameter stability*

Using the hypothetical regression model used in 6.16, let:

$$V_t = Y_t - (\hat{\beta}_{1t-1} + \hat{\beta}_{2t-1}X_{2t} + \hat{\beta}_{3t-1}X_{3t}) \tag{6.22}$$

for t = k+1,. . ., n.

where: $\hat{\beta}_1, \hat{\beta}_2, \hat{\beta}_3$ are the OLS estimates obtained from k observations.

It can be shown that a normalised form of the recursive residuals has the following distribution:

W$_t \sim$ NID(0,σ^2)

Where W$_t$ is a standardised recursive residual, based on Vt.

The CUSUM test is based on:

$$\text{CUSUM}t = (1/s) \sum_{i=k+1}^{t} W_i \tag{6.23}$$

Where S is the full sample estimation of the standard error of regression i.e.

$$s = \sqrt{\frac{\sum_{i=1}^{n} e_i}{n-k}}$$

If the residuals are random and small in magnitude we would expect the CUSUM statistic to remain close to zero; any systematic departure from zero is taken to indicate parameter instability/misspecification. Microfit 4/5 produces a graph of CUSUM statistic against time. In practice, a systematic trend in the graph of CUSUM statistic against time is taken to indicate a break/failure in the regression.

The CUSUM Q statistic is defined as:

$$\text{CUSUM Q} = \left(\sum_{i=k+1}^{t} W_i^2 \, / \sum_{t=k+1}^{n} W_t^2 \right) = RSS_t \, / \, RSS_n \tag{6.24}$$

Where RSS_t = residual sum of squares of the recursive residuals

RSS_n = residual sum of squares of the OLS residuals for the full sample period.

The CUSUM Q statistic lies between 0 and 1. A random dispersion of the CUSUM Q statistic, close to zero, within the band of zero and one, is indicative of parameter stability. However, both CUSUM and CUSUM Q statistics are essentially used in practice as diagnostics indicative of parameter stability. Tests based on these statistics have low power (are not reliable for small samples). It is advisable to complement these parameter stability indicators with a formal Chow test.

6.5 Testing for measurement errors and errors in the variables: the Hausman specification test

In regression analysis, in many instances, variables are likely to be measured with errors. In this case, the OLS estimators are biased and inconsistent and the regression would be unreliable. It is therefore, advisable to test for measurement errors if measurement errors are suspected. In this section we will explain this issue and illustrate, via an example, the application of the J. A. Hausman (1978) specification test to this problem.

Consider the following regression model of the UK food exports:

$$y_t = \alpha + \beta \, q_t + \gamma p_t + u_t$$
$$u_t \sim \text{NID}(0, \sigma^2) \tag{6.25}$$

where:

Y_t = level of UK food exports

q_t = level of world food output

p_t = an index of world food prices relative to the UK food prices

On theoretical grounds we expect the slope parameters β and γ to be positive, implying that Y_t will change in the same direction with both q_t and p_t.

Examining the data requirements of the model, it is likely that all three variables are measured with errors. Does this matter? As far as the dependent variable of the model is concerned, the measurement errors of calculating/gathering data on these variables are captured by the disturbance term, u_t. As long as these errors are normally and independently distributed, the OLS method is still BLUE and so we should not encounter specific problems. The story, however, is different as far for the regressors are concerned. Here, the OLS estimators are biased, inconsistent and unreliable.

To fix these ideas, let:

$q_t^* = $ true value of q_t

$p_t^* = $ true value of p_t

We assume that both q_t and p_t are measured with random measurement errors; under this framework, the observed values of the regressors may be expressed as follows:

$$q_t = q_t^* + u_{1t} \qquad (6.26)$$

and

$$p_t = p_t^* + u_{2t}$$

where u_{1t} and u_{2t} are normally and independently distributed random measurement errors with the following characteristics:

$$u_{1t} \sim NID\ (0, \sigma^2_{u1t}) \text{ and } u_{2t} \sim NID\ (0,\ \sigma^2_{u2t}) \text{ also } cov(u_{1t}u_{2t}) = 0$$

The 'true' regression model is as follows:

$$y_t = \alpha + \beta q_t^* + \gamma\gamma p_t^* + u_t$$

Substitution for the observed values of the regressors into the above equation yields:

$$y_t = \alpha + \beta(q_t - u_{1t}) + \gamma(p_t - u_{2t}) + u_t \qquad (6.27)$$

or

$$y_t = \alpha + \beta q_t + \gamma p_t + u_t - \beta u_{1t} - \gamma u_{2t} \qquad (6.28)$$

let $Wt = u_t - \beta u_{1t} - \gamma u_{2t}$, a composite error term.

The regression model may therefore be expressed as follows:

$$y_t = \alpha + \beta q_t + \gamma p_t + W_t \qquad (6.29)$$

Is it possible to estimate this model by the OLS method? The OLS method is appropriate only if all standard assumptions are valid. If there are indeed random measurement errors in the regressors, the regressors cannot be assumed to be fixed under repeated sampling procedures. In fact, they are stochastic/random variables. Moreover, the regressors are correlated with the composite error term W_t, violating a standard assumption of the classical linear regression model. In this case, it can be shown that OLS estimators are biased and inconsistent. Applying the OLS method, therefore, results in unreliable estimates and faulty inference. In applied work, when dealing with regressors which are likely to have been measured with errors, it is crucial that we undertake a test for measurement errors. If measurement errors are present, we should use an alternative estimation method.

6.5.1 Instrumental variable (IV) estimation methods

The problem with the regression model under consideration is that it includes regressors, q_t and p_t, each containing random measurement errors, resulting in inconsistent OLS estimators. The inconsistency of the OLS estimation is due to the existence of correlation between each regressor and the composite error term, W_t. Within the framework of the IV method we replace each one of the stochastic regressors with an 'instrument'. An instrument for a stochastic/random regressor is a variable which is highly correlated with the regressor, but not correlated with the disturbance term. With regard to the regression model under consideration, we need two instruments, one for q_t and one for p_t, with the following characteristics:

Instrumental for q_t:

A variable, highly correlated with q_t, but not correlated with W_t

Instrumental for p_t:

A variable, highly correlated with p_t but not correlated with W_t

Finding an instrument for stochastic variables appearing in the model is a difficult task in practice. However, with respect to the model under consideration, we use the lagged values of q_t and p_t as the respective instruments.

Since $Cov(q_t q_{1t-1})$ is likely to be high,

and

$$Cov\left(q_{t-1}W_t\right) = 0, \text{because } Cov\left(u_{1t}u_{1t-1}\right) = 0 \tag{6.30}$$

also

$Cov\left(p_t p_{t-1}\right)$ is likely to be high,

and

$Cov\left(p_{t-1}W_t\right) = 0$, because $Cov\left(u_{2t}u_{2t-1}\right) = 0$.

Notice that q_{t-1} and p_{t-1} are chosen as instruments, because measurement errors are assumed to be random. This assumption implies zero covariance between each of the instruments and the composite error term.

Given the instruments, the regression model is then estimated by the IV method. This method is similar to the OLS, in that the estimators are obtained such that the residual sum of squares is minimised. This procedure generates so-called 'normal' equations, as follows:

$$\sum y_t = n\alpha + \beta \sum q_t + \gamma \sum p_t \tag{6.31}$$

$$\sum y_t q_{t-1} = \alpha \sum q_{t-1} + \beta \sum q_t q_{t-1} + \gamma \sum p_t q_{t-1} \tag{6.32}$$

$$\sum y_t p_{t-1} = \alpha \sum p_{t-1} + \beta \sum q_t p_{t-1} + \gamma \sum p_t p_{t-1} \tag{6.33}$$

The solution to these three simultaneous equations generates the instrumental variable estimators. Most econometric regression packages have a sub-routine for IV estimation. In practice, once the instruments are identified, the estimation process itself is done by the appropriate regression packages.

6.5.2 The Hausman test for measurement errors

To develop a diagnostic test for measurement errors, we consider the model for the food exports:

$$y_t = \alpha + \beta q_{1t} + \gamma p_t + w_t \tag{6.34}$$

The OLS estimators of the parameters are denoted as follows:

$$\hat{\alpha}_{OLS}, \hat{\beta}_{OLS}, \hat{\gamma}_{OLS}$$

If random measurement errors are present, these estimators are inconsistent.

Using q_{t-1} and p_{t-1} as instrument of q_t and p_t, respectively, we can generate the IV estimators of parameters. These are denoted as follows:

$$\hat{\alpha}_{IV}, \hat{\beta}_{IV}, \hat{\gamma}_{IV}$$

If measurement errors are not present, both methods of estimation would generate consistent estimators. This observation enables us to formulate the null and alternative hypotheses of the test as follows:

H_0: no measurement error is regressor/independent variables

H_1: H_0 is not true

or:

H_0: $u_{1t} = u_{2t} = 0$

H_1: H_0 is not true

or

$$p \lim(\hat{a}_{IV} - \hat{a}_{OLS}) = 0;$$

$$H_0 \ p \lim(\hat{\beta}_{IV} - \hat{a}_{OLS}) = 0;$$

$$p \lim(\hat{\gamma}_{IV} - \hat{\gamma}_{OLS}) = 0;$$

H_1: H_0 is not true

The final format of H_0 makes the point that, in the absence of measurement errors, the OLS and the IV estimators are both consistent estimators. In the absence of measurement errors, the two estimators are asymptotically identical. It can be shown that the difference between the OLS and IV estimators is zero, if the instruments and the OLS residuals are uncorrelated. To carry out a diagnostic test for the measurement errors, the instruments are added to the regression model to generate an expanded equation. The joint significance of instruments are then tested by the familiar F-test for parameter restrictions. If the instruments are found to be not significant, it is taken to mean that they are uncorrelated with the OLS residuals. Therefore, the IV and the OLS estimators are essentially the same, implying that there is no measurement errors in the regressors. In this situation IV and OLS estimators are consistent, however, the OLS estimators have smaller variances. We now illustrate the Hausman diagnostic test for the measurement error.

6.5.3 *Key steps in the Hausman test for measurement errors*

1   State the null and alternative hypotheses.

   H_0: there are no measurement errors in the regressors

   H_1: H_0 is not true

   or

   H_0: $u_{1t} = u_{2t} = 0$

   H_1: H_0 is not true

2   Estimate the expanded equation by the OLS.

   $$y_t = \alpha + \beta q_t + \gamma p_t + \beta_1 q_{t-1} + \beta_2 p_{t-1} + w_t \tag{6.35}$$

   Using n = 45 observations, the OLS estimate of the expanded equation is:

   $$y_t = \underset{(5.8)}{29.6} + \underset{(0.14)}{0.48 q_t} + \underset{(0.51)}{0.30 p_t} + \underset{(1.01)}{0.20 q_{t-1}} + \underset{(0.02)}{0.30 p_{t-1}}; R^2 = 0.90 \tag{6.36}$$

3   Test for the joint significance of the instruments, that is:

   $$H_0: \beta_1 = \beta_2 = 0$$

   No measurement errors [i.e. instrument and the OLS residuals (w_t) are not correlated].

H_1: H_0 is not true

Measurement errors are present.

4   Estimate the restricted model by OLS:

$$y_t = d + \beta q_t + \gamma p_t + w_t \tag{6.37}$$

$$\hat{y}_t = 38.0 + 0.71 q_t + 0.95 p_t \tag{6.38}$$
$$\quad\;\;(5.0)\quad\;(0.12)\quad\;\;(0.42)$$

$R^2 = 0.86$

$n = 45$

5   Test statistic.

$$F = \frac{[R_u^2 - R_R^2]/d}{[1 - R_u^2]/n - k} \sim Fd, n - k \tag{6.39}$$

Using the numerical values, we have:

$$F = (\frac{0.9 - 0.86}{1 - 0.9}) \times (\frac{45 - 5}{2}) = 8 \tag{6.40}$$

Notice that $n = 45$; $k = 5$ and $d = 2$

Decision rule: if $F > F_{d,n-k}^{\alpha}$ reject H_0 at α level of significance, concluding that H_0 is not consistent with the data. Measurement errors are present in the regressors. Rejection of the null hypothesis implies that OLS estimators are biased and inconsistent and IV method should be employed.
    In our example:

$$F_{2,40}^{0.05} = 3.23$$

Because $F = 8 > F_{2,40}^{0.05} = 3.23$ we reject H_0 concluding that measurement errors are present in the regressors. This implies that The OLS estimators are unbiased and inconsistent and the IV estimators should be used.
    The Hausman test outlined above is an important diagnostic testing procedure used frequently in practice, whenever it is suspected that one or more of the regressors might be correlated with the disturbance term. This is a frequent event in applied work and occurs when working with simultaneous equations models and Panel data regression. We will use this test again in subsequent chapters.

6.6 A summary of key issues

*   Spurious regression is a frequent occurrence when estimating single-equation time series regression models, using SG methodology.

- Spurious regression implies that there is no underlying data generation process to support the long-run static model. In this situation the regression results are spurious, meaningless, and should be discarded.
- A good indication of spurious regression is when the DW test value is low, indicating the presence of autocorrelation, the R^2 value is inflated, and t and F-tests are significant, all because of the presence of autocorrelation.
- As a rule of thumb, if R^2 is greater than the DW test value, the regression is spurious.
- The SG approach to 'solving' the spurious regression problem has been to focus on the model specification, assuming, without further investigation, that each variable is stationary.
- The data generation process of a stationary variable and its key characteristics (mean, variance, covariances) remain the same over time and are time invariant.
- In attempting to correct the model, SG methodology focuses on short-run dynamics, frequently imposing on the static models a short-run partial adjustment model (or an alternative dynamic adjustment process), without an underlying theoretical framework to support such processes. The short-run model is estimated by the OLS or an alternative procedure deemed efficient. The long-run parameter estimates are typically derived from the short-run estimates.
- This is a hit and miss procedure often resulting in a model which is not specified correctly. The regression results, although may seem adequate, are often incorrect and misleading.
- This is the point of departure for the modern time series econometrics based on cointegration methodology.
- It is useful to test for structural breaks and parameter stability when using relatively long time series data. The structural break manifests itself via changing parameters. Regression models breakdown due to some drastic events, such as political upheavals, general strikes and the like. In this situation the assumption that the parameters of the regression model would remain constant over time cannot be maintained, the model is misspecified and the regression is spurious.
- The Chow test for parameter stability is a popular test for the detection of parameter stability. It is carried out when one can identify a particular data point within the sample period as the breaking point of the relationship. It also requires that the error variance remains constant over the sample period. CUSUM and CUSUM Q tests are alternatives to the Chow test. These tests do not require the conditions of the Chow test and are routinely reported by time series regression packages, for example, Microfit 5.
- Measuring independent variables with errors (measurement errors) can often cause serious problems in regression analysis. In this case, the OLS estimators are biased and inconsistent and regression results are misleading. The Hausman test is a popular test used for the detection of measurement errors.

Review questions

1   Explain what you understand by the term 'spurious regression'. How does the traditional approach (SG) deal with this problem in practice?
2   Explain why there is a need to modify the static long-run regression models. How does this modification usually take place in practice? What are the shortcomings of this methodology?

3   Explain the partial adjustment mechanism and discuss how this mechanism might be used to make a regression model dynamic. What are the shortcomings of this adjustment process.
4   Explain the Durbin h-test. Why is there a need for this test?
5   Explain how you would use each of the following diagnostic tests in practice:

   a   the Chow test for parameter stability
   b   the CUSUM and CUSUM Q tests
   c   the Hausman test for measurement error.

Key terms: Chapters 4–6

* *Specification tests* These involve specific alternative forms of the regression model, for example, 't' and 'F' tests of parameter restrictions.
* *Misspecification tests* These tests do not involve specific alternative forms of the model. They are used to detect inadequate specification. For example, the Durbin-Watson test, and the Lagrange multiplier tests for autocorrelation.
* *Serial correlation/autocorrelation* The values of the same random variable are correlated over time/space.
* *The Durbin-Watson test* A misspecification test designed to be used with a first-order autoregressive process to detect autocorrelation.
* *The Lagrange multiplier test* A misspecification test designed to detect higher order autocorrelation (large sample test).
* *The Ramsey regression specification error test (RESET)* A misspecification test designed to detect inadequate specification, including omitted variables and incorrect functional forms.
* *Heteroscedasticity* A breakdown of homoscedasticity assumption. The variance of the disturbance term/dependent variable changes over cross-sectional units/time.
* *The Koenker-Basset test* A test commonly used to confirm the assumption of homoscedasticity.
* *The Chow test for a structural break* A test used to detect parameter stability over time.
* *CUSUM and CUSUM Q tests* diagnostic tests for parameter stability.
* *Measurement errors* Measurement errors in regressors, resulting in inconsistent OLS estimators.
* *The Hausman test for measurement errors* A general misspecification test for measurement errors/exogeneity.
* *Instrumental variable (IV) estimation* Estimation method used when the OLS method is inconsistent, for example, when measurement errors are present.
* *The spurious regression phenomenon* A regression model with no underlying stationary data generation process to support the theory. The regression results are spurious and meaningless.

7 Dynamic econometric modelling
The distributed lag models

INTRODUCTION

In the previous chapter we introduced the partial adjustment model, a popular method used in practice to approximate the short-run dynamic adjustments and hence the data generation process. This chapter continues with the SG methodology and explains in detail how this methodology deals with the short-run dynamic adjustments via the introduction of various lag structures into the regression models.

7.1 A review of the classical normal linear multiple regression model

We begin by considering the classical normal linear multiple regression model and its assumptions:

Linearity of the model The general form of the linear-in-parameters multiple regression model is:

$$Y_t = \beta_0 + \beta_1 X_{1t} + \beta_2 X_{2t} + \cdots + \beta_k X_{kt} + \varepsilon_t, \qquad \text{for} \quad t = 1, 2, \ldots, N, \tag{7.1}$$

where Y_t is the dependent variable; X_{jt} (for j=1, 2,..., k) are k independent, or explanatory, variables; ε_t is the stochastic disturbance, or error term; β_j (for j = 0, 1,..., k) are k+1 unknown parameters to be estimated, the so-called (partial) regression coefficients, with β_0 being the intercept; and t indicates the t-th observation, N being the size of the sample.

Assumptions involving the disturbance term

Zero mean $E(\varepsilon_t) = 0$, for all t. $\tag{7.2}$

Homoscedasticity $\text{var}(\varepsilon_t) = E(\varepsilon_t^2) = \sigma^2$, for all t. $\tag{7.3}$

Serial independence, or no autocorrelation $\text{cov}(\varepsilon_t, \varepsilon_s) = E(\varepsilon_t, \varepsilon_s) = 0$, for $t \neq s$. $\tag{7.4}$

Normality $\varepsilon_t \sim N(0, \sigma^2)$, for all t, $\tag{7.5}$

Assumptions involving the explanatory variables

> *Non-stochastic independent variables* Each independent variable X_j is fixed, or given, in repeated samples of size n, with its variance being a finite positive number. (7.6)

> *Adequate sample size* $N > k + 1$. (7.7)

> *No multicollinearity* There is no exact linear relationship between any of the independent variables. (7.8)

> *No specification bias* The regression model is correctly specified in terms of variables and functional form. (7.9)

Under these assumptions the OLS estimators β_j (for $j = 0, 1,. . ., k$) of the corresponding unknown parameters (for $\hat{\beta}_j = 0, 1,. . ., k$) are best linear unbiased estimators (BLUE).

In the case that t indicates time, or, in other words, the regression model involves time series variables, model (7.1) assumes that the current value of variable Y_t depends on the current values of all explanatory variables included in the model. However, this is not always true. In various economic phenomena the current value of a variable may depend on the current values and/or on past values of some explanatory variables as well. This is because the adjustment towards an equilibrium state might well be sluggish, requiring a number of periods to be completed. In this situation, within the framework of the traditional approach, the regression model is modified to capture the short-run dynamic adjustment process contained in the time series data. These modifications are carried out in an *ad hoc* fashion and then imposed on the regression model, resulting in the so-called distributed lag models. In this chapter we will examine this type of model, explaining applications in economics, estimation procedures and diagnostic testing. A number of diagnostic tests will be revisited to show their applications to the evaluation of the distributed lag models. All procedures will be demonstrated with examples.

Key topics

- Finite distributed lag (DL) models
- Infinite distributed lag (DL) models
- Partial adjustment and adaptive expectation models

7.2 Cases from economic theory

In almost all economic phenomena, the adjustment process between corresponding variables is rarely instantaneous. The process takes time to fully develop its effects, depending on the characteristics and complexity of the phenomenon. Let us examine some simple economic cases.

Case 7.1 The consumption function The simplest linear formulation of the consumption function is:

$$C_t = \alpha_0 + \beta_0 Y_t + u_t \qquad (7.10)$$

where C_t = private consumption, Y_t = personal disposable income, u_t = disturbance term, $\alpha_0 > 0$, and $0 < \beta_0 < 1$. The ratio C_t/Y_t is the 'average propensity to consume' and the first derivative $\partial C_t/\partial Y_t = \beta_0$ is the 'marginal propensity to consume'.

From (7.10) it is seen that the current value of consumption depends on the current value of income only, and not on the current values of any other variable. However, this may be untrue, taking into account that current consumption may also depend on the current level of savings. In such a case, the consumption function could be written as

$$C_t = \alpha_0 + \beta_0 Y_t + \gamma_0 S_t + u_t \tag{7.11}$$

where S_t = private savings, and $\alpha_0 > 0$ parameter.

Following the theory that the current level of savings depends on the past levels of income, a savings function could be written as:

$$S_t = \delta_0 + \delta_1 Y_{t-1} + \delta_2 Y_{t-2} + \cdots + v_t \tag{7.12}$$

where δ_0 (for $j = 0, 1, 2, \ldots$) = parameters, and v_t = disturbance term.

Inserting Equation (7.12) in Equation (7.11), the following equation is produced:

$$C_t = (\alpha_0 + \gamma_0 \delta_0) + \beta_0 Y_t + \gamma_0 \delta_1 Y_{t-1} + \gamma_0 \delta_2 Y_{t-2} + \cdots + (\gamma_0 v_t + u_t), \text{ or}$$
$$C_t = \alpha + \beta_0 Y_t + \beta_1 Y_{t-1} + \beta_2 Y_{t-2} + \cdots + \varepsilon_t \tag{7.13}$$

where the substitution is obvious.

Although Equation (7.13) states that the current level of consumption depends on current income and past levels of income, other models, referring to the so-called 'habit persistence', postulate that the current level of consumption depends on past levels of consumption as well, as is seen in the following equation:

$$C_t = \alpha + \beta_0 Y_t + \beta_1 Y_{t-1} + \beta_2 Y_{t-2} + \cdots + \alpha_1 C_{t-1} + \alpha_2 C_{t-2} + \cdots + \varepsilon_t \tag{7.14}$$

Case 7.2 The accelerator model of investment The accelerator model of investment, in its simplest form, asserts that there exists a fixed relationship between net investment and change in output. This relationship is written as:

$$I_t = \beta_0 X_t + \varepsilon_t \tag{7.15}$$

where I_t = net investment, $X_t = Q_t - Q_{t-1}$ with Q_t = output, and $\beta_0 > 0$ parameter.

This model predicts that investment will fluctuate considerably. Investment will be positive when the economy is in a recovery ($Q_t - Q_{t-1} > 0$) and investment will be negative when the economy is in a recession ($Q_t - Q_{t-1} < 0$). However, the fluctuation of investment depends on other factors, such as the timing of investment decisions.

By assuming that investment decisions can be delayed for various reasons, the response of investment to change in output will spread out over time. In this case, Equation (7.15) is written as:

$$I_t = \beta_0 X_t + \beta_1 X_{t-1} + \beta_2 X_{t-2} + \cdots + \beta_k X_{t-k} + \varepsilon_t \tag{7.16}$$

Case 7.3 The quantity theory of money The quantity theory of money asserts that the price level in an economy is proportional to the quantity of money of this economy. This can be derived from Irving Fisher's (1867–1947) equation:

$$M_t V_t = P_t Q_t \qquad (7.17)$$

where M_t = nominal money stock, V_t = velocity of money, P_t = overall price level, and Q_t = real output, which can be written in natural logarithms as:

$$InM_t + InV_t = InP_t + InQ_t \qquad (7.18)$$

By differentiating the last equation with respect to time we get:

$$m_t + v_t = p_t + q_t \qquad (7.19)$$

where $x_t = \dfrac{d}{dt} In X_t = \dfrac{1}{X_t} \dfrac{dX_t}{dt}$, which in discrete time corresponds to percentage changes over time.

By rewriting (7.19) we get the following equation, which decomposes inflation into three sources: nominal money changes, real output changes, and money velocity changes.

$$p_t = m_t - q_t - v_t \qquad (7.20)$$

Monetarists argue that money changes is the major factor in determining inflation, treating the other two factors as being negligible. Moreover, (7.20) implies that:

1 inflation rate is less than the nominal money changes when the combined effect of output and velocity changes is positive;
2 inflation rate is equal to nominal money changes when the combined effect of output and velocity changes is zero;
3 inflation rate is higher than nominal money changes when the combined effect of output and velocity changes is negative.

Therefore, according to the monetarists view the 'money-inflation' link is written:

$$p_t = \alpha + \beta_0 m_t + \varepsilon_t \qquad (7.21)$$

Although Equation (7.21) assumes that the change of money stock affects inflation instantaneously, in reality, the response of inflation to changes in money stock is spread over time, and thus Equation (7.21) is written as:

$$p_t = \alpha + \beta_0 m_t + \beta_1 m_{t-1} + \beta_2 m_{t-2} + \cdots + \beta_k m_{t-k} + \varepsilon_t \qquad (7.22)$$

Case 7.4 The Phillips curve The original Phillips (1958) curve describes an empirical relationship between the rate of change in money wages and the rate of unemployment as a percentage of labour force. The higher the rate of unemployment, the lower the rate of change in money wages. This relationship is written as:

$$w_t = \alpha U_t^\beta e^{\varepsilon_t} \tag{7.23}$$

where $w_t = (W_t - W_{t-1})/W_{t-1}$ with W_t = monetary wage level, U_t = unemployment rate (per cent), ε_t = disturbance term, e = base of natural logarithm, and $\alpha > 0$ and $\beta < 0$ parameters.

Assuming that wages depend also on past prices, and allowing for some time adjustment between unemployment and wages, the wage determination Equation (7.23) has been augmented to:

$$w_t = \alpha U_t^{\beta_0} ... U_{t-m}^{\beta_m} p_{t-1}^{\gamma_1} ... p_{t-k}^{\gamma_k} e^{\varepsilon_t} \tag{7.24}$$

where $p_t = (P_t - P_{t-1})/P_{t-1}$ with P_t = overall price level, and $\beta_j < 0$ and $\gamma_j > 0$ parameters.

In all these cases we saw that the dependent variable of the economic phenomenon (function) was not only determined by variables of the current time point with the dependent variable (instantaneous adjustment) but from variables of past time points (continuous or dynamic adjustment) as well. The difference between the current time point and a past time point is called 'time lag', or, simply, 'lag', and the corresponding variable is called the 'lagged variable'.

7.3 The definitions

Regression models including lagged variables can be categorised into the following types:

Distributed lag models In these models the explanatory variables include only current and lagged values of the independent variables. For example, if we consider one dependent and one independent variable, the model is of the form:

$$Y_t = \alpha + \beta_0 X_t + \beta_1 X_{t-1} + \cdots + \beta_k X_{t-k} + \varepsilon_t \tag{7.25}$$

Equations (7.13), (7.16), (7.22) and (7.24) are examples of distributed lag models.

Autoregressive or dynamic models In these models the explanatory variables include one or more lagged values of the dependent variable. For example:

$$Y_t = \alpha + \beta X_t + \gamma_1 Y_{t-1} + \gamma_2 Y_{t-2} + \varepsilon_t \tag{7.26}$$

Equation (7.14) is an example of a (distributed lag) autoregressive model.

In distributed lag models the influence of the independent variable X_t on $E(Y_t)$ is distributed over a number, k, of past (lagged) values of X_t. According to the value of this number k, these models are categorised into the following types:

Infinite lag models This is the case when k is infinite. The model is written:

$$Y_t = \alpha + \sum_{i=0}^{k=\infty} \beta_i X_{t-i} + \varepsilon_t \tag{7.27}$$

Finite lag models This is the case when k is finite. The model is written:

$$Y_t = \alpha + \sum_{i=0}^{k<\infty} \beta_i X_{t-i} + \varepsilon_t \tag{7.28}$$

In both cases, infinite or finite lag models, to avoid cases of explosive values of E(Y), we make the assumption that the sum of the β_j coefficients is finite, i.e.

$$\beta_0 + \beta_1 + \beta_2 + ... + \beta_k = \sum_{i=0}^{k} \beta_i = \beta < \infty \qquad (7.29)$$

Let us explain the regression coefficients of a distributed lag model, say model (7.25). In this model, under the assumption of ceteris paribus, if the independent variable X_t is increased by one unit in period t, the impact of this change on $E(Y_t)$ will be β_0 in time t, β_1 in time t+1, β_2 in time t+2, and so on. We define this impact as follows:

Partial multipliers of order i It is the marginal effect of X_{t-i} on Y_t; i.e. it is equal to $\partial Y_t / \partial X_{t-i} = \beta_j$. In other words, these multipliers show the effect on $E(Y_t)$ of a unit increase in X_t made in periods prior to period t.

Short-run or impact multiplier It is the partial multiplier of order i = 0, i.e. it is equal to β_0. In words, this multiplier shows the effect on $E(Y_t)$ of a unit increase in X_t made in the same period t.

Interim or intermediate multipliers of order i It is the sum of the first i partial multipliers, i.e. it is equal to $\beta_0 + \beta_1 + ... + \beta_i$. In other words, these multipliers show the effect on $E(Y_t)$ of a maintained unit increase in X_t for i periods prior to period t.

Long-run or total or equilibrium multiplier It is the sum of all partial multipliers of the distributed lag model, i.e. it is equal to β, as defined in (7.29). In words, this multiplier shows the effect on $E(Y_t)$ of a maintained unit increase in X_t for all periods.

Since the partial multipliers are actually the corresponding partial regression coefficients, these coefficients depend on the units of measurement of the independent variable X_t. A method for expressing these coefficients of free units of measurement values is their transformation into the following:

Standardised coefficients or lag weights They are the coefficients that are derived from the transformation:

$$w_i = \frac{\beta_i}{\sum_{i=0}^{k} \beta_i} = \frac{\beta_i}{\beta}, \text{ for i } = 0, 1, 2, ..., k \qquad (7.30)$$

and they show the proportion of the equilibrium multiplier realised by a specific time period. Inserting (7.30) into (7.27) or (7.28), these models are written as:

$$Y_t = \alpha + \beta \sum_{i=0}^{k} w_i X_{t-i} + \varepsilon_t \qquad (7.31)$$

Having defined the lag weights, the following statistics that characterise the nature of the lag distribution can be also defined:

Mean or average lag It is the weighted average of all lags involved, with the weights being the standardised coefficients:

$$\overline{w} = \sum_{i=1}^{k} i \cdot w_i \tag{7.32}$$

and it shows the average speed with which Y_t responds to a unit sustained change in X_t, provided that all regression coefficients are positive.

Median lag It is the statistic that shows the time required for 50 per cent of the total change in Y_t is realised after a unit sustained change in X_t, and is given by:

$$\text{median lag} = w, \text{ such that } \sum_{i=0}^{w-1} w_i = 0.50 \tag{7.33}$$

7.4 Estimation of distributed lag models

Let us consider, for convenience, the one dependent and one independent variable distributed lag model:

$$Y_t = \alpha + \sum_{i=0}^{k} \beta_i X_{t-i} + \varepsilon_t \tag{7.34}$$

The approaches for estimating this model are usually grouped into the following two categories:

Unrestricted approaches These approaches refer to the case where the lag length is finite and no specific restrictions about the nature of the lag pattern are imposed on the β coefficients of the model. We can distinguish two cases: known lag length, and unknown lag length.

Restricted approaches These approaches refer to the case where specific restrictions about the nature of the lag pattern are imposed on the β coefficients of the model. We can distinguish two cases: finite lag length, and infinite lag length.

7.4.1 Unrestricted estimation of distributed lag models when the lag length is known

According to this approach we consider that the model satisfies the classical assumptions presented in Section 7.1. In principle, the ordinary least squares method can be applied to Equation (7.34) and the corresponding estimator is the best linear unbiased estimator of the β coefficients of the model.

Example 7.1 The quantity theory of money for Greece, 1960–1995 (known lag length)

Suppose that the response of inflation to changes in money stock in Greece is spread over three years. Therefore, Equation (7.22) of the quantity theory of money is written:

$$p_t = \alpha + \beta_0 m_t + \beta_1 m_{t-1} + \beta_2 m_{t-2} + \beta_k m_{t-3} + \varepsilon_t \tag{7.35}$$

Table 7.1 presents annual data on the implicit price deflator for GNP (P) and nominal money stock (M1) from 1960 to 1995. By first computing the rate of inflation

Table 7.1 GNP price deflator and nominal money stock for Greece

Year	Deflator 1970:100	Money (Billion Drs)	Year	Deflator 1970:100	Money (Billion Drs)
1960	73.6	13.8	1980	364.4	267.9
1961	74.8	16.1	1981	435.5	335.3
1962	78.1	18.5	1982	544.0	389.7
1963	79.2	21.3	1983	646.1	449.4
1964	82.0	25.4	1984	775.6	542.5
1965	85.3	28.4	1985	912.6	675.1
1966	89.4	32.1	1986	1073.9	738.8
1967	91.5	39.5	1987	1227.7	843.4
1968	93.2	40.5	1988	1419.4	973.2
1969	96.2	43.7	1989	1595.2	1265.0
1970	100.0	48.7	1990	1920.4	1583.5
1971	103.2	54.5	1991	2265.8	1742.9
1972	108.5	67.2	1992	2599.5	1968.2
1973	129.5	83.9	1993	2958.5	2223.7
1974	157.6	100.2	1994	3272.3	2793.5
1975	177.3	115.7	1995	3600.5	3149.0
1976	204.5	140.2			
1977	230.5	165.6			
1978	260.3	202.9			
1979	309.3	235.4			

Sources: Epilogi (1998). The Greek Economy in Figures.

as $p_t = (P_t - P_{t-1})/P_{t-1}$ and the rate of money change as $m_t = (M1_t - M1_{t-1})/M1_{t-1}$, OLS produces the following results. (The values in the parentheses below the estimated coefficients are asymptotic t-ratios.)

$$\hat{p}_t = -0.153 + 0375m_t + 0.549m_{t-1} + 0.343m_{t-2} + 0.390m_{t-3} \quad (7.36)$$
$$\quad\; (3.15) \quad (2.72) \quad\; (3.92) \qquad (2.36) \qquad (2.68)$$

$$\bar{R}^2 = 05122 \; DW = 0.7980 \; F = 9.1381$$

where $\bar{R}^2$ = adjusted for degrees of freedom determination coefficient, DW = Durbin-Watson d-statistic, and F = F-statistic.

Apart from the low Durbin-Watson statistic, which suggests some autocorrelation, the results in (7.36) suggest that the response of inflation to changes in money stock in Greece is significantly spread over three years.

7.4.2 Unrestricted estimation of distributed lag models when the lag length is unknown

In most cases the true lag length k of model (7.34) is rarely known and thus it must be determined. Although there are various procedures for determining the lag length of a model, the approach adopted in this section is based on searches for model specification.

These approaches choose to optimise a criterion. Among the most common criteria used may be the following:

Maximise adjusted R^2: $\bar{R}^2 = 1 - \left(\dfrac{n-1}{n-q}\right)(1-R^2)$ \qquad (7.37)

Minimise Akaike's $\left(1973\right)$ information criterion : $\text{AIC} = \ln\left(\dfrac{\text{SSR}}{n}\right) + \dfrac{2q}{n}$ (7.38)

Minimise Schwartz's $\left(1978\right)$ criterion: $\text{SC} = \ln\left(\dfrac{\text{SSR}}{n}\right) + \dfrac{q}{n}\ln(n)$ (7.39)

where n = sample size, q = total number of coefficients in the regression model, and SSR = sum of squared residuals.

Although these criteria reward good fit, but place a penalty for extra coefficients to be included in the model, it is very possible that conclusions based on these (and other) criteria will be different. A model could be ranked superior under one criterion and inferior under another.

Example 7.2 The quantity theory of money for Greece, 1960–1995 (unknown lag length)

Suppose that the spread of the response of inflation to changes in money stock in Greece is not known. In this case we will try to estimate the lag length of the distributed lag model (7.34) by optimising the three criteria (7.37) to (7.39).

Table 7.2 presents the values of the three criteria by applying OLS to Equation (7.34) for various lag lengths. According to these values it looks like criteria $\bar{R}^2$ and AIC favour the 5-period lag length, whilst SC favours the 4-period lag length. However, the differences between these values are very small, thus, it looks like a 5-period lag length is acceptable for the distributed lag model. The estimation of this model is presented below:

$$\hat{p}_t = -0.149 + 0361m_t + 0.554m_{t-1} + 0.342m_{t-2} + 0.340m_{t-3} + 0.144m_{t-4} - 0.079m_{t-5}$$

$$\quad (2.61)\quad (2.71)\quad\ (4.16)\quad\quad (2.45)\quad\quad\ (2.38)\quad\quad\ (1.03)\quad\quad\ (0.55)$$

$$\bar{R}^2 = 0.5369 \quad DW = 0.8335 \quad F = 6.6041 \quad\quad\quad (7.40)$$

Although the various criteria indicate that the 'best' model is that with a 5-period distributed lag pattern, the actual estimation of this model in (7.40) shows that as the lag length increases, the t-ratios of the estimated coefficients corresponding to the lag variables decrease, indicating that these coefficients are statistically insignificant. This may possibly be due to the fact that as the lag length increases, the degrees of freedom decrease, and the introduction of more lagged variables will possibly introduce some multicollinearity between the independent variables.

Table 7.2 Estimation results for the inflation-money growth equation for Greece

Lag length	$\bar{R}^2$	AIC	SC
0	0.0681	−5.3096	−5.2198
1	0.2797	−5.5748	−5.4401
2	0.3913	−5.7241	−5.5427
3	0.5122	−5.9712	−5.7422
4	0.5368	−6.0256	−5.7481*
5	0.5369*	−6.0308*	−5.7038
6	0.5174	−5.9919	−5.6147

Notes: estimates from EViews
* Denotes 'best' model for the criterion

Taking into consideration that most time series data are short, two of the most serious problems arise in estimations made by the introduction of high lag lengths:

1 *Low degrees of freedom* The higher the lag length, the lower the degrees of freedom. Lower degrees of freedom imply lower precision (lower efficiency) of the estimates, and therefore lower precision of the tests of hypotheses.
2 *Multicollinearity* The higher the lag length, the higher the chance of successive lagged variables to be correlated. Multicollinearity leads to lower precision of the estimates (higher standard errors) and therefore lower precision of the tests of hypotheses.

In summary, the introduction of higher lag lengths may erroneously lead to the rejection of estimated coefficients as being statistically insignificant, due to the lower precision of the tests of hypotheses. In order to bypass this problem of lower precision of estimates, specific restrictions about the nature of the lag pattern must be imposed on the β coefficients of the distributed lag model. These specific restrictions are discussed in the following sections.

7.5 Restricted estimation of finite distributed lag models

Two of the most common methods for imposing a lag scheme on the β coefficients of a finite distributed lag model, are the arbitrary weights distributed lag schemes and the polynomial distributed lag schemes.

7.5.1 *Arbitrary weights distributed lag schemes*

This approach assigns arbitrary weights to each lagged variable according to a perceived influence of the lagged variable in determining the dependent variable. Various schemes can be used in this assignment exercise. The following are the most commonly used:

Arithmetic lag scheme This is the case (Fisher, 1937) when the weights linearly decrease according to the scheme:

$$\beta_i = \begin{cases} (k+1-i)\beta & \text{for } i = 0,1,2,...,k \\ 0 & \text{for } i > k \end{cases} \tag{7.41}$$

The rationale of this scheme is that more recent values of the dependent variable have greater influence on the independent variable than more remote values. Similarly, an increasing arithmetic scheme can be constructed. By inserting (7.41) into (7.34) the distributed lag model is written:

$$Y_t = \alpha + \beta \sum_{i=0}^{k} (k+1-i)X_{t-i} + \varepsilon_t = \alpha + \beta Z_t + \varepsilon_t \tag{7.42}$$

where the substitution for Z_t is obvious. By applying OLS in (7.42) the estimate b of β is obtained and, therefore, the estimates $b_i = (k+1-i)$ b, for $i = 0, 1, 2,. . ., k$, for the parameters β_i can be correspondingly calculated.

Inverted V lag scheme According to this case (DeLeeuw, 1962), the weights linearly increase for most recent lags and then they decrease for more remote lags. The scheme, for k being even, is the following:

$$\beta_i = \begin{cases} (1+i)\beta & \text{for } 0 \le i \le k/2 \\ (k+1-i)\beta & \text{for } k/2 + 1 \le i \le k \\ 0 & \text{for } i > k \end{cases} \tag{7.43}$$

By inserting (7.43) into (7.34) the distributed lag model is written:

$$Y_i = \alpha + \beta \left[\sum_{i=0}^{k/2}(1+i)X_{t-i} + \sum_{i=k/2+1}^{k}(k+1-i)X_{t-i} \right] + \varepsilon_t = \alpha + \beta Z_t + \varepsilon_t \tag{7.44}$$

where the substitution for Z_t is obvious. By applying OLS in (7.44) the estimate b of β is obtained and, therefore, the estimates $b_i = (1+i)$ b, for $i = 0, 1, 2,\ldots, k/2$, and $b_i = (k+1-i)$ b, for $i = k/2+1,\ldots, k$, for the parameters β_i can be correspondingly calculated.

The approach of arbitrarily assigning weights suffers from the following limitations:

1   The actual scheme of the lag structure must be known, following a theoretical basis, i.e. if it increases or decreases, as per the inverted V scheme.
2   The mechanism for assigning specific weights to the lags must be also known, according to previous information, i.e. if the weights come from a linear, or exponential mechanism, etc.

The advantages of this approach might be the following:

1   The actual regression is a simple two-variable regression.
2   The 'best' lag scheme and weights mechanism is determined by simply optimising statistical criteria, such as those of (7.37) to (7.39).

Example 7.3 The quantity theory of money for Greece, 1960–1995 (arbitrary weights)

Using the data of Table 7.1 the estimates for each arbitrary weights distributed lag scheme, say for a 6-period distributed lag equation, are the following:

Decreasing arithmetic lag scheme Applying (7.41), the Z_t variable is:

$$z_t = 7m_t + 6m_{t-1} + 5m_{t-2} + 4m_{t-3} + 3m_{t-4} + 2m_{t-5} + m_{t-6}$$

The corresponding to (7.42) OLS estimates are the following:

$$\hat{p}_t = -0.169 + 0.064z_t \tag{7.45}$$

$$(3.07) \qquad (5.63)$$

$$\bar{R}^2 = 0.5226 \; DW = 1.1313 \; AC = -6.1650 \; SC = -6.0707$$

Increasing arithmetic lag scheme Applying (7.41) in an increasing order, the Z_t variable is:

$$z_t = m_t + 2m_{t-1} + 3m_{t-2} + 4m_{t-3} + 5m_{t-4} + 6m_{t-5} + 7m_{t-6}$$

The corresponding to (7.42) OLS estimates are the following:

$$\hat{p}_t = -0.024 + 0.034z_t$$

$$(0.32) \quad (2.18)$$

$$\bar{R}^2 = 0.1177 \text{ DW} = 0.6380 \text{ AIC} = -5.5509 \text{ SC} = -5.4566 \qquad (7.46)$$

Inverted V lag scheme Applying (7.43), the Z_t variable is:

$$z_t = m_t + 2m_{t-1} + 3m_{t-2} + 4m_{t-3} + 3m_{t-4} + 2m_{t-5} + m_{t-6}$$

The corresponding to (7.44) OLS estimates are the following:

$$\hat{p}_t = -0.114 + 0.092z_t$$
$$\quad (1.69) \quad (3.78)$$
$$\bar{R}^2 = 0.3215 \text{ DW} = 0.7663 \text{ AIC} = -5.8136 \text{ SC} = -5.7193 \qquad (7.47)$$

Although all three estimates suffer from a considerable autocorrelation, the results of the decreasing arithmetic lag scheme (7.45) are preferable, according to all statistical criteria. Therefore, by applying the formula (7.41), and considering that:

$$\text{var}(b_i) = (k + 1 - i)^2 \text{ var}(b), \text{ for } i = 0, 1, 2, ..., k \qquad (7.48)$$

The final estimated model is the following:

$$\hat{p}_t = -0.169 + 0.448m_t + 0.384m_{t-1} + 0.320m_{t-2} + 0.256m_{t-3}$$
$$+ 0.192m_{t-4} + 0.128m_{t-5} + 0.064m_{t-6} \qquad (7.49)$$

7.5.2 Polynomial distributed lag schemes

Given the lag length, k, the lag schemes in (7.41) and (7.43) assume that the β_i coefficients follow a specific function of the lag index i. However, this constitutes the major limitation of the arbitrary weights distributed lag schemes. The a priori restriction of the coefficients to follow a specific distribution function may be too arbitrary.

Shirley Almon (1965) proposed a method that generalises the arbitrary weights distributed lag schemes by relaxing the specific distribution function. Taking into consideration that a continuous function can generally be approximated by a polynomial, her method suggests that a true smooth distribution of the β_i coefficients can be traced and approximated by a polynomial, $\beta_i = f(i)$, of the lag index i of a fairly low degree r, such as the following:

$$\beta_i = f(i) = \alpha_0 + \alpha_1 i + \alpha_2 i^2 + \cdots + \alpha_r i^r, \quad \text{for } i = 0, 1, 2, ..., k > r \qquad (7.50)$$

According to (7.50), a second degree polynomial could approximate the lag structure shown in Figure 7.1(a), and a third degree polynomial could approximate the lag structure shown in Figure 7.1(b). Generally, the degree of the polynomial is greater by one from the number of turning points shown by the lag structure.

Substituting (7.50) into (7.34) we obtain:

$$Y_t = \alpha + \sum_{i=0}^{k} \beta_i X_{t-i} + \varepsilon_t = \alpha + \sum_{i=0}^{k} (\alpha_0 + \alpha_1 i + \alpha_2 i^2 + \cdots + \alpha_r i^r) X_{t-i} + \varepsilon_t$$

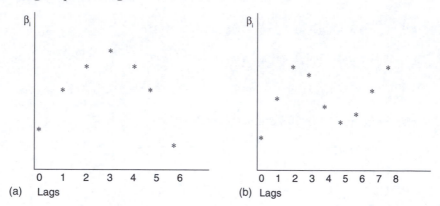

Figure 7.1 Second (a) and third (b) order polynomial approximation of distributed lag structures.

or

$$Y_t = \alpha$$
$$+\alpha_0(X_t + X_{t-1} + X_{t-2} + X_{t-3} + \cdots + X_{t-k})$$
$$+\alpha_1(X_{t-1} + 2X_{t-2} + 3X_{t-3} + \cdots + kX_{t-k})$$
$$+\alpha_2(X_{t-1} + 2^2X_{t-2} + 3^2X_{t-3} + \cdots + k^2X_{t-k})$$
$$+\cdots\cdots\cdots\cdots\cdots\cdots\cdots$$
$$+\alpha_r(X_{t-1} + 2^rX_{t-2} + 3^rX_{t-3} + \cdots + k^rX_{t-k})$$
$$+\varepsilon_t$$

or finally:

$$Y_t = \alpha + \alpha_0 Z_{0t} + \alpha_1 Z_{1t} + \alpha_2 Z_{2t} + \cdots + \alpha_r Z_{rt} + \varepsilon_t \tag{7.51}$$

where the substitution of the Z's is obvious. By considering that (7.51) satisfies the classical assumptions presented in Section 7.1, OLS can be applied to this equation and the best linear unbiased estimates, a and a_i, of the a and a_i coefficients, will correspondingly be obtained.

Having estimated with a_i the α_i coefficients, the actual estimates, b_i, of the β_i coefficients can be calculated by using (7.50), as follows:

$$b_i = f(i) = a_0 + a_1 i + a_2 i^2 + \cdots + a_r i^r, \quad \text{for } i = 0, 1, 2, \ldots, k \tag{7.52}$$

Analytically, the estimates of the β_i coefficients are written:

$$b_0 = f(0) = a_0$$
$$b_1 = f(1) = a_0 + a_1 + a_2 + a_3 + \cdots + a_r$$
$$b_2 = f(2) = a_0 + 2a_1 + 2^2 a_2 + 2^3 a_3 + \cdots + 2^r a_r$$
$$b_3 = f(3) = a_0 + 3a_1 + 3^2 a_2 + 3^3 a_3 + \cdots + 3^r a_r \tag{7.53}$$
$$\cdots\cdots\cdots$$
$$b_k = f(k) = a_0 + ka_1 + k^2 a_2 + k^3 a_3 + \cdots + k^r a_r$$

The estimates in (7.52) or (7.53) are 'restricted least squares estimates', according to the Almon distributed lag approach, because they are restricted to fall on a polynomial of degree r.

Since the variances, var(a_i), and the covariances, cov(a_j,a_h), of the estimated coefficients, a_i, can be derived by applying the OLS method to Equation (7.51), the variances, var(b_i), of the estimated coefficients, b_i, can be derived by the following formula:

$$var(b_i) = var(a_0 + a_1 i + a_2 i^2 + a_3 i^3 + \cdots + a_r i^r)$$

$$= \sum_{j=0}^{r} i^{2j} var(a_j) + 2 \sum_{j<h} i^{(j+h)} cov(a_j a_h) \text{ for } i = 0, 1, 2,...,k \tag{7.54}$$

The last variances are used in the significance tests referring to the β_i coefficients. Therefore, it is very possible some of the β_i coefficients were significant although some of the α_i coefficients were insignificant.

Apart from the restriction of the β_i coefficients falling on the polynomial, it is common in some cases to impose extra restrictions on the coefficients. These extra restrictions, which are called 'endpoint restrictions' push the endpoint β_i coefficients to be equal to zero, i.e., $\beta_{-1} = 0$ and $\beta_{k+1} = 0$, or using (7.50) the endpoint restrictions are written:

$$\beta_{-1} = f(-1) = \alpha_0 - \alpha_1 + \alpha_2 + \cdots + (-1)^r \alpha_r = 0 \tag{7.55}$$

$$\beta_{k+1} = f(k+1) = \alpha_0 + \alpha_1(k+1) + \alpha_2(k+1)^2 + \cdots + \alpha_r(k+1)^r = 0 \tag{7.56}$$

By incorporating these restrictions (both, or either) into Equation (7.51), the OLS method on the 'endpoint restricted equation' can be applied. However, it must be noted here that the endpoint restrictions must be used with caution because these restrictions will have an impact not only on the endpoint coefficients but also on all the coefficients of the model.

In the discussion till now about the polynomial, or Almon, distributed lag models we assumed that we know both the lag length of the model and the degree of the polynomial. However, in most cases these two parameters are unknown, and, thus, have to be approximated.

Determining the lag length This approach has been presented in Section 7.4.2. In summary, searching for the lag length is a problem of testing nested hypotheses. We start by running a regression with a very large value of k. Then, by lowering the value of k by one at a time, we run the corresponding regressions and seek to optimise a criterion, such as $\bar{R}^2 =$, AIC, or SC (see (7.37) to (7.39)).

Determining the degree of the polynomial Similar to determining the lag length, searching for the degree of the polynomial is a problem of testing nested hypotheses. Given the lag length k, we start by running a regression with a large value of r. Then, by lowering the value of r by one at a time, we run the corresponding regressions and seek to optimise a criterion $\bar{R}^2 =$, such as, AIC, or SC. In practice, fairly low degrees of the polynomial ($r = 2$ or $r = 3$) give good results.

Misspecification problems In cases when the lag length, or the degree of the polynomial, or both, have been incorrectly determined, specification problems arise. Although these problems depend on various specific cases, they may be generally summarised as follows:

If k^* is the true lag length of the distributed lag model, then if $k > k^*$ (inclusion of irrelevant variables) the estimates are unbiased and consistent, but inefficient; if $k < k^*$ (exclusion of relevant variables) the estimates are generally biased, inconsistent and inefficient.

If r^* is the true degree of the polynomial, then if $r < r^*$ (imposing invalid restrictions) the estimates are generally biased and inefficient; if $r > r^*$ (over-imposing restrictions) the estimates are unbiased but inefficient.

Example 7.4 The quantity theory of money for Greece, 1960–1995 (polynomial distributed lag model)

Using the data of Table 7.1, the steps involved in applying the polynomial distributed lag model are the following:

1   *Determining the lag length* The lag length of this model has been determined in Example 7.2 to be equal to $k = 5$. Therefore, the distributed lag model is:

$$p_t = \alpha + \beta_0 m_t + \beta_1 m_{t-1} + \beta_2 m_{t-2} + \beta_3 m_{t-3} + \beta_4 m_{t-4} + \beta_5 m_{t-5} + \varepsilon_t \qquad (7.57)$$

2   *Calculating the Z variables* Using various assumed degrees of the polynomial, preferably $r \leq k$, say $k = 5$ in our case, calculate the corresponding Z variables, such as:

$$Z_{0t} = \sum_{i=0}^{5} m_{t-i}$$

$$Z_{1t} = \sum_{i=0}^{5} i m_{t-i}$$

$$Z_{2t} = \sum_{i=0}^{5} i^2 m_{t-i}$$

$$\cdots\cdots\cdots\cdots$$

$$Z_{5t} = \sum_{i=0}^{5} i^5 m_{t-i} \qquad (7.58)$$

3   *Determining the degree of the polynomial* Starting from $r = 5$ and lowering this assumed degree of the polynomial by one at a time, we run the corresponding regression equations, starting from:

$$Y_t = \alpha + \alpha_0 Z_{0t} + \alpha_1 Z_{1t} + \alpha_2 Z_{2t} + \alpha_3 Z_{3t} + \alpha_4 Z_{4t} + \alpha_5 Z_{5t} + \varepsilon_t \qquad (7.59)$$

Table 7.3 presents the values of the three criteria by applying OLS to Equation (7.59) for various degrees of the polynomial. All criteria agree that the degree of the polynomial is equal to 2.

4   *Estimates of the α's* Having determined that the lag length is $k = 5$ and the degree of the polynomial is $r = 2$, the actual estimates are given by:

$$\hat{p}_t = -0.1488 + 0.4207 Z_{0t} - 0.0681 Z_{1t} - 0.0346 Z_{2t}$$
$$\text{se} = (0.0545) \quad (0.0747) \quad\;\; (0.0345) \quad\;\; (0.0179) \qquad (7.60)$$
$$t = (2.7292) \quad (5.6305) \quad\;\; (1.9705) \quad\;\; (1.9336)$$

Table 7.3 Determining the polynomial degree for the inflation-money growth equation for Greece

Degree	$\bar{R}^2$	AIC	SC
1	0.5323	−6.1272	−5.9871
2	0.5754*	−6.1949*	−6.0081*
3	0.5604	−6.1326	−5.8991
4	0.5496	−6.0827	−5.8024
5	0.5369	−6.0308	−5.7038

Notes: estimates from EViews
* Denotes 'best' model for the criterion

$\bar{R}^2 = 0.5754$ DW $= 0.9690$ F $= 14.0993$ AIC $= -6.1949$ SC $= -6.0081$

5 *Estimates of the β's* Having estimated the a coefficients as $a_0 = 0.4207$, $a_1 = -0.0681$, and $a_2 = -0.0346$, considering (7.53), the estimates of the β coefficients are the following:

$b_0 = f(0) = a_0 = 0.4186$
$b_1 = f(1) = a_0 + a_1 + a_2 = 0.4542$
$b_2 = f(2) = a_0 + 2a_1 + 4a_2 = 0.4207$
$b_3 = f(3) = a_0 + 3a_1 + 9a_2 = 0.3181$
$b_4 = f(4) = a_0 + 4a_1 + 16a_2 = 0.1463$
$b_5 = f(5) = a_0 + 5a_1 + 25a_2 = 0.0946$

6 *The estimated model* The estimated distributed lag model corresponding to (7.57), considering also the formula (7.54) for estimating the standard errors of the coefficients, is the following:

$\hat{p}t = -0.1488 + 0.4186m_t + 0.4542m_{t-1} + 0.4207m_{t-2} + 0.3181m_{t-3} + 0.1463m_{t-4} - 0.0946m_{t-5}$
se $= (0.0545)$ (0.1056) (0.0706) (0.0747) (0.0745) (0.0715) (0.1106)
t $= (2.7292)$ (3.9647) (6.4370) (5.6305) (4.2725) (2.0454) (0.8556)
(7.61)

7 *The endpoint restrictions* For comparison purposes, Table 7.4 presents the results from the unrestricted distributed lag estimation in (7.40), from the polynomial distributed lag estimation in (7.61) and for the polynomial distributed lag estimation where both endpoint restrictions (7.55) and (7.56) have been applied. Obviously, other estimations could also been presented, such as polynomial distributed lag estimations with one endpoint restriction only, or with the sum of the distributed lag weights being equal to one, and so on.

Figure 7.2 shows the three estimates presented in Table 7.4. The distribution of the lag weights of the unrestricted distributed lag estimation (UNR) indicates one substantial turning point, and, thus, the polynomial for the polynomial distributed lag estimation (PDL) has been determined as degree equal to two. Finally, the polynomial distributed

Table 7.4 Various estimated models for the inflation-money growth equation for Greece

Variable statistic	Unrestricted (UNR)	Polynomial lag (PDL)	Polynomial lag with endpoint restrictions (EPR)
Constant	−0.1487	−0.1488	−0.1548
m_t	0.3612	0.4186	0.1818
m_{t-1}	0.5539	0.4542	0.3030
m_{t-2}	0.3425	0.4207	0.3636
m_{t-3}	0.3396	0.3181	0.3636
m_{t-4}	0.1438	0.1463	0.3030
m_{t-5}	−0.0790	−0.0946	0.1818
Adjust. R^2	0.5369	0.5754	0.4312
DW	0.8335	0.9690	0.8489
F	6.6041	14.0993	22.9862
AIC	−6.0308	−6.1949	−5.9618
SC	−5.7038	−6.0081	−5.8684

Notes: estimates from EViews
For brevity, standard errors or t-ratios are not reported

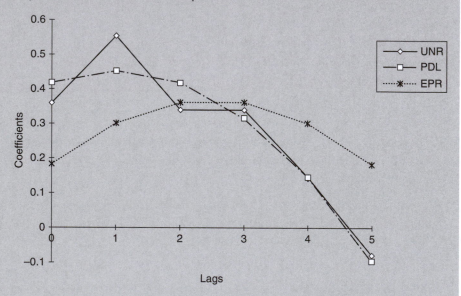

Figure 7.2 Distributed lag estimates for the inflation-money growth equation for Greece.

lag estimation with both endpoint restrictions restricts the distribution of the lag weights to a smooth, symmetric quadratic curve.

7.6 Restricted estimation of infinite distributed lag models

The major assumption in the finite distributed lag models is that the influence of the explanatory variable X_t on the dependent variable Y_t is negligible after a specific point in time and, thus, it should be treated as being zero. However, we saw in the previous section the problems in the estimation of the model, which arise through the wrong determination of that specific point in time, or the lag length, after which any influence is negligible. Of course, these problems will disappear if we accept that the influence of the explanatory variable X_t on the dependent variable Y_t after a specific point in time, in spite of being small, is still present in the model. The result of this consideration is the infinite distributed lag model met in (7.27), or the model:

$$Y_t = \alpha + \sum_{i=0}^{\infty} \beta_i X_{t-i} + \varepsilon_i \tag{7.62}$$

In introducing model (7.62), although there is no problem in determining the lag length, there is now a new problem: the problem of estimating an infinite number of parameters, the β_i, using a finite number of observations. Therefore, methods should be employed in order to lower from infinite to finite the number of estimable parameters. In this section we will present several such methods.

7.6.1 The geometric or Koyck's distributed lag model

This model, introduced by Koyck (1954), is possibly the most popular distributed lag model in empirical research. Koyck proposed that the influence of X_t on Y_t declines continuously with the lag coefficients (weights) following the geometric scheme:

$$\beta_i = \beta_0 \lambda^i, \; 0 < \lambda < 1, \text{ for } i = 0, 1, 2, \ldots \tag{7.63}$$

With the λ parameter, which is known as the 'rate of change', being positive and less than one, it is guaranteed that the values of the β.'s corresponding to greater lags will be smaller than those corresponding to smaller lags; with infinite time, lag weight tends to be zero. Taking into account that β_0 is common to all coefficients, the declining nature of the geometric scheme towards zero can be seen numerically and graphically in Table 7.5 and Figure 7.3 respectively. It can also be seen that the greater the value of λ, the slower the decline of the series.

Substituting (7.63) into (7.62) we get:

$$Y_t = \alpha + \beta_0 \sum_{i=0}^{\infty} \lambda^i X_{t-i} + \varepsilon_i$$

or

$$Y_t = \alpha + \beta_0 X_t + \beta_0 \lambda X_{t-1} + \beta_0 \lambda^2 X_{t-2} + \beta_0 \lambda^3 X_{t-3} + \cdots + \varepsilon_t \tag{7.64}$$

By lagging (7.64) by one period we get:

$$Y_{t-1} = \alpha + \beta_0 X_{t-1} + \beta_0 \lambda X_{t-2} + \beta_0 \lambda^2 X_{t-3} + \beta_0 \lambda^3 X_{t-4} + \cdots + \varepsilon_{t-1} \tag{7.65}$$

Table 7.5 Geometric distribution: successive values of λ^i

Lag λ	0	1	2	3	4	5	6	7	8	9	10
0.25	1	0.250	0.063	0.016	0.004	0.001	0.000	0.000	0.000	0.000	0.000
0.50	1	0.050	0.250	0.125	0.063	0.031	0.016	0.008	0.004	0.002	0.001
0.75	1	0.750	0.563	0.422	0.316	0.237	0.178	0.133	0.100	0.075	0.056

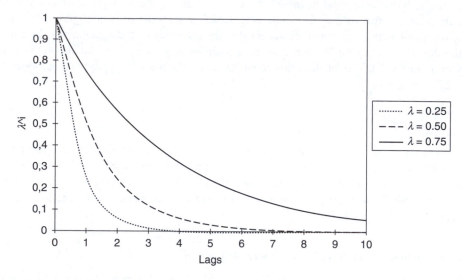

Figure 7.3 Geometric distribution: successive values of λ^i.

Multiplying both terms of (7.65) by λ and subtracting the result from (7.64) we obtain:

$$Y_t - \lambda Y_{t-1} = \alpha(1-\lambda) + \beta_0 X_t + \varepsilon_t - \lambda \varepsilon_{t-1} \tag{7.66}$$

Finally, by rearranging (7.66) we get:

$$Y_t = \alpha_0 + \beta_0 X_t + \lambda Y_{t-1} + \upsilon_t \tag{7.67}$$

where $\alpha_0 = \alpha(1-\lambda)$ and $\upsilon_t = \varepsilon_t - \lambda \varepsilon_{t-1}$.

Ignoring here all the possible problems that the estimation of (7.67) creates, we could say that Koyck, by introducing the geometric scheme (7.63) into model (7.62), managed to reduce the infinite number of coefficients of model (7.62) to three: α_0, β_0 and λ.

Model (7.67), by including the lagged dependent variable Y_{t-1} among its explanatory variables, is an autoregressive, or dynamic, model. Therefore, we see that the application of the geometric scheme to model (7.62) transformed this infinite distributed lag model into an autoregressive model. Furthermore, the disturbance term ε_t of model (7.62) has been transformed into the disturbance term $\upsilon_t = \varepsilon_t - \lambda \varepsilon_{t-1}$ of model (7.67), which is known as a *moving average* of the first order.

The properties of the geometric distributed lag model (7.64) can be summarised as follows:

Mean lag Using formulas (7.30) and (7.32,) the mean lag is equal to:

$$\text{mean lag} = \bar{w} = \frac{\sum_{i=0}^{\infty} i\beta_i}{\sum_{i=0}^{\infty} \beta_i} = \frac{\beta_0(0 + \lambda + 2\lambda^2 + 3\lambda^3 + \cdots)}{\beta_0(1 + \lambda + \lambda^2 + \lambda^3 + \cdots)} = \frac{\lambda/(1-\lambda)^2}{1/(1-\lambda)} = \frac{\lambda}{1-\lambda} \tag{7.68}$$

Median lag Using formula (7.33), and taking into account that:

$$\sum_{i=0}^{k} \lambda^i = \frac{1-\lambda^{k+1}}{1-\lambda}$$

the median lag is equal to:

$$\text{median lag} = w = \frac{\ln(0.5)}{\ln(\lambda)} \tag{7.69}$$

Impact multiplier This is equal to β_0.

Equilibrium multiplier By using formula (7.29) the long-run multiplier is equal to:

$$\beta = \sum_{i=0}^{\infty} \beta_i = \beta_0(1+\lambda+\lambda^2+\lambda^3+\cdots) = \beta_0 \left(\frac{1}{1-\lambda} \right) \tag{7.70}$$

This is why some authors, instead of the geometric scheme (7.63), use the following scheme:

$$\beta_i = \beta(1-\lambda)\lambda^i, \quad 0<\lambda<1 \text{ , for } i=0, 1, 2,... \tag{7.71}$$

7.6.2 The Pascal distributed lag models

One characteristic of the geometric distributed lag model is that its lag weights continuously decrease with time. We also met this characteristic in the decreasing arithmetic lag schemes. To avoid the continuously decreasing lag weights, Solow (1960) proposed the Pascal lag scheme, which resembles the inverted V lag scheme. This lag scheme is the following:

$$\beta_i = \beta w_i, \text{ for } i=0, 1, 2,... \tag{7.72}$$

where, for $i = 0, 1, 2,...$ the weights are given by:

$$w_i = \binom{i+r-1}{i}(1-\lambda)^r \lambda^i = \frac{(i+r-1)!}{i!(r-1)!}(1-\lambda)^r \lambda^i, \quad r = \text{positve integer, } 0<\lambda<1 \tag{7.73}$$

Substituting (7.72) into (7.62) we get the Pascal distributed lag model:

$$Y_t = \alpha + \beta(1-\lambda)^r \left[X_t + r\lambda X_{t-1} + \frac{r(r+1)}{2!}\lambda^2 X_{t-2} + \cdots \right] + \varepsilon_t \tag{7.74}$$

This model has four unknown parameters: α, β, λ, and r. In the case when $r=1$, formula (7.73) is written $w_i = (1-\lambda)\lambda^i$ and, thus, the Pascal distributed lag model is reduced to the geometric distributed lag model. This means that by giving various values for the r parameter we can shape the distribution of the lag weights in a way which seems more suitable for the case. Figure 7.4 shows the distribution of these weights for $\lambda = 0.4$ and $r = 1, 3, 5$, respectively.

In the case that $r = 2$, (7.74) is written:

$$Y_t = \alpha + \beta(1-\lambda)^2(X_t + 2\lambda X_{t-1} + 3\lambda^2 X_{t-2} + \cdots) + \varepsilon_t \tag{7.75}$$

Firstly, by multiplying both terms of the once-lagged Equation (7.75) with -2λ, secondly, by multiplying both terms of the twice-lagged Equation (7.75) with λ^2, thirdly, by adding these two results to Equation (7.75), and, finally, by rearranging we get:

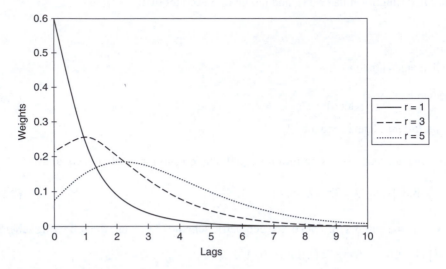

Figure 7.4 Pascal distribution of weights.

$$Y_t = \alpha(1-\lambda)^2 + \beta(1-\lambda)^2 X_t + 2\lambda Y_{t-1} - \lambda^2 Y_{t-2} + (\varepsilon_t - 2\lambda\varepsilon_{t-1} + \lambda^2\varepsilon_{t-2}) \qquad (7.76)$$

Ignoring here all the possible problems that the estimation of (7.76) creates, including the problem of overidentification of the parameters, we could say that by introducing the Pascal scheme with $r = 2$ into model (7.62), this infinite distributed lag model has been transformed into an autoregressive model, where three parameters only have to be estimated: α, β and λ.

Although not very practical for empirical research, generalising (7.76) to include any positive integer value of r, we get:

$$Y_t = \alpha(1-\lambda)^r + \beta(1-\lambda)^r X_t - \sum_{i=1}^r \binom{r}{i}(-\lambda)^i Y_{t-i} + \sum_{i=0}^r \binom{r}{i}(-\lambda)^i \varepsilon_{t-i} \qquad (7.77)$$

7.6.3 The lag operator and the rational distributed lag models

The manipulations of distributed lag models can be simplified by introducing the lag operator L. This operator is defined by $Lx_t = x_{t-1}$.

Some useful algebraic operations with the lag operator are the following:

$$L(Lx_t) = L^2 x_t = x_{t-2}, \quad L^p x_t = x_{t-p}, \quad L^q(L^p x_t) = L^{p+q} x_t = x_{t-p-q},$$

$$L^0 x_t = 1x_t = x_t, \quad L^p(ax_t) = aL^p x_t = ax_{t-p} \quad \text{where } a = \text{constant}$$

Under the lag operator, the infinite distributed lag model (7.62) can be written:

$$Y_t = \alpha + \sum_{i=0}^\infty \beta_i X_{t-i} + \varepsilon_i = \alpha + \sum_{i=0}^\infty \beta_i L^i X_t + \varepsilon_t = \alpha + \beta(L)X_t + \varepsilon_t \qquad (7.78)$$

where

$$\beta(L) = \sum_{i=0}^\infty \beta_i L^i = \beta_0 + \beta_1 L + \beta_2 L^2 + \beta_3 L^3 + \cdots \qquad (7.79)$$

is a polynomial in L.

Jorgenson (1963) approximated the infinite polynomial (7.79) by the ratio of two finite polynomials in L, as:

$$\beta(L) = \frac{\gamma(L)}{\delta(L)} = \frac{\gamma_0 + \gamma_1 L + \gamma_2 L^2 + \cdots + \gamma_p L^p}{\delta_0 + \delta_1 L + \delta_2 L^2 + \cdots \delta_q L^q} \tag{7.80}$$

which is known as the *rational lag function*.

Substituting (7.80) into (7.78), putting $\delta_0 = 1$ for normalisation, and, after rearranging, we get the finite distributed lag autoregressive model:

$$Y_t = \alpha_0 + \gamma_0 X_t + \gamma_1 X_{t-1} + \cdots + \gamma_p X_{t-p} - \delta_1 Y_{t-1} - \cdots - \delta_q Y_{t-q} + \upsilon_t \tag{7.81}$$

where

$$\alpha_0 = \alpha\delta(L) = \alpha(1 + \delta_1 + \cdots + \delta_q) \text{ and } \upsilon_t = \delta(L)\varepsilon_t = \varepsilon_t + \delta_1\varepsilon_{t-1} + \cdots + \delta_q\varepsilon_{t-q} \tag{7.82}$$

Equation (7.81) is the generalisation of all the distributed lag models we have seen till now. If, for example, $\gamma(L) = \gamma_0$ and $\delta(L) = 1 - \lambda L$, then (7.81) becomes the geometric distributed lag model, and if $\gamma(L) = \gamma(1-\lambda)^r$ and $\delta(L) = (1-\delta L)^r$, then (7.81) becomes the Pascal distributed lag model.

7.7 Infinite distributed lag models and economic theory

We saw in the previous section that by imposing restrictions on the coefficients to fall on a specific distribution, the infinite distributed lag model becomes an autoregressive model. In the case, for example, of the geometric distributed lag model (7.64), it becomes model (7.67), or:

$$Y_t = \alpha(1-\lambda) + \beta_0 X_t + \lambda Y_{t-1} + \varepsilon_t - \lambda\varepsilon_{t-1} \tag{7.83}$$

Although this transformation of the models was a mechanical one, seeking just to reduce the infinite number of the coefficients to be estimated, in this section we will try to connect the infinite distributed lag models with specific models of economic theory.

7.7.1 The partial adjustment model

We introduced this model briefly in the previous chapter. According to the partial adjustment model, introduced by Marc Nerlove (1956, 1958), the current level of an explanatory variable, X_t, determines the 'desired' level of the dependent variable, Y_t^*, given by:

$$Y_t^* = \alpha + \beta X_t \tag{7.84}$$

The desired level of inventories of a firm being a function of its sales, or the desired level of capital stock in an economy being a function of its output, might be examples of this model.

However, because a 'desired' level is not an 'observable' level, and thus cannot be used in estimation, Nerlove assumed that due to various reasons in the phenomenon there is a difference between the actual and the desired levels of the dependent variable. In fact he assumed that, apart from random disturbances, the actual change in the dependent variable, $Y_t - Y_{t-1}$, is only a fraction of the desired change, $Y_t^* - Y_{t-1}$, in any period t, i.e.

$$Y_t - Y_{t-1} = \gamma(Y_t^* - Y_{t-1}) + \varepsilon_t, \ 0 < \gamma \le 1 \tag{7.85}$$

Equation (7.85) is known as the *partial adjustment equation*, and fraction γ is known as the adjustment coefficient. The greater the value of γ, the greater the adjustment of the actual to the desired level of the dependent variable takes place in period t. In the extreme case where $\gamma = 1$ the adjustment is instantaneous, or, in other words, all the adjustment takes place in the same time period.

Equation (7.85) can be written as:

$$Y_t = \gamma Y_t^* + (1-\gamma)Y_{t-1} + \varepsilon_t \tag{7.86}$$

which expresses the actual value at time t of the dependent variable as a weighted average of its desired value at time t and its actual value at time t – 1, with γ and $(1-\gamma)$ being respectively the weights. Substituting (7.84) into (7.86) and rearranging, we get:

$$Y_t = \alpha\gamma + \beta\gamma X_t + (1-\gamma)Y_{t-1} + \varepsilon_t \tag{7.87}$$

Equation (7.87) is similar to Equation (7.83), which corresponds to the geometric distributed lag model. In fact, by using the lag operator, (7.87) can be written as:

$$Y_t = \alpha + \frac{\beta\gamma}{1-(1-\gamma)L}X_t + \frac{1}{1-(1-\gamma)L}\varepsilon_t \tag{7.88}$$

or knowing that the inverse of the operator is:

$$\frac{1}{1-(1-\gamma)L} = 1 + (1-\gamma)L + (1-\gamma)^2 L^2 + (1-\gamma)^3 L^3 + \cdots \tag{7.89}$$

Equation (7.88) expands to:

$$Y_t = \alpha + \beta\gamma X_t + \beta\gamma(1-\gamma)X_{t-1} + \beta\gamma(1-\gamma)^2 X_{t-2} + \cdots + \upsilon_t \tag{7.90}$$

where $\upsilon_t = \sum_{i=0}^{\infty}(1-\gamma)^i \varepsilon_{t-i}$. Equation (7.90) is nothing else but an infinite geometric distributed lag model.

7.7.2 *Adaptive expectations models*

According to the adaptive expectations model, introduced by Cagan (1956), the 'expected' level of an explanatory variable, X_t^*, determines the current level of the dependent variable, Y_t, given by:

$$Y_t = \alpha + \beta X_t^* + \varepsilon_t \tag{7.91}$$

The demand for money in an economy being a function of its expected long-run interest rate, the quantity demanded being a function of the expected price, or the level of consumption being a function of the expected, or permanent, income (Friedman, 1957), might be examples of this model.

Similar to the partial adjustment model, since the 'expected' level is not an 'observable' level, and thus cannot be used in estimation, Cagan assumed that the interested agents revise their expectations according to the level from their earlier expectations. In fact he assumed that the change in expectations, $X_t^* - X_{t-1}^*$, is only a fraction δ of the distance between the actual level of the explanatory variable X_t and its expected level X_{t-1}^*, in any period t, i.e.

$$X_t^* - X_{t-1}^* = \delta(X_t - X_{t-1}^*), \quad 0 < \delta \leq 1 \tag{7.92}$$

Equation (7.92) is known as the *adaptive expectations equation*, or due to its error searching nature, the *error learning equation*, and fraction δ is known as the *expectation coefficient*. The greater the value of δ, the greater the realisation of expectations in period t. In the extreme case where $\delta = 1$ expectations are fully and instantaneously realised, or, in other words, all expectations are realised in the same time period.

Equation (7.92) can be written as:

$$X_t^* = \delta X_t + (1 - \delta)X_{t-1}^* \tag{7.93}$$

which expresses the expected value at time t of the explanatory variable as a weighted average of its actual value at time t and its expected value at time $t - 1$, with δ and $(1 - \delta)$ being respectively the weights. Substituting (7.93) into (7.91), we get:

$$Y_t = \alpha + \beta\delta X_t + \beta(1 - \delta)X_{t-1}^* + \varepsilon_t \tag{7.94}$$

By multiplying the lagged-once Equation (7.91) by $(1 - \delta)$ and subtracting the result from Equation (7.94), and, after rearranging, we get:

$$Y_t = \alpha\delta + \beta\delta X_t + (1 - \delta)Y_{t-1} + (\varepsilon_t - (1 - \delta)\varepsilon_{t-1}) \tag{7.95}$$

Equation (7.95) is similar to Equation (7.83), which corresponds to the geometric distributed lag model. In fact, by using the lag operator, (7.95) can be written as:

$$Y_t = \alpha + \frac{\beta\delta}{1 - (1 - \delta)L} X_t + \varepsilon_t \tag{7.96}$$

By now using (7.89) we can expand (7.96) as follows:

$$Y_t = \alpha + \beta\delta X_t + \beta\delta(1 - \delta)X_{t-1} + \beta\delta(1 - \delta)^2 X_{t-2} + \cdots + \varepsilon_t \tag{7.97}$$

Equation (7.97) is nothing else but an infinite geometric distributed lag model. Therefore, we saw that the adaptive expectations model, like the partial adjustment model, is a realisation of the geometric distributed lag model.

7.7.3 The mixed model: partial adjustment and adaptive expectations

By combining the partial adjustment and the adaptive expectations models, we obtain the following mixed model:

$$Y_t^* = \alpha + \beta X_t^* \tag{7.98}$$

$$Y_t - Y_{t-1} = \gamma(Y_t^* - Y_{t-1}) + \varepsilon_t, \quad 0 < \gamma \leq 1 \tag{7.99}$$

$$X_t^* - X_{t-1}^* = \delta(X_t - X_{t-1}^*), \quad 0 < \delta \leq 1 \tag{7.100}$$

where $Y_t^* =$ desired level of the dependent variable, and $X_t^* =$ expected level of the explanatory variable.

The most representative example of this model is Friedman's (1957) permanent income hypothesis, according to which hypothesis, 'permanent consumption' depends on 'permanent income'.

Solving the system of the three equations (7.98) to (7.100), using the hints presented in the two previous sections, we obtain the following equation (Johnston, 1984):

$$Y_t = \alpha\gamma\delta + \beta\gamma\delta X_t + [(1-\delta) + (1-\gamma)]Y_{t-1} - (1-\delta)(1-\gamma)Y_{t-2} + [\varepsilon_t - (1-\delta)\,\varepsilon_{t-1}] \quad (7.101)$$

Equation (7.101) is not similar to those of the partial adjustment and the adaptive expectations because it includes Y_{t-2} among its explanatory variables. This equation, ignoring the identification problems of the parameters involved, reminds us of Equation (7.76) of the Pascal distributed lag models.

7.8 Estimation methods of infinite distributed lag models

We saw, till now, that an infinite distributed lag model:

$$Y_t = \alpha + \beta_0 X_t + \beta_1 X_{t-1} + \beta_2 X_{t-2} + \cdots + \varepsilon_t \quad (7.102)$$

can be reduced into a dynamic model by imposing restrictions on its coefficients to fall on specific schemes. The most popular of such restrictions is that of the geometric lag scheme:

$$\beta_i = \beta_0\lambda^i, \quad 0 < \lambda < 1, \text{ for } i = 0,\ 1,\ 2,\ \ldots \quad (7.103)$$

which substitutes model (7.102) into:

$$Y_t = \alpha + \beta_0 \sum_{i=0}^{\infty} \lambda^i X_{t-i} + \varepsilon_t \quad (7.104)$$

or reduces (7.102) into:

$$Y_t = \alpha_0 + \beta_0 X_t + \lambda Y_{t-1} + \upsilon_t \quad (7.105)$$

where $\alpha_0 = \delta(1-\lambda)$ and $\upsilon_t = \varepsilon_t - \lambda\varepsilon_{t-1}$

In estimating (7.102) under the restriction of (7.103), i.e. in estimating the parameters α, λ, and the β's, we can use either Equation (7.104) – transformed form estimation – or Equation (7.105) – reduced form estimation. However, in both cases, the specification of the disturbances must be considered.

7.8.1 Transformed form estimation of the geometric distributed lag model

Equation (7.104), as it stands, cannot be used for direct estimation because it has an infinite number of coefficients to be estimated. Therefore, it has to be transformed into an equation suitable for estimation purposes. This transformation is the following:

$$\begin{aligned}
Y_t &= \alpha + \beta_0 \sum_{i=0}^{\infty} \lambda^i X_{t-i} + \varepsilon_t \\
&= \alpha + \beta_0(X_t + \lambda X_{t-1} + \cdots + \lambda^{t-1}X_1) + \beta_0\lambda^t(X_0 + \lambda X_{-1} + \cdots) + \varepsilon_t \quad (7.106)
\end{aligned}$$

or

$$Y_t = \alpha + \beta_0 W_t + \theta_0 \lambda^t + \varepsilon_t \tag{7.107}$$

where

$$W_t = X_t + \lambda X_{t-1} + \cdots + \lambda^{t-1} X_1 \tag{7.108}$$

and

$$\theta_0 = \beta_0 \sum_{i=0}^{\infty} \lambda^i X_{-i} = E(Y_0 - \alpha) \tag{7.109}$$

is the so-called 'truncation remainder', which is treated as an unknown parameter.

Equation (7.107) has four unknown parameters to be estimated: α, β_0, θ_0, and λ. If we knew the specification of the error term ε_t we could apply various methods in estimating the equation. Without loss of generality we will consider the following specifications of the disturbances (for other specifications the reader is referred to Kmenta (1986), Judge *et al.* (1988), Greene (1993) and Griffiths *et al.* (1993)).

1   The error term ε_t is *non-autocorrelated*: that is, it satisfies all the classical assumptions stated in Section 7.1.
2   The error term ε_t is *autoregressive of the first order*: that is, it has the form $\varepsilon_t = \rho \varepsilon_{t-1} + \eta_t$, or it is AR(1), where η_t satisfies all the classical assumptions and ρ is the correlation coefficient.
3   The error term ε_t is *moving average of the first order*: that is, it has the form $\varepsilon_t = \eta_t - \mu \eta_{t-1}$, or it is MA(1), where η_t satisfies all the classical assumptions, and μ is the moving average coefficient.

7.8.1.1 Transformed form estimation with non-autocorrelated disturbances

This is the case where for the disturbances we have:

$$E(\varepsilon_t) = 0, \quad var(\varepsilon_t) = \sigma^2, \quad cov(\varepsilon_t, \varepsilon_s) = 0 \text{ for } t \neq s, \ \varepsilon_t \sim N(0, \sigma^2) \tag{7.110}$$

This means that if we knew the value of λ we could compute variables W_t and λ^t and then we could apply OLS to Equation (7.107). For applied purposes, the values of variable W_t could be computed recursively by:

$$\begin{aligned} W_1 &= X_1 \\ W_t &= W_t + \lambda W_{t-1} \quad \text{for } t = 2, 3, ..., n \end{aligned} \tag{7.111}$$

However, the value of λ is not known and thus a search procedure similar to that of Hildreth and Lu (1960) could be used. According to this procedure the sum of squared residuals from the regression Equation (7.107) is estimated for various values of λ between zero and one. The estimates of the parameters α, β_0, θ_0 and λ that correspond to the minimum sum of the squared residuals of the searching regressions have the maximum likelihood properties of consistency and asymptotic efficiency, because minimising the sum of the squared residuals is equivalent to maximising the logarithmic likelihood function Y_1, Y_2,. . ., Y_n, with respect to α, β_0, θ_0 and λ, which is:

$$L = -\frac{n}{2}\log(2\pi\sigma^2) - \frac{1}{2\sigma^2}\sum_{t=1}^{n}\left[Y_t - \alpha - \beta_0 W_t - \theta_0\lambda^t\right]^2 \tag{7.112}$$

7.8.1.2 Transformed form estimation with AR(1) disturbances

This is the case where for the disturbances we have:

$$\varepsilon_t = \rho\varepsilon_{t-1} + \eta_t$$

$$E(\eta_t) = 0, \quad \text{var}(\eta_t) = \sigma_\eta^2, \quad \text{cov}(\eta_t, \eta_s) = 0 \text{ for } t \neq s, \quad \eta_t \sim N(0, \sigma_\eta^2)$$

$$E(\varepsilon_t) = 0, \quad \text{var}(\varepsilon_t) = \sigma^2 = \frac{\sigma_\eta^2}{1-\rho^2}, \quad \text{cov}(\varepsilon_t, \varepsilon_{t-s}) = \rho^s\sigma^2, \quad \varepsilon_t \sim N(0, \sigma^2) \tag{7.113}$$

If we knew the value of the autocorrelation coefficient ρ, then Equation (7.107) could be written as:

$$Y_t - \rho Y_{t-1} = \alpha(1-\rho) + \beta_0(W_t - \rho W_{t-1}) + \theta_0(\lambda^t - \rho\lambda^{t-1}) + \eta_t \tag{7.114}$$

Because the error term in this equation satisfies all the classical assumptions, the OLS method could be applied if, of course, we knew the value of λ. However, we do not know either the value of ρ or the value of λ. Therefore, a similar searching method with the method described in the previous section could be used, with the difference now that this method will be two-dimensional. In other words, we will be searching for values of ρ between -1 and 1, and for values of λ between 0 and 1. The estimates of this methodology will have all the properties of the maximum likelihood estimation because minimising the sum of the squared residuals is equivalent to maximising the corresponding logarithmic likelihood function with respect to α, β_0, θ_0, λ and ρ, which is:

$$L = -\frac{n-1}{2}\log(2\pi\sigma_\eta^2) - \frac{1}{2\sigma_\eta^2}\sum_{t=1}^{n}\left[Y_t^* - \alpha(1-\rho) - \beta_0 W_t^* - \theta_0\lambda_*^t\right]^2 \tag{7.115}$$

where

$$Y_t^* = Y_t - \rho Y_{t-1}, \quad W_t^* = W_t - \rho W_{t-1}, \quad \lambda_*^t = \lambda^t - \rho\lambda^{t-1} \tag{7.116}$$

7.8.1.3 Transformed form estimation with MA(1) disturbances

This is the case where for the disturbances we have:

$$\varepsilon_t = \eta_t - \mu\eta_{t-1}$$

$$E(\eta_t) = 0, \quad \text{var}(\eta_t) = \sigma_\eta^2, \quad \text{cov}(\eta_t, \eta_s) = 0 \text{ for } t \neq s, \quad \eta_t \sim N(0, \sigma_\eta^2)$$

$$E(\varepsilon_t) = 0, \quad \text{var}(\varepsilon_t) = \sigma^2 = \sigma_\eta^2(1+\mu^2), \quad \text{cov}(\varepsilon_t, \varepsilon_{t-s}) = \begin{cases} \mu & \text{(for } s = 1) \\ 0 & \text{(otherwise)} \end{cases}, \varepsilon_t \sim N(0, \sigma^2) \tag{7.117}$$

Taking into account that the error term is written as:

$$\eta_t = \sum_{s=0}^{\infty}(-\mu)^s\varepsilon_{t-s}^s = \varepsilon_t - \mu\varepsilon_{t-1} + \cdots + (-\mu)^{t-1}\varepsilon_1 + (-\mu)^t\eta_0 \tag{7.118}$$

and further assuming that the value of η_0 is negligible, i.e., $\eta_0 = 0$, then if we knew the value of the moving average coefficient μ Equation (7.107) could be written as:

$$Y_t^* = \alpha[1 - \mu + \cdots + (-\mu)^{t-1}] + \beta_0 W_t^* + \theta_0 \lambda_*^t + \eta_t \qquad (7.119)$$

where

$$Y_t^* = Y_t - \mu Y_{t-1} + \cdots + (-\mu)^{t-1} Y_1$$
$$W_t^* = W_t - \mu W_{t-1} + \cdots + (-\mu)^{t-1} W_1$$
$$\lambda_*^t = \lambda^t - \mu \lambda^{t-1} + \cdots + (-\mu)^{t-1} \lambda \qquad (7.120)$$

Because the error term in Equation (7.119) satisfies all the classical assumptions, the OLS method could be applied if, of course, we knew the value of λ. However, we do not know either the value of μ or the value of λ. Therefore, a similar two-dimensional searching method with the method described in the previous section could be used. In other words, we will be searching for values of μ between -1 and 1, and for values of λ between 0 and 1. The estimates of this methodology will have all the properties of the maximum likelihood estimation because minimising the sum of the squared residuals is equivalent to maximising the corresponding logarithmic likelihood function (under the assumption that $\eta_0 = 0$) with respect to α, β_0, θ_0, λ and μ, which is:

$$L = -\frac{n}{2} \log(2\pi\sigma_\eta^2) - \frac{1}{2\sigma_\eta^2} \sum_{t=1}^{n} \left[Y_t^* - \alpha[1 - \mu + \cdots + (-\mu)^{t-1}] - \beta_0 W_t^* - \theta_0 \lambda_*^t \right]^2 \qquad (7.121)$$

The method just described is an 'approximate maximum likelihood method' because it involves the assumption that $\eta_0 = 0$. For the maximum likelihood method, the interested reader is referred to Pesaran (1973) and Balestra (1980).

7.8.2 Reduced form estimation of the geometric distributed lag model

This is the case where estimation is applied to Equation (7.105), i.e.

$$Y_t = \alpha_0 + \beta_0 X_t + \lambda Y_{t-1} + \upsilon_t \qquad (7.122)$$

where $\alpha_0 = \alpha(1 - \lambda)$ and $\upsilon_t = \varepsilon_t - \lambda\varepsilon_{t-1}$

In trying to estimate (7.122) we have to take into account two things: that the equation is *dynamic*, i.e. it contains a lagged dependent variable among its explanatory variables, and that its error term can take various specifications. These specifications can be summarised as follows:

1   The error term u_t is *non-autocorrelated*: that is, it has the form $\upsilon_t = \varepsilon_t$, where ε_t satisfies all the classical assumptions. This is the case of the partial adjustment model (7.87).
2   The error term u_t is *autoregressive of the first order*: that is, it has the form $\upsilon_t = \rho u_{t-1} + \varepsilon_t$, where ε_t satisfies all the classical assumptions and ñ is the correlation coefficient. This case is common in most models with time series data.
3   The error term u_t is *moving average of the first order*: that is, it has the form $\upsilon_t = \varepsilon_t - \lambda\varepsilon_{t-1}$, where ε_t satisfies all the classical assumptions. This is the case of the adaptive expectations model (7.95).

7.8.2.1 Reduced form estimation with non-autocorrelated disturbances

This is the case of the partial adjustment model (7.87):

$$Y_t = \alpha\gamma + \beta\gamma X_t + (1-\gamma)Y_{t-1} + \varepsilon_t \tag{7.123}$$

or

$$Y_t = \alpha_0 + \beta_0 X_t + \gamma_1 Y_{t-1} + \varepsilon_t \tag{7.124}$$

where

$$\alpha_0 = \alpha\gamma, \ \beta_0 = \beta\gamma, \ \gamma_1 = (1-\gamma),$$

$$E(\varepsilon_t) = 0, \ \text{var}(\varepsilon_t) = \sigma^2, \ \text{cov}(\varepsilon_t, \varepsilon_s) = 0 \ \text{for t} \neq \text{s}, \ \varepsilon_t \sim N(0, \sigma^2) \tag{7.125}$$

In this model, the lagged dependent variable Y_{t-1} is a stochastic regressor which is uncorrelated with ε_t, but is correlated with past values of ε_t, i.e.

$$\text{cov}(Y_{t-1}, \varepsilon_t) = 0 \quad \text{and} \quad \text{cov}(Y_{t-1}, \varepsilon_{t-s}) \neq 0 \ \text{ for s} = 1, 2, \ldots \tag{7.126}$$

or, in other words, the stochastic explanatory variable Y_{t-1} is distributed independently of the error term ε_t. In this case, Equation (7.124) may be estimated by OLS. However, the OLS estimates of the coefficients and their standard errors will be consistent and asymptotically efficient, but will be biased in small samples. Thus, these estimates are not BLUE, and therefore the tests of hypotheses will be valid for large samples and invalid for small samples.

In summary, we could apply the OLS methodology to Equation (7.124) as long as the sample size is large enough. In this case, the OLS estimates a_0, b_0 and c_1 of the coefficients α_0, β_0 and γ_1, respectively, could be used to estimate the initial parameters α, β and γ of the model, with the corresponding consistent estimates a, b and c, using (7.125), as follows:

$$c = 1 - c_1, \quad b = \frac{b_0}{1 - c_1}, \quad a = \frac{a_0}{1 - c_1} \tag{7.127}$$

7.8.2.2 Reduced form estimation with AR(1) disturbances

This is the most common case with time series data. This model could be written as:

$$Y_t = \alpha_0 + \beta_0 X_t + \gamma_1 Y_{t-1} + \upsilon_t \tag{7.128}$$

where

$$\upsilon_t = \rho\upsilon_{t-1} + \varepsilon_t$$

$$E(\varepsilon_t) = 0, \quad \text{var}(\varepsilon_t) = \sigma^2, \quad \text{cov}(\varepsilon_t, \varepsilon_s) = 0 \ \text{for t} \neq \text{s}, \ \varepsilon_t \sim N(0, \sigma^2)$$

$$E(\upsilon_t) = 0, \quad \text{var}(\upsilon_t) = \sigma_\upsilon^2 = \frac{\sigma^2}{1 - \rho^2}, \quad \text{cov}(\upsilon_t, \upsilon_{t-s}) = \rho^s \sigma^2, \ \upsilon_t \sim N(0, \sigma_\upsilon^2) \tag{7.129}$$

Given (7.129), it can be proved that:

$$\text{cov}(Y_{t-1}, \upsilon_t) = \frac{\rho\sigma_\upsilon^2}{1 - \gamma_1\rho} \neq 0 \tag{7.130}$$

which means that because u_t is correlated with u_{t-1} and the stochastic explanatory variable Y_{t-1} is correlated with u_{t-1}, then Y_{t-1} will be correlated with u_t. In other words, the application of OLS in Equation (7.110) will give biased and inconsistent estimates of the coefficients and their standard errors. Thus, the corresponding tests of hypotheses will be invalid for small or even for large samples. Therefore, another alternative for OLS estimation is needed. In what follows we will present such alternative methods.

a. The method of instrumental variables (IV)

Having in mind that in Equation (7.128), the cause of the problem was that the stochastic regressor Y_{t-1} was correlated with the error term u_t, Liviatan (1963) tried to eliminate this problem by introducing another variable Z_t, called the 'instrumental variable', in the place of Y_{t-1}, which had the following properties:

1   The instrumental variable Z_t is an approximation of variable Y_{t-1}.
2   Variable Z_t is not correlated with the error term u_t.
3   Variable Z_t is highly correlated with variable Y_{t-1}.

Liviatan used X_{t-1} as an instrumental variable for the estimation of (7.128). X_{t-1} being non-stochastic was definitely not correlated with u_t, and being one of the explanatory variables of Y_{t-1}, was likely to be correlated with Y_{t-1}. The estimates a_0, b_0 and c_1 of the coefficients α_0, β_0 and γ_1 of Equation (7.128), respectively, could be obtained by solving the system of the usual 'normal equations' shown below:

$$\left. \begin{array}{l} \sum Y_t = na_0 + b_0 \sum X_t + c_1 \sum Y_{t-1} \\ \sum Y_t X_t = a_0 \sum X_t + b_0 \sum X_t^2 + c_1 \sum Y_{t-1} X_t \\ \sum Y_t X_{t-1} = a_0 \sum X_{t-1} + b_0 \sum X_t X_{t-1} + c_1 \sum Y_{t-1} X_{t-1} \end{array} \right\} \tag{7.131}$$

Although these estimates will be biased for small samples, as long as the sample increases the solution of system (7.131) will yield consistent estimates.

As another type of instrumental variable for Y_{t-1} in Equation (7.128) could be the lagged dependent predicted variable, $\hat{Y}_{t-1}$, obtained by the following regression:

$$\hat{Y}_t = d_0 + d_1 X_{t-1} + \cdots + d_h X_{t-h} \tag{7.132}$$

i.e. by the regression of the dependent Y_t on lagged variables of X_t. The proper lag length in regression (7.132) could be determined by optimising a criterion, such as those in (7.37) to (7.39). Having obtained $\hat{Y}_{t-1}$ from (7.132), the OLS estimation applied to the following equation:

$$Y_t = \alpha_0 + \beta_0 X_t + \gamma_1 \hat{Y}_{t-1} + \upsilon_t \tag{7.133}$$

which has been derived from Equation (7.128) after substituting Y_{t-1} with $\hat{Y}_{t-1}$,
    will give, as before, consistent estimates. The method just described, i.e. the method where as a first step we get $\hat{Y}_{t-1}$ from (7.132) and as a second step we get the final estimates from (7.133), is called the method of 'two stages least squares' (2SLS). Of course, $\hat{Y}_{t-1}$ could

also be derived from the regression of Y_t on any other set of legitimate instruments and not just on the set of lagged values of X_t.

However, the instrumental variables methodology deals only with the problem of correlation between the stochastic regressor Y_{t-1} and the error term N_t and not with the problem of autocorrelation of the error term. In fact this method is free of the autocorrelation scheme. Therefore, the application of instrumental variables in Equation (7.128) will give consistent but asymptotically inefficient estimates. In other words, a method for dealing with the autocorrelation in the error term must be used. Such a method could be the following Hatanaka's (1976) 'two-step' method, which has the same asymptotic properties as the maximum likelihood estimator (MLE) of normally distributed and serially correlated disturbances.

Step 1 Having estimated from the IV method consistent estimates a_0, b_0 and c_1 of the parameters α_0, β_0 and γ_1, respectively, estimate the residuals $u_t = Y_t - a_0 - b_0 X_t - c_1 Y_{t-1}$, and use them in order to get the estimate $\hat{\rho}$ for the autoregressive coefficient ρ, by regressing u_t against its own lagged value u_{t-1}.

Step 2 By regressing against a constant, and u_{t-1}, where $Y_t^* = Y_t - \hat{\rho} Y_{t-1}$, and $X_t^* = Y_t \hat{\rho} X_{t-1}$, and $Y_{t-1}^* = Y_{t-1} - \hat{\rho} Y_{t-2}$, we get the consistent and asymptotically efficient estimates a_0, b_0 and c_1, of the parameters α_0, β_0 and γ_1. If ϕ denotes the regression coefficient of u_{t-1}, then the two-step estimator of ρ is $\hat{\rho} + \phi$.

Generally, the instrumental variable maximum likelihood with AR(1) estimates could be obtained by maximising the function:

$$L = -\frac{n-1}{2}\log(2\pi\sigma^2) - \frac{1}{2\sigma^2}\sum_{t=1}^{n}\left[Y_t^* - \alpha_0(1-\rho) - \beta_0 X_t^* - \gamma_1 \hat{Y}_{t-1}^* \right]^2 \qquad (7.134)$$

where

$$Y_t^* = Y_t - \rho Y_{t-1}, \quad X_t^* = X_t - \rho X_{t-1}, \quad \hat{Y}_{t-1}^* = \hat{Y}_{t-1} - \rho \hat{Y}_{t-2} \qquad (7.135)$$

with $\hat{Y}_{t-1}$ having been obtained from (7.132), or any other similar estimation. This method is based on the philosophy of the Cochrane and Orcutt method that we will see next.

b. The method of Cochrane and Orcutt (CORC)

The method of Cochrane and Orcutt (1949) refers to the application of OLS to the equation:

$$(Y_t - \rho Y_{t-1}) = \alpha_0(1-\rho) + \beta_0(X_t - \rho X_{t-1}) + \gamma_1(Y_{t-1} - \rho Y_{t-2}) + (\upsilon_t - \rho \upsilon_{t-1}) \qquad (7.136)$$

or

$$Y_t^* = \alpha^* + \beta_0 X_t^* + \gamma_1 Y_{t-1}^* + \varepsilon_t$$
$$\text{where } Y_t^* = Y_t - \rho Y_{t-1}, \ X_t^* = X_t - \rho X_{t-1}, \ Y_{t-1}^* = Y_{t-1} - \rho Y_{t-2}, \ \varepsilon_t = \upsilon_t - \rho \upsilon_{t-1},$$
$$\text{and } \quad \alpha^* = \alpha_0(1-\rho) \qquad (7.137)$$

which is a transformation of Equation (7.128), under the assumption that ρ is known. The application of OLS to Equation (7.137) is nothing else but the method of generalised least squares (GLS) under the assumption that the value of ρ is known. However, in most cases, ρ is unknown and thus it has to be approximated by an estimate. The iterative steps of the CORC methodology are, in this case, the following:

Iteration 1

Step 1.1 Arrange for use the following variables: Y_t, X_t and Y_{t-1}.

Step 1.2 Apply OLS to Equation (7.128) and get estimates a_0, b_0 and c_1, of the parameters α_0, β_0 and γ_1, respectively.

Step 1.3 Use the estimates from step 1.2, in order to estimate the corresponding residuals u_t, i.e. $u_t = Y_t - a_0 - b_0 X_t - c_1 Y_{t-1}$

Step 1.4 Using the estimated residuals u_t, from step 1.3, regress u_t against its own lagged value u_{t-1}, and get the estimate for the autoregressive coefficient ρ.

Iteration 2

Step 2.1 Compute the following variables: $Y_t^* = Y_t - \hat{\rho} Y_{t-1}$, and $X_t^* = Y_t - \hat{\rho} X_{t-1}$

$$Y_{t-1}^* = Y_{t-1} - \hat{\rho} Y_{t-2}$$

Step 2.2 By regressing against a constant, get new estimates a_0, b_0 and c_1, of the parameters α_0, β_0 and γ_1.

Step 2.3 Using the estimates from step 2.2, estimate a new set of residuals, u_t, i.e. $u_t = Y_t - a_0 - b_0 X_t - c_1 Y_{t-1}$.

Step 2.4 Using the estimated residuals u_t, from step 2.3, regress u_t against its own lagged value u_{t-1}, and get the new estimate for the autoregressive coefficient ρ.

Iteration x

By following the four steps x.1 to x.4 in each iteration x, continue this iterative procedure until two successive estimates of the autoregressive coefficient ρ may not differ by more than a predetermined value, say 0.0001. The estimates a_0, b_0 and c_1 of this final iteration will be consistent although their standard errors will be inconsistent. To correct for this inconsistency, the following two-step method may be followed (Harvey, 1990):

Step 1 Having estimated from the CORC method consistent estimates a_0, b_0, c_1 and the parameters α_0, β_0, γ_1 and ρ, respectively, estimate the residuals of the initial model (7.128) and the residuals of the reduced model (7.137).

Step 2 By regressing e_t against a constant, and u_{t-1}, get the consistent and asymptotically efficient estimates a_0, b_0 and c_1 of the parameters α_0, β_0 and γ_1.

Equation (7.136), or (7.137), could also be used in obtaining consistent and asymptotically efficient estimates by maximising the corresponding logarithmic likelihood function with respect to α_0, β_0, γ_1 and ρ, which is:

$$L = \frac{n-1}{2}\log(2\pi\sigma^2) - \frac{1}{2\sigma^2}\sum_{t=1}^{n}[(Y_t - \rho Y_{t-1}) - \alpha_0(1-\rho)$$
$$- \beta_0(X_t - \rho X_{t-1}) - \gamma_1(Y_{t-1} - \rho Y_{t-2})]^2 \tag{7.138}$$

This methodology is called the 'maximum likelihood with AR(1)'.

7.8.2.3 Reduced form estimation with MA(1) disturbances

This is the case of the Koyck infinite distributed lag model (7.102) to (7.105), or:

$$Y_t = \alpha_0 + \beta_0 X_t + \lambda Y_{t-1} + \upsilon_t \tag{7.139}$$

where

$$\upsilon_t = \varepsilon_t - \lambda\varepsilon_{t-1}$$

$$E(\varepsilon_t) = 0, \quad \mathrm{var}(\varepsilon_t) = \sigma^2, \quad \mathrm{cov}(\varepsilon_t, \varepsilon_s) = 0 \text{ for } t \neq s, \quad \varepsilon_t \sim N(0, \sigma^2)$$

$$E(\upsilon_t) = 0, \quad \mathrm{var}(\upsilon_t) = \sigma_\upsilon^2 = \sigma^2(1+\lambda^2), \quad \mathrm{cov}(\upsilon_t, \upsilon_{t-s}) = \begin{cases} \lambda & \text{(for s=1)} \\ 0 & \text{(otherwise)} \end{cases}, \upsilon_t \sim N(0, \sigma_\upsilon^2)$$

$$\tag{7.140}$$

We also met this case in the adaptive expectations model (7.95):

$$Y_t = \alpha\delta + \beta\delta X_t + (1-\delta)Y_{t-1} + (\varepsilon_t + (1-\delta)\varepsilon_{t-1}) \tag{7.141}$$

or

$$Y_t = \alpha_0 + \beta_0 X_t + \delta_1 Y_{t-1} + \upsilon_t \tag{7.142}$$

where

$$\alpha_0 = \alpha\delta, \ \beta_0 = \beta\delta, \ \delta_1 = (1-\delta), \ \upsilon_t = \varepsilon_t - (1-\delta)\varepsilon_{t-1} \tag{7.143}$$

Given (7.140) it can be proved that:

$$\mathrm{cov}(Y_{t-1}, \upsilon_t) = -\lambda\sigma^2 \tag{7.144}$$

which means that u_t is autocorrelated (for $\lambda \neq 0$), and taking into account that the stochastic explanatory variable Y_{t-1} is correlated with ε_{t-1}, this variable is also correlated with υ_t, because υ_t includes ε_{t-1}. In other words, the autocorrelation of the error term and the correlation between an explanatory variable (Y_{t-1}) and the error term makes the application of OLS in Equation (7.139) to give biased and inconsistent estimates of the coefficients and their standard errors. Thus, the corresponding tests of hypotheses will be invalid for small or even large samples.

In order to estimate (7.139) various methods could be used. The instrumental variable method, for example, could be used to obtain consistent estimates of the coefficients because this method does not require any specific assumptions regarding the error term. However, knowing that the error term in (7.139) is of the moving average scheme, the method that will incorporate this information into the estimation methodology may improve the asymptotic efficiency of its estimates. Such methods are the following:

a. *Zellner and Geisel search procedure*

Zellner and Geisel (1970), starting from Equation (7.139) defined $W_t = Y_t - \varepsilon_t$, and using that:

$$W_t - \lambda W_{t-1} = (Y_t - \varepsilon_t) - \lambda(Y_{t-1} - \varepsilon_{t-1}) = \alpha(1 - \lambda) + \beta_0 X_t$$

they obtained:

$$W_t = \alpha(1 - \lambda) + \beta_0 X_t + \lambda W_{t-1} \tag{7.145}$$

Lagging repeatedly (7.145) and substituting the result into the same Equation (7.145) we get:

$$W_t = \alpha(1 - \lambda)(1 + \lambda + \lambda^2 + \cdots + \lambda^{t-1}) + \beta_0(X_t + \lambda X_{t-1} + \lambda^2 X_{t-2} + \cdots + \lambda^{t-1}X_1) + \lambda^t W_0$$

$$\text{or} \quad W_t = \alpha(1 - \lambda)\frac{1 - \lambda^t}{1 - \lambda} + \beta_0 Z_t + \lambda^t W_0$$

where $Z_t = X_t + \lambda X_{t-1} + \lambda^2 X_{t-2} + \ldots + \lambda^{t-1}X_1$ or finally

$$Y_t = \alpha + \beta_0 Z_t + (W_0 - \alpha)\lambda^t + \varepsilon_t \tag{7.146}$$

If we knew the value of λ we could apply OLS in Equation (7.146) because all the variables involved are either known or they could be computed, and the error term ε_t is white noise. However, the value of λ is not known and thus a search procedure similar to that of Hildreth and Lu could be used. According to this procedure, the sum of squared residuals from the regression Equation (7.146) is estimated for various values of λ between zero and one. The estimates of the parameters α, β_0 and λ that correspond to the minimum sum of the squared residuals of the searching regressions have the maximum likelihood properties of consistency and asymptotic efficiency, because minimising the sum of the squared residuals is equivalent to maximising the logarithmic likelihood function $Y_1, Y_2, \ldots, Y_n$, with respect to α, β_0, W_0 and λ, which is:

$$L = -\frac{n}{2}\log(2\pi\sigma^2) - \frac{1}{2\sigma^2}\sum_{t=1}^{n}\left[Y_t - \alpha - \beta_0 Z_t - (W_0 - \alpha)\lambda^t\right]^2 \tag{7.147}$$

b. *Instrumental variable maximum likelihood method with MA(1)*

The procedure just described is based on the assumption that the moving average coefficient (μ) of the error term is equal to the Koyck coefficient (λ). In the case that these two coefficients were different $(\lambda \neq \mu)$ function (7.115) could be used in the estimation instead of function (7.147). This would be the method of approximate maximum likelihood with MA(1), as we saw in section 7.8.1.3.

However, by applying to equation:

$$Y_t = \alpha_0 + \beta_0 X_t + \lambda \hat{Y}_{t-1} + \upsilon_t \tag{7.148}$$

the methodology described in section 7.8.1.3, we could get:

$$Y_t^* = \alpha_0^* + \beta_0 X_t^* + \lambda \hat{Y}_{t-1}^* + \varepsilon_t \tag{7.149}$$

where

$$\alpha_0^* = \alpha_0 [1 - \mu + \cdots + (-\mu)^{t-1}]$$
$$X_t^* = X_t - \mu X_{t-1} + \cdots + (-\mu)^{t-1} X_1$$
$$\hat{Y}_{t-1}^* = \hat{Y}_{t-1} - \mu \hat{Y}_{t-2} + \cdots + (-\mu)^{t-1} \hat{Y}_0 \tag{7.150}$$

with $\hat{Y}_{t-1}$ having been obtained from (7.132), or any other similar estimation.

The estimates of Equation (7.148) could be obtained by maximising the corresponding logarithmic function, which is the following:

$$L = -\frac{n-1}{2}\log(2\pi\sigma^2) - \frac{1}{2\sigma^2}\sum_{t=1}^{n}\left[Y_t^* - \alpha_0^* - \beta_0 X_t^* - \lambda \hat{Y}_{t-1}^*\right]^2 \tag{7.151}$$

The method just described is an 'instrumental variable approximate maximum likelihood method with MA(1)', because it involves assumptions about the 'zero' observations.

7.9 Diagnostic tests for models with lagged dependent variables

We saw in the previous sections that the existence of lagged dependent variables among the explanatory variables of a model violates a basic assumption of the regression model, that the explanatory variables are not correlated with the error term. Furthermore, we saw that in trying to transform the infinite distributed lag model to a model with an estimable number of coefficients, no one guarantees us that the error term of the transformed model will not be autocorrelated. In this section we will present some diagnostic tests which refer to the preceding observations.

7.9.1 The Durbin h-statistic for first-order autocorrelation

The most common statistic used for detecting first-order serial correlation in the error term of the classical regression model is the Durbin-Watson (1950, 1951) d or DW statistic, given by:

$$d = \frac{\sum\limits_{t=2}^{n}(\hat{u}_t - \hat{u}_{t-1})^2}{\sum\limits_{t=1}^{n}\hat{u}_t^2} \tag{7.152}$$

where $\hat{u}_t$ are the residuals of the disturbances u_t, given by $u_t = \rho u_{t-1} + \varepsilon_t$, with ε_t being well behaved. This statistic takes the value of 2 when there is no autocorrelation in the disturbances, and the values of 0 and 4 when there exists a perfectly positive or a perfectly negative autocorrelation, respectively.

The estimate $\hat{\rho}$ of the autocorrelation coefficient ρ in the disturbances is given by:

$$\hat{\rho} = \frac{\sum\limits_{t=2}^{n} u_t u_{t-1}}{\sum\limits_{t=1}^{n} u_t^2} \tag{7.153}$$

It can be shown that between the Durbin-Watson d-statistic and $\hat{\rho}$ it approximately holds that:

$$d \cong 2(1 - \hat{\rho}) \tag{7.154}$$

However, in the presence of lagged dependent variables in the regression model, the Durbin-Watson d-statistic is biased because it tends toward 2, suggesting, thus, that there is no autocorrelation, although autocorrelation may be present. Therefore, in such cases, another test for detecting autocorrelation should be employed.

Durbin (1970) developed a 'large-sample statistic' for detecting first-order serial correlation in models when lagged dependent variables are present. This statistic is called the 'h-statistic' and is given by:

$$h = \hat{\rho} \sqrt{\frac{n}{1 - n[\text{var}(c_1)]}} \cong (1 - \frac{1}{2}d) \sqrt{\frac{n}{1 - n[\text{var}(c_1)]}} \tag{7.155}$$

where n = sample size, $\hat{\rho}$ = estimate of the autocorrelation coefficient according to (7.153), d = Durbin-Watson d-statistic according to (7.154), and $\text{var}(c_1)$ = estimated variance of the coefficient of the lagged dependent variable Y_{t-1} in Equation (7.128).

Durbin showed that for large sample sizes and if $\rho = 0$, then the h-statistic follows the normal distribution with zero mean and unit variance (standardised normal distribution). Therefore, the actual h-test for detecting first-order serial correlation in the disturbances of models with lagged dependent variables is the following:

$$\begin{aligned} H_0 &: \rho = 0 \quad , \quad \text{accept when } h < |\text{ critical value }| \text{ of } N(0,1) \\ H_a &: \rho \neq 0 \quad , \quad \text{accept when } h > |\text{ critical value }| \text{ of } N(0,1) \end{aligned} \tag{7.156}$$

In summary, the steps for this test are the following:

Step 1 Estimate Equation (7.128) and get the residuals and the estimated variance of the coefficient of the lagged dependent variable Y_{t-1}.

Step 2 Compute either d from (7.152) or $\hat{\rho}$ from (7.153).

Step 3 Compute h from (7.155).

Step 4 Apply the hypotheses testing of (7.156).

One could detect the following disadvantages in using the h-test:

1   The h-test is not applicable if $var(c_1) > 1$, because then the denominator in (7.155) becomes negative;
2   The test refers to large sample sizes only;
3   The test is not applicable for higher than first-order serial correlations.

7.9.2 The Breusch-Godfrey, or Lagrange multiplier test for autocorrelation of any order

Breusch (1978) and Godfrey (1978) developed a test (BG) to detect higher-order autocorrelation, which can be also used when longer than one lags of the dependent variable are present in the model, and which is valid for large or small sample sizes. The steps of this test, which follows a Lagrange multiplier test procedure, can be constructed as follows:

Step 1 Properly define the model. The model could be of the following form:

$$Y_t = \alpha + \beta_1 X_{1t} + \beta_2 X_{2t} + \cdots + \beta_p X_{pt} + \gamma_1 Y_{t-1} + \gamma_2 Y_{t-2} + \cdots + \gamma_q Y_{qt} + \upsilon_t$$
$$\upsilon_t = \rho_1 \upsilon_{t-1} + \rho_2 \upsilon_{t-2} + \cdots + \rho_m \upsilon_{t-m} + \varepsilon_t \tag{7.157}$$

where the number of the regression coefficients is $k + 1$, with $k = p + q$ and $n > k + 1$, p is the number of the independent variables, q is the order of the lagged dependent variable, and m is the order of the autoregressive error term, with $m < q$.

Step 2 Apply OLS to Equation (7.157) and obtain the corresponding residuals u_t.

Step 3 Regress u_t against all the regressors of the model, i.e. against the constant, X_{1t}, ..., X_{pt}, Y_{t-1}, ... , Y_{t-q}, plus all the lagged residuals till order m, i.e. u_{t-1}, ..., u_{t-m}, and obtain the corresponding R^2.

Step 4 Calculate the statistic BG as:

$$BG = (n - q) R^2 \tag{7.158}$$

This statistic follows the χ^2 distribution with m degrees of freedom, i.e. it is $BG = (n - q) R^2 \sim \chi^2(m)$.

Step 5 Apply the following test of hypotheses:

$$H_0: \text{ all } \rho_i = 0, \quad \text{accept if BG} < \text{critical value of } \chi^2(m)$$
$$H_a: \text{ not all } \rho_i = 0, \text{ accept if BG} > \text{critical value of } \chi^2(m) \tag{7.159}$$

This test can be used also in the case when the error term follows a moving average process of order m, i.e. it is:

$$\upsilon_t = \varepsilon_t + \lambda_1 \varepsilon_{t-1} + \lambda_2 \varepsilon_{t-2} + \cdots + \lambda_m \varepsilon_{t-m} \tag{7.160}$$

7.9.3 The Sargan test for testing instrument validity

We saw in Section 7.8.2 that the general idea of the instrumental variable methodology was to take a set of instrumental variables which were not correlated with the error term, and to use them in order to construct a new variable that will be used in place of the lagged dependent variable which was correlated with the error term. In estimating, for example, Equation (7.128) we used instead Equation (7.133). In Equation (7.133), variable X_t was used as an instrument for itself, but variable $\hat{Y}_{t-1}$ was used as a 'proxy' for variable $\hat{Y}_{t-1}$. The instruments used in order to construct $\hat{Y}_{t-1}$ were those shown in (7.134), i.e. they were $X_{t-1}, X_{t-2}, \ldots, X_{t-h}$.

Sargan (1964) developed a statistic (SARG) in order to test the validity of the instruments used in the IV estimation, or, in other words, to test if from the set of all possible instrumental variables the subset of instruments used in the estimation is independent of the error term. The steps of this test are the following:

Step 1 Divide the variables included in the structural equation to those which are independent of the error term, say, $X_{1t}, X_{2t}, \ldots, X_{pt}$, and to those which are not independent of the error term, say, $Z_{1t}, Z_{2t}, \ldots, Z_{qt}$.

Step 2 Define the set of instruments, say, $W_{1t}, W_{2t}, \ldots, W_{st}$, where $s \geq q$.

Step 3 Apply the IV estimation to the original equation and obtain the corresponding residuals u_t.

Step 4 Regress u_t against all the independent of the error term variables, i.e. the constant, $X_{1t}, \ldots, X_{pt}$, plus the instruments $W_{t-1}, \ldots, W_{t-q}$, and obtain the corresponding R^2.

Step 5 Calculate the statistic SARG as:

$$SARG = (n-k)R^2 \tag{7.161}$$

where n = number of observations, k = number of coefficients in the original structural model. This statistic follows the χ^2 distribution with $r = s - q$ degrees of freedom, i.e. it is $SARG = (n-k) R^2 \sim \chi^2(r)$.

Step 6 Apply the following test of hypotheses:

H_0: all instruments valid,   if $SARG <$ critical value of $\chi^2(r)$

H_a: not all instruments valid,   if $SARG >$ critical value of $\chi^2(r)$

$$\tag{7.162}$$

In the case that the alternative hypothesis is accepted, at least one of the instrumental variables is correlated with the error term, and, therefore, not all instruments are valid. This means that the IV estimates of the coefficients are also not valid.

7.10 Illustrative examples of infinite distributed lag models

Having completed the theoretical presentation of infinite distributed lag models in the previous sections, we will present in this section some examples applying in real cases to the theory presented.

Example 7.5 The private consumption function for Greece, 1960–1995 Assume that the expected, or permanent, private disposable income Y^* determines private consumption C in Greece, according to the linear function:

$$C_t = \alpha + \beta Y_t^* + \varepsilon_t \tag{7.163}$$

Considering the adaptive expectations model, the mechanism used to transform the unobserved permanent level of the private disposable income into an observable level is:

$$Y_t^* - Y_{t-1}^* = \delta(Y_t - Y_{t-1}^*), \quad 0 < \delta \le 1 \tag{7.164}$$

Following the methodology in 7.7.2, the private consumption function in observable levels is the following:

$$C_t = \alpha\delta + \beta\delta Y_t + (1-\delta)C_{t-1} + (\varepsilon_t + (1-\delta)\varepsilon_{t-1}) \tag{7.165}$$

or in estimable form:

$$C_t = \alpha_0 + \beta_0 Y_t + \delta_1 C_{t-1} + \upsilon_t \tag{7.166}$$

where

$$\alpha_0 = \alpha\delta, \ \beta_0 = \beta\delta, \ \delta_1 = (1-\delta), \ \upsilon_t = \varepsilon_t - (1-\delta)\varepsilon_{t-1} \tag{7.167}$$

Finally, we saw that Equation (7.165) can be expanded in a geometric (or Koyck) infinite distributed lag model, as follows:

$$C_t = \alpha + \beta\delta Y_t + \beta\delta(1-\delta)Y_{t-1} + \beta\delta(1-\delta)^2 Y_{t-2} + \cdots + \varepsilon_t \tag{7.168}$$

Equation (7.168) is nothing else but Equation (7.13), which we saw in the beginning of this chapter.

Table 7.6 presents annual data from 1960 to 1995 for private consumption and private disposable income of the Greek economy, for the estimation of Equation (7.166). Furthermore, this table presents data for gross investment, gross national product, and long-term interest rates, which are necessary for the estimation purposes of the next example. All nominal data are expressed at constant market prices of the year 1970, and in millions of drachmas. Private disposable income is deflated using the consumption price deflator.

Applying the techniques described in Section 7.8 to Equation (7.166), Table 7.7 presents the obtained estimates. The instruments used for the IV estimation are a constant, Y_t, Y_{t-1} and Y_{t-2}. For the application of the Zellner-Geisel method to the corresponding Equation (7.146), we computed Z_t by the recursion:

$$Z_1 = PDI_1$$
$$Z_t = PDI_t + \lambda Z_{t-1}, \quad \text{for } t = 2,3,\dots,n$$
$$\text{where PDI} = \text{Private Disposable Income} \tag{7.169}$$

Applying OLS to Equation (7.146), having first computed Z_t using (7.169) and λ^t, for different values of λ between zero and one, the sum of the squared residuals (SSR) has been estimated. Figure 7.5 presents these results. It is seen in this figure that the value of λ, or the

Table 7.6 Data for the Greek economy referring to consumption and investment

Year	Private consumption	Private disposable income	Gross investment	Gross national product	Long-term interest rate (%)
1960	107808	117179	29121	145458	8.00
1961	115147	127599	31476	161802	8.00
1962	120050	135007	34128	164674	8.00
1963	126115	142128	35996	181534	8.25
1964	137192	159649	43445	196586	9.00
1965	147707	172756	49003	214922	9.00
1966	157687	182366	50567	228040	9.00
1967	167528	195611	49770	240791	9.00
1968	179025	204470	60397	257226	8.75
1969	190089	222638	71653	282168	8.00
1970	206813	246819	70663	304420	8.00
1971	217212	269249	80558	327723	8.00
1972	232312	297266	92977	356886	8.00
1973	250057	335522	10009	383916	9.00
1974	251650	310231	74500	369325	11.83
1975	266884	327521	74660	390000	11.88
1976	281066	350427	79750	415491	11.50
1977	293928	366730	85950	431164	12.00
1978	310640	390189	91100	458675	13.46
1979	318817	406857	99121	476048	16.71
1980	319341	401942	92705	485108	21.25
1981	325851	419669	85750	484259	21.33
1982	338507	421716	84100	483879	20.50
1983	339425	417930	83000	481198	20.50
1984	345194	434696	78300	490881	20.50
1985	358671	456576	82360	502258	20.50
1986	361026	439654	77234	507199	20.50
1987	365473	438454	73315	505713	21.82
1988	378488	476345	79831	529460	22.89
1989	394942	492334	87873	546572	23.26
1990	403194	495939	96139	546982	27.62
1991	412458	513173	91726	566586	29.45
1992	420028	502520	93140	568582	28.71
1993	420585	523066	91292	569724	28.56
1994	426893	520728	93073	579846	27.44
1995	433723	518407	98470	588691	23.05

Sources: Epilogi (1998). The Greek Economy in Figures.

value of $(1-\delta)$ in the adaptive expectations specification, that minimises the sum of squared residuals is 0.65. In our experimentation the steps used for the change of λ had the quite large value of 0.05. However, having found that the value of λ that globally minimises the SSR is 0.65, the precise value of λ could be found by decreasing the steps of change to very small values and repeating the procedure in the neighbourhood of 0.65. The final results are shown in Table 7.6, obtained by using the maximum likelihood routine of Microfit, where we can see that the exact estimate of λ is 0.65879, i.e. not different from the value of 0.65 found earlier.

Taking into account that autocorrelation in Equation (7.166) is of the moving average scheme (although not significant in the actual estimates) the ML with MA(1) estimates

Table 7.7 Estimates of the consumption function for Greece, 1960–1995

	OLS	Instrumental variables	Maximum likelihood with MA(1)
Constant	11282.2 (6.4971)	11307.1 (5.8371)	11199.7 (5.6583)
Income (Yt)	0.24718 (5.6352)	0.30976 (5.6481)	0.26311 (5.9379)
Lagged consumption(Ct−1)	0.67864 (12.2495)	0.59902 (8.6738)	0.65879 (11.7678)
Adjusted R²	0.99881	0.99861	0.99883
DW	1.5349	1.3383	1.9478
h	1.4563[0.145]		
Breusch-Godfrey LM(1)	1.5630 [0.211]	2.6140 [0.106]	
SARGAN		0.0826 [0.774]	
MA(1)			0.24113[0.197]

Notes: estimates from Microfit
() t-ratios in parentheses
[ ] significant levels in brackets

in Table 7.7 have generally the highest asymptotic efficiency compared to the other two estimates in the same table. The estimated adaptive expectations model is written as:

$$\hat{C}_t = 11199.7 + 0.26311Y_t + 0.65879C_{t-1} \tag{7.170}$$

or using (7.167) as:

$$\hat{C}_t = 32823.5 + 0.77111Y_t^*$$

with

$$Y_t^* - Y_{t-1}^* = 0.34121(Y_t - Y_{t-1}^*) \tag{7.171}$$

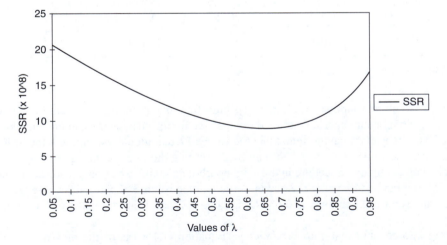

Figure 7.5 Sum of squared residuals with respect to λ.

Finally, the consumption function in the form of a geometric infinite distributed lag model, using (7.168), is written as:

$$\hat{C}_t = 32823.5 + 0.26311X_t + 0.17333X_{t-1} + 0.11419X_{t-2} + \cdots \qquad (7.172)$$

Estimates from (7.170) yield a marginal propensity to consume (MPC) equal to 0.26, implying that a 100 drachmas increase in the current income would increase current consumption by 26 drachmas. However, if this increase in income is sustained, then from Equation (7.144) we see that the marginal propensity to consume out of permanent income will be 0.77, implying that a 100 drachmas increase in permanent income would increase current consumption by 26 drachmas. By comparing these two marginal propensities to consume (the short-run MPC = 0.26 and the long-run MPC = 0.77) and because the expectation coefficient is estimated to be 0.34, this implies that about one-third of the expectations of the consumers are realised in any given period.

Finally, using the estimates in (7.172) and formulas (7.68) to (7.70) we find, respectively, the mean lag, the median lag, the impact multiplier, and the equilibrium multiplier as:

$$\text{mean lag} = \frac{\lambda}{1-\lambda} = \frac{0.65879}{1-0.65879} = 1.93$$

$$\text{median lag} = \frac{\ln(0.5)}{\ln(\lambda)} = \frac{\ln(0.5)}{\ln(0.65879)} = 1.66$$

$$\text{impact multiplier} = \beta_0 = 0.26$$

$$\text{equilibrium multiplier} = \beta_0 \frac{1}{1-\lambda} = 0.26311 \frac{1}{1-0.65879} = 0.77$$

We saw above that the short-run MPC is the impact multiplier and the long-run MPC is the equilibrium multiplier. Furthermore, the mean lag is 1.93, showing that it takes on average about two years for the effect of changes in income to be transmitted to consumption changes. Finally, the medial lag is 1.66, meaning that 50 per cent of the total change in consumption is accomplished in about one and a half years. In summary, consumption adjusts to income within a relatively long time.

Example 7.6 The accelerator model of investment for Greece, 1960–1995
According to this model the desired level of capital stock K^*_t is a linear function of the level of output Q_t in the economy. This is written as:

$$K^*_t = \alpha + \beta Q_t \qquad (7.173)$$

Considering the partial adjustment model, the mechanism used to transform the unobserved level of the desired capital stock into an observed one is:

$$K_t - K_{t-1} = \gamma(K^*_t - K_{t-1}) + \varepsilon_t, \quad 0 < \gamma \le 1 \qquad (7.174)$$

or

$$K_t = \gamma K^*_t + (1-\gamma)K_{t-1} + \varepsilon_t \qquad (7.175)$$

meaning that the actual net investment is only a fraction of the investment required to achieve the desired capital stock. Following the methodology in 7.7.1, the capital stock function in observable levels is the following:

$$K_t = \alpha\gamma + \beta\gamma Q_t + (1-\gamma)K_{t-1} + \varepsilon_t \tag{7.176}$$

Although Equation (7.176) is in an estimable form, in fact the partial adjustment form, this equation produces some estimation problems because the data for the capital stock variable is not usually very reliable. However, by taking into account that capital stock K_t at the end of a period is equal to the capital stock K_{t-1} at the beginning of the period plus gross investment I_t less depreciation D_t, i.e.

$$K_t = K_{t-1} + I_t - D_t \tag{7.177}$$

and assuming that depreciation in period t is proportional to the existing capital stock in period t − 1, i.e.

$$D_t = \delta K_{t-1} + \eta_t \tag{7.178}$$

where δ = depreciation rate and η_t = error term, then Equation (7.176) can be expressed in variables which may be more reliable in terms of data.

Substituting (7.178) into (7.177), and then substituting in the result (7.175), and then rearranging, we obtain that:

$$I_t = \gamma K_t^* - (\gamma - \delta)K_{t-1} + (\varepsilon_t + \eta_t) \tag{7.179}$$

Multiplying both terms of the lagged-once Equation (7.179) times $(1-\delta)$, adding the result to Equation (7.179), and rearranging, we get that:

$$I_t = \gamma K_t^* - \gamma(1-\delta)K_{t-1}^* + (1-\gamma)I_{t-1} + \{[\varepsilon_t - (1-\delta)\varepsilon_{t-1}] + [\eta_t - (1-\delta)\eta_{t-1}]\} \tag{7.180}$$

Finally, substituting (7.173) into (7.180), we obtain:

$$I_t = \alpha\gamma\delta + \beta\gamma Q_t - \beta\gamma(1-\delta)Q_{t-1} + (1-\gamma)I_{t-1} + \upsilon_t$$
$$\text{where} \quad \upsilon_t = \{[\varepsilon_t - (1-\delta)\varepsilon_{t-1}] + [\eta_t - (1-\delta)\eta_{t-1}]\} \tag{7.181}$$

or

$$I_t = \alpha_0 + \beta_0 Q_t + \beta_1 Q_{t-1} + \gamma_1 I_{t-1} + \upsilon_t \tag{7.182}$$

where

$$\alpha_0 = \alpha\gamma\delta, \ \ \beta_0 = \beta\gamma, \ \ \beta_1 = -\beta\gamma(1-\delta), \ \ \gamma_1 = 1-\gamma \tag{7.183}$$

The good thing about the specification of Equation (7.183) (for more specifications see Wallis (1973) and Desai (1976)) is that by estimating it we can estimate all the parameters of the partial adjustment model in Equation (7.176) plus the depreciation rate, without even having data on the capital stock and/or depreciation.

Table 7.8 Estimates of the investment function for Greece, 1960–1995.

	OLS	IV	CORC	Maximum likelihood with AR(1)	Maximum likelihood with MA(1)
Constant	565.7277 (0.1635)	−608.6250 (0.15899)	−280.8577 (0.09640)	−278.5964 (0.09564)	−945.8745 (2.2135)
Q_t	0.50091 (6.0105)	0.49435 (5.8521)	0.55709 (7.2828)	0.55702 (7.2823)	0.55788 (9.9300)
Q_{t-1}	−0.46599 (5.7579)	−0.46723 (5.7235)	−0.52420 (7.1150)	−0.52413 (7.1145)	−0.52697 (9.9701)
I_{t-1}	0.74733 (9.2742)	0.80591 (7.2558)	0.76090 (11.3840)	0.76088 (11.3861)	0.77908 (17.2404)
Adjust. R^2	0.94212	0.94113	0.93642	0.93642	0.94709
DW	2.4427	2.4942	2.0362	2.0368	1.8726
H	−1.4898 [0.136]				
BG	2.6856 [0.101]	2.1146 [0.146]			
SARGAN		0.44211 [0.506]			
AR(1)			−0.31511 [0.097]	−0.31462 [0.097]	
MA(1)					−0.44233 [0.037]

Notes: estimates from Microfit
() t-ratios in parentheses
[ ] significant levels in brackets

Using the data in Table 7.6, I_t = gross investment and Q_t = gross national product, Table 7.8 presents the estimates by applying to Equation (7.182) techniques described in section 7.8. The instruments used for the IV estimation are a constant, Q_t, Q_{t-1}, r_t and r_{t-1}, where r_t = long-term interest rate.

Although all estimates in Table 7.8 are generally acceptable, with the coefficients having the proper a priori signs that Equation (7.181) predicts, the question is which of these estimates is the 'best'. In order to answer this question we should look at the specification of Equation (7.181). Because the error term in (7.181) is of the first-order moving average type it seems that the ML with MA(1) estimates in Table 7.8 are more appropriate. Therefore, using these estimates (a0, b0, b1, c1) of the corresponding regression coefficients ($\alpha 0$, $\beta 0$, $\beta 1$, $\gamma 1$) the estimated parameters (a, b, c, d) of the corresponding parameters (α, β, γ, δ) of the accelerator model of investment for Greece are given by the formulas (7.183), i.e.

$$c_1 = 1 - c \Rightarrow c = 1 - c_1 \Rightarrow c = 0.22092$$

$$b_0 = bc \Rightarrow b = \frac{b_0}{c} \Rightarrow b = 2.52526$$

$$b_1 = -bc(1-d) \Rightarrow d = 1 + \frac{b_1}{bc} = 0.05541$$

$$a_0 = acd \Rightarrow a = \frac{a_0}{cd} = -77269.9 \qquad (7.184)$$

These estimated parameters seem plausible, with the implicit desired capital stock/ GNP ratio being 2.52526 (neglecting the constant term), the depreciation rate being 0.05541, and the adjustment coefficient being 0.22092. The adjustment coefficient is quite small, showing that the adjustment of the current level of capital stock to the desired level of capital stock is rather slow.

7.11 A summary of key issues

- Within the framework of the specific to general approach (SG), econometric models are developed on the basis of economic theory. Given that economic theories are essentially developed to explain the state of rest of variables, that is, their equilibrium values, regression models are also static, lacking dynamic characteristics. Economic time series data, on the other hand, contain all the information on the dynamic adjustments of the variables over time towards the equilibrium state. There is, therefore, a big gap between the static regression models and the time series data to be used for their estimation.
- The static regression models are seldom capable of explaining the data generation process without modification to take into account the dynamic structure of the data generation process. Typically, when a static regression model is estimated with time series data, the results indicate spurious regression and misspecification.
- To explain the data generation process, the static models are modified via inclusion of lags of variables as additional regressors in the regression models.
- A specific form of lag structure gives rise to a specific regression model: Koyck and Almon distributed lag models are the most popular forms of lag structures.
- Note that this modification is not based on theory, it is simply assumed that the dynamic adjustment follows a particular pattern (for example, follows a partial adjustment process). It is therefore likely that these adjustment mechanisms are not consistent with the dynamic adjustments of the data. In this case the 'dynamic' regression model is misspecified.
- The estimation and diagnostic testing of the distributed lag models gives rise to additional problems, typically resolved via modified forms of the OLS methods and new diagnostic testing procedures. The focus of this approach is on applying correct estimation and testing procedures, rather than on finding the data generation process consistent with the observed data.

Review questions

1   In a multiple linear regression model of your choice, show that a partial adjustment model implies a Koyck-type lag structure. What are the implications of this result?

2   The impact of advertising expenditure on sales is assumed to first increase, reach a peak and then decline. Formulate an appropriate finite lag model of the relationship between sales and advertising expenditure, assuming that the lag length is k. What are the consequences of an incorrect order of polynomial? How would you decide on the order of polynomial?

3   Consider the regression model $C_t = \beta_1 + \beta_2 Y^e_t + u_t$, where $u_t \sim \text{nid}(0, \sigma^2)$, and $(Y^e_t - Y^e_{t-1}) = \gamma(Y_t - Y^e_{t-1})$; $0 \leq \gamma \leq 1$. Explain how the regression model might be estimated. What are the problems with the OLS estimation?

4   Explain each of the following:

    a   the Pascal distributed lag model
    b   the partial adjustment model
    c   the adaptive expectation model
    d   the mixed partial and adaptive expectation model.

5   Explain the estimation methods of infinite distributed lag models. Give examples to illustrate your answer.

Key terms: Chapter 7

- *Distributed lag models* Models in which the impact of regressor/s on the dependent variable are distributed over time.
- *Infinite (DL) models* The impact of regressor/regressors on the dependent variable is distributed over infinite time periods.
- *Autoregressive dynamic models* Lagged value/s of the dependent variable appears as a regressor/s.
- *The Almon polynomial model* The influences of the regressors on the dependent variable are constrained to lie on polynomials.
- *The Koyck DL model* The impact of regressor on the dependent variable declines geometrically over time.
- *Partial adjustment models* Used in the SG approach to generate a short-run dynamic model. The desired change is a fraction of actual change.
- *Adaptive expectations model* Used to replace expectational variables in the SG approach. Expectations are formed by assuming agents make systematic mistakes. Agents revise expectations according to a fraction of previous period expectation errors.
- *The Sargan test* A test carried out to confirm instrument validity.

General notes and bibliography: Unit 1

There are many key contributions to econometrics literature closely related to the material in this unit. These contributions show many attempts by the proponents of the traditional approach, since the mid-twentieth century, to improve SG methodology and to make static models dynamic to explain the data generation process (DGP). We list below some of the classical contributions related, cited and used in this unit.

Akaike, H. (1973). 'Information theory and an extension of the maximum likelihood principle' in B. Petrov and F. Csake (eds), *2nd International Symposium on Information Theory*, Budapest: Akademiai Kiado.

Almon, S. (1965). 'The distributed lag between capital appropriations and expenditures', *Econometrica*, 30, 178–196.

Balestra, P. (1980). 'A note on the exact transformation associated with the first-order moving average process', *Econometrica*, 14, 381–394.

Berndt, E. R. (1991). *The Practice of Econometrics: Classic and contemporary*, Reading, MA: Addison Wesley.

Breusch, T. (1978). 'Testing for autocorrelation in dynamic linear models', *Australian Economic Papers*, 17, 334–355.

Cagan, P. (1956). 'The monetary dynamics of hyper inflations' in M. A. Friedman (ed.) *Studies in the Quantity Theory of Money*, Chicago, IL: Chicago University Press.

Chow, C. C. (1960). 'Tests of equity between sets of coefficients in two linear regressions', *Econometrics*, 28(3): 591–605.

Cochrane, D. and Orcutt, G. (1949). 'Application of least squares regression to relationships containing autocorrelated error terms', *Journal of the American Statistical Association*, 44, 32–61.

Darnell, A. C. and Evans, J. L. (1990). *The Limits of Econometrics*, Cheltenham: Edward Elgar.

DeLeeuw, F. (1962). 'The demand for capital goods by manufacturers: A study of quarterly time series', *Econometrica*, 30, 407–423.

Desai, M. (1976). *Applied Econometrics*, London: Philip Allan.

Durbin, J. (1970). 'Testing for serial correlation in least squares regression when some of the regressors are lagged dependent variables', *Econometrica*, 38, 410–421.

Durbin, J. and Watson, G. (1950). 'Testing for serial correlation in least squares regression-I', *Biometrica*, 37, 409–428.

Durbin, J. and Watson, G. (1951). 'Testing for serial correlation in least squares regression-II', *Biometrica*, 38, 159–178.

Fisher, I. (1937). 'Note on a short-cut method for calculating distributed lags', *International Statistical Bulletin*, 29, 323–328.

Friedman, M. A. (1957). *Theory of the Consumption Function*, Princeton, N. J.: Princeton University Press.

Godfrey, L. (1978). 'Testing against general autoregressive and moving average error models when the regressors include lagged dependent variables', *Econometrica*, 46, 1293–1302.

Greene, W. H. (1993). *Econometric Analysis*, New York: Macmillan.

Griffiths, W. E., Hill, R. C. and Judge, G. G. (1993). *Learning and Practicing Econometrics*, New York: John Wiley.

Harvey, A. C. (1990). *The Econometric Analysis of Time Series,* 2nd edn, Cambridge, MA: MIT Press.

Hatanaka, M. (1976). 'Several efficient two-step estimators for dynamic simultaneous equations models with autoregressive disturbances', *Journal of Econometrics*, 4, 189–204.

Hendry, D. F. (1995). *Dynamic Econometrics*, Oxford: Oxford University Press.

Hildreth, G. and Lu, T. (1960). 'Demand relations with autocorrelated disturbances', *Technical Bulletin 276*, Michigan State University Agricultural Experiment Station.

Jarque, M. and Bera, A. K. (1987). 'A test for Normality of observations and regression residuals', *International Statistical Review*, 55, 163–172.

Johnston, J. (1984). *Econometric Methods*, 3rd edn, New York: McGraw-Hill.

Jorgenson, D. W. (1963) 'Capital theory and investment behaviour', *American Economic Review*, 53, 247–259.

Judge, G. G., Griffiths, W. E., Hill, R. C., Lutkepohl, H. and Lee, T. C. (1985). *The Theory and Practice of Econometrics*, 2nd edn, New York: Wiley.

Kennedy, P. (2009). *A Guide to Econometrics*. Cambridge, MA: MIT Press,

Kmenta, J. (1986). *Elements of Econometrics*. New York: Macmillan.

Koyck, L. M. (1954). *Distributed Lags and Investment Analysis*, Amsterdam: North-Holland.

Koenker, R. and Bassett, G. (1982). 'Robust tests for hetroscedasticity based on regression quantiles', *Econometrica*, 50, 43–61.

Liviatan, N. (1963). 'Consistent estimation of distributed lags', *International Economic Review*, 4, 44–52.

Nerlove, M. (1956). 'Estimates of the elasticities of supply of selected agricultural commodities', *Journal of Farm Economics*, 38, 496–509.

Nerlove, M. (1958). 'Distributed lags and Demand Analysis for Agricultural and other Commodities', *Agricultural Handbook No. 141*, US Department of Agriculture.

Pesaran, M. H. (1973). 'The small sample problem of truncation remainders in the estimation of distribution lag models with autocorrelated errors', *International Economic Review*, 14, 120–131.

Phillips, A. W. (1958). 'The relation between unemployment and the rate of change of money wages in the United Kingdom, 1861–1957', *Economica*, XXV, 283–299.

Ramsey, J. B. (1969) 'Tests for specification errors in classical linear least squares regression analysis', *Journal of the Royal Statistical Society*, series B, 31, 350–371.

Sargan, J. D. (1964) 'Wages and prices in the United Kingdom: A study in econometric methodology' in P. E. Hart, G. Mills and J. K. Whitaker (eds) *Econometrics Analysis for National Economic Planning*, London: Butterworths.

Schwarz, R. (1978). 'Estimating the dimension of a model', *Annals of Statistics*, 6, 461–464.

Solow, R. M. (1960). 'On a family of lag distributions', *Econometrica*, 28, 393–406.

Tinter, G. (1968). *Methodology of Mathematical Economics and Econometrics*, Chicago, IL: University of Chicago Press.

Theil, H. (1971). *Principles of Econometrics*, New York: John Wiley and Sons.

Wallis, K. F. (1973). *Topics in Applied Econometrics*, London: Gray-Mills.

White, H. (1980). 'A heteroscedasticity consistent covariance matrix estimator and a direct test of heteroscedasticity', *Econometrica*, 48(4): 187–838.

Zellner, A. and Geisel, M. (1970). 'Analysis of distributed lag models with application to the consumption function', *Econometrica*, 38, 865–888.

Unit 2

Simultaneous equation regression models

- This unit provides detailed coverage of simultaneous equation econometric models. These models typically contain many interrelated linear equations; some variables in the behavioural equations appear as both regressands and regressors, leading to interesting identification and estimation problems. Because of the special nature of these models, this unit is entirely devoted to an explanation of key issues relating to identification of structural parameters, single and systems of equations estimation methods, diagnostic testing, and evaluation of regression results.
- This unit shows the progression of the SG methodology from single-equation to the formulation and estimation of large-scale interrelated systems of linear equations for macroeconomic policy simulation and analysis. Many developments in traditional (SG) methodology stem from the challenges of dealing with special problems associated with the material in this unit.

8 Simultaneous equation models and econometric analysis

INTRODUCTION

Most books on econometrics start with, and exert considerable efforts investigating, single-equation models, such as demand functions, consumption functions, wage rate functions, and so on, similar to those considered in detailed in the previous chapters. However, economic phenomena are not unique. In most cases the single equations under investigation are either related with other single equations, or they are part of a wider phenomenon which may be explained by a system of equations. This chapter will introduce you to regression models with a number of interrelated equations, within which a number of variables are determined simultaneously. We will introduce the concepts step by step using a number of examples to demonstrate key issues. We need to use a bit of matrix algebra here to present some of the results in a compact fashion; however, we will keep the use of matrix algebra to a minimum and instead rely more on practical examples to illustrate key concepts.

Key topics

- Simultaneous equation bias
- Identification
- Estimation methods (single equation/system of equations)

Case 8.1 A demand-supply model for a commodity In many introductory textbooks in economics the market equilibrium model for a commodity is given by the following equations in systemic form:

The demand function: $Q_t^d = \alpha_0 + \alpha_1 P_t + \alpha_2 Y_t + \varepsilon_{dt}$; $\alpha_1 < 0$, $\alpha_2 > 0$ (8.1)

The supply function: $Q_t^s = \beta_0 + \beta_1 P_t + \varepsilon_{st}$; $\beta_1 > 0$ (8.2)

The equilibrium condition: $Q_t^d = Q_t^s = Q_t$ (8.3)

Where Q_t^d = quantity demanded, Q_t^s = quantity supplied, Q_t = quantity sold, P_t = price of commodity, Y_t = income of consumers, α's and β's = parameters, ε's = random disturbances also representing other factors not included in each equation, and t = specific time period. The rationale of the system of Equations (8.1) to (8.3) is that given income, the equilibrium quantity and the equilibrium price can be jointly and interdependently found by solving the system of three equations. This means that different pairs of equilibrium prices and equilibrium quantities correspond to different levels of income. In other words, although income is an explanatory variable for the demand equation only, changes in income causes effects in both the price and quantity sold.

Case 8.2 Income determination in a closed economy without government The simple Keynesian model of income determination in an economy without transactions with the rest of the world (closed economy) and without any government activity can be written as:

The consumption function : $C_t = \alpha_0 + \alpha_1 Y_t + \varepsilon_t; \alpha_1 > 0$ (8.4)

The income accounting identity: $Y_t = C_t + I_t$ (8.5)

where C_t = aggregate consumption, I_t = aggregate investment, Y_t = aggregate income, α's = parameters, ε_t = random disturbances representing other factors not included in the consumption function, and t = a specific time period. The rationale of the system of Equations (8.4) and (8.5) is that, given investment, the levels of consumption and income can be jointly and interdependently found by the solution of this system. This means that different pairs of equilibrium consumption and equilibrium income correspond to different levels of investment. In other words, although investment enters the macroeconomic accounting income identity only, changes in investment causes effects in both equilibrium consumption and equilibrium income.

Case 8.3 The wages-prices link The basic Phillips (1958) curve can be augmented into the following model:

Wages inflation function: $w_t = \alpha_0 + \alpha_1 p_t + \alpha_2 U_t + \varepsilon_{wt}; \alpha_1 > 0, \alpha_2 < 0$ (8.6)

Prices inflation function: $p_t = \beta_0 + \beta_1 w_t + \beta_2 Y_t + \varepsilon_{pt}; \beta_1 > 0, \beta_2 > 0$ (8.7)

where $w_t = (W_t - W_{t-1})/W_{t-1}$ with W_t = monetary wage level, U_t = unemployment rate (per cent), $p_t = (P_t - P_{t-1})/P_{t-1}$, with P_t = price level, Y_t = aggregate demand (income), α's and β's = parameters, ε's = random disturbances also representing other factors not included in each equation, and t = specific time period. The rationale of the system of Equations (8.6) and (8.7) is that given the unemployment rate and aggregate demand levels, then wage inflation and price inflation can be jointly and interdependently found by solution of this system. This means that different pairs of money wage inflation and price inflation correspond to different levels of unemployment rate and aggregate demand. In other words, although the unemployment rate enters the wages function only and aggregate demand enters the prices function only, changes in both or any of these two explanatory variables causes effects in both the money wages inflation and prices inflation.

   A common property of the three cases here is that, in each case, some of the variables included are *jointly and interdependently determined* by the corresponding system of equations that represents the economic phenomenon. In the first case, for example, price P_t and quantity Q_t are jointly and interdependently determined, whilst income Y_t and the disturbances ε_{dt} and ε_{st} affect P_t and Q_t but they are not affected by them. In the second case, consumption C_t and income Y_t are jointly and interdependently determined, whilst investment I_t and the disturbances ε_t affect C_t and Y_t but they are not affected by them. In the third case, money wage inflation w_t and price inflation p_t are jointly and interdependently determined, whilst the unemployment rate U_t, aggregate demand Y_t and the disturbances ε_{wt} and ε_{pt} affect w_t and p_t but they are not affected by them.

Since some of the variables in these systems of equations are jointly and interdependently determined, changes in other variables in the same systems of equations that are not determined by these systems, but are determined outside the systems, are nonetheless transmitted to the jointly and interdependently determined variables. This transmission takes place as an *instantaneous adjustment*, or *feedback*, and we say that the system is a *system of simultaneous equations*. In the first case, for example, the initial result of an increase in income at the existing price level will be increases in demand. The result of a higher demand will be an increase in the price level, which pushes demand to lower levels and supply to higher levels. This feedback between changes in price levels and changes in quantities continues till the system is again in equilibrium, i.e. till quantity demanded is equal to the quantity supplied.

Generally, we say that a set of equations is a simultaneous equations system, or model, if all its equations are needed for determining the level of at least one of its jointly and interdependently determined variables. In what follows we investigate models of simultaneous linear equations.

8.1 Definitions and notation

The variables in a simultaneous equations model may be classified as follows:

Endogenous variables These are the jointly and interdependently determined random variables of the model. Consumption and income, for example, of Case 8.2 are endogenous variables.

Exogenous variables These are the variables that are determined outside the model and independently of the endogenous variables. Although these variables can affect the levels of the endogenous variables, there is no feedback effect. In other words, the endogenous variables cannot affect the levels of the exogenous variables. Unemployment rate and aggregate demand, for example, in Case 3, are exogenous variables.

Lagged dependent variables These are the lagged endogenous variables of any lag length. Because these values are predetermined due to lags for the current period t, their status is considered similar to the status of the exogenous variables.

Predetermined variables These constitute the set of the exogenous variables and the lagged endogenous variables.

Structural disturbances These variables refer to the usual random error variables, or disturbances, or random shocks.

Because the equations in a simultaneous equations model describe the structure of an economic phenomenon they are called *structural equations*. The parameters of a structural equation are called *structural parameters*. Equations (8.1) to (8.3) are, for example, the structural equations representing the simultaneous equations model of Case 8.1, with the α's and β's being the corresponding structural parameters of the model. The structural equations may be classified as follows:

Behavioural equations These are the equations that are determined by the behaviour of economic agents. The demand and supply functions, for example, of Case 8.1, are behavioural equations.

Technical equations These are the equations that describe a technical situation. A production function, for example, that describes the relationship between input and output is a technical equation.

Identities The identities, or definitional equations, express fixed relationships between various variables involved. Equation (8.5), for example, of Case 8.2, is a macroeconomic accounting identity. Identities, being deterministic, do not contain either structural parameters, or error terms.

Equilibrium conditions These are equations which specify the conditions under which some variables may be determined in the model. Equation (8.3), for example, in Case 8.1, is an equilibrium condition specifying how the levels of price and quantity are determined. Equilibrium conditions, being also deterministic, do not contain either structural parameters, or error terms.

A system of simultaneous equations is *complete* if the total number of equations is equal to the total number of the endogenous variables it contains.

Given these definitions, the *structural form* of a simultaneous equations model may be written as follows:

$$\gamma_{11}Y_{1t} + \gamma_{12}Y_{2t} + \cdots + \gamma_{1G}Y_{Gt} + \beta_{11}X_{1t} + \beta_{12}X_{2t} + \cdots + \beta_{1K}X_{Kt} = \varepsilon_{1t}$$

$$\gamma_{21}Y_{1t} + \gamma_{22}Y_{2t} + \cdots + \gamma_{2G}Y_{Gt} + \beta_{21}X_{1t} + \beta_{22}X_{2t} + \cdots + \beta_{2K}X_{Kt} = \varepsilon_{2t} :$$

$$\cdot$$

$$\cdot \tag{8.8}$$

$$\cdot$$

$$\gamma_{G1}Y_{1t} + \gamma_{G2}Y_{2t} + \cdots + \gamma_{GG}Y_{Gt} + \beta_{G1}X_{1t} + \beta_{G2}X_{2t} + \cdots + \beta_{GK}X_{Kt} = \varepsilon_{Gt}$$

where the Y's are G endogenous variables, the X's are K predetermined variables (exogenous and lagged dependent variables), the ε's are the disturbances, the γ's and β's are the structural parameters, and t = 1, 2, ..., n. This structural model is complete because the number of equations is G as it is the number of endogenous variables. Of course, the equations in this model may contain any type of equations. Furthermore, some of the structural coefficients may equal zero, indicating that not all equations involve the same exact variables. The inclusion of a constant term is indicated by the unitary values of one for the X variables. Normally, the γ_{ii} coefficients (diagonal coefficients) are set equal to one to indicate the dependent variable of the corresponding equation.

Model (8.8) may be written in matrix form as:

$$\begin{bmatrix} \gamma_{11} & \gamma_{12} & \cdots & \gamma_{1G} \\ \gamma_{21} & \gamma_{22} & \cdots & \gamma_{2G} \\ \vdots & \vdots & \ddots & \vdots \\ \gamma_{G1} & \gamma_{G2} & \cdots & \gamma_{GG} \end{bmatrix} \begin{bmatrix} Y_{1t} \\ Y_{2t} \\ \vdots \\ Y_{Gt} \end{bmatrix} + \begin{bmatrix} \beta_{11} & \beta_{12} & \cdots & \beta_{1K} \\ \beta_{21} & \beta_{22} & \cdots & \beta_{2K} \\ \vdots & \vdots & \ddots & \vdots \\ \beta_{G1} & \beta_{G2} & \cdots & \beta_{GK} \end{bmatrix} \begin{bmatrix} X_{1t} \\ X_{2t} \\ \vdots \\ X_{Kt} \end{bmatrix} = \begin{bmatrix} \varepsilon_{1t} \\ \varepsilon_{2t} \\ \vdots \\ \varepsilon_{Gt} \end{bmatrix} \tag{8.9}$$

or

$$\Gamma Y_t + BX_t = \varepsilon_t, \quad t = 1, 2, ..., n \tag{8.10}$$

where Γ is a $G \times G$ matrix of the γ coefficients, B is a $G \times K$ matrix of the β coefficients, Y_t is a $G \times 1$ vector of the G endogenous variables for time t, X_t is a $K \times 1$ vector of the K predetermined variables for time t, and ε_t is a $G \times 1$ vector of the structural disturbances for time t.

The assumptions underlying structural disturbances are those of the classical normal linear regression model. These assumptions are written as:

$$\varepsilon_{it} \sim N(0, \sigma_{ii}), \text{ for all t, and } i = 1, 2,..., G, \text{ where } \sigma_{ii} = var(\varepsilon_{it})$$

$$E(\varepsilon_{it}\varepsilon_{is}) = 0, \text{ for } t \neq s, \text{ and } i = 1, 2, ..., G \qquad (8.11)$$

$$E(\varepsilon_{it}\varepsilon_{jt}) = \sigma_{ij}, \text{ for all t, and } i, j = 1, 2, ..., G, \text{ where } \sigma_{ij} = cov(\varepsilon_{it}, \varepsilon_{jt})$$

or in matrix form:

$$\varepsilon_t \sim N(\mathbf{0}, \mathbf{\Sigma}), \text{ with } E(\varepsilon_t \varepsilon_s') = \mathbf{0}, \text{ and } E(\varepsilon_t \varepsilon_t') = \mathbf{\Sigma} = \begin{bmatrix} \sigma_{11} & \sigma_{12} & .. & \sigma_{1G} \\ \sigma_{21} & \sigma_{22} & .. & \sigma_{2G} \\ : & : & :: & : \\ \sigma_{G1} & \sigma_{G2} & .. & \sigma_{GG} \end{bmatrix} \qquad (8.12)$$

where symbol (') indicates 'transpose', and Σ is the so-called variance-covariance matrix of disturbances.

Since model (8.8) is complete, it may be generally solved for endogenous variables. This solution is called the *reduced form model* and it is written as:

$$Y_{1t} = \pi_{11}X_{1t} + \pi_{12}X_{2t} + \cdots + \pi_{1K}X_{Kt} + \upsilon_{1t}$$

$$Y_{2t} = \pi_{21}X_{1t} + \pi_{22}X_{2t} + \cdots + \pi_{2K}X_{Kt} + \upsilon_{2t}$$

$$: \qquad (8.13)$$

$$:$$

$$Y_{Gt} = \pi_{G1}X_{1t} + \pi_{G2}X_{2t} + \cdots + \pi_{GK}X_{Kt} + \upsilon_{Gt}$$

where the π's are the *reduced form coefficients*, and the u's are the *reduced form disturbances*. The reduced form coefficients show the effects on the equilibrium values of the endogenous variables from a change in the corresponding exogenous variables after all feedbacks have taken place.

Model (8.13) may be written in matrix form as:

$$\begin{bmatrix} Y_{1t} \\ Y_{2t} \\ : \\ Y_{Gt} \end{bmatrix} = \begin{bmatrix} \pi_{11} & \pi_{12} & .. & \pi_{1K} \\ \pi_{21} & \pi_{22} & .. & \pi_{2K} \\ : & : & :: & : \\ \pi_{G1} & \pi_{G2} & .. & \pi_{GK} \end{bmatrix} \begin{bmatrix} X_{1t} \\ X_{2t} \\ : \\ X_{Kt} \end{bmatrix} + \begin{bmatrix} \upsilon_{1t} \\ \upsilon_{2t} \\ : \\ \upsilon_{Gt} \end{bmatrix} \qquad (8.14)$$

or

$$\mathbf{Y}_t = \Pi \mathbf{X}_t + \upsilon_t, t = 1, 2, ..., n \qquad (8.15)$$

where Π is a $G \times K$ matrix of the π coefficients, and υ_t is a $G \times 1$ vector of the reduced form disturbances for time t.

If we now return to the structural model (8.10), this can be written as:

$$\mathbf{Y}_t = -\Gamma^{-1}\mathbf{B}\mathbf{X}_t + \Gamma^{-1}\varepsilon_t \tag{8.16}$$

which is the explicit solution for the endogenous variables it contains, under the assumption that the inverse matrix Γ^{-1} exists, or that matrix Γ is nonsingular. In other words, solution (8.16) is the *reduced form model* corresponding to the structural form model (8.10).

By comparing (8.16) with (8.15), we obtain:

$$\Pi = -\Gamma^{-1}\mathbf{B} \tag{8.17}$$

and

$$\upsilon_t = \Gamma^{-1}\varepsilon_t \tag{8.18}$$

From (8.17) it is seen that the reduced form coefficients are functions of the structural coefficients. Furthermore, from (8.18) it is seen that each reduced form disturbance is a linear function of all structural disturbances, and, therefore, the stochastic properties of the reduced form disturbances depend on the stochastic properties of the structural disturbances. These properties are written as:

$$\upsilon_{it} \sim N(0,\omega_{ii}), \text{ for all t, and i=1, 2, ..., G, where } \omega_{ii} = \text{var}(\upsilon_{it})$$
$$E(\upsilon_{it}\upsilon_{is}) = 0, \text{ for } t \neq s, \text{ and i=1, 2, ..., G} \tag{8.19}$$
$$E(\upsilon_{it}\upsilon_{jt}) = \omega_{ij}, \text{ for all t, and i,j = 1, 2, ..., G, where } \omega_{ij} = \text{cov}(\upsilon_{it},\upsilon_{jt})$$

or, in matrix form:

$$\upsilon_t \sim N(\mathbf{0},\mathbf{\Omega}), \text{ with } E(\upsilon_t\upsilon_s') = \mathbf{0}, \text{ and}$$

$$E(\upsilon_t\upsilon_t') = E[\Gamma^{-1}\varepsilon_t\varepsilon_t'(\Gamma^{-1})'] = \Omega = \Gamma^{-1}\Sigma(\Gamma^{-1})' = \begin{bmatrix} \omega_{11} & \omega_{12} & .. & \omega_{1G} \\ \omega_{21} & \omega_{22} & .. & \omega_{2G} \\ \vdots & \vdots & \vdots\vdots & \vdots \\ \omega_{G1} & \omega_{G2} & .. & \omega_{GG} \end{bmatrix} \tag{8.20}$$

Having established the notation and the properties of the general structural model and the corresponding reduced form model, we distinguish two important cases of specific models, according to the values of the γ coefficients in matrix Γ.

1 *Seemingly unrelated equations* This is the case where matrix Γ is diagonal, i.e. it has the following form:

$$\Gamma = \begin{bmatrix} \gamma_{11} & 0 & .. & 0 \\ 0 & \gamma_{22} & .. & 0 \\ \vdots & \vdots & \vdots\vdots & \vdots \\ 0 & 0 & .. & \gamma_{GG} \end{bmatrix} \tag{8.21}$$

In this case each endogenous variable appears in one and only one equation. In fact, we do not have a system of simultaneous equations, but instead we have a set of seemingly unrelated equations.

2   *Recursive equations model* This is the case where matrix Γ is triangular, i.e. it has the following form:

$$\Gamma = \begin{bmatrix} \gamma_{11} & 0 & .. & 0 \\ \gamma_{21} & \gamma_{22} & .. & 0 \\ : & : & :: & : \\ \gamma_{G1} & \gamma_{G2} & .. & \gamma_{GG} \end{bmatrix} \tag{8.22}$$

In this case the first equation contains one only endogenous variable, let us say the first endogenous variable. The second equation contains the first endogenous variable plus a new one, let us say the second endogenous variable, and so on. The final equation contains all the endogenous variables of the system. In other words, the solution for the first endogenous variable is completely determined by the first equation of the system. The solution for the second endogenous variable is completely determined by the first and the second equations of the system, and so on. The solution for the final endogenous variable is completely determined by all equations of the system.

8.2 Simultaneous equation bias

Let us return to the simple macroeconomic model of Case 8.2 presented in Section 8.1, i.e. to the model:

The consumption function: $C_t = \alpha_0 + \alpha_1 Y_t + \varepsilon_t$; $\alpha_1 > 0$ (8.23)

The income accounting identity: $Y_t = C_t + I_t$ (8.24)

According to the notation established in Section 2, and having classified variables C_t and Y_t as being endogenous and variable I_t as being exogenous, the structural model of Equations (8.23) and (8.24) is written in standard form as:

$$\begin{aligned} C_t - \alpha_1 Y_t - \alpha_0 + 0 I_t &= \varepsilon_t \\ -C_t + Y_t + 0 - I_t &= 0 \end{aligned} \tag{8.25}$$

or, in matrix form as:

$$\begin{bmatrix} 1 & -\alpha_1 \\ -1 & 1 \end{bmatrix} \begin{bmatrix} C_t \\ Y_t \end{bmatrix} + \begin{bmatrix} -\alpha_0 & 0 \\ 0 & -1 \end{bmatrix} \begin{bmatrix} i_t \\ I_t \end{bmatrix} = \begin{bmatrix} \varepsilon_t \\ 0 \end{bmatrix} \tag{8.26}$$

where I is the unitary variable (a $n \times 1$ vector, all values being one) and the disturbance term ε_t follows the assumptions of the classical normal linear model, i.e.

$$E(\varepsilon_t) = 0, \ \text{var}(\varepsilon_t) = \sigma^2, \ \text{cov}(\varepsilon_t, \varepsilon_s) = 0 \ \text{for } t \neq s, \ \varepsilon_t \sim N(0, \sigma^2) \tag{8.27}$$

According to (8.10), (8.26) can be written as:

$$\Gamma Y_t + BX_t = \varepsilon_t, \qquad t = 1, 2, ..., n \tag{8.28}$$

where

$$\Gamma = \begin{bmatrix} 1 & -\alpha_1 \\ -1 & 1 \end{bmatrix}, \; B = \begin{bmatrix} -\alpha_0 & 0 \\ 0 & -1 \end{bmatrix}, \; Y_t = \begin{bmatrix} C_t \\ Y_t \end{bmatrix}, \; X_t = \begin{bmatrix} i_t \\ I_t \end{bmatrix}, \; \varepsilon_t = \begin{bmatrix} \varepsilon_t \\ 0 \end{bmatrix} \tag{8.29}$$

Solving the model of Equations (8.23) and (8.24) for endogenous variables we obtain the explicit solution:

$$C_t = \frac{\alpha_0}{1-\alpha_1} + \frac{\alpha_1}{1-\alpha_1} I_t + \frac{1}{1-\alpha_1} \varepsilon_t$$
$$Y_t = \frac{\alpha_0}{1-\alpha_1} + \frac{1}{1-\alpha_1} I_t + \frac{1}{1-\alpha_1} \varepsilon_t \tag{8.30}$$

which, according to (8.14) and (8.15), in matrix form is written as:

$$\begin{bmatrix} C_t \\ Y_t \end{bmatrix} = \begin{bmatrix} \dfrac{\alpha_0}{1-\alpha_1} & \dfrac{\alpha_1}{1-\alpha_1} \\ \dfrac{\alpha_0}{1-\alpha_1} & \dfrac{1}{1-\alpha_1} \end{bmatrix} \begin{bmatrix} i_t \\ I_t \end{bmatrix} + \begin{bmatrix} \dfrac{1}{1-\alpha_1} \varepsilon_t \\ \dfrac{1}{1-\alpha_1} \varepsilon_t \end{bmatrix} \tag{8.31}$$

or

$$Y_t = \Pi X_t + \upsilon_t, \, t = 1, 2, ..., n \tag{8.32}$$

where

$$\Pi = \begin{bmatrix} \pi_{11} & \pi_{12} \\ \pi_{21} & \pi_{22} \end{bmatrix} = \begin{bmatrix} \dfrac{\alpha_0}{1-\alpha_1} & \dfrac{\alpha_1}{1-\alpha_1} \\ \dfrac{\alpha_0}{1-\alpha_1} & \dfrac{1}{1-\alpha_1} \end{bmatrix} \text{ and } \upsilon_t = \begin{bmatrix} \upsilon_{1t} \\ \upsilon_{2t} \end{bmatrix} = \begin{bmatrix} \dfrac{1}{1-\alpha_1} \varepsilon_t \\ \dfrac{1}{1-\alpha_1} \varepsilon_t \end{bmatrix} \tag{8.33}$$

Solution (8.30), or equivalently (8.32), is the reduced form model of the structural model of the two simultaneous equations: (8.23) and (8.24). If fact, this solution can be verified by applying (8.17) and (8.18) respectively as:

$$\Pi = \begin{bmatrix} \pi_{11} & \pi_{12} \\ \pi_{21} & \pi_{22} \end{bmatrix} = -\Gamma^{-1}B = -\frac{1}{1-\alpha_1} \begin{bmatrix} 1 & \alpha_1 \\ 1 & 1 \end{bmatrix} \begin{bmatrix} -\alpha_0 & 0 \\ 0 & -1 \end{bmatrix} = \begin{bmatrix} \dfrac{\alpha_0}{1-\alpha_1} & \dfrac{\alpha_1}{1-\alpha_1} \\ \dfrac{\alpha_0}{1-\alpha_1} & \dfrac{1}{1-\alpha_1} \end{bmatrix} \tag{8.34}$$

and

$$v_t = \begin{bmatrix} v_{1t} \\ v_{2t} \end{bmatrix} = \Gamma^{-1}\varepsilon_t = \frac{1}{1-\alpha_1}\begin{bmatrix} 1 & \alpha_1 \\ 1 & 1 \end{bmatrix}\begin{bmatrix} \varepsilon_t \\ 0 \end{bmatrix} = \begin{bmatrix} \dfrac{1}{1-\alpha_1}\varepsilon_t \\ \dfrac{1}{1-\alpha_1}\varepsilon_t \end{bmatrix} \tag{8.35}$$

Of course, for the existence of the inverse of matrix Γ it must be $1-\alpha_1 \neq 0$. Furthermore, from (8.19) it can be derived that the properties of the reduced form disturbances $v_{1t} = v_{2t} = v_t$ are given by:

$$E(v_t) = 0, \quad \mathrm{var}(v_t) = \sigma_v^2 = \frac{1}{(1-\alpha_1)^2}\sigma^2, \quad \mathrm{cov}(v_t, v_s) = 0 \text{ for } t \neq s, \; v_t \sim N(0, \sigma_v^2) \tag{8.36}$$

We said in section 8.1 that the reduced form coefficients show the effects on the equilibrium values of the endogenous variables from a change in the corresponding exogenous variables after all feedbacks have taken place. Coefficients $\pi_{22} = 1/(1-\alpha_1)$ and $\pi_{12} = \alpha_1/(1-\alpha_1)$, for example, in (8.33), show the 'total effects' on Y_t and on C_t respectively, of a change in I_t. By analysing, for example, coefficient π_{22}, we obtain:

$$\pi_{22} = \frac{1}{1-\alpha_1} = 1 + \frac{\alpha_1}{1-\alpha_1} \tag{8.37}$$

In other words, (8.37) shows that the 'total effect' $1/(1-\alpha_1)$ on Y_t of a change in I_t, i.e. the investment multiplier, may be divided between a 'direct effect' equal to 1, and an 'indirect effect' equal to $\alpha_1/(1-\alpha_1)$. The direct effect, 1, is the direct increase in Y_t, shown in the income accounting identity (8.24), as the coefficient of I_t, and the indirect effect is the indirect increase in Y_t through the increase in consumption C_t, $\alpha_1/(1-\alpha_1)$, in Equation (8.30), transmitted to the income accounting identity.

In the structural model of Equations (8.23) and (8.24) it is assumed that the exogenous variable I_t is independent of the error term ε_t. However, this is not true for the endogenous variable Y_t, although this variable appears as an explanatory variable in Equation (8.23). This is because this variable is jointly and interdependently determined by variables I_t and ε_t, as shown in the reduced form model in (8.30) or (8.32), and, therefore, it can be proved that:

$$\mathrm{cov}(Y_t, \varepsilon_t) = \frac{1}{1-\alpha_1}\sigma^2 \neq 0 \tag{8.38}$$

(8.38) shows that the explanatory variable Y_t in Equation (8.23) is not independent of the error term ε_t, and, therefore, this equation does not satisfy the assumptions of the classical regression model. Thus, the application of OLS to this equation would yield biased and inconsistent estimates.

Generally, because the endogenous variables of a simultaneous equations model are all correlated with the disturbances, the application of OLS to equations in which endogenous variables appear as explanatory variables yields biased and inconsistent estimates. This failure of OLS is called *simultaneous equation bias*.

This simultaneous equation bias does not disappear by increasing the size of the sample, because it can be proved that:

$$p\lim(a_1) = \alpha_1 + \frac{1}{1-\alpha_1}\left(\frac{\sigma^2}{\text{var}(Y_t)}\right) \tag{8.39}$$

where a_1 is the OLS estimator of α_1. (8.39) shows that the probability limit of a_1 is not equal to the true population parameter α_1, and thus the estimator is inconsistent. In fact, (8.39) shows that the $p\lim(a_1)$ will be always greater than α_1 because $\alpha_1 < 1$ and the variances are positive numbers.

8.3 Coping with simultaneous equation bias

We saw earlier that the problem of the simultaneous equation bias arises when we apply the OLS method to the structural model, because, due to the correlation between the endogenous variables of the system and its error terms, the OLS estimator is biased and inconsistent. But we also saw in the previous section that the reduced form model contains only predeter-mined variables on the right hand side of its equations, which are not correlated with the reduced form disturbances. Therefore, by assuming that the reduced form disturbances satisfy the classical linear regression model assumptions, the application of the OLS method to the structural form equations generally gives unbiased and consistent estimates.

The question that now arises is, can we estimate the structural parameters of the model by using the consistent estimates of the reduced form parameters? The answer to this question is that there may be a solution to this problem by employing (8.17), which connects the parameters of the reduced form model with the parameters of the structural model. Let us consider the following examples.

Example 8.1 Estimating a simple income determination model

Assume a structural model of Equations (8.23) and (8.24). The corresponding reduced form model in its specific form is that given in (8.30), and in general form is that given in (8.32). From the specific and general structural forms we saw in the previous section that:

$$\pi_{11} = \pi_{21} = \frac{\alpha_0}{1-\alpha_1}, \quad \pi_{12} = \frac{\alpha_1}{1-\alpha_1}, \quad \pi_{22} = \frac{1}{1-\alpha_1} \tag{8.40}$$

This means that if we had consistent estimates of the π's, then we could get consistent estimates of the α's by solving the system of equations in (8.40). By denoting with $\wedge$ the estimates of the π's and with 'a' the estimates of the α's, the estimates of the struc-tural coefficients are:

$$\frac{\hat{\pi}_{21}}{\hat{\pi}_{22}} = \frac{a_0/(1-a_1)}{1/(1-a_1)} = a_0 \quad \text{and} \quad \frac{\hat{\pi}_{12}}{\hat{\pi}_{22}} = \frac{a_1/(1-a_1)}{1/(1-a_1)} = a_1 \tag{8.41}$$

This technique, by which we first estimate the reduced form parameters and then obtain through the system (8.40) estimates of the structural parameters, is called *indirect least squares* (ILS).

Table 7.6 in chapter 7 contains data referring to the private consumption (C_t) and to private disposable income (Y_t) for an EU member, Greece. Furthermore, regarding private savings ($S_t = Y_t - C_t$), it assumed that all are invested (I_t). In other words, we have the simple structural model of Equations (8.23) and (8.24) and the corresponding reduced form model (8.30), or (8.33).

Using the data in Table 7.6, the OLS estimates of the reduced form equations of the model are (s.e. = standard errors and t = t-ratio in absolute values):

$$\hat{C}_t = 74218.71 + 3.22239 I_t \quad \bar{R}^2 = 0.883$$

s.e. (14013.2) (0.19763)

t   [5.29635] [16.30515]

(8.42)

and

$$\hat{Y}_t = 74218.71 + 4.22239 I_t \quad \bar{R}^2 = 0.929$$

s.e. (14013.2) (0.19763)

t   [5.29635] [21.36510]

(8.43)

Corresponding to (8.40), we have:

$$\hat{\pi}_{11} = \hat{\pi}_{21} = \frac{a_0}{1-a_1} = 74218.71 \;, \; \hat{\pi}_{12} = \frac{a_1}{1-a_1} = 3.22239 \;, \; \hat{\pi}_{22} = \frac{1}{1-a_1} = 4.22239$$

and, therefore, from (8.41) we obtain the estimates of the structural coefficients, using the method of indirect least squares, as:

$$a_0 = \frac{\hat{\pi}_{21}}{\hat{\pi}_{22}} = 17577.39 \quad \text{and} \quad a_1 = \frac{\hat{\pi}_{12}}{\hat{\pi}_{22}} = 0.76317$$

(8.44)

In summary, we have managed to get *unique estimates* of the structural coefficients by applying the method of indirect least squares.

Ignoring the problem of the simultaneous equation bias, if we apply the method of OLS directly to the structural equation of private consumption we get the following estimates:

$$\hat{C}_t = 11907.23 + 0.77958 Y_t, \quad \bar{R}^2 = 0.994$$

s.e. (3812.87) (0.01032)

t   [3.12291] [75.5662]

(8.45)

By comparing (8.45) with (8.44) we see that $a_{1,OLS} = 0.77958 > a_{1,ILS} = 0.76317$. This result verifies, in a sense, the theoretical result stated in (8.39).

Example 8.2 Estimating a demand-supply model for meat

Considering the market equilibrium condition $Q^d_t = Q^s_t$, a model describing the demand and supply equations for meat could be:

The demand function : $Q_t = \alpha_0 + \alpha_1 P_t + \alpha_2 P_{ft} + \alpha_3 Y_t + \varepsilon_{1t}$

(8.46)

The supply function: $Q_t = \beta_0 + \beta_1 P_t + \beta_2 w_t + \varepsilon_{2t}$

(8.47)

where Q_t = the quantity of meat, P_t = the price of meat, P_{ft} = the price of fish as a substitute for meat, Y_t = income, w_t = cost of labour as a main factor of production, and ε_t's are the error terms. According to the laws of demand and supply we expect $\alpha_1 < 0$ and $\beta_1 > 0$, respectively. We expect $\alpha_2 > 0$ because fish is a substitute for meat and $\alpha_3 > 0$ because the higher the income, the greater the meat demanded. Finally, we expect $\beta_2 < 0$ because the higher the prices of the factors of production, the lower the production.

By solving the system of two structural equations (8.46) and (8.47) for the two endogenous variables P_t and Q_t, we get the following reduced form model:

$$P_t = \pi_{11} + \pi_{12}w_t + \pi_{13}P_{ft} + \pi_{14}Y_t + \upsilon_{1t} \tag{8.48}$$

$$Q_t = \pi_{21} + \pi_{22}w_t + \pi_{23}P_{ft} + \pi_{24}Y_t + \upsilon_{2t} \tag{8.49}$$

where

$$\pi_{11} = \frac{\beta_0 - \alpha_0}{\alpha_1 - \beta_1}, \; \pi_{12} = \frac{\beta_2}{\alpha_1 - \beta_1}, \; \pi_{13} = -\frac{\alpha_2}{\alpha_1 - \beta_1}, \; \pi_{14} = -\frac{\alpha_3}{\alpha_1 - \beta_1} \tag{8.50}$$

$$\pi_{21} = \frac{\beta_0\alpha_1 - \alpha_0\beta_1}{\alpha_1 - \beta_1}, \; \pi_{22} = \frac{\alpha_1\beta_2}{\alpha_1 - \beta_1}, \; \pi_{23} = -\frac{\alpha_2\beta_1}{\alpha_1 - \beta_1}, \; \pi_{24} = -\frac{\alpha_3\beta_1}{\alpha_1 - \beta_1} \tag{8.51}$$

and

$$\upsilon_{1t} = \frac{\varepsilon_{2t} - \varepsilon_{1t}}{\alpha_1 - \beta_1}, \; \upsilon_{2t} = \frac{\alpha_1\varepsilon_{2t} - \beta_1\varepsilon_{1t}}{\alpha_1 - \beta_1} \tag{8.52}$$

If we make use of the data in Table 8.1 where Q_t = meat consumption, Y_t = personal disposable income, P_t = the meat consumption price index, P_t = the fish consumption price index, and w_t = real unit labour cost, the OLS estimates of the two reduced form equations (8.48) and (8.49) are:

$$\hat{P}_t = -4.08811 + 3.15485w_t + 0.46503P_{ft} + 5.97E - 06Y_t \quad \bar{R}^2 = 0.996$$

$$\text{s.e.} \quad (1.8931) \quad (1.6274) \quad (0.0082) \quad (1.37E - 06) \tag{8.53}$$

$$\text{t} \quad [2.1595] \quad [1.9385] \quad [56.5939] \quad [4.3701]$$

and

$$\hat{Q}_t = 8501.874 - 6367.821w_t + 19.37733P_{ft} + 0.05726Y_t \quad \bar{R}^2 = 0.974$$

$$\text{s.e.} \quad (3991.87) \quad (3431.64) \quad (17.3266) \quad (0.0029) \tag{8.54}$$

$$\text{t} \quad [2.1298] \quad [1.8556] \quad [1.1184] \quad [19.8658]$$

Having obtained the reduced form estimates in (8.53) and (8.54), let us try, following the methodology of the previous example, to find the indirect least squares estimates of the structural form model. Let us try, for example, to find an estimate b_1 of β_1. From (8.50) and (8.51) we get:

Table 8.1 Meat consumption data for an EU member

Year	Meat consumption (constant 1970 prices, million drs)	Personal disposable income (constant 1970 prices, million drs)	Meat consumption price index (base year: 1970)	Fish consumption price index (base year: 1970)	Real unit labour cost* (total economy, base year: 1970)
1960	6978.000	117179.2	0.730582	0.631294	1.245935
1961	7901.000	127598.9	0.687128	0.643396	1.160569
1962	8660.000	135007.1	0.668129	0.664978	1.153455
1963	9220.000	142128.3	0.705857	0.686165	1.096545
1964	9298.000	159648.7	0.825554	0.723415	1.092480
1965	11718.00	172755.9	0.844342	0.793698	1.070122
1966	12858.00	182365.5	0.874242	0.854387	1.073171
1967	13686.00	195611.0	0.886746	0.878201	1.074187
1968	14468.00	204470.4	0.871924	0.890306	1.074187
1969	15041.00	222637.5	0.888305	0.913162	1.032520
1970	16273.00	246819.0	1.000000	1.000000	1.000000
1971	17538.00	269248.9	1.088836	1.109464	0.980691
1972	18632.00	297266.0	1.139330	1.181059	0.969512
1973	19789.00	335521.7	1.421598	1.398077	0.895325
1974	20333.00	310231.1	1.642847	1.600000	0.917683
1975	21508.00	327521.3	1.809792	1.993345	0.927846
1976	22736.00	350427.4	2.100325	2.158964	0.942073
1977	25379.00	366730.0	2.294023	2.390215	0.991870
1978	26151.00	390188.5	2.498719	3.168778	1.018293
1979	26143.00	406857.2	3.243239	3.794650	1.021341
1980	26324.00	401942.8	3.861875	6.849719	1.000000
1981	24324.00	419669.1	5.269651	9.000263	1.065041
1982	26155.00	421715.6	6.708813	10.17698	1.073171
1983	27098.00	417930.3	7.873865	11.63759	1.101626
1984	27043.00	434695.7	8.948711	13.95143	1.077236
1985	27047.00	456576.2	10.54561	18.22986	1.104675
1986	27136.00	439654.1	12.26179	23.00331	1.046748
1987	28616.00	438453.5	13.43940	27.15239	1.026423
1988	29624.00	476344.7	15.09249	29.46009	1.033537
1989	30020.00	492334.4	18.44444	33.97218	1.081301
1990	29754.00	495939.2	21.63215	40.39124	1.116870
1991	29332.00	513173.0	23.91613	45.39971	1.016260
1992	30665.00	502520.1	27.24601	51.81363	0.969512
1993	31278.00	523066.1	30.08261	57.15542	0.965447
1994	35192.00	520727.5	31.82757	63.53983	0.977642
1995	36505.00	518406.9	33.60107	72.49126	0.997967

Sources: Epilogi (1998)
* EC (1997), Annual Economic Report for 1997, *European Economy*.

$$\frac{\hat{\pi}_{23}}{\hat{\pi}_{13}} = \frac{-a_2 b_1 / (a_1 - b_1)}{-a_2 / (a_1 - b_1)} = b_1 = \frac{19.3773}{0.46503} = 41.6689 \tag{8.55}$$

However, from the same system of (8.50) and (8.51) we can also get that:

$$\frac{\hat{\pi}_{24}}{\hat{\pi}_{14}} = \frac{-a_3 b_1 / (a_1 - b_1)}{-a_3 / (a_1 - b_1)} = b_1 = \frac{0.05726}{5.97E-06} = 9591.62 \tag{8.56}$$

By comparing the two values of the estimate b_1 in (8.55) and (8.56) we see that these values are very different. This means that by applying, in this example, the same methodology of indirect least squares as we did in example 8.1 we get two consistent but different estimates of β_1. This result is due to the fact that, in estimating Equations (8.48) and (8.49) we did not take into account the restriction of $\pi_{23}/\pi_{13} = \pi_{24}/\pi_{14}$. In other words, the use of the indirect least squares method does not always give unique estimates. This creates a problem which is known as the *problem of identification*.

8.4 Identification

Let us summarise the simultaneous equations models used till now as follows:
  Structural equations model:

$$\Gamma Y_t + BX_t = \varepsilon_t \tag{8.56a}$$

$$\text{with} \qquad \varepsilon_t \sim N(0, \Sigma) \tag{8.56b}$$

where

  Yt = is a G×1 vector of the endogenous variables in time t.
  Xt = is a K×1 vector of the predetermined variables in time t.
  εt = is a G×1 vector of the structural disturbances in time t.
  Γ = is a G×G nonsingular matrix of the γ's structural coefficients.
  B = is a G×K matrix of the β's structural coefficients.
  Σ = is a G×G symmetric positive definite matrix of the variance-covariance parameters of the structural disturbances.

The specific solution, or restricted reduced form model, being:

$$Y_t = -\Gamma^{-1}BX_t + \Gamma^{-1}\varepsilon_t \tag{8.57}$$

The general solution, or unrestricted reduced form model, being:

$$Y_t = \Pi X_t + \upsilon_t \tag{8.58}$$

With: $\upsilon_t \sim N(0, \Omega)$ $\tag{8.59}$

Where: $\Omega = \Gamma - 1\Sigma(\Gamma - 1)'$ $\tag{8.60}$

And υ_t = is a G×1 vector of the reduced form disturbances in time t.
Π = is a G × K matrix of the π's reduced form coefficients. Ω = is a G × G matrix of the variance-covariance parameters of structural disturbances.

The coefficients system:

$$\Pi = -\Gamma^{-1}B \tag{8.61}$$

The variance-covariance system:

$$v_t = \Gamma^{-1}\varepsilon_t \qquad (8.62)$$

Furthermore, we saw that if we apply an OLS estimator to the structural model, then we have the problem of simultaneous equation bias, i.e. we will get inconsistent estimates of the structural coefficients B and Γ, because the endogenous variables of the model, Y_t, are not independent of the structural error term, ε_t. We also saw that we can apply the OLS estimator to the unrestricted reduced form model, in order to obtain consistent estimates of the reduced form coefficients Π, because the predetermined variables, X_t, are independent of the reduced form error term, v_t. Finally, we saw that using the indirect least squares method, i.e. having first estimated the reduced form coefficients consistently with OLS and secondly obtaining consistent estimates of the structural coefficients through the coefficients system, there are cases where we can get unique estimates. Of course, there are other cases where we cannot obtain unique estimates of the structural coefficients, or estimates at all. This brings the problem of identification.

Equations in simultaneous equations models may be grouped into the following two categories:

Identified equations These are the equations for which estimates of the structural coefficients can be obtained from the estimates of the reduced form coefficients.

Unidentified or underidentified equations These are the equations for which estimates of the structural coefficients cannot be obtained from the estimates of the reduced form coefficients.

The identified equations may be further grouped into the following two categories:

Exactly or just or fully identified equations These are the identified equations for which a unique estimate of the structural coefficients can be obtained.

Overidentified equations These are the identified equations for which more than one estimate of at least one of their structural coefficients can be obtained.

Generally, the problem of identification arises because the same reduced form model may be compatible with more than one structural model, or, in other words, with more than one theory. We say then that we have *observationally equivalent relations* and we cannot distinguish them without more information.

8.4.1 Observationally equivalent relations

We shall investigate the problem of identification by using the concept of the observationally equivalent relations in various cases.

Case 8.4 Underidentified equations If Q = quantity and P = price, assume the simple structural demand-supply model under equilibrium conditions:

where

$$\text{demand} = Q_t = \alpha_0 + \alpha_1 P_t + \varepsilon_{1t} \qquad (8.63)$$

$$\text{supply} = Q_t = \beta_0 + \beta_1 P_t + \varepsilon_{2t} \tag{8.64}$$

The reduced form model is:

$$P_t = \frac{\beta_0 - \alpha_0}{\alpha_1 - \beta_1} + \frac{\varepsilon_{2t} - \varepsilon_{1t}}{\alpha_1 - \beta_1} = \pi_1 + \upsilon_{1t} \tag{8.65}$$

$$Q_t = \frac{\alpha_1\beta_0 - \alpha_0\beta_1}{\alpha_1 - \beta_1} + \frac{\alpha_1\varepsilon_{2t} - \beta_1\varepsilon_{1t}}{\alpha_1 - \beta_1} = \pi_2 + \upsilon_{2t} \tag{8.66}$$

where

$$\pi_1 = \frac{\beta_0 - \alpha_0}{\alpha_1 - \beta_1} \text{ and } \pi_2 = \frac{\alpha_1\beta_0 - \alpha_0\beta_1}{\alpha_1 - \beta_1} \tag{8.67}$$

By counting the coefficients of the structural and reduced form models we see that the structural model has four coefficients and the reduced form model has two coefficients. Furthermore, each of the two equations in the coefficients system (8.67) contains all four structural coefficients. Therefore, it is not possible from system (8.67) to find solutions for the structural coefficients and, thus, both structural equations are underidentified.

The problem of underidentification of both equations in this model is shown in Figure 8.1. Figure 8.1(a) represents some scatter points of pairs of equilibrium prices and quantities data. Figure 8.1(b) shows the scatter points plus some different structures of demand (D, d) and supply (S, s) curves. The reduced scatter points of Figure 8.1(a) may be the result of the intersection of the demand (D) and supply (S) curves, or of the demand (d) and supply (s) curves, or of any other demand or supply curves in Figure 8.1(b). In other words, having only the information included in the scatter points, it is impossible to distinguish which structure of demand and supply curves corresponds to these scatter points. Thus, more than one structure (theories) are consistent with the same scatter points (data) and there is no way of distinguishing them without further information. These structures are underidentified.

Let us see the same problem presented in Figure 8.1 from another point of view. If we multiply Equation (8.63) by λ, where $1 \geq \lambda \geq 0$, and Equation (8.64) by $(1 - \lambda)$ and add the two results, we obtain the following combined equation, which is a linear combination of the two original equations:

$$Q_t = \gamma_0 + \gamma_1 P_t + \varepsilon_t \tag{8.68}$$

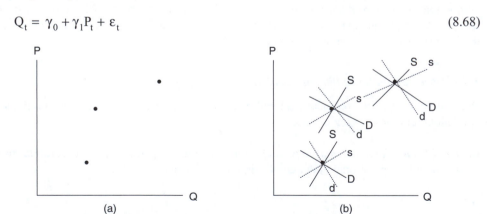

Figure 8.1 Market equilibria and underidentification.

where

$$\gamma_0 = \lambda\alpha_0 + (1-\lambda)\beta_0, \quad \gamma_1 = \lambda\alpha_1 + (1-\lambda)\beta_1, \quad \varepsilon_t = \lambda\varepsilon_{1t} + (1-\lambda)\varepsilon_{2t} \tag{8.69}$$

Observing the combined Equation (8.68) we see that it has the exact same form as the forms of the original Equations (8.63) and (8.64). We say that these three equations are *observationally equivalent*. Therefore, if we just have pairs of data on Q_t and P_t, we do not know if that by regressing Q_t on P_t the underlying relation is that of the demand Equation (8.63), or of the supply Equation (8.64), or of the combined Equation (8.68). In other words, more than one structure (relation) are consistent with the same data and there is no way of distinguishing them without further information. These structures are underidentified.

Case 8.5 Exactly or just identified equations Assume a structural demand-supply model under the equilibrium conditions as:

The demand : $Q_t = \alpha_0 + \alpha_1 P_t + \alpha_2 Y_t + \varepsilon_{1t}$ $\hspace{2cm}$ (8.70)

The supply : $Q_t = \beta_0 + \beta_1 P_t + \varepsilon_{2t}$ $\hspace{2cm}$ (8.71)

This model differs from that of Case 8.4 because the demand equation now contains more information. The quantity demanded depends now not only on prices but on income, Y_t, as well. The reduced form model is:

$$P_t = \frac{\beta_0 - \alpha_0}{\alpha_1 - \beta_1} - \frac{\alpha_2}{\alpha_1 - \beta_1} Y_t + \frac{\varepsilon_{2t} - \varepsilon_{1t}}{\alpha_1 - \beta_1} = \pi_{11} + \pi_{12} Y_t + \upsilon_{1t} \tag{8.72}$$

$$Q_t = \frac{\alpha_1\beta_0 - \alpha_0\beta_1}{\alpha_1 - \beta_1} - \frac{\alpha_2\beta_1}{\alpha_1 - \beta_1} Y_t + \frac{\alpha_1\varepsilon_{2t} - \beta_1\varepsilon_{1t}}{\alpha_1 - \beta_1} = \pi_{21} + \pi_{22} Y_t + \upsilon_{2t} \tag{8.73}$$

where:

$$\pi_{11} = \frac{\beta_0 - \alpha_0}{\alpha_1 - \beta_1}, \quad \pi_{12} = -\frac{\alpha_2}{\alpha_1 - \beta_1}, \quad \pi_{21} = \frac{\alpha_1\beta_0 - \alpha_0\beta_1}{\alpha_1 - \beta_1}, \quad \pi_{22} = -\frac{\alpha_2\beta_1}{\alpha_1 - \beta_1} \tag{8.74}$$

By counting the coefficients of the structural and of the reduced form models we see that the structural model has five coefficients and the reduced form model has four coefficients. Therefore, it is not possible from the coefficients system (8.74) to find solutions for all of the structural coefficients. In fact, we see that from system (8.74) we can find a unique solution for the coefficients of the supply function as:

$$\beta_1 = \pi_{22}/\pi_{12} \text{ and } \beta_0 = \pi_{21} - \beta_1\pi_{11} \tag{8.75}$$

Unfortunately, we cannot find, from the same system, solutions for all coefficients of the demand function. Therefore, the supply function is exactly identified, whilst the demand function is not identified.

The exact identification of the supply equation and the non-identification of the demand equation in this model is shown in Figure 8.2. Figure 8.2(a) represents some scatter points of pairs of equilibrium prices and quantities. Figure 8.2(b) shows the scatter points plus the information that the demand curve shifts over time to the right, from D_1 to D_3, because of

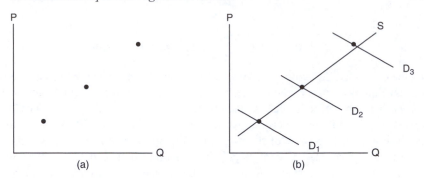

Figure 8.2 Market equilibria and exact identification of the supply function.

increasing income, and the supply curve remains stable, or relatively stable. Therefore, the introduction of this new information in this model, with respect to the model in Case 8.4, distinguishes a unique supply curve, but it is impossible to distinguish a unique demand curve. The observed values of Q_t and P_t, i.e. the intersection points of demand and supply curves, trace (identify) the supply curve. Thus, the supply equation is exactly identified, whilst the demand equation is not identified.

This can be also seen in the following combined equation, which is a linear combination of the two original Equations (8.70) and (8.71):

$$Q_t = \gamma_0 + \gamma_1 P_t + \gamma_2 Y_t + \varepsilon_t \tag{8.76}$$

where

$$\gamma_0 = \lambda\alpha_0 + (1-\lambda)\beta_0, \ \gamma_1 = \lambda\alpha_1 + (1-\lambda)\beta_1, \ \gamma_2 = \lambda\alpha_2, \ \varepsilon_t = \lambda\varepsilon_{1t} + (1-\lambda)\varepsilon_{2t} \tag{8.77}$$

Observing the combined Equation (8.76) we see that it has the same exact form to that of the demand Equation (8.70) and different form from that of the supply Equation (8.71). We say, therefore, that the combined and the demand equations are *observationally equivalent*, meaning that the demand function is not identified, and the combined and the supply equations are *not observationally equivalent*, meaning that the supply function is identified.

Case 8.6 An exactly or just identified model Assume a structural demand-supply model under the equilibrium conditions as:

$$\text{The demand} = Q_t = \alpha_0 + \alpha_1 P_t + \alpha_2 Y_t + \varepsilon_{1t} \tag{8.78}$$

$$\text{The supply} = Q_t = \beta_0 + \beta_1 P_t + \beta_2 W_t + \varepsilon_{2t} \tag{8.79}$$

This model differs from the model in Case 8.5 because the supply equation now contains more information. The quantity supplied depends now not only on prices, but on wages, W_t, as well, depicting the negative effect of the cost of a major factor of production to the quantity produced and supplied. The reduced form model is:

$$P_t = \frac{\beta_0 - \alpha_0}{\alpha_1 - \beta_1} - \frac{\alpha_2}{\alpha_1 - \beta_1}Y_t + \frac{\beta_2}{\alpha_1 - \beta_1}W_t + \frac{\varepsilon_{2t} - \varepsilon_{1t}}{\alpha_1 - \beta_1} \tag{8.80}$$

$$= \pi_{11} + \pi_{12}Y_t + \pi_{13}W_t + \upsilon_{1t}$$

$$Q_t = \frac{\alpha_1\beta_0 - \alpha_0\beta_1}{\alpha_1 - \beta_1} - \frac{\alpha_2\beta_1}{\alpha_1 - \beta_1}Y_t + \frac{\alpha_1\beta_2}{\alpha_1 - \beta_1}W_t + \frac{\alpha_1\varepsilon_{2t} - \beta_1\varepsilon_{1t}}{\alpha_1 - \beta_1}$$

$$= \pi_{21} + \pi_{22}Y_t + \pi_{23}W_t + \upsilon_{2t}$$

(8.81)

where

$$\pi_{11} = \frac{\beta_0 - \alpha_0}{\alpha_1 - \beta_1}, \ \pi_{12} = -\frac{\alpha_2}{\alpha_1 - \beta_1}, \ \pi_{13} = \frac{\beta_2}{\alpha_1 - \beta_1}$$

$$\pi_{21} = \frac{\alpha_1\beta_0 - \alpha_0\beta_1}{\alpha_1 - \beta_1}, \ \pi_{22} = -\frac{\alpha_2\beta_1}{\alpha_1 - \beta_1}, \ \pi_{23} = \frac{\alpha_1\beta_2}{\alpha_1 - \beta_1}$$

(8.82)

By counting the coefficients of the structural and the reduced form models we see that the structural model has six coefficients and the reduced form model also has six coefficients. Therefore, it is generally possible from the coefficients system (8.82) to find a unique solution for all structural coefficients, and, thus, both equations are exactly identified. In this case the model as a whole is exactly identified.

We can derive the same results using the following combined equation, which is a linear combination of the two original Equations (8.78) and (8.79):

$$Q_t = \gamma_0 + \gamma_1 P_t + \gamma_2 Y_t + \gamma_3 W_t + \varepsilon_t$$

(8.83)

where:

$$\gamma_0 = \lambda\alpha_0 + (1-\lambda)\beta_0, \ \gamma_1 = \lambda\alpha_1 + (1-\lambda)\beta_1,$$

$$\gamma_2 = \lambda\alpha_2, \ \gamma_3 = (1-\lambda)\beta_2, \ \varepsilon_t = \lambda\varepsilon_{1t} + (1-\lambda)\varepsilon_{2t}$$

(8.84)

Observing the combined Equation (8.84) we see that it has a different form from the forms of both the demand Equation (8.78) and the supply Equation (8.79). We say, therefore, that the combined and the demand and supply equations are *not observationally equivalent*, meaning that both the demand and the supply functions are identified.

Case 8.7 Overidentified equations Assume a structural demand-supply model under the equilibrium conditions as:

$$\text{The demand} = Q_t = \alpha_0 + \alpha_1 P_t + \alpha_2 Y_t + \alpha_3 P_{ft} + \varepsilon_{1t}$$

(8.85)

$$\text{The supply} = Q_t = \beta_0 + \beta_1 P_t + \beta_2 W_t + \varepsilon_{2t}$$

(8.86)

This model differs from the model of Case 8.6 because the demand equation now contains even more information. The quantity demanded depends now not only on prices and income but on the prices of a substitute good, P_{ft}, as well, thus depicting the positive effect on the quantity demanded by an increase in the price of the substitute good. We met this case in Case 8.2. The reduced form model is:

$$P_t = \frac{\beta_0 - \alpha_0}{\alpha_1 - \beta_1} - \frac{\alpha_2}{\alpha_1 - \beta_1}Y_t - \frac{\alpha_3}{\alpha_1 - \beta_1}P_{ft} + \frac{\beta_2}{\alpha_1 - \beta_1}W_t + \frac{\varepsilon_{2t} - \varepsilon_{1t}}{\alpha_1 - \beta_1}$$

$$= \pi_{11} + \pi_{12}Y_t + \pi_{13}P_{ft} + \pi_{14}W_t + \upsilon_{1t}$$

(8.87)

$$Q_t = \frac{\alpha_1\beta_0 - \alpha_0\beta_1}{\alpha_1 - \beta_1} - \frac{\alpha_2\beta_1}{\alpha_1 - \beta_1}Y_t - \frac{\alpha_3\beta_1}{\alpha_1 - \beta_1}P_{ft} + \frac{\alpha_1\beta_2}{\alpha_1 - \beta_1}W_t + \frac{\alpha_1\varepsilon_{2t} - \beta_1\varepsilon_{1t}}{\alpha_1 - \beta_1}$$

$$= \pi_{21} + \pi_{22}Y_t + \pi_{23}P_{ft} + \pi_{14}W_t + \upsilon_{2t}$$

(8.88)

where

$$\pi_{11} = \frac{\beta_0 - \alpha_0}{\alpha_1 - \beta_1}, \ \pi_{12} = -\frac{\alpha_2}{\alpha_1 - \beta_1}, \ \pi_{13} = -\frac{\alpha_3}{\alpha_1 - \beta_1}, \ \pi_{14} = \frac{\beta_2}{\alpha_1 - \beta_1}$$

$$\pi_{21} = \frac{\alpha_1\beta_0 - \alpha_0\beta_1}{\alpha_1 - \beta_1}, \ \pi_{22} = -\frac{\alpha_2\beta_1}{\alpha_1 - \beta_1}, \ \pi_{23} = -\frac{\alpha_3\beta_1}{\alpha_1 - \beta_1}, \ \pi_{24} = \frac{\alpha_1\beta_2}{\alpha_1 - \beta_1}$$

(8.89)

By counting the coefficients of the structural and of the reduced form models we see that the structural model has seven coefficients and the reduced form model has eight coefficients. Therefore, it is not possible from the coefficients system (8.89) to find a unique solution for all of the structural coefficients. In fact, we see that from system (8.89) we can obtain:

$$\beta_1 = \pi_{23}/\pi_{13} \text{ or } \beta_1 = \pi_{22}/\pi_{12}$$

(8.90)

meaning that from the same data we can get two generally different estimates of β_1. Furthermore, because β_1 appears in all the equations of system (8.89), for each estimate of β_1 in (8.90) we get a set of estimates of the other structural coefficients as well. Therefore, the two equations are overidentified.

We can derive the same results by using the following combined equation, which is a linear combination of the two original Equations (8.85) and (8.86):

$$Q_t = \gamma_0 + \gamma_1 P_t + \gamma_2 Y_t + \gamma_3 W_t + \gamma_4 P_{ft} + \varepsilon_t$$

(8.91)

where

$$\gamma_0 = \lambda\alpha_0 + (1-\lambda)\beta_0, \ \gamma_1 = \lambda\alpha_1 + (1-\lambda)\beta_1,$$

$$\gamma_2 = \lambda\alpha_2, \ \gamma_3 = (1-\lambda)\beta_2, \ \gamma_4 = \lambda\alpha_3, \ \varepsilon_t = \lambda\varepsilon_{1t} + (1-\lambda)\varepsilon_{2t}$$

(8.92)

Observing the combined Equation (8.91) we see that it has a different form from that of the demand Equation (8.85) and the supply Equation (8.86). We say, therefore, that the combined and the demand and supply equations are *not observationally equivalent*, meaning that both the demand and supply functions are identified.

Summarising the cases, we can say that if an equation has an omitted variable, in a two simultaneous equations system, then this equation is identified. This 'condition' is the general topic of investigation in the next section.

8.5 Conditions for identification

Counting the parameters in the structural model (8.55) and (8.56) we see that there are $G \times G = G2$ parameters in matrix Γ, $G \times K$ parameters in matrix B, and $G \times (G + 1)/2$ in matrix Σ. Similarly, counting the parameters in the reduced form model (8.58) and (8.59) we see that there are $G \times K$ parameters in matrix Π, and $G \times (G + 1)/2$ parameters in matrix Ω.

Comparing the number of parameters of the structural and of the reduced form models we see that the structural model has

$$G^2 + G \times K + G \times (G+1)/2 - G \times K - G \times (G+1)/2 = G^2 \tag{8.93}$$

more parameters than the reduced from model. Therefore, the indirect least squares method is not generally successful in providing unique estimates of the structural parameters, because the parameters of the structural model are in excess of G^2 with respect to the parameters of the reduced form model. For obtaining unique estimates, i.e. for identification, we need further prior information in the form of G^2 a priori restrictions on the parameters.

This prior information referring to the parameters of the $\tilde{A}$, $\hat{A}$ and $\acute{O}$ matrices comes in several forms, as follows:

Normalisation This is the case in each equation when the coefficient of one of the G endogenous variables is normalised to be equal to one. Usually it is set that $\tilde{a}_{ii} = 1$, for $I = 1, 2, \ldots, G$. It corresponds, in other words, to the endogenous variable that appears on the left hand side of the equation. Therefore, with normalisation, the G^2 a priori restrictions reduce to $G(G-1)$ restrictions.

Zero restrictions This is the case when some of the endogenous or predetermined variables do not appear in each of the equations. The corresponding coefficients of the *excluded variables* are set equal to zero.

Identity restrictions This refers to the inclusion of identities in the model. The identities do not carry any coefficients to be estimated, but they aid in the identification of other equations.

Parameter restrictions within equations This refers to certain relationships among parameters within equations. If the Cobb-Douglas production function, for example, is of constant returns of scale, the sum of the elasticities of the factors of production must equal one.

Parameter restrictions across equations This refers to certain relationships among parameters across equations. If consumer behaviour in the European Union member states, for example, is the same, then the marginal propensity to consume across the member states consumption functions must be set as equal across equations.

Disturbance variance-covariance parameter restrictions By assuming, for example, that the structural disturbances among equations are not correlated, then the off-diagonal elements of matrix Σ are set equal to zero.

Let us now write the coefficients system (8.61) as:

$$\Gamma\Pi = -B \tag{8.94}$$

For a single equation of the system (8.55), say equation i, (8.94) becomes:

$$\gamma_i \Pi = -\beta_i \tag{8.95}$$

where

$$\gamma_i = \begin{bmatrix} \gamma_{i1} & \gamma_{i2} & \cdots & \gamma_{iG} \end{bmatrix}, \; \beta_i = \begin{bmatrix} \beta_{i1} & \beta_{i2} & \cdots & \beta_{iK} \end{bmatrix} \tag{8.96}$$

For this new writing of the coefficients system, let as introduce the following notation:

G = number of all the endogenous variables of the system.

g = number of the endogenous variables appearing in the *i*th equation
      (i.e. number of non-zero elements in γ_i).

g* = G − g = number of endogenous variables not appearing in the *i*th equation.

K = number of all the predetermined variables of the system.

k = the number of the predetermined variables appearing in the *i*th equation.
      (i.e. number of non-zero elements in β_i).

k* = K − k = the number of predetermined variables not appearing in the *i*th equation.

Under this notation, and without loss of generality, (8.96) is written as:

$$\gamma_i = \left[\underbrace{\gamma_{i1} \quad \gamma_{i2} \quad \cdots \quad \gamma_{ig}}_{g} \quad \underbrace{0 \quad 0 \quad \cdots \quad 0}_{g*} \right] = \left[\underbrace{\gamma_g}_{1 \times g} \quad \underbrace{0_{g*}}_{1 \times g*} \right] \tag{8.97}$$

and

$$\beta_i = \left[\underbrace{\beta_{i1} \quad \beta_{i2} \quad \cdots \quad \beta_{ik}}_{k} \quad \underbrace{0 \quad 0 \quad \cdots \quad 0}_{k*} \right] = \left[\underbrace{\beta_k}_{1 \times k} \quad \underbrace{0_{k*}}_{1 \times k*} \right] \tag{8.98}$$

By substituting (8.97) and (8.98) into (8.95) and by partitioning matrix Π appropriately, (8.95) is written as follows:

$$\left[\gamma_g \quad 0_{g*} \right] \left[\begin{array}{cc} \underbrace{\Pi_{gk}}_{g \times k} & \underbrace{\Pi_{gk*}}_{g \times k*} \\ \underbrace{\Pi_{g*k}}_{g* \times k} & \underbrace{\Pi_{g*k*}}_{g* \times k*} \end{array} \right] = -\left[\beta_k \quad 0_{k*} \right] \tag{8.99}$$

System (8.99) can be analysed into the following two subsystems:

$$\gamma_g \Pi_{gk} = -\beta_k \tag{8.100}$$

$$\gamma_g \Pi_{gk*} = 0_{k*} \tag{8.101}$$

In these two subsystems we observe that (8.101) contains γ coefficients only, which are g in number and correspond to the coefficients of all the endogenous variables included in equation i. By normalisation we can put one of these coefficients equal to 1 and, therefore, the number of the unknown coefficients in (8.101) reduces to g − 1. Subsystem (8.100) contains both the γ coefficients that are also contained in subsystem (8.101) plus the β coefficients, which are k in number and correspond to the coefficients of all the predetermined variables included in equation i. Therefore, if we first estimate the γ coefficients from subsystem (8.101) then we can estimate the β coefficients by substituting the estimated γ coefficients in subsystem (8.100).

Because subsystem (8.101) now contains g − 1 unknown coefficients, therefore, for the existence of a solution this subsystem must have at least g − 1 equations, or it must be that:

$$k* \geq g - 1 \qquad (8.102)$$

In words, (8.102) says that in order for equation i to be identified, the number of predetermined variables excluded (not appearing) forming this equation i ($k*$) must be greater or equal to the number of the endogenous variables included (appearing) in this equation I, less one ($g - 1$). (8.102) is known as the *order condition*.

However, it is possible some of the equations in subsystem (8.101) are not independent with respect to the γ and π coefficients. Therefore, the order condition is only a *necessary* condition for identification and not a sufficient condition. Thus, a *necessary and sufficient* condition for identification requires that the number of independent equations in subsystem (8.101) to be equal to $g - 1$. This, of course, will happen if, and only if, by forming all square submatrices of matrix Π_{gk*}, the order corresponding to the submatrices largest non-zero determinant is equal to $g - 1$, or, in other words, if, and only if, it is true that:

$$\text{rank}\left(\Pi_{gk*}\right) = g - 1 \qquad (8.103)$$

(8.103) is known as the *rank condition*, because it can be proved (see Kmenta, 1971) that:

$$\text{rank}\left(\Pi_{gk*}\right) = \text{rank}(\Delta) - g* \qquad (8.104)$$

where Δ is the matrix which consists of all the structural coefficients for the variables of the system excluded from the *i*th structural equation but included in the other structural equations. The rank condition (8.103) may be also written as:

$$\text{rank}(\Delta) = G - 1 \qquad (8.105)$$

Let us now summarise the order and rank conditions for identification of an equation in a simultaneous equations model.

The order condition of identification In a model of G simultaneous equations with G endogenous variables and K predetermined variables, an equation which includes g endogenous variables and k predetermined variables is identified if the number of predetermined variables excluded from the equation ($K - k$) is not less than the number of endogenous variables included in that equation, less one ($g - 1$), i.e.

$$K - k \geq g - 1 \qquad (8.106)$$

The rank condition of identification In a model of G simultaneous equations an equation is identified if, and only if, the rank of matrix Δ, which is constructed from the coefficients of all the variables excluded from that specific equation but included in the other equations of the model, has a rank equal to the number of equations, less one, i.e.

$$\text{rank}(\Delta) = G - 1 \qquad (8.107)$$

The properties of the conditions for identification The order condition for identification is a necessary condition, whilst the rank condition for identification is a necessary and sufficient condition. In other words, for an equation to be identified, the rank condition must be satisfied, but if the equation is exactly identified or overidentified this is determined by the order condition according to whether it is $K - k = g - 1$ or $K - k > g - 1$, respectively.

Furthermore, let us state the identification possibilities for an equation:

- *Overidentified equation* If $K - k > g - 1$ and rank$(\Delta) = G - 1$.
- *Exactly identified equation* If $K - k = g - 1$ and rank$(\Delta) = G - 1$.
- *Underidentified equation* If $K - k \geq g - 1$ and rank$(\Delta) < G - 1$, or if $K - k < g - 1$.

In what follows we apply the preceding theory in investigating identification in two simple models of simultaneous equations.

Example 8.3 Investigating identification of the demand-supply model of Case 8.5

Consider the demand-supply model of Case 8.5, which under equilibrium conditions is written in Equations (8.70) and (8.71), or

$$The\ Demand = \ Q_t = \alpha_0 + \alpha_1 P_t + \alpha_2 Y_t + \varepsilon_{1t}$$
$$The\ Supply = \ Q_t = \beta_0 + \beta_1 P_t + \varepsilon_{2t} \tag{8.108}$$

Where Q_t = quantity, P_t = prices, Y_t = income, and ε_t's = disturbances. This model is complete because it has two equations and two endogenous variables. The endogenous variables are Q_t and P_t, and the exogenous variable is Y_t.

According to (8.55), model (8.108) can be written in the following form.

$$Demand: \ Q_t - \alpha_1 P_t - \alpha_0 - \alpha_2 Y_t = \varepsilon_{1t}$$
$$Supply: \ Q_t - \beta_1 P_t - \beta_0 + 0 Y_t = \varepsilon_{2t} \tag{8.109}$$

Investigating the demand function In this function there are $k = 1$ exogenous variables (Y_t) and $g = 2$ endogenous variables (Q_t, P_t). Therefore, the order condition $K - k = 1 - 1 = 0 < g - 1 = 2 - 1 = 1$ is 'satisfied' for underidentification.

Investigating the supply function In this function there are $k = 0$ exogenous variables and $g = 2$ endogenous variables (Q_t, P_t). Therefore, the order condition $K - k = 1 - 0 = 1 = g - 1 = 2 - 1 = 1$ is satisfied for exact identification.

The rank condition can be investigated by forming matrix Δ from (8.109), which is:

$$\Delta = [-\alpha_2]$$

Evaluating the $(G - 1) \times (G - 1) = (2 - 1) \times (2 - 1) = 1 \times 1$ determinants of matrix Δ we get that:

$$|\Delta_1| = |-\alpha_2| = -\alpha_2 \neq 0$$

Therefore, the rank condition is satisfied since we can construct at least one non-zero determinant of order 1, i.e. rank$(\Delta) = G - 1 = 1$. In summary, by taking into account both the order and rank conditions, the supply function is exactly identified.

Example 8.4 Investigating identification in a simple macroeconomic model

Given the following macroeconomic model:

Consumption: $C_t = \alpha_0 + \alpha_1 Y_t + \alpha_2 C_{t-1} + \varepsilon_{1t}$

Investment: $I_t = \beta_0 + \beta_1 Y_t + \beta_2 Y_{t-1} + \beta_3 I_{t-1} + \varepsilon_{2t}$

Taxes: $T_t = \gamma_0 + \gamma_1 Y_t + \varepsilon_{3t}$

Income: $Y_t = C_t + I_t + G_t$ (8.110)

Where C_t = consumption, Y_t = income, I_t = investment, T_t = taxes, G_t = government spending, and ε_t's = disturbances. This model is complete because it has four equations and four endogenous variables. The endogenous variables are C_t, I_t, T_t and Y_t and the predetermined variables are C_{t-1}, Y_{t-1}, I_{t-1} and G_t.

According to (8.55), model (8.110) can be written in the following way:

Consumption: $C_t - \alpha_1 Y_t + 0 I_t + 0 T_t - \alpha_0 - \alpha_2 C_{t-1} + 0 Y_{t-1} + 0 I_{t-1} + 0 G_t = \varepsilon_{1t}$

Investment: $0 C_t - \beta_1 Y_t + I_t + 0 T_t - \beta_0 + 0 C_{t-1} - \beta_2 Y_{t-1} - \beta_3 I_{t-1} + 0 G_t = \varepsilon_{2t}$

Taxes: $0 C_t - \gamma_1 Y_t + 0 I_t + T_t - \gamma_0 + 0 C_{t-1} + 0 Y_{t-1} + 0 I_{t-1} + 0 G_t = \varepsilon_{3t}$

Income: $-C_t + Y_t - I_t + 0 T_t + 0 + 0 C_{t-1} + 0 Y_{t-1} + 0 I_{t-1} - G_t = 0$ (8.111)

Investigating the consumption function In this function there are $k = 1$ predetermined variables (C_{t-1}) and $g = 2$ endogenous variables (C_t, Y_t). Therefore, the order condition $K - k = 4 - 1 = 3 > g - 1 = 2 - 1 = 1$ is satisfied for overidentification.

The rank condition can be investigated by forming matrix Δ from (8.111), which is:

$$\Delta = \begin{bmatrix} 1 & 0 & -\beta_2 & -\beta_3 & 0 \\ 0 & 1 & 0 & 0 & 0 \\ -1 & 0 & 0 & 0 & -1 \end{bmatrix}$$

Evaluating the $(G - 1) \times (G - 1) = (4 - 1) \times (4 - 1) = 3 \times 3$ determinants of matrix Δ we get that:

$$|\Delta_1| = \begin{vmatrix} 1 & 0 & -\beta_2 \\ 0 & 1 & 0 \\ -1 & 0 & 0 \end{vmatrix} = -\beta_2 \neq 0$$

Therefore, the rank condition is satisfied since we can construct at least one non-zero determinant of order 3, i.e. rank(Δ) = G − 1 = 3. In summary, by taking into account both the order and rank conditions, the consumption function is overidentified.

Investigating the investment function In this function there are $k = 2$ predetermined variables (Y_{t-1}, I_{t-1}) and $g = 2$ endogenous variables (I_t, Y_t). Therefore, the order condition $K - k = 4 - 2 = 2 > g - 1 = 2 - 1 = 1$ is satisfied for overidentification.

The rank condition can be investigated by forming matrix Δ from (8.111), which is:

$$\Delta = \begin{bmatrix} 1 & 0 & -\alpha_2 & 0 \\ 0 & 1 & 0 & 0 \\ -1 & 0 & 0 & -1 \end{bmatrix}$$

Evaluating the $(G-1) \times (G-1) = (4-1) \times (4-1) = 3 \times 3$ determinants of matrix Δ we get that:

$$|\Delta_1| = \begin{vmatrix} 1 & 0 & -\alpha_2 \\ 0 & 1 & 0 \\ -1 & 0 & 0 \end{vmatrix} = -\alpha_2 \neq 0$$

Therefore, the rank condition is satisfied since we can construct at least one non-zero determinant of order 3, i.e., rank$(\Delta) = G - 1 = 3$. In summary, by taking into account both the order and rank conditions, the investment function is overidentified.

Investigating the taxes function In this function there are $k = 0$ predetermined variables and $g = 2$ endogenous variables (T_t, Y_t). Therefore, the order condition $K - k = 4 - 0 = 4 > g - 1 = 2 - 1 = 1$ is satisfied for overidentification.

The rank condition can be investigated by forming matrix Δ from (8.111), which is:

$$\Delta = \begin{bmatrix} 1 & 0 & -\alpha_2 & 0 & 0 & 0 \\ 0 & 1 & 0 & -\beta_2 & -\beta_3 & 0 \\ -1 & -1 & 0 & 0 & 0 & -1 \end{bmatrix}$$

Evaluating the $(G-1) \times (G-1) = (4-1) \times (4-1) = 3 \times 3$ determinants of matrix Δ we get that:

$$|\Delta_1| = \begin{vmatrix} 1 & 0 & -\alpha_2 \\ 0 & 1 & 0 \\ -1 & -1 & 0 \end{vmatrix} = -\alpha_2 \neq 0$$

Therefore, the rank condition is satisfied since we can construct at least one non-zero determinant of order 3, i.e. rank$(\Delta) = G - 1 = 3$. In summary, by taking into account both the order and rank conditions, the taxes function is overidentified.

8.6 Methods of estimation

In the beginning of Section 8.5 we noted that if we apply the OLS method to the structural equations of a simultaneous equation system we will get inconsistent estimates because the endogenous variables of the system's equations are not independent by the structural error terms. Furthermore, we saw that there are cases where we can obtain indirectly consistent estimates of the structural coefficients of the system by applying the OLS methodology to the reduced form equations of the system, because the predetermined variables of the system are independent of the reduced form error terms. However, there are specific simultaneous equations models where the direct application of OLS to the structural equations leads to consistent estimates of the structural parameters.

The methods for estimating the structural parameters of a simultaneous equations model may be grouped into the following two categories:

1 *Single-equation methods of estimation* These are the methods where each equation in the model is estimated individually, taking into account only the information included in the specific equation and without considering all the other information included in the rest of the equations of the system. For this reason, these methods are known as limited information methods. We present the following such methods:

  a   Ordinary least squares method (OLS), for fully recursive models.
  b   Indirect least squares (ILS) method, for exactly identified equations.
  c   Instrumental variables (IV) method.
  d   Two-stage least squares (2SLS) method.
  e   Limited information maximum likelihood (LIML) method.

2 *System methods of estimation* These are the methods where all the equations of the model are estimated simultaneously, taking into account all the information included in all equations simultaneously. For this reason, these methods are known as full information methods. We present the following such methods:

  a   Three-stage least squares (3SLS) method.
  b   Full information maximum likelihood (FIML) method.

8.6.1 Single-equation methods of estimation

8.6.1.1 Ordinary least squares method (OLS), for fully recursive models

We saw in Section 8.2 that a recursive equations model is that where matrix Γ, in the structural model (8.10), is triangular, i.e. it is of the form shown in (8.22). Specifically, by normalising with respect to the coefficient of each endogenous dependent variable in the corresponding equation, the recursive equations model may be written as follows:

$$
\begin{aligned}
Y_{1t} &= \beta_{11}X_{1t} +_{12} X_{2t} +...+ \beta_{1K}X_{Kt} + \epsilon_{1t} \\
Y_{2t} &= \gamma_{21}Y_{1t} + \beta_{21}X_{1t} + \beta_{22}X_{2t} +...+ \beta_{2K}X_{Kt} + \epsilon_{2t} \\
Y_{3t} &= \gamma_{31}Y_{1t} + \gamma_{32}Y_{2t} + \beta_{31}X_{1t} + \beta_{32}X_{2t} +...+ \beta_{3K}X_{Kt} + \epsilon_{3t} \\
&... \\
Y_{Gt} &= \gamma_{G1}Y_{1t} + \gamma_{G2}Y_{2t} +...+ \gamma_{G,G-1}Y_{G-1,t} + \beta_{G1}X_{1t} + \beta_{G2}X_{2t} +...+ \beta_{GK}X_{Kt} + \epsilon_{Gt}
\end{aligned} \tag{8.112}
$$

If we now assume that the variance-covariance matrix Σ of the structural disturbances is diagonal, i.e.

$$
E(\varepsilon_t \varepsilon_t') = \Sigma =
\begin{bmatrix}
\sigma_{11} & \sigma_{12} & .. & \sigma_{1G} \\
\sigma_{21} & \sigma_{22} & .. & \sigma_{2G} \\
: & : & :: & : \\
\sigma_{G1} & \sigma_{G2} & .. & \sigma_{GG}
\end{bmatrix}
=
\begin{bmatrix}
\sigma_{11} & 0 & .. & 0 \\
0 & \sigma_{22} & .. & 0 \\
: & : & :: & : \\
0 & 0 & .. & \sigma_{GG}
\end{bmatrix} \tag{8.113}
$$

then the model is called a *fully recursive model*. In this case we can apply the OLS estimation in the first equation of the model because the predetermined variables in this equation are uncorrelated with the error term ε_{1t}. We can also apply the OLS estimation in the second equation of the model because both the predetermined variables in this equation are uncorrelated with the error term ε_{2t}, and the endogenous variable Y_{1t} is also uncorrelated with ε_{2t}. This is because the endogenous variable Y_{1t}, which is also an explanatory variable in the second equation, although it is a function of ε_{1t}, is still not correlated with ε_{2t} due to (8.113), which assumes that ε_{1t} and ε_{2t} are not correlated. For exactly the same reasons, we can apply OLS to all equations of the fully recursive model. In other words, the structural parameters of the fully recursive model can be estimated consistently and asymptotically efficiently with OLS. Of course, in cases where the structural disturbances are correlated among equations, then the OLS approach is not applicable and therefore other methods have to be used.

Example 8.5 The wages-prices link for an EU member

Assume the following revised version of the wages-prices link model of Case 8.3. The prices inflation function:

$$p_t = \alpha_0 + \alpha_1 w_{t-1} + \alpha_2 Y_t + \alpha_3 p_{t-1} + \varepsilon_{1t}, \; \alpha_1 > 0, \; \alpha_2 > 0, \; 0 < \alpha_3 < 1 \qquad (8.114)$$

The wages inflation function:

$$w_t = \beta_0 + \beta_1 p_t + \beta_2 U_t + \beta_3 w_{t-1} + \varepsilon_{2t}, \; \beta_1 > 0, \; \beta_2 < 0, \; 0 < \beta_3 < 1 \qquad (8.115)$$

where w_t = percentage change of money wage level, p_t = percentage change of the general level of prices, Y_t = aggregate demand, and U_t = the unemployment rate. The model of Equations (8.114) and (8.115) is a recursive model because the dependent (endogenous) variable p_t of the first equation is a function of exogenous (Y_t) and lagged endogenous (w_{t-1}, p_{t-1}) variables only. Furthermore, the dependent (endogenous) variable w_t of the second equation is a function of the dependent variable p_t of the first equation plus a function of exogenous (U_t) and lagged endogenous (w_{t-1}) variables. By assuming that the variance-covariance matrix of the structural disturbances is diagonal, we can apply the OLS procedure to the two equations individually.

Using data in Table 8.2, where w_t = the percentage change of nominal compensation per employee, p_t = the annual percentage change of the GNP price deflator, U_t = the unemployment rate as a percentage of civilian labour force, and Y_t = GNP at constant prices, the OLS estimates of the two Equations (8.114) and (8.115) are:

$$\hat{p}_t = -3.29432 + 0.33264 w_{t-1} + 0.01391 Y_t + 0.39320 p_{t-1} \quad \bar{R}^2 = 0.7575$$

s.e.   (2.3883)   (0.1482)   (0.0074)   (0.1755)

t   [1.3794]   [2.2443]   [1.8847]   [2.2402] $\qquad (8.116)$

and

$$\hat{w}_t = 7.59395 + 0.38277 p_t - 0.58217 U_t + 0.40607 w_{t-1} \quad \bar{R}^2 = 0.6941$$

s.e.   (2.1741)   (0.1319)   (0.2714)   (0.1466)

t   [3.4929]   [2.9017]   [2.1449]   [2.7700] $\qquad (8.117)$

Table 8.2 Wages-prices link data of an EU member

Year	GNP price deflator (annual percentage change)	Nominal compensation per employee (annual percentage change)	Unemployment rate (percentage of civilian labour force)	GNP (in constant 1970 prices, billion drs)*
1960	1.2	4.0	6.1	145.458
1961	1.5	4.6	5.9	161.802
1962	4.6	6.6	5.1	164.674
1963	1.4	7.7	5.0	181.534
1964	3.7	13.3	4.6	196.586
1965	4.0	12.2	4.8	214.922
1966	4.9	12.6	5.0	228.040
1967	2.4	9.5	5.4	240.791
1968	1.7	9.8	5.6	257.226
1969	3.4	9.6	5.2	282.168
1970	3.9	8.8	4.2	304.420
1971	3.2	8.0	3.1	327.723
1972	5.0	12.6	2.1	356.886
1973	19.4	17.2	2.0	383.916
1974	20.9	19.3	2.1	369.325
1975	12.3	20.3	2.3	390.000
1976	15.4	23.2	1.9	415.491
1977	13.0	22.0	1.7	431.164
1978	12.9	23.1	1.8	458.675
1979	18.6	22.1	1.9	476.048
1980	17.7	15.7	2.7	485.108
1981	19.8	21.3	4.0	484.259
1982	25.1	27.6	5.8	483.879
1983	19.1	21.5	7.1	481.198
1984	20.3	20.5	7.2	490.881
1985	17.7	23.2	7.0	502.258
1986	17.5	12.8	6.6	507.199
1987	14.3	11.5	6.7	505.713
1988	15.6	18.6	6.8	529.460
1989	14.4	24.0	6.7	546.572
1990	20.6	23.1	6.4	546.982
1991	19.8	14.3	7.0	566.586
1992	14.6	8.2	7.9	568.582
1993	14.1	10.1	8.6	569.724
1994	10.9	11.9	8.9	579.846
1995	9.3	12.7	9.1	588.691

Sources: EC (1997) Annual Economic Report for 1997, *European Economy*.
* Epilogi (1998)

8.6.1.2 *Indirect least squares method (ILS), for exactly identified equations*

Previously, we used this method many times when trying to obtain unique estimates of the structural coefficients using consistent estimates of the reduced form coefficients. In fact, we said there that if an equation is exactly identified then the indirect least squares method yields unique estimates of the structural coefficients of this equation. To summarise, the steps used for this method are:

Step 1 Solve the structural equations system in order to get the reduced form system, i.e. the system of (8.57), or:

$$Y_t = - \Gamma^{-1} B X_t + \Gamma^{-1} \varepsilon_t \qquad (8.118)$$

Step 2 Apply the OLS method to each reduced form equation and get the consistent and asymptotically efficient estimates of the corresponding reduced form coefficients, i.e. apply the OLS method to (8.58), or:

$$Y_t = \Pi X_t + \upsilon_t \tag{8.119}$$

Step 3 Substituting the estimates of the reduced form coefficients to the coefficients system, solve it in order to get consistent and asymptotically efficient estimates of the structural coefficients, i.e. solve the system (8.95), or the two subsystems (8.100) and (8.101), or, finally:

$$c_g P_{gk} = -b_k \tag{8.120}$$

$$c_g P_{gk*} = 0_{k*} \tag{8.121}$$

where c's are the estimates of γ's, b's are the estimates of β's, and P's are the estimates of Π's.

Example 8.6 A wages-prices link model for an EU member

Assume the following revised version of the wages-prices link model of Example 8.5.

A prices inflation function:

$$p_t = \alpha_0 + \alpha_1 w_t + \alpha_2 Y_t + \varepsilon_{1t}, \ \alpha_1 > 0, \ \alpha_2 > 0 \tag{8.122}$$

A wages inflation function:

$$w_t = \beta_0 + \beta_1 p_t + \beta_2 U_t + \varepsilon_{2t}, \ \beta_1 > 0, \beta_2 < 0 \tag{8.123}$$

This model is a simultaneous equations model with $G = 2$ endogenous variables (p_t, w_t) and $K = 2$ exogenous variables (Y_t, U_t). Furthermore, according to the order and rank conditions, both equations are exactly identified. Therefore, the model of Equations (8.122) and (8.123) is an exactly identified model (see Case 8.6).
    According to step 1, the reduced form model is:

$$p_t = \frac{\alpha_0 + \alpha_1 \beta_0}{1 - \alpha_1 \beta_1} + \frac{\alpha_2}{1 - \alpha_1 \beta_1} Y_t + \frac{\alpha_1 \beta_2}{1 - \alpha_1 \beta_1} U_t + \frac{\varepsilon_{1t} + \alpha_1 \varepsilon_{2t}}{1 - \alpha_1 \beta_1}$$

$$w_t = \frac{\beta_0 + \alpha_0 \beta_1}{1 - \alpha_1 \beta_1} + \frac{\alpha_2 \beta_1}{1 - \alpha_1 \beta_1} Y_t + \frac{\beta_2}{1 - \alpha_1 \beta_1} U_t + \frac{\beta_1 \varepsilon_{1t} + \varepsilon_{2t}}{1 - \alpha_1 \beta_1} \tag{8.124}$$

According to step 2 and using the data in Table 8.2, the results of the OLS application to the unrestricted reduced form model:

$$p_t = \pi_{11} + \pi_{12} Y_t + \pi_{13} U_t + \upsilon_{1t}$$
$$w_t = \pi_{21} + \pi_{22} Y_t + \pi_{23} U_t + \upsilon_{2t} \tag{8.125}$$

are the following:

$$\hat{p}_t = -1.68241 + 0.04479 Y_t - 0.87508 U_t \quad \bar{R}^2 = 0.6520$$

s.e.   (2.4202)   (0.0054)   (0.3485)   (8.126)

t   [0.6951]   [8.2165]   [2.5106]

$$\hat{w}_t = 9.37057 + 0.03250Y_t - 1.42523U_t \quad \bar{R}^2 = 0.4923$$

s.e.   (2.5689)   (0.0058)   (0.3700)   (8.127)

t   [3.6476]   [5.6174]   [3.8522]

According to step 3, the estimates of the structural coefficients will be obtained from the solution of the following corresponding coefficients system:

$$\pi_{11} = \frac{\alpha_0 + \alpha_1\beta_0}{1 - \alpha_1\beta_1}, \quad \pi_{12} = \frac{\alpha_2}{1 - \alpha_1\beta_1}, \quad \pi_{13} = \frac{\alpha_1\beta_2}{1 - \alpha_1\beta_1}$$

$$\pi_{21} = \frac{\beta_0 + \alpha_0\beta_1}{1 - \alpha_1\beta_1}, \quad \pi_{22} = \frac{\alpha_2\beta_1}{1 - \alpha_1\beta_1}, \quad \pi_{23} = \frac{\beta_2}{1 - \alpha_1\beta_1}$$

(8.128)

These estimates are given by

$$a_1 = \frac{\hat{\pi}_{13}}{\hat{\pi}_{23}} = 0.61399, \qquad\qquad b_1 = \frac{\hat{\pi}_{22}}{\hat{\pi}_{12}} = 0.72569$$

$$a_2 = (1 - a_1 b_1)\hat{\pi}_{12} = 0.02483, \qquad b_2 = (1 - a_1 b_1)\hat{\pi}_{23} = -0.79019$$

$$a_0 = (1 - a_1 b_1)\hat{\pi}_{11} - a_1 b_0 = -7.43590, \quad b_0 = \hat{\pi}_{21} - b_1\hat{\pi}_{11} = 10.59149$$

(8.129)

8.6.1.3 Instrumental variables (IV) method

Assuming that one equation of the structural model, say the first equation, has g endogenous variables and k predetermined variables, and normalising the coefficient of its dependent (endogenous) variable to be equal to one, this equation may generally be written as:

$$Y_1 = Y_1\ \gamma_1 + X_1\beta_1 + \varepsilon_1$$

(8.130)

where

$$Y_1 = \begin{bmatrix} Y_{11} \\ Y_{12} \\ :: \\ Y_{1n} \end{bmatrix} \quad Y_1 = \begin{bmatrix} Y_{21} & Y_{31} & :: & Y_{g1} \\ Y_{22} & Y_{32} & :: & Y_{g2} \\ :: & :: & :: & :: \\ Y_{2n} & Y_{3n} & :: & Y_{gn} \end{bmatrix} \quad X_1 = \begin{bmatrix} X_{11} & X_{21} & :: & X_{k1} \\ X_{12} & X_{22} & :: & X_{k2} \\ :: & :: & :: & :: \\ X_{1n} & X_{2n} & :: & X_{kn} \end{bmatrix} \quad \varepsilon_1 = \begin{bmatrix} \varepsilon_{11} \\ \varepsilon_{12} \\ :: \\ \varepsilon_{1n} \end{bmatrix}$$

(8.131)

$$\gamma_1 = \begin{bmatrix} \gamma_{12} \\ \gamma_{13} \\ :: \\ \gamma_{1g} \end{bmatrix} \quad \beta_1 = \begin{bmatrix} \beta_{11} \\ \beta_{12} \\ :: \\ \beta_{1k} \end{bmatrix}$$

Equation (8.130) may also be written as:

$$Y_1 = Z_1\ \delta_1 + \varepsilon_1$$

(8.132)

where

$$Z_1 = \left[Y_1 X_1\right] \text{ and } \delta_1' = \left[\gamma_1 \beta_1\right] \tag{8.133}$$

If d_1 denotes an estimator of δ_1, the OLS estimator for Equation (8.132) is:

$$d_{1,OLS} = \left(Z_1' Z_1\right)^{-1} Z_1' Y_1 \tag{8.134}$$

and

$$\text{var-cov}\left(d_{1,OLS}\right) = s_1^2 \left(Z_1' Z_1\right)^{-1} \tag{8.135}$$

where

$$s_1^2 = \left(Y_1 - Z_1 d_{1,OLS}\right)' \left(Y_1 - Z_1 d_{1,OLS}\right) / (n-g-k+1) \tag{8.136}$$

We have argued till now that this estimator yields inconsistent estimates because of the correlation of Z_1 with ε_1, or because of the correlation of Y_1 with ε_1.

If W_1 is now an $n \times (g-1+k)$ matrix that satisfies all the requirements to be considered as an instrumental variables matrix, then the instrumental variables estimator, which gives consistent estimates, is given by:

$$d_{1,IV} = \left(W_1' Z_1\right)^{-1} W_1' Y_1 \tag{8.137}$$

and

$$\text{var} - \text{cov}\left(d_{1,IV}\right) = s_1^2 \left(W_1' Z_1\right)^{-1} \left(W_1' W_1\right)\left(Z_1' W_1\right)^{-1} \tag{8.138}$$

where

$$s_1^2 = (Y_1 - Z_1 d_{1,IV})'(Y_1 - Z_1 d_{1,IV})/(n-g-k+1) \tag{8.139}$$

However, in the case of an exactly identified equation, the number excluded from the equation predetermined variables, $K - k$, is equal to the number included in the right-hand side endogenous variables, $g - 1$. Therefore, these predetermined variables could be used as instruments in the place of Y_1. In this case it can be proved that the ILS estimator is the same as the IV estimator.

Example 8.7 A wages-prices link model for an EU member

Consider the wages-prices link model of Example 8.5. In this model the endogenous variables are p_t and w_t, and the exogenous variables are Y_t and U_t. The Z matrix in the prices equation is $Z_1 = [1 \ w \ Y]$ in which w may be correlated with the error term. The corresponding instrumental variables W matrix is $W_1 = [1 \ U \ Y]$. The Z matrix in the wages equation is $Z_2 = [1 \ p \ U]$ in which p may be correlated with the error term. The corresponding instrumental variables W matrix is $W_2 = [1 \ Y \ U]$.

Using the sample data of Table 8.2, and EViews, the IV estimates of the structural equations of the model are:

$$\hat{p}_t = -7.43590 + 0.61399 w_t + 0.02483 Y_t \quad \bar{R}^2 = 0.7649$$

$$\begin{array}{llll} \text{s.e.} & (2.0600) & (0.2010) & (0.0066) \end{array} \tag{8.140}$$

$$\begin{array}{llll} \text{t} & [3.6097] & [3.0547] & [3.7801] \end{array}$$

$$\hat{w}_t = 10.5915 + 0.72569p_t - 0.79019U_t \qquad \bar{R}^2 = 0.6540$$

s.e.   (2.0076)   (0.1066)   (0.2879)

t   [5.2758]   [6.8051]   [2.7444]

Because both equations are exactly identified, we see that the IV estimates in (8.140) are exactly the same as estimates found with the ILS method in (8.129). However, the estimates in (8.140) also include the standard errors estimated according to (8.138). The corresponding ILS estimates in (8.129) do not include their standard errors because due to non-linear relationships between the structural and the reduced form coefficients the computation of the standard errors of the structural coefficients through standard errors of the reduced form coefficients is awkward.

8.6.1.4 *Two-stage least squares (2SLS) method*

In an identified equation the number of the excluded predetermined variables is equal to the number of the included explanatory endogenous variables. Therefore, in using the IV approach we can use endogenous variables, as many instruments, as the number of the excluded predetermined variables.

For the overidentified equation the number of the excluded exogenous variables is greater than the number of the included explanatory endogenous variables. This means that in using the IV approach we can use, as instruments, any combination of excluded exogenous variables. However, by not using all the exogenous variables as instruments we lose information, a fact that will possibly yield inefficient estimates. Two-stage least squares is an approach that uses as instruments all the exogenous variables to get consistent and efficient estimates.

Assume that the following equation, which has g endogenous and k predetermined variables, is an overidentified equation in a structural model of G endogenous and K predetermined variables.

$$Y_1 = Y_1\gamma_1 + X_1\beta_1 + \varepsilon_1 = Z_1\delta_1 + \varepsilon_1 \tag{8.141}$$

where

$$Z_1 = [Y_1 \ X_1] \text{ and } \delta_1' = [\gamma_1 \ \beta_1]$$

with

$$Y_1 = [Y_2 \ Y_3 \dots Y_g], X_1 = [X_1 \ X_2 \dots X_k] \text{ and } X = [X_1 \ X_{k+1} \ X_{k+2} \dots X_K]$$

If d_1 denotes an estimator of δ_1, the two-stage least squares approach has the following two steps:

Step 1 Apply the OLS method to the following unrestricted reduced form equations:

$$Y_i = X\pi_i + \upsilon_i \text{ for } i = 2, 3, \dots, g \tag{8.142}$$

to obtain the estimates of the reduced form coefficients $p_i = (X'X) - 1X'Yi$, where p_i estimate of π_i, and use these estimates to obtain the predicted sample values of Y_i, i.e. $\hat{Y}_i = Xp_i = X(X'X)^{-1}X'Y_i$.

Step 2 Use the predicted sample values of Y_i, to construct matrix $Z_1 = [\hat{Y}_1 \ X_1]$ where $\hat{Y}_1 = [\hat{Y}_2 \ \hat{Y}_3 \ldots \hat{Y}_g]$ and apply the OLS method to the equation:

$$Y_1 = \hat{Y}_1 \gamma_1 + X_1\beta_1 + \eta_1 = \hat{Z}_1 \delta_1 + \eta_1 \tag{8.143}$$

where $\eta_1 = $ error term, to get to the 2SLS estimator:

$$d_{1,2SLS} = \left(\hat{Z}_1'\hat{Z}_1\right)^{-1}\hat{Z}_1'Y_1 \tag{8.144}$$

The 2SLS estimator (8.144), in terms of the values of the original variables and for the *i*th equation is written as

$$d_{i,2SLS} = \left(\hat{Z}_i'\hat{Z}_i\right)^{-1}\hat{Z}_i'Y_i = \left[(Z_i'X)(X'X)^{-1}(X'Z_i)\right]^{-1}(Z_i'X)(X'X)^{-1}X'Y_i \tag{8.145}$$

and

$$\text{var}-\text{cov}(d_{i,2SLS}) = s_i^2 \left(\hat{Z}_i'\hat{Z}_i\right)^{-1} \tag{8.146}$$

where

$$s_i^2 = \left(Y_i - Z_i d_{i,2SLS}\right)'\left(Y_i - Z_i d_{i,2SLS}\right)/(n-g-k+1) \tag{8.147}$$

For an exactly identified equation, the 2SLS estimator can be shown that it is the same with the ILS estimator, and it can be interpreted as an IV estimator (see Johnston, 1984).

One of the basic assumptions in the analysis above is that the structural error terms were not autoregressive. In the case that the error terms are autoregressive, we use the *two-stage least squares with autoregression* (2SLS/AR). We can distinguish two cases:

a. 2SLS/AR(1) when there are no lagged endogenous variables

This is the simple case where:

$$\varepsilon_{i,t} = \rho_i \varepsilon_{i,t-1} + \upsilon_{i,t} \text{ for } i = 1, 2, ..., G \tag{8.148}$$

For the *i*th equation and the t*th observation the usual quasi-differenced equation is the following:

$$Y_{i,t} - \rho_i Y_{i,t-1} = (Y_{i,t}' - \rho_i Y_{i,t-1}')\gamma_i + (X_{i,t}' - \rho_i X_{i,t-1}')\beta_i + \upsilon_{i,t} \tag{8.149}$$

Because the problem of autoregression is a problem of efficiency and not of consistency, any consistent estimate of ρ_i, let us say an estimate based on the residuals of the 2SLS method, can be used in (8.149). Therefore, the steps for the 2SLS/AR(1) method may be the following:

Step 1 The same as step 1 of the 2SLS method. In other words, regress all the endogenous variables on all the exogenous variables of the model and keep their predictions, $\hat{Y}_{i,t}$.

Step 2 The same as step 2 of the 2SLS method. In words, substitute the predictions of the endogenous variables found in step 1 in place of the corresponding endogenous variables on the right-hand side of each equation and apply OLS. Having estimated $\mathbf{d}_i$, compute the 2SLS residuals e_i, and then compute the estimate of ρ_i, i.e. compute:

$$\hat{\rho}_i = \frac{\sum e_{i,t} e_{i,t-1}}{\sum e_{i,t}^2} \tag{8.150}$$

Step 3 Take the results of steps 1 and 2 formulate the following model:

$$Y_{i,t} - \hat{\rho}_i Y_{i,t-1} = (\hat{\mathbf{Y}}'_{i,t} - \hat{\rho}_i \mathbf{Y}'_{i,t-1}) \gamma_i + (\mathbf{X}'_{i,t} - \hat{\rho}_i \mathbf{X}'_{i,t-1}) \beta_i + \upsilon_{i,t} \tag{8.151}$$

and estimate it with OLS.

Step 4: The Cochrane-Orcutt iterative procedure may be used in step 3.

b. 2SLS/AR(1) when there are lagged endogenous variables

In the presence of lagged endogenous variables the estimate of ρ_i is not consistent. In this case the steps for the 2SLS/AR(1) method may be modified as follows:

Step 1 Treat all lagged endogenous variables as the current endogenous variables, regress all the current endogenous variables on all the (strictly) exogenous variables of the model and keep their predictions, $\hat{\mathbf{Y}}_{i,t}$.

Step 2 The same as step 2 of the 2SLS method. In other words, substitute the predictions of the current and the lagged endogenous variables found in step 1 in place of the corresponding endogenous variables on the right-hand side of each equation and apply OLS. Having estimated $\mathbf{d}_i$, compute the 2SLS residuals e_i, and then compute the estimate of ρ_i, using (8.150).

Step 3 Take the results of steps 1 and 2 formulate the following model:

$$Y_{i,t} - \hat{\rho}_i Y_{i,t-1} = (\hat{\mathbf{Y}}'_{i,t} - \hat{\rho}_i \mathbf{Y}'_{i,t-1}) \gamma_i + (\mathbf{X}'_{i,t} - \hat{\rho}_i \mathbf{X}'_{i,t-1}) \beta_i + \upsilon_{i,t} \tag{8.152}$$

and estimate it with OLS.

Step 4 The Cochrane-Orcutt iterative procedure may be used in step 3.

Example 8.8 A simple macroeconomic model for an EU member (2SLS)

Consider the following macroeconomic model for an EU member:

Private consumption function:

$$C_t = \alpha_0 + \alpha_1 Y_t + \alpha_2 C_{t-1} + \varepsilon_{1t} \quad \alpha_1 > 0, \quad 0 < \alpha_2 < 1 \tag{8.153}$$

Private gross investment function:

$$I_t = \beta_0 + \beta_1 Y_t + \beta_2 r_t + \beta_3 I_{t-1} + \varepsilon_{2t}, \quad \beta_1 > 0, \quad \beta_2 < 0, \quad 0 < \beta_3 < 1 \tag{8.154}$$

A money demand function:

$$r_t = \gamma_0 + \gamma_1 Y_t + \gamma_2 M_{t-1} + \gamma_3 P_t + \gamma_4 r_{t-1} + \varepsilon_{3t}, \gamma_1 > 0, \ \gamma_2 < 0, \gamma_3 > 0, 0 < \gamma_4 < 1 \quad (8.155)$$

Income identity:

$$Y_t = C_t + I_t + G_t \qquad (8.156)$$

where, using data from Table 8.3:

C_t = private consumption at constant market prices of year 1970 (million dr),
I_t = gross private investment at constant market prices of year 1970 (million dr),
G_t = government spending at constant market prices of year 1970 (million dr),
Y_t = total financial resources at constant market prices of year 1970 (million dr),
M_t = money supply (M1) at current prices (billion dr),
r_t = long-term interest rate (%),
P_t = consumer price index (base year 1970 = 1).

The structural model of Equations (8.153)–(8.156) has four endogenous variables (C_t, I_t, r_t, Y_t) and six predetermined variables (C_{t-1}, I_{t-1}, M_{t-1}, P_t, r_{t-1}, G_t, plus the constant). According to the order and rank conditions, all structural equations are overidentified. The estimated equations with the 2SLS method, using EViews, are shown below:

Private consumption function:

$$\hat{C}_t = 7519.307 + 0.17415 Y_t + 0.73293 C_{t-1}$$

s.e.   (2121.6)   (0.0479)   (0.0706)

t   [3.5441]   [3.6384]   [10.377]

(8.157)

$\bar{R}^2 = 0.999$ DW $= 1.895$ BG $= 0.092\ [0.762]$ SARGAN $= 6.668\ [0.155]$

where the figures in brackets next to the diagnostic tests show the level of significance.

Private gross investment function:

$$\hat{I}_t = 6232.39 + 0.07278 Y_t - 1097.613 r_t + 0.64325 I_{t-1}$$

s.e. (2932.5) (0.0223)   (347.874)   (0.1019)

t   [2.1252] [3.2685]   [3.1552]   [6.3115]

(8.158)

$\bar{R}^2 = 0.895$ DW $= 1.642$ BG $= 1.502\ [0.220]$ SARGAN $= 2.486\ [0.478]$

The money demand function:

$$r_t = -1.46373 + 9.12(E-06) Y_t - 0.00839 M_{t-1} + 0.53795 P_t + 0.88081 r_{t-1}$$

s.e.   (0.9257) (3.73(E-06))   (0.0039)   (0.3058)   (0.1046)

t   [1.5812] [2.4472]   [2.1520]   [1.7591]   [8.4230]

(8.159)

$\bar{R}^2 = 0.967$ DW $= 1.322$ BG $= 5.206\ [0.023]$ SARGAN $= 7.1344\ [0.028]$

Although the estimates of the three structural equations are generally acceptable in terms of the a priori restrictions (signs of coefficients) and the statistical and diagnostic tests, the money demand function shows some autocorrelation in the residuals (DW and BG

Table 8.3 Basic macroeconomic data of an EU member.

Year	Private consumption	Gross private investment	Government spending	Total financial resources	Money supply (M1)	Long-term interest rate	Consumer price index
1960	107808	19264	24548	151620	13.8	8.00	0.783142
1961	115147	19703	33606	168456	16.1	8.00	0.791684
1962	120050	22216	29571	171837	18.5	8.00	0.801758
1963	126115	24557	40299	190971	21.3	8.25	0.828688
1964	137192	30826	41594	209612	25.4	9.00	0.847185
1965	147707	35072	49745	232524	28.4	9.00	0.885828
1966	157687	36610	45184	239481	32.1	9.00	0.916505
1967	167528	34315	51488	253331	39.5	9.00	0.934232
1968	179025	43863	50624	273512	40.5	8.75	0.941193
1969	190089	51091	60825	302005	43.7	8.00	0.969630
1970	206813	50737	66375	323925	48.7	8.00	1.000000
1971	217212	55112	73528	345852	54.5	8.00	1.033727
1972	232312	64122	79300	375734	67.2	8.00	1.068064
1973	250057	72187	91421	413665	83.9	9.00	1.228156
1974	251650	52211	82892	386753	100.2	11.83	1.517795
1975	266884	53702	85850	406436	115.7	11.88	1.701147
1976	281066	58380	87023	426469	140.2	11.50	1.929906
1977	293928	66750	85376	446054	165.6	12.00	2.159872
1978	310640	70600	88636	469876	202.9	13.46	2.436364
1979	318817	76385	93148	488350	235.4	16.71	2.838453
1980	319341	70465	92514	482320	267.9	21.25	3.459030
1981	325851	63495	102037	491383	335.3	21.33	4.081844
1982	338507	60300	107530	506337	389.7	20.50	5.114169
1983	339425	56000	113748	509173	449.4	20.50	6.067835
1984	345194	48570	114654	508418	542.5	20.50	7.130602
1985	358671	49670	128908	537249	675.1	20.50	8.435285
1986	361026	50525	124963	536514	738.8	20.50	10.30081
1987	365473	52436	120587	538496	843.4	21.82	11.91950
1988	378488	58335	125348	562171	973.2	22.89	13.61448
1989	394942	64027	138583	597552	1265.0	23.26	15.59285
1990	403194	73412	136965	613571	1583.5	27.62	18.59539
1991	412458	65774	157460	635692	1742.9	29.45	22.09116
1992	420028	64324	155635	639987	1968.2	28.71	25.40122
1993	420585	62671	156887	640143	2223.7	28.56	28.88346
1994	426893	64308	156524	647725	2793.5	27.44	32.00385
1995	433723	67324	144978	646025	3149.0	23.05	34.98085

Sources: Epilogi (1998)

tests) and that the instruments are not all valid (SARGAN test). Therefore, we present below the estimates of the money demand function with the method of 2SLS/AR(1).

$$r_t = -1.86465 + 1.38(E-05)Y_t - 0.00837M_{t-1} + 0.55770P_t + 0.76147r_{t-1}$$

s.e. (1.8378) (1.06(E−05)) (0.0041) (0.3450) (0.2669)

t [1.0146] [1.2998] [2.0483] [1.6165] [2.8525] (8.160)

$$\bar{R}^2 = 0.968 \quad DW = 1.799 \quad e_t = 0.40808e_{t-1}$$

$$(0.3326) \ [1.2271]$$

In (8.160) the estimated correlation coefficient is not significant, as can be seen from the low t-ratio.

8.6.1.5 Limited information maximum likelihood (LIML) method

This method utilises the likelihood of the endogenous variables included in the structural equation to be estimated only, and not all the endogenous variables of the model, and thus the name 'limited'. Assume, for example, that we want to estimate the following first equation of the model:

$$Y_1 = Y_1\gamma_1 + X_1\beta_1 + \varepsilon_1 \tag{8.161}$$

where

$$Y_1 = [Y_2\ Y_3\ \dots\ Y_g]\ \text{and}\ X_1 = [X_1\ X_2\ \dots\ X_k]$$

or the equation

$$Y_{1g}\gamma_{1g} - X_1\beta_1 = \varepsilon_1 \tag{8.162}$$

where

$$Y_{1g} = [Y_1\ Y_1]\ \text{and}\ \gamma'_{1g} = [1 - \gamma_1]$$

The unrestricted reduced form equations for the endogenous variables included in the first structural equation is given by:

$$Y_i = X\pi_i + \upsilon_i \qquad \text{for i = 1, 2, ..., g} \tag{8.163}$$

where

$$X = [X_1\ X_{k+1}\ X_{k+2}\ \dots\ X_K]\ \text{and}\ \pi_i = [\pi_{i1}\ \pi_{i2}\ \dots\ \pi_{iK}]$$

Under the assumption that the reduced form disturbances are normally distributed, the log of their joint distribution L_1 is:

$$\text{In}\,L_1 = -\frac{n}{2}\Big[g\,\text{In}(2\pi) + \text{In}\,|\Omega_1|\Big] - \frac{1}{2}\sum_t \mathbf{v}'_{1t}\Omega_1^{-1}\mathbf{v}_{1t}$$

where

$$
\mathbf{v}_{1t} = \begin{bmatrix} \upsilon_{1t} \\ \upsilon_{2t} \\ :: \\ \upsilon_{gt} \end{bmatrix}
\quad \text{and} \quad
\Omega_1 = E(\mathbf{v}_1\mathbf{v}'_1) = \begin{bmatrix} \omega_{11} & \omega_{12} & :: & \omega_{1g} \\ \omega_{21} & \omega_{22} & :: & \omega_{2g} \\ :: & :: & :: & :: \\ \omega_{g1} & \omega_{g2} & :: & \omega_{gg} \end{bmatrix}
\tag{8.164}
$$

According to Anderson and Rubin (1949), the limited information maximum likelihood approach refers to the maximisation of (8.164) subject to the restriction that rank (Ω_{gk*}) = $g - 1$, where Ω_{gk*} is given in (8.103). However, it can be proved (see Johnston (1984), Kmenta (1986)) that the maximisation of (8.164) is equivalent with the minimisation of the *least variance ratio*, given by:

$$\ell = \frac{\gamma'_{1g} W^*_{1g} \gamma_{1g}}{\gamma'_{1g} W_{1g} \gamma_{1g}}$$

where $W^*_{1g} = Y'_{1g} Y_{1g} - Y'_{1g} X_1 (X'_1 X_1)^{-1} X'_1 Y_{1g}$

and $W_{1g} = Y'_{1g} Y_{1g} - Y'_{1g} X (X'X)^{-1} X'Y_{1g}$

(8.165)

By noting that c_{1g} is an estimate of γ_{1g}, b_1 is an estimate of β_1, and λ is the smallest characteristic root of the determinantal equation:

$| W^*_{1g} - \ell W_{1g} | = 0$, which is a polynomial in ℓ, (8.166)

then the LIML estimator is given by

$$(W^*_{1g} - \lambda W_{1g}) c_{1g} = 0$$ (8.167)

and

$$b_1 = (X'_1 X_1)^{-1} (X'_1 Y_{1g}) c_{1g}$$ (8.168)

The LIML estimator given in (8.167) and (8.168) has the same asymptotic variance-covariance matrix with the estimator of 2SLS. Furthermore, in the case of an exactly identified equation it can be shown that $\lambda = 1$, and, therefore, the LIML estimator produces the ILS estimator.

Example 8.9 A simple macroeconomic model for an EU member (LIML)

Consider the macroeconomic model for an EU member presented in Example 8.8. The estimated equations with the LIML method, using TSP, are shown below:

Private consumption function:

$\hat{C}_t = 8423.51 + 0.14142 Y_t + 0.78107 C_{t-1}$

s.e. (2304.6) (0.0538) (0.0794)

t [3.6551] [2.6283] [9.8403]

$\bar{R}^2 = 0.999$ DW $= 1.923$ $\lambda = 1.247$

(8.169)

where λ is the variance ratio.

Private gross investment function:

$\hat{I}_t = 6254.74 + 0.0719 Y_t - 1089.52 r_t + 0.64687 I_{t-1}$

s.e. (2935.7) (0.0225) (352.45) (0.10239)

t [2.1306] [3.1951] [3.0912] [6.3175]

$\bar{R}^2 = 0.895$ DW $= 1.649$ $\lambda = 1.087$

(8.170)

Money demand function:

$\hat{r}_t = -1.48583 + 9.28(E - 06) Y_t - 0.00841 M_{t-1} + 0.53967 P_t + 0.8775 lr_{t-1}$

s.e. (0.9266) (3.74(E - 06)) (0.0039) (0.3059) (0.1047)

t [1.6036] [2.4843] [2.1566] [1.7643] [8.3785]

$\bar{R}^2 = 0.968$ DW $= 1.312$ $\lambda = 1.312$

(8.171)

8.6.2 System methods of estimation

The common factor in the single-equation estimation methods proposed till now is that in all methods we tried to bypass the correlation between the explanatory endogenous variables in the structural equations under estimation and their error terms. These single-equation estimation techniques did not consider the possible correlation of disturbances among equations. Thus, although the single-equation methods estimators were consistent, they were not asymptotically efficient. In this section we will present two methods of estimation of the structural parameters of a model that treat all equations simultaneously, and thus they are increasing the efficiency of the corresponding estimators, because they contain all possible information among equations, as such, for example, of the correlation among their error terms.

8.6.2.1 Three-stage least squares (3SLS) method

Repeating Equation (8.130), a structural model may be written for all its structural equations as:

$$Y_1 = Y_1\gamma_1 + X_1\beta_1 + \varepsilon_1 = Z_1\delta_1 + \varepsilon_1$$
$$Y_2 = Y_2\gamma_2 + X_2\beta_2 + \varepsilon_2 = Z_2\delta_2 + \varepsilon_2$$
$$\ldots\ldots$$
$$Y_G = Y_G\gamma_G + X_G\beta_G + \varepsilon_G = Z_G\delta_G + \varepsilon_G$$

(8.172)

where $Z_i = [Y_i X_i]$ and $\delta_i = [\gamma_i \beta_i]$

System (8.172) can be also written as:

$$Y = Z\delta + \varepsilon$$

where

$$Y = \begin{bmatrix} Y_1 \\ Y_2 \\ :: \\ Y_G \end{bmatrix}, \quad Z = \begin{bmatrix} Z_1 & 0 & :: & 0 \\ 0 & Z_2 & :: & 0 \\ :: & :: & :: & :: \\ 0 & 0 & :: & Z_G \end{bmatrix}, \quad \delta = \begin{bmatrix} \delta_1 \\ \delta_2 \\ :: \\ \delta_G \end{bmatrix}, \quad \varepsilon = \begin{bmatrix} \varepsilon_1 \\ \varepsilon_2 \\ :: \\ \varepsilon_G \end{bmatrix}$$

(8.173)

To avoid the problem of correlation between the explanatory endogenous variables Y_i and ε_i, for $i = 1, 2, \ldots, G$, we saw in the previous sections that we can use the predicted values of Y_i, from the regression of Y_i on all the predetermined variables of the model, in the place of the corresponding explanatory endogenous variables. Then, system (8.172) is written as:

$$Y_1 = \hat{Y}_1\gamma_1 + X_1\beta_1 + \eta_1 = \hat{Z}_1\delta_1 + \eta_1$$
$$Y_2 = \hat{Y}_2\gamma_2 + X_2\beta_2 + \eta_2 = \hat{Z}_2\delta_2 + \eta_2$$
$$\ldots\ldots$$
$$Y_G = \hat{Y}_G\gamma_G + X_G\beta_G + \eta_G = \hat{Z}_G\delta_G + \eta_G$$

(8.174)

where $\hat{Z}_i = [\hat{Y}_i X_i]$ and $\delta_i = \begin{bmatrix} \gamma_i \\ \beta_i \end{bmatrix}$

and respectively system (8.174), in which the various possible identities are not included, is written as:

$$\mathbf{Y} = \hat{\mathbf{Z}}\,\delta + \eta$$

where (8.175)

$$\mathbf{Y} = \begin{bmatrix} Y_1 \\ Y_2 \\ :: \\ Y_G \end{bmatrix}, \quad \hat{\mathbf{Z}} = \begin{bmatrix} \hat{Z}_1 & 0 & :: & 0 \\ 0 & \hat{Z}_2 & :: & 0 \\ :: & :: & :: & :: \\ 0 & 0 & :: & \hat{Z}_G \end{bmatrix}, \quad \delta = \begin{bmatrix} \delta_1 \\ \delta_2 \\ :: \\ \delta_G \end{bmatrix}, \quad \eta = \begin{bmatrix} \eta_1 \\ \eta_2 \\ :: \\ \eta_G \end{bmatrix}$$

System (8.175) leads to the consistent 2SLS estimator, which, according to (8.144), is the following:

$$\mathbf{d}_{2SLS} = \left(\hat{\mathbf{Z}}'\hat{\mathbf{Z}}\right)^{-1}\hat{\mathbf{Z}}'\mathbf{Y}$$ (8.176)

If we knew a consistent estimate of matrix $\Omega = E(\eta,\eta')$, i.e. an estimate of the variance-covariance matrix of the disturbances in (8.175), then we could apply Aitken's (1935) generalised least squares (GLS) estimator, which is:

$$\mathbf{d}_{GLS} = \left(\hat{\mathbf{Z}}'\Omega^{-1}\hat{\mathbf{Z}}\right)^{-1}\hat{\mathbf{Z}}'\Omega^{-1}\mathbf{Y}$$ (8.177)

However, knowing the 2SLS consistent estimator in (8.176), we use it in order to compute a consistent estimate W of Ω, as follows:

$$\mathbf{W} = \begin{bmatrix} w_{11}\mathbf{I}_n & w_{12}\mathbf{I}_n & :: & w_{1G}\mathbf{I}_n \\ w_{21}\mathbf{I}_n & w_{22}\mathbf{I}_n & :: & w_{2G}\mathbf{I}_n \\ :: & :: & :: & :: \\ w_{G1}\mathbf{I}_n & w_{G2}\mathbf{I}_n & :: & w_{GG}\mathbf{I}_n \end{bmatrix}$$

where (8.178)

$$w_{ij} = \frac{1}{n - g_i + 1 - k_i}\left(Y_i - Z_i d_{i,\,2SLS}\right)'\left(Y_i - Z_i d_{i,\,2SLS}\right)$$

for $i, j = 1, 2, ..., G$ and $g_i + k_i \geq g_j + k_j$

By substituting (8.178) into (8.177) we obtain the 3SLS estimator, which is:

$$\mathbf{d}_{3SLS} = \left(\hat{\mathbf{Z}}'\mathbf{W}^{-1}\mathbf{Z}\right)^{-1}\hat{\mathbf{Z}}'\mathbf{W}^{-1}\mathbf{Y}$$ (8.179)

with

$$var - cov(\mathbf{d}_{3SLS}) = \left(\hat{\mathbf{Z}}'\mathbf{W}^{-1}\hat{\mathbf{Z}}\right)^{-1}$$ (8.180)

In summary, the three steps in the 3SLS method are the following:

Step 1 The same as step 1 of the 2SLS method. In words, regress all the endogenous variables on all the exogenous variables of the model and keep their predictions, $\hat{Y}_{i,t}$.

Step 2 The same as step 2 of the 2SLS method. In other words, substitute the predictions of the endogenous variables found in step 1 in place of the corresponding endogenous variables on the right-hand side of each equation and apply OLS. Having estimated $d_{i,2SLS}$, compute matrix W in (8.178).

Step 3 Using the results of steps 1 and 2, apply the GLS estimator, i.e. compute the 3SLS estimator according to (8.179) and (8.180).

If in place of the estimates $d_{i,2SLS}$ of step 2, the estimates $d_{i,3SLS}$ of step 3 are used, then the whole procedure may be iterated, to produce the *iterative three-stage least squares*. However, it has been proved (Madansky, 1964) that this iterative procedure does not improve the asymptotic efficiency and does not provide the maximum likelihood estimator. Furthermore, it has been proved (Zellner and Theil, 1962) that the exactly identified equations do not add relevant information in the estimation of the overidentified equations.

Example 8.10 A simple macroeconomic model for an EU member (3SLS)

Consider the macroeconomic model for an EU member presented in Example 8.8. The estimated equations with the 3SLS method, using EViews, are shown below:

Private consumption function:

$$\hat{C}_t = 7835.32 + 0.16152Y_t + 0.75162C_{t-1}$$

s.e.   (1976.1)   (0.0419)   (0.0618)   (8.181)

t   [3.9651]   [3.8522]   [12.1551]

$\bar{R}^2 = 0.999$ DW $= 1.911$

Private gross investment function:

$$\hat{I}_t = 6442.75 + 0.07281Y_t - 1080.57r_t + 0.63380I_{t-1}$$

s.e. (2745.7)   (0.0197)   (314.13)   (0.0893)   (8.182)

t   [2.3465]   [3.6876]   [3.4399]   [7.0979]

$\bar{R}^2 = 0.896$ DW $= 1.911$

A money demand function:

$$\hat{r}_t = -1.8292 + 1.02(E-05)Y_t - 0.00775M_{t-1} + 0.46344P_t + 0.88864r_{t-1}$$

s.e.   (0.8089) (3.25(E-06))   (0.0031)   (0.2401)   (0.0884)

t   [2.2614] [3.1498]   [2.5383]   [1.9301]   [10.0569]   (8.183)

$\bar{R}^2 = 0.966$ DW $= 1.304$

Finally, the corresponding variance-covariance matrix **W** of the disturbances used in the estimation is the following:

$$\mathbf{W} = \begin{bmatrix} w_{C,C} & w_{C,I} & w_{C,r} \\ w_{I,C} & w_{I,I} & w_{I,r} \\ w_{r,C} & w_{r,I} & w_{r,r} \end{bmatrix} = \begin{bmatrix} 10806587 & 3119375 & -1949.103 \\ 3119375 & 21008012 & 1403.266 \\ -1949.103 & 1403.266 & 1.641795 \end{bmatrix}$$

8.6.2.1 Full information maximum likelihood (FIML) method

Let us write the simultaneous equations model in the form of (8.10) and (8.12), which is:

$$\mathbf{\Gamma Y}_t + \mathbf{BX}_t = \varepsilon_t, \quad t = 1, 2, \ldots, n \tag{8.184}$$

and

$$\varepsilon_t \sim N(\mathbf{0}, \Sigma) \quad E(\varepsilon_t \varepsilon_s') = 0 \quad E(\varepsilon_t \varepsilon_t') = \Sigma \tag{8.185}$$

The full information maximum likelihood estimator is based on the entire system of equations and can be found by maximising the following log of the likelihood function (Kmenta, 1986):

$$L = -\frac{Gn}{2}\ln(2\pi) - \frac{n}{2}\ln|\Sigma| + n\ln|\Gamma| - \frac{1}{2}\sum_{t=1}^{n}(\mathbf{\Gamma Y}_t + \mathbf{BX}_t)'\Sigma^{-1}(\mathbf{\Gamma Y}_t + \mathbf{BX}_t) \tag{8.186}$$

with respect to Γ, B and Σ. This estimator is consistent and asymptotically efficient. In the case that the simultaneous equations model contains identities, the variance-covariance matrix of the structural disturbances Σ is singular and, therefore, its inverse Σ^{-1} does not exist. In this case, and before constructing the likelihood function, the identities of the system can be eliminated by substituting them into the other equations.

Example 8.11 A simple macroeconomic model for an EU member (FIML)

Consider the macroeconomic model for an EU member presented in Example 8.8. The estimated equations with the FIML method, using TSP, are shown below:

Private consumption function:

$$\hat{C}_t = 8261.57 + 0.14666Y_t + 0.77342C_{t-1}$$

$$\text{s.e.} \quad (4670.5) \quad (0.0860) \quad (0.1236) \tag{8.187}$$

$$t \quad [1.7689] \quad [1.7050] \quad [6.2582]$$

$$\bar{R}^2 = 0.999 \quad DW = 1.921$$

Private gross investment function:

$$\hat{I}_t = 6365.42 + 0.07923Y_t - 1184.43r_t + 0.61406I_{t-1}$$

$$\text{s.e.} \quad (5512.6) \quad (0.0740) \quad (1148.4) \quad (0.2976) \tag{8.188}$$

$$t \quad [1.1547] \quad [1.0708] \quad [1.0314] \quad [2.0635]$$

$$\bar{R}^2 = 0.905 \quad DW = 1.584$$

Money demand function:

$$\hat{r}_t = -1.88352 + 10.6(E-06)Y_t - 0.00772M_{t-1} + 0.46338P_t + 0.87237r_{t-1}$$

s.e.   (1.8536) (6.91(E-06))   (0.0095)   (0.6965)   (0.1684)   (8.189)

t   [1.0161] [1.5796]   [0.8110]   [0.6653]   [5.1812]

$$\bar{R}^2 = 0.970 \quad DW = 1.2842$$

8.7 Seemingly unrelated equations

We saw in Section 8.2 that in the case where matrix $\tilde{A}$, in the structural form of a system of equations, is diagonal, i.e. it has the form:

$$\Gamma = \begin{bmatrix} \gamma_{11} & 0 & .. & 0 \\ 0 & \gamma_{22} & .. & 0 \\ : & : & :: & : \\ 0 & 0 & .. & \gamma_{GG} \end{bmatrix} \tag{8.190}$$

the system of the structural equations is not a system of simultaneous equations but instead it is a *set of equations*. In this case each equation contains one, and only one, endogenous variable, e.g. its dependent variable.

Generally speaking, this set of equations may be written analytically as:

$$Y_{1t} = \beta_{11}X_{11,t} + \beta_{12}X_{12,t} + \cdots + \beta_{1K_1,t}X_{1K_1 t} + \varepsilon_{1t}$$

$$Y_{2t} = \beta_{21}X_{21,t} + \beta_{22}X_{22,t} + \cdots + \beta_{2K_2,t}X_{2K_2 t} + \varepsilon_{2t}$$

$$\cdots\cdots\cdots\cdots\cdots\cdots\cdots\cdots\cdots\cdots\cdots\cdots\cdots\cdots\cdots\cdots\cdots\cdots\cdots\cdots \tag{8.191}$$

$$Y_{Gt} = \beta_{G1}X_{G1,t} + \beta_{G2}X_{G2,t} + \cdots + \beta_{GK_G,t}X_{GK_G t} + \varepsilon_{Gt}$$

for t = 1, 2, ..., n, or in matrix form as

$$\mathbf{Y}_i = \mathbf{X}_i\beta_i + \varepsilon_i \quad \text{for } i = 1,2,...,G \tag{8.192}$$

where for the *i*th equation, Y_i is a n × 1 vector of the values of the dependent variable, X_i is a n × K_i matrix of the values of the explanatory variables, ε_i is a n × 1 vector of the values of the error variable, and β_i is a K_i × 1 vector of the corresponding regression coefficients. The equations in (8.192) may be also written together as:

$$\underbrace{\begin{bmatrix} \mathbf{Y}_1 \\ \mathbf{Y}_2 \\ :: \\ \mathbf{Y}_G \end{bmatrix}}_{Gn \times 1} = \underbrace{\begin{bmatrix} \mathbf{X}_1 & \mathbf{0} & :: & \mathbf{0} \\ \mathbf{0} & \mathbf{X}_2 & :: & \mathbf{0} \\ :: & :: & :: & :: \\ \mathbf{0} & \mathbf{0} & :: & \mathbf{X}_G \end{bmatrix}}_{Gn \times K} \underbrace{\begin{bmatrix} \beta_1 \\ \beta_2 \\ :: \\ \beta_G \end{bmatrix}}_{K \times 1} + \underbrace{\begin{bmatrix} \varepsilon_1 \\ \varepsilon_2 \\ :: \\ \varepsilon_G \end{bmatrix}}_{Gn \times 1} \tag{8.193}$$

where K = K_1 + K_2 + ... + K_G, or finally as:

$$\mathbf{Y} = \mathbf{X}\beta + \varepsilon \tag{8.194}$$

where the substitution is obvious.

With respect to the error terms, we employ the following assumptions:

1. The error terms have zero mean:

$$E(\varepsilon_{it}) = 0, \quad t = 1, 2, ..., n, \quad i = 1, 2, ..., G \tag{8.195}$$

2. For each equation i (=1,2,...,G), the error terms have constant variance over time:

$$var(\varepsilon_{it}) = E(\varepsilon_{it}^2) = \sigma_i^2 = \sigma_{ii}, \quad t = 1, 2, ..., n \tag{8.196}$$

These variances may be different for different equations.

3. For each equation i (=1,2,...,G) and for two different time periods $t \neq s$ (=1,2,...,n), the error terms are not autocorrelated:

$$cov(\varepsilon_{it}\varepsilon_{is}) = E(\varepsilon_{it}\varepsilon_{is}) = 0, \quad t \neq s \tag{8.197}$$

4. For the same time period t (=1,2,...,n), the error terms of two different equations $I \neq j$ (=1,2,...,G) may be correlated (*contemporaneous correlation*):

$$cov(\varepsilon_{it}\varepsilon_{jt}) = E(\varepsilon_{it}\varepsilon_{jt}) = \sigma_{ij}, \quad i \neq j \tag{8.198}$$

5. For two different equations $I \neq j$ (=1,2,...,G) and for two different time periods $t \neq s$ (=1,2,...,n), the error terms are not correlated:

$$cov(\varepsilon_{it}\varepsilon_{js}) = E(\varepsilon_{it}\varepsilon_{js}) = 0, \quad t \neq s, \quad i \neq j \tag{8.199}$$

In matrix form the assumptions above may be written as:

$$E(\varepsilon_i) = \mathbf{0}, \quad E(\varepsilon_i\varepsilon_i') = \sigma_{ii}\mathbf{I}, \quad E(\varepsilon_i\varepsilon_j') = \sigma_{ij}\mathbf{I} \tag{8.200}$$

or

$$E(\varepsilon) = \mathbf{0}, \quad E(\varepsilon\varepsilon') = \Omega = \Sigma \otimes \mathbf{I} \tag{8.201}$$

where I is an identity matrix of order n×n, $\otimes$ is the Kronecker product, and

$$\Sigma = \begin{bmatrix} \sigma_{11} & \sigma_{12} & .. & \sigma_{1G} \\ \sigma_{21} & \sigma_{22} & .. & \sigma_{2G} \\ :: & :: & :: & :: \\ \sigma_{G1} & \sigma_{G2} & .. & \sigma_{GG} \end{bmatrix} \quad \text{with } \Omega = \Sigma \otimes \mathbf{I} = \begin{bmatrix} \sigma_{11}\mathbf{I} & \sigma_{12}\mathbf{I} & .. & \sigma_{1G}\mathbf{I} \\ \sigma_{21}\mathbf{I} & \sigma_{22}\mathbf{I} & .. & \sigma_{2G}\mathbf{I} \\ :: & :: & :: & :: \\ \sigma_{G1}\mathbf{I} & \sigma_{G2}\mathbf{I} & .. & \sigma_{GG}\mathbf{I} \end{bmatrix} \tag{8.202}$$

From the discussion it is seen that the only link between the equations of the set of equations in (8.191), or in (8.192), is the contemporaneous correlation. In other words, the only link is through the covariance σ_{ij} of the error terms of the *i*th and the *j*th equations. For this reason Zellner (1962) gave the name *seemingly unrelated regression equations* (SURE) to these equations.

The methods used in order to estimate the set of equations in (8.191), or in (8.192), depend on the assumptions about the error terms. These methods are the following:

8.7.1 Ordinary least squares (OLS)

If we assume that from the five assumptions (8.195) to (8.199), only the assumptions (8.195) and (8.196) hold, then each equation in the set of equations in (8.191) could be estimated individually by the classical ordinary least squares method. The least squares estimator in this case is the best linear unbiased estimator, and is given by:

$$\mathbf{b}_{i,OLS} = (\mathbf{X}_i'\mathbf{X}_i)^{-1}\mathbf{X}_i'\mathbf{Y}_i \qquad (8.203)$$

with

$$\text{var} - \text{cov}(\mathbf{b}_{i,OLS}) = s_i^2(\mathbf{X}_i'\mathbf{X}_i)^{-1} \qquad (8.204)$$

where

$$s_i^2 = \frac{1}{n - K_i}\sum_{j=1}^{n}e_j^2 = \frac{1}{n - K_i}\mathbf{e}_i'\mathbf{e}_i \qquad (8.205)$$

Example 8.12 Food demand equations for an EU member (OLS)

Consider the following set of three linear demand equations for specific food products:

$$
\begin{aligned}
meat: &\quad Q_{m,t} = \beta_{10} + \beta_{11}P_{m,t} + \beta_{12}P_{f,t} + \beta_{13}Y_t + \varepsilon_{1t} \\
vegetables: &\quad Q_{v,t} = \beta_{20} + \beta_{21}P_{v,t} + \beta_{22}P_{d,t} + \beta_{23}Y_t + \varepsilon_{2t} \\
oil: &\quad Q_{o,t} = \beta_{30} + \beta_{31}P_{o,t} + \beta_{33}Y_t + \varepsilon_{3t}
\end{aligned}
\qquad (8.206)
$$

where (actual data for estimation purposes in parentheses):

Q_m = quantity demanded (consumption) of meat
Q_v = quantity demanded (consumption) of fruit and vegetables
Q_o = quantity demanded (consumption) of oils and fats
P_m = price (index) of meat
P_f = price (index) of fish
P_v = price (index) of fruit and vegetables
P_d = price (index) of dairy goods
P_o = price (index) of oils and fats
Y = personal disposable income

The a priori restrictions for the coefficients in the three demand equations are the following:

meat: $\beta_{11}<0$ (normal good), $\beta_{12}>0$ (substitute good), $\beta_{13}>0$ (superior good)
vegetables: $\beta_{21}<0$ (normal good), $\beta_{22}>0$ (substitute good), $\beta_{23}>0$ (superior good)
oils: $\beta_{31}<0$ (normal good), $\beta_{33}>0$ (superior good)

Assuming that there is no contemporaneous correlation between the error terms of the three demand equations, we can apply the OLS method. The corresponding results, using the data in Table 8.4, are shown below:

Table 8.4 Consumption expenditure for specific food products (at constant 1970 market prices, million drs), price indices for specific food products (base year 1970), and personal disposable income (at constant 1970 market prices, million drs) of an EU member.

Year	Q_m	Q_v	Q_o	P_m	P_f	P_v	P_d	P_o	Y
1960	6978	11313	4977	0.730	0.631	0.764	0.727	0.635	117179.2
1961	7901	13094	5300	0.687	0.643	0.766	0.740	0.638	127598.9
1962	8660	12369	5430	0.668	0.665	0.779	0.767	0.647	135007.1
1963	9220	13148	5528	0.706	0.686	0.825	0.778	0.729	142128.3
1964	9298	15564	6186	0.826	0.723	0.778	0.829	0.732	159648.7
1965	11718	15132	6457	0.844	0.794	0.908	0.890	0.772	172755.9
1966	12858	16536	6428	0.874	0.854	0.977	0.946	0.786	182365.5
1967	13686	16659	5559	0.887	0.878	0.996	0.955	0.938	195611.0
1968	14468	18357	6582	0.872	0.890	0.952	0.974	0.857	204470.4
1969	15041	18733	7108	0.888	0.913	1.072	0.989	0.922	222637.5
1970	16273	19692	6681	1.000	1.000	1.000	1.000	1.000	246819.0
1971	17538	18865	7043	1.089	1.109	1.129	1.009	1.003	269248.9
1972	18632	19850	7223	1.139	1.181	1.198	1.016	1.038	297266.0
1973	19789	21311	7439	1.421	1.398	1.531	1.186	1.272	335521.7
1974	20333	21695	7311	1.643	1.600	1.918	1.582	1.696	310231.1
1975	21508	22324	7326	1.810	1.993	2.162	1.788	1.931	327521.3
1976	22736	21906	7638	2.100	2.159	2.709	2.008	1.957	350427.4
1977	25379	20312	6979	2.294	2.390	3.191	2.122	2.140	366730.0
1978	26151	22454	6973	2.499	3.169	3.733	2.504	2.444	390188.5
1979	26143	23269	7287	3.243	3.795	4.241	2.985	2.775	406857.2
1980	26324	24164	8103	3.862	6.850	5.294	3.764	3.440	401942.8
1981	24324	26572	7335	5.270	9.000	6.382	4.898	4.072	419669.1
1982	26155	25051	7591	6.709	10.177	7.450	5.945	4.727	421715.6
1983	27098	25344	8492	7.874	11.637	8.625	6.973	5.537	417930.3
1984	27043	25583	8580	8.949	13.951	10.682	8.319	6.774	434695.7
1985	27047	23402	8303	10.546	18.230	11.960	10.134	8.725	456576.2
1986	27136	23666	7287	12.262	23.003	13.128	12.514	10.254	439654.1
1987	28616	24639	7258	13.439	27.152	15.561	14.254	10.200	438453.5
1988	29624	26857	7328	15.092	29.460	16.553	15.776	11.007	476344.7
1989	30020	26431	7230	18.444	33.972	19.307	18.873	13.585	492334.4
1990	29754	25808	7261	21.632	40.391	23.881	22.757	17.181	495939.2
1991	29332	26409	7596	23.916	45.400	29.734	26.049	22.076	513173.0
1992	30665	26358	7638	27.246	51.814	31.481	29.590	20.751	502520.1
1993	31278	28120	7815	30.083	57.155	32.248	35.182	22.355	523066.1
1994	35192	28405	8126	31.827	63.540	36.397	40.331	26.603	520727.5
1995	36505	28388	8195	33.601	72.491	39.122	42.793	31.090	518406.9

Sources: Epilogi (1998)

The demand equation for meat:

$$\hat{Q}_{m,t} = 627.6114 - 1242.417P_{m,t} + 594.4882P_{f,t} + 0.06553Y_t, \quad \bar{R}^2 = 0.981$$

s.e.	(664.79)	(299.14)	(140.87)	(0.0027)	(8.207)
t	[0.9441]	[4.1532]	[4.2207]	[24.592]	

A demand equation for fruit and vegetables:

$$\hat{Q}_{v,t} = 8364.896 - 397.1046P_{v,t} + 329.6762P_{d,t} + 0.04062Y_t, \quad \bar{R}^2 = 0.948$$

s..e.	(691.59)	(177.43)	(156.88)	(0.0027)	(8.208)
t	[12.081]	[2.2381]	[2.1015]	[15.002]	

A demand equation for oils and fats:

$$\hat{Q}_{o,t} = 4819.17 - 32.6999P_{o,t} + 0.00724Y_t, \quad \bar{R}^2 = 0.721$$

$$\text{s.e.} \quad (269.15) \quad (14.939) \quad (0.00095) \tag{8.209}$$

$$\text{t} \quad [17.905] \quad [2.1890] \quad [7.6547]$$

The estimates of the three demand equations are acceptable in the light of the signs of the regression coefficients and the reported statistics.

8.7.2 Generalised least squares (GLS)

In the case that assumption (8.198) holds then the OLS estimator is not efficient because it does not use information on the contemporaneous correlation. To obtain a more efficient estimator than the OLS estimator, the set of the equations may be written in the form of the 'stacked' model of (8.193), In other words, the G different equations may be viewed as the single equation of (8.193), and the generalised least squares estimator may be used. This estimator, which is a best linear unbiased estimator, is given by (Aitken, 1935).

$$b_{GLS} = (X'\Omega^{-1}X)^{-1}X'\Omega^{-1}Y = \left[X'\left(\Sigma^{-1}\otimes I\right)X\right]^{-1}X'\left(\Sigma^{-1}\otimes I\right)Y \tag{8.210}$$

with

$$\text{var} - \text{cov}(b_{GLS}) = (X'\Omega^{-1}X)^{-1} = \left[X'\left(\Sigma^{-1}\otimes I\right)X\right]^{-1} \tag{8.211}$$

8.7.3 Seemingly unrelated regression estimator (SURE)

For the GLS estimator in (8.210) and (8.211) to have practical meaning we have to know matrices Ω or Σ, or, in other words, we have to know the variances-covariances σ_{ij} in matrix (8.202). In order to obtain consistent estimates of these variances-covariances, the following steps may be used (Zellner, 1962):

Step 1 Apply the OLS method to each of the equations individually and obtain the estimates of the regression coefficients according to (8.203), or:

$$b_{i,OLS} = (X_i'X_i)^{-1}X_i'Y_i \tag{8.212}$$

Step 2 Using these OLS estimates obtain the corresponding residuals according to:

$$e_{i,OLS} = Y_i - X_i b_{i,OLS} \tag{8.213}$$

Step 3 Using the residuals estimated in (8.213) obtain consistent estimates s_{ij} of the variances-covariances σ_{ij} according to:

$$s_{ij} = \frac{1}{\left[(n - K_i)(n - K_j)\right]^{1/2}}e_{i,OLS}'e_{i,OLS} = \frac{1}{\left[(n - K_i)(n - K_j)\right]^{1/2}}\sum_{t=1}^{n}e_{it}e_{jt} \tag{8.214}$$

Step 4 Using the estimates in (8.214) construct the following variance-covariance matrices S and W, as being estimates of the matrices Σ and Ω, respectively:

$$
\mathbf{S} = \begin{bmatrix} s_{11} & s_{12} & \cdot\cdot & s_{1G} \\ s_{21} & s_{22} & \cdot\cdot & s_{2G} \\ :: & :: & :: & :: \\ s_{G1} & s_{G2} & \cdot\cdot & s_{GG} \end{bmatrix} \quad \text{with} \ \ \mathbf{W} = \mathbf{S} \otimes \mathbf{I} = \begin{bmatrix} s_{11}\mathbf{I} & s_{12}\mathbf{I} & \cdot\cdot & s_{1G}\mathbf{I} \\ s_{21}\mathbf{I} & s_{22}\mathbf{I} & \cdot\cdot & s_{2G}\mathbf{I} \\ :: & :: & :: & :: \\ s_{G1}\mathbf{I} & s_{G2}\mathbf{I} & \cdot\cdot & s_{GG}\mathbf{I} \end{bmatrix} \tag{8.215}
$$

Step 5 Substituting the estimates of (8.215) into (8.210) and (8.211) we obtain the *SUR estimator*, as:

$$
\mathbf{b}_{SUR} = (\mathbf{X}'\mathbf{W}^{-1}\mathbf{X})^{-1}\mathbf{X}'\mathbf{W}^{-1}\mathbf{Y} = \left[\mathbf{X}'\left(\mathbf{S}^{-1}\otimes\mathbf{I}\right)\mathbf{X}\right]^{-1}\mathbf{X}'\left(\mathbf{S}^{-1}\otimes\mathbf{I}\right)\mathbf{Y} \tag{8.216}
$$

with

$$
\text{var} - \text{cov}(\mathbf{b}_{SUR}) = (\mathbf{X}'\mathbf{W}^{-1}\mathbf{X})^{-1} = \left[\mathbf{X}'(\mathbf{S}^{-1}\otimes\mathbf{I})\mathbf{X}\right]^{-1} \tag{8.217}
$$

Step 6 Having estimated the regression coefficients in (8.216), the whole process could be iterated by substituting these estimates into step 2 and then continuing to the next steps. This process will yield the *iterated SUR estimates*, which correspond to the *maximum likelihood estimates of a SUR model* (Oberhofer and Kmenta, 1974).

Example 8.13 Food demand equations for an EU member (SUR)

Consider the set (8.206) of the three linear demand equations for specific food products of Example 8.12. Assuming that there exists contemporaneous correlation between the error terms of these equations, the SUR estimates for these equations are derived as follows:

Step 1 The OLS estimates of the regression coefficients of the three equations individually have been obtained in Example 8.12.

Step 2, 3, 4 Using these estimates the residuals for the three equations have been calculated and, furthermore, using these residuals the variance-covariance matrix S have been estimated as follows:

$$
\mathbf{S} = \begin{bmatrix} 1145077 & 22757.26 & 134263.2 \\ 22757.26 & 1108305 & 202239.7 \\ 134263.2 & 202239.7 & 207761.2 \end{bmatrix} \tag{8.218}
$$

Step 5, 6 Using (8.216) and (8.217) the SUR estimates have been obtained to be the following (results from EViews):

The demand for meat:

$$
\hat{Q}_{m,t} = 680.5815 - 1192.477 P_{m,t} + 572.2006 P_{f,t} + 0.06516 Y_t, \ \ \bar{R}^2 = 0.981
$$

s.e.	(625.189)	(269.793)	(4.5010)	(0.0025)	(8.219)
t	[1.0886]	[4.4200]	[4.5010]	[26.2964]	

The demand for fruit and vegetables:

$$\hat{Q}_{v,t} = 8481.553 - 331.7326P_{v,t} + 273.6894P_{d,t} + 0.03992Y_t, \quad \bar{R}^2 = 0.948$$

s.e.	(643.04)	(151.121)	(133.489)	(0.0025)	(8.220)
t	[13.190]	[2.195]	[2.050]	[16.112]	

The demand for oils and fats:

$$\hat{Q}_{o,t} = 4831.429 - 31.4861P_{o,t} + 0.00718Y_t, \quad \bar{R}^2 = 0.721$$

s.e.	(257.48)	(14.266)	(0.0009)	(8.221)
t	[18.764]	[2.207]	[7.942]	

The variance-covariance matrix S used in the final iteration of the iterative SUR estimation (EViews) is the following:

$$S = \begin{bmatrix} 114687 & 51998.11 & 136474.4 \\ 51998.11 & 1113091 & 209501.3 \\ 136474.4 & 209501.3 & 207802.8 \end{bmatrix} \tag{8.222}$$

Comparing the results in Example 8.13 (SUR) with those in Example 8.12 (OLS) we see that the estimates in Example 8.13 are in general more efficient (greater t-ratios) than the corresponding estimates in Example 8.12. Generally, the greater the contemporaneous correlation, the more efficient the SUR estimates are with respect to the OLS estimates.

8.7.4 Hypothesis testing for seemingly unrelated equations

We saw thus far that in the case where there is no contemporaneous correlation, there is no need to apply the SURE methodology, because by applying the OLS methodology in each equation individually we will obtain efficient estimates. Furthermore, having stacked together in model (8.193) the individual equations of a set of G equations, the obvious question that arises is: are these linear restrictions among the regression coefficients of this 'stacked single' equation? Two tests have been suggested to deal with these problems.

a. Testing for contemporaneous correlation

This test is formed as follows:

H_0 : all covariances are zero ($\sigma_{ij} = 0$ for $i \neq j$)

H_a : at least one covariance is nonzero
$$\tag{8.223}$$

Breusch and Pagan (1980) suggested that under the null hypothesis the Lagrange multiplier statistic λ, which is given by:

$$\lambda = n \sum_{i=2}^{G} \sum_{j=1}^{i-1} r_{ij}^2 \tag{8.224}$$

where

$$r_{ij}^2 = \frac{s_{ij}^2}{s_{ii}s_{jj}}$$ (8.225)

follows asymptotically the χ^2 distribution with $G(G-1)/2$ degrees of freedom.

Example 8.14 Food demand equations for an EU member (testing for contemporaneous correlation)

Consider the set (8.206) of the three linear demand equations for specific food products of Example 8.12. According to (8.225), the residual correlation matrix r_{OLS} of the OLS residuals (Example 8.12) and the residual correlation matrix r_{SUR} of the SUR residuals (Example 8.13) are the following:

$$r_{OLS} = \begin{bmatrix} 1.0000 & 0.0202 & 0.2753 \\ 0.0202 & 1.0000 & 0.4215 \\ 0.2753 & 0.4215 & 1.0000 \end{bmatrix}, r_{SUR} = \begin{bmatrix} 1.0000 & 0.0460 & 0.2796 \\ 0.0460 & 1.0000 & 0.4356 \\ 0.2796 & 0.4356 & 1.0000 \end{bmatrix}$$ (8.226)

According now to (8.224), the Lagrange multiplier statistic is:

$$\lambda_{OLS} = n(r_{21}^2 + r_{31}^2 + r_{32}^2) = 9.1390, \quad \lambda_{SUR} = n(r_{21}^2 + r_{31}^2 + r_{32}^2) = 9.7214, \quad n = 36$$ (8.227)

Taking into account that $G = 3$, the degrees of freedom are $G(G-1)/2 = 6$, and for a significant level of 0.05 we get from the tables of the chi-squared distribution that $X^2(3) = 7.81473$. Thus, because the value(s) of the Lagrange multiplier statistic(s) is greater than the critical level of the $X^2(3)$ distribution, the null hypothesis is rejected in favour of the alternative hypothesis. In other words, at least one covariance is non-zero, suggesting that there exists contemporaneous correlation.

---

b. *Testing linear restrictions on the coefficients*

This test is formed as follows:

$$\begin{aligned} H_0 &: \mathbf{R}\beta = \mathbf{r} \\ H_a &: \mathbf{R}\beta \neq \mathbf{r} \end{aligned}$$ (8.228)

where R is a known matrix of dimensions $J \times K$, β is the coefficients vector of dimensions $K \times 1$, and r is a known vector of dimensions $J \times 1$.

Under the null hypothesis, the usual Wald (1943) statistic is written, in this case as:

$$g = (\mathbf{Rb} - \mathbf{r})'(\mathbf{RCR}')^{-1}(\mathbf{Rb} - \mathbf{r}) \sim \chi^2(J)$$ (8.229)

where

$$C = \left[\mathbf{X}'\left(\Sigma^{-1} \otimes \mathbf{I}\right)\mathbf{X} \right]^{-1}$$ (8.230)

or

$$\lambda = \frac{g/J}{(\mathbf{Y} - \mathbf{Xb})'(\Sigma^{-1} \otimes \mathbf{I})(\mathbf{Y} - \mathbf{Xb})/(Gn - K)} \sim F(J, Gn - K) \qquad (8.231)$$

However, for these tests to be operational, matrix Σ in the formulas above must be replaced with its estimate S (see Judge *et al.* 1985).

Example 8.15 Food demand equations for an EU member (testing linear restrictions on the coefficients)

Consider the set (8.206) of the three linear demand equations for specific food products of Example 8.12. According to (8.193) this set of equations may be written as:

$$\begin{bmatrix} Q_m \\ Q_v \\ Q_o \end{bmatrix} = \begin{bmatrix} 1 & P_m & P_f & Y & 0 & 0 & 0 & 0 & 0 & 0 & 0 \\ 0 & 0 & 0 & 0 & 1 & P_v & P_d & Y & 0 & 0 & 0 \\ 0 & 0 & 0 & 0 & 0 & 0 & 0 & 0 & 1 & P_o & Y \end{bmatrix} \begin{bmatrix} \beta_{10} \\ \vdots \\ \beta_{13} \\ \vdots \\ \beta_{23} \\ \vdots \\ \beta_{33} \end{bmatrix} = \begin{bmatrix} \varepsilon_1 \\ \varepsilon_2 \\ \varepsilon_3 \end{bmatrix} \qquad (8.232)$$

Assume now that we want to test if the marginal propensity to consume (demand) with respect to income is the same for all food commodities. In other words, we want to test if the restrictions $\beta_{13} = \beta_{23} = \beta_{33}$, or, equivalently, the restrictions $\beta_{13} - \beta_{33} = 0$ and $\beta_{23} - \beta_{33} = 0$, are correct. According to (8.228) these restrictions are written:

$$\mathbf{R\beta} = \begin{bmatrix} 0 & 0 & 0 & 1 & 0 & 0 & 0 & 0 & 0 & 0 & -1 \\ 0 & 0 & 0 & 0 & 0 & 0 & 0 & 1 & 0 & 0 & -1 \end{bmatrix} \begin{bmatrix} \beta_{10} \\ \vdots \\ \beta_{13} \\ \vdots \\ \beta_{23} \\ \vdots \\ \beta_{33} \end{bmatrix} = \begin{bmatrix} 0 \\ 0 \end{bmatrix} = \mathbf{r} \qquad (8.233)$$

Taking into account (8.233) and using the SUR estimation in Example 8.13, statistic (8.229) is equal to (estimation with EViews) g = 834.2011. Because this value is greater than the 0.05 significant level critical value of $\chi^2(2) = 5.99146$, the null hypothesis is rejected in favour of the alternative hypothesis. In other words, at least one of the marginal propensities to consume is not equal to the other propensities to consume.

8.7.5 *Seemingly unrelated regression estimator with autocorrelation in the disturbances (SURE/AR)*

Until now we assumed, according to (8.197), that there is no autocorrelation in the disturbances. However, in the case where there is autocorrelation in the disturbances, assumption (8.200) is written as:

$$E(\varepsilon_i \varepsilon_i') = \begin{bmatrix} 1 & \rho_i & .. & \rho_i^{n-1} \\ \rho_i & 1 & .. & \rho_i^{n-2} \\ :: & :: & :: & :: \\ \rho_i^{n-1} & \rho_i^{n-2} & .. & 1 \end{bmatrix} \quad E(\varepsilon_i \varepsilon_j') = \begin{bmatrix} 1 & \rho_j & .. & \rho_j^{n-1} \\ \rho_i & 1 & .. & \rho_j^{n-2} \\ :: & :: & :: & :: \\ \rho_i^{n-1} & \rho_i^{n-2} & .. & 1 \end{bmatrix} \quad (8.234)$$

where ρ_i is the autocorrelation coefficient of the disturbances in the *i*th equation.

Park (1967) suggested the following steps in order to estimate a seemingly unrelated equations model with autocorrelation in the disturbances:

Step 1 Apply the OLS method to each of the equations individually and obtain the estimates of the regression coefficients.

Step 2 Using these OLS estimates obtain the corresponding residuals e_i and estimate the autocorrelation coefficients $\hat{\rho}_i$ for each equation individually, by regressing $e_{i,t}$ on $e_{i,t-1}$.

Step 3 Using the estimated autocorrelation coefficients transform the data according to the following transformations:

$$Y_{i,t}^* = Y_{i,t} - \rho_i Y_{i,t-1} \;,\; X_{i,t}^* = X_{i,t} - \rho_i X_{i,t-1} \quad \text{for } t = 2,3,...,n$$
$$Y_{i,t}^* = \sqrt{1 - r_i^2} \, Y_{i,t} \;,\; X_{i,t}^* = \sqrt{1 - r_i^2} \, X_{i,t} \quad \text{for } t = 1 \quad (8.235)$$

Step 4 Apply the SUR estimator to the transformed data of step 3, i.e. apply the steps 3, 4, 5 and 6 of the methodology in Section 8.7.3.

Example 8.16   Food demand equations for an EU member (SURE/AR)

Consider the set (8.206) of the three linear demand equations for specific food products in Example 8.12. Having estimated in Example 8.11 each equation individually by OLS, Table 8.5 presents the Durbin-Watson statistics and the corresponding estimated autocorrelation coefficients according to step 2.

Table 8.5 Durbin-Watson statistics and autocorrelation coefficients

	Demand for meat	Demand for fruits and vegetables	Demand for oils and fats
Durbin-Watson	1.42144	1.13530	0.98065
Autocorrelation	0.27993	0.39407	0.47848
(s.e.)	(0.16393)	(0.15077)	(0.15000)
[t-ratio]	[1.70759]	[2.61379]	[3.18986]

Notes: estimates with EViews

Having transformed all data according to the estimated autocorrelation coefficients in Table 8.5 and the transformations in (8.235), the application of the SURE methodology to these transformed data yields the following results:

The demand for meat:

$$\hat{Q}^*_{m,t} = 851.5305 - 1092.406P^*_{m,t} + 529.8507P^*_{f,t} + 0.06410Y^*_t$$

s.e. (797.29) (284.02) (132.23) (0.0031)

t [1.0680] [3.8462] [4.0071] [20.781]

$\bar{R}^2 = 0.966$ DW $= 1.835$

(8.236)

The demand for fruits and vegetables:

$$\hat{Q}^*_{v,t} = 8436.796 - 318.4453P^*_{v,t} + 266.7486P^*_{d,t} + 0.03979Y^*_t$$

s.e. (876.388) (167.744) (147.342) (0.0033)

t [9.6268] [1.8984] [1.8104] [12.1737]

$\bar{R}^2 = 0.871$ DW $= 1.757$

(8.237)

The demand for oils and fats:

$$\hat{Q}^*_{o,t} = 4851.646 - 20.50658P^*_t + 0.00690Y^*_t$$

s.e. (389.834) (20.060) (0.00135)

t [12.4454] [1.0222] [5.1100]

$\bar{R}^2 = 0.350$ DW $= 1.717$

(8.238)

Finally, the residual covariance matrix S and the residual correlation matrix r used in the estimation are the following:

$$S = \begin{bmatrix} 1047576 & -24074.4 & 109603.4 \\ -24074.4 & 916728 & 134899 \\ 109603.4 & 134899 & 158488.4 \end{bmatrix} \quad r = \begin{bmatrix} 1.00000 & -0.02457 & 0.26899 \\ -0.02457 & 1.00000 & 0.35391 \\ 0.26899 & 0.35391 & 1.00000 \end{bmatrix}$$

(8.239)

From (8.224), using the estimated residual correlation matrix r in (8.239), it can be calculated that $\lambda = 7.1356$. This value is less than the 0.05 significant level critical value of $\chi^2(3) = 7.81473$ and, thus, it can be argued that it was not necessary to use the SURE methodology to the transformed data, but an OLS application to these transformed data would yield efficient results.

8.8 Diagnostic tests for simultaneous equation models

The diagnostic tests in a simultaneous equation model may be classified into the following categories:

1 Tests investigating the omission of predetermined variables from specific equations;
2 Tests investigating the serial correlation in the disturbances of the equations of the model;
3 Tests investigating the simultaneity of the variables involved in a simultaneous equations model;
4 Tests investigating the exogeneity of the variables involved in a simultaneous equations model.

8.8.1   Tests for omitted variables

These tests, which generally test the restrictions that overidentify an equation, may be formed as follows:

H_0 : appropriately omitted exogenous variables

H_a : inappropriately omitted exogenous variables
(8.240)

Two such tests considered here are:

a. Likelihood ratio tests (LR)

Anderson and Rubin (1950) suggested a likelihood ratio statistic, which is given by:

$$LR = n(\lambda_i - 1) \sim \chi^2(K - k_i - g_i) \tag{8.241}$$

where λ_i is the smallest characteristic root of the determinantal equation of the LIML estimation (see Section 8.6.1.4). In the case that the value of the statistic LR is greater than the critical value of the χ^2 distribution for a given significance level, then this means that exogenous variables have been inappropriately omitted from the equation under examination.

Example 8.17 A simple macroeconomic model for an EU member (testing overidentifying restrictions, LR)

Using the model estimated in Example 8.9 with LIML. This model has $G = 4$ endogenous variables and $K = 6$ (excluding the constant) predetermined variables. For each equation we have the following information:

A private consumption function: $k_1 = 1$ $g_1 = 2$ $\lambda_1 = 1.247$

A private gross investment function: $k_2 = 2$ $g_2 = 2$ $\lambda_2 = 1.087$

A money demand function: $k_3 = 3$ $g_3 = 2$ $\lambda_3 = 1.312$

Taking into account that $n = 35$, we can get from (8.241) and from tables of the chi-squared distribution, for 0.05 significance level yields:

$LR_1 = 8.645 > \chi^2(3) = 7.82$, meaning that H_0 is rejected,

$LR_2 = 3.045 < \chi^2(2) = 5.99$, meaning that H_0 is accepted, and

$LR_3 = 10.92 > \chi^2(1) = 3.84$, meaning that H_0 is rejected.

In other words, the LR test suggests that from the private consumption function and from the money demand function exogenous variables have been inappropriately omitted. However, Basmann (1960) found that this test rejects the null hypothesis too often.

b. Lagrange multiplier tests (LM)

Hausman (1983) suggested the following steps in order to test omitted variables from an equation (see also Wooldridge, 1990):

Step 1 Estimate the specific equation with one of the single-equation methods of estimation and save the residuals.

Step 2 Regress the saved residuals in step 1 on all the predetermined variables of the model plus the constant and note R^2.

Step 3 Use the Lagrange multiplier statistic LM, which is given by:

$$LM = nR^2 \sim \chi^2(K - k_i - g_i) \tag{8.242}$$

in order to test the hypotheses in (8.240).

Example 8.18 A simple macroeconomic model for an EU member (testing overidentifying restrictions, LM)

Using the model estimated in Example 8.8 with 2SLS. From the regression of the saved residuals for each equation on all the predetermined variables of the model, we obtained the following determination coefficients:

A private consumption function: $R^2 = 0.208369$
A private gross investment function: $R^2 = 0.080182$
A money demand function: $R^2 = 0.117510$

Taking into account that n = 35, we can get from (8.242) and from tables of the chi-squared distribution, for 0.05 significance level, yields:

$LM_1 = 7.293 < \chi^2(3) = 7.82$, meaning that H_0 is accepted,
$LM_2 = 2.806 < \chi^2(2) = 5.99$, meaning that H_0 is accepted, and
$LM_3 = 4.113 > \chi^2(1) = 3.84$, meaning that H_0 is rejected.

In other words, the LM test suggests that from the money demand function only exogenous variables have been inappropriately omitted.

8.8.2 Tests for serial correlation

The *i*th equation of a structural model according to (8.130) can be written as:

$$Y_{i,t} = Y_{i,t}\gamma_i + X_{i,t}\beta_i + \varepsilon_{i,t} \tag{8.243}$$

with matrix $Z_t = [X_{1t}\ X_{2t} \ldots X_{Kt}]$ being the matrix of all the predetermined variables and matrix $Y_t = [Y_{1t}\ Y_{2t} \ldots Y_{Gt}]$ being the matrix of all the endogenous variables in the model.

Wooldridge (1991) suggested the following procedure in order to test the serial correlation of any order in the disturbances of the *i*th equation of the model:

Step 1 Estimate the *i*th Equation (8.243) by 2SLS and save the corresponding residuals $e_{i,t}$.

Step 2 Estimate the reduced form equations of the simultaneous equations model, i.e. regress each endogenous variable of the model on $\mathbf{Z}_t$, and save the fitted values of all the endogenous variables $\hat{\mathbf{Y}}_t$.

Step 3 Regress $e_{i,t}$ against, $\hat{\mathbf{Y}}_{i,t}$, $\mathbf{X}_{i,t}$ and $e_{i,t-1}$, $e_{i,t-2}$, . . ., $e_{i,t-p}$ and note R^2.

Step 4 Use the Lagrange multiplier statistic LM, which is given by:

$$LM = (n-p)R^2 \sim \chi^2(p) \tag{8.244}$$

in order to test the null hypothesis of no serial correlation.

Example 8.19 A simple macroeconomic model for an EU member (testing serial correlation, LM)

Using the model estimated in Example 8.8 with 2SLS. From the regression of the saved residuals for each equation against the fitted values of its explanatory endogenous variables, its predetermined variables and the lagged values of the saved residuals, we obtained the following results using also the LM statistic in (8.244):

Private consumption function:

$R^2 = 0.002963$ for $p = 1$ with $n = 34$ and $R^2 = 0.057579$ for $p = 2$ with $n = 33$,
$LM_1 = 0.098 < \chi^2(1) = 3.84$ and $LM_2 = 1.785 < \chi^2(2) = 5.99$.

Private gross investment function:

$R^2 = 0.046305$ for $p = 1$ with $n = 34$ and $R2 = 0.047381$ for $p = 2$ with $n = 33$,
$LM_1 = 1.528 < \chi^2(1) = 3.84$ and $LM2 = 1.469 < \chi^2(2) = 5.99$.

Money demand function:

$R^2 = 0.098102$ for $p = 1$ with $n = 34$ and $R^2 = 0.194614$ for $p = 2$ with $n = 33$,
$LM_1 = 3.237 < \chi^2(1) = 3.84$ and $LM_2 = 6.033 > \chi^2(2) = 5.99$.

In other words, the LM test suggests that the disturbances in the money demand function exhibit some serial correlation of the second order (compare with results in (8.159)).

8.8.3 Simultaneity tests

We saw in previous sections that because the endogenous variables in a simultaneous equations model are correlated with the disturbances, the application of OLS to equations in which endogenous variables appear as explanatory variables, will yield biased and inconsistent estimates. This failure of OLS, which is called simultaneous equation bias, becomes the starting point for investigating methods (alternative to OLS) of estimation which could yield consistent and efficient estimates. However, in the case where an explanatory endogenous variable is not correlated with the error term, there is no need to use alternative methods of estimation. In fact, if we use these methods when we should not, the estimates may be still consistent but inefficient. Therefore, there is a need for checking if the explanatory endogenous variables were correlated with the error terms becoming apparent.

Accordingly, the test for simultaneous equation bias, or simultaneity, or the test for investigating the correlation between the explanatory endogenous variables and the error term, may be formed as follows:

H_0 : there is no simultaneity (there is no correlation)

H_a : there is simultaneity (there is correlation)

(8.245)

Considering Equation (8.243), Hausman (1976) suggested the following steps for testing the hypotheses in (8.245):

Step 1 Estimate the reduced form equations of the simultaneous equations model, i.e. regress each endogenous variable of the model on Z_t, and save the fitted values of all the endogenous variables $\hat{Y}_t$ and also save the corresponding reduced form residuals u_t.

Step 2 Because $Y_t = \hat{Y}_t + u_t$, substitute this expression of the explanatory endogenous variables into Equation (8.243) and estimate by OLS the following equation:

$$Y_{i,t} = \hat{Y}_{i,t}\gamma_i + u_{i,t}\gamma_i + X_{i,t}\beta_i + \varepsilon_{i,t}$$

(8.246)

For efficient estimation, Pindyck and Rubinfeld (1991) suggest the following equation, instead of Equation (8.246):

$$Y_{i,t} = Y_{i,t}\gamma_i + u_{i,t}\gamma_i + X_{i,t}\beta_i + \varepsilon_{i,t}$$

(8.247)

Step 3 Use the F-test (or the t-test for one regression coefficient) to test the significance of the regression coefficients of the $u_{i,t}$ variables. If the test shows significant coefficients, accept the alternative hypothesis in (8.245), i.e. accept that there is simultaneity. If the test shows non-significant coefficients, accept the null hypothesis in (8.245), i.e. accept that there is no simultaneity.

Example 8.20 A simple macroeconomic model for an EU member (testing simultaneity)

Using the model estimated in Example 8.8.

Denoting with $u_{C,t}$, $u_{I,t}$, $u_{r,t}$ and $u_{Y,t}$ the reduced form residuals corresponding to the reduced form equations with respect to C, I, r and Y, and following the steps of the Hausman test, the estimated equations of the model in step 2 are the following, where sign { } denotes the significance level of the corresponding estimate:

The private consumption function:

$$\hat{C}_t = 7519.307 + 0.17415\hat{Y}_t + 0.44296u_{Y,t} + 0.73293C_{t-1}$$

sign. {0.0001}   {0.0000}   {0.0000}   {0.0000}

(8.248)

$\bar{R}^2 = 0.999$

The private gross investment function:

$$\hat{I}_t = 5579.631 + 0.06765\hat{Y}_t + 0.53513u_{Y,t} - 1025.758\hat{r}_t - 596.8422u_{r,t} + 0.67607I_{t-1}$$

sign. $\{0.0087\}$ $\{0.0001\}$ $\{0.0000\}$ $\{0.0004\}$ $\{0.0404\}$ $\{0.0000\}$ $\quad$ (8.249)

$\bar{R}^2 = 0.962$ $\quad$ F(for redundant $u_{Y,t}$ and $u_{r,t}$) = 38.549 $\{0.0000\}$

The money demand function:

$$\hat{r}_t = -1.46373 + 9.12(E-06)\hat{Y}_t - 2.35(E-05)u_{Y,t} - 0.00839M_{t-1} + 0.53795P_t + 0.88081r_{t-1}$$

sign. $\{0.1233\}$ $\{0.0202\}$ $\{0.4299\}$ $\{0.0391\}$ $\{0.0879\}$ $\{0.0000\}$ $\quad$ (8.250)

$\bar{R}^2 = 0.967$

According to step 3, the significance level for the regression coefficient of $u_{Y,t}$ in Equation (8.248) using the t-test is $\{0.0000\}$, the significance level for the regression coefficients of $u_{Y,t}$ and $u_{r,t}$ in Equation (8.248) using the F-test is $\{0.000\}$, and the significance level for the regression coefficient of $u_{Y,t}$ in Equation (8.249) using the t-test is $\{0.4299\}$. In other words, the simultaneity problem is present in the private consumption function and in the private gross investment function, whilst there is no simultaneity problem in the money demand function.

8.8.4 *Exogeneity tests*

Although the categorisation of the variables of a simultaneous equations model into endogenous and exogenous variables depends mainly on the theory that the model is trying to represent, Hausman (1976) extended his simultaneity test to be able to test if the predetermined endogenous variables are really endogenous variables. Considering the ith Equation (8.243), with respect to variables $Y_{i,t}$, the test may be formed as follows:

$\quad$ H_0 : variables $Y_{i,t}$ are exogenous

$\quad$ H_a : variables $Y_{i,t}$ are endogenous $\qquad\qquad\qquad\qquad\qquad$ (8.251)

The steps of the test are given below:

Step 1 Estimate the reduced form equations of the simultaneous equations model, i.e. regress each endogenous variable of the model on Z_t, and save the fitted values of all the endogenous variables $\hat{Y}_t$.

Step 2 Estimate by OLS the following equation:

$$Y_{i,t} = Y_{i,t}\gamma_i + \hat{Y}_{i,t}\lambda_i + X_{i,t}\beta_i + \varepsilon_{i,t} \qquad\qquad (8.252)$$

Step 3 Use the F-test (or the t-test for one regression coefficient) to test the significance of the regression coefficients of the $\hat{Y}_t$ variables. If the test shows significant coefficients, accept the alternative hypothesis in (8.251), i.e. accept that the corresponding variables are endogenous. If the test shows not significant coefficients, accept the null hypothesis in (8.251), i.e. accept that the corresponding variables are exogenous.

Example 8.21 A simple macroeconomic model for an EU member (testing exogeneity)

Assume the model estimated in Example 8.8.

Following the steps of the Hausman test for exogeneity, the estimated equations of the model in step 2 are:

A private consumption function:

$$\hat{C}_t = 7519.307 + 0.44296Y_t - 0.26881\hat{Y}_t + 0.73293C_{t-1}$$

$$\text{sign } \{0.0001\} \quad \{0.0000\} \quad \{0.0003\} \quad \{0.0000\} \tag{8.253}$$

$$\bar{R}^2 = 0.999$$

A private gross investment function:

$$\hat{I}_t = 5579.631 + 0.53513Y_t - 0.46747\hat{Y}_t - 596.8422r_t - 428.916\hat{r}_t + 0.67607I_{t-1}$$

$$\text{sign } \{0.0087\} \quad \{0.0000\} \quad \{0.0000\} \quad \{0.0404\} \quad \{0.2596\} \quad \{0.0000\} \tag{8.254}$$

$$\bar{R}^2 = 0.962 \quad \text{F (for redundant } \hat{Y}_t \text{ and } \hat{r}_t) = 27.803 \ \{0.0000\}$$

A money demand function:

$$r_t = -1.46374 - 2.35(E-05)Y_t + 3.26(E-05)\hat{Y}_t - 0.00839M_t + 0.53795P_t + 0.88081r_{t-1}$$

$$\text{sign } \{0.1233\} \quad \{0.4299\} \quad \quad \{0.2793\} \quad \quad \{0.0391\} \quad \{0.0879\} \quad \{0.0000\} \tag{8.255}$$

$$\bar{R}^2 = 0.967$$

According to step 3, the significance level for the regression coefficient of $\hat{Y}_t$ in Equation (8.253) using the t-test is $\{0.0003\}$, the significance level for the regression coefficients of $\hat{Y}_t$ and $\hat{r}_t$ in Equation (8.254) using the F-test is $\{0.0000\}$, and the significance level for the regression coefficient of $\hat{Y}_t$ in Equation (8.255) using the t-test is $\{0.2793\}$. In other words, in the private consumption function, variable Y_t behaves as an endogenous variable, in the private gross investment function, at least one of the variables, Y_t and r_t, behave as an endogenous variable, and, finally, in the money demand function, variable Y_t behaves as an exogenous variable (this final result is parallel with the result referring to the problem of no simultaneity in Equation (8.250)).

8.9 A comparison of methods of estimation

Table 8.6 briefly presents the results obtained in the preceding sections of this chapter, referring to the estimation of a simple macroeconomic model for an EU member. The methods of estimation involve OLS, from single-equation methods, including 2SLS and FIML, and from systems methods of estimation, including 3SLS and FIML. The obvious question is which of the estimates in Table 8.6 are 'preferable'.

Although a quick answer could be that the systems methods of estimation are preferable, because these possibly involve more information than the single-equation methods of estimation, the answer is usually not as quick or as simple. Starting with OLS, we saw that this method, if applied to a simultaneous equations model, produces biased and inconsistent

Table 8.6 Estimates of a simple macroeconomic model for an EU member

	OLS	2SLS	LIML	3SLS	FIML
Consumption					
Constant	5250.619	7519.307	8423.51	7835.32	8261.57
	[2.8302]	[3.554]	[3.6551]	[3.9651]	[1.7689]
Y_t	0.25626	0.17415	0.14142	0.16152	0.14666
	[6.8976]	[3.6384]	[2.6283]	[3.8522]	[1.7050]
C_{t-1}	0.61213	0.73293	0.78107	0.75162	0.77342
	[11.1495]	[10.377]	[9.8403]	[12.1551]	[6.2582]
Investment					
Constant	6014.662	6232.39	6254.74	6442.75	6365.42
	[2.0652]	[2.1252]	[2.1306]	[2.3465]	[1.1547]
Y_t	0.08032	0.07278	0.07190	0.07281	0.07923
	[4.0370]	[3.2685]	[3.1951]	[3.6876]	[1.0708]
r_t	−1165.609	−1097.613	−1089.52	−1080.57	−1184.43
	[3.8046]	[3.1552]	[3.0912]	[3.4399]	[1.0314]
I_{t-1}	0.60591	0.64325	0.64687	0.63380	0.61406
	[6.1879]	[6.3115]	[6.3175]	[7.0979]	[2.0635]
Money					
Constant	−1.39435	−1.46373	−1.48583	−1.8292	−1.88352
	[1.5103]	[1.5812]	[1.6036]	[2.2614]	[1.0161]
Y_t	8.6(E-06)	9.12(E-06)	9.28(E-06)	1.02(E-05)	10.6(E-06)
	[2.3285]	[2.4472]	[2.4843]	[3.1498]	[1.5796]
M_{t-1}	−0.00833	−0.00839	−0.00841	−0.00775	−0.00772
	[2.1367]	[2.1520]	[2.1566]	[2.5383]	[0.8110]
P_t	0.53255	0.53795	0.53967	0.46344	0.46338
	[1.7422]	[1.7591]	[1.7643]	[1.9301]	[0.6653]
r_{t-1}	0.89118	0.88081	0.87751	0.88864	0.87237
	[8.5598]	[8.4230]	[8.3785]	[10.0569]	[5.1812]

Notes: t-ratios in brackets

estimates. Going to single-equation methods of estimation we saw that 2SLS and LIML are preferable to OLS because they produce consistent estimates. Furthermore, the systems methods of estimation, 3SLS and FIML, are preferable to 2SLS and LIML, because they produce more efficient estimates than the single methods of estimation. However, the preceding discussion refers to the asymptotic properties of the estimates of the various methods and not to their finite-sample properties. But, in most applications, the sample sizes are not infinite but finite and generally small.

Although, in theory, the systems methods look to be asymptotically more preferable than the single-equation methods, in practice we have to take into account the following disadvantages of systems methods:

1 Even in these days of high-speed computers, the computational burden for a moderate or large econometric model is quite large.
2 Possible specification errors in one or more equations of the system are transmitted to the other equations of the system, although these equations were correctly specified. Therefore, the systems methods of estimation are very sensitive to specification errors, whilst the single-equation methods of estimation are not as sensitive. For the latter

methods, any specification error in one equation is stacked with that equation and does not affect the estimates of the rest of the equations.

Returning to the three-equation small macroeconomic model of an EU member, with 36 annually aggregate observations per variable, we see in Table 8.6 that the estimates of the regression coefficients are not very different from the methods of estimation. Furthermore, assuming that the t-ratio is a consistent statistic to be used for hypothesis testing (because the sample size is greater than 30), and taking into account all the diagnostic tests performed in the previous sections, we believe that the 3SLS estimates are preferable for this simple model. This is because the 3SLS method yielded estimates of the regression coefficients which are similar in value to the other methods of estimation, but at the same time the 3SLS estimates are more efficient than the estimates by other methods as can be seen from the higher t-ratios.

8.10 A summary of key issues

* Simultaneous equations models allow for economic variables to be determined jointly within a consistent framework. A key feature of this type of model is that variables may change role from one equation to the next; a regressand in one equation may be treated as a regressor in another.
* Large-scale simultaneous equations models containing hundreds of equations are constructed for policy simulation and policy analysis by public and private sectors agencies.
* A particular problem associated with this type of model is the simultaneous equation bias problem. This problem arises because, within the framework of the model, regressors are stochastic and correlated with the disturbance terms. This is similar to the errors in a variable problem, and would lead to biased and inconsistent OLS estimators.
* The identification problem is concerned with whether it is possible to find estimates of structural form parameters from the estimates of the reduced form parameters. It should be checked and solved before estimation to ensure that structural form parameters can in fact be identified.
* The order and rank conditions are applied to check the identification status of an equation/system. The order condition is a necessary condition, whilst the rank condition is necessary and sufficient. That is, if the rank condition is satisfied, the order condition is also satisfied. The rank condition must therefore be satisfied for an equation/system to be identified.
* There are various estimation methods available. The method of indirect least squares is used with exactly identified equations. For overidentified and exactly identified equations, the 2SLS method is commonly used in practice.
* 3SLS and FIML methods estimate equations simultaneously and are more efficient compared to single-equation estimation methods. These methods are routinely used in practice for the estimation of the simultaneous equations systems.

Review questions

1   Explain what you understand by the 'identification problem'. Why should identification problems be dealt with prior to estimation?

2 'An equation is identified if the "rank" condition is satisfied.' Discuss.
3 Discuss the advantages of the 2SLS method. Under what circumstances might indirect least squares be used?
4 Explain the full information maximum likelihood method. Illustrated your answer with reference to a model of your own choice.
5 Explain what you understand by each of the following:

    a   simultaneous equation bias
    b   identification problem
    c   seemingly unrelated equations.

6 Explain the types of diagnostic tests for the simultaneous equation systems. Explain each of the following:

    a   tests for omitted variables
    b   likelihood ratio tests
    c   Lagrange multiplier tests
    d   tests for serial correlation
    e   simultaneity tests.

Key terms: Unit 2

- *Simultaneous equation bias* OLS estimators are biased and inconsistent due to interrelationships between variables.
- *Identification problem* A problem concerning simultaneous equations models where one or more equations may not have unique statistical forms (not identified).
- *Order condition* A necessary but not sufficient condition for an equation to be identified.
- *Rank condition* A necessary and sufficient condition for an equation to be identified.
- *Indirect least squares* A single method of estimation based on the OLS method used on an exactly identified equation. The reduced form model is estimated by the OLS.
- *Two-stage least squares (2SLS)* A method of estimation for exactly or overidentified equations.
- *Three-stage least squares (3SLS) and full information maximum likelihood (FIML) methods* Two popular methods for estimating simultaneous equation systems. Within their respective frameworks, all equations are simultaneously estimated, unlike single-equation methods, for example, 2SLS.

General notes and bibliography: Unit 2

Many contributions to econometric theory and applied econometrics have been carried out within the subject matter of the simultaneous equations systems. We have cited some of the key contributions in this chapter to show the development of this important topic in econometrics. We list below these key contributions.

Aitken, A. (1935). 'On least squares and linear combinations of observations', *Proceedings of the Royal Statistical Society*, 55, 42–48.
Anderson, T. and Rubin, H. (1949). 'Estimation of the parameters of a single equation in a complete system of stochastic equations', *Annals of Mathematical Statistics*, 20, 46–63.

Anderson, T. and Rubin, H. (1950). 'The asymptotic properties of estimators of the parameters of a single equation in a complete system of stochastic equations', *Annals of Mathematical Statistics*, 21, 570–582.

Basmann, R. (1960). 'On finite sample distributions of generalised classical linear identifiability test statistics', *Journal of the American Statistical Association*, 55, 650–659.

Breusch, T. and Pagan, A. (1980). 'The LM test and its applications to model specification in econometrics', *Review of Economic Studies*, 47, 239–254.

Hausman, J. A. (1976). 'Specification tests in Econometrics', *Econometrica*, 46, 1251–1271.

Hausman, J. A. (1983). 'Specification and estimation of simultaneous equations models', in Z. Griliches and M. Intriligator (eds) *Handbook of Econometrics*, Amsterdam: North Holland.

Johnston, J. (1984). *Econometric Methods*, 3rd edn, New York: McGraw-Hill.

Judge, G. G., Griffiths, W. E., Hill, R. C., Lutkepohl, H. and Lee, T. C. (1985). *The Theory and Practice of Econometrics*, 2nd edn, New York: Wiley.

Kmenta, J. (1986). *Elements of Econometrics*, New York: McGraw-Hill.

Madansky, A. (1964). 'On the efficiency of three-stage least squares estimation', *Econometrica*, 32, 55.

Oberhofer, W. and Kmenta, J. (1974). 'A general procedure for obtaining maximum likelihood estimates in generalised regression models', *Econometrica*, 42, 579–590.

Park, R. (1967). 'Efficient estimation of a system of regression equations when disturbances are both serially and contemporaneously correlated', *Journal of the American Statistical Association*, 62, 500–509.

Phillips, A. W. (1958). 'The relation between unemployment and the rate of change of money wages in the United Kingdom, 1861–1957', *Economica*, XXV, 283–299.

Pindyck, R. S. and Rubinfeld, D. L. (1991). *Econometric Models and Economic Forecasts*, 3rd edn, New York: McGraw-Hill.

Wald, A. (1943). 'A note on the consistency of the maximum likelihood estimator', *Annals of Mathematical Statistics*, 20, 595–601.

Wooldridge, J. (1990). 'A note on the Lagrange multiplier and F-statistics for two stage least squares regression', *Economic Letters*, 34, 151–155.

Wooldridge, J. (1991). 'On the application of robust regression-rooted diagnostics to models of conditional means and conditional variables', *Journal of Econometrics*, 47, 5–46.

Zellner, A. (1962). 'An efficient method of estimating seemingly unrelated regressions and tests for aggregation bias', *Journal of the American Statistical Association*, 57, 348–368.

Zellner, A. and Theil, H. (1962). 'Three stage least squares: Simultaneous estimation of simultaneous equations', *Econometrica*, 30, 63–68.

Unit 3

Qualitative variables in econometric models – panel data regression models

- This unit covers regression models involving cross-section data and panel data analysis. The common trait is the availability, in recent years, of these types of data for regression. This availability of data has made it possible for regression analysis to be carried out on many interesting applied issues involving large-scale cross-section and panel data sets.
- Cross-section data sets are typically collected via surveys and questionnaires. They contain information on many qualitative variables, which are key in explaining the decision-making process by individual economic units. This unit provides an introduction to the treatment of qualitative variables in regression models, as both regressors or regressands.
- The unit contains three chapters. Chapter 9 explains the inclusion of qualitative variables via dummy variables as regressors in the regression models. Chapter 10 provides an introductory coverage of qualitative response models. In this type of model the dependent variable is a categorical qualitative variable representing an individual's response to a particular question of interest. The qualitative response models can deal with many interesting applied issues involving an individual decision-making process.
- Chapter 11 provides introductory coverage of panel data regression analysis. This type of data are used to eliminate the omitted variable problem inherent in cross-section data studies, as well as dealing with many interesting empirical issues which can only be investigated via a panel data set containing data on the same cross-sectional units over time.

9 Dummy variable regression models

INTRODUCTION

Econometric models are derived on the basis of deductive reasoning, which identifies inter-relationships among a number of variables. These variables are measured by conventional time series or cross-section data. However, qualitative variables, those variables which cannot be measured by quantitative data, can also have a significant impact on the dependent variable under consideration. For example, in cross-sectional analysis of household consumption expenditure, qualitative variables, such as location, the level of education of household members, and the gender mix of the household, can influence the household consumption. Dummy variables are introduced into regression models to capture the impact of these qualitative variables on household consumption expenditure.

Qualitative variables can also appear as dependent variables in regression models. For example, in a study of incidence of private health insurance, based on cross-section data, the dependent variable of the model is expressed as either an individual possessing private insurance, or not, given his/her characteristics, including income and occupation. In this type of model, the dependent variable essentially represents the response of an individual to a particular question being asked. The answer to the question is either positive or negative, representing qualitative variables. In recent years, due to the availability of large-scale micro-econometric data, these models have become popular, particularly in the area of market research.

This introductory chapter deals with the qualitative variables as regressors in regression models, while the next chapter provides an introductory discussion of the qualitative dependent variable models.

Key topics

- Dummy variables
- Seasonal adjustment of data using dummy variables
- Pooling time series and cross-section data
- Testing for the structural break using dummy variables

9.1 Dummy variables and regression analysis

Dummy variables are used in regression analysis to take account of the impact of qualitative variables on the dependent variable. They are binary variables taking only the values of unity and zero. Unity is used to denote the occurrence of an event/characteristic, while zero signifies the absence of a qualitative characteristic.

Dummy variables are used in cross-section and time series regression models. In a time series model they are frequently employed for seasonal adjustments of data. In a cross-section analysis they are normally employed to capture the impact of a qualitative variable, such as gender or level of education, on the dependent variable.

We now demonstrate the application of the dummy variables in regression/econometric models, using a number of examples.

9.1.1. A model of household consumption expenditure, cross section data: measuring the impact of location on household consumption expenditure

The location of households can have a significant impact on household consumption. Location is a qualitative variable and to capture its impacts, we need to employ dummy variables. In the example of family consumption expenditure, to bring the location variable into the analysis, we distinguish between two locations: south and north. We define the following location dummy variable:

$Di = 1$, if the household is located in the south

$= 0$, if the household is located in the north

Suppose the regression model is specified as:

$$C_i = \beta_1 + \beta_2 Y_i + u_i \qquad\qquad u_i \sim NID(0, \sigma^2)$$

C_i = the ith household consumption expenditure

Y_i = the ith household income

How does location of the household influence consumption expenditure? We can distinguish between three types of impact:

1   Location only influences the level of autonomous expenditure: the intercept term β_1.
2   Location only influences the marginal propensity to consume: the slope parameter β_2.
3   Location influences both the intercept term and the slope parameters of the regression model.

Figure 9.1 depicts the population regression of the two different locations under 1, above.

Notice that β_2 is the marginal propensity to consume in both locations. The slope of the lines are the same, while the level of autonomous consumption expenditure is assumed to be higher in the south. Thus, households with the same level of income, on average, have higher autonomous expenditure in the south, because the cost of living in the south might be higher. The location variable is, therefore, assumed to shift the southern household's consumption function upwards, as depicted in Figure 9.1. Note that the basic idea is that location of the

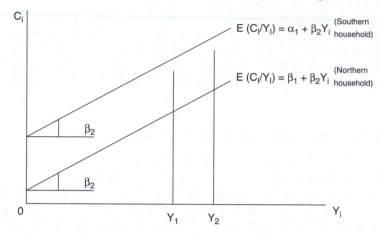

Figure 9.1 Intercept dummies: southern and northern locations.

household is a relevant regressor in cross-section studies of the type we are studying. This is a hypothesis and should be tested later. We have two regression models:

$$C_i = \alpha_1 + \beta_2 Y_i + u_i \qquad \text{southern household} \tag{9.1}$$

$$C_i = \beta_1 + \beta_2 Y_i + u_i \qquad \text{northern household} \tag{9.2}$$

A way of proceeding would be to run two regressions, one for the south and one for the north, then test to see if the difference between α_1 and β_1 is statistically significant. This procedure, however, is seldom done in practice, since it involves two regressions. The 'correct' way is to use the location dummy variable to combine the two models and then run one regression to test the significance of location. This can be done in two ways: regression with or without the intercept term. We consider the regression with the intercept term here and regression without the intercept term in 9.2.

(i) BASE groups: regression with an intercept term

The basic idea here is to combine the two models, using one as a base group. For example, we can use the 'northern household group' as a base/reference group and compare the southern households with this group.

Combined model

Using the northern group as a 'base' group, the location dummy may be used to derive the combined model, as follows:

$$C_i = \beta_1 + \beta_2 Y_i + (\alpha_1 - \beta_1) D_i + u_i; \quad i = 1,....n \tag{9.3}$$

Base group   Deviation from
(northern   the base group
household)

If the household is located in the north, Di = 0, and the regression model will be $C_i = \beta_1 + \beta_2 Y_i + u_i$, which is the northern household group regression equation. If the household is located in the south, then $D_1 = 1$ and the regression model will be $C_i = \alpha_1 + \beta_2 Y_i + u_i$. In this example, the location variable only affects the intercept terms of the model, i.e. the level of autonomous expenditure. The location variables can, however, also influence the slope parameter.

9.1.2 Dummy variable trap and multicollinearity problem

Before we go further with this topic, it is important to deal with a key issue concerning the use of dummy variables in regression models. The number of dummy variables should always be one minus the number of categories represented by a qualitative variable. In the above example, the qualitative variable is the location of the household, with two categories: northern households (those living in the north of the country) and southern households (those living in the south of the country). Following this rule we need only one location dummy variable, as defined above. If by mistake we introduce two location dummy variables, one for the north and one for the south, we would fall into the so-called *dummy variable trap*. In this situation, the estimation of each individual parameter would not be possible. This is because by introducing two location dummy variables instead of one, we have created a perfect linear relationship between some of the regressors of this model. This type of linear relationship is called perfect multicollinearity, and if this situation arises it would not be possible to estimate each individual parameter separately, rendering the OLS regression meaningless. To illustrate this problem, we introduce below two location dummy variables, as follows:

S_i = 1 if ith observation is a southern household
   = 0 otherwise

and

N_i = 1 if ith observation is a northern household
   = 0 otherwise

The regression model may be specified as follows:

$$C_i = \beta_1 + \beta_2 Y_i + \beta_3 S_i + \beta_4 N_i + u_i$$

When the ith household is from the south, $S_i = 1$ and $N_i = 0$, therefore the intercept term would be $\beta_1 + \beta_3$, therefore neither β_1 nor β_3 can be separately estimated, as what we are estimating is their sum. When the household is from the north, $N_i = 1$ and $S_i = 0$, and in this case the intercept term of the regression model would be $\beta_1 + \beta_4$. Again, we are estimating the sum of two parameters. This is what is meant by the dummy variable trap, where too many dummy variables are introduced into the regression model, making the estimation of each individual parameter impossible. Note that the value of the regressor of the intercept term is always set equal to unity. Also, the sum of $S_i + N_i$ is equal to unity. There is, therefore, a perfect linear relationship (perfect multicollinearity) between the intercept term's regressor and S_i and N_i, as this regressor's value is now equal to the sum of Si and Ni. Estimation of each individual parameter is not possible due to perfect multicollinearity inherent in this regression model.

To avoid the dummy variable trap we have two options:

- Allow for the intercept term in the regression model but use one of the alternatives as a base/reference group. In this case we need to introduce dummy variables for all the other groups. This approach works best in practice as most regression packages require the regression equation to include an intercept term.
  or
- Do not allow for the intercept term (no base/reference group), and introduce dummy variables for each group. This option requires regression without an intercept term. We discuss both of these techniques below.

9.1.3 Location variable affects the intercept term and the slope parameters

It can be argued that not only is the level of autonomous expenditure influenced by the location but also the marginal propensity to consume. In this case, the regression model for each region may be written as follows:

$$C_i = \alpha_1 + \alpha_2 Y_i + u_i \quad \text{southern} \tag{9.4}$$

$$C_i = \beta_1 + \beta_2 Y_i + u_i \quad \text{northern} \tag{9.5}$$

Combined model

Using the northern group as a 'base/reference' group, the location dummy may be used to derive the combined model, as follows:

$$C_i = \beta_1 + \beta_2 Y_i + (\alpha_1 - \beta_1)D_i + (\alpha_2 - \beta_2) D_i Y_i + u_i \tag{9.6}$$

Base group

How does this combined model work? We start with the northern household; in this case $D_i = 0$ and the model is:

$$C_i = \beta_1 + \beta_2 Y_i + u_i \quad \text{northern household / base group} \tag{9.7}$$

If the household is located in the south, $D_i = 1$ and:

$$C_i = \beta_1 + \beta_2 Y_i + (\alpha_1 - \beta_1) + (\alpha_2 - \beta_2)Y_i + u_i \tag{9.8}$$

or, $\quad C_i = \alpha_1 + \alpha_2 Y_i + u_i \quad \text{Southern households} \tag{9.9}$

The combined model may then be estimated by the OLS method using a cross-section data set. The model can be used to test the hypothesis that location makes a difference to household consumption. We can conduct the following test:

9.1.4 Significance tests for location on autonomous expenditure

We set the null hypothesis as:

Ho: $\alpha_1 - \beta_1 = 0$

H_1: $\alpha_1 - \beta_1 \neq 0$

The level of autonomous expenditure is the same for both northern and southern households.

Let $\gamma = \alpha_1 - \beta_1$, where γ is the parameter of the dummy variable, D_i, in the combined equation. The test statistic may be written as:

$$t = \frac{\gamma - \hat{\gamma}}{SE(\hat{\gamma})} \sim t_{n-k} \tag{9.10}$$

To proceed with the test, we estimate the equation by OLS and calculate the value of the 't' statistic. If the calculated value of t falls in the rejection region, we do not reject H_0 at $\alpha = 5\%$, concluding that the difference in the level of autonomous expenditure in the two regions is statistically significant. We conduct a similar test of significance on the slope parameter, $(\alpha_2 - \beta_2)$, to see if there are differences between the marginal propensity to consume in the two regions. Finally, we can conduct a joint test of significance.

H_0: $(\alpha_1 - \beta_1) = 0$; $(\alpha_2 - \beta_2) = 0$

H_1: H_0 is not true

Test statistic:

$$F = \frac{[RSS_R - RSS_U]/d}{RSS_U/(n-k)} \sim F_{d,n-k} \tag{9.11}$$

where RSSR = residual sum of squares of the restricted model, RSS_U = residual sum of squares of the unrestricted model, d is the number of restriction (i.e. d = 2) and n – k is the degrees of freedom of the unrestricted regression equation. To proceed with the test, we need to estimate the unrestricted and the restricted equation, calculate the value of the test statistic and compare the value with the critical value of the test, say at the 5% level of significance; if:

$$F \geq F_{n-k}^{0.05}$$

$$-t_{n-k}^{0.025} \leq t \leq -t_{n-k}^{0.085}$$

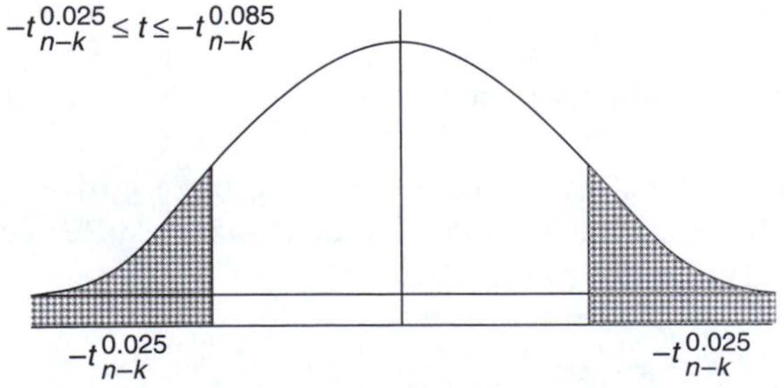

Figure 9.2 Critical region for t-distribution.

we reject the null hypothesis, at $\alpha = 5\%$, concluding that the location of household has a significant impact on household consumption.

9.2 No base group: regression with no intercept term

We can combine various groups, without using a particular group as a base/reference, as follows:

Assuming that location only influences the level of autonomous expenditure, we may write:

$C_i = \alpha_1 + \alpha_2 Y_i + u_i$ southern households

$C_i = \beta_1 + \beta_2 Y_i + u_i$ northern households

There is no base group, so we need to define two dummy variables, one for each group:

Let D_{1i} = 1 if the ith household is located in the north
= 0 otherwise

and

Let D_{2i} = 1 if the ith household is located in the south
= 0 otherwise

The combined regression model may now be written as:

$$C_i = \alpha_1 D_{1i} + \beta_2 Y_i + \beta_1 D_{2i} + u_i \qquad i = 1,..., n \tag{9.12}$$

Let us now see how it works. If a household is located in the north, $D_{1i} = 1$ and $D_{2i} = 0$, we get:

$$C_i = \alpha_1 D_{1i} + \beta_2 Y_i + u_i \qquad \text{northern household} \tag{9.13}$$

If a household is located in the south, $D_{1i} = 0$ and $D_{2i} = 1$, and we get the southern household model. Note that within this framework the regression model is estimated with no intercept term to avoid the dummy variable trap and the problem of perfect multicollinearity discussed above. The lack of an intercept term can cause problems for some regression packages. It is therefore advisable to select a base group and run a model with an intercept term in applied work.

9.3. More than one qualitative variable influencing household consumption expenditure

In addition to the location of households, suppose we have information on more qualitative variables, for example:

1 The gender of the head of household: female; male;

2 the age of the head of household: below 25 years; between 25 and 50; above 50;
3 the level of education of household: no university degrees; university degrees.

There are now, therefore, four qualitative variables, including the location of the household. In practice, we are interested to see whether any one, or all, of the variables influence consumption. To this end we need to introduce a number of dummy variables, as follows:

D_{1i} = 1 if the ith household is located in the south
　　= 0 otherwise
D_{2i} = 1 if the ith head of household is female
　　= 0 otherwise
D_{3i} = 1 if the head of the household is 25 or less
　　= 0 otherwise
D_{4i} = 1 if the age of the head of household is more than 25 but less than 50
　　= 0 otherwise
D_{5i} = 1 if the ith head of household has a degree
　　= 0 otherwise

To proceed we choose a 'base/reference group'. We define the 'base group' to be the one for which the values of each dummy variable is zero. Within this framework the base/reference group household is defined as being located in the north, the head of the household is male, the age of the head of household is 50 years or over, and the head of household has not got a university degree. The regression model of the base group may, therefore, be written as follows:

$$C_i = \beta_1 + \beta_2 Y_i + u_i \qquad\qquad i = 1,...n \qquad\qquad (9.14)$$

The above regression model is then used to estimate the difference between autonomous expenditure for each group of households and that of the base group, as follows:

$$C_i = \beta_1 + \beta_2 Y_i \qquad + (\alpha_1 - \beta_1)D_i \qquad + (\alpha_2 - b_1)D_{i2i}$$

| Base group | The difference in autonomous expenditure due to location | Difference due to gender |

$$+ (\alpha_3 - \beta_1)D_{3i} \qquad + (\alpha_4 - \beta_1)D_{4i} \qquad + (\alpha_5 - \beta_1)D_{5i} + u_i \qquad (9.15)$$

| Difference due to age (less than 25 yrs) | Difference due to age (25 yrs < age < 50 yrs) | Difference due to education level |

Having estimated the model, we undertake 't' and 'F' tests to test the significance of each qualitative variable (t-test) as well as to test their collective significance (F-test).

　　Note that, when we choose a base group, the regression model has an intercept term. Moreover, the number of dummy variables needed in each category is one minus the number of categorical variables. For example, taking into account the three categories of age, as defined above, we need to define only two dummy variables, when a base group is used.

9.4. Seasonal adjustments of data using seasonal dummies

Many economic variables exhibit seasonal variations over time. Therefore, values change with the seasons. For example, consumer expenditure tends to increase in the last quarter of the year, compared with others. Dummy variables are frequently used to capture seasonal components. To illustrate the methodology, we consider the following example.

9.4.1 Example: demand for textiles and seasonal adjustment of data

The demand equation for textiles may be specified as:

$$Y_t = \beta_1 + \beta_2 X_{2t} + \beta_3 X_{3t} + u_t \tag{9.16}$$

where

Y_t = real per capita expenditure on textiles
X_{2t} = real per capita income
X_{3t} = relative prices of textiles

All variables are measured in natural logs. Based on 28 quarterly seasonally unadjusted observations, we obtain the following OLS results:

$$Y_t = 1.370 + 1.140 \; X_{2t} - 0.830 \; X_{3t} \tag{9.17}$$
$$\quad (0.310) \; (0.160) \quad\;\; (0.140)$$

Where the figures in the parentheses are the estimated standard errors.
Residual sum of squares: RSS = 0.75, n = 28 number of observations.
To see if the demand for textiles has seasonal components, we use the fourth quarter of the year as the 'base/reference' period. We then use seasonal dummy variables to compare other quarters with the fourth quarter:

D_{1t} = 1   if t is the 1st quarter
         = 0   otherwise
D_{2t} = 1   if t is the 2nd quarter
         = 0   otherwise
D_{3t} = 1   if t is the 3rd quarter
         = 0   otherwise

The regression model, including these dummy variables is specified as:

$$Y_t = \underbrace{\beta_1 + \beta_2 X_{2t} + \beta_3 X_{3t}}_{\text{Base period}} \quad + \underbrace{(\alpha_1 - \beta_1)D_{1t}}_{\substack{\text{Deviation of the} \\ \text{first quarter from} \\ \text{'base period'}}}$$

$$+ \underbrace{(\alpha_2 - \beta_2)D_{2t}}_{\substack{\text{Second quarter} \\ \text{compared with the} \\ \text{base quarter}}} \qquad + \underbrace{(\alpha_3 - \beta_3)D_{3t}}_{\substack{\text{Third quarter} \\ \text{compared with} \\ \text{the base quarter}}} + u_t \tag{9.18}$$

Now consider how the regression model works. When the observations relate to the first quarter of the year, $D_{1t} = 1$ and $D_{2t} = D_{3t} = 0$; we get the following model, corresponding to the first quarter:

$$Y_t = \alpha_1 + \beta_2 X_{2t} + \beta_3 X_{3t} + u_t \tag{9.19}$$

1st quarter:

$D_{1t} = 1$
$D_{2t} = 0$
$D_{3t} = 0$

The regressions for the second and the third quarter of the year are obtained similarly as:

$$Y_t = \alpha_2 + \beta_2 X_{2t} + \beta_3 X_{3t} + u_t \tag{9.20}$$

2nd quarter:

$D_{1t} = 0$
$D_{2t} = 1$
$D_{3t} = 0$

and

$$Y_t = \alpha_3 + \beta_2 X_{2t} + \beta_3 X_{3t} + u_t \tag{9.21}$$

3rd quarter:

$D_{1t} = 0$
$D_{2t} = 0$
$D_{3t} = 1$

The seasonal regression model was estimated by OLS, generating the following results:

$$Yt = 1.20 \quad + \quad 1.10\, X_{2t} - 0.75 X_{3t} + 0.28\, D_{1t} - 0.38\, D_{2t} - 0.45 D_{3t} + u_t \tag{9.22}$$
$$(0.210) \quad (0.245) \quad (0.0620) \quad (0.028) \quad (0.031) \quad (0.042)$$

RSS = 0.65
n = 28

From these results, the impact of autonomous expenditure on textiles goods in the fourth quarter of the year is estimated at 1.20 per capita. The coefficient of D_{1t}, 0.28, shows how much this figure changes in the first quarter of the year, compared to the fourth quarter. It appears, therefore, that autonomous per capita expenditure in the first quarter, compared to the fourth quarter, rises by 0.28. Then in the second and third quarters, compared to the fourth, it falls by 0.38 and 0.45, respectively. We also notice that each seasonal component is statistically significant. To check if there is a statistically significant seasonal variation in expenditure on textiles, we perform a joint test of significance:

$H_0: (\alpha_1 - \beta_1) = (\alpha_2 - \beta_1) = (\alpha_3 - \beta_1) = 0$

(no seasonal variation)

$H_1: H_0$ is not true

Test statistic:

$$F = \frac{[RSS_R - RSS_U]/d}{RSS_U/(n-k)} \sim F_{d,n-k} \tag{9.23}$$

Substitution of values in (9.23) yields:

$$F = \frac{[0.75 - 0.65]/3}{0.65/[28-6]} \tag{9.24}$$

$$= 14/39$$

$$\cong 0.3$$

Comparing this figure with the theoretical value of:

$$F_{3,22}^{0.05} = 23$$

we cannot reject the null hypothesis. Therefore, there are no seasonal effects present in the data. Note, in this example, seasonal variation is assumed to only impact the intercept term, leaving slope parameters unchanged over time.

9.5 Pooling cross-section data with time series data

Occasionally, in order to improve the precision of the parameter estimates, it is useful to combine various data sets to increase the number of observations. For example, suppose we have a cross-sectional data set for three years on the annual consumption expenditure of n households, randomly selected from a large population, as follows:

Data set on consumption and income year one: 1 . . . n observations on a group of randomly selected households.

Date set on consumption and income year two: 1 . . . n observations on a group of randomly selected households.

Data set on consumption and income year three: 1 . . . n observations on a group of randomly selected households.

There are n cross-section data over three years. If n is small, estimation on the basis of cross-section data alone is not possible. Pooling cross-section data with time series data is a simple method to increase the number of observations and, hence, the degrees of freedom of the regression. Note that the households are randomly selected and therefore are not the same n households for each year. If they were the same households, the data set is called a panel data set, requiring panel data regression. This type of regression will be discussed in Chapter 10. Normally, the precision of OLS estimators will improve as more observations are used in the estimation. We can increase the number of observations and, hence, improve degrees of freedom by pooling random samples drawn from the same population at different points in time. This is frequently done in practice by introducing dummy variables in the regression models. Typically, to pool a cross-section data set with a time series data set it is assumed that the intercept term of the regression model changes, both across households and over time, whilst the slope parameters remain constant. Within this framework, to pool the above data sets we select one household and one year as the base, and compare all the other households with the base household group, as follows:

$$C_{it} = \beta_1 + \beta_2 Y_{it} + \alpha_2 z_{2t} + \alpha_3 z_{3t} + \ldots + \alpha_{10} z_{nt} + \gamma_2 d_{i2} + \gamma_3 d_{i3} + u_{it} \tag{9.25}$$

Where the dummy variables are defined as:

$z_{it} = 1$ for i = 2, . . ., n

   = 0 otherwise

and

$d_{it} = 1$ for t = 2,3

   = 0 otherwise $\tag{9.26}$

C_{it} and Y_{it} are, respectively, consumption and income of the *i*th household in period t. In this regression model a randomly selected cross-section data set consisting of n observations are being pooled with the time series data to increase the number of observations via the dummy variable technique. Note that household one is the base group and the changes in the intercept term across households and time are compared to this household's intercept term β_1. The number of observations is now n × 3 = 3n for this pooled regression model.

9.6 Using dummy variables to test for parameter stability

The dummy variable technique can be used to test for a structural break and parameter stability, providing a simple alternative to the Chow test introduced in Chapter 6. To illustrate this method we consider the following:
   Consumption-income model:

for the period t = 1981–1996

$$C_t = \alpha + \beta Y_t + u_t \tag{9.27}$$

for the period t = 1998–2011

$$C_t = \gamma + \delta Y_t + u_t \tag{9.28}$$

Assuming that all standard conditions are satisfied.
   It is thought that a structural break might have occurred in the economy in 1997, changing both intercept term and slope parameters of the relationship, as shown above. To test for the structural break and parameter stability, we use one of the above regression models as the base regression and introduce one dummy variable to combine the two periods, as follows:

Combined model

$$C_t = \alpha + \beta Y_t + (\gamma - \alpha)D_t + (\delta - \beta) D_t Y_t + u_t \qquad (9.29)$$

$D_t = 1$ for observations over the period 1998–2011
$\quad = 0$ otherwise (for observations 1981–1996)

The above regression model may be used to test for the parameter stability, as follows:

$$H_0:(\alpha - \gamma) = (\beta - \delta) = 0$$
$$H_1: H_0 \text{ is not true} \qquad (9.30)$$

The test statistic is the familiar F-test for testing linear restrictions on the parameters of the regression model:

$$F = \frac{[RSS_R - RSS_U]/d}{RSS_U /(n-k)} \sim Fd, n-k \qquad (9.31)$$

Decision rule: if the F-test value is greater than the corresponding critical value at a pre-set level of significance, reject the null, concluding that the break occurred in 1997. Note that the number of restrictions is only two, as there are two restrictions on the parameters of the combined model. This procedure provides a simple alternative to the Chow test, and is used frequently in practice to test for structural breaks in the time series and to check the parameters' stability.

9.7 A summary of key issues

- Dummy variables are used in regression models to capture the influence of qualitative variables and the occurrence of sudden events in regression analysis.
- Dummy variables are particularly useful for estimating seasonal effects and pooling time series data with cross-section data.
- Dummy variables can be introduced in regression models to test restrictions on the parameters, including testing for the parameter stability. This technique provides a simple alternative to the Chow test.
- When using dummy variables it is advisable to use one category as a base or reference group, and introduce dummy variables for other groups. In this way the problem of the dummy variable trap and perfect multicollinearity are avoided.

Review questions

1 Explain how dummy variables may be employed in regression models to account for the impact of qualitative variables on the dependent variables. Give examples to illustrate your answer.
2 Explain what you understand by the dummy variable trap. How can this problem be avoided in practice?
3 It is thought that the stock prices are relatively low on Mondays, the so-called 'Monday effect'. Explain how this effect on stock prices might be captured via the dummy variable technique.

4   Explain how dummy variables might be employed to capture seasonal variations in the data. Why are there normally only three seasonal dummies used when there are four seasons?

5   Give an example and demonstrate the use of dummy variables for testing parameter stability and for structural break in regression models.

10 Qualitative response regression models

INTRODUCTION

In recent years large-scale cross-section data sets containing several hundred and even thousands of observations on the characteristics of individuals, firms and even towns/cities/regions have become available. The availability of this type of data, and software advances, has made it possible for practitioners to perform empirical investigations in the fields of social science, economics and marketing. A distinguishing feature of this type of investigation involving regression models is that the dependent variable is specified as a qualitative variable, representing the response of an individual, or firm, to particular questions. For example, in an investigation on the incidence of R&D activities by firms, a firm is either undertaking R&D activities, or not, given its characteristics (e.g. sales, exports, etc.) The dependent variable, the R&D status of the firm, is dichotomous, representing the response of the firm to the question: are you undertaking R&D activities? The response is either positive or negative. The dependent variable is therefore a categorical variable, represented by a dummy variable taking two values: if the answer is positive, it takes a value of one, otherwise it takes a value of zero. Alternatively, in a study of incidence of private health insurance, using a large sample of cross-section of data on the characteristics of individuals, an individual either has private health insurance, or not, given his or her characteristics (e.g. income, occupation, age, etc.). The question being asked of each individual is: do you have private health insurance? The response is either positive or negative. If it is found to be positive, the dependent variable, the insurance ownership status of an individual, takes a value of one, otherwise it takes a value of zero. In these examples, the dependent variable is defined on the characteristics of individuals/firms. It is a dichotomous qualitative variable eliciting a 'yes' or a 'no' response. Qualitative response models lead to a number of interesting problems concerning estimation, interpretation and analysis. In this introductory chapter we deal with binary qualitative dependent variable regression models, as well as multinomial and ordered logit regression models.

Key topics

- The linear probability model (LPM)
- The logit and probit models
- The multinomial logit model
- The ordered logit/probit models

10.1 The linear probability model (LPM)

We introduce the LPM by considering the incidence of private health ownership.

Let Y = an individual's status of private health insurance. The binary response may be presented as follows:

if Y_i = 1   the ith individual has private health insurance
      = 0   the ith individual does not have private health insurance

It is assumed that Y depends on income, thus:

$$Y_i = \beta_1 + \beta_2 X_i$$

In addition, we introduce a disturbance term u_i, to take into account the influence of other factors, so:

$$Y_i = \beta_1 + \beta_2 X_i + u_i \qquad (10.1)$$

where $E(u_i) = 0$, Var $(u_i) = \delta^2$, cov = $(u_i \, u_j) = 0$ for all i and j

A model, where a dichotomous dependent variable is expressed as a linear function of one, or a number of regressors, is called a linear probability model. This is because the expected value of Y_i is the conditional probability that the individual has private health insurance (i.e. $Y_1 = 1$, given the individual's income (given x_i)). To see this, let P_i = probability that $Y_i = 1$ (the response is positive). In this case, $1 - P_i$ = probability that $Y_i = 0$, the response is negative. The probability distribution of Y_i is:

Y_i	Probability
$Y_i = 1$	P_i
$Y_i = 0$	$1-P_i$

The mathematical expectation of Y_i is therefore: $E(Y_i/X_i) = P_i$, hence the conditional expectation of Y_i, given X_i is the probability of a positive response, given income. Note also that, under $E(u_i) = 0$, using LPM, we have:

$$E\left(Y_i/X_i\right) = \beta_1 + \beta_2 X_i \qquad (10.2)$$

Therefore, within a LPM model, we have:

$$E\left(Y_i / X_i\right) = \beta_1 + \beta_2 X_i = P_i \qquad (10.3)$$

In a LPM, a key objective is to estimate the conditional probability of a positive response of an event occurring, given certain characteristics. This is done by estimating two unknown parameters, β_1 and β_2. In this specification, the slope parameter shows the impact of a one unit change in the individual's income on the probability of the individual having private health insurance.

10.1.1 Problems associated with the LPM

Given a LPM model, $Y_i = \beta_1 + \beta_2 X_i + u_i$, our aim is to estimate the conditional probability of a positive response. That is, $P_i = E(Y_1 = 1) = \beta_1 + \beta_2 X_i$;

where $0 \leq P_i \leq 1$.

This is done by estimating β_1 and β_2, using data on X_i and Y_i. However, there is no mechanism in the model to ensure that the estimated probabilities obtained from the estimate of β_1 and β_2 are within the permissible range of zero and one. This is an obvious problem in the use of LPMs. In addition, the assumption of linearity may be considered to be rather unrealistic. To see this, notice that β_2 can be expressed as:

$$\beta_2 = \Delta P_i / \Delta X_i$$

That is, β_2 measures the change in probability due to a unit change in income. Since parameter β_2 is a constant, the change in the probability, at all levels of income, is in fact assumed to be constant. This feature is rather unrealistic. At low levels of income, up to a certain level of income, it is reasonable to assume that incremental changes in income have no effect on the probability. Once income reaches a certain level, however, there is a strong probability that it will change at an increasing rate with income. Once a certain high level of income is reached, there is no effect on the probability as a result of the change in income. This type of non-linear relationship between the probability P_i and income may be depicted as follows:

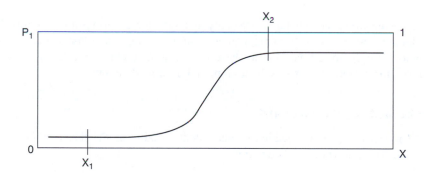

Figure 10.1 Non-linear probabilities of health insurance on income.

The S-shaped curve depicted in Figure 10.1 can be approximated mathematically by a logistical function as:

$$P_i = E(Y_i = 1) = 1/(1 + e^{-(\beta_1 + \beta_2 X_i)})$$

For all values of X_i, the logistical function falls between zero and one. Given this property and non-linearity, the logistical function is frequently used to estimate conditional probabilities in models involving qualitative dependent variables.

In addition to the above problems, another issue arises with LPMs.

10.1.2 Heteroscedasticity

LPM is associated with heteroscedasticity in the disturbance term. In other words, under LPM specification, the distribution of disturbance terms of the model are inevitably heteroscedastic. The estimation of the model by OLS therefore results in inefficient estimators. To see why the disturbance term is heteroscedastic, we derive the variance:

The disturbance term takes only two values with the following probabilities:

when $Y_i = 1$

$$u_i = 1 - \beta_1 - \beta_2 X_i \qquad\qquad \text{Probability}\left(P_i\right) \qquad\qquad (10.4)$$

when $Y_i = 0$

$$u_i = -\beta_1 - \beta_2 X_i \qquad\qquad \text{Probability}\left(1 - P_i\right) \qquad\qquad (10.5)$$

$$\text{Var}(u_i) = (1 - \beta_1 - \beta_2 X_i)^2 P_i + (-\beta_1 - \beta_2 X_i)^2 (1 - P_i)$$

Also, we know that $P_i = E(Y_i/X_i) = \beta_1 + \beta_2 X_i$

Substitution for P_i into the above, results in:

$$\begin{aligned}
\text{Var}\left(u_i\right) &= (1 - \beta_1 - \beta_2 X_i)^2(\beta_1 + \beta_2 X_i) + (-\beta_1 - \beta_2 X_i)^2(1 - \beta_1 - \beta_2 X_i) \\
&= (1 - \beta_1 - \beta_2 X_i)(\beta_1 + \beta_2 X_i)[1 - \beta_1 - \beta_2 X_{i+} \beta_1 + \beta_2 X_i] \qquad (10.6) \\
&= \left(1 - P_i\right)P_i \qquad \textit{Heteroscedastic}
\end{aligned}$$

In addition to the presence of heteroscedasticity, the disturbance term is not normally distributed and, unless large observations are available, statistical tests based on a normal distribution cannot be used in LPMs. Due to these problems inherent in the LPM, in practical applications the preferred choice is the logit model described below:

10.2 The logit regression model

The logit model is a popular qualitative dependent variable model that is widely used in practice. The attractions of the model are:

1   Being based on the logistical curve, for all values of the regressors, the value of the dependent variable (the probability of positive response) falls between zero and one.
2   The probability function is a non-linear function following a logistical curve. This is a more realistic pattern of change in the probability when compared to LPMs.
3   The estimation of the logit model is quick and easy and there are many packages available for the estimation of logit-type models (SHAZAM, EViews, LIMDEP, Microfit 4/5).

10.2.1 Estimation of the logit model

To illustrate the technique, we consider the example of private health insurance once again. We have:

$$P_i = P_i(Y_i = 1) = E(Y_i / X_i) = 1/(1 + e^{-(\beta_1 + \beta_2 X_i)}) \tag{10.7}$$

Equation (10.7) gives the probability of a positive response. Under this specification, the probability of a negative response is:

$$1 - P_i = 1 - (1/(1 + e^{-(\beta_1 + \beta_2 X_i)})) = e^{-(\beta_1 + \beta_2 X_i)} / (1 + e^{-(\beta_1 + \beta_2 X_i)}) \tag{10.8}$$

Division of P_i by $1 - P_i$ gives the odds ratio in favour of an individual possessing private health insurance, as follows:

$$\text{odds ratio} = P_i / (1 - P_i) = e^{\beta_1 + \beta_2 X_i} \tag{10.9}$$

To estimate the model, we take the natural log of both sides, hence:

$$\log (P_i / 1 - P_i) = \log e^{\beta_1 + \beta_2 X_i} \tag{10.10}$$

or

$$L_i = \log(P_i / 1 - P_i) = \beta_1 + \beta_2 X_i \tag{10.11}$$

where, L_i is the logit function. In practice, the model is usually estimated by maximum likelihood methods. However, in principle, it may be estimated by the OLS method, provided that a large data set is available. To illustrate the OLS estimation using group data, we use the following steps:

Step 1 A large cross-section data set is typically collected via questionnaires. The data is arranged into different categories of income.

Step 2 For each category, the number of people with a positive response to the binary question are recorded. To generate estimates/proxies for P_i, the probability of a positive response, this number is then divided by the total number of respondents in each income category.

Step 3 These calculated probabilities are then used in the regression model to allow estimation. This procedure is shown below:

Income category	N	Number of people with positive response	Frequency
X_1	N_1	n_1	$P_1 = n_1/N_1$
X_2	N_2	n_2	$P_2 = n_2/N_2$
....	....	....	....
....	....	....	....
	....	....	....

Step 4 The relative frequencies from the above are used as proxies for the probabilities in the logit model:

$$L_i = \ln\left(P_i / 1 - P_i\right) = \beta_1 + \beta_2 X_i + u_i; \qquad \text{for } i = 1, 2 \ldots n \qquad (10.12)$$

Where u_i is a disturbance term added to (10.11) to capture the net influence of variables other than income on the dependent variable. Given a large data set, the distribution of the disturbance term can be shown to approach a normal distribution, as follows:

$$u_i \sim N\left\{0, 1 / \left[N_1 P_i \left(1 - P_i\right)\right]\right\} \qquad (10.13)$$

Note that the variance of this distribution changes with each observation, and the assumption of homoscedasticity cannot be maintained. To generate efficient estimates, the logit model is usually divided by $1/\ [N_1 P_i(1 - P_i)]$ (multiply the dependent/independent variable by $N_1 P_i(1 - P_i)$), using estimated relative frequencies instead of the probabilities. This procedure usually succeeds in removing heteroscedasticity. The model can then be estimated by the OLS method.

The estimated slope coefficient shows the impact of a unit change in a regressor (a partial change if there is more than one regressor) on the log of odds ratio. This concept, however, is seldom used in applied work as the focus of attention in many studies is on the estimated conditional probabilities. Computing packages (e.g. Microfit, EViews) routinely report the fitted conditional probabilities associated with any given set of values of the regressors. The use of these fitted values will be illustrated in an example of logit model estimation given below.

10.3 The probit/normit model

The logit model provides a convenient way of estimating the dummy dependent variable models. This model is based on the cumulative logistical function, which is S-shaped and falls between zero and one. Another cumulated density function (CDF), which has similar characteristics to those of a logistical function, is the normal cumulative density function. This is another S-shaped curve lying between zero and one. The normal CDF is also frequently used by practitioners for estimation of the dummy dependent variable models. The dummy dependent variable regression models based on the normal cumulative density function are called 'probit' or, sometimes, 'normit' models. Thus, for the incidence of private health insurance, the corresponding normal cumulative density function may be written as:

$$P_i = pr(y_i = 1) = \frac{1}{\sqrt{2\pi}} \int_{-\infty}^{\beta + \beta_2 x_i} e^{-t^2/2} dt \qquad (10.14)$$

where t is a standardised normal variable that is $t \sim n(0,1)$, P_i = probability of a positive response, given X_i. The Figure 10.2 presents a normal CDF, which is depicted against a logistical CDF.

As seen in Figure 10.2, there is little difference between the two CDFs. Normally, a logit model has flatter tails compared to probit models. That is, the conditional probability P_i approaches one or zero at a slower rate in logit models compared to probit models. Given

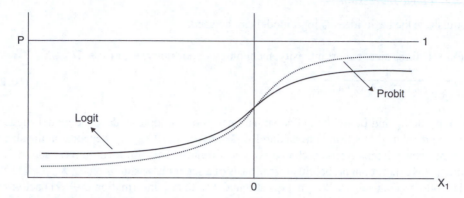

Figure 10.2 A normal CDF plotted against a logistical CDF.

slight differences between the two CDFs, the choice between probit and logit models is essentially a matter of convenience.

10.4 Logit/probit regression models in practice

In regressions involving a binary response/dichotomous dependent variable, logit/probit models are used to estimate the conditional probability that a particular characteristic is present. For example, in a study of whether or not a firm is engaged in research and development (R&D) activities, we can identify the main characteristics, and, based on these estimates, the conditional probability that a firm is active in R&D. To illustrate the methodology, we consider the following example:

The dependent variable:

$y_i = 1$ if the ith firm is engaged in R&D
$y_i = 0$ otherwise

In order to specify a regression model, we need to use theory to identify the key factors influencing a firm's R&D activities. According to theoretical reasoning (see, for example, Seddighi and Hunly (2007)), some of these factors may be listed as:

- X_1 = firm size. We distinguish between small, medium and large firms, so:
  large firms are where turnover/sales exceeds $1 million
  medium firms are where turnover/sales exceeds $100,000
  small firms are where turnover/sales are less than $100,000
- X_2 = export intensity. We distinguish the following categories:
  high: where 50%, or more, of sales are for exports
  medium: where export intensity is between 10–50% of sales
  low: where export intensity is less than 10% (less than 10% of sales are exported)
- X_3 = technological opportunity. Here we consider the following two categories:
  high: where a firm operates in a high/modern technological sector (software firms, etc.)
  low: where a firm operates in a low technological sector (metal work, etc.)

10.4.1 A logic regression

To illustrate the basic ideas, a logit model can be used:

$$Pr\ (Y_i = 1/\ \text{firms size, export intensity, technology opportunity}) = pr\ (Y_i = 1/X_1, X_2, X_3) = \frac{1}{1+e^{-(\beta_0 + \beta_1 X_{ii} + \beta_2 X_{2i} + \beta_3 X_{3i})}} \tag{10.15}$$

where β_0, β_1, β_2, and β_3 are the unknown parameters of the logit model. The model suggests that the probability of a firm undertaking R&D activities, $Pr\ (Y_i = 1)$, depends on the size of the firm, export intensity and technological opportunity. The aim of the investigation is to estimate this conditional probability on the basis of a set of observations on Y_i, X_{ii}, X_{2i} and X_{3i}.

To collect a data set, we design a questionnaire to obtain information on R&D activities, size of firm, export intensity and technological opportunities. By doing this we obtain sample data of, say 130 firms, containing information on these variables. Given that all regressors are categorical variables, we assign the following values to each variable as:

- X_{1i} = 1 if firm is small
  = 2 if firm is medium
  = 3 if firm is large
- X_{2i} = 1 if export intensity is low
  = 2 if export intensity is medium
  = 3 if export intensity is high
- X_{3i} = 1 if in a low technology sector
  = 2 if in a high technology sector

Finally:

- Y_i = 1 if firm is R&D active
  = 0 if firm is not R&D active

There are $3 \times 3 \times 2 = 18$ different types of firm. For each type we calculate the conditional probability of a firm being engaged in R&D activities.

In practice, the estimation is carried out using the likelihood method via a regression package, such as Microfit 4/5, EViews or LIMDEP. A typical output for our example may be listed as follows:

Table 10.1 Regression results

Variable/parameter	Estimated coefficient	Standard error	t-ratio
X_1: β_1	0.0458	0.34055	0.13477
X_2: β_2	1.1050	0.34939	3.1628
X_3: β_3	1.3548	0.48041	2.8201
constant: β_0	−4.7311	0.98294	−4.8132

We notice that X_2 and X_3 are statistically significant (relatively high t-ratios), whereas X_1 appears to be statistically insignificant. However, recall that a firm is identified by all three variables jointly. Therefore, we are interested in the estimates of all slope coefficients

(β_1, β_2, β_3) rather than each individual coefficient. To test for the joint significance of the regressors, a likelihood ratio (LR) test is usually performed in logit/probit regression. This test statistic has a chi-squared distribution with a degrees of freedom equal to the number of regressors of the model. An appropriate regression software package (e.g. Microfit 4/5 LIMDEP, EViews) routinely reports the LR test value. In the above example, the LR = 16.32 and Df = 3. The 5% critical value of the test is 12.83, we can, therefore, reject the null hypothesis and conclude that the three regressors are jointly significant. The estimated coefficients are then used in the logit model to generate predicted probabilities. In practical applications, the change in the probability of a positive response due to a unit change in any one of the regressors is usually calculated via the difference in the corresponding fitted probabilities reported by the regression packages. Table 10.2 presents the predicted probabilities of a selection of firms corresponding to the above example.

Table 10.2 Logit probability of R&D activity and firm characteristics

Firm	Probability	X_1			X_2			X_3		
		3	2	1	3	2	1	3	2	1
1	0.80710	*			*				*	
2	0.58085	*				*			*	
3	0.56964		*				*		*	
4	0.51912	*			*					*
5	0.50765		*		*					*
6	0.49618			*	*					*
7	0.31439			*			*		*	
8	0.10588			*			*			*
9	0.10161		*				*			*
10	0.09749		*				*			*

According to these results, firms with the highest predicted probability of undertaking R&D are those with high turnovers, high export intensities and high technological opportunity (firm 1). Firms with low turnovers, low export intensity and low technological opportunity, have the lowest predicted probability of undertaking R&D (only 9%). Analysing the top six firms, that is those firms with a predicted probability of approximately 50% and more, it can be seen that all such firms have high or medium export intensities, while five have high sales and three operate within a high technological environment. The analysis clearly identifies exporting firms as being likely to be involved in R&D activities.

With reference to the *goodness of fit* measure, because the logit/probit models are non-linear in the parameters, the conventional coefficient of determination is not applicable. Unfortunately, there is no universally accepted measure of goodness of fit for these type of models. Most computing packages routinely report a pseudo R-squared value called the *McFadden R-squared*, which ranges between 0 and 1, with a value close to unity indicating a good fit. In the above example, this measure of goodness of fit is reported at 0.5612, indicating a fairly good fit, according to this measure.

In most applications, the logit and probit models typically generate similar results. The probit results for this example are essentially the same. If a researcher considers that movement towards a probability of one or zero, after certain values of the regressors have been reached, occurs quickly, then a probit model provides a better approximation to the data generation process. Otherwise, the logit model is preferred and more commonly used in practice.

10.5 Multi-response qualitative dependent variable regression models

In the above examples the dependent variable was specified as a binary variable representing choice between two alternatives. In many applications there are more than two options facing economic units, such as individuals, household, firms and governments. Qualitative dependent variable models representing the choice between more than two options facing an economic agent are called multi-response/polychotomous dependent variable models. In applying this type of model, the focus is on estimating the probability of choosing a particular option given the economic agent's key characteristics. The estimation is carried out via generalised logit/probit models; in practice, the logit specification is the preferred choice, as in the case of binary response models. Depending on the type of qualitative data collected, these regression models go under the names of *multinomial logit* and *ordered logit/probit* models. To introduce some of the key ideas, we consider the following examples:

10.5.1 Multinomial logit regression

We begin by considering some simple examples:

- R&D and firms clustering
  Firms are often faced with choosing between various options regarding the type of R&D activities to carry out, as follows:
  Option 1. R&D on product development
  Option 2. R&D on process development
  Option 3. R&D on basic research
  Option 4. R&D on an informal basis
  Given information on a set of firms' characteristics (sales, types of activity and products, extent of competition faced by the firm, exporting activities, etc.) and a large data set, one can estimate the probability of a firm choosing one of the above options for its R&D activity. This type of information is often reviewed by policy makers to help establish various kinds of clusters of firms, to help to enhance firms' R&D efforts, and, hence, their growth.
- Marketing tourism destination choices
  One of the main areas of applications of multinomial logit models is in the area of consumer marketing. In this type of study, typically, an individual faces a number of options, and the aim is to estimate the probability that an individual with a certain set of characteristics chooses one of the available options. To illustrate, suppose an individual can choose between three holiday destinations, as follows:
  Option 1. Destination A
  Option 2. Destination B
  Option 3. Destination C
  Suppose the individual characteristic influencing the decision making process is the individual's *income*. The aim is to estimate the probability that the individual chooses each one of the available options, given his/her level of income. In a marketing exercise of this kind, knowledge of the estimated conditional probabilities are used for targeting advertisement on individuals with a comparatively high probability of choosing any one of the available options. For example, if it is found that individuals with *income* = £30,000 per annum

choose option 1, with the fitted probability of 35%, option 2 with the fitted probability of 25%, and option 3 with the fitted probability of 40%, then clearly option 3 is the preferred choice for this group of individuals. This type of information is of significant potential value in target marketing and advertising campaigns for tourism destination options.

10.5.2 Specification and estimation

To go a bit further, touching on the model's specification and estimation, using the above example, we define:

P_{ij} = P(individual i chooses Option j); j = 1,2 and 3.

where P_{ij} is the probability that individual i chooses Option j; and three binary dummy variables, Y_{i1}, Y_{i2}, and Y_{i3}, as follows:

Y_{i1} = 1 if individual i chooses Option 1; Y_{i2} = 0 and Y_{i3} = 0
Y_{i2} = 1 if individual i chooses Option 2; Y_{i1} = 0 and Y_{i3} = 0
Y_{i3} = 1 if individual i chooses Option 3; Y_{i1} = 0 and Y_{i2} = 0

The probability that individual i chooses each one of the above options, within the framework of a multinomial logit, can be expressed as follows:

Probability of choosing Option 1:

$$P_{i1} = 1/1 + exp[\alpha + \beta xi] + exp[\gamma + \delta xi], \qquad (10.16)$$

Where x_i = individual *i*th income.

Probability of choosing Option 2:

$$P_{i2} = \frac{exp(\alpha + \beta xi)}{1 + exp(\alpha + \beta xi) exp(\gamma + \delta xi)} \qquad (10.17)$$

and

Probability of choosing option 3:

$$P_{i3} = \frac{exp(\gamma + \delta xi)}{1 + exp(\alpha + \beta xi) exp(\gamma + \delta xi)} \qquad (10.18)$$

Notice that parameters α *and* β are specific to choosing Option 2 and parameters γ *and* δ are specific to choosing Option 3. The parameters for choosing Option 1 is set to zero to ensure that $P_{i1} + P_{i2} + P_{i3} = 1$ (the sum of probabilities must add up to unity). The objective is to estimate the above unknown parameters on the basis of a large sample of data on individuals and their income: X_i. The estimation is carried out via the maximum likelihood method (ML) using computer software (e.g. LIMDEP). Once the parameters are estimated, the fitted probabilities are then generated for comparison and target marketing, as explained above.

10.6 Ordered logit/probit regression models

Often when collecting survey data via questionnaires a Likert Scale (a scale used to indicate the extent of preferences) is used to collect information on the opinion of people concerning a particular issue or option. For example, when collecting data on the quality of provision of a service via questionnaires, for example, on banking services, hotel services, etc., a customer is typically asked to select one of the following options about the service quality:

Question/statement: I find the quality of service to be good.

Options:

1   Strongly disagree
2   Disagree
3   Neutral
4   Agree
5   Strongly agree

For the purpose of computer modelling, numerical data/codes are assigned to each option. These numerical values are ordinal only, reflecting the ranking of each option. This type of ordinal data, based on a Likert scale, are frequently collected via surveys seeking opinions on various issues and subjects. They are used in quality improvement surveys, marketing surveys, by credit rating agencies, by government agencies, and by financial organisations.

10.6.1 Modelling ordered/ranked data: some basic ideas

To model this type of ranked data we need a data generation process, that is, we need to explain how a typical individual ranks and chooses a particular option. The conventional method for this purpose is based on the consumer choice theory and is borrowed from microeconomics. The basic idea is this: in assigning ranking position to each alternative, an individual has and uses a utility index. This index is, of course, unobservable and depends on a set of variables pertinent to the individual. Furthermore, this utility index converts individual preferences into ranking positions for various options facing the individual.

To illustrate this idea, let us assume that there is only one explanatory variable, *time*, which is important to the individual when the quality of a banking service is to be ranked. *Time* is measured in minutes, showing the time taken for provision of a banking service. For the purpose of modelling, the ith individual utility index may be expressed as follows:

$$Y_i^* = \alpha \left(TIME \right)_i + u_i \qquad \text{for } i = 1, 2\ldots \qquad (10.19)$$

where Y* is the unobservable utility index (this type of unobservable variable is called a latent variable), α is an unknown parameter, and u is a disturbance term. The relationship suggests that in ranking the quality of service, the individual takes into consideration the time taken to provide the service, as well as some other less important random factors captured by the error term, u. Notice that this is not a regression model, as the dependent variable is not observable. To make this type of conceptual model operational, it is then assumed that each option is chosen according to some threshold values. Given that in the above example the individual is faced with five options, four threshold values in minutes, T1, T2, T3 and T4, may be specific, as follows:

Option 1 is chosen $\left(\text{strongly disagree}\right)$ if $Y^* \geq T4$

Option 2 is chosen $\left(\text{disagree}\right)$ if $T3 \leq Y^* < T4$

Option 3 is chosen $\left(\text{neutral}\right)$ if $T2 \leq Y* < T3$ (1.20)

Option 4 is chosen $\left(\text{agree}\right)$ if $T1 \leq Y* < T2$

Option 5 is chosen $\left(\text{strongly agree}\right)$ if $Y* < T1$

In principle, the probability of each of the above options can be calculated, provided the distribution of the Y* or the error term is known. In applied work, practitioners either assume a standard normal distribution or a logistic distribution for the latent variable in this type of modelling. The ordered probit model is based on the standard normal distribution, while the ordered logit model uses a logistic distribution as its foundation. Both models tend to produce very similar results. Estimation is carried out using maximum likelihood estimation via appropriate software, such as LIMDEP. On the basis of a large data set, this procedure generates the estimates of the unknown threshold parameters, T1, T2, T3 and T4, as well as the utility index parameter, α, such that the corresponding likelihood function is maximised. Once these parameters are estimated, one can determine the thresholds for various available options and accordingly improve the quality of the provision of a service. For example, suppose in the above example we estimate that T1 = 10, T2 = 15, T3 = 25 and T4 = 45 minutes. To improve service quality, attention should be on reducing the time taken to provide the service to below the T2 level of 15 minutes. This type of information enables service providers to improve the quality of service provision, on a systematic cost-based framework.

The qualitative dependent variable models in different forms have become increasingly more popular in recent years. This is because large-scale survey data on all sorts of issues are nowadays collected to help decision-making processes. In addition, regression packages, such as LIMDEP, are now readily available, and are capable of handling this type of data set and modelling, allowing estimation and inference to be carried out efficiently and with relative ease.

10.7 A summary of key issues

- Qualitative dependent variable regression models are used with large-scale cross-sectional data sets normally collected via questionnaires and surveys.
- In these types of models, the dependent variable is a categorical variable representing the economic unit's response to a particular question being asked. The response can be binary, more than two categories (multi-response), or an ordered response.
- Binary response models are typically estimated by the logit/probit regression models. The LPM is not a popular choice because of problems inherent in this linear specification.
- Dummy variables are used to specify the dependent variable of the multi-response and ordered logit models. The focus is on estimating the conditional probability of a particular response, given economic unit characteristics.
- Maximum likelihood methods are used to estimate the qualitative response models. The estimation is typically carried out with a specialist regression package, for example, LIMDEP.

Review questions

1 What are the shortcomings of the LPM? Under what circumstances would you employ this model?
2 Explain how a logit model might be estimated. How would you interpret the regression results of a logit model?
3 Explain the main differences between a logit model and a probit model.
4 Explain how an ordered logit model might be constructed to improve the provision of teaching quality in a university of your own choice.
5 Give examples of each of the following models:

   a   binary logit regression model
   b   multinomial logit regression model
   c   ordered/ranked logit regression model.

In each case explain how you would specify and estimate a regression model (assume a large cross-section data set for each case).

11　Panel data regression models

INTRODUCTION

Panel data sets provide a rich environment for researchers to investigate issues which could not be studied in either cross-sectional or time series settings alone. A key attribute of this type of data is that it provides a methodology to correct for the omitted variable problem inherent in cross-sectional data analysis. In a typical panel data study there are a large number of cross-sectional units, for example, a large number of individuals, firms or even regions/countries, and only a few periods of time. Researchers collect data on the characteristics of the cross-sectional units over a relatively short period of time, to investigate changes in behaviour or potential of a typical cross-section unit. A key feature of the panel data set is that it provides *observation over time on the same cross-sectional units*. This is in contrast to a pooled cross-section/time series data set, discussed in Chapter 9, where, typically, a randomly selected cross-section data set is observed a number of times over time, in order to increase the number of observations and to improve the degrees of freedom of the regression. This chapter focuses discussion on panel data of the type described above, providing an introduction to their applications and estimation in practice.

Key topics

- The nature of panel data and its applications
- Using panel data to correct for the omitted variable problem
- The fixed-effects regression models
- The random-effects regression models
- Panel data regression in practice

11.1　Examples of panel data regression

11.1.1　Earning potential of university graduates

In a panel study of earning potential of university graduates, researchers collect data on the characteristics of a large number of graduates, say 1,000. These characteristics can include gender, age, type of degree, employment, etc. These graduates are then followed over time (usually over a short span of time, i.e. 1–3 years). The researchers then collect data on the graduates' earnings, promotions, etc., to investigate the impact of each one of the above characteristics on earning potential. Such a panel data set consists of

1,000 observations on the same cross-sectional units (graduates), over a relatively short period of time, 1–3 years.

11.1.2 Effectiveness of negative income tax

A frequently cited panel data study is a series of investigations on the effectiveness of negative income tax in the USA in the early 1970s. In this type of panel data investigation, researchers collected data on thousands of individuals/families over 8–13 quarters. The information included in the panel data consisted of individuals' characteristics, including consumption expenditure, age, gender, number of children, etc. The focus of the investigation was whether or not negative income tax had influenced the consumption expenditure of a typical individual/family over time.

11.1.3 The neoclassical growth theory and the 'convergence hypothesis'

A frequently debated topic in neoclassical growth theory is the issue of convergence, first put forward by Solow (1956). According to the convergence hypothesis, the per capita growth rate of GDP of the poorer nations will converge to that of richer nations over time. In particular, the lower the initial level of productivity, the faster the economy will grow. This process will eventually result in an absolute convergence. To test this hypothesis one needs a panel data set consisting of a sample of a large number of countries over a specific period of time. The panel data set provides information on the characteristics of a large number of countries (the cross-sectional units) over a specific period of time. The convergence hypothesis cannot be investigated either in cross-sectional or time series settings alone.

11.1.4 Firms' R&D expenditure

A panel data set consisting of a large number of firms can be used to investigate factors influencing the rate of growth of the firms' R&D expenditure. Such a panel data set could consist of observations on the characteristics of a large number of firms over a relatively short period of time, 4–5 years. Again, this type of issue cannot be investigated by either time series or cross-section data alone.

11.2 The nature of panel data regression and analysis

In the above examples panel data sets typically provide information on a large number of cross-sectional units over a relatively short period of time. They are typically wide but short. Panel data sets are therefore more oriented towards cross-section regression analysis. In such analysis the main focus of investigation is usually on the issue of heterogeneity across cross-sectional units. Heterogeneity implies that there are individual/unit effects present in the data. That is, there are *unmeasured variables* influencing each individual/unit, giving rise to differences in individuals and, hence, heterogeneity. Ignoring these differences in regression models, where they are present in the data, gives rise to the *omitted variable problem* and biased and inconsistent OLS estimators due to the fact that these individual effects tend to be correlated with the regressors. Therefore, if one uses a cross-section data set on its own to estimate a cross-sectional regression model, ignoring these unmeasured individual differences, one typically obtains biased OLS estimates and misleading regression results due to the omitted variable problem. In many applications the omitted variables are difficult to model by the dummy variable methodology discussed in Chapter 9, moreover, as there are many cross-sectional units, each requiring a number of dummy variables, often, in practice, there are insufficient degrees of freedom for estimation and analysis. The focus of a panel data regression is often on capturing these unmeasured individual effects *to correct for the omitted variables problem.* As we shall see below, this correction can be carried out in a number of different ways, depending on whether the panel data are collected via a *non-random* or a *random* sampling method/procedure.

We distinguish between two types of panel data sets, as follows:

1   Panel data sets collected via a *non-random sampling/selection procedure* consisting of a relatively large number of cross-sectional units observed over several periods of time. In this type of panel data the unmeasured omitted variables are assumed to be fixed over time, giving rise to the *fixed-effects model.*
2   Panel data sets collected via a *random sampling/selection procedure* consisting of a relatively large number of cross-sectional units over several periods of time. In this type of panel data the unmeasured variables are randomly distributed, giving rise to the *random-effects model.*

11.3 The fixed-effects model

The fixed-effects model is normally used with a non-randomly selected cross-section data set containing observations on the same cross-sectional units over a relatively short period of time. Many applications of panel data involving the use of published economic data sets fall into this category. For example, studies involving panel data on a number of firms, or regions, or countries, over time. These data sets are usually collected from published secondary sources in a non-random fashion. It is therefore appropriate to assume that the impact of unmeasured variables, for example, ability and culture, associated with each cross-section unit, is fixed, and this impact is to remain constant over a short period of time. Following this line of reasoning, it is often assumed that the individual differences or hetero-geneity across cross-sectional units can be best captured by the differences in the intercept terms of the regression models. That is, the unmeasured omitted variables are assumed to change the intercept term of the regression model, shifting the regression line parallel to itself but leaving the slope parameters unchanged. Within this framework, the intercept term of the regression line varies across the cross-sectional units but remains the same over time, the slope parameters remaining fixed across individuals and time. In order to illustrate some of the basic ideas of this type of modelling, consider the following regression model where, for ease of presentation, only two regressors are included:

$$Y_{it} = \beta_1 + \beta_2 X_{2it} + \beta_3 X_{3it} + \alpha_i + u_{it}; \quad \text{where } i = 1,2 \dots \text{N and } t = 1,2 \dots \text{T} \tag{11.1}$$

Y_{it} denotes the dependent variable corresponding to the cross-sectional unit i at the time t; β_1 is the intercept term; β_2 and β_3 are the slope parameters fixed over time and across cross-sectional units; X_2 and X_3 are the two regressors changing values across cross-sectional units and over time, hence, subscripts i and t; α_i is the *i*th individual/cross-sectional unit effect; and, finally, u_{it} is a disturbance term satisfying the standard conditions.

The focus of attention of the panel data analysis is on the individual effect term α_i. This term is supposed to capture all unmeasured and unobserved variables that influence each cross-section unit in a different fashion, for example, such variables as the cross-sectional unit's ability, common sense and culture. These are likely to be correlated with the regressors of the model, and if ignored, that is, left in the disturbance term of the model, would cause the OLS estimators to be biased and inconsistent. Note that as one moves from one cross-section unit to the other, the intercept term of the regression model would change, but the slope parameters would remain unchanged. To go a bit further with this discussion, we consider below an example of panel data regression analysis in practice.

11.3.1 The neoclassical convergence hypothesis

Panel data set A panel data set collected from published sources (for example, from the OECD publications online) containing observations on a cross-section of countries over time.

To study the neoclassical convergence hypothesis, a researcher collects cross-sectional data on 20 countries from a published online data bank, for example, the OECD publications, over a 5-year period. Note that the key requirement of the fixed-effects model, that the data should be non-random and be collected in a non-random fashion is satisfied here. The relevant variables of the regression model are per capita annual growth rate of GDP, G $\dot{D}$ P, (dependent variable) and per capita GDP (independent variable). The following simple regression model is specified:

$$GĊP_{it} = \beta_1 + \alpha_i + \beta GDP_{it} + u_{it}; \qquad u_{it} \sim NID\ (0,\ \sigma_u^2)$$
$$i = 1,..., 20; \ \ t = 1,..., 5 \tag{11.2}$$

Altogether, the study has $(N \times T)$ $20 \times 5 = 100$ panel data observations.

Notice that each variable is identified by two subscripts: i to denote the *i*th cross-sectional unit (country i), and t to denote period of time (period t). For example, GDP_{it} is the per capita income of country i in period t. We have retained all standard assumptions concerning the disturbance term, as indicated.

α_i is the individual fixed-effect term representing the fixed country effect. This term represents the combined influence on the dependent variable of many qualitative and unmeasured variables specific to each country. For example, the combined impact on the rate of growth of per capita GDP of variables such as geographical location of the country; the level of openness of the country; whether the country has natural resources, such as oil and gas; race; religion; and other unmeasured variables, such as people's ability and culture. Within the framework of a fixed-effects model, it is assumed that the intercept term of the regression model ($\beta_1 + \alpha_i$) varies across 20 countries in response to these variables, but the slope parameter remains fixed. In what follows we discuss two alternative approaches to estimating this fixed-effects model.

11.3.2 Approach (i): removing the individual fixed-effect term from the regression model to correct for the omitted variable problem

(a) Within-groups fixed-effects regression model

Despite the attention given to the individual fixed-effect term α_i, to correct for the omitted variable problem, the focus of panel data analysis is often on how to remove this term from the regression model. In many applied econometric cross-sectional studies researchers are interested in estimating the slope parameters of the regression models and the estimates of the intercept terms are not the focus of research. This is the case in the above example, where the focus of the economic theory is on the slope parameter β and its sign. More specifically, the convergence hypothesis suggests an inverse relationship between the rate of growth of per capita GDP and the per capita GDP and, therefore, a negative sign for the slope parameter β. Within the fixed-effects model framework, the fixed-effect term of this regression model captures the combined influence of the unmeasured variables identified above. But, because these variables are not explicitly considered in the regression model, their omission typically leads to biased OLS estimators, incorrect parameter estimates and signs, and faulty statistical inference. This problem is normally solved via a data transformation procedure designed to remove the fixed-effect term from the regression equation. The transformed model is estimated via the OLS to generate unbiased and consistent estimators. This is a popular approach for eliminating the omitted variable problem from the regression model.

The key steps of the data transformation procedure are as follows:

Step 1 Find the average value of each variable over the period of the data set for each cross-sectional unit specified in the model. In the above example, this method requires that for each one of the 20 countries we first find the average value of per capita GDP growth rate, and the GDP per capita over a 5-year period. Using the regression model, this step implies:

$$\frac{1}{T}\sum_{t=1}^{t=T}(\dot{GDP}_{it} = \beta_1 + \alpha_i + \beta GDP_{it} + u_{it}), \text{ where } t = 1,2,3,4,5 \text{ and } i = 1,2....,20;$$

$$T = 5, \text{ and } N = 20.$$

(11.3)

Using the fact that under the fixed-effects framework the parameters do not change over time, we can write this equation in terms of average/mean value of each variable, as follows:

$$\overline{\dot{GDP}_i} = \beta_1 + \alpha_i + \beta\overline{GDP}_i + \bar{u}_i, \qquad \text{where } i = 1,2....20 \tag{11.4}$$

Step 2 Find the deviation of each individual cross-section observation from its respective average/mean value calculated in step 1. Because the intercept term for each cross-sectional unit is assumed to be constant over time, this data transformation eliminates the regression intercept term. Also, each of the country-specific fixed-term effects are eliminated. This data transformation, therefore, removes the omitted variables implicitly captured by these terms. Using our example, this step implies:

$$(\dot{GDP}_{it} - \overline{\dot{GDP}_i}) = \beta(GDP_{it} - \overline{GDP}_i) + (u_{it} - \bar{u}_i); \text{ for } i = 1,2....20$$

$$\text{and } t = 1,2,3,4,5$$

(11.5)

Note that the data transformation is carried out for each country and for each year. For example, for country 1 (i = 1), each variable is expressed in each year (t = 1,2. . .5) in deviation form from its average value of 5 years. For each one of the countries in the sample, we have 5 observations, and the total number of observations is N × T = 20 × 5 = 100. The transformed data set is said to be in 'deviation from the individual mean form' and the regression is known as the *within-groups regression model*.

Step 3 Estimate the within-groups regression model above by the OLS using a regression package designed to carry out fixed-effects estimation (for example, EViews and Stata). These regression packages carry out the required transformation of the data automatically and use appropriate regression through origin to estimate the model. This data transformation removes the omitted variable problem, and the OLS estimators of the transformed model are unbiased and consistent. These estimators are sometimes called the *fixed-effects estimators*.

Step 4 Analysis: following this procedure, suppose that in the above example, the slope parameter estimate is $\hat{\beta} = -0.003$. This value implies that for every one unit change in per capita income, it is estimated that the rate of growth of per capita GDP, on average, will fall by 0.003 of 1%. This is a rather small change, but the sign of the parameter estimate is consistent with the prediction of the convergence hypothesis.

Step 5 Having obtained the OLS estimate of the slope parameter we can now *recover* the estimate of the intercept term of each country's regression model $(\beta_1 + \alpha_i)$ using the fact that the OLS regression line passes through the point of the means, as follows:

$$\beta_1 + \alpha_i = \overline{G\dot{D}P_i} - \hat{\beta}\,\overline{GDP_i}; \qquad \text{for } i = 1,2,3...20 \ (N = 20) \qquad (11.6)$$

Note that, if we specify the original model without intercept term and only specify the fixed country effect in the regression model, this procedure generates the OLS estimates of the fixed-effects terms.

Comments

The above data transformation significantly reduces the available degrees of freedom of the regression. In transforming the data for each cross-sectional unit, we lose one degree of freedom, reducing the available degrees of freedom by n. In general, the degrees of freedom of the within-group fixed regression model is NT-N-K, where K is the number of parameters to be estimated. Applying this to our example, the degrees of freedom of the regression is now only $100-20-2 = 78$. In addition to a significant loss of degrees of freedom, this transformation also eliminates all time-invariant variables from the regression. For example, variables such as geographical position of the country, or race and religion, normally taken into account via the dummy variable technique, will all be eliminated. Moreover, the residual sum of squares of this type of transformed model is normally more than that of the original model, giving rise to imprecise parameter estimates. Despite these issues and shortcomings, the within-groups fixed-effects regression model is a popular method and is often the preferred choice, in practice, for removing the omitted variable problem.

(b) *First differences fixed-effects regression model*

This is another approach for the correction of the omitted variable problem inherent in cross-section data regression. In this approach the individual fixed-effect terms are removed via the first differencing method. This approach uses the first difference of each variable to correct for the omitted variable problem. Typically, in practice, a cross-section data set is collected for only two periods. To correct for the omitted variable problem, the data is transformed into first difference form and then is used in a OLS regression model to generate the OLS estimates of the slope parameters. Provided standard conditions concerning the disturbance term are satisfied, this method is capable of generating efficient estimators.

This method is illustrated below:

Current period:

$$(1) \quad G\dot{D}P_{it} = \beta_1 + \alpha_i + \beta GDP_{it} + u_{it}; \qquad\qquad i = 1,2...20. \quad t = 1,2... \qquad (11.7)$$

Previous period:

$$(2) \quad G\dot{D}P_{it-1} = \beta 1 + \alpha_i + \beta GDP_{it-1} + u_{it-1}; \qquad i = 1,2...20, \quad t = 1,2 \tag{11.8}$$

First difference form (1)–(2)

$$\Delta G\dot{D}P_{it} = \beta \Delta GDP_{it} + \Delta u_{it}; \qquad \text{for all t.} \tag{11.9}$$

This type of data transformation removes the fixed-effect terms, α_i, but the intercept term of the regression model is also removed. Moreover, the disturbance term of the transformed model would now be autocorrelated under the above conditions. This is because the successive values of the disturbance terms now have a common term. In this case the OLS estimators would be inefficient and the regression would not be reliable. Only when the first differencing removes the autocorrelation from the data would this method be useful. Because of these issues, the within-groups fixed-effects regression model is preferred to this method for removing the omitted variables from the regression models.

11.3.3 Approach (ii): capturing the individual fixed effects – the least squares dummy variable (LSDV) regression

When the number of non-randomly selected cross-sectional units is relatively small, one can use dummy variable methodology to allow for different individual fixed effects. To avoid the dummy variable trap, the regression model is usually specified without the intercept term. For each individual unit, a dummy variable is then specified to capture explicitly the impact of each individual fixed effect on the dependent variable. Note that this approach does need panel data. With only cross-section data, we need a dummy variable for each cross-section unit, thereby depleting the degrees of freedom. For instance, in the above example, if we use only cross-section data on 20 countries, we need 20 individual country-effect dummy variables, leaving the regression model without any degrees of freedom.

To demonstrate the dummy variable regression methodology we return to the above example and include a number of dummy variables in the regression model, as follows:

$D_i = 1$ if ith country for i = 1,2...20

$D_i = 0$ otherwise

The dummy variable regression model is as follows:

$$G\dot{D}P_{it} = \sum_{i=1}^{i=n} \alpha_i D_i + \beta GDP_{it} + u_{it}; \qquad t = 1,2,3,4,5 \text{ and } i = 1,2,...20; \tag{11.10}$$

The coefficients of the dummy variables change across countries but remain constant over time. The dummy variable regression model is estimated by the OLS using an appropriate regression package (for example, EViews) to generate estimates of the country effects, α_i, and the slope parameter β. This type of fixed-effects model is referred to as a *least squares dummy variables (LSDV) model*. This procedure generates efficient estimators provided that all standard conditions are satisfied. It can be shown that mathematically this method is identical to the within-groups regression model, however, both methods suffer from similar limitations. In particular, as in the case of within-groups regression, one cannot estimate the coefficients of the variables that are fixed for each cross-section unit. For example, suppose for country one, we want to look at the impact of membership of the WTO via a dummy variable method. This would not be possible due to perfect multicollinearity as the sum of the country-specific dummy variables would always be unity, which is equal to the value of the regressor of this new dummy variable, introduced to take account of the status of the country one membership of the WTO. Thus, there is an exact linear relationship between variables that are fixed for each cross-sectional unit, and the fixed-effect dummy variables and this type of variable cannot be included in the LSDV models.

11.3.4 Testing for heterogeneity within the framework of the LSDV model

The assumption of heterogeneity (different country effects) can be tested as follows:

$$H_0: \alpha_1 = ..., = \alpha_{20} = \alpha \qquad \text{no specific fixed country effects}$$
$$H_1: H_0 \text{ is not true} \tag{11.11}$$

The appropriate test statistic is the familiar F-test for parameter restrictions:

$$F = \frac{[RSS_R - RSS_U]/d}{RSS_U/(TN - k)} \sim Fd,(TN - k) \tag{11.12}$$

where
   RSS_R = residual sum of squares of the restricted model (no country effect) corresponding to the regression model below:

$$GDP_{it} = \alpha + + \beta \; GDP_{it} + u_{it}; \qquad i = 1,2...20 \text{ and } t = 1,2...,5 \tag{11.13}$$

This restricted regression model is estimated by the OLS from the pooled cross–section/time series data set to generate the residual sum of squares, RSS_R.
   RSS_U = residual sum of squares corresponding to the unrestricted LSDV regression model.

   d = no. of parameter restrictions (d = 19)
   TN = 5 × 20 = 100
   k = 21 (20 = country effects parameters + one slope parameter)

   If the value of the F-test statistic is greater than the corresponding theoretical value of F at say 5% level of significance, we reject H_0 and conclude that there are significant country effects in the data. In this situation the LSDV method is consistent with evidence and it generates linear unbiased and efficient estimators, provided that the usual assumptions concerning the disturbance term are satisfied.
   In cases when N is large, as it typically is in a panel study of families and individuals, the LSDV method is not appropriate, because of the degrees of freedom problem. In practice, when N is large the within-groups fixed-effects regression model is often the preferred option.

11.3.5 Shortcomings of the fixed-effects methodology

The fixed-effects regression models are characterised by three basic problems:

1 The degrees of freedom problem, due to a large number of cross-sectional units.
2 They are unable to deal with variables which change across individual cross-sectional units but remain fixed over time.
3 Inference about the population from which the cross-sectional units are sampled is not possible since these methods produce results conditional on the units in the data set. Because the selection of the cross-sectional units is non-random, a fixed-effects methodology can only explain information contained in the collected data set. In a typical panel data study, because of the above reasons, researchers tend to use a random-effects model. We briefly consider this model below.

11.4 The random-effects model

In a typical panel data study, researchers deal with a very large population consisting of thousands of individuals. For example, a panel data study of university graduates' employment prospects would consist of thousands of new graduates. In this type of study a cross-section data set is selected from the population on the basis of a random sampling method. Because of this selection procedure, it is possible to treat the individual effects as being randomly drawn from a given population. They are random terms giving rise to the random-effects model.

In a random-effects model it is assumed that the individual effects are randomly distributed across cross-sectional units. To capture the individual effects, the regression model is specified, with an intercept term representing an overall constant term. The unobserved individual effects are subsumed into the disturbance term of the model. In this framework the disturbance term of the regression model has two components: an error term associated with each observation and a random term representing each individual effect. To illustrate the basic ideas, consider the following model (11.1) presented above:

$$Y_{it} = \beta_1 + \beta_2 X_{2it} + \beta_3 X_{3it} + \alpha_i + u_{it}; \text{ where } i = 1,2...,n \text{ and} \\ t = 1,2...,t \tag{11.14}$$

Within the framework of the random effect, α_i is a random variable representing unobserved individual effects. Let W_{it} denote the disturbance term of the random-effect regression model, that is:

$$W_{it} = \alpha_i + u_{it} \tag{11.15}$$

and

$$Y_{it} = \beta_1 + \beta_2 X_{2it} + \beta_3 X_{3it} + W_{it} \text{ for } i = 1,2...n \text{ and } t = 1,2...t \tag{11.16}$$

This innovation subsumed all relevant omitted variables into the composite error term of the regression model, effectively dealing with each one of the problems associated with the fixed-effects methodology identified above. However, the random-effects methodology is also problematic. In particular, if α_i, the individual random-effect term, is correlated with any one of the regressors, the OLS estimators would be unbiased and inconsistent.

Accordingly, for the random-effects methodology to work, the following two conditions must be met:

1   The cross-sectional units are selected randomly.
2   The individual random-effects terms are distributed independently of the regressors of the model.

If these conditions are met, in practice, the random-effects regression model is typically preferred to the fixed-effects model. Let us assume for the moment that these two conditions are satisfied. Can this model be estimated by the OLS? The answer to this question depends on the properties of the composite disturbance term, W_{it}. To check these, we assume that each individual effect is distributed independently around the mean of zero with a constant variance of $\sigma^2\alpha$. Let us look at these properties one by one below:

$$E(W_{it}) = E(\alpha_i + u_{it}) = E(\alpha_i) + E(u_{it}) = 0 \text{ for all i and t} \tag{11.17}$$

$$\text{Var}(W_{it}) = \text{Var}(\alpha_i + u_{it}) = \text{Var}(\alpha_i) + \text{Var}(u_{it}) + 2Cov(\alpha_i\, u_{it}) = \sigma_\alpha^2 + \sigma_u^2 \tag{11.18}$$

Next we need to check for autocorrelation in the composite error term:

$$W_{it} = \alpha_i + u_{it} \quad \text{for I} = 1,2...n \text{ and } t = 1,2...t \tag{11.19}$$

Note that α_i, the individual effect, is random but is time-invariant. Therefore, as we go forward in time, this term remains in each of the future error terms of the individual i. In other words, each individual's composite error term will have a common term over time and would therefore be autocorrelated. This is shown below:

$$cov(w_{it}w_{it+1}) = E(\alpha_i + u_{it})(\alpha_i + u_{it+!}) = \sigma_a^2 \text{ for all i and t} \tag{11.20}$$

This type of autocorrelation is due to the nature of the panel data set, which provides observations on the same individuals over time. Note that there is no autocorrelation between different randomly selected individuals, but there is autocorrelation between observations of the same individual over time. The unmeasured random individual effects captured by the composite error term are correlated for each individual over time, generating autocorrelation in the disturbance term of the random-effects regression model. In this situation OLS estimators are inefficient and the OLS regression is unreliable. In the case of the random-effects model, the efficient estimator is generalised least squares. For estimation purposes, in practice, we use appropriate regression software (for example, EViews). A two-step estimation procedure is used to transform the data to eliminate autocorrelation from the panel data set. The various components are first estimated by using the residuals from OLS regression. Then, the feasible generalised least squares (FGLS) estimates are computed using the estimated variances.

11.4.1 Using the random-effects regression model

Working with the random-effects regression models in practice requires a careful step by step approach. These steps are briefly summarised below.

Step 1 Make sure the cross-section data is randomly selected from the population.

Step 2 Perform a version of the Hausman test to see whether the unobservable individual effects are independently distributed of the regressors. This is a critical step for the use of the random-effects regression model. The appropriate test statistic for this purpose is a version of the Hausman measurement error test already encountered in the previous chapters. This version of the test is known as the Durbin-Wu-Hausman (DWH) test and it is routinely carried out and reported by regression packages (for example, EViews). The null hypothesis of this test is:

$H_{0:}$ individual random effects are independently distributed of the regressors

$H_{1:}$ H_0 is not true

Step 3 If this null is *not* rejected then the random-effects regression is appropriate and the random-effects estimators are unbiased, consistent and efficient. The DWH test can be carried out in a similar fashion to the Hausman measurement error test demonstrated in Chapter 6. To do this test, the fixed-effects estimates are obtained (these can be considered to be instruments for the random-effects regression model), and are then compared to the random-effects estimates. Under the null hypothesis these two types of estimators should generate similar results. The DWH test is designed to determine whether the differences between these two types of parameter estimates, taken jointly, are statistically significant. The test statistic has an F/chi-squared distribution. In general, as a rule of thumb, a relatively large value of the DWH test statistic implies rejection of the null hypothesis. The degrees of freedom of this test are shown to be lower than the number of the parameter restrictions of the test, and are calculated and reported by the regression software.

Step 4 If the null hypothesis is rejected, the random-effects regression is unreliable and the parameter estimates are invalid. In this situation, practitioners tend to use the fixed-effects regression results, despite its shortcomings.

11.5 Panel data regression analysis in practice

To illustrate the key steps of estimating a panel data regression model, we use a hypothetical example of a kind used frequently in the panel data regression analysis of economic data. Suppose a researcher is wishing to investigate the determinants of the per capita GDP growth rate using a country-wide panel data set. Having reviewed the relevant academic literature, the researcher specifies the following regression model:

$$Y_{it} = \beta_1 + \beta_2 X_{2it} + \beta_3 X_{3it} + \alpha_i + u_{it}; \quad \text{where} \quad i = 1,\dots,n; \quad t = 1,2\dots,t \tag{11.21}$$

Where Y_{it} is the *i*th country real per capita growth rate in period t, X_{2i} is the *i*th country's level of exports, and X_{3it} is the *i*th country's level of fixed capital formation. According to the literature, one expects a positive sign for both of the slope parameters, β_2 and β_3. The parameter α_i is the individual country effect, capturing the combined influence of such variables as culture and ability on the dependent variable, and u_{it} is a disturbance term satisfying all standard assumptions. To estimate this model a researcher obtains data over a 10-year period on 15 countries 'randomly' selected from the OECD (Organisation of Economic Cooperation and Development) year book, available online. There are, altogether, nxt = 15 × 10 = 150 cross-section/time series data on each variable. The focus of analysis is typically on the slope parameters β_2 and β_3. In a panel data study of this kind, there are a number of questions that need to be answered before the regression analysis is carried out, as follows:

- Can the data be treated as randomly selected data?
- Should the country effect be specified as a fixed-effects model or a random-effects model?
- What type of estimation method should be used?
- To answer these questions we follow the methodology set out above.

Step 1 Although the data are said to be randomly collected, given the nature of the economic data and the fact that a published data bank is used, it is advisable to carry out the DWH test before estimation.

Step 2 This test requires the estimation of the model:

a   under the fixed-effects specification, α_i are non–random;

and

b   under the random-effects specification, α_i are randomly distributed.

The DWH test null and alternative hypotheses are:

$H_0 : \alpha_i$ are independently distributed of X_2 and X_3

$H_1 : H_0$ is not true

$$(11.22)$$

This test determines whether the estimates of the parameters taken jointly are significantly different in the two regressions.

Step 3 If H_0 is not rejected the random-effects specification is the preferred option. This test has a chi-squared distribution, with the degrees of freedom equal to the number of parameters being compared, but occasionally a lower number is reported. For this example the test statistic is computed by the EViews regression package as chi-squared = 18.76, with 2 degrees of freedom. The corresponding critical value at a 5% level of significance is 5.99; the test statistic falls into the critical region of the test, we therefore reject H_0 and conclude that, for this example, the appropriate specification of the country effect is the fixed-effects model.

Step 4 The fixed-effects model regression using the within-groups regression method generates the OLS estimates of β_2 *and* β_3, respectively, as 0.024 and 0.045. These parameter estimates are consistent with the theoretical prediction. Moreover, the OLS estimators are unbiased and consistent under the fixed-effects specification. The fixed-effects regression appears to be the appropriate panel data analysis in this example.

11.6 A summary of key issues

- Panel data sets typically contain observations on a large number of cross-sectional units over a relatively short period of time.
- Panel data regression is mainly concerned with removing the 'omitted variable problem' from the regression to avoid biased and inconsistent OLS estimators.
- The omitted variable problem is due to individual effects inherent in cross-section data. If the cross-section data set is collected using non-random sampling procedures, the regression model is called the fixed-effects model. In this case, the individual fixed effect changes across individuals but is assumed to be fixed over time.
- A popular method of estimating fixed-effects models is the within-groups fixed-effects model. Within the framework of this model, data are transformed to eliminate the omitted variable problem. The estimation of the transformed model is undertaken by the OLS method. OLS estimators are unbiased and consistent.
- If the cross-sectional units are collected via a random sampling procedure, the individual effects are randomly distributed and are subsumed within the disturbance term. This type of panel data gives rise to the random-effects models.
- Estimation of the random-effects models is not straightforward as there are likely to be two key problems present: (a) disturbance terms are correlated with the regressors of the model, and (b) disturbance terms are likely to be autocorrelated due to individual effects. OLS estimators are biased, inconsistent and inefficient.
- To estimate a random-effects regression model, first check to see whether the disturbance terms are correlated with the regressors using the DWH testing procedures. If the results suggest correlation (the null hypothesis is rejected) report the fixed-effects within-groups regression results.
- If the null hypothesis of the DWH is not rejected, report the random-effects regression results, as the corresponding estimators are more efficient compared to the fixed-effects estimators.

Review questions

1 Explain what you understand by a panel data set. What are the key features of this type of data set? What type of studies can be carried out with this type of data? Give examples to illustrate your answer.

2 Explain what you understand by the 'omitted variable problem'. How is this problem resolved via panel data analysis?

3 Explain what you understand by the fixed-effects model. Under what conditions should this model be used? What are the limitations of fixed-effects panel data studies?

4 Explain the within-groups fixed-effects regression model. How does this model overcome the omitted variable problem? Use an example to illustrate your answer.

5 Explain the least squares dummy variable model (LSDV). How does this model deal with the individual fixed effects? How can this model be used for testing for heterogeneity of the cross-sectional units?

6 Explain the random-effects model. Under what conditions might this model be employed in practice? What are the limitations of this type of panel data analysis?

7 Collect a panel data set consisting of the average annual stock prices of 60 manufacturing companies over 5 years and the level of annual investment expenditures by each

company over this 5-year period (you can collect this type of data from the online sources, for example, from the London Stock Exchange website). It is thought that the average annual stock price is positively related to the annual investment expenditure. Use an appropriate regression package (EViews) to carry out each one of the following steps in this panel data study.

a　Specify a panel data regression equation and explain its underlying assumptions.

b　Compare and contrast the fixed-effects model and the random-effects model and explain which of these two alternatives is appropriate in this regression.

c　Use the DWH test to select the appropriate model for the panel data regression. Explain the DWH test and specify the null and alternative hypotheses of this test.

d　Carry out a panel data regression analysis consistent with the result of the DWH test. Explain and evaluate the regression results.

Key terms: Unit 3

- *Dummy variables* Used to capture the impact of qualitative variables on the dependent variable of a regression model.
- *A shift dummy* Used to capture the impact of a qualitative variable on the intercept term of a regression model.
- *Qualitative dependent variable models* Models in which the dependent variable is qualitative/dichotomous.
- *Linear probability model (LPM)* A linear model designed to estimate the conditional probability of a positive response/presence of a characteristic.
- *The logit model* A non-linear probability model based on a logistic curve, designed to estimate the conditional probability of a positive response/presence of a characteristic.
- *The probit/normit model* A non-linear probability model based on the normal cumulative distribution, designed to estimate the conditional probability of a positive response/presence of a characteristic.
- *Multinomial logit model* A qualitative dependent variables model dealing with multi-response qualitative variables using a logistic probability distribution.
- *Ordered logit regression model* A qualitative dependent variable model dealing with ordered preferences using logit probability distribution.
- *Panel data* A data set normally consisting of a large number of observations on cross-sectional units over a relatively short period of time.
- *A panel data study* A study based on a panel data set to capture individual cross-sectional effects.
- *Fixed-effects model* Individual effects are fixed over time and are captured by shifts in the intercept term of the model.
- *Least squares dummy variable model (LSDV)* Used with a fixed-effects model.
- *Random-effects model (REM)* Individual effects are randomly distributed over cross-sectional units.
- *The Durbin-Wu-Hausman (DWH) test* A variant of the Hausman test (1978). A statistical test used to test the existence of correlation between individual effects and the regressors of the model. Use in practice to select between the fixed-effects and the random-effects specifications in panel data analysis.

General notes and bibliography: Unit 3

The qualitative response regression models and panel data regression are relatively new topics in econometrics, but there are many classic contributions already in these fields. A classic reference for the former topic is Maddala (1983), *Limited Dependent and Qualitative Variables in Economics*. Also, Baltagi (2005), *Econometric Analysis of Panel Data*, provides an excellent exposition of panel data analysis. We list these below, along with some additional accessible references for this unit.

Baltagi, B. H. (2005). *Econometric Analysis of Panel Data*, 3rd edn, New York: Wiley.

Greene, W. (2003). *Econometric analysis*, 5th edn, Prentice-Hall.

Hans Franses, P. and Paap, R. (2001). *Qualitative Models in Marketing Research*, Cambridge: Cambridge University Press.

Hausman, J. A. (1978). 'Specification tests in econometrics', *Econometrica*, 46, 1251–71.

Hausman, J. A. and McFadden, D. (1984). 'Specification tests for the multinomial logit model', *Econometrica*, 52, 1219–40.

Kennedy, P. (2008). *A Guide to Econometrics*, 6th edn, Blackwell Publishing.

Maddala, G. S. (1983). *Limited Dependent and Qualitative Variables in Economics*, Cambridge: Cambridge University Press.

Scott Long, J. (1997). *Regression Models for Categorical and Limited Dependent Variables*, Sage Publications.

Wooldridge, J. (2002). *Economic Analysis of Cross Section and Panel Data*, MIT Press.

Unit 4

Time series econometrics

- This unit provides an introduction to modern time series regression analysis. It explains how the phenomenon of the spurious regression led to the development of a new methodology for time series regression analysis, replacing the SG methodology in the early 1980s.
- The unit provides introductory coverage of the concept of stationary time series and discusses its key role in modern time series econometrics and cointegration analysis.
- This unit has four key chapters: Chapter 12 covers key definitions and concepts. Chapter 13 provides a detailed explanation of the unit root tests and their applications. Chapter 14 introduces the methodology of cointegration and applies this methodology to a number of bivariate econometric models. Finally, Chapter 14 provides introductory coverage of multivariate cointegration analysis.
- This unit provides a rigorous but non-technical approach to the key topics, using many applied examples to illustrate the use of unit root tests and cointegration analysis in practice.

12 Stationary and non-stationary time series

INTRODUCTION

The specific to general (SG) approach to time series analysis implicitly assumes that the means and the variances of the economic variables in a regression model remain constant over time. That is, they are time-invariant, and when these assumptions break down, alternative methods of estimation to the OLS are used to generate efficient estimators. Within this framework the underlying reasons for the breakdown of these assumptions are seldom systematically investigated. The mean and variances of many economic and financial variables are, however, time-variant and their time series are non-stationary. The non-stationary time series and their treatment have given rise to some important contributions in econometrics in recent years, including unit root tests and cointegration analysis. In the next three chapters we will focus attention on these topics. Each chapter will include an extended summary of key issues to help with better understanding of techniques and applications.

This introductory chapter provides a discussion on the basic definitions, concepts and ideas of time series econometrics. Key procedures are illustrated via examples using actual time series data.

Key topics

- Stationary and non-stationary time series
- Models with deterministic and stochastic trends
- Integrated time series
- Testing for stationarity: the autocorrelation function

12.1 The definitions

The most common definitions in time series analysis are the following:

Stochastic process A family of real valued random variables, $X_1, X_2, X_3, \ldots$, where the subscripts refer to successive time periods, is called a 'stochastic process' and is denoted with $\{X_t\}$. Each random variable in the stochastic process generally has its own probability distribution and is not independent of others in the series.

Time series Consider that for each time period we get a sample of size one (one observation) on each of the random variables of a stochastic process. Therefore, we get a series of observations corresponding to each time period and to each different random variable. This series of observations is called a 'time series' and is denoted with X_t.

Realisation The time series X_t is a 'single realisation' of the stochastic process $\{X_t\}$ because of lack of replication in sampling, or, in other words, because it is impossible to get another observation from the same random variable. We could say that the stochastic process is regarded as the 'population' and the time series is regarded as its realisation, i.e. as a 'sample' in cross-sectional data (one observation from each section, each random variable). For convenience, we will use the terms 'stochastic process' and 'time series' synonymously, and we will use the common notation of X_t to represent them.

Strict stationarity Because each of the random variables X_t in a stochastic process has a probability distribution, a stochastic process can be specified by the joint probability distribution of its random variables. A stochastic process, and, correspondingly, a time series, is said to be 'strictly stationary' if its joint distribution is unchanged if displaced in time, or, in other words, if its joint distribution of any set of n variables, $X_1, X_2, \ldots, X_n$, is the same as the joint distribution of $X_{1+k}, X_{2+k}, \ldots, X_{n+k}$ for all n and k.

Weak stationarity Because it is generally difficult in practice to determine the joint distribution of a stochastic process, we can instead use the means, the variances, and the covariances of its random variables X_t, for $t = 1,2,\ldots$. A stochastic process, and, correspondingly, a time series, is said to be 'weakly stationary' if:

1. The mean $E(X_t) = \mu$ is constant for all t. $\qquad\qquad$ (12.1)

2. The variance $\text{var}(X_t) = E(X_t - \mu)^2 = \sigma^2$ is constant for all t. $\qquad$ (12.2)

3. The covariance $\text{cov}(X_t, X_{t+k}) = E\left[(X_t - \mu)(X_{t+k} - \mu)\right] = \gamma_k$

   is constant for all t and $k \neq 0$. $\qquad\qquad$ (12.3)

Stationarity In this chapter when we use the term 'stationary', we will refer to weak stationarity. Generally speaking, a stochastic process, and, correspondingly, a time series, is stationary if the means and variances are constant over time and the (auto) covariances between two time periods, t and t+k, depend only on the distance (gap or lag) k between these two time periods and not on the actual time period t at which these covariances are considered.

Non-stationarity If one or more of the three conditions for stationarity are not fulfilled, the stochastic process, and, correspondingly, the time series, is called 'non-stationary'. In fact, most time series in economics are non-stationary. In Figure 12.1, for example, the time series of private consumption (CP) and personal disposable income (PDI) for an EU member, since they are all trending consistently upwards, are almost certain not to satisfy condition (12.1) for stationarity, and, therefore, they are non-stationary (actual data for these series can be found in Table 12.1).

Having defined stationarity, in what follows we present some useful time series models:

12.2 Models with deterministic and stochastic trends

White noise This is a purely random process $\{\varepsilon_t\}$, for t taking values from $-\infty$ to $+\infty$, where the ε_t are all identically and independently distributed (IID) with:

1. mean $E(\varepsilon_t) = 0$ for all t $\qquad\qquad$ (12.4)

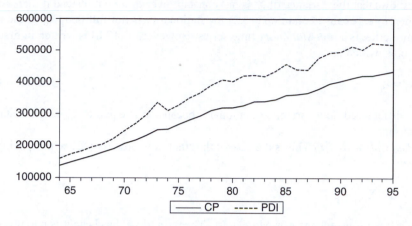

Figure 12.1 Private consumption and personal disposable income for an EU member, 1960–1995, annual data, millions of 1970 (drs).

2. variance $\operatorname{var}\left(\varepsilon_t\right) = \sigma 2$ for all t, and $\qquad$ (12.5)

3. covariance $\operatorname{cov}\left(\varepsilon_t, \varepsilon_{t+k}\right) = 0$ for all t and $k \neq 0$. $\qquad$ (12.6)

The white noise time series, which is also written as:

$$\varepsilon_t \sim \text{NID}\left(0, \sigma 2\right) \qquad (12.7)$$

is *stationary by definition*, since its means are zero, its variances are σ^2, and its covariances are zero, being therefore constant over time.

Random walk This is a simple stochastic process $\{X_t\}$ with X_t being determined by:

$$X_t = X_{t-1} + \varepsilon_t \qquad (12.8)$$

where ε_t is white noise.

The mean of X_t in (7.8) is given by:

$$E\left(X_t\right) = E\left(X_{t-1} + \varepsilon_t\right) = E\left(X_{t-1}\right) + E\left(\varepsilon_t\right) = E\left(X_{t-1}\right), \text{ due to } \left(12.4\right), \qquad (12.9)$$

implying that the mean of X_t is constant over time. In order to find the variance of X_t, we use (12.8), which after successive substitutions is written as:

$$X_t = X_0 + \varepsilon_1 + \varepsilon_2 + \cdots + \varepsilon_t = X_0 + \sum_{t=1}^{t} \varepsilon_t \qquad (12.10)$$

where X_0 is the initial value of X_t, which is assumed to be any constant or could be also taken to be equal to zero. The variance of (12.10), taking into account (12.7), is given by:

$$\operatorname{var}\left(X_t\right) = \sum_{t=1}^{t} \operatorname{var}\left(\varepsilon_t\right) = t\sigma^2 \qquad (12.11)$$

(12.11) shows that the variance of X_t is not constant over time, but instead it increases with time. Therefore, because condition (12.2) for stationarity is not fulfilled, X_t, or the random walk time series, is a *non-stationary* time series. However, if (12.8) is written in first differences, i.e. is written as:

$$\Delta X_t = \varepsilon_t \tag{12.12}$$

this first differenced new variable is stationary, because it is equal to ε_t, which is stationary by definition.

Random walk with drift This is the case of the stochastic process $\{X_t\}$ with X_t being determined by:

$$X_t = \mu + X_{t-1} + \varepsilon_t \tag{12.13}$$

where $\mu \neq 0$ is a constant and ε_t is white noise. The term 'drift' has been given to this process because if we write (12.13) as the first difference:

$$\Delta X_t = X_t - X_{t-1} = \mu + \varepsilon_t \tag{12.14}$$

this shows that the time series X_t 'drifts' upwards or downwards, depending on the sign of μ being positive or negative. The random walk with drift time series is also a non-stationary time series. The processes in (12.8) and in (12.13) are no longer 'random walks' if the assumption of white noise is relaxed to allow for autocorrelation in ε_t. However, even in cases of autocorrelation in ε_t, time series X_t will still be non-stationary.

Time trends We call 'time trend' the tendency of a non-stationary series to move in one direction. Let us consider the following model:

$$X_t = \alpha + \beta t + \phi X_{t-1} + \varepsilon_t \ , \ \alpha \neq 0 \tag{12.15}$$

where ε_t is white noise and t is a time trend.

Using model (12.15) we can distinguish the following cases:

Case 1. Stochastic trend This is the case where $\beta = 0$ and $\phi = 1$. Model (12.15) is written in this case as:

$$X_t = \alpha + X_{t-1} + \varepsilon_t \tag{12.16}$$

or

$$\Delta X_t = \alpha + \varepsilon_t \tag{12.17}$$

From (12.17) it is seen that X_t trends upwards or downwards according to the sign of α being positive or negative, respectively. This type of trend is known as 'stochastic trend'. Model (12.16) is called a *difference-stationary process* (DSP) because the non-stationarity in X_t can be eliminated by taking first differences of the time series (Nelson and Plosser, 1982).

Case 2. Deterministic trend This is the case where $\beta \neq 0$ and $\phi = 0$. Model (12.15) is written in this case as:

$$X_t = \alpha + \beta t + \varepsilon_t \qquad (12.18)$$

From (12.18) it is seen that X_t trends upwards or downwards according to the sign of β being positive or negative, respectively. This type of trend is known as a 'deterministic trend'. Model (12.18) is called a *trend-stationary process* (TSP) because the non-stationarity in X_t can be eliminated by subtracting the trend ($\alpha + \beta t$) from the time series.

Case 3. Combined stochastic and deterministic trend This is the case where $\beta \neq 0$ and $\phi = 1$. Model (12.15) is written in this case as:

$$X_t = \alpha + \beta t + X_{t-1} + \varepsilon_t \qquad (12.19)$$

From (12.19) it is seen that X_t trends upwards or downwards according to the combined effect of the parameters α and β. This type of trend is known as 'combined stochastic and deterministic trend'. To test the hypothesis that a time series is of a DSP type against being of a TSP type, specific tests have to be employed, such as those developed by Dickey and Fuller (1979, 1981).

Generalisations We saw in (12.8) that the random walk process is the simplest non-stationary process. However, this process is a special case of:

$$X_t = \phi X_{t-1} + \varepsilon_t \qquad (12.20)$$

which is called a *first-order autoregressive process* (AR$_1$). This process is stationary if the parameter ϕ holds that $-1 < \phi < 1$. If it is either $\phi < -1$ or $\phi > 1$ then the process will be non-stationary.

Generalising, equation (12.20) is a special case of:

$$X_t = \phi_1 X_{t-1} + \phi_2 X_{t-2} + \phi_3 X_{t-3} + \dots + \phi_q X_{t-q} + \varepsilon_t \qquad (12.21)$$

which is called a *qth-order autoregressive process* (AR$_q$). It can be proved (Greene, 1999) that this process is stationary if the roots of the *characteristic equation*:

$$1 - \phi_1 L - \phi_2 L^2 - \phi_3 L^3 - \dots - \phi_q L^q = 0 \qquad (12.22)$$

where L is the lag operator, are all greater than unity in absolute values. Otherwise, the process in (12.21) is non-stationary.

12.3 Integrated time series

We saw in (12.12) that if the random walk series is differenced once, the differenced series $\Delta X_t = X_t - X_{t-1}$ is stationary. In this case we say that the original non-stationary series X_t is *integrated of order 1*, and is denoted with I(1). Similarly, if a non-stationary series has to be differenced twice ($\Delta^2 X_t = \Delta X_t - \Delta X_{t-1}$) before it becomes stationary, the original series X_t is *integrated of order 2*, and is denoted with I(2). Generally, if a non-stationary series has to be differenced d times before it becomes stationary, the original series X_t is *integrated of order d*, and is denoted with I(d). By definition, I(0) denotes a stationary series, which means that this series is stationary without any differencing. However, if a series does not become stationary, irrespective of how many times it is differenced, it is called *non-integrated*.

In the special case where the time series X_t is subject to 's' seasonality (say quarterly ($s = 4$), monthly ($s = 12$), etc.), the definition of an integrated series is modified respectively (Engle *et al.* (1989), Charemza and Deadman (1997)). Thus, a non-stationary series is said to be *s-seasonally integrated of order* (d,D), and is denoted with $SI_s(d,D)$, if in order to be transformed to a stationary series, it has to be s-differenced D times and then the resulting series has to be first differenced d times.

12.3.1 The properties of integrated series

If a series X_t is integrated of order d, then this is written as:

$$X_t \sim I\left(d\right) \tag{12.23}$$

Generally, we distinguish the following properties of integrated series:

1   If $X_t \sim I(0)$ and $Y_t \sim I(1)$ then $Z_t = (X_t + Y_t) \sim I(1)$.

2   If $X_t \sim I(d)$ then $Z_t = (a + bX_t) \sim I(d)$, where a and b are constants.

3   If $X_t \sim I(0)$ then $Z_t = (a + bX_t) \sim I(0)$.

4   If $X_t \sim I(d_1)$ and $Y_t \sim I(d_2)$, then $Z_t = (a\,X_t + b\,Y_t) \sim I(d_2)$, where $d_1 < d_2$.

5   If $X_t \sim I(d)$ and $Y_t \sim I(d)$, then $Z_t = (a\,X_t + b\,Y_t) \sim I(d^*)$, where d^* in most cases is equal to d. However, there are special cases, which we will see later in this chapter, where d^* is less than d.

12.4 Testing for stationarity: the autocorrelation function

Tests for stationarity may be divided into two groups: the traditional and the modern. The first group that uses the autocorrelation function is presented in this section, and the second group that uses the unit roots we present in the next chapter.

For a stochastic process we know that it is:

mean : $E(X_t) = \mu$ $\qquad\qquad\qquad$ (12.24)

variance : $\text{var}\left(X_t\right) = E\left(X_t - \mu\right)^2 = \gamma_0$ $\qquad$ (12.25)

covariance : $\text{cov}\left(X_t, X_{t+k}\right) = E\left[\left(X_t - \mu\right)\left(X_{t+k} - \mu\right)\right] = \gamma_k$ $\qquad$ (12.26)

hence the population autocorrelation function (P_ACF) is given by:

$$\rho_k = \frac{\gamma_k}{\gamma_0} = \frac{\text{cov}(X_t, X_{t+k})}{\text{var}(X_t)} \tag{12.27}$$

where ρ_k is the autocorrelation coefficient (AC) between X_t and X_{t-k}. The autocorrelation coefficient ρ_k takes values between -1 and $+1$, as verifiable from (12.27). The plot of ρ_k against k is called the *population correlogram*. One basic property of the autocorrelation function is that it is an even function of lag k, i.e. it is $\rho_k = \rho_{-k}$. For other properties see Jenkins and Watts (1968).

For a realisation of a stochastic process, i.e. for a time series X_t, we know that it is:

$$\text{mean}: \quad \overline{X} = \frac{1}{n}\sum X_t \tag{12.28}$$

$$\text{variance}: \quad \hat{\gamma}_0 = \frac{1}{n}\sum\left(X_t - \overline{X}\right)^2 \tag{12.29}$$

$$\text{covariance}: \quad \hat{\gamma}_k = \frac{1}{n}\sum\left(X_t - \overline{X}\right)\left(X_{t+k} - \overline{X}\right) \tag{12.30}$$

hence the *sample autocorrelation function* (S_ACF) is given by:

$$\rho_k = \frac{\hat{\gamma}_k}{\hat{\gamma}_0} = \frac{\sum\left(X_t - \overline{X}\right)\left(X_{t+k} - \overline{X}\right)}{\sum\left(X_t - \overline{X}\right)^2} \tag{12.31}$$

where $\hat{\rho}_k$ is the estimated autocorrelation coefficient between X_t and X_{t-k}. The estimated autocorrelation coefficient $\hat{\rho}_k$ takes values between -1 and $+1$, as verifiable from (12.31). The plot of $\hat{\rho}_k$ against k is called the *sample correlogram*. In what follows, when we refer to autocorrelation functions or correlograms, we mean the sample equivalent.

As a rule of thumb, the correlogram can be used for detecting non-stationarity in a time series. As an example, let us consider the time series of private consumption for an EU member, as presented in Table 12.1. We have seen already in Figure 12.1 that this time series may be non-stationary. In Table 12.2 the estimated autocorrelation coefficients (AC) for this time series are reported, and the corresponding correlogram is presented in Figure 12.2. Furthermore, in Table 12.2 the estimated autocorrelation coefficients for the

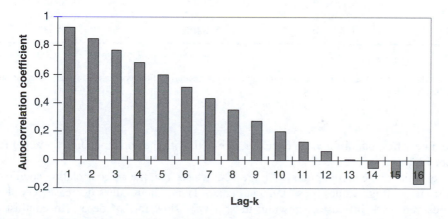

Figure 12.2 Correlogram for private consumption of an EU member.

Table 12.1 Private consumption and personal disposable income for an EU member (1970 constant prices)

Year	Private consumption	Personal disposable income	Consumption price index
1960	107808.0	117179.2	0.783142
1961	115147.0	127598.9	0.791684
1962	120050.0	135007.1	0.801758
1963	126115.0	142128.3	0.828688
1964	137192.0	159648.7	0.847185
1965	147707.0	172755.9	0.885828
1966	157687.0	182365.5	0.916505
1967	167528.0	195611.0	0.934232
1968	179025.0	204470.4	0.941193
1969	190089.0	222637.5	0.969630
1970	206813.0	246819.0	1.000000
1971	217212.0	269248.9	1.033727
1972	232312.0	297266.0	1.068064
1973	250057.0	335521.7	1.228156
1974	251650.0	310231.1	1.517795
1975	266884.0	327521.3	1.701147
1976	281066.0	350427.4	1.929906
1977	293928.0	366730.0	2.159872
1978	310640.0	390188.5	2.436364
1979	318817.0	406857.2	2.838453
1980	319341.0	401942.8	3.459030
1981	325851.0	419669.1	4.081844
1982	338507.0	421715.6	5.114169
1983	339425.0	417930.3	6.067835
1984	345194.0	434695.7	7.130602
1985	358671.0	456576.2	8.435285
1986	361026.0	439654.1	10.30081
1987	365473.0	438453.5	11.91950
1988	378488.0	476344.7	13.61448
1989	394942.0	492334.4	15.59285
1990	403194.0	495939.2	18.59539
1991	412458.0	513173.0	22.09116
1992	420028.0	502520.1	25.40122
1993	420585.0	523066.1	28.88346
1994	426893.0	520727.5	32.00385
1995	433723.0	518406.9	34.98085

Sources: Epilogi (1998)

Note: the data in this table will be used to demonstrate key procedures of the cointegration analysis in the subsequent chapters

same time series, but differenced once, are reported, with the corresponding correlogram in Figure 12.3.

By examining the correlogram in Figure 12.2 we see that the autocorrelation coefficients start from very high values ($\hat{\rho}_k = 0.925$ at lag $k = 1$) and their values decrease very slowly towards zero as k increases, showing, thus, a very slow rate of decay. In contrast, the correlogram in Figure 12.3 shows that all autocorrelation coefficients are close to zero. The

Table 12.2 Autocorrelation coefficients (AC), Ljung-Box Q-Statistic (LB_Q), and probability level (Prob) for the private consumption time series for an EU member

Lag	Original series of private consumption			Differenced series of private consumption		
k	AC	LB_Q	Prob	AC	LB_Q	Prob
1	0.925	33.440	0.000	0.148	0.8333	0.361
2	0.848	62.362	0.000	−0.068	1.0138	0.602
3	0.768	86.800	0.000	0.291	4.4489	0.217
4	0.682	106.70	0.000	−0.058	4.5876	0.332
5	0.597	122.44	0.000	−0.119	5.1938	0.393
6	0.514	134.47	0.000	0.166	6.4184	0.378
7	0.430	143.21	0.000	0.122	7.1072	0.418
8	0.351	149.24	0.000	−0.245	9.9972	0.265
9	0.276	153.11	0.000	−0.026	10.032	0.348
10	0.202	155.27	0.000	−0.078	10.347	0.411
11	0.131	156.21	0.000	−0.163	11.778	0.381
12	0.065	156.45	0.000	0.161	13.237	0.352
13	0.002	156.45	0.000	0.062	13.465	0.413
14	−0.058	156.66	0.000	−0.136	14.604	0.406
15	−0.117	157.54	0.000	−0.203	17.279	0.302
16	−0.170	159.52	0.000	−0.102	17.983	0.325

Notes: estimates via EViews

correlogram in Figure 12.2 is a typical correlogram for a non-stationary time series, whilst the correlogram in Figure 12.3 is a typical correlogram for a stationary time series. Generally, as a rule of thumb:

If, in the correlogram of a time series, the estimated autocorrelation coefficient $\hat{\rho}_k$ does not fall quickly as the lag k increases, this is an indication that the time series is non-stationary. By contrast, if in the correlogram of a time series, the estimated

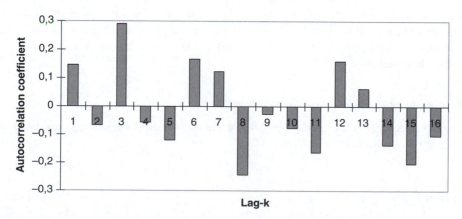

Figure 12.3 Correlogram for differenced private consumption of an EU member.

autocorrelation coefficient $\hat{\rho}_k$ does fall quickly as the lag k increases then, this is an indication that the time series is stationary.

12.5 Using autocorrelation coefficients to test for stationarity

We have argued that the correlogram is a rule of thumb in detecting non-stationarity of a time series. More objective measures should be used for detecting the non-stationarity of a time series. Some of these are as follows:

a. *Testing autocorrelation coefficients individually*

Bartlett (1946) has shown that the sample autocorrelation coefficients approximately follow the normal distribution with zero mean and variance equal to 1/n, where n is the sample size. Therefore, the hypotheses for testing autocorrelation coefficients individually may be formulated as:

$$\left. \begin{array}{l} H_0 : \rho_k = 0 \ , \ \text{if} \ |\hat{\rho}_k| < t_{\alpha/2} \dfrac{1}{\sqrt{n}} \ , \text{i.e.,} \qquad \text{stationary} \\[3mm] H_a : \rho_k \neq 0 \ , \ \text{if} \ |\hat{\rho}_k| > t_{\alpha/2} \dfrac{1}{\sqrt{n}} \ , \ \text{i.e., non-stationary} \end{array} \right\} \qquad (12.32)$$

where $t_{\frac{\alpha}{2}}(m)$ is the critical value of the t-distribution (normal distribution) for an α level of significance.

   In our case, of the time series of the private consumption in Table 12.1, the sample size is n = 36 and therefore $1/\sqrt{36}$ = 0.167. If we assume that the level of significance is α = 0.05 then $t_{\alpha/2}$ = 1.96, and, thus, $t_{\alpha/2}1/\sqrt{n}$ = 0.327. Comparing this value of 0.327 with the estimated autocorrelation coefficients in Table 12.2 of the original private consumption series, we see that all the AC up to lag k = 8 are greater than the critical value of 0.327. Therefore, we accept the alternative hypothesis in (12.32), i.e. we accept the hypothesis that private consumption is a non-stationary time series. Furthermore, comparing this value of 0.327 with the estimated autocorrelation coefficients in Table 12.2 of the once differenced private consumption series, we see that the absolute values of all the AC are less than the critical value of 0.327. Therefore, we accept the null hypothesis in (12.32), i.e. we accept the hypothesis that the once differenced once private consumption is a stationary time series.

b. *Testing autocorrelation coefficients jointly*

Box and Pierce (1970), in testing the autocorrelation coefficients jointly, developed the so-called *Q-statistic*, which is given by:

$$Q = n \sum_{k=1}^{m} \hat{\rho}_k^2 \sim \chi^2(m) \qquad (12.33)$$

where n is the sample size and m is the lag length used. Because this statistic is not valid for small samples, Ljung and Box (1978) proposed a variation of the statistic in (12.33), the LB_Q statistic, as follows:

$$LB\_Q = n(n+2)\sum_{k=1}^{m}\left(\frac{\hat{\rho}_k^2}{n-k}\right) \sim \chi^2(m) \tag{12.34}$$

The statistic in (12.34) is more powerful, both in small and large samples, than the statistic in (12.33), which may be used in large samples only. The hypotheses for testing autocorrelation coefficients jointly may be formulated as:

$$\left.\begin{array}{l} H_0: \text{ all } \rho_k = 0 \quad , \text{ if } LB\_Q < \chi_\alpha^2(m) \text{ , i.e.,} \quad\quad \text{stationary} \\ H_a: \text{ not all } \rho_k = 0 \text{ , if } LB\_Q > \chi_\alpha^2(m) \text{ , i.e., non-stationary} \end{array}\right\} \tag{12.35}$$

where: $\chi_\alpha^2(m)$ is the critical value of the χ^2 distribution for an a level of significance and m degrees of freedom.

In this time series of the private consumption in Table 12.1, the sample size is n = 36 and the estimated autocorrelation coefficients reported in Table 12.2 extend up to lag length k = 16. Furthermore, in the same Table 12.2, the Ljung-Box Q-statistics (LB_Q) are reported for the specific lag lengths autocorrelation coefficients and with the corresponding probability levels for significance (Prob). We see in Table 12.2 that all the Probs are 0.000 for the autocorrelation coefficients of the original private consumption series. Therefore, we accept the alternative hypothesis in (12.35), i.e. we accept the hypothesis that private consumption is a non-stationary time series. Finally, none of the Probs in Table 12.2 are less than the 0.05 significance level for the autocorrelation coefficients of the once differenced private consumption series. Therefore, we accept the null hypothesis in (12.35), i.e. we accept the hypothesis that the once differenced private consumption is a stationary time series.

12.6 A summary of key issues

- Given a time series, $Y_1, Y_2, \ldots Y_t$, it is assumed that each value in this series is drawn randomly from a probability distribution (each Y is a random variable with a probability distribution). More specifically, the set of series $(Y_1, Y_2, \ldots Y_t)$ is a set of *jointly* distributed random variables. That is, there exists some joint probability function P $(Y_1, Y_2, \ldots Y_t)$ that assigns probabilities to all possible values of the time series, $Y_1, Y_2, \ldots Y_t$. This type of data generation process is called a stochastic process.
- A set of observed time series values of Y's is a realisation set of this joint probability distribution.
- This joint probability function is difficult to model and needs simplifying assumptions concerning its characteristics over time. When modelling the time series, the first issue to be resolved is whether or not the joint probability distribution that generated the data series can be assumed to be invariant with respect to time.
- If this data generation process is time-invariant, we have a stationary time series. In this case we can model the data and forecast on the basis of its characteristics. This is similar

to the requirement of SG modelling that the parameters are to remain constant over time (no structural break).

- If the joint probability function changes with time we have a non-stationary stochastic process generating data. Modelling of data on the basis of past values is not possible. Regression analysis is inappropriate in this situation.
- In economics and finance, most time series are generated by non-stationary stochastic processes: GDP, prices, profits, dividends, stock prices, etc. Each appear to be generated by a non-stationary process closely approximated by a random walk process.
- Although it is difficult to model non-stationary series, certain classes of non-stationary stochastic processes (e.g. RW models) can easily be converted, via differencing of the data, to stationary time-invariant stochastic processes for the purpose of analysis. This is the normal procedure in the univariate time series analysis of the Box and Jenkins type. It is also now the standard procedure in time series econometrics via the cointegration procedure.
- Let y_t y_{t+1} ..y_{t+k} be a realisation set from a stochastic process corresponding to the random variables $(Y_t, Y_{t+1}, \ldots, Y_{t+k})$ with the joint probability function $P(Y_t, Y_{t+1}, \ldots, Y_{t+k})$, a future set of realisation, m periods ahead, conditional on this current probability function is generated by $P(Y_{t+m}, Y_{t+1+m}, \ldots, Y_{t+K+m}/Y_t \ldots Y_{t+k})$. We define a stationary process, as one whose joint probability distribution and conditional joint probability distribution are both invariant with respect to displacement in time, that is:

$$P(y_t, y_{t+1}, \ldots, y_{t+k}) = P(y_{t+m}, y_{t+1+m}, \ldots, y_{t+k+m}), \text{ for any t, k and m}$$

- It is possible for the shape of the joint probability distribution/stochastic process to change over time, but its mean, variance and covariances remain time-invariant. In this case the series is termed 'weak form stationary'.
- If the joint probability distributions are time-invariant/stationary, then the series is said to be a 'strict sense/strong form stationary'.
- In most analysis, weak form is used for modelling purposes.

Review questions

1   Explain what you understand by each one of the following:

    a   a stochastic time series process
    b   a stationary time series process
    c   a non-stationary time series.

In each case give an example to illustrate your answer.

2   Distinguish between conditions for a weak form and a strong form stationarity. Explain what you understand by a joint probability function of a time series data generation process.

3   Collect a time series data set on aggregate imports for the period 1980–2010, relating to a country of your own choice.

    a   Plot your data in actual figures and in 1st difference form. What can you infer from these plots?

b   Plot the associated correlogram and explain what it implies.
c   Test for the non-stationarity using relevant individual and joint tests of significance.

4   Explain the specific to general (SG) approach to the analysis of time series regression models. How does this approach normally deal with the problem of spurious regression? Give examples to illustrate your answer.

13 Testing for stationarity
The unit root tests

INTRODUCTION

The concept of stationarity is of crucial importance in modern time series econometrics. If variables of interest are found to be stationary then it is meaningful to include them in a regression model for the purpose of short- and long-run analysis using the cointegration methodology. On the other hand, if one or more of the variables are found to be non-stationary, their inclusion into a regression model typically results in spurious regression and faulty analysis. It is therefore important to first test for the stationarity of time series variables to establish their status. This testing procedure is carried out via the unit root testing methodology, which constitutes a key stage in modern time series econometrics. This chapter provides an introduction to the unit root testing methodology, using a number of examples to illustrate the applications of key procedures in practice.

Key topics

- Dickey-Fuller unit root tests
- Problems with the unit root tests

13.1 The unit root methodology

Consider the first-order autoregressive process introduced in Chapter 12.

$$X_t = \phi X_{t-1} + \varepsilon_t \tag{13.1}$$

where ε_t is white noise. This process may also be written in a first-order difference equation form as:

$$X_t - \phi X_{t-1} = \varepsilon_t \quad \text{or as} \quad \left(1 - \phi L\right) X_t = \varepsilon_t \tag{13.2}$$

For (13.2) to be stationary the root of the characteristic equation $1 - \phi L = 0$ must be greater than unity in absolute values. This equation has one root only, which is $L = 1/\phi$, and, thus, stationarity requires $-1 < \phi < 1$. Therefore, the hypotheses for testing the stationarity of X_t may be written as:

$$\left. \begin{array}{l} H_0: |\phi| \geq 1, \text{ for non-stationarity} \\ H_a: |\phi| < 1, \text{ for stationarity} \end{array} \right\} \tag{13.3}$$

In the case that $\phi = 1$, i.e. if the null hypothesis is true, then (13.2) is the random walk process, which we saw was non-stationary. This unity of ϕ is known as the *unit root* problem, i.e. the problem of the non-stationarity of the corresponding process. In other words, a unit root is another way to express non-stationarity.

By subtracting X_{t-1} from both sides of (13.1), we get that:

$$X_t - X_{t-1} = \phi X_{t-1} - X_{t-1} + \varepsilon_t$$

which is also written as:

$$\Delta X_t = \delta X_{t-1} + \varepsilon_t \qquad (13.4)$$

where Δ is the difference operator and $\delta = \phi - 1$. In other words, (13.4) is another way to write (13.1). Assuming that ϕ is positive (this is true for most economic time series) the hypotheses in (13.3) may be written equivalently as:

$$\left. \begin{array}{l} H_0: \ \delta \geq 0, \ \text{for non-stationarity} \\ H_a: \ \delta < 0, \ \text{for stationarity} \end{array} \right\} \qquad (13.5)$$

In the case that $\delta = 0$, or, equivalently, $\phi = 1$, i.e. if the null hypothesis is true, the corresponding process is non-stationary. In other words, non-stationarity, or the unit root problem, may be expressed either as $\phi = 1$, or as $\delta = 0$. One could then suggest that the problem of testing for non-stationarity of time series X_t reduces to testing if parameter $\phi = 1$ in the regression of Equation (13.1), or if parameter $\delta = 0$ in the regression of Equation (13.4). Such testing could be performed by using the two t-tests respectively:

$$t_\phi = \frac{\hat{\phi} - 1}{S_{\hat{\phi}}} \quad \text{or} \quad t_\delta = \frac{\hat{\delta}}{S_{\hat{\delta}}} \qquad (13.6)$$

where $S_{\hat{\phi}}$ and $S_{\hat{\delta}}$ are the estimated standard errors of the estimated parameters $\hat{\phi}$ and $\hat{\delta}$ respectively. However, the situation is more complex. Under the null hypothesis of non-stationarity, i.e. under $\phi = 1$ or $\delta = 0$, the t-values computed in (13.6) do not follow the usual Student's t-distribution, but they follow a non-standard and even asymmetrical distribution. Therefore, other distribution tables should be employed.

13.2 The Dickey-Fuller (DF) test

Dickey and Fuller (1979), on the basis of Monte Carlo simulations, and under the null hypothesis of the existence of a unit root in the process generating of time series, have tabulated critical values for the t_δ-statistic in (13.6), which they called τ *(tau) statistics*. These critical values are presented in Table 13.1. More recently, these critical values have been extended by MacKinnon (1991) through Monte Carlo simulations. Comparing the critical values in Table 13.1 with those of the standard t-distribution we see that the τ values are much greater (in absolute values) than the corresponding t-values. The Dickey-Fuller test for a unit root may then be constructed in the following two steps:

Step 1 Run the OLS regression in (13.4), i.e.

$$\Delta X_t = \delta X_{t-1} + \varepsilon_t \qquad (13.7)$$

and save the usual t_δ-ratio in (13.6).

Step 2 Decide about the existence of a unit root in the process generating the time series X_t, according to the following hypothesis:

$$H_0: \ \delta = 0, \ \text{for non-stationarity, if } t_\delta > \tau \Bigg\}$$
$$H_a: \ \delta < 0, \ \text{for stationarity,} \qquad \text{if } t_\delta < \tau \Bigg\} \tag{13.8}$$

where τ is the critical value from Table 13.1 for a given significance level. In other words, for a time series to be stationary, the t_δ value must be *much negative*. Otherwise, the time series is non-stationary.

Dickey and Fuller noticed that the τ critical values depend on the type of the regression Equation (13.7). Therefore they tabulated τ critical values when the regression equation contains a constant also, i.e. when Equation (13.7) becomes:

$$\Delta X_t = \alpha + \delta \, X_{t-1} + \varepsilon_t \tag{13.9}$$

Table 13.1 Critical values for the Dickey-Fuller τ-statistics

Sample size	Probability of a smaller value							
	0.01	*0.025*	*0.05*	*0.10*	*0.90*	*0.95*	*0.975*	*0.99*
No constant No time (statistic-τ)								
25	−2.66	−2.26	−1.95	−1.60	0.92	1.33	1.70	2.16
50	−2.62	−2.25	−1.95	−1.61	0.91	1.31	1.66	2.08
100	−2.60	−2.24	−1.95	−1.61	0.90	1.29	1.64	2.03
250	−2.58	−2.23	−1.95	−1.62	0.89	1.29	1.63	2.01
500	−2.58	−2.23	−1.95	−1.62	0.89	1.28	1.62	2.00
∞	−2.58	−2.23	−1.95	−1.62	0.89	1.28	1.62	2.00
Constant No time (statistic-τ_μ)								
25	−3.75	−3.33	−3.00	−2.62	−0.37	0.00	0.34	0.72
50	−3.58	−3.22	−2.93	−2.60	−0.40	−0.03	0.29	0.66
100	−3.51	−3.17	−2.89	−2.58	−0.42	−0.05	0.26	0.63
250	−3.46	−3.14	−2.88	−2.57	−0.42	−0.06	0.24	0.62
500	−3.44	−3.13	−2.87	−2.57	−0.43	−0.07	0.24	0.61
∞	−3.43	−3.12	−2.86	−2.57	−0.44	−0.07	0.23	0.60
Constant Time (statistic-τ_τ)								
25	−4.38	−3.95	−3.60	−3.24	−1.14	−0.80	−0.50	−0.15
50	−4.15	−3.80	−3.50	−3.18	−1.19	−0.87	−0.58	−0.24
100	−4.04	−3.73	−3.45	−3.15	−1.22	−0.90	−0.62	−0.28
250	−3.99	−3.69	−3.43	−3.13	−1.23	−0.92	−0.64	−0.31
500	−3.98	−3.68	−3.42	−3.13	−1.24	−0.93	−0.65	−0.32
∞	−3.96	−3.66	−3.41	−3.12	−1.25	−0.94	−0.66	−0.33

Source: Fuller, W. (1976) *Introduction to Statistical Time Series*, New York: John Wiley.

and when the regression equation contains a constant and a linear trend, i.e. when Equation (13.4) becomes:

$$\Delta X_t = \alpha + \beta t + \delta X_{t-1} + \varepsilon_t \qquad (13.10)$$

For Equation (13.9) the corresponding τ critical values are called τ_μ, and for Equation (13.10) the corresponding τ critical values are called τ_τ. These critical values are also presented in Table 13.1. However, the test about the stationarity of a time series always depends on the coefficient δ of the regressor X_{t-1}.

Example 13.1 Testing the stationarity of the private consumption time series of an EU member (DF)

In Table 12.1 the private consumption (C_t) time series for an EU member is presented. We saw in Chapter 12 that using the autocorrelation function methodology, this time series is non-stationary. Let us now apply the DF test on the same data. Corresponding to Equations (13.9) and (13.10), the OLS estimates for C_t are, respectively, the following:

$$\Delta \hat{C}_t = 12330.48 - 0.01091 C_{t-1}$$

$$t \qquad [5.138] \qquad [-1.339] \qquad\qquad\qquad (13.11)$$

$$R^2 = 0.052 \quad DW = 1.765$$

$$\Delta \hat{C}_t = 15630.83 + 346.4522t - 0.04536 C_{t-1}$$

$$t \qquad [1.966] \qquad [0.436] \qquad [-0.571] \qquad\qquad (13.12)$$

$$R^2 = 0.057 \quad DW = 1.716$$

In Table 13.2 the MacKinnon critical values for the rejection of the hypothesis of a unit root, evaluated from EViews for Equations (13.11) and (13.12), are reported.

Considering the hypotheses testing specified above, we see that for Equation (13.11) the $t_\delta = -1.339$ value is greater than all the τ_μ critical values in Table 13.2 and, thus, the null hypothesis is not rejected. Therefore, the private consumption time series exhibits a unit root, or, in other words, is a non-stationary time series. Similarly, for Equation (13.12) the $t_\delta = -0.571$ value is greater than all the τ_τ critical values in Table 13.2 and, thus, the null hypothesis is again not rejected. Therefore, the private consumption (C_t) time series exhibits a unit root, or, in other words, is a non-stationary time series.

Table 13.2 MacKinnon critical values for Equations (13.11) and (13.12) and the DF t_δ ratios

Significance level	Equation (13.11)	Equation (13.12)
	Constant, no trend (τ_μ) [$t_\delta = -1.339$]	Constant and trend (τ_τ) [$t_\delta = -0.571$]
0.01	−3.6289	−4.2412
0.05	−2.9472	−3.5426
0.10	−2.6118	−3.2032

Table 13.3 MacKinnon critical values for Equations (13.13) and (13.14) and the DF t_δ ratios

Significance level	Equation (13.13)	Equation (13.14)
	Constant, no trend (τ_μ) [$t_\delta = -4.862$]	Constant and trend (τ_τ) [$t_\delta = -5.073$]
0.01	−3.6353	−4.2505
0.05	−2.9499	−3.5468
0.10	−2.6133	−3.2056

Having found that the C_t time series is non-stationary, let us see how the first difference of this series (δC_t) behaves in terms of non-stationarity. By repeating the same exercise, as we did with C_t, we get for ΔC_t the following results:

$$\Delta^2 \hat{C}_t = 7972.671 - 0.85112 \Delta C_{t-1}$$

t   [4.301]   [−4.862]   (13.13)

$$R^2 = 0.425 \quad DW = 1.967$$

$$\Delta^2 \hat{C}_t = 10524.35 - 114.4611t - 0.89738 \Delta C_{t-1}$$

t   [3.908]   [−1.294]   [−5.073]   (13.14)

$$R^2 = 0.454 \quad DW = 1.988$$

where $\Delta^2 X_t = \Delta X_t - \Delta X_{t-1}$. In Table 13.3 the MacKinnon critical values for the rejection of the hypothesis of a unit root, evaluated from EViews for Equations (13.13) and (13.14), are reported.

Considering the hypotheses testing specified above, we see that for Equation (13.13) the $t_d = -4.862$ value is much less than all the τ_μ critical values in Table 13.3 and, thus, the alternative hypothesis is accepted. Therefore, the private consumption differenced once time series is not exhibiting a unit root, or, in other words, is a stationary time series. Similarly, for Equation (13.14) the $t_\delta = -5.073$ value is much less than all the τ_τ critical values in Table 13.3 and, thus, the alternative hypothesis is again accepted. Therefore, the private consumption differenced once time series does not exhibit a unit root, or, in other words, is a stationary time series.

Summarising the results of this example, we can say that since ΔC_t is stationary, i.e. using the terminology in Chapter 12 it is an I(0) stochastic process, and C_t is non-stationary, the private consumption time series is an I(1) stochastic process. When the terminology of integration is used in examining the non-stationarity of a stochastic process, the Dickey-Fuller tests are also known as *tests of integration* of a stochastic process.

13.3 The augmented Dickey-Fuller (ADF) test

We can generalise the DF test, if we consider the general case of an autoregressive process as follows:

$$X_t = \phi_1 X_{t-1} + \phi_2 X_{t-2} + \phi_3 X_{t-3} + \cdots + \phi_q X_{t-q} + \varepsilon_t \tag{13.15}$$

which is a qth-order autoregressive process.

We can express this equation in first difference form to generate:

$$\Delta X_t = \delta X_{t-1} + \delta_1 \Delta X_{t-1} + \delta_2 \Delta X_{t-2} + \cdots + \delta_{q-1} \Delta X_{t-q+1} + \varepsilon_t$$

where $\delta = \phi_1 + \phi_2 + \phi_3 + \ldots + \phi_q - 1$ and the δ_js are general functions of the ϕs. The corresponding ADF equations are the following equations, respectively:

$$\Delta X_t = \delta X_{t-1} + \sum_{j=2}^{q} \delta_j \Delta X_{t-j+1} + \varepsilon_t \tag{13.16}$$

$$\Delta X_t = \alpha + \delta X_{t-1} + \sum_{j=2}^{q} \delta_j \Delta X_{t-j+1} + \varepsilon_t \tag{13.17}$$

$$\Delta X_t = \alpha + \beta t + \delta X_{t-1} + \sum_{j=2}^{q} \delta_j \Delta X_{t-j+1} + \varepsilon_t \tag{13.18}$$

Because the original Dickey-Fuller equations have been 'augmented' with the lagged differenced terms to produce Equations (13.16), (13.17) and (13.18), respectively, the usual DF test applied to the latter equations takes the name of the *augmented Dickey-Fuller (ADF) test*. In fact, both the critical values for the Dickey-Fuller τ-statistics in Table 13.3 still hold for the ADF test and the testing of hypotheses is still that in (13.8). In other words, if t_δ, which it is generated from the OLS regressions of Equations (13.16), (13.17) or (13.18) is negative enough, then the corresponding times series will be stationary. Otherwise, it will be non-stationary.

Note that the key reason for augmenting the initial Dickey-Fuller equations with extra lagged differenced terms is to eliminate possible autocorrelation from the disturbances. The DF test is not valid if the disturbance terms are autocorrelated, and, in practice, typically the ADF test procedure, designed to eliminate autocorrelation, is the preferred option. In order to see how many extra terms we have to include in the equations, the usual Akaike's information criterion (AIC) and Schwartz criterion (SC) could be employed. Furthermore, in order to test if the disturbances were not autocorrelated, the usual Breusch-Godfrey, or Lagrange multiplier (LM) test could be used. We demonstrate these key issues via an example below.

Example 13.2 Testing the stationarity of the consumer price index time series of an EU member (ADF) test

To illustrate the ADF procedures we use the data set on consumer price index first encountered in Chapter 12, which is presented in Table 12.1. Table 13.4 presents the AIC, SC, and LM statistics for the consumer price index, P_t, using the augmented Dickey-Fuller Equations (13.17) and (13.18).

From the results in Table 13.4 it is seen that the estimated equations, with no extended differenced terms of P_t (q = 0), show that autocorrelation exists in the residuals. Therefore, this equation is discarded. There is no autocorrelation in the residuals when the equations are extended with one (q = 1) or two (q = 2) differenced terms of P_t, given low values of the LM test statistics. Furthermore, comparing the AIC and SC statistics between the various estimated versions of the equations, it is seen that for Equation (13.17) the minimum statistics are for q = 1, and for Equation (13.18) the minimum statistics are also for q = 1. Note these are larger negative values, therefore smaller AIC and SC statistics. These 'best' estimated equations are the following:

Table 13.4 AIC, SC and LM statistics for the P_t Equations (13.17) and (13.18)

	q = 0			q = 1			q = 2		
	AIC	SC	LM(1)	AIC	SC	LM(1)	AIC	SC	LM(1)
eq. (13.17)	−1.766	−1.677	21.329 (0.000)	−2.647	−2.513	0.527 (0.468)	−2.571	−2.389	0.133 (0.715)
eq. (13.18)	−2.101	−1.967	16.607 (0.000)	−2.717	−2.537	1.185 (0.276)	−2.670	−2.444	0.217 (0.641)

Notes: estimates with EViews, probabilities in parentheses

Table 13.5 MacKinnon critical values for Equations (13.19) and (13.20) and the DF t_δ ratios

Significance level	Equation (13.19)	Equation (13.20)
	Constant, no trend (τ_μ) [$t_\delta = -0.809$]	Constant and trend (τ_τ) [$t_\delta = -0.582$]
0.01	−3.6353	−4.2505
0.05	−2.9499	−3.5468
0.10	−2.6133	−3.2056

$$\Delta \hat{P}_t = 0.07860 - 0.01692 P_{t-1} + 1.13822 \Delta P_{t-1}$$

$$\text{t} \qquad [1.398] \quad [-0.809] \qquad [7.099] \tag{13.19}$$

$$R^2 = 0.957 \quad DW = 1.817$$

$$\Delta \hat{P}_t = -0.13369 + 0.01831t - 0.01171 P_{t-1} + 0.96093 \Delta P_{t-1}$$

$$\text{t} \qquad [-1.134] \quad [2.023] \quad [-0.582] \qquad [5.453] \tag{13.20}$$

$$R^2 = 0.962 \quad DW = 1.746$$

Using these 'best' estimated equations, in Table 13.5 the MacKinnon critical values for the rejection of the hypothesis of a unit root, evaluated from EViews for Equations (13.19) and (13.20), are reported. These critical values are the same critical values as those in Table 13.3, showing, thus, that the MacKinnon critical values are not affected by the number of the extra differenced terms in the equations.

Considering the same hypotheses as those for the DF test in (13.8), we see that for Equation (13.19) the $t_\delta = -0.809$ value is greater than all the τ_μ critical values in Table 13.5 and, thus, the null hypothesis is not rejected. Therefore, the consumer price index time series exhibits a unit root, or, in other words, is a non-stationary time series. Similarly, for Equation (13.20) the $t_\delta = -0.582$ value is greater than all the τ_τ critical values in Table 13.5 and, thus, the null hypothesis is again not rejected. Therefore, the consumer price index (P_t) time series exhibits a unit root, or, in other words, is a non-stationary time series.

By repeating the same exercise as we did with P_t, we observe that the differenced once time series, i.e. ΔP_t, is also a non-stationary time series. If we do the same for the differenced twice time series, i.e. $\Delta^2 P_t$, we find that it is a stationary time series. In other words, the consumer price index (P_t) is an I(2) stochastic process.

13.4 Testing joint hypotheses with the Dickey-Fuller tests

In DF or ADF tests we have seen till now the null hypothesis was with respect to parameter δ. Nothing was said for the other two deterministic parameters of the Dickey-Fuller regression equations, i.e. of the parameters α, referring to the constant, or drift, and β, referring to the linear deterministic trend, or time trend. Dickey and Fuller (1981) provided tests for testing jointly the parameters α, β and δ. The F-test, given by:

$$F = \frac{(SSR_r - SSR_u)/r}{SSR_u/(n-k)} \tag{13.21}$$

where:

SSR$_r$ = sum of squared residuals from the restricted equation
SSR$_u$ = sum of squared residuals from the unrestricted equation
n = number of usable observations
k = number of the coefficients in the unrestricted equation
r = number of restrictions

could be used in order to test joint hypotheses, following the usual Wald methodology for testing restrictions. However, because the F-distribution is not standard, for these tests Dickey and Fuller provided three additional F-statistics, called Φ_1, Φ_2 and Φ_3, according to the joint hypotheses to be tested. These three statistics are reported in Table 13.6.
    The joint hypotheses are the following:

1 When Dickey-Fuller regression equations of the form (13.18) are used:

$$\left.\begin{aligned} &H_0: \ \alpha = \beta = \delta = 0, && \text{if } F < \Phi_2 \\ &H_a: \ \text{not all } \alpha, \beta, \delta = 0, && \text{if } F > \Phi_2 \end{aligned}\right\} \tag{13.22}$$

2 When Dickey-Fuller regression equations of the form (13.18) are used:

$$\left.\begin{aligned} &H_0: \ \beta = \delta = 0, && \text{, if } F < \Phi_3 \\ &H_a: \ \text{not both } \beta \text{ and } \delta = 0, && \text{, if } F > \Phi_3 \end{aligned}\right\} \tag{13.23}$$

3 When Dickey-Fuller regression equations of the form (13.17) are used:

$$\left.\begin{aligned} &H_0: \ \alpha = \delta = 0, && \text{, if } F < \Phi_1 \\ &H_a: \ \text{not both } \alpha \text{ and } \delta = 0, && \text{, if } F > \Phi_1 \end{aligned}\right\} \tag{13.24}$$

Example 13.3 Testing joint hypotheses for the non-stationarity of the consumer price index time series of an EU member (ADF)

We found in the above Example (13.2) that the consumer price index (P_t) is non-stationary. In this example we will illustrate the Dickey-Fuller joint hypotheses tests with the time series below.
    Using the estimated Equation (13.20) we can test the joint hypotheses in (13.22) and in (13.23). In other words, for (13.22) we test that:

$$H_0: \text{ data are generated by } \Delta P_t = \delta_1 \Delta P_{t-1} + \varepsilon_t \quad \text{if } F < \Phi_2$$
$$H_a: \text{ data not generated by } \Delta P_t = \delta_1 \Delta P_{t-1} + \varepsilon_t \quad \text{if } F > \Phi_2$$

(13.25)

and for (13.23) we test that:

$$H_0: \text{ data are generated by } \Delta P_t = \alpha + \delta_1 \Delta P_{t-1} + \varepsilon_t \quad \text{if } F < \Phi_3$$
$$H_a: \text{ data are not generated by } \Delta P_t = \alpha + \delta_1 \Delta P_{t-1} + \varepsilon_t \quad \text{if } F > \Phi_3$$

(13.26)

From the estimated Equation (13.20), using the usual Wald statistic for redundant variables, for $n = 34$ usable observations, $k = 4$ estimated coefficients and $r = 3$ restrictions, we get that $F_2(\alpha = 0, \beta = 0, \delta = 0) = 2.277$. The value of this statistic $F_2 = 2.277$ is less than the critical value $\Phi_2(n = 25) = 5.68$ and $\Phi_2(n = 50) = 5.13$, for 0.05 significance level, reported in Table 13.6. Therefore, we accept the null hypothesis, i.e. we accept that P_t is random walk, since $\alpha = 0$ means the absence of a stochastic trend, $\beta = 0$ means the absence of a deterministic trend also and $\delta = 0$ means non-stationarity.

From the estimated Equation (13.20), using the usual Wald statistic for redundant variables, for $n = 34$ usable observations, $k = 4$ estimated coefficients and $r = 2$ restrictions, we get that $\Phi_3(\beta = 0, \delta = 0) = 2.406$. The value of this statistic $F_3 = 2.406$ is less than the critical value $\Phi_3(n = 25) = 7.24$ and $\Phi_3(n = 50) = 6.73$, for 0.05 significance level, reported in Table 13.6. Therefore, we accept the null hypothesis, i.e. we accept that P_t is subject to a stochastic trend only, since $\beta = 0$ means the absence of a deterministic trend and $\delta = 0$ means non-stationarity.

Table 13.6 Critical values for the Dickey-Fuller Φ-statistics

Sample size	Probability of a smaller value							
	0.01	0.025	0.05	0.10	0.90	0.95	0.975	0.99
Statistic $\Phi 1$								
25	0.29	0.38	0.49	0.65	4.12	5.18	6.30	7.88
50	0.29	0.39	0.50	0.66	3.94	4.86	5.80	7.06
100	0.29	0.39	0.50	0.67	3.86	4.71	5.57	6.70
250	0.30	0.39	0.51	0.67	3.81	4.63	5.45	6.52
500	0.30	0.39	0.51	0.67	3.79	4.61	5.41	6.47
∞	0.30	0.40	0.51	0.67	3.78	4.59	5.38	6.43
Statistic $\Phi 2$								
25	0.61	0.75	0.89	1.10	4.67	5.68	6.75	8.21
50	0.62	0.77	0.91	1.12	4.31	5.13	5.94	7.02
100	0.63	0.77	0.92	1.12	4.16	4.88	5.59	6.50
250	0.63	0.77	0.92	1.13	4.07	4.75	5.40	6.22
500	0.63	0.77	0.92	1.13	4.05	4.71	5.35	6.15
∞	0.63	0.77	0.92	1.13	4.03	4.68	5.31	6.09
Statistic $\Phi 3$								
25	0.74	0.90	1.08	1.33	5.91	7.24	8.65	10.61
50	0.76	0.93	1.11	1.37	5.61	6.73	7.81	9.31
100	0.76	0.94	1.12	1.38	5.47	6.49	7.44	8.73
250	0.76	0.94	1.13	1.39	5.39	6.34	7.25	8.43
500	0.76	0.94	1.13	1.39	5.36	6.30	7.20	8.34
∞	0.77	0.94	1.13	1.39	5.34	6.25	7.16	8.27

Source: Dickey, D.A. and W.A. Fuller (1981) 'Likelihood ratio statistics for autoregressive time series with a unit root', *Econometrica*, 49, 4, 1057–1072.

Using the estimated Equation (13.19) we can test the joint hypotheses in (13.24). In other words, for (13.24) we test that:

$$H_0: \text{data are generated by } \Delta P_t = \delta_1 \Delta P_{t-1} + \varepsilon_t \text{ if } F < \Phi_1$$
$$H_a: \text{data are not generated by } \Delta P_t = \delta_1 \Delta P_{t-1} + \varepsilon_t \text{ if } F > \Phi_1$$ (13.27)

From the estimated Equation (13.19), using the usual Wald statistic for redundant variables, for $n = 34$ usable observations, $k = 3$ estimated coefficients and $r = 2$ restrictions, we get that $F_1(\alpha = 0, \delta = 0) = 1.246$. The value of this statistic $F_1 = 1.246$ is less than the critical value $\Phi_1(n = 25) = 5.18$ and $\Phi_1(n = 50) = 4.86$, for 0.05 significance level, reported in Table 13.6. Therefore, we accept the null hypothesis, i.e. we accept that P_t is random walk, since $\alpha = 0$ means the absence of a stochastic trend and $\delta = 0$ means non-stationarity.

13.5 Testing conditional hypotheses with the Dickey-Fuller tests

Dickey and Fuller (1981) provided us with three symmetric critical τ_{ij} values, called $\tau_{\alpha\mu}$, $\tau_{\alpha\tau}$, and $\tau_{\beta\mu}$, reported in Table 13.7, for testing the drift parameter α and the linear time trend parameter β, conditionally upon $\delta = 0$.

Table 13.7 Critical values for the Dickey-Fuller τ_{ij}-statistics (symmetric distributions)

Sample size	Probability of a smaller value			
	0.90	0.95	0.975	0.99
Statistic – $\tau_{\alpha\mu}$				
25	2.20	2.61	2.97	3.41
50	2.18	2.56	2.89	3.28
100	2.17	2.54	2.86	3.22
250	2.16	2.53	2.84	3.19
500	2.16	2.52	2.83	3.18
∞	2.16	2.52	2.83	3.18
Statistic – $\tau_{\alpha\tau}$				
25	2.77	3.20	3.59	4.05
50	2.75	3.14	3.47	3.87
100	2.73	3.11	3.42	3.78
250	2.73	3.09	3.39	3.74
500	2.72	3.08	3.38	3.72
∞	2.72	3.08	3.38	3.71
Statistic – $\tau_{\beta\tau}$				
25	2.39	2.85	3.25	3.74
50	2.38	2.81	3.18	3.60
100	2.38	2.79	3.14	3.53
250	2.38	2.79	3.12	3.49
500	2.38	2.78	3.11	3.48
∞	2.38	2.78	3.11	3.46

Source: Dickey, D.A. and W.A. Fuller (1981) 'Likelihood ratio statistics for autoregressive time series with a unit root', *Econometrica*, 49, 4, 1057–1072.

The conditional hypotheses are the following:

1 When Dickey-Fuller regression equations of the form (13.18) are used:

$$H_0: \ \alpha = 0 \text{ given that } \delta = 0, \quad \text{if } |t| < |\tau_{\alpha\tau}| \left.\right\} \atop H_a: \ \alpha \neq 0 \text{ given that } \delta = 0, \quad \text{if } |t| > |\tau_{\alpha\tau}| \quad (13.28)$$

2 When Dickey-Fuller regression equations of the form (13.18) are used:

$$H_0: \ \beta = 0 \text{ given that } \delta = 0, \quad \text{if } |t| < |\tau_{\beta\tau}| \left.\right\} \atop H_a: \ \beta \neq 0 \text{ given that } \delta = 0, \quad \text{if } |t| > |\tau_{\beta\tau}| \quad (13.29)$$

3 When Dickey-Fuller regression equations of the form (13.17) are used:

$$H_0: \ \alpha = 0 \text{ given that } \delta = 0, \quad \text{if } |t| < |\tau_{\alpha\mu}| \left.\right\} \atop H_a: \ \alpha \neq 0 \text{ given that } \delta = 0, \quad \text{if } |t| > |\tau_{\alpha\mu}| \quad (13.30)$$

Example 13.4 Testing conditional hypotheses for the non-stationarity of the consumer price index time series of an EU member (ADF)

We found in Examples 13.2 and 13.3 that the consumer price index (P_t) time series for an EU member is non-stationary. In this example we will illustrate the Dickey-Fuller conditional hypotheses tests presented just above.

From the estimated Equation (13.20) with n = 34 usable observations we get that $t_\alpha = -1.134$ and $t_\beta = 2.023$. For testing hypotheses (13.28) and (13.29) we have to compare these t-values with the corresponding τ_{ij} critical values in Table 13.7. From Table 13.7 we have that $\tau_{\alpha\tau}(n = 25) = 3.20$ and $\tau_{\alpha\tau}(n = 50) = 3.14$, and $\tau_{\beta\tau}(25) = 2.85$ and $\tau_{\beta\tau}(50) = 2.81$. Therefore, since $|t_\alpha| < |\tau_{\alpha\tau}|$ and $|t_\beta| < |\tau_{\beta\tau}|$ we accept the null hypotheses in (13.28) and (13.29), respectively, i.e. we accept that given that P_t is non-stationary, there is neither a stochastic trend nor a deterministic trend generating the series.

From the estimated Equation (13.19) with n = 34 usable observations we get that $t_\alpha = 1.398$. For testing hypotheses (13.30) we have to compare this t-value with the corresponding τ_{ij} critical value in Table 13.7. From Table 13.7 we have that $\tau_{\alpha\mu}(n = 25) = 2.61$ and $\tau_{\alpha\mu}(n = 50) = 2.56$. Therefore, since $|t_\alpha| < |\tau_{\alpha\mu}|$ we accept the null hypotheses in (13.30), i.e. we accept that given that P_t is non-stationary, there is no stochastic trend generating the time series.

In summary, we see that the results in Example 13.4 do not contradict the results obtained in Example 13.3. In other words, we could say that in the process of generating the non-stationary time series of the price consumer index of an EU member, both stochastic trends and deterministic trends are absent.

13.5.1 A sequential procedure in the Dickey-Fuller tests when the data generating process is unknown

The tests for unit roots of a time series are not as simple as the tests presented in the previous sections suggest. Unfortunately, the tests for the presence of unit roots in a time series are conditional on the presence of deterministic drifts and trends. The tests for the presence of deterministic drifts and trends in a time series are conditional on the presence of unit roots (Campbell and Perron, 1991; Enders, 2010). Doldado *et al.* (1990), Holden and Perman (1994) and Enders (1995) presented sequential procedures for testing the unit roots in a time series if the data generating process is not known. These procedures are based on the following points:

1   The 'top to bottom' philosophy, meaning that the top (starting) point of the procedure should be the most general case and then, step by step, to move towards the lowest (finishing) point, which should be the most specific case.
2   If it is known that the time series under investigation contains a drift or trend, then the null hypothesis of a unit root can be tested using the standard normal distribution.
3   Because the unit roots tests have low power in rejecting the null hypothesis of a unit root, if, at any step of the sequential procedure of testing, the null hypothesis is rejected, then the whole procedure ends, concluding that the time series under investigation is stationary.

A modified mixture of these sequential procedures could be the following:

Step 1 Estimate the following equation with OLS:

$$\Delta X_t = \alpha + \beta t + \delta X_{t-1} + \sum_{j=2}^{q} \delta_j \Delta X_{t-j+1} + \varepsilon_t \tag{13.31}$$

- Use statistics AIC and SC to find the proper number of differenced terms to be included in the equation.
- Use statistic LM to test for autocorrelation in the residuals.

Step 2 Use statistic τ_τ to test the null hypothesis $\delta = 0$ in Equation (13.31).

- If the null hypothesis is rejected then time series X_t does not contain a unit root. You may stop the whole process, concluding that the time series is stationary.
- If the null hypothesis is not rejected you must continue, in order to test the drift and trend terms.

Step 3 Use statistic $\tau_{\beta\tau}$ to test the conditional null hypothesis $\beta = 0$, given $\delta = 0$, i.e. to test the significance of the trend term given that the time series contains a unit root. You may verify this test by using statistic Φ_3 to test the joint null hypothesis $\beta = \delta = 0$.

- If the null hypothesis is not rejected, i.e. if β is not significant, you may continue.
- If the null hypothesis is rejected, i.e. if β is significant, you have to perform the following test:

Use the standard normal distribution to retest the null hypothesis $\delta = 0$.

- If the null hypothesis is rejected, i.e. if time series X_t does not contain a unit root, you may stop the process, concluding that the time series is stationary.
- If the null hypothesis is not rejected, i.e. if time series X_t contains a unit root, you conclude that $\beta \neq 0$ and $\delta = 0$.

Step 4 Use statistic $\tau_{\alpha\tau}$ to test the conditional null hypothesis $\alpha = 0$, given $\delta = 0$, i.e. to test the significance of the drift term given that the time series contains a unit root. You may verify this test by using statistic Φ_2 to test the joint null hypothesis $\alpha = \beta = \delta = 0$.

- If the null hypothesis is not rejected, i.e. if α is not significant, you may continue.
- If the null hypothesis is rejected, i.e. if α is significant, you have to perform the following test:
- Use the standard normal distribution to retest the null hypothesis $\delta = 0$.
- If the null hypothesis is rejected, i.e. if time series X_t does not contain a unit root, you may stop the process, concluding that the time series is stationary.
- If the null hypothesis is not rejected, i.e. if time series X_t contains a unit root, you conclude that $\alpha \neq 0$ and $\delta = 0$.

Step 5 Estimate the following equation with OLS:

$$\Delta X_t = \alpha + \delta X_{t-1} + \sum_{j=2}^{q} \delta_j \Delta X_{t-j+1} + \varepsilon_t \tag{13.32}$$

Step 6 Use statistic τ_μ to test the null hypothesis $\delta = 0$ in Equation (13.32).

- If the null hypothesis is rejected, then time series X_t does not contain a unit root. You may stop the whole process, concluding that the time series is stationary.
- If the null hypothesis is not rejected, you must continue, in order to test the drift term.

Step 7 Use statistic $\tau\alpha\mu$ to test the conditional null hypothesis $\alpha = 0$, given $\delta = 0$, i.e. to test the significance of the drift term, given that the time series contains a unit root. You may verify this test by using statistic $\Phi1$ to test the joint null hypothesis $\alpha = \delta = 0$.

- If the null hypothesis is not rejected, i.e. if α is not significant, you may continue.
- If the null hypothesis is rejected, i.e. if α is significant, you have to perform the following test:

Use the standard normal distribution to retest the null hypothesis $\delta = 0$.

- If the null hypothesis is rejected, i.e. if time series X_t does not contain a unit root, you may stop the process, concluding that the time series is stationary.
- If the null hypothesis is not rejected, i.e. if time series X_t contains a unit root, you conclude that $\alpha \neq 0$ and $\delta = 0$.

Step 8 Estimate the following equation with OLS:

$$\Delta X_t = \delta X_{t-1} + \sum_{j=2}^{q} \delta_j \Delta X_{t-j+1} + \varepsilon_t \tag{13.33}$$

Step 9 Use statistic τ to test the null hypothesis $\delta = 0$ in Equation (13.33).

- If the null hypothesis is rejected, you conclude that time series X_t does not contain a unit root, i.e. it is stationary.
- If the null hypothesis is not rejected, you conclude that time series X_t contains a unit root, i.e. it is non-stationary.

Example 13.5 Using a sequential procedure for testing the non-stationarity of the consumer price index time series of an EU member (ADF)

This example is in fact a summary of the tests performed in Examples 13.2, 13.3 and 13.4. Table 13.8 summarises relevant results from these examples.

Table 13.8 Results of a sequential procedure for testing unit roots of the consumer price index time series (P) of an EU member

Equation	Intercept	Trend	P_{t-1}	ΔP_{t-1}	LM(1)	$F_3 (\Phi_3)$	$F_2(\Phi_2)$	$F_1(\Phi_1)$
(7.67)	−0.1337	0.0183	−0.0117	0.9609	1.185	2.406	2.277	
	[−1.134]	[2.023]	[−0.582]	[5.453]	(0.276)			
(7.68)	0.0786		−0.0169	1.1382	0.527			1.246
	[1.398]		[−0.809]	[7.099]	(0.468)			
(7.69)			−0.0153	1.1597	0.919			
			[−0.723]	[7.161]	(0.345)			

Notes: t-ratios in brackets; probabilities in parentheses

According to the steps presented above, a brief explanation of these results is as follows:

Step 1 The results for Equation (13.31) are shown. There is no autocorrelation in the residuals.

Step 2 Because $t_\delta = -0.582 > \tau_\tau = -3.5468$ the time series contains a unit root.

Step 3 Because $|t_\beta| = 2.023 < |\tau_{\beta\tau}| = 2.81$ it may be $\beta = 0$. This result is also verified by $F_3 = 2.406 < \Phi_3 = 6.73$.

Step 4 Because $|t_\alpha| = 1.134 < |\tau_{\alpha\tau}| = 3.14$ it may be $\alpha = 0$. This result is also verified by $F_2 = 2.277 < \Phi_2 = 5.13$.

Step 5 The results for Equation (13.32) are shown. There is no autocorrelation in the residuals.

Step 6 Because $t_\delta = -0.809 > \tau_\mu = -2.9499$ the time series contains a unit root.

Step 7 Because $|t_\alpha| = 1.398 < |\tau_{\alpha\mu}| = 2.56$ it may be $\alpha = 0$. This result is also verified by $F_1 = 1.246 < \Phi_1 = 4.86$.

Step 8 The results for Equation (13.33) are shown. There is no autocorrelation in the residuals.

Step 9 Because $t_\delta = -0.723 > \tau = -1.95$ the time series contains a unit root.

Final conclusion: the consumer price index (P_t) time series for an EU member contains a unit root without drift and without trend.

13.6 The multiple unit roots, the seasonal unit roots and the panel data unit root tests

Since the original Dickey-Fuller and the augmented Dickey-Fuller test were developed, various modifications and/or extensions of this test have been proposed. We have already seen some of these tests in the previous sections. However, we will now refer briefly to some of these and other tests.

a. The multiple roots tests

Dickey and Pantula (1987), in order to test if a time series has more than one unit root, proposed the successive testing of the time series, differenced accordingly. In other words, if a time series has possibly one unit root, a simple version of the estimated equation we saw is the following:

$$\Delta X_t = \alpha + \delta X_{t-1} + \varepsilon_t \tag{13.34}$$

If the time series has possibly two roots, the estimated equation is the following:

$$\Delta^2 X_t = \alpha + \delta \Delta X_{t-1} + \varepsilon_t \tag{13.35}$$

If the time series has possibly three roots, the estimated equation is the following:

$$\Delta^3 X_t = \alpha + \delta \Delta^2 X_{t-1} + \varepsilon_t \tag{13.36}$$

and so on. For each equation the usual DF or ADF procedure should be applied (see Examples 13.1 and 13.2).

b. The seasonal unit root tests

When a time series X_t is measured s times per year, Dickey *et al.* (1984) proposed that the following regression equation be used:

$$\Delta_s Z_t = \delta Z_{t-s} + \sum_{j=1}^{q} \delta_j \Delta_s X_{t-j} + \varepsilon_t \tag{13.37}$$

where $\Delta_s Z_t = Z_t - Z_{t-s}$, and

$$Z_t = X_t - \sum_{j=1}^{h} \hat{\lambda}_j X_{t-j} \tag{13.38}$$

with the $\hat{\lambda}_j$s being the estimates of the λ_js obtained from the following regression:

$$\Delta_s X_t = \sum_{j=1}^{h} \lambda_j \Delta_s X_{t-j} + \eta_t \tag{13.39}$$

The test on unit roots could be based on the Student's t-statistic of the δ coefficient in the regression (13.37). Osborn *et al.* (1988), instead of using $\Delta_s Z_t$ as the dependent variable in the regression Equation (13.37), proposed variable $\Delta_s X_t$. Furthermore, Hylleberg *et al.* (1990) proposed a more general test to deal with cyclical movements at different frequencies, and, therefore, to test the corresponding unit roots (for more see Charemza and Deadman, 1997).

In the simple case where the seasonal pattern of a time series X_t measured s times per time period is purely deterministic, the following regression equation could be used:

$$\Delta\hat{\eta}_t = \delta\hat{\eta}_{t-1} + \sum_{j=1}^{q}\delta_j\Delta\hat{\eta}_{t-j} + \varepsilon_t \tag{13.40}$$

where $\hat{\eta}_t$ are the estimated residuals of η_t derived from the following regression equation:

$$X_t = \alpha_s + \sum_{j=1}^{s-1}\alpha_j D_{jt} + \eta_t \tag{13.41}$$

where D_{jt} are $s - 1$ dummy variables. In other words, $\hat{\eta}_t$ could be considered as a deseasonalised time series in the place of X_t. For the testing of unit roots the usual DF or ADF procedure could be used for coefficient δ of the regression Equation (13.40) (Dickey *et al.* (1986), Enders (2010)).

c. The Phillips-Perron test

One of the basic assumptions of the DF tests is that the disturbances are independently and identically distributed (IID). Phillips and Perron (1988) proposed statistics, named the Z-statistics, where the assumption of IID is relaxed. However, because the modifications to the DF tests proposed by Phillips-Perron are nonparametric, we believe that this test, although popular, is beyond the scope of this book.

d. The Schmidt-Phillips test

Schmidt and Phillips (1992) have shown that a unit root test based on a detrended time series has more power compared to the DF tests, but it is more involved to use in practice. The key steps are as follows:

Step 1 Use a random walk with a drift model:

$$Y_t = a + \beta t + \sum u_{t-i}, \text{ summation is from } i = 1 \text{ to } t. \tag{13.42}$$

The basic idea is to remove the deterministic trend by estimating the trend coefficient β. Using this estimate the series is then detrended.

Step 2 Use the detrended series, $\det(Y_{t-1})$, in the following DF/ADF type equation:

$$\Delta Y_t = a + \gamma \det(Y_{t-1}) + u_t \tag{13.43}$$

Step 3 The null of the unit root ($H_0:\gamma = 0$) can be rejected, if the absolute value of the corresponding 'test statistic' is larger than the critical value. The CV of this test for $n = 200$ at 5% is -3.04 (S-P test critical values). It can be shown that this test has more power compared to DF/ADF tests and can better distinguish between a TS and a DS time series.

e. The IPS panel data unit root test

In recent years, because of the popularity of the panel data regression modelling, it has become common practice to test for the unit root when working with panel data/pooled data sets. A popular unit root test for panel data/pooled data is recommended by Im, Pesaran and Shin (2003), and is known as the (IPS) test. Suppose we have n series, each having T observations. The basic idea of the test is to perform an ADF test on each n series, pool the estimates together, and then carry out a unit root test on the pooled estimated test value. Key steps may be summarised as follows:

Step 1 For each n time series run an ADF test (use the same model in each case, for example, run a random walk with a drift parameter model in a ADF form).

Step 2 Let the t_{ADFi} to denote the unit root test static value for each of n series.

Step 3 Obtain the average value of the test statistic in step 2 as follows:

$$t_{IPS} = (1/n)(t_{ADF1} + t_{ADF2} + t_{ADF3} + \dots t_{ADFn})$$ (13.44)

Step 4 The test statistic is a Z-statistic, as follows:

$$Z_{IPS} = \frac{n^{1/2}(t_{IPS} - E(t_{IPS}))}{\sqrt{var(t_{IPS})}}$$ (13.45)

Im, Pesaran and Shin (2003) showed that Z_{IPS} has a standard normal distribution when sample size is large. Moreover, they calculated the critical values of this test for various levels of n and T. For example, for n = 5 and T = 50, at a 5% level of significance, the critical value is calculated at −2.18.

Step 5 If the absolute value of test statistic Z_{IPS} is greater than the critical value, reject the null hypothesis that each of the n series has a unit root, or that all n series are I(1) series. Note that this is a large sample test and the lowest permissible value for n is calculated at 5.

f. A quick test for non-stationarity

Sargan and Bhargava (1983) suggested a quick test, although it is now very popular, for testing the possible non-stationarity of a time series X_t. Their test uses the same formula as the known formula for computing the Durbin-Watson statistic, which is:

$$IDW = \frac{\Sigma(X_t - X_{t-1})^2}{\Sigma(X_t - \bar{X})^2}$$ (13.46)

where $\bar{X}$ = arithmetic mean of X_t. Due to the formula (13.46) this statistic is called the *integration Durbin-Watson (IDW) statistic*. However, if the time series X_t is regressed on a constant, the estimate of the constant is the arithmetic mean of the time series X_t, and the one corresponding to this DW regression statistic is the IDW statistic computed in (13.46). In this regression, if the time series X_t is non-stationary, so will the corresponding residuals, because:

$$X_t = a + e_t$$ (13.47)

where a = estimated intercept and e_t = residuals. If the value of IDW is low, say lower than 0.5, time series X_t is suspected to be non-stationary. If the value of IDW is close to 2, time series X_t is stationary.

As an example, the value of IDW for the private consumption (C_t) time series of an EU member is equal to 0.010, indicating that this time series is non-stationary, as we found in Example 7.1. Furthermore, for the same time series differenced once (ΔC_t) it is IDW = 1.692, indicating that time series ΔC_t is stationary, as we also found in Example 7.1.

13.7 Problems of the unit root tests and recommendations

The basic problem that is encountered in the use of the Dickey-Fuller tests is the *lack of power* of the tests. The power of a test is its ability to detect a false null hypothesis and it is measured by the probability of rejecting the null hypothesis when it is false. It has been proved, using Monte Carlo simulations, that the power of the unit root tests is very low. In other words, although a time series may be stationary, the unit root tests may fail to detect this, and suggest that the time series is non-stationary.

Because most macroeconomic time series X_t are trended upwards, the unit root tests often indicate that these series are non-stationary. A usual procedure to transform the trended upwards time series to roughly remaining constant over time, is to consider their percentage growth, i.e. to consider the time series $(X_t - X_{t-1})/X_{t-1}$. When the values of a time series are positive, by getting the natural logarithms of the series, i.e. $x_t = \ln(X_t)$, we can use the 'lower case' series x_t in the unit root tests. In trying to detect if the time series x_t has a unit root we use the difference $\Delta x_t = x_t - x_{t-1}$. However, because it is approximately true that:

$$\Delta x_t = \ln X_t - \ln X_{t-1} = \ln\left(\frac{X_t}{X_{t-1}}\right) \approx \frac{X_t - X_{t-1}}{X_{t-1}} \tag{13.48}$$

in the unit root tests the time series are often taken in logarithms instead of natural levels. To see this, assume the upwards trending time series of the consumer price index (P_t), for example, which is given by:

$$P_t = P_0 e^{gt + \eta_t} \tag{13.49}$$

where g = constant rate of growth and η_t = error term. If we take the logarithms of both sides of (13.49) we obtain that:

$$\ln P_t = \ln P_0 + gt + \eta_t \tag{13.50}$$

which can be written as:

$$\ln P_t - \ln P_{t-1} = gt - g(t-1) + \eta_t - \eta_{t-1}$$

or

$$p_t - p_{t-1} = g + \varepsilon_t \tag{13.51}$$

where $p_t = \ln P_t$ and $\varepsilon_t = \eta_t - \eta_{t-1}$. In the case that ε_t is white noise, Equation (13.51) is a random walk process with a drift parameter.

13.8 A summary of key issues

- The starting point in modern time series econometrics is the phenomenon of the spurious regression. That is, a high level of autocorrelation, significant t and F-ratios and high R^2, all in the same regression, signifying serious specification problems. The traditional approach to econometric analysis fails to provide an adequate answer/solution to this problem.
- The problem is due to the fact that economic/financial variables are seldom stationary over time. That is, the joint probability functions generating the realised values of each variable (data set) change over time, therefore when they combine in a regression model, the result is a meaningless spurious regression.
- The modern approach to the problem of the spurious regression is as follows:

Step 1 Check the characteristics of the data generation processes (DGP) of each variable under consideration. The potential DGP for most macroeconomic and also financial time series could be any one of the following non-stationary stochastic processes (Nelson and Plosser, 1982):

A simple random walk – changes over time according to $\Delta y_t = u_t$ (DS series).
A random walk with drift – changes over time according to $(\Delta y_t = a + u_t)$ (DS series).
A random walk plus noise – changes over time according to $(\Delta y_t = u_t + \Delta \eta_t)$, (DS Series).

These DGPs have stochastic trends and are non-stationary; in particular, each series variance will increase/changes rapidly over time. The DGP could be trend stationary, that is $\Delta y_t = a$ (TS – needs detrending).

Step 2 Having gone through the first step for each variable (say Y and X, for example) plot the data for each variable – check the pattern of change for each variable over time.

Step 3 Test for the unit root to examine the order of the integration of each of the variables under consideration, as follows:

Dickey and Fuller (1979) consider three different regression models that can be used to test for the presence of a unit root:

Model 1 A pure/simple random walk (RW) of the form:

$Y_t = \alpha Y_{t-1} + ut$
$H_0: \alpha = 1$ i.e. Y_t is I(1) – DS (difference stationary)
$H_1: \alpha < 1$ (strictly less than unity) – Y_t is I(0) – stationary

Problem: if $\alpha = 1$, then a regression in levels is likely to be biased, and in particular bias α towards zero. Therefore, the RW model is re-parameterised by subtracting Y_{t-1} from both sides as, $Y_t - Y_{t-1} = \Delta Yt = \gamma Y_{t-1} + u_t$; where $\gamma = \alpha - 1$

$H0: \gamma = 0$; Y_t is I(1) – DS
$H1: \gamma < 0$; Y_t is I(1) – a stationary series

Model 2 A random walk model with a drift:

$\Delta Y_t = a + \gamma Y_{t-1} + u_t$ (a = intercept term/drift parameter).
$H_0: \gamma = 0$; Y_t is I(1) – DS
$H_1: \gamma < 0$; Y_{t-1} is I(1) – a stationary process

Model 3 RW with a drift and a linear time trend:

$\Delta Y_t = a + \gamma Y_{t-1} + \beta t + u_t$
$H_0: \gamma = 0$; Y_t is I(1) – DS
$H_1: \gamma < 0$; Y_{t-1} is I(0) – a stationary process

- The DF test involves estimating one (or more) of the DF equations (models 1, 2 or 3), using OLS in order to obtain the estimated value of γ and the associated standard error. Compare the resulting 't-ratio' with the appropriate value reported in the DF tables to determine whether to reject or not reject the null H_0.
- Note that the above methodology is the same regardless of which of the three forms/models is estimated. However, you should take into account the following key points:
- The DF distribution is not exactly the same as a t-distribution and the critical values for $H_0: \gamma = 0$ depends on the form of the model and on the sample size.
- The DF statistics are called τ, tau. For no constant or time trend – Model 1: CV for n = 500 at 5% is −1.96. For constant but no time trend – Model 2: CV for n = 500, at 5% is −2.87. For constant and time trend – Model 3: CV for n = 500, at 5% is −3.42τ.
- The augmented Dicky-Fuller (ADF) tests are used if autocorrelation is detected. In this case, add lags of the dependent variables to the RHS of each model to remove autocorrelation, as follows:

Model 1

$$\Delta Y_t = \gamma Y_{t-1} + \Sigma \, \delta j \, \Delta Y_{t-k} + u_t$$

Model 2

$$\Delta Y_t = a + \gamma Y_{t-1} + \Sigma \, \delta j \Delta \, Y_{t-k} + u_t$$

Model 3

$$\Delta Y_t = a + \gamma Y_{t-1} + \beta \, t + \Sigma \delta j \, \Delta Y_{t-k} + u_t$$

In each case the H_0 and H_1 are:

$H_0: \gamma = 0 \ldots Y$ is I(1)
$H_1: \gamma < 0 \ldots Y$ is I(0)

The critical values of the ADF tests are the same as those for the DF tests.

- Note that the correct lag length is important in an ADF test, and incorrect lag length could lead to misleading results. The lag length selection can be determined by individual significance (t tests on δ parameter, autocorrelation tests, and model selection criteria (e.g. AIC and BIC) produced by regression software).

- In practice, to remove autocorrelation, start with a relatively large lag (two/three lags), then test down using a t-test of significance. In many applications one or two lags will normally remove the autocorrelation. Be aware that an increased number of parameters will reduce the power of an ADF test.
- Dickey and Fuller (1981) provided three additional F-statistics (called $\phi 1$, $\phi 2$ and $\phi 3$) to test joint hypotheses on the parameters (this procedure helps in finding the DGP). The tests are as follows:

Model 2 (RW with drift – DF/ADF form)

H_0: $a = \gamma = 0$; Y is I(1)

Use $\phi 1$.

Model 3 (drift + a linear tend- DF/ADF forms)

H_0: $a = \gamma = \beta = 0$; Y_t is I(1)

Use $\phi 2$.

Or H_0: $\gamma = \beta = 0$; Y_t is I(1)

Use $\phi 3$.

- Test statistics are called $\phi 1$ (test one), $\phi 2$ (test two) and $\phi 3$ (test three). These are calculated in exactly the same way as ordinary F-tests:

$$\phi i = \frac{(\text{RSS(restricted)} - \text{RSS(unrestricted)})/r}{\text{RSS(unrestricted)}/(\text{T-K})}$$

i = 1,2,3.
RSS = residual sum of squares
r = is the number of parameter restrictions (for the first test r = 2, second test r = 3, and for the third test r = 2)

- Large values of ϕ suggest a rejection of the null hypothesis.
- Dickey and Fuller (1981) have provided critical values for different sample sizes. For example, for a sample size of 100, the critical values at a 5% level of significance are:

for $\phi 1$ CV = 4.71
for $\phi 2$ Cv = 4.88
for $\phi 3$ Cv = 6.49

In each case, if the value of ϕ is less than CV, do not reject H_0 at a 5% level of significance, Y_t is I(1) and the restrictions are binding.

Review questions

1   Explain what you understand by a unit root test. Why are unit root tests necessary when dealing with time series regressions?

2   Explain the Dicky-Fuller (DF) and the augmented Dicky-Fuller (ADF) unit root tests. Why is the ADF test more popular in applied work?

3   Explain how you would determine the correct lag length when using an ADF test. What are the consequences of incorrect lag length for the ADF test?

4   What are the problems and limitations of the unit root tests. How would you overcome these problems?

5   Collect UK annual time series data for the period 1970–2008 from the Economic Trends Annual Supplement (available online) on each of the following:

   a   GDP in constant prices
   b   aggregate consumption expenditure in constant prices
   c   gross fixed capital formation in constant prices.

   Use a regression package to plot each variable in level and in 1st difference form. Are these variables stationary? For each variable carry out an ADF test, explaining all procedures and techniques. What are the limitations of these procedures? Explain.

6   'The basic problem with unit root tests is lack of "power".' Discuss.

14 Cointegration analysis
Two-variable case

INTRODUCTION

Cointegration analysis is perhaps the most significant development in econometrics since the mid 1980s. In simple words, cointegration analysis refers to groups of variables that drift together, although each is individually non-stationary in the sense that they tend upwards or downwards over time. This common drifting of variables makes linear relationships between these variables exist over long periods of time, thereby giving us insight into equilibrium relationships of economic variables. Cointegration analysis is a technique used in the estimation of the long-run or equilibrium parameters in a relationship with non-stationary variables. It is a new method popularised in response to the problems inherent in the specific to general approach to time series analysis. It is used for specifying, estimating and testing dynamic models, and it can be used for testing the validity of underlying economic theories. Furthermore, the usefulness of cointegration analysis is also seen in the estimation of the short-run or disequilibrium parameters in a relationship, because the latter estimation can utilise the estimated long-run parameters through cointegration methods. In this chapter we provide an introduction to the methodology of cointegration, focusing on two-variable regression models.

Key topics

- Spurious regression and modern time series econometrics
- The concept of cointegration
- The Engle-Granger (EG) methodology
- The estimation of the error correction short-run models

14.1 Spurious regression and cointegration analysis

To illustrate key issues let us consider Friedman's permanent income hypothesis in the simple version that total private consumption (C_t) is the sum of permanent private consumption ($C_{p,t}$) and transitory private consumption (ε_t). Assuming that permanent private consumption is proportional to permanent personal disposable income (Y_t), we could write that the private consumption function by:

$$C_t = C_{p,t} + \varepsilon_t = \beta_1 Y_t + \varepsilon_t \tag{14.1}$$

where $1 \leq \beta_1$ (= proportionality parameter) > 0. In estimating this function with OLS, using the data for an EU member presented in Table 12.1, and under the assumption that permanent personal disposable income is equal to personal disposable income, we will get:

$$\hat{C}_t = 0.80969Y_t \quad R^2 = 0.9924 \quad DW = 0.8667$$
$$t \quad [75.5662]$$

(14.2)

The estimates in (14.2), apart from the low Durbin-Watson statistic, are very good. The t-statistic is very high, showing that the regression coefficient is significant, and the R^2 is also very high, indicating a very good fit. However, these estimates may be misleading because the two time series involved in the equation are trended or non-stationary random processes, as can be seen in Figure 12.1. As a consequence, the OLS estimator is not consistent and the corresponding usual inference procedures are not valid. As we explained in Chapter 6, these regressions where the results look very good in terms of R^2 and t-statistics, but the variables involved are trended time series, have been called *spurious regressions* by Granger and Newbold (1974). In fact, Granger and Newbold suggested that if in a regression with trended time series variables, the DW statistic is low and the coefficient of determination R^2 is high, we should suspect that the estimated equation possibly suffers from spurious regression. As a rule of thumb, if $R^2 > DW$, spurious regression should be suspected, as in Equation (14.2), for example, where $R^2 = 0.9924 > DW = 0.8667$.

Taking into account that most time series in economics are non-stationary (Nelson and Plosser, 1982) then the situation of getting spurious regression results is normally the case in regression analysis. The SG methodology response to this problem has been to develop and use alternative estimation methods to the OLS to deal with the changing means and variances, ignoring the underlying cause of the problem. An alternative practical methodology to avoid the problem of non-stationarity of the time series has been to use regressions in the first differences of the time series. However, using relationships where the variables are expressed in differences is like referring to the short-run or disequilibrium state of the phenomenon under investigation and not to its long-run or equilibrium state, where the variables are expressed in their original levels, as most economic theories suggest.

14.1.1 The modern econometrics response to the phenomenon of spurious regression

Given the problem of spurious regression, non-stationary stochastic processes cannot be mixed together in regression models and they must first be converted into stationary series. The question is how can this conversion be done? The answer depends on the form that a stochastic process is assumed to have. Random walk models/autoregressive processes of low orders appear to provide a good approximation to data generation processes. These type of series are normally termed difference stationary (DS), this is because by differencing the series it can be converted from a non-stationary to a weak form stationary series. The number of times a series must be differenced to generate a stationary series is called the order of integration of the series. Most financial/economic time series are integrated of order one. That is, by differencing the series only once, we can generate a stationary time-invariant time series. There are exceptions to this generalisation. For example, nominal wages in most countries are found to be integrated of order two. That is, the relevant time series has to be differenced twice to yield a stationary time series.

The modern approach

- The first step in modern time series econometrics is, therefore, to find the order of integration of each time series for econometric analysis. This is done via a series of *unit root tests* (DF/ADF) discussed in Chapter 13. If the two series have the same order of integration then they can be mixed together, however, note that this may again result in a spurious regression. Most economic/financial series are integrated of order one, therefore, if mixed in level forms, the result is spurious regression. This is the case as a linear combination of them (i.e. the disturbance term) will also be a non-stationary integrated of order one series. There is no tendency for the two non-stationary series to move together and there is no stationary/equilibrium state for the model. Note that this key step is totally ignored in SG methodology.
- There is, however, *a rather special occurrence*, not falling into the normal case outlined above, as follows:

  In certain cases, due to economic/financial market characteristics, when the two or more non-stationary stochastic processes are combined they result in a stationary stochastic process, that is, the two/more joint probability distributions, when mixed together, generate a linear combination which has a stationary probability distribution with white noise characteristics. In this special case, the variables are said to be cointegrated and there exists a long-run equilibrium solution. In addition, the adjustment towards this long-run state is taking place via an error correction model (ECM).
- Within the framework of cointegration methodology, key problems and issues arising from SG methodology may therefore be resolved by a careful step by step analysis of the time series data. This is how the modern approach to time series econometrics identifies and deals with the real cause of spurious regressions, which are so frequently encountered in time series regression analysis. In what follows we discuss in detail each key step in cointegration analysis.

14.2 Cointegration: definition and concept

In the case of Equation (14.1), the permanent income hypothesis, where the transitory private consumption (ε_t) is by definition a stationary time series, requires that the linear combination of the two time series, C_t and Y_t (i.e. the time series $C_t - \beta_1 Y_t$), must be stationary because this series is equal to the stationary series ε_t. However, it is more than certain that both time series C_t and Y_t are non-stationary. In fact, these series are integrated of order one, i.e. it is $C_t \sim I(1)$ and $Y_t \sim I(1)$. In other words, although $C_t \sim I(1)$ and $Y_t \sim I(1)$, the permanent income hypothesis requires that their linear combination $\varepsilon_t = C_t - \beta_1 Y_t$ to be stationary, i.e. to be $\varepsilon_t = C_t - \beta_1 Y_t \sim I(0)$. In such a special case we say that the time series C_t and Y_t are cointegrated. But, let us formulate this result more generally. Engle and Granger (1987) developed the following definition:

Cointegration of two variables Two time series, Y_t and X_t, are said to be cointegrated of order (d,b), where $d \geq b \geq 0$, if both time series are integrated of order d, and there exists a linear combination of these two time series, say $a_1 Y_t + a_2 X_t$, which is integrated of order (d − b). In mathematical terms, this definition is written as:

$$\text{If } Y_t \sim I(d) \text{ and } X_t \sim I(d), \text{ then } Y_t, X_t \sim CI(d,b) \text{ if } a_1 Y_t + a_2 X_t \sim I(d-b) \qquad (14.3)$$

where CI is the symbol of cointegration. The vector of the coefficients that constitutes the linear combination of the two series, i.e. $[a_1, a_2]$ in (14.3), is called the *cointegrating vector*.

We can distinguish the following two special cases, which we will investigate in this chapter:

1 The case where $d = b$, resulting in $a_1Y_t + a_2X_t \sim I(0)$, which means that the linear combination of the two time series is stationary, and, therefore, $Y_t, X_t \sim CI(d,d)$.
2 The case where $d = b = 1$, resulting in $a_1Y_t + a_2X_t \sim I(0)$, which means that the linear combination of the two time series is stationary, and, therefore, $Y_t, X_t \sim CI(1,1)$.

Let us consider the following relationship where $Y_t \sim I(1)$ and $X_t \sim I(1)$:

$$Y_t = \beta_0 + \beta_1 X_t \tag{14.4}$$

This relationship is in a *long-run equilibrium* when:

$$0 = Y_t - \beta_0 - \beta_1 X_t \tag{14.5}$$

The deviation from the long-run equilibrium, called the *equilibrium error*, ε_t, is given by:

$$\varepsilon_t = Y_t - \beta_0 - \beta_1 X_t \tag{14.6}$$

For the long-run equilibrium to have meaning, i.e. to exist, the equilibrium error in (14.6) should fluctuate around the equilibrating zero value, as shown in (14.5). In other words, the equilibrium error ε_t should be a stationary time series, i.e. it should be $\varepsilon_t \sim I(0)$ with $E(\varepsilon_t) = 0$. According to the definition in (14.3), because $Y_t \sim I(1)$ and $X_t \sim I(1)$, and the linear combination $\varepsilon_t = Y_t - \beta_0 - \beta_1 X_t \sim I(0)$, we can say that Y_t and X_t are cointegrated of order $(1,1)$, i.e. it is $Y_t, X_t \sim CI(1,1)$. The cointegrating vector is $[1, -\beta_0, -\beta_1]$. It can be proved that in the two-variable case, and under the assumption that the coefficient of one of the variables is normalised to equal unity, the cointegrating vector, i.e. the linear combination of the two time series, *is unique*.

Combining the results above we could say that the cointegration between two time series is another way to express the existence of a long-run equilibrium relationship between these two time series. Therefore, by considering that Y_t and X_t are cointegrated and that the equilibrium error ε_t is stationary with zero mean, we can write that:

$$Y_t = \beta_0 + \beta_1 X_t + \varepsilon_t \tag{14.7}$$

and be sure that Equation (14.7) will not produce spurious results. Stock (1987) proved that for large samples the OLS estimator for Equation (14.7) is *super-consistent*, i.e. it is consistent and very efficient, because it converges faster to the true values of the regression coefficients than the OLS estimator involving stationary variables. However, Banerjee *et al.* (1986) showed that for small samples the OLS estimator is biased and the level of bias depends on the value of R^2; the higher the R^2 the lower the level of bias. Finally, according to Granger (1986), if we want to avoid spurious regression situations we should test before any regression if the variables involved are cointegrated, something that we present in the next section.

14.3 Testing for cointegration

In this section we will present two simple methods for testing for cointegration between two variables.

a. The Engle-Granger approach

Suppose that we want to test if the two variables Y_t and X_t are cointegrated. This approach, which is called the Engle-Granger (EG) test, or the augmented Engle-Granger (AEG) test, suggests the following steps:

Step 1 Find the order of integration of both variables using the unit root methodology presented in Chapter 13. There are three cases: (1) If the order of integration of the two variables is the same, something that the concept of cointegration requires, continue to the next step. (2) If the order of integration of the two variables is different, you may conclude that the two variables are not cointegrated. (3) If the two variables are stationary the whole testing process stops because you can use the standard regression techniques for stationary variables.

Step 2 If the two variables are integrated of the same order, say I(1), estimate the long-run equilibrium equation with OLS:

$$Y_t = \beta_0 + \beta_1 X_t + \varepsilon_t \tag{14.8}$$

which in this case is called the potential *cointegrating regression*, and save the residuals, e_t, as an estimate of the equilibrium error, ε_t. Although the estimated cointegrating vector $[1, -b_0, -b_1]$ is a consistent estimate of the true cointegrating vector $[1, \beta_0, -\beta_1]$, this is not true for the estimated standard errors of these coefficients. For this reason the estimated standard errors are often not quoted with the cointegrating regression.

Step 3 For the two variables to be cointegrated the equilibrium errors must be stationary. To test this stationarity apply the unit root methodology presented in Chapter 13 to the estimated equilibrium errors saved in the previous step. You could use, for example, the Dickey-Fuller test, or the augmented Dickey-Fuller test, to time series e_t, which involves the estimation of a version of the following equation with OLS:

$$\Delta e_t = \delta e_{t-1} + \sum_{j=2}^{q} \delta_j \Delta e_{t-j+1} + \upsilon_t \tag{14.9}$$

Two things we should take into account in applying the DF or ADF tests:

1   Equation (14.9) does not include a constant term, because, by construction, the OLS residuals e_t are centred around zero.
2   Because the estimate of δ in (14.9) is downward biased, due to the fact that, by construction, the OLS methodology seeks to produce stationary residuals e_t, the usual Dickey-Fuller τ statistics are not appropriate for this test. Engle and Granger (1987), Engle and Yoo (1987), MacKinnon (1991), and Davinson and MacKinnon (1993) presented critical values for this test, which are even more negative that the usual Dickey-Fuller τ statistics. In Table 14.1 critical values for this cointegration test are presented.

Table 14.1 Critical values for the EG or AEG cointegration tests

No. of variables	m = 2			m = 3			m = 4		
Significance levels									
Sample size	0.01	0.05	0.10	0.01	0.05	0.10	0.01	0.05	0.10
25	−4.37	−3.59	−3.22	−4.92	−4.10	−3.71	−5.43	−4.56	−4.15
50	−4.12	−3.46	−3.13	−4.59	−3.92	−3.58	−5.02	−4.32	−3.98
100	−4.01	−3.39	−3.09	−4.44	−3.83	−3.51	−4.83	−4.21	−3.89
∞	−3.90	−3.33	−3.05	−4.30	−3.74	−3.45	−4.65	−4.10	−3.81

Source: Thomas, R. L. (1997), based on MacKinnon (1991).
m = number of variables in the cointegrating regression.

Step 4 Arrive at conclusions about the cointegration of the two variables according to the following hypotheses:

$$H_0: \delta = 0, \text{ for non-stationarity of } e_t, \text{ i.e. for non-cointegration, if } t_\delta > \tau$$
$$H_a: \delta < 0, \text{ for stationarity of } e_t, \text{ i.e. for cointegration, if } t_\delta < \tau$$

(14.10)

Example 14.1 Cointegration between private consumption and personal disposable income for an EU member (EG, or AEG)

To illustrate the above steps, we continue to use the data presented in Chapter 12, Table 12.1, on the private consumption (C_t) and the personal disposable income (Y_t) for an EU member state. Following the steps above we will try to find if these two variables are cointegrated.

Step 1 Finding the order of integration of the two variables: taking into account criteria AIC, SC and LM(1), we obtained:

For the private consumption variable (see Example 12.1):

$$\Delta\hat{C}_t = 12330.48 - 0.01091C_{t-1}$$
$$t \quad [5.138] \quad [-1.339]$$
$$R^2 = 0.052 \quad DW = 1.765$$

(14.11)

and

$$\Delta^2\hat{C}_t = 7972.671 - 0.85112\Delta C_{t-1}$$
$$t \quad [4.301] \quad [-4.862]$$
$$R^2 = 0.425 \quad DW = 1.967$$

(14.12)

For the personal disposable income variable:

$$\Delta\hat{Y}_t = 19903.93 - 0.02479Y_{t-1}$$
$$t \quad [3.054] \quad [-1.387]$$
$$R^2 = 0.055 \quad DW = 2.270$$

(14.13)

and

$$\Delta^2\hat{Y}_t = 12889.39 - 1.11754\Delta Y_{t-1}$$

t   [3.983]   [−6.270]   (14.14)

$$R^2 = 0.551 \quad DW = 2.014$$

Table 14.2 presents the MacKinnon critical values for the rejection of the hypothesis of a unit root, evaluated from EViews for equations (14.11) to (14.14).

From the figures in Table 14.2 it is seen that both C_t and Y_t are non-stationary and that both ΔC_t and ΔY_t are stationary. In other words, both C_t and Y_t are integrated of order one, i.e. it is $C_t \sim I(1)$ and $Y_t \sim I(1)$. Therefore, we can proceed to step 2.

Table 14.2 MacKinnon critical values for Equations (14.11) to (14.14) and the DF t_δ ratios

Significance level	Critical values for Equations (14.11) and (14.13) [eq. (14.11) $t_\delta = -1.339$] [eq. (14.13) $t_\delta = -1.387$]	Critical values for Equations (14.12) and (14.14) [eq. (14.12) $t_\delta = -4.862$] [eq. (14.14) $t_\delta = -6.272$]
0.01	−3.6289	−3.6353
0.05	−2.9472	−2.9499
0.10	−2.6118	−2.6133

Step 2 The long-run estimated equilibrium relationship, or the cointegrating regression, is the following:

$$\hat{C}_t = 11907.23 + 0.779585Y_t$$

t   [3.123]   [75.566]   (14.15)

$$R^2 = 0.994 \quad DW = 1.021$$

Using the estimated cointegrating vector [1, −11907.23, −0.779585] we have estimated and saved the estimated equilibrium errors e_t.

Step 3 Testing the stationarity of e_t. Taking into account the criteria AIC, SC and LM(1), we obtained:

$$\Delta\hat{e}_t = -0.51739e_{t-1} \quad R^2 = 0.224 \quad DW = 1.948$$

t   [−3.150]   (14.16)

Step 4 Comparing the $t_\delta = -3.150$ value from Equation (14.16) with the critical values in Table 14.1 for m = 2, we see that this value is more or less equal to the critical values for a 0.10 level of significance. In other words, if we assume a significance level equal to 0.10, or 0.11, then we 'accept' the alternative hypothesis that e_t is stationary, meaning, thus, that variables C_t and Y_t are cointegrated, or that there exists a long-run equilibrium relationship between these two variables. However, if we work with a significance level of less than 0.10, then these two variables are not cointegrated and we cannot say that there exists a long-run equilibrium relationship between private consumption and personal disposable income for an EU member.

b. The Durbin-Watson approach

This approach is very simple and is based on the following two steps:

Step 1 Estimate the cointegrating regression (14.8), save the residuals e_t, and compute the Durbin-Watson statistic, which now is called the *cointegrating regression Durbin-Watson (CRDW) statistic*, as:

$$\text{CRDW} = \frac{\sum(e_t - e_{t-1})^2}{\sum(e_t - \bar{e})^2}, \quad \text{where } \bar{e} = \text{arithmetic mean} \tag{14.17}$$

Step 2 Arrive at a decision about the cointegration of the two variables according to the following hypotheses:

$$\left.\begin{array}{l} H_0: \text{ non-stationarity of } e_t, \text{ i.e. non-cointegration, if CRDW} < d \\ H_a: \text{ stationarity of } e_t, \text{ i.e. cointegration, if CRDW} > d \end{array}\right\} \tag{14.18}$$

The critical d values, with the null hypothesis being $d = 0$, have been computed by Sargan and Bhargava (1983) and by Engle and Granger (1987). These critical values are 0.511, 0.386 and 0.322 for significance levels of 0.01, 0.05 and 0.10, respectively.

Example 14.2 Cointegration between private consumption and personal disposable income for an EU member (CRDW)

Here we repeat Example 14.1 using the methodology of the CRDW.

Step 1 From the estimated cointegrating regression we see that CRDW = 1.021.

Step 2 Because the CRDW = 1.021 and is greater than the critical values noted above, the alternative hypothesis of stationarity is accepted, and, thus, we can conclude that private consumption and personal disposable income are cointegrated.

---

c. The autoregressive distributed lag (ADL) model approach

The Engle-Granger approach for testing cointegration between two variables, Y_t and X_t, depends crucially on the estimated equilibrium error e_t, or, in other words, on the estimation of the long-run equilibrium relationship. Phillips and Loretan (1991) suggested that instead of the cointegrating equation (14.8), which is possibly misspecified due to the omission of lagged variables, we could use the autoregressive distributed lag (ADL) equation:

$$Y_t = \alpha + \sum_{j=1}^{k} \alpha_j Y_{t-j} + \sum_{j=0}^{k} \beta_j X_{t-j} + \varepsilon_t \tag{14.19}$$

In the steady-state long-run equilibrium, the variables take the same values for all periods, i.e. it is $Y_t = Y_{t-1} = Y_{t-2} = \ldots = Y^*$ and $X_t = X_{t-1} = X_{t-2} = \ldots = X^*$, and, therefore, the steady-state long-run equilibrium relationship becomes:

$$Y^* = \frac{\alpha}{1 - \sum\limits_{j=1}^{k} \alpha_j} + \frac{\sum\limits_{j=0}^{k} \beta_j}{1 - \sum\limits_{j=1}^{k} \alpha_j} X^* = \alpha^* + \beta^* X^* \tag{14.20}$$

where the cointegrating vector is $[1, -\alpha^*, -\beta^*]$. Using this cointegrating vector the equilibrium error is $\varepsilon^* = Y^* - \alpha^* - \beta^* X^*$. If $[1, -a^*, -b^*]$ is the estimated cointegrating vector, obtained by estimating firstly (14.19) with OLS and secondly by substituting the estimates into (14.20), the estimated equilibrium error is given by $e_t = Y_t - a^* - b^* X_t$. This estimated equilibrium error could be used in testing for cointegration between the two variables, Y_t and X_t, following the steps of the Engle-Granger approach presented above.

Example 14.3 Cointegration between private consumption and personal disposable income for an EU member (ADL)

Here we repeat Example 14.1 using the methodology of the ADL.

Step 1 It has been shown in the above examples that both variables, private consumption and personal disposable income, are integrated of order one.

Step 2 An estimate with OLS of a version of equation (14.19) is shown below:

$$\hat{C}_t = 9254.83 + 0.79945C_{t-1} + 0.27887Y_t - 0.12502Y_{t-1}$$

$$t \quad [4.725] \quad [9.832] \quad\quad [6.193] \quad\quad [-1.962] \tag{14.21}$$

$$R^2 = 0.999 \quad DW = 1.947$$

Substituting the estimates from (14.21) into the corresponding parameters of (14.22) we get that:

$$a^* = \frac{a}{1-a_1} = \frac{9254.83}{1-0.79945} = 46147.25,$$

$$b^* = \frac{b_0 + b_1}{1-a_1} = \frac{0.27887 - 0.12502}{1-0.79945} = 0.76714$$

and therefore the estimated cointegrating vector is $[1, -46147.25, -0.76714]$. This cointegrating vector is used to construct the estimated equilibrium error $e_t = Y_t - 46147.25 - 0.76714X_t$.

Step 3 Testing the stationarity of e_t. Taking into account the criteria AIC, SC and LM(1), we obtained:

$$\Delta\hat{e}_t = -0.03202e_{t-1} - 0.41477\Delta e_{t-1} - 0.36552\Delta e_{t-2}$$

$$t \quad\quad [-0.759] \quad\quad [-2.362] \quad\quad [-2.059] \tag{14.22}$$

$$R^2 = 0.217 \quad DW = 2.047$$

Step 4 Comparing the $t_8 = -0.759$ value from Equation (14.22) with the critical values in Table 7.11 for $m = 2$, we see that this value is much less than all the critical values noted in the table. This means that the equilibrium error is non-stationary, indicating, thus, that private consumption and personal disposable income are not cointegrated.

Summarising the last three examples we could say that in Example 14.1 we found that variables C_t and Y_t were on the borderline of being cointegrated, in Example 14.2 we found that these variables are cointegrated, and, finally, in Example 14.3 we found that the same two variables are not cointegrated. The results of these examples show that cointegration tests *lack power* and fail to recover cointegration between two variables, even when these variables are cointegrated. Therefore, we should use cointegration tests with great caution.

14.4 Cointegration: the estimation of error correction models (ECM)

The most important result in cointegration analysis is the so-called *Granger representation theorem* (Granger, 1986; Engle and Granger, 1987). According to this theorem, if two variables, Y_t and X_t, are cointegrated then there is a long-run relationship between them. Of course, in the short-run these variables may be in disequilibrium, with the disturbances being the equilibrating error ε_t. The dynamics of this short-run disequilibrium relationship between these two variables can always be described by an *error correction model* (ECM), which was first introduced by Sargan (1964). This error correction model, which connects the short-run and the long-run behaviour of the two variables is given by:

$$\Delta Y_t = \text{lagged}(\Delta Y_t, \Delta X_t) + \lambda \varepsilon_{t-1} + \upsilon_t, \ -1 < \lambda < 0 \tag{14.23}$$

where $Y_t \sim I(1)$, $X_t \sim (1)$, $Y_t, X_t \sim CI(1,1)$, $\varepsilon_t = Y_t - \beta_0 - \beta_1 X_t \sim I(0)$, u_t = white noise disturbance term and λ = short-run adjustment coefficient.

In (14.23) all variables are stationary because Y_t and X_t being integrated of order one, their differences ΔY_t and ΔX_t are integrated of order zero. Furthermore, the equilibrium error ε_t is integrated of order zero because variables Y_t and X_t are cointegrated. In other words, one could say that Equation (14.23) could be estimated by OLS. However, this is not the case, because the equilibrium error ε_t is not an observable variable. Therefore, before any estimation of Equation (14.23), values of this error should be obtained.

Engle and Granger (1987) proposed the following two-step methodology in estimating Equation (14.23):

Step 1 Estimate the potential cointegrating regression (14.8), then get the consistent estimated cointegrating vector $[1, -b_0, -b_1]$ and use it in order to obtain the estimated equilibrium error $e_t = Y_t - b_0 - b_1 X_t$.

Step 2 Estimate the following equation by OLS:

$$\Delta Y_t = \text{lagged}(\Delta Y_t, \Delta X_t) + \lambda e_{t-1} + \upsilon_t \tag{14.24}$$

In estimating (14.24) we should take care about the following:

1   Use appropriate statistics, such as AIC, SC and LM, for example, in order to decide about the proper number of lags for the differenced variables to be used.

2   Use, if appropriate, the non-lagged differenced variable X_t.
3   Include in the equation other differenced 'exogenous' variables, as long as they are integrated of order one, in order to improve fit.

Example 14.4 Estimating an error correction model between private consumption and personal disposable income for an EU member (ECM)

Let us consider from Example 14.1 that the two variables C_t and Y_t are cointegrated.

Step 1 From the cointegrating regression estimated in (14.15), or:

$$\hat{C}_t = 11907.23 + 0.779585Y_t$$

t   [3.123]   [75.566]   (14.25)

$R^2 = 0.994$ DW $= 1.021$

we get the residuals, e_t.

Step 2 According to (14.24), using the criteria AIC, SC and t-ratios, a version of an estimated error correction model is the following:

$$\Delta\hat{C}_t = 5951.557 + 0.28432\Delta Y_t - 0.19996e_{t-1}$$

t   [7.822]   [6.538]   [−2.486]   (14.26)

$R^2 = 0.572$ DW $= 1.941$ LM(1) $= 0.007\{p = 0.934\}$

The results in (14.26) show that short-run changes in personal disposable income Y_t positively affect private consumption C_t. Furthermore, because the short-run adjustment coefficient is significant, it shows that 0.19996 of the deviation of the actual private consumption from its long-run equilibrium level is corrected each year. The above cointegration analysis has identified that there is a long-run relationship between C and Y; in addition it has shown that the adjustment towards this equilibrium is uniquely determined via an ECM regression model (14.26). Note that this procedure is a significant improvement over the SG methodology, with the latter seldom being able to correctly identify the short-run dynamic adjustment process.

14.5 A summary of key issues

- Suppose two variables, Y and X (for example, spot and future prices of an asset), are believed to be integrated of order one and we want to determine whether there exists an equilibrium relationship between the two variables. The theory suggests that there is a long-run relationship between Y and X. We therefore wish to test the long-run relationship suggested by a long-run theory.
- Engle and Granger (1987) proposed a five-step procedure to determine if two I(1) variables are cointegrated of order CI(1,1), as follows:
- *Step 1* Use DF/ADF tests to determine the order of integration of each variable. ADF tests are more commonly used here due to autocorrelation in the data. Make sure the lag

length is 'correct' based on AIC, t and F-test values. Three types of results might emerge from the unit root tests, as follows:

- Case 1: Y is I(0) and X is I(0) – it is not necessary to proceed further with a cointegration test – use standard regression methods.
- Case 2: Y is (1), X is I(2) or Y is I (0), X is I(1). That is, the two variables are integrated of different orders. In this case, it is possible to conclude that they are not cointegrated. Note: if there are more than two variables with different order of integrations, it is possible that they are multicointegrated.
- Case 3: if both variables are I(1) go to the next step.
- *Step 2* If the results of step 1 indicate that both Y and X are I(1), the next step is to estimate, by the OLS, the long-run equilibrium relationship suggested by the economic/ finance theory:

$$Y_t = a + bX_t + u_t.$$

Note that $u_t = Y_t - (a + b X_t)$. If Y and X are cointegrated then u_t, a linear combination of them, must be I(0), that is, a white noise process.

- Using the OLS residuals, e_t, from the potential regression model, use them as a proxy for u_t, to test to see whether e_t series is I (0).
- *Step 3* Perform a DF/ADF test on the OLS residuals from step 2, as follows:

$$\Delta e_t = \gamma e_{t-1} + \Sigma\, a_i\, \Delta\, e_{t-i} + \varepsilon_t,$$ where ε_t is a white noise process.

There is no need to include an intercept term in the above ADF equation, since the time series is a residual sequence.

Again use AIC, t and F-tests to determine the appropriate lag length for the ADF. The parameter of interest is γ and the null and alternative hypotheses are as follows:

$$H_0: \gamma = 0$$
$$H_1: \gamma < 0$$

If you can reject H_0, e_t series is I(0), stationary. Hence, conclude that Y and X are cointegrated and there exists a long-run equilibrium relationship between them, as the theory suggests.

- Since the OLS method used to estimate the potential cointegration equation minimises the RSS and the residual variance is made as small as possible, the testing procedure based on the DF critical values is inclined towards rejecting H_0. To overcome this problem, Engle and Granger developed their own CV values for the above tests. The CVs depend on the sample size and number of variables used in the analysis. For example, to test for cointegration between Y and X, using 100 observations, at a 5% level of significance, the CV is −3.398. If the absolute value of t is greater than 3.398, reject H_0 – conclude cointegration. If the two variables are cointegrated, then the adjustment towards equilibrium takes place via an ECM process.
- The Granger representation theorem states that if two variables, Y and X, are cointegrated then the relationship between them can be expressed as ECM, which in turn shows how adjustment towards a long-run equilibrium takes place. Moreover, for any set of I(1) variables, error correction and cointegration are equivalent. That is ECM presentation implies cointegration.

- *Step 4* From the cointegration regression the 'equilibrium error' is $u_t = Y_t - (a + bX_t)$, a proxy for this is the OLS residual, e_t. The ECM implies that in each period a fraction of this error, corresponding to the previous time period, is corrected for. This process will move the model towards equilibrium given sufficient time. The estimation of the ECM representation is the step 4 of the EG methodology, as follows:

$$\Delta Y_t = \alpha + \beta e_{t-1} + \Sigma a_i \Delta Y_{t-i} + \Sigma b_i \Delta X_{t-i} + \varepsilon_t$$

This is the ECM representation. It shows the adjustment towards equilibrium via the ECM term, βe_{t-1}. β is termed the speed of adjustment coefficient. It shows how ΔY_t reacts to the previous time period 'equilibrium error'.

- *Step 5* Assess the adequacy of the ECM regression. Carry out diagnostic checks to ensure the disturbance term is white noise. Again ensure that the lag length is chosen correctly. The equilibrium solution is given by the ECM term, when all changes in the variables are set to zero.
- Note: the EG methodology cannot deal with the general case of more than two variables.
- The normalisation procedure is not clear. That is, there might be an ECM between Y and X as well as X and Y (X as the dependent variable in this case).
- In practice, it is possible to find that one regression indicates that the variables are cointegrated, whereas reversing the order indicates no cointegration.
- Use economic/financial theory/knowledge to specify the ECM regression.
- For the general case of more than two variables, use the Johansen (1988) procedure.

Review questions

1 Explain how the modern approach to time series econometrics deals with the problem of spurious regression.
2 Explain what you understand by the concept of cointegration. What are the key steps in the Engle-Granger approach to cointegration analysis?
3 Explain what you understand by [a] $I \sim (0)$, [b] $I \sim (1)$ and [c] $I(2)$ time series. What are the consequences of mixing an $I \sim (0)$ time series with an $I(1)$?
4 'Cointegration methodology is basically an "inductive" method lacking a theoretical foundation.' Discuss.
5 Collect a time series data for levels of aggregate imports and gross domestic product (GDP) covering at least 50 annual/quarterly periods, for a country of your own choice. Carry out each one of the following steps using an appropriate regression package (e.g. Microfit 5, EViews).

   a Plot each of the variables in level and first difference form and explain your plots. Are these time series integrated of order one?
   b Use an ADF test on each variable to establish the order of integration. Explain how you would determine the order of lag length in each case. On the basis of your results explain whether it would be correct to include both variables in a regression model.
   c Run a potential cointegrating regression, using economic theory to specify the equation.
   d Obtain the residuals from the above regression and plot these residuals in both the level and 1st difference form. Explain the implications of your plots.

e   Use an ADF test on the residuals of the potential cointegrating equation, determine the lag length, and explain the implications of your results. Are the two time series cointegrated?

f   Assume that the two variables under consideration are cointegrated, specify a short-run ECM model, and determine the correct dynamic specification to ensure a white noise error term. Explain the implications of your results, paying particular attention to the speed of adjustment.

6   Explain the Engel-Granger (EG) cointegration methodology. What are the shortcomings of this method? Can the Engel-Granger causality test overcome these shortcomings?

7   Collect annual time series data on UK real disposable income and real aggregate personal consumption expenditure for the period 1974–2006, from the Economic Trends Annual Supplement (available online).Use a regression package (e.g. Microfit 5 or EViews) to carry out each task stated below.

a   Plot the data on each variable in level and in 1st difference form. Explain your plots.

b   Carry out ADF tests on each variable. In each case pay particular attention to the determination of the lag length.

c   Use the Engel-Granger methodology to investigate cointegration between these two variables. Explain each step carefully.

d   Assume that the two variables are cointegrated, and specify an ECM short-run model. Estimate the ECM model ensuring that the error term is white noise.

e   Explain the implications of the ECM regression results.

15 Cointegration analysis
The multivariate case

INTRODUCTION

This chapter provides an introductory coverage of cointegration analysis when more than two variables are investigated. The multivariate case is a bit more complex and it does require the use of matrix algebra to derive results. However, the methodology is now routinely carried out via time series econometric packages (e.g. Microfit 5 and EViews) and is straightforward to use in practice. In what follows we have tried to keep the level of mathematics to a minimum and have used a number of examples to illustrate key ideas and procedures.

Key topics

- The Engle-Granger (EG) methodology
- Vector autoregression and cointegration
- The Johansen approach
- Granger causality test

15.1 Cointegration of more than two variables: key ideas and concepts

Engle and Granger (1987) developed the following general definition:

Cointegration of more than two variables k time series, X_{1t}, X_{2t}, . . ., X_{kt}, are said to be cointegrated of order (d,b), where $d \geq b \geq 0$, if all time series are integrated of order d, and there exists a linear combination of these k time series, say $a_1 X_{1t} + a_2 X_{2t} + \ldots + a_k X_{kt}$, which is integrated of order (d−b). In mathematical terms, this definition is written:

$$\text{If } X_{1t} \sim I(d),\ X_{2t} \sim I(d), ..., X_{kt} \sim I(d) \quad \text{then } X_{1t},\ X_{2t}, ..., X_{kt} \sim CI(d, b)$$

$$\text{if } a_1 X_{1t} + a_2 X_{2t} + ... + a_k X_{kt} \sim I(d - b) \tag{15.1}$$

The vector of the coefficients that constitute the linear combination of the k time series, i.e. $[a_1, a_2, . . ., a_k]$ in (15.1), is the *cointegrating vector*.

We can distinguish the following two special cases which we will investigate in this chapter:

1   The case where $d = b$, resulting in $a_1X_{1t} + a_2X_{2t} + \ldots + a_kX_{kt} \sim I(0)$, which means that the linear combination of the k time series is stationary, and therefore, $X_{1t}, X_{2t}, \ldots, X_{kt} \sim CI(d,d)$.

2   The case where $d = b = 1$, resulting in $a_1X_{1t} + a_2X_{2t} + \ldots + a_kX_{kt} \sim I(0)$, which means that the linear combination of the k time series is stationary, and therefore, $X_{1t}, X_{2t}, \ldots, X_{kt} \sim CI(1,1)$.

To demonstrate basic ideas let us consider the following three-variable relationship where $Y_t \sim I(1)$, $X_t \sim I(1)$ and $Z_t \sim I(1)$:

$$Y_t = \beta_0 + \beta_1 X_t + \beta_2 Z_t \tag{15.2}$$

This relationship is in a *long-run equilibrium* when:

$$0 = Y_t - \beta_0 - \beta_1 X_t - \beta_2 Z_t \tag{15.3}$$

The deviation from the long-run equilibrium, i.e. the *equilibrium error*, ε_t, is given by:

$$\varepsilon_t = Y_t - \beta_0 - \beta_1 X_t - \beta_2 Z_t \tag{15.4}$$

As in the two-variable case, for the long-run equilibrium to have meaning, i.e. to exist, the equilibrium error in (15.4) should fluctuate around the equilibrating zero value, as shown in (15.3). In other words, the equilibrium error ε_t should be a stationary time series, i.e. it should be $\varepsilon_t \sim I(0)$ with $E(\varepsilon_t) = 0$. According to the definition in (15.1), because $Y_t \sim I(1)$, $X_t \sim I(1)$ and $Z_t \sim I(1)$, and the linear combination $\varepsilon_t = Y_t - \beta_0 - \beta_1 X_t - \beta_2 Z_t \sim I(0)$, we can say that Y_t, X_t and Z_t are cointegrated of order $(1,1)$, i.e. it is $Y_t, X_t, Z_t \sim CI(1,1)$. The cointegrating vector in this case is $[1, -\beta_0, -\beta_1, -\beta_2]$.

In the two-variables case and under the assumption that the coefficient of one of the variables is normalised to equal unity, we said in Chapter 14 that the cointegrating vector, is unique. However, in the multivariable case this is not true. It has been shown that if a long-run equilibrium relationship exists between k variables, then these variables are cointegrated, whilst if k variables are cointegrated, then there exists at least one long-run equilibrium relationship between these variables. In other words, in the multivariate case the cointegrating vector is *not unique*.

It can be proved (Greene, 1999) that in the case of k variables, there can only be up to $k-1$ linearly independent cointegrating vectors. The number of these linearly independent cointegrating vectors is called the *cointegrating rank*. Therefore, the cointegrating rank in the case of k variables may range from 1 to $k - 1$. As a consequence, in the case where more than one cointegrating vectors exist, it may be impossible without out-of-sample information to identify the long-run equilibrium relationship (Enders, 2010). This is the case because cointegration is a purely statistical concept and it is in fact 'a-theoretical' in the sense that cointegrated relationships need not have any economic meaning (Maddala, 1992).

15.2 Cointegration tests for the multivariate case

The tests presented in Chapter 14 for cointegration of two variables may be generalised to include k variables. In this section we present the generalisation of the Engle-Granger approach only.

The Engle-Granger approach

Suppose we want to test if the k + 1 variables, Y_t, X_{1t}, X_{2t}, . . ., X_{kt}, are cointegrated. This approach, which is called the Engle-Granger (EG) test, or the augmented Engle-Granger (AEG) test, suggests the following steps:

Step 1 Find the order of integration of all variables using the unit root methodology presented in Chapter 13. If the order of integration of all variables is the same, something that the concept of cointegration requires, continue to the next step. However, it is possible to have a mixture of different-order variables where subsets of the higher-order variables are cointegrated to the order of the lower-order variables (Cuthbertson *et al.*, 1992). We will not consider these possibilities in this book.

Step 2 If all the variables are integrated of the same order, say I(1), estimate the long-run equilibrium equation with OLS:

$$Y_t = \beta_0 + \beta_1 X_{1t} + \beta_2 X_{2t} + \cdots + \beta_k X_{kt} + \varepsilon_t \tag{15.5}$$

which in this case is the *cointegrating regression* and save the residuals, e_t, as an estimate of the equilibrium error, ε_t. Although the estimated cointegrating vector $[1, -b_0, -b_1, -b_2, . . ., -b_k]$ is a consistent estimate of the true cointegrating vector $[1, -\beta_0, -\beta_1, -\beta_2, . . ., -\beta_k]$, this is not true for the estimated standard errors of these coefficients.

Step 3 For the variables to be cointegrated the equilibrium errors must be stationary. To test this stationarity, apply the unit root methodology presented in Chapter 13 to the estimated equilibrium errors saved in the previous step. You could use, for example, the Dickey-Fuller test, or the augmented Dickey-Fuller test, to time series e_t, which involves the estimation of a version of the following equation with OLS:

$$\Delta e_t = \delta e_{t-1} + \sum_{j=2}^{q} \delta_j \Delta e_{t-j+1} + \upsilon_t \tag{15.6}$$

Two things we should take into account in applying the DF, or ADF, tests:

1   Equation (15.6) does not include a constant term, because, by construction, the OLS residuals e_t are centred around zero.
2   Because the estimate of δ in (15.6) is downward biased, due to the fact that, by construction, the OLS methodology seeks to produce stationary residuals e_t, the usual Dickey-Fuller τ statistics are not appropriate for this test. Critical values, such as those presented in Table 14.1 should be used. All these critical values depend on the number of variables included in the cointegrating regression.

Step 4 Arrive at a decision about the cointegration of the variables according to the following hypotheses:

$$\left. \begin{array}{ll} H_0: \ \delta = 0, & \text{for non-stationarity of } e_t, \ \text{i.e. for non-cointegration, if } t_\delta > \tau \\ H_a: \ \delta < 0, & \text{for stationarity of } e_t, \ \text{i.e. for cointegration, if } t_\delta < \tau \end{array} \right\} \tag{15.7}$$

Example 15.1 Cointegration between private consumption, personal disposable income, and inflation rate for an EU member (EG, or AEG)

In Table 12.1 private consumption (C_t), personal disposable income (Y_t) and the consumer price index (P_t) for an EU member are presented. We used formula (13.48) in order to compute the inflation rate (Z_t). Following these steps we can determine if these three variables are cointegrated.

Step 1 Finding the order of integration of the three variables: taking into account criteria AIC, SC and LM(1), we obtained:

Variables C_t and Y_t are integrated of order one, i.e. it is $C_t \sim I(1)$ and $Y_t \sim I(1)$
For the inflation rate variable:

$$\Delta \hat{Z}_t = 0.02233 - 0.18357 Z_{t-1}$$

$$t \qquad [1.889] \quad [-1.991] \tag{15.8}$$

$$R^2 = 0.110 \quad DW = 2.097$$

and

$$\Delta^2 Z_t = 0.00266 - 1.12517 \Delta Z_{t-1}$$

$$t \qquad [0.394] \quad [-6.296] \tag{15.9}$$

$$R^2 = 0.561 \quad DW = 2.031$$

Table 15.1 presents the MacKinnon critical values for the rejection of the hypothesis of a unit root, evaluated from EViews for Equations (15.8) to (15.9).

Table 15.1 MacKinnon critical values for Equations (15.8) to (15.9) and the DF t_δ ratios

Significance level	Critical values for Equation (15.8)[$t_\delta=-1.991$]	Critical values for Equation (15.9) [$t_\delta=-6.296$]
0.01	−3.6353	−3.6422
0.05	−2.9499	−2.9527
0.10	−2.6133	−2.6148

From the figures in Table 15.1 it is seen that Z_t is non-stationary and that δZ_t is stationary, i.e. it is $Z_t \sim I(1)$. In summary, all the three variables are integrated of order one and we can therefore proceed to step 2.

Step 2 The long-run estimated equilibrium relationship, or the cointegrating regression, is the following:

$$\hat{C}_t = 8746.662 + 0.81087 Y_t - 73481.43 Z_t$$

$$t \quad [2.220] \quad [50.831] \quad [-2.396] \tag{15.10}$$

$$R^2 = 0.995 \quad DW = 1.518$$

Using the estimated cointegrating vector [1, −8746.662, −0.81087, −73481.43] we have estimated and saved the estimated equilibrium errors e_t.

Step 3 Testing the stationarity of e_t. Taking into account the criteria AIC, SC and LM(1) we obtained:

$$\Delta \hat{e}_t = -0.78108 e_{t-1} \quad R^2 = 0.375 \quad DW = 1.900$$
$$t \quad [-4.455]$$

$$(15.11)$$

Step 4 Comparing the $t_\delta = -4.455$ value from Equation (15.11) with the critical values in Table 14.1 for m = 3, we see that this value is less than the critical values for a 0.05 level of significance. In other words, we accept the alternative hypothesis in (15.7) i.e. we accept that e_t is stationary, meaning, thus, that variables C_t, Y_t and Z_t are cointegrated.

If we go back to the similar example in Chapter 14, we saw there that by using the Engel-Granger cointegration test we were not sure if variables C_t and Y_t were cointegrated. In this example, using the exactly same methodology, we found that variables C_t, Y_t and Z_t are cointegrated. This should not be surprising if we consider that in the two-variable Example of chapter 14 we possibly made a specification error in assuming that, in the long-run, private consumption was dependent on personal disposable income only. In this example, having possibly corrected this specification error, by also including the level of inflation rate of the economy, we were able to reach more definite conclusions.

15.3 Cointegration: estimation of error correction models (ECM)

In the case of more than two variables, the Granger two-step estimation methodology for the error correction equation, that we have seen in the previous chapter, still holds under the assumption that one cointegrating vector exists. In this case, the error correction model which connects the short-run and the long-run behaviour of the k+1 variables is given by:

$$\Delta Y_t = \text{lagged}(\Delta Y_t, \Delta X_{1t}, \Delta X_{2t}, ..., \Delta X_{kt}) + \lambda \varepsilon_{t-1} + \upsilon_t, \quad -1 < \lambda < 0 \qquad (15.12)$$

where $Y_t \sim I(1)$, $X_{1t} \sim I(1)$,. . ., $X_{kt} \sim I(1)$, Y_t, X_{1t},. . ., $X_{kt} \sim CI(1,1)$, $\varepsilon_t = Y_t - \beta_0 - \beta_1 X_{1t} - ... - \beta_k X_{kt} \sim I(0)$, υ_t = white noise disturbance term and λ = short-run adjustment coefficient.

Under the assumption of the existence of only one cointegrating vector that connects the cointegrated variables, the OLS estimation applicable to the cointegrating equation will give consistent estimates. In the case where there are more than one cointegrating vectors, the Engle-Granger methodology is no longer valid because it is not producing consistent estimates. In this case we have to use the methods presented in the next section.

The Engle and Granger (1987) two-step methodology in estimating Equation (15.12), under the assumption of the existence of only one cointegrating vector, is the following:

Step 1 Estimate the cointegrating regression (15.5), get the consistent estimated cointegrating vector [1, − b_0, − b_1, . . ., − b_k] and use it in order to obtain the estimated equilibrium error $e_t = Y_t - b_0 - b_1 X_{1t} - ... b_k X_{kt}$.

Step 2 Estimate the following equation by OLS:

$$\Delta Y_t = \text{lagged}(\Delta Y_t, \Delta X_{1t}, \Delta X_{2t}, ..., \Delta X_{kt}) + \lambda e_{t-1} + \upsilon_t \tag{15.13}$$

In estimating (15.13) we should take care about the following:

1   Use appropriate statistics, such as AIC, SC and LM, for example, in order to decide about the proper number of lags for the differenced variables to be used.
2   Use, if appropriate, the non-lagged differenced variables X_t.
3   Include in the equation other differenced 'exogenous' variables, as long as they are integrated of order one, in order to improve fit.

Example 15.2 Estimating an error correction model between private consumption, personal disposable income and inflation rate for an EU member (ECM)

Let us consider from the above example that the three variables C_t, Y_t and Z_t are cointegrated. Furthermore, assume that there exists one cointegrating vector only.

Step 1 From the cointegrating regression estimated in (15.10), or:

$$\hat{C}_t = 8746.662 + 0.81087Y_t - 73481.43Z_t$$

$$t \quad [2.220] \qquad [50.831] \qquad [-2.396] \tag{15.14}$$

$$R^2 = 0.995 \quad DW = 1.518$$

we get the residuals, e_t.

Step 2 According to (15.13), using the criteria AIC, SC and t-ratios, a version of an estimated error correction model is the following:

$$\Delta\hat{C}_t = 0.50572\Delta C_{t-1} + 0.34563\Delta Y_t - 76297.96\Delta Z_t - 0.37675e_{t-1}$$

$$t \quad [6.370] \qquad\qquad [7.479] \qquad\quad [-3.107] \qquad\quad [-2.786] \tag{15.15}$$

$$R^2 = 0.511 \quad DW = 2.254 \quad LM(1) = 0.264\{p = 0.607\}$$

The results in (15.15) show that short-run changes in personal disposable income, Y_t, and in the inflation rate, affect private consumption, C_t, positively and negatively, respectively. Furthermore, because the short-run adjustment coefficient is significant, it shows that 0.37675 of the deviation of the actual private consumption from its long-run equilibrium level is corrected each year.

15.4 Vector autoregressions and cointegration

The Engle-Granger methodology produces some problems when more than two variables are involved in the cointegrating exercise. In this case, the Johansen (1988) and Stock and Watson (1998) approaches to cointegration may be considered. Because these approaches make use of the vector autoregression models, we will very briefly present them in this section.

15.4.1 Vector autoregression (VAR) models

Assume the following simultaneous equation model in its structural form:

$$C_t = \alpha_0 + \alpha_1 Y_t + \alpha_2 C_{t-1} + \varepsilon_{1t}$$
$$Y_t = \beta_0 + \beta_1 Y_{t-1} + \beta_2 C_{t-1} + \varepsilon_{2t} \tag{15.16}$$

where C = consumption and Y = income. The rationale of the first equation of this model could be that current consumption depends on current income and on lagged consumption due to habit persistence. The rationale of the second equation may be that current income depends on lagged income and on lagged consumption, because higher consumption indicates higher demand, which produces higher economic growth and, therefore, higher income.

Corresponding to model (15.16), a reduced-form model can be found to be the following:

$$C_t = \pi_{10} + \pi_{11} C_{t-1} + \pi_{12} Y_{t-1} + \upsilon_{1t}$$
$$Y_t = \pi_{20} + \pi_{21} C_{t-1} + \pi_{22} Y_{t-1} + \upsilon_{2t} \tag{15.17}$$

A distinctive property of the reduced-form model (15.17) is that all its endogenous variables are expressed in terms of its lagged endogenous variables only. In this model there are no other 'exogenous' variables. This model constitutes of a *vector autoregressive model of order 1*, because the highest lag length of its variables is one, and is denoted with *VAR(1)*.

Generally, a system of m variables of the form:

$$Y_{1t} = \alpha_{10} + \alpha_{11,1} Y_{1,t-1} + \alpha_{12,1} Y_{1,t-2} + \cdots \alpha_{1k,1} Y_{1,t-k} + \cdots$$
$$+ \alpha_{11,m} Y_{m,t-1} + \alpha_{12,m} Y_{m,t-2} + \cdots \alpha_{1k,m} Y_{m,t-k} + \upsilon_{1t}$$
$$\cdots\cdots\cdots\cdots\cdots\cdots\cdots\cdots\cdots\cdots\cdots\cdots\cdots\cdots\cdots\cdots\cdots\cdots\cdots\cdots\cdots \tag{15.18}$$
$$Y_{mt} = \alpha_{m0} + \alpha_{m1,1} Y_{1,t-1} + \alpha_{m2,1} Y_{1,t-2} + \cdots \alpha_{mk,1} Y_{1,t-k} + \cdots$$
$$+ \alpha_{m1,m} Y_{m,t-1} + \alpha_{m2,m} Y_{m,t-2} + \cdots \alpha_{mk,m} Y_{m,t-k} + \upsilon_{mt}$$

is called a *vector autoregressive model, or process, of order k, or VAR(k)*. In matrix form (15.18) is written:

$$Y_t = \delta + A_1 Y_{t-1} + \cdots + A_k Y_{t-k} + \upsilon_t = \delta + \sum_{j=1}^{k} A_j Y_{t-j} + \upsilon_t \tag{15.19}$$

where

$$Y_t = \begin{bmatrix} Y_{1t} \\ Y_{2t} \\ \vdots \\ Y_{mt} \end{bmatrix} \quad \delta = \begin{bmatrix} \alpha_{10} \\ \alpha_{20} \\ \vdots \\ \alpha_{m0} \end{bmatrix} \quad A_j = \begin{bmatrix} \alpha_{11,j} & \alpha_{12,j} & \vdots\vdots & \alpha_{1m,j} \\ \alpha_{21,j} & \alpha_{22,j} & \vdots\vdots & \alpha_{2m,j} \\ \vdots\vdots & \vdots\vdots & \vdots\vdots & \vdots\vdots \\ \alpha_{m1,j} & \alpha_{m2,j} & \vdots\vdots & \alpha_{mm,j} \end{bmatrix} \quad \upsilon_t = \begin{bmatrix} \upsilon_{1t} \\ \upsilon_{2t} \\ \vdots \\ \upsilon_{mt} \end{bmatrix} \tag{15.20}$$

In the cases where in the system (15.18) the lag lengths are not the same in all the equations of the system, this model is called *near-vector autoregressive, or near VAR*.

The assumptions that usually follow a VAR model are the assumptions of a reduced-form simultaneous equation model, i.e.:

$\upsilon_{it} \sim N(0, \omega_{ii})$, for all t, and $i = 1, 2, ..., m$, where $\omega_{ii} = \text{var}(\upsilon_{it})$

$E(\upsilon_{it}\upsilon_{is}) = 0$, for $t \neq s$, and $i = 1, 2, ..., m$ (15.21)

$E(\upsilon_{it}\upsilon_{jt}) = \omega_{ij}$, for all t, and i, $j = 1, 2, ..., m$, where $\omega_{ij} = \text{cov}(\upsilon_{it}, \upsilon_{jt})$

or in matrix form

$$\upsilon_t \sim N(\mathbf{0}, \mathbf{\Omega}), \text{ with } E(\upsilon_t\upsilon_t') = \mathbf{0} \text{ and } \mathbf{\Omega} = E(\upsilon_t\upsilon_t') = \begin{bmatrix} \omega_{11} & \omega_{12} & .. & \omega_{1m} \\ \omega_{21} & \omega_{22} & .. & \omega_{2m} \\ : & : & :: & : \\ \omega_{m1} & \omega_{m2} & : & \omega_{mm} \end{bmatrix} \quad (15.22)$$

A vector stochastic process $\{Y_t\}$ is called stationary if (Judge *et al.* 1988):

$$\left.\begin{aligned} &E(\mathbf{Y}_t) = \mathbf{\mu} \text{ for all t} \\ &\text{var}(Y_{jt}) < \infty \text{ for } j = 1,2,...,m \text{ and all t} \\ &\text{cov}(\mathbf{Y}_t, \mathbf{Y}_{t+k}) = E\left[(\mathbf{Y}_t - \mathbf{\mu})(\mathbf{Y}_{t+k} - \mathbf{\mu})'\right] = \mathbf{\Gamma}_k \text{ for all t} \end{aligned}\right\} \quad (15.23)$$

Furthermore, a VAR(k) process is stationary if its means and covariance matrices are bounded and the polynomial defined by the determinant

$$|\mathbf{I} - \mathbf{A}_1\lambda - \mathbf{A}_2\lambda^2 - \cdots - \mathbf{A}_k\lambda^k| = 0 \quad (15.24)$$

has all it roots outside the complex unit circle (Judge *et al.* 1988).

Under the assumptions written above, the parameters of a VAR(k) model can be consistently estimated with OLS. Therefore, for the ith equation, the OLS estimator is given by:

$$\mathbf{a}_i = (\mathbf{X}'\mathbf{X})^{-1}\mathbf{X}'\mathbf{Y}_i \sim N(\alpha_i, \omega_{ii}(\mathbf{X}'\mathbf{X})^{-1}) \quad (15.25)$$

where

$$\mathbf{a}_i = \begin{bmatrix} a_{i0} & a_{i1,1} & ... & a_{ik,m} \end{bmatrix} \text{ is an estimate of } \alpha_i = \begin{bmatrix} \alpha_{i0} & \alpha_{i1,1} & ... & \alpha_{ik,m} \end{bmatrix}$$

$$\mathbf{Y}_i = \begin{bmatrix} Y_{i1} & Y_{i2} & ... & Y_{in} \end{bmatrix}' \text{ and } \mathbf{X}_i = \begin{bmatrix} \mathbf{1} & \mathbf{Y}_{1,-1} & ... & \mathbf{Y}_{m,-k} \end{bmatrix} \quad (15.26)$$

Consistent estimates w_{ij} of the parameters ω_{ii} in (15.22) are given by:

$$w_{ij} = \frac{(\mathbf{Y}_i - \mathbf{Xa}_i)'(\mathbf{Y}_i - \mathbf{Xa}_i)}{n} \text{ or } \frac{(\mathbf{Y}_i - \mathbf{Xa}_i)'(\mathbf{Y}_i - \mathbf{Xa}_i)}{n - mk - 1} \quad (15.27)$$

We have to note here that the generalised least squares (GLS) estimator, if applied to (15.18), will give the exact same results as the OLS estimator because matrix X is the same for all equations. The seemingly unrelated regressions (SUR) estimator could be applied to the near VAR model to improve efficiency.

The preceding estimation method assumes that the lag length, i.e. the order of the VAR, is known. In cases where the VAR order is large we have a major problem in VAR analysis: the problem of *over-parameterisation*. However, in most cases, the VAR order is not known and therefore it has to be selected. Common tests for selecting the VAR order are the following. In all these tests it is assumed that the number of observations is n, and thus k pre-sample values for all the variables must be considered:

a. The likelihood ratio (LR) test

This test depends on the usual likelihood ratio statistic given by:

$$LR = 2\left[\ln \ell_u - \ln \ell_r\right] \sim \chi^2(v) \tag{15.28}$$

where
$\ln \ell_u$ = log of likelihood of the complete in coefficients (unrestricted) equation
$\ln \ell_r$ = log of likelihood of the smaller in coefficients (unrestricted) equation
v = number of restrictions imposed

Assuming that the coefficients of a VAR(k) model corresponding to the lagged variables are given by the matrix $A = [A_1\ A_2 \dots A_k]$, the test works by testing in a sequence the following hypotheses, starting from a large assumed lag length k.

$$H_0: A_k \quad = 0 \text{ vs. } H_a: \ A_k \neq 0$$
$$H_0: A_{k-1} = 0 \text{ vs. } H_a: \ A_{k-1} \neq 0 \text{ given that } A_k = 0$$
$$H_0: A_{k-2} = 0 \text{ vs. } H_a: \ A_{k-2} \neq 0 \text{ given that } A_k = A_{k-1} = 0 \tag{15.29}$$

....

$$H_0: A_1 = 0 \text{ vs. } H_a: \ A_1 \neq 0 \text{ given that } A_k = A_{k-1} = \dots = A_2 = 0$$

The test stops when a null hypothesis is rejected using the LR statistic and the VAR order q, for $k \geq q \geq 1$, is selected accordingly. However, since estimation methods require white noise errors, a higher value of q might finally be used in the estimations (Holden and Perman, 1994).

The Akaike information criterion (AIC) and Schwartz criterion (SC)

The usual Akaike's information criterion and Schwartz criterion in the VAR context are defined as follows:

$$AIC(q) = \ln |\mathbf{W}_q| + \frac{2m^2q}{n} \tag{15.30}$$

and

$$SC(q) = \ln |\mathbf{W}_q| + \frac{m^2q}{n} \ln(n) \tag{15.31}$$

where m = number of equations, n = common sample size, q = lag length, and W is the estimated residual covariance matrix Ω evaluated for VAR(q). The VAR order q is selected for the corresponding minimum value of the criterion.

Example 15.3 Estimating a VAR model for the private consumption and personal disposable income for an EU member (VAR)

Suppose that we want to estimate a VAR model for the variables of private consumption (C_t) and personal disposable income (Y_t) of an EU member, as discussed in the previous examples.

The first thing that we have to do is to specify the VAR order. Because the data are annual it seems unlikely that the lag length will be more than $k = 3$. Therefore, keeping the values of the variables for the first three years as pre-sample values, Table 15.3 presents the statistics from the estimation of the model for various lag lengths ranging from k = 1 to k = 3.

Table 15.2 Statistics for the consumption-income VAR model for an EU member

Lag length (q)	Log likelihood (ln$^\ell$)	AIC(q)	SC(q)	LR
1	−619.1697	35.20985	35.34726	–
2	−617.4926	35.23003	35.45905	3.3542
3	−616.0448	35.26455	35.58518	2.8956

Notes: Estimates with EViews

For the LR test it is v = 4, because going down from one lag length to an immediately lower lag length, we exclude one lag on each of the two variables in each of the two equations. For a 0.05 significance level, the critical value for the $\chi^2(4)$ distribution is 9.4877. Because of going down from q = 3 to q = 1, none of the LR values in Table 15.2 is greater that $\chi^2(4) = 9.4877$, this means that none of the null hypotheses in (15.29) are rejected. Therefore, this test indicates that the proper VAR order of this model is q = 1. The same VAR order, q = 1, is indicated by the other two statistics, AIC and SC, because these statistics take their minimum value for q = 1.

Estimates of the VAR(1) model are given below:

$$\hat{C}_t = 12581.43 + 0.96780C_{t-1} + 0.01657Y_{t-1} \quad R^2 = 0.9978$$

$$t \quad [4.537] \quad [8.579] \quad [0.189] \tag{15.32}$$

and

$$\hat{Y}_t = 11929.05 + 0.60371C_{t-1} + 0.50776Y_{t-1} \quad R^2 = 0.9903$$

$$t \quad [1.613] \quad [2.007] \quad [2.174] \tag{15.33}$$

15.5 VAR and cointegration

Let us consider the VAR model of (15.18), with m variables, or:

$$Y_t = \sum_{j=1}^{k} A_j Y_{t-j} + \upsilon_t \tag{15.34}$$

where, for simplicity, the intercept has been excluded. Assume also that all its m variables are either simultaneously integrated of order one, or of order zero.

Model (15.34) can be rewritten as

$$\Delta Y_t = BY_{t-1} + \sum_{j=1}^{k-1} B_j \Delta Y_{t-j} + \upsilon_t \tag{15.35}$$

where

$$B = -\left(I - A_1 - A_2 - ... - A_k\right) \tag{15.36}$$

and

$$B_j = -\left(A_{j+1} - A_{j+2} - ... - A_{j+k}\right) \quad \text{for } j = 1, 2,..., k-1 \tag{15.37}$$

Model (15.35) looks like an *error correction model*, and if all its m variables are integrated of order one, then variables ΔY_{t-j} are stationary. This model can consistently be estimated under the assumption that its variables are cointegrated, so BY_{t-1} is also stationary.

It can be proved that (see Engle and Granger (1987) and Johansen (1989) for the original works, or Enders (2010) and Charemza and Deadman (1997) for good presentations):

1 If the rank of matrix B is zero, then all the elements in this matrix are zero. Therefore, in (15.35) the error correction mechanism BY_{t-1} does not exist, meaning that there is no long-run equilibrium relationship between the variables of the model. Thus, these variables are not cointegrated. The VAR model could be formulated in terms of the first differences of the variables.

2 If the rank of matrix B is equal to m, i.e. its rows are linearly independent, the vector process $\{Y_t\}$ is stationary, meaning that all variables are integrated of order zero, and, therefore, the question of cointegration does not arise. The VAR model could be formulated in terms of the levels of all variables.

3 If the rank of matrix B is r, where $r < m$, i.e. its rows are not linearly independent, it can be shown that this matrix can be written as:

$$B = D \times C' \tag{15.38}$$

where D and C are matrices of m×r dimensions. Matrix C is called the *cointegrating matrix*, and matrix D is called the *adjustment matrix*. In the case where $Y_t \sim I(1)$ then $C'Y_t \sim I(0)$, i.e. the variables in Y_t are cointegrated. The cointegrating vectors are the corresponding columns in C, say $c_1, c_2, ..., c_r$. In other words, the rank r of matrix B defines the number of *cointegrating vectors*, i.e. the *cointegrating rank*. The VAR model could be formulated in terms of a *vector error correction* (VEC) model.

The three findings above constitute the generalisation of the *Granger representation theorem*. The work of Johansen (1988), and, similarly, of Stock and Watson (1988), was to identify the cointegrating rank r and to provide estimates of the cointegrating and adjustment matrices, using the maximum likelihood method. The steps of the Johansen approach may be formulated as follows (Dickey *et al.* (1994), Charemza and Deadman (1997)):

Step 1 Using unit roots tests, say ADF, find the order of integration of the variables involved, say m in number.

Step 2 Using the variables in level terms formulate a VAR model and select the VAR order, say k, by using LR, AIC, SC, or other tests.

Step 3 Regress ΔY_t on $\Delta Y_{t-1}, \Delta Y_{t-2}, ..., \Delta Y_{t-k+1}$ and save the residuals. From these residuals, construct the m×1 vector R_{0t} taking the tth element from the saved residuals from each one of the assumed regressions of the m variables.

Step 4 Regress Y_{t-k} on $\Delta Y_{t-1}, \Delta Y_{t-2}, ..., \Delta Y_{t-k+1}$ and save the residuals. From these residuals, construct the m×1 vector R_{kt}, taking the tth element from the saved residuals from each one of the assumed regressions of the m variables.

Step 5 If n is the sample size, using the following formula:

$$S_{ij} = \frac{1}{n} \sum_{t=1}^{n} R_{it} R'_{jt} \quad \text{for i, j} = 0,k \tag{15.39}$$

compute the four m × m matrices S_{00}, S_{0k}, S_{k0}, and S_{kk}.

Step 6 Find the squared canonical correlations which correspond to the ordered character-istic roots of the matrix:

$$S = S_{00}^{-1/2} S_{0k} S_{kk}^{-1} S_{k0} S_{00}^{-1/2} \tag{15.40}$$

or find the characteristic roots, or eigenvalues, of the polynomial equation in μ:

$$|\mu S_{kk} - S_{k0} S_{00}^{-1} S_{0k}| = 0 \tag{15.41}$$

Having m variables, m is also the maximum number of characteristic roots that can be found. Let us denote these roots, ordered in decreasing value, as $\hat{\mu}_1 > \hat{\mu}_2 > \hat{\mu}_3 > \ldots > \hat{\mu}_m$.

Step 7 Recall that, if rank(**B**) = 0, the variables are not cointegrated, if rank(**B**) = m, the vari-ables are stationary, and if rank(**B**) = r, where 0 < r < m, the variables are cointegrated. Furthermore, it is known that the rank of matrix **B** is equal to the number of the characteristic roots that are significantly different from zero. Therefore, the exercise of finding the rank of matrix **B** reduces to the testing of the significance of the characteristic roots $\hat{\mu}_1 > \hat{\mu}_2 > \hat{\mu}_3 > \ldots > \hat{\mu}_m$, or of the insignificance of $1 - \hat{\mu}_j$ (for j = 1, 2, .., m) from unity. The test is based on the following two likelihood ratio (LR) statistics:

$$\lambda_{trace}(r) = -n \sum_{j=r+1}^{m} \ln(1 - \hat{\mu}_j) \tag{15.42}$$

and/or

$$\lambda_{max}(r, r+1) = -n \cdot In(1 - \hat{\mu}_{r+1}) \tag{15.43}$$

For the statistic (15.42) the hypotheses to be tested are in the following sequence:

H_0: r = 0 vs. H_a: r ≥ 1 (if $\lambda_{trace}(r)$ > critical value)
H_0: r ≤ 1 vs. H_a: r ≥ 2 (if $\lambda_{trace}(r)$ > critical value)
.... (15.44)
H_0: r ≤ m − 1 vs. H_a: r = m (if $\lambda_{trace}(r)$ > critical value)

For the statistic (15.43) the hypotheses to be tested are in the following sequence:

H_0: r = 0 vs. H_a: r = 1 (if $\lambda_{max}(r)$ > critical value)
H_0: r ≤ 1 vs. H_a: r = 2 (if $\lambda_{max}(r)$ > critical value)
.... (15.45)
H_0: r ≤ m − 1 vs. H_a: r = m (if $\lambda_{max}(r)$ > critical value)

Critical values for these statistics can be found in Johansen (1988), Johansen and Juselius (1990), Osterwald-Lenum (1992) and in Enders (2010). Table 15.3 presents critical values

Table 15.3 Critical values of the λ_{max} and λ_{trace} statistics

	80%	90%	95%	97.5%	99%
λ_{max} and λ_{trace} statistics with trend drift					
m-r			λ_{max}		
1	1.699	2.816	3.962	5.332	6.936
2	10.125	12.099	14.036	15.810	17.936
3	16.324	18.697	20.778	23.002	25.521
4	22.113	24.712	27.169	29.335	31.943
5	27.889	30.774	33.178	35.546	38.341
			λ_{trace}		
1	1.699	2.816	3.962	5.332	6.936
2	11.164	13.338	15.197	17.299	19.310
3	23.868	26.791	29.509	32.313	35.397
4	40.250	43.964	47.181	50.424	53.792
5	60.215	65.063	68.905	72.140	76.955
λ_{max} and λ_{trace} statistics without trend or constant					
m-r			λ_{max}		
1	4.905	6.691	8.083	9.658	11.576
2	10.666	12.783	14.595	16.403	18.782
3	16.521	18.959	21.279	23.362	26.154
4	22.341	24.917	27.341	29.599	32.616
5	27.953	30.818	33.262	35.700	38.858
			λ_{trace}		
1	4.905	6.691	8.083	9.658	11.576
2	13.038	15.583	17.844	19.611	21.962
3	25.445	28.436	31.256	34.062	37.291
4	41.623	45.248	48.419	51.801	55.551
5	61.566	65.956	69.977	73.031	77.911
λ_{max} and λ_{trace} statistics a constant in cointegrating vector					
m-r			λ_{max}		
1	5.877	7.563	9.094	10.709	12.740
2	11.628	13.781	15.752	17.622	19.834
3	17.474	19.796	21.894	23.836	26.409
4	22.938	25.611	28.167	30.262	33.121
5	28.643	31.592	34.397	36.625	39.672
			λ_{trace}		
1	5.877	7.563	9.094	10.709	12.741
2	15.359	17.957	20.168	22.202	24.988
3	28.768	32.093	35.068	37.603	40.198
4	45.635	49.925	53.347	56.449	60.054
5	66.624	71.472	75.328	78.857	82.969

Source: Enders, W. (2010), (reproduced from Johansen, S. and K. Juselius (1990).

reproduced from Enders (2010) for various specifications of the VAR model and of the cointegrating vector. However, in both trace and max tests, (15.44) and (15.45), the testing of the hypotheses stops when, going from top to bottom, we encounter the first non-significant result. For this case, the rank r of matrix **B** is that shown by the corresponding null hypothesis.

Step 8 To each of the characteristic roots there corresponds an eigenvector, say $v_1, v_2, \ldots, v_m$, which can constitute the eigenmatrix $V = [v_1 \, v_2 \ldots v_m]$. These eigenvectors can be normalised by using $V'S_{kk}V = I$. If in step 7 it has been found that r is the order of matrix B, then the first r eigenvectors in V are the r cointegrating vectors that constitute the cointegrating matrix $C = [v_1 \, v_2 \ldots v_r]$. The adjustment matrix is found by $D = S_{0k}C$. These are the ML estimators of C and D.

Example 15.4 Testing cointegration between the log of private consumption, the log of personal disposable income and inflation rate for an EU member (The Johansen approach)

Suppose that we want to test cointegration between the variables of the log of private consumption ($c_t = \log C_t$), the log of personal disposable income ($y_t = \log Y_t$) and inflation ($z_t = \log P_t - \log P_{t-1}$) of an EU member, for which the original values are presented in Chapter 12, Table 12.1.

Following the steps presented above, and using for comparisons the common sample 1964–1995, treating, thus, the initial values of the variables as pre-sample values, we get:

Step 1 Using the ADF test we found that all m = 3 variables are integrated of order one, i.e. it is $c_t \sim I(1)$, $y_t \sim I(1)$ and $z_t \sim I(1)$.

Step 2 Using the variables in level terms, i.e. as c_t, y_t and z_t, we have formulated a VAR model and selected the VAR order, say k, by using the LR, AIC, and SC statistics, presented in Table 15.4.

For the LR test, the degrees of freedom are v = 9, because going down from one lag length to an immediately lower lag length, we exclude one lag on each of the three variables in each of the three equations. For a 0.05 significance level, the critical value for the $\chi^2(9)$ distribution is 16.919. Because going down from q = 3 to q = 1, none of the LR values in Table 15.4 are greater than $\chi^2(9) = 16.919$; this means that none of the null hypotheses in (15.29) are rejected. Therefore, this test indicates that the proper VAR order of this model is q = 1. However, the other two statistics, AIC and SC, indicate an order of q = 2, because these statistics take their minimum value for q = 2.

Steps 3–8 There is no need to go through, one by one, all the other steps presented above. Econometric packages like Microfit and EViews include the Johansen test as a standard procedure. In what follows we made use of EViews.

Assuming that the correct VAR order is k = 2, according to AIC and SC, and assuming further that the time series have means and linear trends, but the cointe-

Table 15.4 Statistics for the consumption-income VAR model for an EU member

Lag length (q)	Log likelihood (ln^f)	AIC(q)	SC(q)	LR
1	290.9015	−23.44498	−23.26176	–
2	297.2352	−23.65333	−23.33270	12.6674
3	300.0237	−23.64011	−23.18207	2.7885

Notes: estimates with EViews

grating equations have only intercepts, Table 15.5 presents statistics of the Johansen tests based on the λ_{trace} LR statistic (15.42).

On the basis of the statistics in Table 15.5, or taking into account the critical values reported in Table 15.3, and for the 5% significance level, we see that the hypothesised cointegrating equations are at most one, because according to the hypotheses testing in (15.44) the LR ratio statistic cannot reject the H_0: $r \leq 1$, because this statistic is less than the corresponding critical value.

The estimate of the single cointegrating vector in normalised form has been estimated with EViews to be [1.000000 −0.802239 0.786507 −2.404530] and the corresponding long-run relationship is given by:

$$c_t = 0.802239 y_t - 0.76507 z_t + 2.404530$$

s.e.　(0.0858)　　　(0.3689) $\qquad\qquad\qquad\qquad$ (15.46)

t　　[9.3467]　　　[−2.1319]

Let us assume now that the correct VAR order is k = 1, according to LR, and let us also consider, as before, that the time series have means and linear trends, but the cointegrating equations have only intercepts. Table 15.6 presents statistics of the Johansen tests based on the λ_{trace} LR statistic (15.46).

On the basis of the statistics in Table 15.6, and for the 5% significance level, we see that the hypothesised cointegrating equations are at most two, because according to the hypotheses testing in (15.44) the LR ratio statistic cannot reject the H_0: $r \leq 2$, because this statistic is less than the corresponding critical value.

The estimates of the two cointegrating vectors in normalised forms have been estimated with EViews to be [1.000000 0.00000 1.869601 −12.74157], with the corresponding long-run relationship:

$$c_t = -1.869601 z_t + 12.74157$$

s.e.　(1.7578) $\qquad\qquad\qquad\qquad\qquad\qquad\qquad\qquad$ (15.47)

t　　[−1.0636]

Table 15.5 Test statistics for cointegration of c_t, y_t, and z_t. VAR(k = 2) and n = 32 (linear deterministic trend in the data)

Eigenvalue	LR	5% critical value	1% critical value	Hypothesised No. of CE(s)
0.518647	37.04098	29.68	35.65	None
0.317653	13.64407	15.41	20.04	At most 1
0.043199	1.413110	3.76	6.65	At most 2

Notes: estimates with EViews

Table 15.6 Test statistics for cointegration of c_t, y_t, and z_t. VAR(k = 1) and n = 32 (linear deterministic trend in the data)

Eigenvalue	LR	5% critical value	1% critical value	Hypothesised no. of CE(s)
0.601504	46.95860	29.68	35.65	None
0.375848	17.51672	15.41	20.04	At most 1
0.073218	2.433170	3.76	6.65	At most 2

Notes: estimates with EViews

and [0.00000 1.00000 1.467762 −12.89880] with the corresponding long-run relationship:

$$y_t = -1.467762z_t + 12.89880$$

s.e.   (1.8557)   (15.48)

t   [−0.7910]

Comparing the two results above for VAR(2) and VAR(1) we see that our conclusions changed completely with respect to the number of the long-run relationships that exist between these two variables. Furthermore, if we change the assumptions referring to the data generating process (DGP), i.e. assuming linear trends, or not, in the data and/ or intercepts or trends in the cointegrating equations, we may obtain altogether different results. Table 15.7 presents the conclusions reached with the Johansen approach assuming different initial conditions for testing cointegration between these three variables.

The contradicting results presented in Table 15.7 about the cointegration between the three variables, c_t, y_t and z_t, show that although cointegration tests are very valuable in distinguishing between spurious and meaningful regressions, we should not rely only on cointegration methods. We should use economic theory and all the a priori knowledge that is associated with this theory, in order to decide the number and the form of the cointegrating regressions. From the three long-run equilibrium relationships estimated in (15.46), (15.47) and (15.48), it seems that the cointegrating equation (15.46) is very reasonable, taking into account that the long-run income elasticity of consumption is 0.80, a highly acceptable value, and the coefficient of the inflation variable is negative, showing, thus, the negative effect of rising inflation on consumption.

Finally, for the case of VAR(2) and one cointegrating regression, the estimated first equation of the vector error correction model is shown below (the other two equations or the other estimated terms are not shown here):

$$\Delta \hat{c}_t = -0.317084 \left(c_{t-1} - 0.802239 y_{t-1} + 0.786507 z_{t-1} - 2.40453 \right) + \text{other terms}$$

t   [−5.0259]   [−9.3467]   [2.1319]   (15.49)

$$R^2 = 0.6740$$

In Equation (15.49) the coefficient of the estimated equilibrium error is negative (−0.317084) and significant, showing, thus, that it is using the hypothesis of the error correction mechanism.

Table 15.7 Number of cointegrating regressions by VAR order and DGP assumptions

	No linear trends in series		Linear trends in series	
	No intercept – no trend in CEs	*Intercept – no trend in CEs*	*Intercept – no trend in CEs*	*Intercept – trend in CEs*
VAR(1)	2	2	2	2
VAR(2)	2	1	1	1

Notes: Estimates with EViews

A final point on cointegration analysis, identified by the above worked examples, is worth re-emphasising here before we close this coverage of cointegration methodology. Note that cointegration is essentially an inductive methodology. That is, it is a statistical method of data analysis and is not based on economic theory. It is basically a statistical methodology. Therefore, in practice, as was pointed out above, it is always good practice to use knowledge of economic theory to specify potential cointegrating regression and to carry out normalisation procedures when using cointegration analysis.

15.6 The Granger causality test

We close this chapter by briefly explaining the Granger causality test. This is a useful practical method for determining the direction of the causation between variables and it may therefore be used in cointegration analysis when there is a lack of clear theoretical framework concerning the variables under investigation. When in a regression equation we say that the 'explanatory' variable X_t affects the 'dependent' variable Y_t, we indirectly accept that variable X_t *causes* variable Y_t, in the sense that changes in variable X_t induce changes in variable Y_t. This is, in simple terms, the concept of *causality*. With respect to the direction of causality, we can distinguish the following cases:

1   *Unidirectional causality* This is the case when X_t causes Y_t, but Y_t does not cause X_t.
2   *Bilateral or feedback causality* This is the case when variables X_t and Y_t are jointly determined.

Because, in most cases, in the absence of theoretical models, the direction of causality is not known, various tests have been suggested to identify this direction. The most well-known test is the one proposed by Granger (1969). This test being based on the premise that 'the future cannot cause the present or the past', utilises the concept of the VAR models. Let us therefore consider the two-variable, X_t and Y_t, VAR(k) model:

$$Y_t = \alpha_{10} + \sum_{j=1}^{k} \alpha_{1j} X_{t-j} + \sum_{j=1}^{k} \beta_{1j} Y_{t-j} + \varepsilon_{1t} \tag{15.50}$$

$$X_t = \alpha_{20} + \sum_{j=1}^{k} \alpha_{2j} X_{t-j} + \sum_{j=1}^{k} \beta_{2j} Y_{t-j} + \varepsilon_{2t} \tag{15.51}$$

With respect to this model we can distinguish the following cases:

1   If $\{\alpha_{11}, \alpha_{12}, \ldots, \alpha_{1k}\} \neq 0$ and $\{\beta_{21}, \beta_{22}, \ldots, \beta_{2k}\} = 0$, there exists a unidirectional causality from X_t to Y_t, denoted as $X \to Y$.
2   If $\{\alpha_{11}, \alpha_{12}, \ldots, \alpha_{1k}\} = 0$ and $\{\beta_{21}, \beta_{22}, \ldots, \beta_{2k}\} \neq 0$, there exists a unidirectional causality from Y_t to X_t, denoted as $Y \to X$.
3   If $\{\alpha_{11}, \alpha_{12}, \ldots, \alpha_{1k}\} \neq 0$, and $\{\beta_{21}, \beta_{22}, \ldots, \beta_{2k}\} \neq 0$, there exists a bilateral causality between Y_t and X_t, denoted as $X \Leftrightarrow Y$.

In order to test the hypotheses referring to the significance or not of the sets of the coefficients of the VAR model of Equations (15.50) and (15.51), the usual Wald F-statistic could be utilised, which is the following:

$$F_c = \frac{(SSR_r - SSR_u)/k}{SSR_u/(n-2k-1)} \sim F(k, n-2k-1) \tag{15.52}$$

where: SSR_u = sum of squared residuals from the complete equation (unrestricted)

SSR_r = sum of squared residuals from the equation under the assumption that a set of variables is redundant (restricted)

The hypotheses in this test may be formed as follows:

H_0: X does not Granger cause Y, i.e. $\{\alpha_{11},...,\alpha_{1k}\} = 0$, if $F_c <$ critical value of F

H_a: X does Granger cause Y, i.e. $\{\alpha_{11},...,\alpha_{1k}\} \neq 0$, if $F_c >$ critical value of F

(15.53)

and

H_0: Y does not Granger cause X, i.e. $\{\beta_{11},...,\beta_{1k}\} = 0$, if $F_c <$ critical value of F

H_a: Y does Granger cause X, i.e. $\{\beta_{11},...,\beta_{1k}\} \neq 0$, if $F_c >$ critical value of F

(15.54)

It has to be noted here that in the hypotheses (15.53) and (15.54) it is not tested if 'X causes Y', but instead it is tested if 'X causes Y according to the Granger type'. This is because the Granger test is just a statistical test based not on a specific theory of causation but based on the ability of the equation to better predict the dependent variable. Furthermore, the validity of the test depends on the order of the VAR model and on the stationarity or not of the variables. The validity of the test is reduced if the variables involved are non-stationary (Geweke, 1984). Finally, other tests have been proposed, such as those of Sims (1972) and Geweke *et al.* (1983), for example, and, moreover, Granger (1988) extended his test to also consider the concept of cointegration.

Example 15.6 Testing Granger causality between the log of private consumption and inflation rate for an EU member (the Granger test)

Consider the following two assumptions: (1) demand (consumption) depends on the level of prices (inflation rate), and (2) the level of prices (inflation rate) depends on demand (consumption), because it is formed by a 'pull-type inflation mechanism'. Anyone, or both, of these assumptions may be correct. We will use the Granger causality test between the variables of the log of private consumption ($c_t = logC_t$) and inflation rate ($z_t = logP_t - logP_{t-1}$) of an EU member, for which the original values are presented in Table 12.1. Let us consider the case of a VAR(2) model because our data are annual.

In Table 15.8 we present the calculated F_c statistics according to formula (15.52) for all the possible cases of redundant variables in the two equations of the VAR(2) model.

Table 15.8 F-statistics for testing the redundancy of variables

	Redundant: z_t, z_{t-1}	Redundant: c_t, c_{t-1}
Dependent, c_t	$\{\alpha_{11}, \alpha_{12}\} = 0$ vs. $\{\alpha_{11}, \alpha_{12}\} \neq 0$ 3.9359 (0.0316)	$\{\beta_{11}, \beta_{12}\} = 0$ vs. $\{\beta_{11}, \beta_{12}\} \neq 0$ 2767.940 (0.0000)
Dependent, z_t	$\{\alpha_{21}, \alpha_{22}\} = 0$ vs. $\{\alpha_{21}, \alpha_{22}\}\alpha0$ 12.5418 (0.0001)	$\{\beta_{21}, \beta_{22}\} = 0$ vs. $\{\beta_{21}, \beta_{22}\}\alpha0$ 5.6961 (0.0086)

Notes: significance levels in parentheses

From the results in Table 15.8 we are interested in those referring to the testing of the set of coefficients $\{\alpha_{11}, \alpha_{12}\}$ and $\{\beta_{21}, \beta_{22}\}$. We see that in both cases the F-statistics are significant (significance levels less than 0.05) meaning that $\{\alpha_{11}, \alpha_{12}\} \neq 0$ and $\{\beta_{21}, \beta_{22}\} \neq 0$, or that z Granger cause c, and c Granger cause z, respectively. In other words, the Granger causation between consumption and inflation in an EU member is of the bilateral type, i.e. $c \Leftrightarrow z$, something which was possibly expected. Note that in a cointegration analysis this type of information is useful, particularly when there is no theoretical framework to guide specification of potential cointegrating regressions and subsequent normalisation procedures.

15.7 A summary of key issues

- The Johansen procedure can deal with the general case of more than two variables and also provides procedures to test parameter restrictions, which are useful for testing theoretical restrictions.
- The Johansen method relies heavily on the relationship between the rank of a matrix and its characteristics roots/eigenvalues. The rank of a matrix is equal to the number of independent cointegrated relationships/vectors. If rank is one there is one single cointegrated relationship. The rank of a matrix is equal to the number of its non-zero characteristic roots.
- The number of distinct cointegrated vectors/relationships can be obtained by checking the significance of the characteristic roots, using the trace and the max. tests.
- The Johansen procedure may be viewed as a multivariate DF test, in which unit root tests and cointegration tests are carried out on n variables.
- There are two key test statistics. These are called trace and max. test statistics.
- Trace statistic test the null hypothesis that the number of distinct cointegrated relationships is less than or equal to r (1,2,3, etc.). In general, with k variables there could be $k-1$ cointegrating relationships.
- The max. test statistic tests the null hypothesis that the number of cointegrated relationships is r against the alternative of $r + 1$. The critical values are usually reported by the regression packages (e.g. Microfit 5).
- Using the Johansen procedure, with five variables, suppose we obtain the following results:

Characteristics roots	max. statistic	trace statistic
$\lambda 1 = 0.43$	30.09	49.14
$\lambda 2 = 0.1776$	10.36	19.05
$\lambda 3 = 0.1128$	6.34	8.69
$\lambda 4 = 0.0434$	2.35	2.35

- Analysis: in contrast to the trace test, the max. test has a specific form and is easier to carry out. Using this test, we test for $r = 0$, against $r = 1$ (r is the no. of cointegrated relationships). The calculated value of max. (0,1) is 30.09, and the CV of the test at 5% is reported to be 28.14, hence it is possible to reject $r = 0$ in favour of $r = 1$: it seems that there is only one cointegrating relationship. However, it is advisable to test $r = 1$ against $r = 2$, using max. (1, 2), before concluding cointegration. The calculated value of max. (1, 2) is 10.36, the critical value at 5%, and $(n - r = 5 - 2 = 3)$ is 22.0, therefore we cannot reject H_0. We conclude that there is potentially one cointegrated relationship between five variables. The trace test usually is consistent with the max. test, but the max. text is more specific and easier to apply.

• Once a unique cointegrated vector/relationship is found, the ECM regression can be carried out to t estimate the short-run adjustment via an ECM process.

Review questions

1   Explain the shortcomings of the Engle-Granger methodology when dealing with cointegration analysis of a multivariate case.
2   Explain the Granger causality test and discuss why this test might be useful in cointegration analysis.
3   Explain the type of cointegration analysis to be employed when dealing with several variables. How would you use knowledge of theory to help with the specification and analysis?
4   Collect a time series data set (quarterly) for the period 1985–2010, for a country of your own choice, consisting of the following variables:

• Gross domestic product (GDP)
• sum of public, G, and private consumption expenditure, C: CG
• investment expenditure (gross capital formation): INV
• exports of goods and services: E
• aggregate imports: M
• relative price of Imports to the price of domestically produced: Pm/Pd.

Use a relevant economic theory to explain how M, imports, might be determined by the above variables (for example, see Abbott and Seddighi, 1996). Based on theory, explain how you would define your variables for the purpose of a regression analysis. Consider the theoretical model:

M = F(CG, INV, E, Pm/pd)

Use an appropriate regression package (e.g. Microfit 5 or EViews) to investigate cointegration of the above model. With reference to the material covered in this chapter explain each step of this investigation.

Key terms: Unit 4

• *Spurious regression* Misleading results due to non-stationarity of the variables.
• *Weak stationarity* The mean, variance and the covariances of a time series are time-invariant (constant over time).
• *Unit root test* A statistical test designed to detect non-stationarity.
• *IDW* Integration Durbin-Watson statistic used to detect non-stationarity.
• *Cointegration* An econometric methodology employed to confirm the existence of a long-run relationship among economic variables, as postulated by economic theory.
• *VAR (model)* Vector autoregression model.
• *ECM: error correction model* In each period a fraction of the previous period error is corrected. If variables are found to be cointegrated, the adjustment towards equilibrium takes place via an ECM process. An ECM process implies cointegration (EG representation theorem).

General notes and bibliography: Unit 4

The concepts of stationarity, unit root testing and cointegration analysis are of crucial importance in the development of the modern time series econometrics. There have been many notable contributions in this area in recent years. We list below a number of key contributions.

Abbott, A. and Seddighi, H.R. (1996). 'Aggregate imports and expenditure components in the U.K.', *Applied Economics*, September 1996, 28, 98–110.

Bartlett, M. S. (1946). 'On the theoretical specification of sampling properties of autocorrelated time series', *Journal of the Royal Statistical Society*, Series B, 27, 27–41.

Box, G. E. P. and Piece, D. A. (1970). 'Distribution of residual autocorrelations in autoregressive integrated moving average time series models', *Journal of the American Statistical Association*, 65, 1509–1525.

Campbell, J. Y. and Perron, P. (1991). 'Pitfalls and opportunities: What macroeconomists should now about unit roots', *Technical Working Paper 100*, NBER Working Papers Series.

Charemza, W. W. and Readman, D. F. (1997). *New Directions in Econometric Practice: General to Specific Modelling, Cointegration and Vector Autoregression*, 2nd edn, Cheltenham: Edward Elgar.

Cuthbertson, K., Hall, S. G., and Taylor, M. P. (1992). *Applied Econometric Techniques*, New York: Philip Allan.

Davinson, R. and MacKinnon, J. G. (1993). *Estimation and Inference in Econometrics*, New York: Oxford University Press.

Dickey, D. A. and Fuller, W. A. (1979). 'Distributions of the estimators for autoregressive time series with a unit root', *Journal of the American Statistical Association*, 74, 427–431.

Dickey, D. A. and Fuller, W. A. (1981). 'Likelihood ratio statistics for autoregressive time series with a unit root', *Econometrica*, 49, 1057–1072.

Dickey, D. A. and Pantula, S. (1987). 'Determining the order of differencing in autoregressive processes', *Journal of Business and Economic Statistics*, 15, 455–461.

Dickey, D. A., Bell, W., and Miller, R. (1986). 'Unit roots in time series models: Tests and implications', *American Statistician*, 40, 12–26.

Dickey, D. A., Hasza, D. P., and Fuller, W. A. (1984). 'Testing for unit roots in seasonal time series', *Journal of the American Statistical Association*, 79, 355–367.

Dickey, D. A., Jansen, D. W., and Thornton, D. L. (1994). 'A primer on cointegration with an application to money and income', in B. B. Rao, (ed), *Cointegration for the Applied Economist*, New York: St. Martin's Press.

Doldado, J., Jenkinson, T., and Sosvilla-Rivero, S. (1990). 'Cointegration and unit roots', *Journal of Econometric Surveys*, 4: 249–273.

Enders, W. (2010). *Applied Econometric Time Series*, 3rd edn, New York: John Wiley.

Engle, R. F. and Granger, C. W. J. (1987). 'Cointegration and error correction: Representation, estimation and testing', *Econometrica*, 55, 251–276.

Engle, R. F. and Yoo, B. S. (1987). 'Forecasting and testing cointegrated systems', *Journal of Econometrics*, 35, 145–159.

Engle, R. F., Granger, C. W. J., and Hallman, J. J. (1989). 'Merging short- and long-run forecasts: an application of seasonal cointegration to monthly electricity sales forecasting', *Journal of Econometrics*, 40, 45–62.

Fuller, W. (1976). *Introduction to Statistical Time Series*, New York: John Wiley.

Geweke, J. (1984). 'Inference and causality in economic time series models', in Z. Griliches and M. D. Intriligator (eds), *Handbook of Econometrics*, vol. 2, Amsterdam: North Holland.

Geweke, J., Meese, R. and Dent, W. (1983). 'Comparing alternative tests of causality in temporal systems', *Journal of Econometrics*, 77, 161–194.

Granger, C. W. J. (1969). 'Investigating casual relations by econometric models and cross-spectral models', *Econometrica*, 37, 424–438.

Granger, C. W. J. (1986). 'Developments in the study of cointegrated economic variables', *Oxford Bulletin of Economics and Statistics*, 48, 213–228.

Granger, C. W. J. (1988). 'Some recent developments in a concept of causality', *Journal of Econometrics*, 39, 199–221.

Granger, C. W. J. and Newbold, P. (1974). 'Spurious regressions in econometrics', *Journal of Econometrics*, 35, 143–159.

Greene, W. H. (1999). *Econometric Analysis*, 4th edn, New Jersey: Prentice-Hall.

Gujarati, D. N. (1995). *Basic Econometrics*, 3rd edn, New York: McGraw-Hill.

Holden, D. and Perman, R. (1994). 'Unit roots and cointegration for the economist' in B. B. Rao (ed), *Cointegration for the Applied Economist*, New York: St. Martin's Press.

Hylleberg, S., Engle, R. F., Granger, C. W. J., and Yoo, B. S. (1990). 'Seasonal integration and cointegration', *Journal of Econometrics*, 44, 215–238.

Im, K., Pesaran, M. H., and Shin, Y. (2003). 'Testing for unit roots in heterogeneous panels', *Journal of Econometrics*, 115, 29–52.

Jenkins, G. M. and Watts, D. G. (1968). *Spectral Analysis and Its Applications*, San Francisco: Holden-Day.

Johansen, S. (1988). 'Statistical analysis of cointegration vectors', *Journal of Economic Dynamics and Control*, 12, 213–254.

Johansen, S. and Juselius, K. (1990). 'Maximal likelihood estimation and inference on cointegration – with applications to the demand of money', *Oxford Bulletin of Economics and Statistics*, 52, 169–210.

Judge, G. G., Hill, R. C., Griffiths, W. E., Lutkepohl, H. and Lee, T. C. (1988). *Introduction to Theory and Practice of Econometrics*, 2nd edn, New York: John Wiley.

Ljung, G. M. and Box, G. P. E. (1978). 'On a measure of lack of fit in time series models', *Biometrica*, 66, 66–72.

MacKinnon, J. G. (1991). 'Critical values of cointegration tests', in R. F. Engle and C. W. J. Granger (eds), *Long-Run Econometric Relationships: Readings in Cointegration*, New York: Oxford University Press.

Maddala, G. S. (1992). *Introduction to Econometrics*, 2nd edn, New Jersey: Prentice-Hall.

Nelson, C. R. and Plosser, C. I. (1982). 'Trends and random walks in macroeconomic time series', *Journal of Monetary Economics*, 10, 139–162.

Osborn, D. R., Chui, A. P. L., Smith, J. P. and Birchenhall, C. R. (1988). 'Seasonality and the order of integration in consumption', *Oxford Bulletin of Economics and Statistics*, 50, 361–377.

Osterwald-Lenum, M. (1992). 'A note with qualities of the asymptotic distribution of the maximum likelihood cointegration rank test statistics', *Oxford Bulletin of Economics and Statistics*, 54, 461–472.

Phillips, P. C. B. and Loretan, M. (1991). 'Estimating long-run economic equilibria', *Review of Economic Studies*, 5, 407–436.

Phillips, P. and Perron, P. (1988). 'Testing for a unit root in time series regression', *Biometrica*, 75, 335–346.

Sargan, J. D. (1964). 'Wages and prices in the United Kingdom: A study of econometric methodology', in P. E. Hart, G. Mills and J. K. Whitaker (eds), *Econometric Analysis for National Economic Planning*, London: Butterworths.

Sargan, J. D. and Bhargava, A. (1983). 'Testing residuals from least squares regression for being generated by the Gaussian random walk', *Econometrica*, 51, 153–174.

Schmidt, P. and Phillips, P. (1992). 'LM tests for a unit root in the presence of deterministic trends', *Oxford Bulletin of Economics and Statistics*, 54, 257–87.

Seddighi, H. R. and Shearing, D. (1998). 'The demand for tourism in the North East of England with special reference to Northumbria: an empirical study', *Tourism Management*, 18(8), December 1997, 499–511.

Sims, C. (1972). 'Money, income, and causality', *American Economic Review*, 62, 540–552.

Stock, J. H. (1987). 'Asymptotic properties of least squares estimators of cointegrating vectors', *Econometrica*, 55, 1035–1056.

Stock, J. H. and Watson, M. (1988). 'Testing for common trends', *Journal of the American Statistical Association*, 83, 1097–1107.

Thomas, R. L. (1997). *Modern Econometrics: an introduction*, Harlow: Addison-Wesley.

Unit 5

Aspects of financial time series econometrics

- Time series data on financial variables, such as stock/share prices, asset prices and exchange rates, are known as financial time series. Data sets on financial time series are collected by financial institutions, for example, the London Stock Exchange and *Financial Times*, and are normally available online.
- Two key characteristics of financial time series are: (a) high frequency of the data and (b) volatility of the data. High frequency of data reflects the way financial markets operate in practice. In these markets prices change rapidly due to continuous changes in supply and demand for financial assets, in response to news and changes in market conditions. Data sets are available on an hourly and daily basis, in contrast to low-frequency economic data.
- Volatility of financial data reflects uncertainty about the market valuation of financial assets and corresponding continuous adjustments in financial prices.
- Volatility in the time series give rise to time-variant variance and covariances of the time series. These key characteristics are inherently unstable over time, giving rise to non-stationary financial time series. They are not a sign of misspecification, rather they are inherent characteristics of financial time series.

This unit focuses on modelling volatility and correlation of financial time series. This is an important aspect of econometric analysis of financial data and it needs to be tackled first as part of the modelling exercise, before the start of estimation and regression analysis. The unit will also explain in detail the relevant estimation and regression procedures of financial time series.

16 Modelling volatility and correlations in financial time series

Dennis Philip
Durham Business School

INTRODUCTION

Econometric modelling of time series, discussed in the previous chapters, was mainly centred around modelling the conditional first moment (or conditional mean). Temporal dependencies in the variances and covariances were considered as model misspecifications. To this effect, researchers had developed ways of correcting such misspecifications and time series were studied in the context of homoscedasticity. However, developments in financial econometrics noted that most of the financial time series showed time-varying variances and covariances that captured the risk or the uncertainty element in financial assets. This meant that heteroscedasticity was not to be considered as model misspecification but as an important feature present in financial time series that should be modelled and not corrected.

In this chapter we will discuss the important methodologies commonly employed to explain the dynamics in the variances and covariances of financial assets. In this, we will review the popular frameworks introduced for modelling the volatility and correlations in financial time series. The interest in modelling these higher moments stems from the fact that such estimates have been used as inputs to several financial applications in asset pricing and for risk management purposes.

This chapter begins by defining volatility and its features. We then introduce the parametric estimators of volatility that have been developed in the literature, such as exponentially weighted moving average (EWMA), and autoregressive conditional heteroscedastic (ARCH) type models. Then we introduce non-parametric estimators of volatility, such as range estimators and realised volatility that have been widely used in recent years due to the availability of high-frequency financial data. Finally, we outline the multivariate specifications developed for modelling conditional volatility and conditional correlations.

Key topics

- Volatility features in financial time series
- (G)ARCH models
- Asymmetric volatility models
- Non-parametric estimators of volatility
- Multivariate volatility and correlation models

16.1 Defining volatility and its features

Volatility can be defined as the variations in returns that are observed for a unit of time. Volatility, if assumed to be constant, can be measured by sample standard deviations when the returns are normally distributed. Suppose returns $r_t \sim N(\mu, \sigma^2)$. The sample standard deviation is given by:

$$\hat{\sigma} = \sqrt{\frac{1}{T-1}\sum_{t=1}^{T}(r_t - \mu)^2} \tag{16.1}$$

where μ is the average return over the $T-$ day period. If we consider $T = 252$ trading days per year, $\hat{\sigma}$ measures volatility per year. And, if we assume that the returns are uncorrelated over time:

$$\hat{\sigma}_{yearly} = \sqrt{\sum_{t=1}^{T}Var(r_t)}$$
$$= \sqrt{T}\sigma_{daily} \tag{16.2}$$

This shows that if returns are uncorrelated, we can approximate uncertainty for several horizons as volatility is a function of time. For example, if volatility is 25% per year, then weekly volatility is approximately $25/\sqrt{52} = 3.47\%$.

In the above case, since the second moment of a normally distributed random variable fully summarises the dispersion characteristics of the variable, standard deviation is a good measure of volatility. However, since returns distributions of financial time series commonly show fat tails and are non-normal, standard deviations are no longer a good measure of volatility. For skewed financial data, a better measure of volatility could be the interquartile range.

However, it is typically the case that the volatility we observe in returns is not constant but time-varying. Figure 16.1 plots daily log-returns of the FTSE 100 from Jan 1, 1990 to Dec 31, 2010.

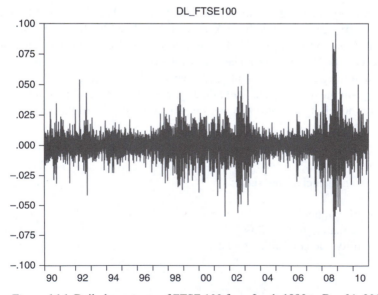

Figure 16.1 Daily log-returns of FTSE 100 from Jan 1, 1990 to Dec 31, 2010.

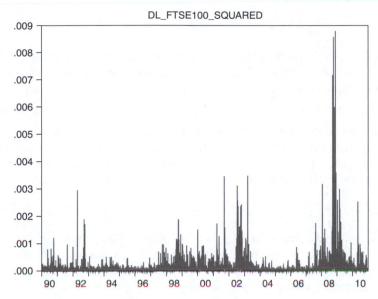

Figure 16.2 Squared daily returns for FTSE 100.

We can see that volatility is certainly not constant. There are periods of high volatility, such as during the 2007–08 financial crisis and there are periods of low volatility, such as the mid-1990s. We also see that volatility tends to cluster where we observe large (small) movements in one period, these are being followed by large (small) movements. This can be graphically seen in Figure 16.2 where we plot the squared daily returns for the FTSE 100. Volatility tends to persist. The effect of shocks on stock returns tends to extend during several subsequent periods and such features of volatility have been referred to as long memory. Studying the autocorrelation functions for squared returns would show significant correlations over extended lag lengths.

A further feature of volatility documented in the literature is known as leverage effects. This feature refers to the asymmetric relationship between volatility and news. Bad news in one period tends to increase subsequent volatility to a much greater extent than good news of the same magnitude. Here, news is often proxied by unexpected returns and volatility by daily squared returns (see Black (1976), Engle and Ng (1993), among others).

16.2 Parametric estimators of volatility

In order to capture the stylised features of volatility that are observed empirically, researchers have devised several types of parametric models. In this section we will discuss some of the main developments in the literature.

16.2.1 Autoregressive conditional heteroscedastic (ARCH) models

Engle (1982) developed the autoregressive conditional heteroscedastic (ARCH) framework that allows for the conditional variance to be time-varying (that is, heteroscedastic rather than homoscedastic). The persistence in volatility is captured by an autoregressive model for conditional volatility. In this, the variance of the residuals from the mean equation are allowed to depend on the past shocks (proxied by lagged squared residuals).

Consider the mean equation:

$$Y_t = \beta' X_t + \varepsilon_t \tag{16.3}$$

where β is an $n \times 1$ vector of coefficients and X is an $n \times 1$ vector of regressors and $\varepsilon_t \sim iidN(0, \sigma_t^2)$. In this case, the variance of the residuals is allowed to be time-varying.

If the previous q day's squared residuals or shocks ($\varepsilon_{t-1}^2, \varepsilon_{t-2}^2, \ldots, \varepsilon_{t-q}^2$) cumulatively influence the volatility today then we can write $\sigma_t^2 = \sum_{j=1}^{q} \varepsilon_{t-j}^2$. However, recent shocks influence volatility much more than shocks that have happened further in the past. Therefore, it makes sense to use the weighted average of the shocks (more weight to recent shocks and less weight to shocks in the distant past). Also, if we assign some weight to the long-run average variance rate, we have the ARCH (q) model:

$$\sigma_t^2 = \alpha_0 + \alpha_1 \varepsilon_{t-1}^2 + \ldots + \alpha_q \varepsilon_{t-q}^2 \tag{16.4}$$

where α_0 captures the long-run average variance, and $\alpha_i \geq 0$ for $i = 0, 1, \ldots, q$ in order for the variance equation to be positive. In this specification, the shocks up to q periods ago affect the current volatility of the process.

A simple case of this model is the ARCH(1) model:

$$\sigma_t^2 = \alpha_0 + \alpha_1 \varepsilon_{t-1}^2 \tag{16.5}$$

where we assume that last period shocks affect the variance of this period. The size and the impact of the shocks depend on the size and sign of α_1. The estimated coefficients have to be positive as σ_t^2 cannot be negative.

Testing for ARCH effects

Before estimating an ARCH(q) model, we have to examine the possible presence of changing variance among the residuals (heteroscedasticity). This is commonly known as testing for ARCH effects in residuals. Engle's (1982) ARCH LM test involves first estimating the residuals from the mean equation. We then regress the squared residuals on p of its own lags and test the joint null hypothesis that all the estimated p coefficients are zero (that is, no presence of autocorrelation in the squared residuals). More specifically, consider the postulated mean equation for returns:

$$r_t = \beta_0 + \beta_1 X_{1t} + \beta_2 X_{2t} + \varepsilon_t \tag{16.6}$$

We square the estimated residuals $\hat{\varepsilon}_t$ from the above regression and run an auxiliary regression:

$$\hat{\varepsilon}_t^2 = \alpha_0 + \alpha_1 \hat{\varepsilon}_{t-1}^2 + \ldots + \alpha_q \hat{\varepsilon}_{t-q}^2 + v_t \tag{16.7}$$

and test the joint null hypothesis:

$$H_0 : \alpha_1 = \ldots = \alpha_q = 0 \text{ (i.e. no ARCH effect)} \tag{16.8}$$

against the alternative hypothesis that at least one of the coefficients is non-zero. The q lags in the auxiliary regression tests for the presence of an ARCH(q) variance process. The test statistic is based on the R^2 (squared correlation coefficient) from the auxiliary regression, which is chi-squared distributed:

$$TR^2 \sim \chi^2(q) \tag{16.9}$$

where T is the number of observations. If the test statistics exceed the critical values from a chi-squared distribution, we reject the null and conclude that ARCH effects are present in the returns. This test can also be written in terms of the F-statistic and usually reported alongside with the LM-statistic in most econometric software packages. Engle's ARCH LM test validates the use of ARCH type models for modelling the variance process of returns.

16.2.2 Generalised ARCH (GARCH) model

This model generalises the ARCH(q) specification introduced in Section 16.2.1. As we increase the lags in an ARCH(q) model for capturing the higher-order ARCH effects present in the data, we lose parsimony. This is because we have a lot of parameters to estimate and we lose degrees of freedom. Bollerslev (1986) and Taylor (1986) independently proposed a generalised ARCH (GARCH) model that would include the p lagged conditional variance terms in the variance equation.

More specifically, the GARCH(p, q) specification is given by:

$$\sigma_t^2 = \alpha_0 + \sum_{i=1}^{q} \alpha_i \varepsilon_{t-i}^2 + \sum_{j=1}^{p} \beta_j \sigma_{t-j}^2 \tag{16.10}$$

where the current period volatility is explained by the long-run average variance, the past values of the shocks, and the past history of volatility. A simple case of this model is the GARCH (1,1) specification:

$$\sigma_t^2 = \alpha_0 + \alpha_1 \varepsilon_{t-1}^2 + \beta_1 \sigma_{t-1}^2 \tag{16.11}$$

which has been widely implemented in practice. In this model, the volatility is influenced by the last period estimate of volatility and shocks observed in the last period. The GARCH process assigns geometrically decaying weights to past shocks. In order to illustrate this, consider a GARCH (1,1) process in Equation 11.

If we substitute for the conditional variance equation at $t-1$ (σ_{t-1}^2) in Equation 16.11:

$$\sigma_t^2 = \alpha_0 + \alpha_1 \varepsilon_{t-1}^2 + \beta_1 \left[\alpha_0 + \alpha_1 \varepsilon_{t-2}^2 + \beta_1 \sigma_{t-2}^2 \right]$$
$$= \alpha_0 + \alpha_0 \beta_1 + \alpha_1 \varepsilon_{t-1}^2 + \alpha_1 \beta_1 \varepsilon_{t-2}^2 + \beta_1^2 \sigma_{t-2}^2 \tag{16.12}$$

Now substituting for the conditional variance equation at $t-2$ (σ_{t-2}^2), we get:

$$\sigma_t^2 = \alpha_0 + \alpha_0 \beta_1 + \alpha_1 \varepsilon_{t-1}^2 + \alpha_1 \beta_1 \varepsilon_{t-2}^2 + \beta_1^2 \left[\alpha_0 + \alpha_1 \varepsilon_{t-3}^2 + \beta_1 \sigma_{t-3}^2 \right]$$
$$= \alpha_0 + \alpha_0 \beta_1 + \alpha_0 \beta_1^2 + \alpha_1 \varepsilon_{t-1}^2 + \alpha_1 \beta_1 \varepsilon_{t-2}^2 + \alpha_1 \beta_1^2 \varepsilon_{t-3}^2 + \beta_1^3 \sigma_{t-3}^2 \tag{16.13}$$

From the above we can see that the weight applied to ε_{t-i}^2 is $\alpha_1 \beta_1^{i-1}$ and the weights decline at rate β. If we further consider an infinite number of successive substitutions for the conditional variance equations (as above), we can see that a GARCH (1,1) specification encapsulates an infinite-order ARCH specification with coefficient weights declining geometrically.

16.2.3 Exponentially weighted moving average (EWMA) model

The exponentially weighted moving average (EWMA) model is the same as the ARCH models, but the weights decrease exponentially as you move back through time. The model can be written as:

$$\sigma_t^2 = \lambda \sigma_{t-1}^2 + (1-\lambda)\varepsilon_{t-1}^2 \tag{16.14}$$

where λ is the constant decay rate, say 0.94.

To see that the weights cause an exponential decay, we substitute for σ_{t-1}^2 in equation 16.14:

$$\begin{aligned} \sigma_t^2 &= \lambda\left[\lambda\sigma_{t-2}^2 + (1-\lambda)\varepsilon_{t-2}^2\right] + (1-\lambda)\varepsilon_{t-1}^2 \\ &= (1-\lambda)\varepsilon_{t-1}^2 + \lambda(1-\lambda)\varepsilon_{t-2}^2 + \lambda^2\sigma_{t-2}^2 \end{aligned} \tag{16.15}$$

Further, substituting for σ_{t-2}^2 in Equation 16.15, we get:

$$\begin{aligned} \sigma_t^2 &= (1-\lambda)\varepsilon_{t-1}^2 + \lambda(1-\lambda)\varepsilon_{t-2}^2 + \lambda^2\left[\lambda\sigma_{t-3}^2 + (1-\lambda)\varepsilon_{t-3}^2\right] \\ &= (1-\lambda)\varepsilon_{t-1}^2 + \lambda(1-\lambda)\varepsilon_{t-2}^2 + \lambda^2(1-\lambda)\varepsilon_{t-3}^2 + \lambda^3\sigma_{t-3}^2 \end{aligned} \tag{16.16}$$

Risk metrics uses EWMA model estimates for volatility with $\lambda = 0.94$. For $\lambda = 0.94$, we see:

$$\sigma_t^2 = (0.06)\,u_{t-1}^2 + (0.056)\,u_{t-2}^2 + (0.053)\,u_{t-3}^2 + (0.83)\,\sigma_{t-3}^2 \tag{16.17}$$

To generalise, if we continue substitution, we can write Equation 16.14 as:

$$\sigma_t^2 = (1-\lambda)\sum_{i=1}^{T}\lambda^{i-1}\varepsilon_{t-i}^2 + \lambda^T\sigma_{t-T}^2 \tag{16.18}$$

where for a large T, the second term $\lambda^T\sigma_{t-T}^2 \to 0$ and we can see that the weight for $\{\varepsilon_{t-i}^2\}_{i=1}^{T}$ declines at rate λ.

GARCH models are the same as the EWMA model in assigning exponentially declining weights to past observations. However, unlike EWMA, GARCH models also assign some weight to the long-run average variance rate. In Equation 16.11, when the intercept parameter $\alpha_0 = 0$ and $\alpha_1 + \beta_1 = 1$, then the GARCH (1,1) model reduces to an EWMA model.

16.2.4 Asymmetric volatility models

Volatility in financial time series show 'leverage effects'; that is to say, there is an asymmetric relationship between news and volatility. This was first documented by Black (1976). Empirically, we observe that positive news and negative news impact subsequent periods' volatility in varying degrees. An unexpected negative shock in the market is observed to cause a higher degree of volatility in prices than an unexpected positive shock of the same magnitude. This asymmetric feature in volatility is not captured by (G)ARCH models, which assume identical effects of positive and negative news. By modelling conditional volatility as a function of squared previous shocks, (G)ARCH models only account for the magnitude of the shocks and not their signs (positive or negative shocks). Therefore, asymmetric volatility models have been introduced in the literature. Below we review two such models: GJR and EGARCH.

Glosten, Jagannathan and Runkle (GJR) model

This asymmetric volatility model was introduced by Glosten, Jagannathan and Runkle (1993) (hence known as the GJR model). In this model, we capture the asymmetries in conditional variances by distinguishing the sign of the shock. We separate the positive and negative shocks in the data and allow for different coefficients in a GARCH framework. A GJR(p,q) model is given by:

$$\sigma_t^2 = \alpha_0 + \sum_{j=1}^{q} \alpha_j^+ \varepsilon_{t-j}^2 + \sum_{j=1}^{q} \delta_j \varepsilon_{t-j}^2 D_{t-j} + \sum_{j=1}^{p} \beta_j \sigma_{t-j}^2 \tag{16.19}$$

where

$$D_{t-j} = \begin{cases} 1 \text{ for } \varepsilon_{t-j} < 0 \\ 0 \text{ for } \varepsilon_{t-j} \geq 0 \end{cases} \tag{16.20}$$

The coefficients $\{\delta_j\}_{j=1}^{q}$ capture the additional volatility components of negative shocks. If $\{\delta_j = 0\}_{j=1}^{q}$ then this reduces to a GARCH(p,q) model.

Consider the simplest case of a GJR(1,1) model:

$$\sigma_t^2 = \alpha_0 + \alpha_1^+ \varepsilon_{t-1}^2 + \delta_T \varepsilon_{t-1}^2 D_{t-1} + \beta_1 \sigma_{t-1}^2 \tag{16.21}$$

where α_1^+ measures the impact of positive shocks and $\alpha_1^+ + \delta_T (= \alpha_1^-)$ measures the impact of negative shocks. For testing symmetry, we consider testing $H_0: \delta_T = 0$. Significant leverage effects can be observed when $\delta_T > 0$. For positivity of the conditional variances, we require $\alpha_0 > 0$, $\alpha_1^+ \geq 0$, and $\alpha_1^+ + \delta_T \geq 0$. Hence, δ_T is allowed to be negative, provided $\alpha_1^+ > |\delta_T|$.

Exponential GARCH (EGARCH) model

Nelson (1991) proposed the popular exponential GARCH (EGARCH) framework that modelled the asymmetries in volatility as well as guaranteeing positivity for the conditional variance. An EGARCH(p,q) model specification is given by:

$$\ln\left(\sigma_t^2\right) = \alpha_0 + \sum_{j=1}^{q} \alpha_j \left[\frac{\varepsilon_{t-j}}{\sigma_{t-j}}\right] + \sum_{j=1}^{q} \alpha_j^* \left[\left|\frac{\varepsilon_{t-j}}{\sigma_{t-j}}\right| - \mu\right] + \sum_{j=1}^{p} \beta_j \ln\left(\sigma_{t-j}^2\right) \tag{16.22}$$

where, if the error terms $\varepsilon_t/\sigma_t \sim N(0,1)$ then $\mu = E\left[\left|\frac{\varepsilon_t}{\sigma_t}\right|\right] = \sqrt{\frac{2}{\pi}}$. In the case of non-normal errors, we can allow for other fat-tailed distributions, such as student t, or GED. In such cases, μ will take other forms. The variable $\left(\dfrac{\varepsilon_{t-j}}{\sigma_{t-j}}\right)$ captures the relative size of the shocks and $\left(\left|\dfrac{\varepsilon_{t-j}}{\sigma_{t-j}}\right| - \mu\right)$ captures the relative magnitude of the shocks. The coefficients $\left\{\alpha_j\right\}_{j=1}^q$ capture the asymmetric impact of sign of the shocks.

Since we model the log of the conditional variance here, we are not required to impose any positivity constraints during the estimation of the conditional variance. Specifying the model as a logarithm ensures positivity of σ^2_t. Therefore, the leverage effect is exponential rather than quadratic.

Consider the case of EGARCH(0,1) specification:

$$\ln\left(\sigma^2_t\right) = \alpha_0 + \alpha_1 \varepsilon_{t-1} + \alpha_1^* \left[\left|\varepsilon_{t-1}\right| - \mu\right] \tag{16.23}$$

where $\varepsilon_{t-1} = \varepsilon_{t-1}/\sigma_{t-1}$.

Suppose the estimated output of the above model is:

$$\ln\left(\hat{\sigma}^2_t\right) = \hat{\alpha}_0 + \hat{\alpha}_1 \varepsilon_{t-1} + \hat{\alpha}_1^* \left[\left|\varepsilon_{t-1}\right| - \mu\right] \tag{16.24}$$

where $\hat{\alpha}_0 = 0$, $\hat{\alpha}_1 = -0.3$, $\hat{\alpha}_1^* = 0.6$, and $\mu = 0.85$. Let us consider the following cases:
Case 1: impact of a positive scaled shock of $+1.0$ at $t-1$

$$\ln(\hat{\sigma}^2_t) = -0.3(1) + 0.6[|1| - 0.85] = -0.21$$

Hence $\hat{\sigma}^2_t = \exp(-0.21) = 0.81$, which is a 0.19 decrease in volatility at time t.
Case 2: impact of a negative scaled shock of -1.0 at $t-1$

$$\ln(\hat{\sigma}^2_t) = -0.3(-1) + 0.6[|-1| - 0.85] = 0.39$$

Hence $\hat{\sigma}^2_t = \exp(0.39) = 1.48$, which is a 0.48 increase in volatility at time t.

We see that the model allows for positive and negative shocks to have different effects on the conditional variance. For $\hat{\alpha}_1$ negative, we observe that a negative shock has a greater impact than a positive shock. This reflects the 'leverage effects' documented in financial markets. If we have $\hat{\alpha}_1$ positive, say $\hat{\alpha}_1 = +0.3$, then a $+1.0$ shock will have an impact of 0.39 and a -1.0 shock will have an impact of -0.21 to the log of conditional variance. Hence, under this model, the coefficient $\hat{\alpha}_1$ allows for the sign of the shock to have an impact on the conditional volatility over and above the magnitude captured by $\hat{\alpha}_1^*$. When $\hat{\alpha}_1 = 0$, positive and negative shocks have the same impact on conditional volatility.

Testing for asymmetric conditional volatility

Formal tests have been proposed by Engle and Ng (1993) to assess the significant presence of asymmetric effects in conditional volatility. These are the sign bias test, the negative sign bias test, and the positive sign bias test. These tests are usually conducted on the (standardised) residuals from a particular volatility model.

If $\hat{\varepsilon}_t$ is the estimated residuals from a volatility model and $\hat{\sigma}_t$ is the estimated volatility, we define the standardised residuals as $\hat{\varepsilon}_t = \hat{\varepsilon}_t/\hat{\sigma}_t$. Let S_t^- be a dummy variable that equals one for $\hat{\varepsilon}_t < 1$ and zero otherwise. Further, we define $S_t^+ = 1 - S_t^-$, which captured positive standardised shocks at time t.

The three tests are based on the significance of the t-statistics for the coefficients from three simple linear regressions of the squared standardised residuals on S^-_{t-1}, $S^-_{t-1}\hat{\varepsilon}_{t-1}$ and $S^+_{t-1}\hat{\varepsilon}_{t-1}$, respectively. A joint test of no asymmetric effects can also be carried out as $\chi^2(3)$ test calculated as $T \cdot R^2$ from the following regression:

$$\hat{\varepsilon}^2_t = \psi_0 + \psi_1 S^-_{t-1} + \psi_2 \left(S^-_{t-1}\hat{\varepsilon}_{t-1} \right) + \psi_3 \left(S^+_{t-1}\hat{\varepsilon}_{t-1} \right) + v_t \qquad (16.25)$$

The coefficient ψ_1 captures the effect of sign of the shocks. ψ_2 and ψ_3 indicate whether the magnitude of the negative and positive shocks differ, respectively.

16.2.5 GARCH-in-mean (GARCH-M) model

GARCH-in-mean or the GARCH-M model introduces conditional variance into the conditional mean equation in order to model the risk-return relationships fundamental to financial applications. Engle *et al.* (1987), who initially introduced the ARCH-M framework, modelled the time-varying risk premia for investors holding long-term bonds. They consider the model:

$$y_t = \mu_t + \varepsilon_t \qquad (16.26)$$

where $\varepsilon_t \sim N(0,\sigma^2_t)$, y_t is the excess returns on the long-term bond relative to a one-period treasury bill and μ_t is the risk premia attached to holding the long-term bond. The risk premia are modelled as:

$$\mu_t = \beta_0 + \beta_1 \sigma_t \qquad (16.27)$$

where σ^2_t is an ARCH(q) process:

$$\sigma^2_t = \alpha_0 + \sum_{j=1}^{q} \alpha_j \varepsilon^2_{t-j} \qquad (16.28)$$

β_1 captures the compensation (time-varying risk premia) that the investors holding long-term bonds receive for bearing the risk of interest rate changes.

The rationale behind such models is that investors are risk-averse and therefore expect an increased proportion of returns for undertaking an increased proportion of risk from the investment. Therefore, expected returns are a function of risk. In the above model, risk is captured by the conditional standard deviations. Alternatively, other functional forms, such as $ln(\sigma^2_t)$ or σ^2_t, can be used in the specifications of the mean equation. Some empirical studies use lagged conditional volatility variables in order to capture the volatility spillovers and contagion observed between financial markets. The above model can also be extended by incorporating other forms of ARCH processes to produce GARCH-M, EGARCH-M, GJR-M and several other ARCH extensions.

16.2.6 Empirical illustration of estimating (G)ARCH models

In this section we illustrate some of the modelling framework discussed so far by using FTSE 100 daily price observations from Jan 1, 1990 to Dec 31, 2010 (a sample of 5,480 observations). We begin by modelling the FTSE 100 returns using an autoregressive model, and testing for the presence of ARCH effects in residuals. Table 16.1 records the results obtained from fitting an ARMA(1,1) model to the FTSE 100 returns.

Table 16.1 ARMA(1,1) model results for FTSE 100 returns $r_t = \phi_0 + \phi_1 r_{t-1} + \theta_1 \varepsilon_{t-1} + \varepsilon_t$

	Coefficient	*Std. error*	*t-statistic*	*Prob.*
ϕ_0	0.000162	0.00013	1.23805	0.2157
ϕ_1	0.719539	0.10371	6.93792	0.0000
θ_1	−0.75908	0.09718	−7.81141	0.0000
Information criteria				
Akaike	−6.13048			
Schwarz	−6.12686			
Hannan-Quinn	−6.12922			
ARCH LM Test				
ARCH(1) test:	F-statistic(1,5475) = 312.5229 [0.0000]			
ARCH(5) test:	F-statistic(5,5467) = 294.0781 [0.0000]			

Table 16.2 ARMA(1,1)-GARCH(1,1) model results for FTSE 100 returns $r_t = \phi_0 + \phi_1 r_{t-1} + \theta_1 \varepsilon_{t-1} + \varepsilon_t$
$\varepsilon_t \sim iidN(0,\sigma_t^2)$ $\sigma_t^2 = \alpha_0 + \alpha_1 \varepsilon_{t-1}^2 + \beta_1 \sigma_{t-1}^2$

	Coefficient	*Std. error*	*t-statistic*	*Prob.*
Mean equation:				
ϕ_0	0.000376	6.86E-05	5.4763	0.0000
ϕ_1	0.961621	0.00324	297.061	0.0000
θ_1	−0.97657	6.34E-05	−15393.3	0.0000
Variance equation:				
α_0	1.21E-06	1.98E-07	6.0899	0.0000
α_1	0.08543	0.00571	14.9719	0.0000
β_1	0.905286	0.0062	146.075	0.0000
Information criteria				
Akaike	−6.4997			
Schwarz	−6.49246			
Hannan-Quinn	−6.49717			
ARCH LM Test				
ARCH(1) test:	F-statistic(1,5475) = 1.487840 [0.2226]			
ARCH(5) test:	F-statistic(5,5467) = 1.035302 [0.3948]			

The AR and MA parameters in the mean equation show strong significance at a 1% level. While testing for the presence of ARCH effects in residuals, we find that the residuals are not homoscedastic and indeed show ARCH effects. Hence, we model the variances of the residuals using (G)ARCH models. We consider estimating the conditional variance using the popular GARCH(1,1) model. Table 16.2 records the results from an ARMA(1,1)-GARCH(1,1) model for the FTSE 100 returns.

The results show that the ARMA(1,1)-GARCH(1,1) model fits the data well and the estimated parameters are all significant. The ARCH LM test indicates no ARCH effects in the residuals. This means that the GARCH(1,1) model has explained all the ARCH effects that were present in the data. The information criteria suggest that the heteroscedastic ARMA(1,1)-GARCH(1,1) model is much preferred over the homoscedastic ARMA(1,1) model.

In order to test for any neglected asymmetries in the volatility model, we conduct the three sign bias tests proposed by Engle and Ng (1993). These tests investigate possible misspecifications of the conditional variance equation. The volatility model under the null hypothesis is the GARCH(1,1) specification. Table 16.3 records the asymmetric test results.

Table 16.3 Engle and Ng (1993) asymmetric test results for FTSE 100 returns

	t-test	Prob.
Sign bias test	0.64143	0.52124
Negative sign bias test	1.15311	0.24887
Positive size bias test	3.22226	0.00127
Joint test	16.33731	0.00097

The results show insignificant coefficient from the sign bias t-test. This means that the positive and negative shocks (in terms of sign) have a similar impact on the next period volatility and that there is no 'sign bias' in the above GARCH(1,1) specification. To test whether the magnitude (or size) of negative and positive shocks impact volatility differently, we conduct the negative sign bias test and the positive sign bias test, respectively. We find that the coefficient associated to the magnitude of last-period negative shocks is insignificant. This means that there is no neglected 'size bias' associated with the negative shocks. However, in the case of positive shocks, we see a significant asymmetric effect uncaptured by the GARCH(1,1) specification. When testing for the overall asymmetric effect, using the joint test for the three effects, we find that the underlying conditional volatility process is asymmetric. Hence, we model the conditional volatility using a GJR(1,1) model. Table 16.4 records the results from the ARMA(1,1)-GJR(1,1) model for the FTSE 100 returns. We also conduct the asymmetric sign bias tests on the residuals from this model and find that the model has captured all the asymmetries in the data.

Table 16.4 ARMA(1,1)-GJR(1,1) model results for FTSE 100 returns $r_t = \phi_0 + \phi_1 r_{t-1} + \theta_1 \varepsilon_{t-1} + \varepsilon_t$

$$\varepsilon_t \sim iidN(0,\sigma_t^2) \quad \sigma_t^2 = \alpha_0 + \alpha^+_1 \varepsilon_{t-1}^2 + \delta_T \varepsilon_{t-1}^2 D_{t-1} + \beta_1 \sigma_{t-1}^2 D_{t-1} = \begin{cases} 1 \text{ for } \varepsilon_{t-1} < 0 \\ 0 \text{ for } \varepsilon_{t-1} \geq 0 \end{cases}$$

	Coefficient	Std. error	t-statistic	Prob.
Mean equation:				
ϕ_0	0.000196	1.12E-04	1.754	0.0794
ϕ_1	0.686473	0.13876	4.947	0.0000
θ_1	−0.698797	0.14743	−4.74	0.0000
Variance equation:				
α_0	1.27E-06	2.75E-07	4.64	0.0000
α_1	0.017011	0.006591	2.581	0.0099
β_1	0.922546	0.009416	97.98	0.0000
δ_T	0.095475	0.014165	6.74	0.0000
Information criteria				
Akaike	−6.516966			
Schwarz	−6.508523			
Hannan-Quinn	−6.51402			
ARCH LM Test				
ARCH(1) test:	F-statistic(1,5475) = 2.461762 [0.1167]			
ARCH(5) test:	F-statistic(5,5467) = 1.143841 [0.3347]			
Engle and Ng (1993) tests				
	t-test	Prob.		
Size bias test	0.38617	0.69937		
Negative size bias test	0.21395	0.83059		
Positive size bias test	2.00322	0.04515		
Joint test	4.60971	0.20271		

Table 16.5 ARMA(1,1)-GJR(1,1)-in-mean model results for FTSE 100 returns $r_t = \phi_0 + \phi_1 r_{t-1} + \theta_1 \varepsilon_{t-1}$

$$+ \lambda \sigma_t + \varepsilon_t, \, \varepsilon_t \sim iidN(0,\sigma_t^2) \, \sigma_t^2 = \alpha_0 + \alpha_1^+ \, \varepsilon_{t-1}^2 + \delta_T \varepsilon_{t-1}^2 D_{t-1} + \beta_1 \sigma_{t-1}^2 \quad D_{t-1} = \begin{cases} 1 \text{ for } \varepsilon_{t-1} < 0 \\ 0 \text{ for } \varepsilon_{t-1} \geq 0 \end{cases}$$

	Coefficient	Std. error	t-statistic	Prob.
Mean equation:				
ϕ_0	−0.000024	3.47E-04	−0.06932	0.9447
ϕ_1	0.664809	0.16297	4.079	0.0000
θ_1	−0.675739	0.17315	−3.903	0.0001
λ	0.027782	0.041109	0.6758	0.4992
Variance equation:				
α_0	1.33E-02	3.07E-03	4.349	0.0000
α_1	0.017156	0.006661	2.575	0.0100
β_1	0.921338	0.009836	93.67	0.0000
δ_T	0.095533	0.01416	6.747	0.0000

In terms of the information criteria, we find that the ARMA(1,1)-GJR(1,1) specification is more preferred than the ARMA(1,1)-GARCH(1,1) or the ARMA(1,1) specification.

Further, in order to study the risk-return relationship in finance, where an increase in risk is required to be compensated with an increase in returns, we fit a GARCH-in-mean model to the FTSE 100 returns. The GARCH-in-mean framework allows the conditional variance to explain the conditional mean and, hence, capture any risk premium or compensation associated with holding the FTSE 100 index. More specifically, we include the conditional standard deviation term into the conditional mean equation of FTSE 100 returns and estimate the ARMA(1,1)-GJR(1,1)-in-mean model. The results are provided in Table 16.5.

In Table 16.5 the parameter of interest is λ. We find that the estimated parameter λ is positive but insignificant. Hence, we do not find any significant functional relationship between the asset returns for the FTSE 100 and its risk (or volatility), as captured by the GJR(1,1) model.

16.3 Non-parametric estimators of volatility

In this section we discuss non-parametric estimators of volatility that use intraday price information. Due to the availability of high-frequency data, we are now able to accurately measure volatility by observing the volatility process almost instantaneously. Below, we discuss two popular approaches developed in the literature: realised volatility and range-based volatility estimators.

16.3.1 Realised volatility

The concept of realised volatility was first introduced by Andersen and Bollerslev (1998) and developed in Andersen, Bollerslev, Diebold and Labys (2001) and Andersen, Bollerslev, Diebold and Ebens (2001). Realised volatility estimates can be simply calculated by summing intraday squared returns at short intervals of time. Since realised volatility can be directly estimated from data (unlike treating volatility as latent and estimating it via econometric models), we can treat volatility as observable and study its properties directly. As sampling frequency is increased, it can be shown that realised volatility is consistent and arbitrarily close to the underlying true continuous-time volatility.

To introduce the theoretical justifications in using realised volatility, suppose that the logarithm of asset prices follows a continuous-time martingale process:

$$dp_t = \sigma_t dW_t \tag{16.29}$$

where W_t is a standard Brownian motion and σ_t is the spot volatility. The conditional variance for one-period returns, $r_{t+1} \equiv p_{t+1} - p_t$ is:

$$\int_t^{t+1} \sigma_s^2 ds \tag{16.30}$$

which is called the integrated volatility (or the true volatility) over the period t to $t + 1$. Since we do not observe this integral, we estimate it using the theory of quadratic variation. Let m be the sampling frequency, such that there are m continuously compounded returns in one unit of time (say, one day). The jth return is given by:

$$r_{t+j/m} \equiv p_{t+j/m} - p_{t+(j-1)/m} \tag{16.31}$$

The realised volatility (in one unit of time) can be defined as:

$$RV_{t+1} = \sum_{j=1}^{m} r_{t+j/m}^2 \tag{16.32}$$

Then, from the theory of quadratic variation, if sample returns are uncorrelated, it follows that:

$$p \lim_{m \to \infty} \left(\int^{+1} \sigma_s^2 ds - RV_{t+1} \right) = 0 \tag{16.33}$$

Hence, as we increase the sampling frequency of intraday returns, we find that realised volatility converges to the integrated volatility. However, increasing the sampling frequency induces market microstructure effects, such as nonsynchronous trading, discrete price observations, intraday periodic volatility patterns and bid-ask bounce (see Campbell *et al.* (1997) for more discussion). Therefore, in actual applications, realised volatility is constructed using high-frequency returns measured above a 5 minute interval. Andersen *et al.* (1999) proposed volatility signature plots as simple graphical tools to determine the optimal sampling frequency. In this, we plot the average realised volatility against sampling frequency and pick the highest frequency where average realised volatility appears to stabilise.

Andersen, Bollerslev, Diebold and Labys (2001) and Andersen, Bollerslev, Diebold and Ebens (2001) documented the distributional features of realised volatility. They found that the distributions of the non-normal asset returns scaled by the realised standard deviations are Gaussian. Further, they found that while the unconditional distributions of the variances and covariances for asset returns were leptokurtic and highly skewed to the right, the logarithmic realised standard deviations and correlations all appear approximately Gaussian. They confirm volatility clustering effects in daily returns and find high volatility persistence even in the monthly returns. The logarithm of realised volatility showed long memory properties and appeared fractionally integrated with very slow mean-reversions. Therefore, several dynamic models, such as the autoregressive fractionally integrated moving average (ARFIMA) model and the heterogeneous autoregressive (HAR) model have been effectively applied to model realised volatility (see Giot and Laurent (2004), Koopman *et al.* (2005), Corsi *et al.* (2008), Corsi (2009), among others).

16.3.2 Range-based volatility

In estimating volatility using intraday price variations, an alternative way would be to use the price range information. Suppose log prices of assets follow a zero-drift Brownian motion. A price range can be defined as the difference between the highest and lowest log asset prices over a fixed sampling period.

To fix notation: if C_t is the closing price on date t, O_t is the opening price on date t, H_t the high price on date t, L_t the low price on date t and σ is the volatility to be estimated, we define the following (notation from Yang and Zhang (2000)):

- $o_t = \ln O_t - \ln C_{t-1}$, the normalised opening price
- $c_t = \ln C_t - \ln O_t$, the normalised closing price
- $h_t = \ln H_t - \ln O_t$, the normalised high price
- $l_t = \ln L_t - \ln O_t$, the normalised low price

Various range-based volatility estimators have been proposed in literature. Parkinson (1980) was the first to introduce a range estimator of daily volatility based on the highest and lowest prices on a particular day. He used the range of log prices to define:

$$\hat{\sigma}_t^2 = \frac{1}{4\ln 2}\left(h_t - l_t\right)^2 \tag{16.34}$$

He showed that a range-based estimator can be around 5.2 times more efficient than using daily closing prices. Garman and Klass (1980) extended Parkinson's estimator by incorporating information about closing prices, as below:

$$\hat{\sigma}_t^2 = 0.5\left(h_t - l_t\right)^2 - \left[2\ln 2 - 1\right]c_t^2 \tag{16.35}$$

Garman and Klass's estimator showed an efficiency of around 7.4, in comparison with using the standard close-to-close prices. Parkinson (1980) and Garman and Klass (1980) assume that the log-price follows a Brownian motion with no drift term. This means that the average return is assumed to be equal to zero. Rogers and Satchell (1991) relaxed this assumption and used daily highest, lowest, opening and closing prices in estimating volatility. The Rogers and Satchell (1991) estimator is given by:

$$\hat{\sigma}_t^2 = h_t\left(h_t - c_t\right) + l_t\left(l_t - c_t\right) \tag{16.36}$$

This estimator performs better than the estimators proposed by Parkinson (1980) and Garman and Klass (1980). Yang and Zhang (2000) proposed a refinement to the Rogers and Satchell (1991) estimator for the presence of opening price jumps. Due to overnight volatility, the opening price and the previous day's closing price are mostly not the same. Estimators that do not incorporate opening price jumps underestimate volatility. The Yang and Zhang (2000) estimator is simply the sum of the estimated overnight volatility, the opening market volatility and the Rogers and Satchell (1991) estimator. Other range-based estimators proposed in the literature include those of Beckers (1983), Kunitomo (1992), Alizadeh et al. (2002), Brunetti and Lildolt (2002), among others.

Despite these theoretical advances in range-based volatility estimators, empirical applications of such models have been few. Chou (2005) claims that the poor empirical performance of such models is due to their failure to capture the dynamic evolution of volatilities.

He therefore proposes a conditional autoregressive range (CARR) model for the price range. A CARR(p,q) model for the daily price range R_t is given by:

$$R_t = \lambda_t \varepsilon_t \quad \text{and} \quad \varepsilon_t \, | \, \Omega_{t-1} \sim f(.) \tag{16.37}$$

$$\lambda_t = \alpha_0 + \sum_{i=1}^{q} \alpha_i R_{t-i}^2 + \sum_{j=1}^{p} \beta_j \lambda_{t-j}^2 \tag{16.38}$$

where λ_t is the conditional mean of the range based on all information up to time t. The coefficients ($\alpha_0, \alpha_i, \beta_j$) must all be positive to ensure positivity of λ_t. The dynamic structure for λ_t captures the persistence of the shocks to the price range. The normalised range $\varepsilon_t = R_t/\lambda_t$ is assumed to have a density function f(·) with unit mean. This model belongs to the family of the multiplicative error model of Engle (2002) and a unit mean exponential density function for ε_t can be used to estimate the parameters in the CARR model (see Engle and Russell (1998)).

Chou (2005) showed that the CARR model provides a better in-sample and out-of-sample performance compared with a standard GARCH model. Brandt and Jones (2006) proposed a range-based EGARCH model, which is essentially Nelson's (1991) EGARCH model, but replaces the 'standardised deviation of the absolute return from its expected value' with the 'standardised deviation of the log range from its expected value'. They showed that range-based estimators provide significant forecastability of volatility as far as one year ahead, contradicting return-based volatility predictions that are only possible for short horizons.

16.4 Multivariate volatility and correlation models

Multivariate modelling of volatilities would mean modelling the variances and covariances among the various assets. These cases naturally arise in financial applications, such as asset pricing and portfolio selection, market linkages and integration between markets, hedging and risk management, etc. Modelling the covariances enables us to study the movements across markets and across assets (co-volatilities). Further, the multivariate framework can also be useful for generating forecasts for covariances and correlations, along with the univariate volatility forecasts in one coherent statistical framework. Several multivariate approaches have been proposed in the literature. Some of the excellent survey articles in this area include Bauwens *et al.* (2006), and Silvennoinen and Teräsvirta (2008). In this section we will only discuss some of the key developments in this area.

Consider a general expression for asset returns:

$$y_t = \mu_t + \varepsilon_t \tag{16.39}$$

$$\varepsilon_t = H_t^{1/2} \cdot z_t \text{ where } z_t \sim iidD\left(0, I_N\right) \tag{16.40}$$

where y_t is a n-dimensional vector of asset returns and μ_t is the conditional mean vector. The matrix H_t is the $N \times N$ positive definite conditional variance matrix of y_t. In this section we will consider the important question: how do we parameterise H_t?

16.4.1 Vech model

In modelling the covariance matrix H_t, Bollerslev *et al.* (1988) were the first to propose a natural multivariate extension of the univariate GARCH(p,q) models known as the *vech* model. The *vech(p,q)* model is given by:

$$vech\left(H_t\right) = C + \sum_{i=1}^{q} A_i^* vech\left(\varepsilon_{t-i}\varepsilon'_{t-i}\right) + \sum_{j=1}^{p} B_j^* vech\left(H_{t-j}\right) \tag{16.41}$$

where *vech* is the vector-half operator, which stacks the lower triangular elements of an $N \times N$ matrix into a $[N(N + 1)/2] \times 1$ vector. The vech model is covariance stationary if all the eigenvalues of A^* and B^* are less than one in modulus.

A challenge in this parameterisation is to ensure H_t is a positive definite covariance matrix. Hence, nonlinear inequality restrictions have to be imposed while estimating the parameters. Further, as the number of assets N increase, the number of parameters to be estimated is very large. For example, if we have 3 assets ($N = 3$), the number of parameters to be estimated in a vech (1,1) framework would be 78. Hence, to simplify, Bollerslev *et al.* (1988) proposed a *diagonal vech* representation where A_i^* and B_j^* are diagonal matrices. For example, for the case of two assets ($N = 2$) and a single-period lag model ($p = q = 1$), we have:

$$
\begin{bmatrix} h_{11,t} \\ h_{21,t} \\ h_{22,t} \end{bmatrix} = \begin{bmatrix} c_1 \\ c_2 \\ c_3 \end{bmatrix} + \begin{bmatrix} a_{11}^* & & \\ & a_{22}^* & \\ & & a_{33}^* \end{bmatrix} \begin{bmatrix} \varepsilon_{1,t-1}^2 \\ \varepsilon_{2,t-1}\cdot\varepsilon_{1,t-1} \\ \varepsilon_{2,t-1}^2 \end{bmatrix}
$$
$$
+ \begin{bmatrix} b_{11}^* & & \\ & b_{22}^* & \\ & & b_{33}^* \end{bmatrix} \begin{bmatrix} h_{11,t-1} \\ h_{21,t-1} \\ h_{22,t-1} \end{bmatrix} \tag{16.42}
$$

The diagonal restriction reduces the number of parameters to be estimated to 9 (from 21 in the case of a full vech representation). However, the diagonal vech representation does not capture the interactions in variances among assets (such as copersistence, causality and asymmetries). The diagonal vech model is stationary if *if* $\sum_{i=1}^{q} a_{ii}^* + \sum_{j=1}^{p} b_{jj}^* < 1$.

16.4.2 BEKK model

Engle and Kroner (1995) proposed a *BEKK (p,q)* representation where:

$$H_t = CC' + \sum_{i=1}^{q} A_i\left(\varepsilon_{t-i}\varepsilon'_{t-i}\right)A_i' + \sum_{j=1}^{p} B_j H_{t-j} B_j' \tag{16.43}$$

where C, $A's$ and $B's$ are matrices of $N \times N$ dimension. C is a lower triangular matrix and therefore CC' will be positive definite. Also, by estimating A and B rather than A^* and B^* (as in the case of the vech model) we can easily ensure positive definiteness. For example, in the case of 2 assets ($N = 2$), we have:

$$\begin{bmatrix} h_{11,t} & h_{12,t} \\ h_{21,t} & h_{22,t} \end{bmatrix} = CC' + \begin{bmatrix} a_{11} & a_{12} \\ a_{21} & a_{22} \end{bmatrix}' \begin{bmatrix} \varepsilon_{1,t-1}^2 & \varepsilon_{1,t-1}, \varepsilon_{2,t-1} \\ \varepsilon_{2,t-1}, \varepsilon_{1,t-1} & \varepsilon_{2,t-1}^2 \end{bmatrix}$$

$$\begin{bmatrix} a_{11} & a_{12} \\ a_{21} & a_{22} \end{bmatrix}' + \begin{bmatrix} b_{11} & b_{12} \\ b_{21} & b_{22} \end{bmatrix}'$$

$$\begin{bmatrix} h_{11,t-1} & h_{12,t-1} \\ h_{21,t-1} & h_{22,t-1} \end{bmatrix} \begin{bmatrix} b_{11} & b_{12} \\ b_{21} & b_{22} \end{bmatrix}$$

(16.44)

A BEKK(p,q) model requires estimation of $N(N + 1)/2$ parameters from matrix C and N^2 $(p + q)$ parameters from matrices $A's$ and $B's$. For example, if we have 3 assets ($N = 3$), the number of parameters to be estimated in a BEKK (1,1) framework would be 24. Hence, to reduce the number of parameters to be estimated, we can impose a *Diagonal BEKK* representation where A_i and B_j are diagonal. Alternatively, we can have A_i and B_j as scalar multiplied by a matrix of ones. In this case, we will have a *Scalar BEKK* model. The Diagonal BEKK and Scalar BEKK models are covariance stationary if $\sum_{i=1}^q a_{nn,i}^2 + \sum_{j=1}^p b_{nn,j}^2 < 1$ $\forall n = 1,2,...,N$ and $\sum_{i=1}^q a_i^2 + \sum_{j=1}^p b_j^2 < 1$, respectively.

16.4.3 *Constant conditional correlation (CCC) model*

Bollerslev (1990), assuming conditional correlations constant, proposed that conditional covariances (H_t) can be parameterised as a product of corresponding conditional standard deviations.

$$H_t = D_t R D_t$$

$$\text{where } D_t = \begin{bmatrix} \sqrt{h_{11,t}} & & \\ & \ddots & \\ & & \sqrt{h_{NN,t}} \end{bmatrix}; R = \begin{bmatrix} 1 & \rho_{12} & \cdots & \rho_{1N} \\ \rho_{21} & 1 & & \vdots \\ \vdots & & \ddots & \\ \rho_{N1} & \cdots & & 1 \end{bmatrix}$$

(16.45)

Each conditional standard deviation can in turn be defined as any univariate GARCH model, such as the GARCH(1,1) specification:

$$h_{ii,t} = c_i + \alpha_i \varepsilon_{i,t-1}^2 + \beta_i h_{ii,t-1} \quad i = 1,2,...,N$$

(16.46)

H_t is positive definite if all N conditional covariances are positive and R is positive definite. The number of parameters to be estimated in a CCC-GARCH(1,1) specification is $N(N + 5)/2$. For the case of 3 assets ($N = 3$), the number of parameters to be estimated in a CCC-GARCH(1,1) framework would be 12.

In most empirical applications, the conditional correlations have been found to be far from constant (see Longin and Solnik (1995), Bera and Kim (2002), among others). Formal tests for constant correlations have been proposed in the literature. Tse (2000) proposes testing the null:

$$h_{ijt} = \rho_{ij}\sqrt{h_{iit}h_{jjt}} \tag{16.47}$$

against the alternative:

$$h_{ijt} = \rho_{ijt}\sqrt{h_{iit}h_{jjt}} \tag{16.48}$$

where the conditional variances, h_{iit} and h_{jjt} are GARCH-type models. The test statistic is a Lagrange multiplier test, which is asymptotically $\chi^2(N(N-1)/2)$. Engle and Sheppard (2001) proposed another test for constant correlations with the null hypothesis:

$$H_0 : R_t = \bar{R} \text{ for all } t \tag{16.49}$$

against the alternative $H_1 : vech(R_t) = vech(\bar{R}) + \beta*_1\ vech(R_{t-1}) + \ldots + \beta*_p vech(R_{t-p})$. This test statistic is again chi-squared distributed.

16.4.4 Dynamic conditional correlation (DCC) model

Since, in most applications, we see the hypothesis of constant conditional correlation is rejected, Engle (2002) and Tse and Tsui (2002) proposed a generalisation of the CCC model by allowing for the conditional correlation matrix to be time-varying. This is the dynamic conditional correlation model. Below we discuss the model introduced by Engle (2002). Engle (2002) proposed the DCC framework:

$$H_t = D_t R_t D_t \tag{16.50}$$

where D_t is the diagonal matrix of conditional standard deviations derived from some univariate GARCH model (as defined in the case of CCC) and R_t is the conditional correlation matrix. We then standardise the residuals by its dynamic standard deviations to get standardised residuals. Let:

$$u_t = D_t^{-1}\varepsilon_t \tag{16.51}$$

be the vector of standardised residuals of N GARCH models. These variables now have standard deviations of one. We now model the conditional correlations of residuals (ε_t) by modelling conditional covariances of standardised residuals (u_t). We define R_t as:

$$R_t = diag\left(Q_t\right)^{-1/2} Q_t diag\left(Q_t\right)^{-1/2} \tag{16.52}$$

or

$$R_t = \begin{bmatrix} \sqrt{q_{11}} & & \\ & \ddots & \\ & & \sqrt{q_{NN}} \end{bmatrix}_t^{-1} \cdot Q_t \cdot \begin{bmatrix} \sqrt{q_{11}} & & \\ & \ddots & \\ & & \sqrt{q_{NN}} \end{bmatrix}_t^{-1}$$

where Q_t is an $N \times N$ symmetric positive definite matrix given by:

$$Q_t = \left(1 - \sum_{i=1}^{q} \alpha_i - \sum_{j=1}^{p} \beta_j\right)\bar{Q} + \sum_{i=1}^{q} \alpha_i\left(u_{t-i}u'_{t-i}\right) + \sum_{j=1}^{p} \beta_j Q_{t-j} \tag{16.53}$$

where $\alpha_i \geq 0, \beta_j \geq 0, \sum_{i=1}^{q}\alpha_i + \sum_{j=1}^{p}\beta_j < 1$ and $\bar{Q} = \frac{1}{T}\sum_{t=1}^{T} u_t u'_t$ is the standardised unconditional covariance matrix. For the case of a single-period lag model (with $p = q = 1$), we can write:

$$Q_t = \bar{Q} + \alpha_1\left[\left(u_{t-1}u'_{t-1}\right) - \bar{Q}\right] + \beta_1\left[Q_{t-1} - \bar{Q}\right] \tag{16.54}$$

We can see that Q, at time t, is a function of three components:

1   unconditional covariance matrix $\bar{Q}$ of standardised residuals;
2   additional persistent component from the covariance matrix of lagged standardised residuals u_{t-1};
3   additional persistent component from Q_{t-1}, i.e. past history of itself.

Two-step estimation of DCC models

Under the assumption of normality of innovations, Engle and Sheppard (2001) showed that the DCC can be estimated in two steps. Let $\varepsilon_t \sim N(0, H_t)$ and let θ be vector of unknown parameters in matrix H_t. The log-likelihood function is given by:

$$\begin{aligned}
l(\theta) &= -\frac{1}{2}\sum_{t=1}^{T}\left(N\log(2\pi) + \log|H_t| + \varepsilon'_t H_t^{-1}\varepsilon_t\right) \\
&= -\frac{1}{2}\sum_{t=1}^{T}\left(N\log(2\pi) + \log|D_t R_t D_t| + \varepsilon'_t D_t^{-1} R_t^{-1} D_t^{-1}\varepsilon_t\right) \\
&= -\frac{1}{2}\sum_{t=1}^{T}\left(N\log(2\pi) + 2\log|D_t| + \log|R_t| + u'_t R_t^{-1}u_t\right)
\end{aligned} \tag{16.55}$$

where $u_t = D_t^{-1}\varepsilon_t$ is the standardised residuals. Adding and subtracting $u'_t u_t$ we get:

$$\begin{aligned}
l(\theta) &= -\frac{1}{2}\sum_{t=1}^{T}(N\log(2\pi) + 2\log|D_t| + \varepsilon'_t D_t^{-1} D_t^{-1}\varepsilon_t \\
&\quad -u'_t u_t + \log|R_t| + u'_t R_t^{-1}u_t)
\end{aligned} \tag{16.56}$$

This representation allows us to decompose the log-likelihood $l(\theta)$ as a sum of the volatility part ($l_v(\phi)$) containing the parameters in matrix D and the correlation part ($l_c(\psi)$) containing the parameters in matrix R. That is, we partition the vector of parameters into two subsets: $\theta = \{\phi, \psi\}$. The log-likelihoods can be written as:

$$l(\theta) = l_V(\phi) + l_C(\psi \mid \phi) \tag{16.57}$$

where

$$l_V(\phi) = -\frac{1}{2}\sum_{t=1}^{T}\left(N\log(2\pi) + \log|D_t|^2 + \varepsilon'_t D_t^{-2}\varepsilon_t\right) \tag{16.58}$$

$$l_C\left(\psi \mid \phi\right) = -\frac{1}{2}\sum_{t=1}^{T}\left(\log|R_t| + u_t' R_t^{-1} u_t - u_t' u_t \right) \tag{16.59}$$

The likelihood of the volatility term $l_v(\phi)$ is apparently the sum of the individual GARCH likelihoods, which is jointly maximised by separately maximising each term. This gives us the parameters ϕ. Then the likelihood of the correlation term $l_c(\psi \mid \phi)$ is maximised, conditional on the volatility parameters that were estimated before. In the likelihood function for the correlation term, R_t takes the DCC form $diag(Q_t)^{-1/2} \cdot Q_t \cdot diag(Q_t)^{-1/2}$.

Therefore, a two-step estimation procedure can be employed to estimate the DCC model. First, we estimate the conditional variances (volatility terms ϕ) using MLE. That is, we maximise the likelihood to find $\hat{\phi}$:

$$\hat{\phi} = \text{argmax}\left\{l_V\left(\phi\right)\right\} \tag{16.60}$$

Second, we compute the standardised residuals $u_t = D_t^{-1}\varepsilon_t$ and we estimate the correlations among the several assets. Here we maximise the likelihood function of the correlation term $\hat{\psi}$.

$$\hat{\psi} = \text{argmax}\left\{l_C\left(\hat{\psi} \mid \hat{\phi}\right)\right\} \tag{16.61}$$

The above DCC estimation methodology employs the assumption of normality in conditional returns, which is generally not the case for financial assets. Other alternative fat-tailed distributions, such as Student-t, Laplace or logistic distributions, can be employed in estimating the DCC model. Alternative model specifications have also been suggested in the literature. An excellent review of such generalisations and alternative specifications to modelling correlations is summarised in Engle (2009).

16.5   A summary of key issues

- Volatility in financial time series is not constant, but time-varying. There is high persistence in volatility where the effects of shocks to asset returns extend during several subsequent periods after the shock.
- An autoregressive conditional heteroscedastic (ARCH) type framework allows for the conditional variances to be time-varying and explains the dynamic relationship in volatility.
- EWMA and GARCH specifications model volatility as a dynamic process where volatility today is a function of past estimates of volatility and past shocks. The past shocks are assigned exponentially, declining weights as you move back through time since recent shocks influence volatility more than shocks that have happened further in the past.
- There is an asymmetric relationship between news and volatility, wherein an unexpected negative shock in the market is observed to cause a higher degree of volatility in prices than an unexpected positive shock of the same magnitude. This is called the leverage effect.
- Due to the availability of high-frequency data, realised volatility and range-based estimates provide attractive non-parametric alternatives to modelling volatility.
- Realised volatility, simply calculated by summing intraday squared returns at short intervals of time, has become a popular benchmark for estimating volatility.
- Multivariate modelling of volatilities naturally arises in financial time series where we have more than one asset. BEKK, CCC and DCC are popular methodologies proposed to model conditional volatilities and conditional correlations between assets.

Review questions

1   *'The alphabet soup of volatility models continually amazes. The most influential models were the first: the GARCH model of Bollerslev (1986), and the EGARCH of Nelson (1991). Asymmetric models of Glosten, Jagannathan and Runkle (1993), Rabemananjara and Zakoian (1993), Engle and Ng (1993) and power models such as Higgins and Bera (1992), Engle and Bollerslev (1986), and Ding, Granger and Engle (1993) joined models such as SWARCH, STARCH, QARCH and many more. The linguistic culmination might be that of Figlewski (conference presentation, UCSD, 1995), the YAARCH model, an acronym for yet another ARCH model. Coupled with these models was a sophisticated analysis of the stochastic process of data generated by such models as well as estimators of the unknown parameters.'*

   The above quote is from Engle (2002, pp. 425–426). Why are researchers in financial econometrics interested in developing several conditional models for the second-order moments?

2   Prove that an ∞ – order ARCH process can be approximated by a GARCH(1,1) model.

3   Why has the model-free 'realised volatility' measure become a simple yet efficient way to aggregate risk?

4   Discuss the salient distributional features of realised asset volatility.

5   Outline the dynamic conditional correlation framework used for the modelling of time-varying variances and correlations.

General notes and bibliography: Unit 5

Alizadeh, S., Brandt, M. W. and Diebold, F. X. (2002). 'Range-based estimation of stochastic volatility models', *Journal of Finance*, 57, 1047–1092.

Andersen, T. G. and Bollerslev, T. (1998). 'Answering the skeptics: yes, standard volatility models do provide accurate forecasts', *International Economic Review*, 39, 885–905.

Andersen, T. G., Bollerslev, T., Diebold, F. X. and Ebens, H. (2001). 'The distribution of realized stock return volatility', *Journal of Financial Economics*, 61, 43–76.

Andersen, T., Bollerslev, T., Diebold, F. X. and Labys, P. (1999). '(Understanding, Optimizing, Using and Forecasting) Realized Volatility and Correlation', Manuscript, Northwestern University, Duke University and University of Pennsylvania. Published in revised form as 'Great realizations', *Risk*, March 2000, 105–108.

Andersen, T., Bollerslev, T., Diebold, F. X. and Labys, P. (2001). 'The distribution of realized exchange rate volatility', *Journal of the American Statistical Association*, 96, 42–55.

Bauwens, L., Laurent, S. and Rombouts, J. (2006). 'Multivariate GARCH models: a survey', *Journal of Applied Econometrics*, 21, 79–109.

Beckers, S. (1983). 'Variance of security price returns based on high, low, and closing prices', *Journal of Business*, 56, 97–112.

Bera, A. K. and Kim, S. (2002). 'Testing constancy of correlation and other specifications of the BGARCH model with an application to international equity returns', *Journal of Empirical Finance*, 9, 171–195.

Black, F. (1976). 'Studies of stock market volatility changes', *Proceedings of the American Statistical Association, Business and Economic Statistics Section*, 177–181.

Bollerslev, T. (1986). 'Generalized autoregressive conditional heteroskedasticity', *Journal of Econometrics*, 31, 307–327.

Bollerslev, T. (1990). 'Modelling the coherence in short-run nominal exchange rates: a multivariate generalized ARCH model', *Review of Economics and Statistics*, 72, 498–505.

Bollerslev, T., Engle, R. F. and Wooldridge, J. M. (1988). 'A capital asset pricing model with time varying covariances', *Journal of Political Economy*, 96, 116–131.

Brandt, M. and Jones, C. (2006). 'Volatility forecasting with range-based EGARCH models', *Journal of Business and Economic Statistics*, 24, 470–486.

Brunetti, C. and Lildolt, P. (2002). 'Return-based and range-based (co)variance estimation, with an application to foreign exchange markets', Technical Report 127, Centre for Analytical Finance, University of Aarhus.

Campbell, J. Y., Lo, A. W. and MacKinlay, A.C. (1997). *The Econometrics of Financial Markets*, NJ: Princeton University Press.

Chou, R. Y. (2005). 'Forecasting financial volatilities with extreme values: the conditional autoregressive range (CARR) model', *Journal of Money Credit and Banking*, 37, 561–582.

Corsi, F. (2009). 'A simple approximate long-memory model of realized volatility', *Journal of Financial Econometrics*, 7, 174–196.

Corsi, F., Kretschmer, U., Mittnik, S. and Pigorsch, C. (2008). 'The volatility of realized volatility', *Econometric Reviews*, 27, 46–78.

Engle, R. F. (1982). 'Autoregressive conditional heteroskedasticity with estimates of the variance of UK inflation', *Econometrica*, 50, 987–1008.

Engle, R. F. (2002a). 'New frontiers for Arch models', *Journal of Applied Econometrics*, 17, 425–446.

Engle, R. F. (2002b). 'Dynamic conditional correlation: a simple class of multivariate generalized autoregressive conditional heteroskedasticity models', *Journal of Business and Economic Statistics*, 20, 339–350.

Engle, R. F. (2009). *Anticipating Correlations: A New Paradigm for Risk Management*, Princeton University Press.

Engle, R. F. and Kroner, F. K. (1995). 'Multivariate simultaneous generalized ARCH', *Econometric Theory*, 11, 122–150.

Engle, R. F., Lilien, D. M. and Robins, R. P. (1987). 'Estimating time-varying risk premia in the term structure: the ARCH-M model', *Econometrica*, 55, 391–408.

Engle, R. F. and Ng, V. K. (1993). 'Measuring and testing the impact of news on volatility', *Journal of Finance*, 48, 1749–1778.

Engle, R. F. and Russell, J. R. (1998). 'Autoregressive conditional duration: a new model for irregular spaced transaction data', *Econometrica*, 66, 1127–1162.

Engle, R. F. and Sheppard, K. (2001). 'Theoretical and empirical properties of dynamic conditional correlation multivariate GARCH', NBER Working Paper 8554.

Garman, M. B. and Klass, M. J. (1980). 'On the estimation of price volatility from historical data', *Journal of Business*, 53, 67–78.

Giot, P. and Laurent, S. (2004). 'Modelling daily value-at-risk using realized volatility and ARCH type models', *Journal of Empirical Finance*, 11, 379–398.

Glosten, L. R., Jagannathan, R. and Runkle, D. (1993). 'On the relation between the expected value and the volatility of the nominal excess return on stocks', *Journal of Finance*, 48, 1779–1801.

Koopman, S., Jungbacker, B. and Hol, E. (2005). 'Forecasting daily variability of the S&P 100 stock index using historical, realised and implied volatility measurements', *Journal of Empirical Finance*, 12, 445–475.

Kunitomo, N. (1992). 'Improving the Parkinson method of estimating security price volatilities', *Journal of Business*, 65, 295–302.

Longin, F. and Solnik, B. (1995). 'Is the correlation in international equity returns constant:1960–1990', *Journal of International Money and Finance*, 14, 3–26.

Nelson, D. (1991). 'Conditional heteroskedasticity in asset returns: a new approach', *Econometrica*, 59, 347–370.

Parkinson, M. (1980). 'The extreme value method for estimating the variance of the rate of return', *Journal of Business*, 53, 61–65.

Rogers, L. C. G. and Satchell, S. E. (1991). 'Estimating variance from high, low and closing prices', *Annals of Applied Probability*, 1, 504–512.

Silvennoinen, A. and Teräsvirta, T. (2008). 'Multivariate GARCH models', In T. G. Andersen, R. A. Davis, J. P. Kreiss and T. Mikosch, (eds), *Handbook of Financial Time Series*, New York: Springer.

Taylor, S. (1986). *Modelling Financial Time Series*, Chichester: Wiley.

Tse, Y. K. (2000) 'A test for constant correlations in a multivariate GARCH model', *Journal of Econometrics*, 98, 107–127.

Tse, Y. K. and Tsui, A. K. C. (2002). 'A multivariate GARCH model with time-varying correlations', *Journal of Business and Economic Statistics*, 20, 351–362.

Yang, D. and Zhang, Q. (2000). 'Drift independent volatility estimation based on high, low, open and close prices', *Journal of Business*, 73, 477–491.

Appendix

YEAR	M (constant. price)	GDP (constant. price)	M (current. price)	GDP (current. price)
1980_Q1	24 675	147 204	15 235	55 221
Q2	23 763	144 506	15 044	56 700
Q3	21 754	144 270	13 729	58 625
Q4	21 244	142 601	13 441	60 149
1981_Q1	20 361	141 529	12 955	61 184
Q2	21 486	141 737	14 155	62 240
Q3	23 908	143 556	16 547	63 926
Q4	23 155	143 426	16 586	65 650
1982_Q1	23 026	143 936	16 358	67 266
Q2	24 007	145 579	17 316	68 592
Q3	23 265	145 485	16 917	69 682
Q4	22 988	146 153	17 040	71 550
1983_Q1	24 084	148 313	18 399	73 801
Q2	24 707	149 408	19 183	74 344
Q3	24 861	151 126	19 478	76 310
Q4	25 741	152 881	20 368	78 319
1984_Q1	26 050	154 253	21 028	78 884
Q2	27 202	153 152	22 659	80 675
Q3	27 421	153 814	23 643	81 325
Q4	28 547	155 977	25 247	83 523
1985_Q1	28 620	157 629	26 339	85 315
Q2	27 865	160 132	25 017	88 597
Q3	27 313	160 163	23 614	89 564
Q4	28 171	161 264	23 753	91 476
1986_Q1	28 926	163 574	24 221	92 842
Q2	29 951	165 429	24 730	94 342
Q3	30 178	166 330	25 279	95 791
Q4	30 595	169 121	26 663	98 342
1987_Q1	30 245	170 036	26 368	100 517
Q2	31 756	171 815	27 266	103 051
Q3	33 220	175 606	28 744	107 011
Q4	33 852	177 251	29 071	109 052
1988_Q1	34 306	180 074	29 058	112 351
Q2	35 757	180 922	30 524	114 777
Q3	36 731	183 433	32 128	118 768
Q4	38 825	184 742	32 947	122 490

1989_Q1	39 413	185 229	34 422	124 886
Q2	38 628	186 403	35 299	126 809
Q3	39 535	186 590	36 665	129 878
Q4	38 890	186 793	36 304	132 595
1990_Q1	39 964	188 321	37 988	135 176
Q2	39 835	189 318	38 099	139 353
Q3	39 107	187 058	36 199	141 463
Q4	38 398	185 977	35 971	141 308
1991_Q1	37 242	185 875	34 563	143 842
Q2	37 334	185 253	35 215	145 806
Q3	37 564	184 538	36 136	147 145
Q4	38 115	184 741	36 147	149 356
1992_Q1	38 850	185 208	36 388	151 142
Q2	40 638	184 568	37 751	152 429
Q3	40 251	185 615	37 391	153 165
Q4	40 733	186 469	40 129	154 118
1993_Q1	41 158	187 536	42 122	156 896
Q2	40 776	188 569	41 877	158 689
Q3	41 649	190 394	42 644	162 113
Q4	42 167	192 644	43 482	164 629
1994_Q1	43 203	194 808	44 638	166 888
Q2	43 581	197 533	45 591	169 183
Q3	43 352	199 449	46 483	170 877
Q4	45 151	200 927	48 543	174 379
1995_Q1	44 411	201 652	48 733	176 144
Q2	46 038	203 350	51 281	178 620
Q3	47 082	204 282	53 290	180 733
Q4	47 507	205 950	53 747	183 679
1996_Q1	49 523	207 343	56 314	186 655
Q2	50 191	207 914	56 974	189 948
Q3	51 119	209 761	56 775	192 475
Q4	52 149	212 140	57 356	194 212

A data set for the model of UK competitive imports- the data are generated from The Economic Trends Annual Supplement 2004, UK. Note that the reference year for this data set is year 2001.

Probabilities (areas) under the standardised normal distribution:

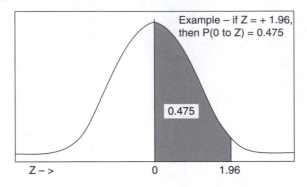

Z	0	0.01	0.02	0.03	0.04	0.05	0.06	0.07	0.08	0.09
0.0	0	0.004	0.008	0.012	0.016	0.0199	0.0239	0.0279	0.0319	0.0359
0.1	0.0398	0.0438	0.0478	0.0517	0.0557	0.0596	0.0636	0.0675	0.0714	0.0753
0.2	0.0793	0.0832	0.0871	0.091	0.0948	0.0987	0.1026	0.1064	0.1103	0.1141
0.3	0.1179	0.1217	0.1255	0.1293	0.1331	0.1368	0.1406	0.1443	0.148	0.1517
0.4	0.1554	0.1591	0.1628	0.1664	0.17	0.1736	0.1772	0.1808	0.1844	0.1879
0.5	0.1915	0.195	0.1985	0.2019	0.2054	0.2088	0.2123	0.2157	0.219	0.2224
0.6	0.2257	0.2291	0.2324	0.2357	0.2389	0.2422	0.2454	0.2486	0.2517	0.2549
0.7	0.258	0.2611	0.2642	0.2673	0.2704	0.2734	0.2764	0.2794	0.2823	0.2852
0.8	0.2881	0.291	0.2939	0.2967	0.2995	0.3023	0.3051	0.3078	0.3106	0.3133
0.9	0.3159	0.3186	0.3212	0.3238	0.3264	0.3289	0.3315	0.334	0.3365	0.3389
1.0	0.3413	0.3438	0.3461	0.3485	0.3508	0.3531	0.3554	0.3577	0.3599	0.3621
1.1	0.3643	0.3665	0.3686	0.3708	0.3729	0.3749	0.377	0.379	0.381	0.383
1.2	0.3849	0.3869	0.3888	0.3907	0.3925	0.3944	0.3962	0.398	0.3997	0.4015
1.3	0.4032	0.4049	0.4066	0.4082	0.4099	0.4115	0.4131	0.4147	0.4162	0.4177
1.4	0.4192	0.4207	0.4222	0.4236	0.4251	0.4265	0.4279	0.4292	0.4306	0.4319
1.5	0.4332	0.4345	0.4357	0.437	0.4382	0.4394	0.4406	0.4418	0.4429	0.4441
1.6	0.4452	0.4463	0.4474	0.4484	0.4495	0.4505	0.4515	0.4525	0.4535	0.4545
1.7	0.4554	0.4564	0.4573	0.4582	0.4591	0.4599	0.4608	0.4616	0.4625	0.4633
1.8	0.4641	0.4649	0.4656	0.4664	0.4671	0.4678	0.4686	0.4693	0.4699	0.4706
1.9	0.4713	0.4719	0.4726	0.4732	0.4738	0.4744	0.475	0.4756	0.4761	0.4767
2.0	0.4772	0.4778	0.4783	0.4788	0.4793	0.4798	0.4803	0.4808	0.4812	0.4817
2.1	0.4821	0.4826	0.483	0.4834	0.4838	0.4842	0.4846	0.485	0.4854	0.4857
2.2	0.4861	0.4864	0.4868	0.4871	0.4875	0.4878	0.4881	0.4884	0.4887	0.489
2.3	0.4893	0.4896	0.4898	0.4901	0.4904	0.4906	0.4909	0.4911	0.4913	0.4916
2.4	0.4918	0.492	0.4922	0.4925	0.4927	0.4929	0.4931	0.4932	0.4934	0.4936
2.5	0.4938	0.494	0.4941	0.4943	0.4945	0.4946	0.4948	0.4949	0.4951	0.4952
2.6	0.4953	0.4955	0.4956	0.4957	0.4959	0.496	0.4961	0.4962	0.4963	0.4964
2.7	0.4965	0.4966	0.4967	0.4968	0.4969	0.497	0.4971	0.4972	0.4973	0.4974
2.8	0.4974	0.4975	0.4976	0.4977	0.4977	0.4978	0.4979	0.4979	0.498	0.4981
2.9	0.4981	0.4982	0.4982	0.4983	0.4984	0.4984	0.4985	0.4985	0.4986	0.4986
3.0	0.4987	0.4987	0.4987	0.4988	0.4988	0.4989	0.4989	0.4989	0.499	0.499

The above (standardised) normal distribution values were generated with MS Excel.

Probabilities (areas) under the 'students' 't' distribution:

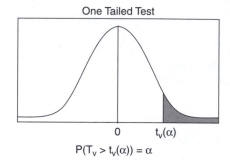

One Tailed Test

$P(T_v > t_v(\alpha)) = \alpha$

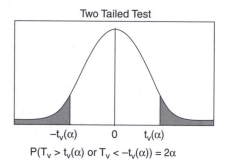

Two Tailed Test

$P(T_v > t_v(\alpha) \text{ or } T_v < -t_v(\alpha)) = 2\alpha$

(for v degrees of freedom (dof))

alpha	0.4	0.25	0.1	0.05	0.025	0.01	0.005	0.0025	0.001	0.0005
2 alpha	0.8	0.5	0.2	0.1	0.05	0.02	0.01	0.005	0.002	0.001
V dof										
1	0.325	1	3.078	6.314	12.706	31.821	63.656	127.321	318.289	636.578
2	0.289	0.816	1.886	2.92	4.303	6.965	9.925	14.089	22.328	31.6
3	0.277	0.765	1.638	2.353	3.182	4.541	5.841	7.453	10.214	12.924
4	0.271	0.741	1.533	2.132	2.776	3.747	4.604	5.598	7.173	8.61
5	0.267	0.727	1.476	2.015	2.571	3.365	4.032	4.773	5.894	6.869
6	0.265	0.718	1.44	1.943	2.447	3.143	3.707	4.317	5.208	5.959
7	0.263	0.711	1.415	1.895	2.365	2.998	3.499	4.029	4.785	5.408
8	0.262	0.706	1.397	1.86	2.306	2.896	3.355	3.833	4.501	5.041
9	0.261	0.703	1.383	1.833	2.262	2.821	3.25	3.69	4.297	4.781
10	0.26	0.7	1.372	1.812	2.228	2.764	3.169	3.581	4.144	4.587
11	0.26	0.697	1.363	1.796	2.201	2.718	3.106	3.497	4.025	4.437
12	0.259	0.695	1.356	1.782	2.179	2.681	3.055	3.428	3.93	4.318
13	0.259	0.694	1.35	1.771	2.16	2.65	3.012	3.372	3.852	4.221
14	0.258	0.692	1.345	1.761	2.145	2.624	2.977	3.326	3.787	4.14
15	0.258	0.691	1.341	1.753	2.131	2.602	2.947	3.286	3.733	4.073
16	0.258	0.69	1.337	1.746	2.12	2.583	2.921	3.252	3.686	4.015
17	0.257	0.689	1.333	1.74	2.11	2.567	2.898	3.222	3.646	3.965
18	0.257	0.688	1.33	1.734	2.101	2.552	2.878	3.197	3.61	3.922
19	0.257	0.688	1.328	1.729	2.093	2.539	2.861	3.174	3.579	3.883
20	0.257	0.687	1.325	1.725	2.086	2.528	2.845	3.153	3.552	3.85
21	0.257	0.686	1.323	1.721	2.08	2.518	2.831	3.135	3.527	3.819
22	0.256	0.686	1.321	1.717	2.074	2.508	2.819	3.119	3.505	3.792
23	0.256	0.685	1.319	1.714	2.069	2.5	2.807	3.104	3.485	3.768
24	0.256	0.685	1.318	1.711	2.064	2.492	2.797	3.091	3.467	3.745
25	0.256	0.684	1.316	1.708	2.06	2.485	2.787	3.078	3.45	3.725
26	0.256	0.684	1.315	1.706	2.056	2.479	2.779	3.067	3.435	3.707
27	0.256	0.684	1.314	1.703	2.052	2.473	2.771	3.057	3.421	3.689
28	0.256	0.683	1.313	1.701	2.048	2.467	2.763	3.047	3.408	3.674
29	0.256	0.683	1.311	1.699	2.045	2.462	2.756	3.038	3.396	3.66
30	0.256	0.683	1.31	1.697	2.042	2.457	2.75	3.03	3.385	3.646
40	0.255	0.681	1.303	1.684	2.021	2.423	2.704	2.971	3.307	3.551
60	0.254	0.679	1.296	1.671	2	2.39	2.66	2.915	3.232	3.46
120	0.254	0.677	1.289	1.658	1.98	2.358	2.617	2.86	3.16	3.373
INF	0.253	0.674	1.282	1.645	1.96	2.326	2.576	2.807	3.09	3.291

The above 'students' 't' distribution values were generated with MS Excel.

Probabilities (areas) under the 'F' distribution values (at α = 0.01) (i.e. the upper 1% points):

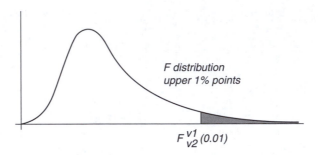

v1	1	2	3	4	5	6	7	8	9	10	15	20	40	60	120	∞
v2																
1	4052	4999	5404	5624	5764	5859	5928	5981	6022	6056	6157	6209	6286	6313	6340	6366
2	98.5	99	99.16	99.25	99.3	99.33	99.36	99.38	99.39	99.4	99.43	99.45	99.48	99.48	99.49	99.5
3	34.12	30.8	29.46	28.71	28.24	27.91	27.67	27.49	27.34	27.23	26.87	26.69	26.41	26.32	26.22	26.13
4	21.2	18	16.69	15.98	15.52	15.21	14.98	14.8	14.66	14.55	14.2	14.02	13.75	13.65	13.56	13.46
5	16.26	13.3	12.06	11.39	10.97	10.67	10.46	10.29	10.16	10.05	9.72	9.55	9.29	9.2	9.11	9.02
6	13.75	10.9	9.78	9.15	8.75	8.47	8.26	8.1	7.98	7.87	7.56	7.4	7.14	7.06	6.97	6.88
7	12.25	9.55	8.45	7.85	7.46	7.19	6.99	6.84	6.72	6.62	6.31	6.16	5.91	5.82	5.74	5.65
8	11.26	8.65	7.59	7.01	6.63	6.37	6.18	6.03	5.91	5.81	5.52	5.36	5.12	5.03	4.95	4.86
9	10.56	8.02	6.99	6.42	6.06	5.8	5.61	5.47	5.35	5.26	4.96	4.81	4.57	4.48	4.4	4.31
10	10.04	7.56	6.55	5.99	5.64	5.39	5.2	5.06	4.94	4.85	4.56	4.41	4.17	4.08	4	3.91
11	9.65	7.21	6.22	5.67	5.32	5.07	4.89	4.74	4.63	4.54	4.25	4.1	3.86	3.78	3.69	3.6
12	9.33	6.93	5.95	5.41	5.06	4.82	4.64	4.5	4.39	4.3	4.01	3.86	3.62	3.54	3.45	3.36
13	9.07	6.7	5.74	5.21	4.86	4.62	4.44	4.3	4.19	4.1	3.82	3.66	3.43	3.34	3.25	3.17
14	8.86	6.51	5.56	5.04	4.69	4.46	4.28	4.14	4.03	3.94	3.66	3.51	3.27	3.18	3.09	3
15	8.68	6.36	5.42	4.89	4.56	4.32	4.14	4	3.89	3.8	3.52	3.37	3.13	3.05	2.96	2.87
16	8.53	6.23	5.29	4.77	4.44	4.2	4.03	3.89	3.78	3.69	3.41	3.26	3.02	2.93	2.84	2.75
17	8.4	6.11	5.19	4.67	4.34	4.1	3.93	3.79	3.68	3.59	3.31	3.16	2.92	2.83	2.75	2.65
18	8.29	6.01	5.09	4.58	4.25	4.01	3.84	3.71	3.6	3.51	3.23	3.08	2.84	2.75	2.66	2.57
19	8.18	5.93	5.01	4.5	4.17	3.94	3.77	3.63	3.52	3.43	3.15	3	2.76	2.67	2.58	2.49
20	8.1	5.85	4.94	4.43	4.1	3.87	3.7	3.56	3.46	3.37	3.09	2.94	2.69	2.61	2.52	2.42
21	8.02	5.78	4.87	4.37	4.04	3.81	3.64	3.51	3.4	3.31	3.03	2.88	2.64	2.55	2.46	2.36
22	7.95	5.72	4.82	4.31	3.99	3.76	3.59	3.45	3.35	3.26	2.98	2.83	2.58	2.5	2.4	2.31
23	7.88	5.66	4.76	4.26	3.94	3.71	3.54	3.41	3.3	3.21	2.93	2.78	2.54	2.45	2.35	2.26
24	7.82	5.61	4.72	4.22	3.9	3.67	3.5	3.36	3.26	3.17	2.89	2.74	2.49	2.4	2.31	2.21
25	7.77	5.57	4.68	4.18	3.85	3.63	3.46	3.32	3.22	3.13	2.85	2.7	2.45	2.36	2.27	2.17
26	7.72	5.53	4.64	4.14	3.82	3.59	3.42	3.29	3.18	3.09	2.81	2.66	2.42	2.33	2.23	2.13
27	7.68	5.49	4.6	4.11	3.78	3.56	3.39	3.26	3.15	3.06	2.78	2.63	2.38	2.29	2.2	2.1
28	7.64	5.45	4.57	4.07	3.75	3.53	3.36	3.23	3.12	3.03	2.75	2.6	2.35	2.26	2.17	2.06
29	7.6	5.42	4.54	4.04	3.73	3.5	3.33	3.2	3.09	3	2.73	2.57	2.33	2.23	2.14	2.03
30	7.56	5.39	4.51	4.02	3.7	3.47	3.3	3.17	3.07	2.98	2.7	2.55	2.3	2.21	2.11	2.01
40	7.31	5.18	4.31	3.83	3.51	3.29	3.12	2.99	2.89	2.8	2.52	2.37	2.11	2.02	1.92	1.8
60	7.08	4.98	4.13	3.65	3.34	3.12	2.95	2.82	2.72	2.63	2.35	2.2	1.94	1.84	1.73	1.6
120	6.85	4.79	3.95	3.48	3.17	2.96	2.79	2.66	2.56	2.47	2.19	2.03	1.76	1.66	1.53	1.38
∞	6.63	4.61	3.78	3.32	3.02	2.8	2.64	2.51	2.41	2.32	2.04	1.88	1.59	1.47	1.32	1

The above 'F' distribution values (at α = 0.01) were generated with MS Excel.

Probabilities (areas) under the 'F' distribution values (at α = 0.05) (i.e. the upper 5% points):

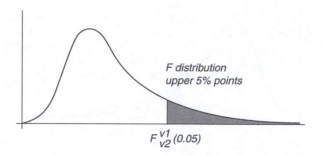

$F^{v1}_{v2}(0.05)$

v1 / v2	1	2	3	4	5	6	7	8	9	10	15	20	40	60	120	∞
1	161.5	200	215.7	224.6	230.2	234	236.8	238.9	240.5	241.9	246	248	251.1	252.2	253.3	254.3
2	18.51	19	19.16	19.25	19.3	19.33	19.35	19.37	19.38	19.4	19.43	19.45	19.47	19.48	19.49	19.5
3	10.13	9.55	9.28	9.12	9.01	8.94	8.89	8.85	8.81	8.79	8.7	8.66	8.59	8.57	8.55	8.53
4	7.71	6.94	6.59	6.39	6.26	6.16	6.09	6.04	6	5.96	5.86	5.8	5.72	5.69	5.66	5.63
5	6.61	5.79	5.41	5.19	5.05	4.95	4.88	4.82	4.77	4.74	4.62	4.56	4.46	4.43	4.4	4.37
6	5.99	5.14	4.76	4.53	4.39	4.28	4.21	4.15	4.1	4.06	3.94	3.87	3.77	3.74	3.7	3.67
7	5.59	4.74	4.35	4.12	3.97	3.87	3.79	3.73	3.68	3.64	3.51	3.44	3.34	3.3	3.27	3.23
8	5.32	4.46	4.07	3.84	3.69	3.58	3.5	3.44	3.39	3.35	3.22	3.15	3.04	3.01	2.97	2.93
9	5.12	4.26	3.86	3.63	3.48	3.37	3.29	3.23	3.18	3.14	3.01	2.94	2.83	2.79	2.75	2.71
10	4.96	4.1	3.71	3.48	3.33	3.22	3.14	3.07	3.02	2.98	2.85	2.77	2.66	2.62	2.58	2.54
11	4.84	3.98	3.59	3.36	3.2	3.09	3.01	2.95	2.9	2.85	2.72	2.65	2.53	2.49	2.45	2.4
12	4.75	3.89	3.49	3.26	3.11	3	2.91	2.85	2.8	2.75	2.62	2.54	2.43	2.38	2.34	2.3
13	4.67	3.81	3.41	3.18	3.03	2.92	2.83	2.77	2.71	2.67	2.53	2.46	2.34	2.3	2.25	2.21
14	4.6	3.74	3.34	3.11	2.96	2.85	2.76	2.7	2.65	2.6	2.46	2.39	2.27	2.22	2.18	2.13
15	4.54	3.68	3.29	3.06	2.9	2.79	2.71	2.64	2.59	2.54	2.4	2.33	2.2	2.16	2.11	2.07
16	4.49	3.63	3.24	3.01	2.85	2.74	2.66	2.59	2.54	2.49	2.35	2.28	2.15	2.11	2.06	2.01
17	4.45	3.59	3.2	2.96	2.81	2.7	2.61	2.55	2.49	2.45	2.31	2.23	2.1	2.06	2.01	1.96
18	4.41	3.55	3.16	2.93	2.77	2.66	2.58	2.51	2.46	2.41	2.27	2.19	2.06	2.02	1.97	1.92
19	4.38	3.52	3.13	2.9	2.74	2.63	2.54	2.48	2.42	2.38	2.23	2.16	2.03	1.98	1.93	1.88
20	4.35	3.49	3.1	2.87	2.71	2.6	2.51	2.45	2.39	2.35	2.2	2.12	1.99	1.95	1.9	1.84
21	4.32	3.47	3.07	2.84	2.68	2.57	2.49	2.42	2.37	2.32	2.18	2.1	1.96	1.92	1.87	1.81
22	4.3	3.44	3.05	2.82	2.66	2.55	2.46	2.4	2.34	2.3	2.15	2.07	1.94	1.89	1.84	1.78
23	4.28	3.42	3.03	2.8	2.64	2.53	2.44	2.37	2.32	2.27	2.13	2.05	1.91	1.86	1.81	1.76
24	4.26	3.4	3.01	2.78	2.62	2.51	2.42	2.36	2.3	2.25	2.11	2.03	1.89	1.84	1.79	1.73
25	4.24	3.39	2.99	2.76	2.6	2.49	2.4	2.34	2.28	2.24	2.09	2.01	1.87	1.82	1.77	1.71
26	4.23	3.37	2.98	2.74	2.59	2.47	2.39	2.32	2.27	2.22	2.07	1.99	1.85	1.8	1.75	1.69
27	4.21	3.35	2.96	2.73	2.57	2.46	2.37	2.31	2.25	2.2	2.06	1.97	1.84	1.79	1.73	1.67
28	4.2	3.34	2.95	2.71	2.56	2.45	2.36	2.29	2.24	2.19	2.04	1.96	1.82	1.77	1.71	1.65
29	4.18	3.33	2.93	2.7	2.55	2.43	2.35	2.28	2.22	2.18	2.03	1.94	1.81	1.75	1.7	1.64
30	4.17	3.32	2.92	2.69	2.53	2.42	2.33	2.27	2.21	2.16	2.01	1.93	1.79	1.74	1.68	1.62
40	4.08	3.23	2.84	2.61	2.45	2.34	2.25	2.18	2.12	2.08	1.92	1.84	1.69	1.64	1.58	1.51
60	4	3.15	2.76	2.53	2.37	2.25	2.17	2.1	2.04	1.99	1.84	1.75	1.59	1.53	1.47	1.39
120	3.92	3.07	2.68	2.45	2.29	2.18	2.09	2.02	1.96	1.91	1.75	1.66	1.5	1.43	1.35	1.25
∞	3.84	3	2.6	2.37	2.21	2.1	2.01	1.94	1.88	1.83	1.67	1.57	1.39	1.32	1.22	1

The above 'F' distribution values (at α = 0.05) were generated with MS Excel.

Probabilities (areas) under the 'F' distribution values (at α = 0.1) (i.e. the upper 10% points):

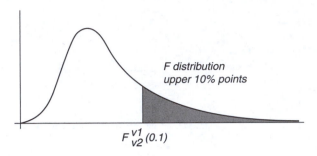

F distribution
upper 10% points

$F_{v2}^{v1}(0.1)$

v1	1	2	3	4	5	6	7	8	9	10	15	20	40	60	120	∞
v2																
1	39.86	49.5	53.59	55.83	57.24	58.2	58.91	59.44	59.86	60.19	61.22	61.74	62.53	62.79	63.06	63.33
2	8.53	9	9.16	9.24	9.29	9.33	9.35	9.37	9.38	9.39	9.42	9.44	9.47	9.47	9.48	9.49
3	5.54	5.46	5.39	5.34	5.31	5.28	5.27	5.25	5.24	5.23	5.2	5.18	5.16	5.15	5.14	5.13
4	4.54	4.32	4.19	4.11	4.05	4.01	3.98	3.95	3.94	3.92	3.87	3.84	3.8	3.79	3.78	3.76
5	4.06	3.78	3.62	3.52	3.45	3.4	3.37	3.34	3.32	3.3	3.24	3.21	3.16	3.14	3.12	3.11
6	3.78	3.46	3.29	3.18	3.11	3.05	3.01	2.98	2.96	2.94	2.87	2.84	2.78	2.76	2.74	2.72
7	3.59	3.26	3.07	2.96	2.88	2.83	2.78	2.75	2.72	2.7	2.63	2.59	2.54	2.51	2.49	2.47
8	3.46	3.11	2.92	2.81	2.73	2.67	2.62	2.59	2.56	2.54	2.46	2.42	2.36	2.34	2.32	2.29
9	3.36	3.01	2.81	2.69	2.61	2.55	2.51	2.47	2.44	2.42	2.34	2.3	2.23	2.21	2.18	2.16
10	3.29	2.92	2.73	2.61	2.52	2.46	2.41	2.38	2.35	2.32	2.24	2.2	2.13	2.11	2.08	2.06
11	3.23	2.86	2.66	2.54	2.45	2.39	2.34	2.3	2.27	2.25	2.17	2.12	2.05	2.03	2	1.97
12	3.18	2.81	2.61	2.48	2.39	2.33	2.28	2.24	2.21	2.19	2.1	2.06	1.99	1.96	1.93	1.9
13	3.14	2.76	2.56	2.43	2.35	2.28	2.23	2.2	2.16	2.14	2.05	2.01	1.93	1.9	1.88	1.85
14	3.1	2.73	2.52	2.39	2.31	2.24	2.19	2.15	2.12	2.1	2.01	1.96	1.89	1.86	1.83	1.8
15	3.07	2.7	2.49	2.36	2.27	2.21	2.16	2.12	2.09	2.06	1.97	1.92	1.85	1.82	1.79	1.76
16	3.05	2.67	2.46	2.33	2.24	2.18	2.13	2.09	2.06	2.03	1.94	1.89	1.81	1.78	1.75	1.72
17	3.03	2.64	2.44	2.31	2.22	2.15	2.1	2.06	2.03	2	1.91	1.86	1.78	1.75	1.72	1.69
18	3.01	2.62	2.42	2.29	2.2	2.13	2.08	2.04	2	1.98	1.89	1.84	1.75	1.72	1.69	1.66
19	2.99	2.61	2.4	2.27	2.18	2.11	2.06	2.02	1.98	1.96	1.86	1.81	1.73	1.7	1.67	1.63
20	2.97	2.59	2.38	2.25	2.16	2.09	2.04	2	1.96	1.94	1.84	1.79	1.71	1.68	1.64	1.61
21	2.96	2.57	2.36	2.23	2.14	2.08	2.02	1.98	1.95	1.92	1.83	1.78	1.69	1.66	1.62	1.59
22	2.95	2.56	2.35	2.22	2.13	2.06	2.01	1.97	1.93	1.9	1.81	1.76	1.67	1.64	1.6	1.57
23	2.94	2.55	2.34	2.21	2.11	2.05	1.99	1.95	1.92	1.89	1.8	1.74	1.66	1.62	1.59	1.55
24	2.93	2.54	2.33	2.19	2.1	2.04	1.98	1.94	1.91	1.88	1.78	1.73	1.64	1.61	1.57	1.53
25	2.92	2.53	2.32	2.18	2.09	2.02	1.97	1.93	1.89	1.87	1.77	1.72	1.63	1.59	1.56	1.52
26	2.91	2.52	2.31	2.17	2.08	2.01	1.96	1.92	1.88	1.86	1.76	1.71	1.61	1.58	1.54	1.5
27	2.9	2.51	2.3	2.17	2.07	2	1.95	1.91	1.87	1.85	1.75	1.7	1.6	1.57	1.53	1.49
28	2.89	2.5	2.29	2.16	2.06	2	1.94	1.9	1.87	1.84	1.74	1.69	1.59	1.56	1.52	1.48
29	2.89	2.5	2.28	2.15	2.06	1.99	1.93	1.89	1.86	1.83	1.73	1.68	1.58	1.55	1.51	1.47
30	2.88	2.49	2.28	2.14	2.05	1.98	1.93	1.88	1.85	1.82	1.72	1.67	1.57	1.54	1.5	1.46
40	2.84	2.44	2.23	2.09	2	1.93	1.87	1.83	1.79	1.76	1.66	1.61	1.51	1.47	1.42	1.38
60	2.79	2.39	2.18	2.04	1.95	1.87	1.82	1.77	1.74	1.71	1.6	1.54	1.44	1.4	1.35	1.29
120	2.75	2.35	2.13	1.99	1.9	1.82	1.77	1.72	1.68	1.65	1.55	1.48	1.37	1.32	1.26	1.19
∞	2.71	2.3	2.08	1.94	1.85	1.77	1.72	1.67	1.63	1.6	1.49	1.42	1.3	1.24	1.17	1

The above 'F' distribution values (at α = 0.1) were generated with MS Excel.

Index